THE **BUSN** SOLUTION

Every 4LTR Press solution includes:

Visually Engaging Textbook + **Online Study Tools** + **Tear-out Review Cards** + **Interactive eBook**

STUDENT RESOURCES:

- Interactive eBook
- Auto-Graded Quizzes
- Flashcards
- Games: Crossword Puzzles, Beat the Clock, & Quiz Bowl
- PowerPoint® Slides
- Videos
- Chapter Review Cards
- Interactive Exhibits
- Interactive Business Decision Making Scenarios
- Podcasts
- Cases & Exercises

Students sign in at **www.cengagebrain.com**

INSTRUCTOR RESOURCES:

- All Student Resources
- Engagement Tracker
- First Day of Class Instructions
- LMS Integration
- Custom Options through 4LTR+ Program
- Instructor's Manual
- Test Bank
- PowerPoint® Slides
- Instructor Prep Cards
- Engagement Tracker
- Videos

Instructors sign in at **www.cengage.com/login**

> "I loved that **BUSN** was available online and all of the different things that are available to students such as flashcards and the quizzes."
>
> – **Ahyde Nieves,** *Tillamook Bay Community College*

SOUTH-WESTERN
CENGAGE Learning

BUSN5
Marce Kelly, Jim McGowen

Executive Vice President and Publisher, Business: Jonathan Hulbert

Vice President of Editorial, Business: Jack W. Calhoun

Publisher: Erin Joyner

Executive Director, 4LTR Press: Neil Marquardt

Acquisitions Editor: Jason Fremder

Developmental Editor: Julie Klooster

Editorial Assistant: Megan Fischer

Associate Project Manager, 4LTR Press: Pierce Denny

Executive Brand Manager, 4LTR Press: Courtney Sheldon

Marketing Manager: Michelle Lockard

Marketing Coordinator: Leigh T. Smith

Sr. Marketing Communications Manager: Sarah Greber

Sr. Content Project Manager: Martha Conway

Sr. Media Editor: Kristen Meere

Manufacturing Planner: Ron Montgomery

Production Service: Macmillan Publishing Services

Sr. Art Director: Stacy Jenkins Shirley

Sr. Rights Acquisition Specialist, Images: Deanna Ettinger

Photo Researcher: Charlotte Goldman

Rights Acquisition Specialist, Text: Sam Marshall

Text Permissions Researcher: Karyn Morrison

Cover and Internal Designer: KeDesign, Mason, OH

Cover Image: © iStockphoto.com/Yunus Arakon

Inside Front Cover Images: © iStockphoto.com/sdominick, © iStockphoto.com/alexsl, © iStockphoto.com/A-Digit

Title Page Images: © iStockphoto.com/CostinT, © iStockphoto.com/photovideostock, © iStockphoto.com/Leontura;

Back cover Image: © iStockphoto.com/René Mansi

Special Feature Images:
Spilled coffee: © iStockphoto.com/Aleksander Krol
Man with feet on desk: © iStockphoto.com/Lise Gagne
Green recycling: © iStockphoto.com/Radovan Marček
Thumbs up: © iStockphoto.com/Lasse Kristensen
Puzzle/iPad: © iStockphoto.com/Alex Slobodkin
Woman with business card: © iStockphoto.com/ Amanda Rohde

For product information and technology assistance, contact us at **Cengage Learning Customer & Sales Support, 1-800-354-9706**

For permission to use material from this text or product, submit all requests online at **www.cengage.com/permissions** Further permissions questions can be emailed to **permissionrequest@cengage.com**

Library of Congress Control Number: 2011942710

Student Edition ISBN 13: 978-1-111-82672-7
Student Edition ISBN 10: 1-111-82672-2

Student Edition with CourseMate ISBN 13: 978-1-111-82673-4
Student Edition with CourseMate ISBN 10: 1-111-82673-0

South-Western
5191 Natorp Boulevard
Mason, OH 45040
USA

Cengage Learning products are represented in Canada by Nelson Education, Ltd.

To learn more about 4LTR Press, visit **4ltr.cengage.com/busn** Purchase any of our products at your local college store or at our preferred online store **www.cengagebrain.com**

Printed in the United States of America
1 2 3 4 5 6 7 16 15 14 13 12

√calculated Risk

BUSN

1 The Business Environment

2 Creating a Business

3 Financing a Business

4 Marketing a Business

5 Managing a Business

CONTENTS

PART 1 — The Business Environment

© iStockphoto.com/studiovision

© Brian A Jackson/Shutterstock.com

Chapter 4

Business Ethics and Social Responsibility: Doing Well by Doing Good

Chapter 5

Business Communication: Creating and Delivering Messages that Matter

PART 2 — Creating a Business

© iStockphoto.com/Catherine Yeulet

PART 3 — Financing a Business

Chapter 10

Financial Markets:
Allocating Financial Resources

© Olga Danylenko/Shutterstock.com

PART 4 Marketing a Business

AP Images/Ross D. Franklin

PART 5 Managing a Business

© Digital Vision/ Jupiterimages

© Jamey Ekins/Shutterstock.com

To my family—
Scot, Justin, Lauren,
Allison, Cathy, and Shel.
You are my greatest blessing.

—Marce Kelly

To my grandsons,
Kyle and Xander.
Grandy loves you!

—Jim McGowen

The idea for this book—a whole new way of learning—began with students like you across the country. We paid attention to students who wanted to learn about business without slogging through endless pages of dry text. We listened to students who wanted to sit through class without craving a triple espresso. We responded to students who wanted to use their favorite gadgets to prepare for tests.

So we are confident that BUSN will meet your needs. The short, lively text covers all the key concepts without the fluff. The examples are relevant and engaging, and the visual style makes the book fun to read. But the text is only part of the package. You can access a rich variety of study tools via computer or iPod—the choice is yours.

We did one other thing we hope you'll like. We paid a lot of attention to students' concerns about the high price of college textbooks. We made it our mission to ensure that our package not only meets your needs but does so without busting your budget!

This innovative, student-focused package was developed by the authors—Marce Kelly and Jim McGowen—and the experienced Cengage Learning publishers. The Cengage team contributed a deep understanding of students and professors across the nation, and the authors brought years of teaching and business experience.

Marce Kelly, who earned her MBA from UCLA's Anderson School of Management, spent the first 14 years of her career in marketing, building brands for Neutrogena and The Walt Disney Corporation. But her true love is teaching, so in 2000 she accepted a full-time teaching position at Santa Monica College. Professor Kelly has received seven Outstanding Instructor awards from the International Education Center and has been named four times to *Who's Who Among American Teachers*.

Jim McGowen is professor emeritus in the Business Division at Southwestern Illinois College. He has taught Introduction to Business for over a quarter of a century, and continues to teach several sections of the course each year. Professor McGowen chaired the Business Transfer Department at Southwestern Illinois College for twelve years, giving him the opportunity to work with faculty teaching a wide range of business courses. This experience gave him a deep appreciation for role the Introduction to Business course plays in a business curriculum. Professor McGowen has a bachelor's degree in business administration and a master's degree in economics, both from Auburn University. He has received the Emerson Prize for Teaching Excellence and been recognized for teaching excellence by the Illinois Community College Trustees Association. He was named Faculty Member of the Year at Southwestern Illinois College in 2007.

We would appreciate any comments or suggestions you want to offer about this package. You can reach Jim McGowen at jmcgowen4@gmail.com and Marce Kelly at marcella.kelly@gmail.com. We wish you a fun, positive, productive term, and look forward to your feedback!

Marce Kelly

© Cengage Learning 2013

Jim McGowen

© Cengage Learning 2013

1 Business Now:
Change Is the Only Constant

> "WHETHER YOU THINK *THAT* YOU CAN, OR THAT YOU CAN'T, *YOU* ARE USUALLY RIGHT."
>
> — HENRY FORD, FOUNDER, FORD MOTOR COMPANY

LO1 Business Now: Moving at Breakneck Speed

Day by day, the business world simply spins faster. Industries rise—and sometimes fall—in the course of a few short months. Technologies forge instant connections across the globe. And powerful new trends surface and submerge, sometimes within less than a year. In this fast-paced, fluid environment, change is the only constant.

Successful firms lean forward and embrace the change. They seek the opportunities and avoid the pitfalls. They carefully evaluate risks. They completely understand their market. And they adhere to ethical practices. Their core goal: to generate long-term profits by delivering unsurpassed **value** to their customers.

Over the past few years, the explosive growth in Facebook and Twitter have played a pivotal part in forging a new role for both businesses and consumers in today's dynamic business environment. In a nod to Twitter, *AdvertisingAge* magazine dug through the most recent Census data and identified a host of trends in a "Twitter-Ready" 140 character format. Among the highlights:

- ➲ The median household income in the U.S. is roughly $50,000.
- ➲ The top 40% of Americans earn 75% of the money.
- ➲ Four in ten kids are born to single moms.
- ➲ By 2010, birthrates had dropped to an all-time record low.

- ➲ 60% of Americans now live in the South and West Regions.
- ➲ 26% of men make six or more cell phone calls a day. [1]

Business Basics: Some Key Definitions

While you can certainly recognize a business when you see one, more formal definitions may help as you read through this book. A **business** is any organization that provides goods and services in an effort to earn a profit. **Profit** is the financial reward that comes from starting and running a business. More specifically, profit is the money that a business earns in sales (or revenue), minus expenses such as the cost of goods and the cost of salaries. But clearly, not every business earns a profit all the time. When a business brings in less money than it needs to cover expenses, it incurs a **loss**. If you launch a music label, for instance, you'll need to pay your artists, buy or lease a studio, and purchase equipment, among other expenses. If your label generates hits, you'll earn more than enough to cover all your expenses and make yourself rich. But a series of duds could leave you holding the bag. Just the possibility of earning a profit provides a powerful incentive for people of all backgrounds to launch their own enterprise. Despite the economic meltdown of 2008, American business start-ups in 2009 reached their highest level in 14 years. [2] You've probably noticed the entrepreneurial ambition among your peers, since more than 40% of college freshmen plan to launch their own business at some point in their career—and many actually begin the process while in college. [3] People who risk their time, money, and other resources to start and manage a business are called **entrepreneurs.**

The *Forbes* list of the richest Americans highlights the astounding ability of the entrepreneurial spirit to build wealth. The top ten—featured in Exhibit 1.1—include multiple members of the Walton family who were not themselves entrepreneurs: their money comes from retail powerhouse Walmart, founded by brilliant, eccentric entrepreneur Sam Walton.

Interestingly, as entrepreneurs create wealth for themselves, they produce a ripple effect that enriches everyone around them. For instance, if your new website becomes

value The relationship between the price of a good or a service and the benefits that it offers its customers.

business Any organization that provides goods and services in an effort to earn a profit.

profit The money that a business earns in sales (or revenue), minus expenses, such as the cost of goods, and the cost of salaries. Revenue—Expenses = Profit (or Loss).

loss When a business incurs expenses that are greater than its revenue.

entrepreneurs People who risk their time, money, and other resources to start and manage a business.

the next Facebook, who will benefit? Clearly, *you* will. And you'll probably spend at least some of that money enriching your local clubs, clothing stores, and car dealerships. But others will benefit, too, including your members, advertisers on your site and the staff who support them, contractors who build your facilities, and the government that collects your taxes. The impact of one successful entrepreneur can extend to the far reaches of the economy. In fact, in the last thirty years, literally all net job creation in this country has taken place in firms less than five years old.[4] Multiply the impact by thousands of entrepreneurs—each working in his or her own self-interest—and you can see how the profit motive benefits virtually everyone.

From a bigger-picture perspective, business drives up the **standard of living** for people worldwide, contributing to a higher **quality of life**. Not only do businesses provide the products and services that people enjoy, but they also provide the jobs that people need. Beyond the obvious, business contributes to society through innovation—think cars, TVs, and personal computers. Business also helps raise the standard of living through taxes, which the government spends on projects that range from streetlights to environmental cleanup. And socially responsible firms contribute even more, actively advocating for the well-being of the society that feeds their success.

LO2 The History of Business: Putting It All in Context

You may be surprised to learn that—unlike today—business hasn't always been focused on what the customer wants. In fact, business in the United States has changed rather dramatically over the past 200–300 years. Most business historians divide the history of American business into five distinct eras, which overlap during the periods of transition:

- ⊙ **The Industrial Revolution:** Technological advances fueled a period of rapid industrialization in America from the mid-1700s to the mid-1800s. As mass production took hold, huge factories replaced skilled artisan workshops. The factories hired large numbers of semiskilled workers, who specialized in a limited number of tasks. The result was unprecedented production efficiency, but also a loss of individual ownership and personal pride in the production process.

EXHIBIT 1.1
The Richest Americans 2010, *Forbes* Magazine

NAME	NET WORTH	SOURCE OF WEALTH
BILL GATES	$54,000,000,000	Microsoft
WARREN BUFFET	$45,000,000,000	Berkshire Hathaway
LAWRENCE ELLISON	$27,000,000,000	Oracle
CHRISTY WALTON AND FAMILY	$24,000,000,000	Walmart
CHARLES KOCH	$21,500,000,000	manufacturing, energy
DAVID KOCH	$21,500,000,000	manufacturing, energy
JIM C. WALTON	$20,100,000,000	Walmart
ALICE WALTON	$20,000,000,000	Walmart
S. ROBSON WALTON	$19,700,000,000	Walmart
MICHAEL BLOOMBERG	$18,000,000,000	Bloomberg
LARRY PAGE	$15,000,000,000	Google
SERGEY BRIN	$15,000,000,000	Google

Source: *The Richest People in America*, September 16, 2010, Forbes magazine website, http://www.forbes.com/wealth/forbes-400, accessed January 15, 2011

Ooops! What were they thinking?

Not Every Dumb Move Is an Utter Disaster...

In the wake of disastrous mistakes and outrageous mismanagement across our economy, it might be tough to remember that some mistakes are actually pretty amusing. But *BNET Website* collected a number of examples that might help remind you.[5] A sampling:

● *"We care—NOT!!"* After shipping nearly 12 million potentially defective computers, a lawsuit against Dell alleges that the firm offered its sales force training that included tips such as: "Don't bring this to customer's attention proactively" and "Emphasize uncertainty."

● *The wrong kind of stimulus:* According to the Social Security Administration's Inspector General, more than 17,000 prison inmates and almost 72,000 dead people received economic stimulus checks from the federal government, totalling $22.3 million.

● *Do those chips come with ear plugs?:* In 2010, PepsiCo, noisily introduced biodegradable packaging for its Sun Chips brand, but soon switched back to its non-recyclable bags, after Facebook groups popped up with names such as: "Sorry but I can't hear you over this Sun Chips bag" and "I wanted Sun Chips but my roommate was sleeping." Testing indicated that the complainers had a legitimate point. Opening the biodegradable bags created more than 100 decibels of noise (similar to the noise level of a jet taking off at a distance of 300 meters).

● *Accidental Cyber-Snooping:* As Google sent its "Street View" cars all over the world collecting panoramic images for uploading into GoogleMaps, the firm "unintentionally" collected and retained, among other things, passwords and complete email messages picked up from unsecured Wi-Fi networks.

● *Wasted time or well worthwhile?* To celebrate the 30th anniversary of Pac-Man in 2010, engineers at Google turned the site's home page into a fully functional version of the game, wasting an estimated 4.8 million hours of the world's time and more than $120 million in lost productivity.

● **The Entrepreneurship Era:** Building on the foundation of the industrial revolution, large-scale entrepreneurs emerged in the second half of the 1800s, building business empires. These industrial titans created enormous wealth, raising the overall standard of living across the country. But many also dominated their markets, forcing out competitors, manipulating prices, exploiting workers, and decimating the environment. Toward the end of the 1800s, the government stepped into the business realm, passing laws to regulate business and protect consumers and workers, creating more balance in the economy.

● **The Production Era:** In the early part of the 1900s, major businesses focused on further refining the production process and creating

greater efficiencies. Jobs became even more specialized, increasing productivity and lowering costs and

© Fotosearch/Archive Photos/Getty Images

When in doubt, we usually don't!

Most of us can probably think of a time when we should have taken some action, but instead we did nothing, because doing nothing was easier. . . . Enter the choice architects, behavioral scientists, who claim that businesses, governments, and other institutions can engineer our options to "nudge" us into making choices that are (ideally) more socially desirable, or (from a business standpoint) more profitable than the choices that we'd make on our own. A couple of examples:

⊙ **Better Aim:** As most women who share toilets with men can attest, even the best-intentioned men don't seem to, uh, aim well when it comes to toilet hygiene. In busy restrooms, this is more than just a gross annoyance; dirty bathrooms increase cleaning costs and undermine brand image. Aad Kiedboom, an economist who worked for the Schiphol International Airport in Amsterdam, tackled this issue by etching the image of a black housefly onto the bowls of the airport's urinals, just to the left of the drain. As a result, "spillage" decreased 80%.

⊙ **Musical Stairs:** In response to rising obesity rates, the city of Stockholm has retrofitted a staircase in its Odenplan subway station to resemble giant piano keys, which produce real sound, to encourage commuters to climb the stairs rather than ride the escalator. Hidden video footage suggests that so far it's been a resounding success—well used and fun for everyone.

Advocates argue that choice architects work for the good of society, encouraging—but never coercing—people to make positive choices. Critics argue that choice architects are manipulative—shoving rather than nudging, which interferes with peoples' freedom of choice. In the wrong hands, that can be dangerous. What is your perspective? In the hands of business, will choice architecture ultimately be positive or negative?[6]

---

prices. In 1913, Henry Ford introduced the assembly line, which quickly became standard across major manufacturing industries. With managers focused on efficiency, the customer was an afterthought. But when customers tightened their belts during the Great Depression and World War II, businesses took notice. The "hard sell" emerged: aggressive persuasion designed to separate consumers from their cash.

⊙ **The Marketing Era:** After WWII, the balance of power shifted away from producers and toward consumers, flooding the market with enticing choices. To differentiate themselves from their competitors, businesses began to develop brands, or distinctive identities, to help consumers understand the differences among various products. The *marketing concept* emerged: a consumer focus that permeates successful companies in every department, at every level. This approach continues to influence business decisions today as global competition heats up to unprecedented levels.

⊙ **The Relationship Era:** Building on the marketing concept, today, leading-edge firms look beyond each immediate transaction with a customer and aim to build long-term relationships. Satisfied customers can become advocates for a business, spreading the word with more speed and credibility than even the best promotional campaign. And cultivating current customers is more profitable than constantly seeking new ones. One key tool is technology. Using the Web and other digital resources, businesses gather detailed information about their customers and use these data to serve them better.

LO3 Nonprofits and the Economy: The Business of Doing Good

Nonprofit organizations play a critical role in the economy, often working hand-in-hand with businesses to improve the quality of life in our society. Focusing on areas such as health, human services, education, art, religion, and culture, **nonprofits** are business-*like* establishments, but their primary goals do not include profits. Chuck Bean, Executive Director of the Nonprofit Roundtable, explains: "By definition, nonprofits are not in the business of financial gain. We're in the business of doing good. However, nonprofits are still businesses in every other sense—they employ people, they take in revenue, they produce goods and services and contribute in significant ways to our region's economic stability and growth." Nationwide, nonprofits employ about one in ten workers, accounting for more paid workers than the entire construction industry and more than the finance, insurance, and real-estate sectors combined. And nonprofit museums, schools, theaters, and orchestras have become economic magnets for many communities, drawing additional investment.[7]

Many businesses work with nonprofits to boost their impact in the community.

AP Images/Tyler Morning Telegraph, Tom Worner

nonprofits Business-*like* establishments that employ people and produce goods and services with the fundamental goal of contributing to the community rather than generating financial gain.

factors of production Four fundamental elements—natural resources, capital, human resources, and entrepreneurship—that businesses need to achieve their objectives.

LO4 Factors of Production: The Basic Building Blocks

Both businesses and nonprofits rely on **factors of production**—four fundamental resources—to achieve their objectives. Some combination of these factors is crucial for an economic system to work and create wealth. As you read through the factors, keep in mind that they don't come free of charge. Human resources, for instance, require wages, while entrepreneurs need a profit incentive.

- ⊃ **Natural resources:** This factor includes all inputs that offer value in their natural state, such as land, fresh water, wind, and mineral deposits. Most natural resources must be extracted, purified, or harnessed; people cannot actually create them. (Note that agricultural products, which people do create through planting and tending, are not a natural resource.) The value of all natural resources tends to rise with high demand, low supply, or both.

- ⊃ **Capital:** This factor includes machines, tools, buildings, information, and technology—the synthetic resources that a business needs to produce goods or services. Computers and telecommunications capability have become pivotal elements of

business environment
The setting in which business operates. The five key components are: economic environment, competitive environment, technological environment, social environment, and global environment.

capital across a surprising range of industries, from financial services to professional sports. You may be surprised to learn that in this context, capital does not include money, but clearly, businesses use money to acquire, maintain, and upgrade their capital.

- **Human Resources:** This factor encompasses the physical, intellectual, and creative contributions of everyone who works within an economy. As technology replaces a growing number of manual labor jobs, education and motivation have become increasingly important to human resource development. Given the importance of knowledge to workforce effectiveness, some business experts, such as management guru Peter Drucker, break out knowledge as its own category, separate from human resources.

- **Entrepreneurship:** Entrepreneurs are people who take the risk of launching and operating their own businesses, largely in response to the profit incentive. They tend to see opportunities where others don't, and they use their own resources to capitalize on that potential. Entrepreneurial enterprises can kick-start an economy, creating a tidal wave of opportunity by harnessing the other factors of production. But entrepreneurs don't thrive in an environment that doesn't support them. The key ingredient is economic freedom: freedom of choice (whom to hire, for instance, or what to produce), freedom from excess regulation, and freedom from too much taxation. Protection from corruption and unfair competition is another entrepreneurial "must."

Clearly, all of these factors must be in place for an economy to thrive. But which factor is *most* important? One way to answer that question is to examine current economies around the world. Russia and China are both rich in natural resources and human resources. And both countries have a solid level of capital (growing in China, and deteriorating in Russia). Yet, neither country is wealthy; both rank relatively low in terms of gross national income per person. The missing ingredient seems to be entrepreneurship, limited in Russia largely through corruption and in China through government interference and taxes. Contrast those examples with, say, Hong Kong. The population is small, and the natural resources are severely limited, yet Hong Kong has consistently ranked among the richest regions in Asia. The

reason: operating for many years under the British legal and economic system, the government actively encouraged entrepreneurship, which fueled the creation of wealth. Recognizing the potential of entrepreneurship, China has recently done more to relax regulations and support free enterprise. The result has been tremendous growth, which may yet bring China into the ranks of the wealthier nations.[8]

LO5 The Business Environment: The Context for Success

No business operates in a vacuum. Outside factors play a vital role in determining whether each individual business succeeds or fails. Likewise, the broader **business environment** can make the critical difference in whether an overall economy thrives or disintegrates. The five key dimensions of the business environment are the economic environment, the competitive environment, the technological environment, the social environment, and the global environment, as shown in Exhibit 1.2.

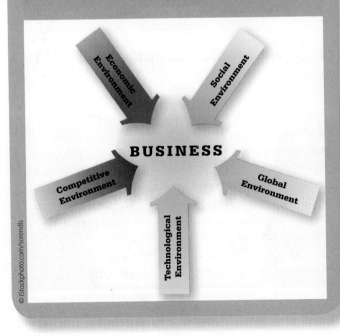

EXHIBIT 1.2
The Business Environment

Each dimension of the business environment affects both individual businesses and the economy in general.

© iStockphoto.com/sorendls

The Economic Environment

In September 2008, the U.S. economy plunged into the worst fiscal crisis since the Great Depression. Huge, venerable financial institutions faced collapse, spurring unprecedented bailouts by the federal government and the Federal Reserve. By the end of the year, the stock market had lost more than a third of its value, and 11.1 million Americans were out of work. Housing prices fell precipitously, and foreclosure rates reached record levels. As fear swept through the banking industry, neither businesses nor individuals could borrow money to meet their needs. Economic turmoil in the United States spread quickly around the world, fueling a global economic crisis.

But through 2009, the U.S. economy began to recover, although unemployment remained high. The Federal Reserve—the U.S. central banking system—took unprecedented, proactive steps to encourage an economic turnaround. And President Barack Obama spearheaded passage of a massive economic stimulus package, designed not only to create jobs, but also to build infrastructure—with a focus on renewable energy—to position the U.S. economy for stability and growth in the decades to come. (The price, of course, will be more national debt, which could counterbalance some of the benefits.)

The government also takes active steps on an ongoing basis to reduce the risks of starting and running a business. The result: free enterprise and fair competition flourish. Despite the economic crisis, research suggests that most budding entrepreneurs still plan to launch their firms in

> ## The bank bailout was about as popular as a root canal.
> —BARACK OBAMA, STATE OF THE UNION ADDRESS, JANUARY 2010

the next three years. One of the government policies that support business is the relatively low federal tax rate, both for individuals and businesses. And President Obama has proposed lowering the tax rate even further for a large swath of individual taxpayers and businesses. A number of states—from Alabama to Nevada—make their local economies even more appealing by providing special tax deals to attract new firms. The federal government also runs entire agencies that support business, such as the Small Business Administration. Other branches of the government, such as the Federal Trade Commission, actively promote fair competitive practices, which help give every enterprise a chance to succeed.

Another key element of the U.S. economic environment is legislation that supports enforceable contracts. For instance, if you contract a company to supply your silk screening business with 1,000 blank tee shirts at $4.00 per piece, that firm must comply or face legal consequences. The firm can't wait until a day before delivery and jack up the price to $8.00 per piece, because you would almost certainly respond with a successful lawsuit. Many U.S. business people take enforceable contracts for granted,

Flex Your Creativity: Use Boredom to Build Your Brain

Next time you're checked out when you really ought to be paying attention, consider that you might be actually building your brainpower rather than melting it. A growing body of research about boredom suggests that boredom "should be recognized as a legitimate human emotion that can be central to learning and creativity." One reason may be that creative problem solving taps into many different parts of our brains. Boredom may give us an opportunity to activate our less-used cerebral resources, triggering those magical "Aha!" moments that seem to happen whenever we're not trying too hard. Experiments in the 1970s suggested that boredom actually "had the power to exert pressure on individuals to stretch their inventive capacity." So, next time you're bored, don't' be too quick to whip out your smartphone—you may be cheating yourself (and the world) of your next big creative breakthrough.[9]

speed-to-market The rate at which a new product moves from conception to commercialization.

but in a number of developing countries—which offer some of today's largest business opportunities—contracts are often not enforceable (at least not in day-to-day practice).

Corruption also affects the economic environment. A low level of corruption and bribery dramatically reduces the risk of running a business by ensuring that everyone plays by the same set of rules—rules that are clearly visible to every player. Fortunately, U.S. laws keep domestic corruption mostly—but not completely—at bay. Other ethical lapses, such as shady accounting, can also increase the cost of doing business for everyone involved. But in the wake of ethical meltdowns at major corporations such as Enron and WorldCom, the federal government has passed tough-minded new regulations to increase corporate accountability. If the new legislation effectively curbs illegal and unethical practices, every business will have a fair chance at success.

Upcoming chapters on economics and ethics will address these economic challenges and their significance in more depth. But bottom line, we have reason for cautious (some would say *very* cautious) optimism. The American economy has a proven track record of flexibility and resilience, which will surely help us navigate this crisis and uncover new opportunity.

The Competitive Environment

As global competition intensifies yet further, leading-edge companies have focused on customer satisfaction like never before. The goal: to develop long-term, mutually beneficial relationships with customers. Getting current customers to buy more of your product is a lot less expensive than convincing potential customers to try your product for the first time. And if you transform your current customers into loyal advocates—vocal promoters of your product or service—they'll get those new customers for you more effectively than any advertising or discount program. Companies such as Dr. Pepper, Olive Garden restaurants, and Northwestern Mutual life insurance lead their industries in customer satisfaction, which translates into higher profits even when the competition is tough.[10]

Customer satisfaction comes in large part from delivering unsurpassed value. The best measure of value is the size of the gap between product benefits and price. A product has value when its benefits to the customer are equal to or greater than the price that the customer pays. Keep in mind that the cheapest product doesn't necessarily represent the best value. If a 99-cent toy from Big Lots breaks in

a day, customers may be willing to pay several dollars more for a similar toy from somewhere else. But if that 99-cent toy lasts all year, customers will be delighted by the value and will likely encourage their friends and family to shop at Big Lots. The key to value is quality, and virtually all successful firms offer top-quality products relative to their direct competitors.

A recent ranking study by consulting firm Interbrand highlights brands that use imagination and innovation to deliver value to their customer. Exhibit 1.3 shows the winners and the up-and-comers in the race to capture the hearts, minds, and dollars of consumers around the world.

Leading Edge versus Bleeding Edge Speed-to-market—the rate at which a firm transforms concepts into actual products—can be another key source of competitive advantage. And the pace of change just keeps getting faster. In this tumultuous setting, companies that stay ahead of the pack often enjoy a distinct advantage. But keep in mind that there's a difference between leading edge and bleeding edge. Bleeding-edge firms launch products that fail because

EXHIBIT 1.3
2010 Global Brand Champions and the Ones to Watch, *BusinessWeek* and Interbrand

MOST VALUABLE	BIGGEST GAINERS/ BRANDS	PERCENTAGE GAIN
1. COCA-COLA	1. Apple	+37%
2. IBM	2. Google	+36%
3. MICROSOFT	3. Blackberry	+32%
4. GOOGLE	4. JP Morgan	+29%
5. GE	5. Allianz	+28%
6. MCDONALD'S		
7. INTEL		
8. NOKIA		
9. DISNEY		
10. HP		

Source: Best Global Brands 2010, Interbrand website, http://issuu.com/interbrand/docs/bgb_report_us_version?viewMode=presentation&mode=embed, accessed January 17, 2011 they're too far ahead of the market. During the late 1990s, for example, in the heart of the dot.com boom, WebVan, a grocery delivery service, launched to huge fanfare. But the firm went bankrupt just a few years later in 2001, partly because customers weren't yet ready to dump traditional grocery stores in favor of cyber-shopping. Leading-edge firms, on the other hand, offer products just as the market becomes ready to embrace them.[11]

Apple provides an excellent example of leading edge. You may be surprised to learn that Apple—which controls about 70%[12] of the digital music player market—did not offer the first MP3 player. Instead, it surveyed the existing market to help develop a new product, the iPod, which was far superior in terms of design and ease-of-use. But Apple didn't stop with one successful MP3 player. Racing to stay ahead, they soon introduced the colorful, more affordable iPod mini. And before sales reached their peak, they launched the iPod Nano, which essentially pulled the rug from under the blockbuster iPod mini just a few short months before the holiday selling season. Why? If they hadn't done it, someone else may well have done it instead. And Apple is almost maniacally focused on maintaining its competitive lead.[13]

The Workforce Advantage

Employees can contribute another key dimension to a firm's competitive edge. Recent research suggests that investing in worker satisfaction yields tangible, bottom-line results. The researchers evaluated the stock price of *Fortune* magazine's annual list of the "100 Best Companies to Work for in America" to the S&P 500, which reflects the overall market. In 2009, the heart of the Great Recession, the firms with the highest employee satisfaction provided a 10.3% annual return, compared to a 2.95% return for the firms in the S&P 500. While the critical difference in performance most likely stemmed from employee satisfaction, other factors—such as excellent product and superb top management—likely *also* played a role in both employee satisfaction and strong stock performance.[14]

Finding and holding the best talent will likely become a crucial competitive issue in the next decade, as the baby boom generation begins to retire. The 500 largest U.S. companies anticipate losing about half of their senior managers over the next five to six years. Since, January 1, 2011, 10,000 baby boomers began to turn 65 (the traditional retirement age) every day, and the Pew Research Center anticipates that this trend will continue for 19 years. Replacing the skills and experience these workers bring to their jobs may be tough: baby boomers include about 77 million people, while the generation that follows includes only 46 million. Firms that cultivate human resources now will find themselves better able to compete as the market for top talent tightens.[15]

business technology
Any tools—especially computers, telecommunications, and other digital products—that businesses can use to become more efficient and effective.

The Technological Environment

The broad definition of **business technology** includes any tools that businesses can use to become more efficient and effective. But more specifically, in today's world, business technology usually refers to computers, telecommunications, and other digital tools. Over the past few decades, the impact of digital technology on business has been utterly transformative. New industries have emerged, while others have disappeared. And some fields—such as travel, banking, and music—have changed dramatically. Even in

Motivated Apple employees help create satisfied Apple customers.

© David Butow/Bloomberg via Getty Images

Innovation: For Better or for Worse

Creativity matters, not just for individual businesses, but also for the overall economy. And with global competition, the stakes are high. The editors of *Encyclopedia Britannica* recently explored creativity over time and across countries, compiling a list of the 100 greatest inventions of all time. The editors chose the winners—which they did not rank—based on how profoundly the innovations have affected human life—for better or for worse. Before you read further, consider which inventions you would place on the list. How have they affected human life? What inventions would you expect to find on the list in the future?

Many of the citations are not surprising, such as the computer, eyeglasses, gunpowder, candles, vaccinations, and the atomic bomb. Others are somewhat amusing, including disposable diapers (which *have* improved the quality of life for millions of parents worldwide!), cat litter, Astroturf (artificial grass), and Post-it notes. A few citations, such as Muzak (generic "elevator music"), and bikinis, are somewhat puzzling, although they have clearly permeated contemporary culture.

While most of the inventions on this top 100 list are fairly recent, some are older than you might think. Flush toilets, for instance, have been around since the 1500s, although toilet tissue wasn't invented until 1857. Vending machines were invented in Egypt sometime between 200 and 100 BC. And the construction nail was invented by the Sumerians in about 3300 BC.

Interestingly, over the last century, corporations, rather than individuals, have been responsible for a growing number of key innovations. Examples include the Camcorder (Sony), the laptop computer (Radio Shack), and Viagra (Pfizer). This trend is only likely to build momentum as global competition intensifies.

The United States, despite our relatively short history, dominates the list of greatest inventions, with 162 of 325 mentions, or just under 50%. One reason may be that our nation celebrates individuality, creativity, and, of course, the profit incentive. If we continue to flex our creative muscles, we could find ourselves with a competitive edge far into the twenty-first century.

Sometimes, accessing creativity is simply a matter of asking the right questions. Nottingham-Spirk, a successful industrial design firm responsible for a string of blockbuster new product hits, constantly asks questions of its own inventors, from the mild (e.g., "What can we so to make this 'NICE' product a 'WOW'?") to the wild (e.g., "What if the candy bar could levitate?"). And the firm uses the answers to all of these questions to drive innovation.[16]

---

categories with relatively unchanged products, companies have leveraged technology to streamline production and create new efficiencies. Examples include new processes such as computerized billing, digital animation, and robotic manufacturing. For fast-moving firms, the technological environment represents a rich source of competitive advantage, but it clearly can be a major threat for companies that are slow to adopt or to integrate new approaches.

The creation of the **World Wide Web** has transformed not only business, but also people's lives. Anyone, anywhere, anytime can use the Web to send and receive images and data (as long as access is available). One result is the rise of **e-commerce** or online sales, which allow businesses to tap into a worldwide community of potential customers. In the wake of the global economic crisis, e-commerce has slowed from the breakneck 20%+ growth rates of the last five years,

but even so, analysts predict that solid single-digit growth will continue. Business-to-business selling comprises the vast majority of total e-commerce sales (and an even larger share of the profits). A growing number of businesses have also connected their digital networks with suppliers and distributors to create a more seamless flow of goods and services.[17]

Within five years, there will probably be more **mobile** Web users than desktop users.

— Bloomberg BusinessWeek

©iStockphoto.com/hohos

Alternative selling strategies thrive on the Internet, giving rise to a more individualized buying experience. If you've browsed seller reviews on eBay or received shopping recommendations from Amazon, you'll have a sense of how personal web marketing can feel. Online technology also allows leading-edge firms to offer customized products at prices that are comparable to standardized products. On the Scion website, for instance, customers can build their own car and "see it inside and out, with full rotation and zooming" while sitting at home in their pajamas.

As technology continues to evolve at breakneck speed, the scope of change—both in everyday life and business operations—is almost unimaginable. In this environment, companies that welcome change and manage it well will clearly be the winners.

The Social Environment

The social environment embodies the values, attitudes, customs, and beliefs shared by groups of people. It also covers **demographics**, or the measurable characteristics of a population. Demographic factors include population size and density and specific traits such as age, gender, race, education, and income. Clearly, given all these influences, the social environment changes dramatically from country to country. And a nation as diverse as the United States features a number of different social environments. Rather than cover the full spectrum, this section will focus on the broad social trends that have the strongest impact on American business. Understanding the various dimensions

of the social environment is crucial, since successful businesses must offer goods and services that respond to it.

Diversity While the American population has always included an array of different cultures, the United States has become more ethnically diverse in recent years. Caucasians continue to represent the largest chunk of the population at 66%, but the Hispanic and Asian populations are growing faster than any other ethnic groups. If current trends continue, according to the Pew Research Center, the overwhelming bulk of growth in the U.S. population in the coming decades will be due to immigration. In fact, by 2050, about 19% of Americans will be immigrants, compared with 12% in 2005. The Latino population will triple in size, and the Caucasian population will drop to less than half the U.S. population.[18] Exhibit 1.4 demonstrates the shifting population breakdown.

But the national statistics are somewhat misleading, since ethnic groups tend to cluster together. African Americans, for example, currently comprise about 38% of the Mississippi population, Asians comprise about 58% of the Hawaii population, and Hispanics comprise about 47% of the New Mexico population.[19]

So what does this mean for business? Growing ethnic populations offer robust profit potential for firms that pursue them. For instance, a number of major corporations such as AutoZone, Kellogg, Anheuser-Busch, PepsiCo, and

World Wide Web The service that allows computer users to easily access and share information on the Internet in the form of text, graphics, video, apps, and animation.

e-commerce Business transactions conducted online, typically via the Internet.

demographics The measurable characteristics of a population. Demographic factors include population size and density and specific traits such as age, gender, and race.

Exhibit 1.4
U.S. Population Estimates

Population Groups (share of total)

Foreign-born: 12% (2005), 19% (2050)
White: 67% (2005), 47% (2050)
Hispanic: 14% (2005), 29% (2050)
Black: 13% (2005), 13% (2050)
Asian: 5% (2005), 9% (2050)

Source: U.S. Population Projections: 2005 – 2050, February 11, 2008, by Jeffrey S. Passel and D'Vera Cohn, Pew Research Center website, http://pewhispanic.org/files/reports/85.pdf, accessed January 17, 2011

Green Jeans: A Fashion Statement that Really Matters"

Environmentalists have known for years that the greenest fashion statements they can make is to buy little, wash less, and keep stuff longer. Eager to head in a different direction, Levi Strauss introduced organic cotton blue jeans in 2007. This seemed to be an eco-friendly move, since cotton represents only a small fraction of the world's crops, yet uses about 25% of the world's pesticides. But more recently, Levi's has taken a more comprehensive look at its production processes and realized that cotton use is only one small part of its overall impact on the environment. In fact, over the lifetime of its famous 501 jeans, from the cotton fields needed to make the fabric to consumers' tossing their dirty dungarees in the washing machine, each pair uses up 3,480 L of water, which is the equivalent of running a garden hose for 106 minutes. To help conserve water, a vital, increasingly scarce resource, Levi's revamped its production process and introduced Water‹Less jeans, in early 2011. On average, the jeans, which cost the same as conventional ones, use 28% less water in the finishing process. Multiply that by the more than 1.5 million pairs of Water‹Less jeans Levi's expects to sell in the first few months on the market, and the savings add up to approximately 16 million L of water. While the Water‹Less jeans come in several different colors, they can all safely be called green jeans.[20]

Procter & Gamble have invested heavily in the Hispanic market over the past five years. A recent study shows that these heavy-hitters have realized an impressive $4 return on each $1 that they invested in Hispanic marketing. Targeting an ethnic market can also yield remarkable results for products that cross over into mainstream culture. Music mogul and entrepreneur Russell Simmons, for example, initially targeted his music and clothing to the African American market, but his success quickly spilled over to mainstream culture, helping him build a hip-hop empire.[21]

Growing diversity also affects the workforce. A diverse staff—one that reflects an increasingly diverse marketplace—can yield a powerful competitive advantage in terms of both innovation and ability to reach a broad customer base. From global behemoths such as General Electric to local corner stores, companies have taken proactive steps to hire and nurture people from a broad range of backgrounds. And that doesn't just reflect racial or ethnic roots. True diversity also includes differences in gender, age, religion, and nationality, among other areas. Leading-edge firms have also taken proactive steps to train their entire workforce to manage diversity for top performance.[22]

Effectively managing diversity should only become easier as time goes by. Multiple studies demonstrate that young American adults are the most tolerant age group, and they are moving in a more tolerant direction than earlier generations regarding racial differences, immigrants, and homosexuality. As this generation gathers influence and experience in the workforce, they are likely to leverage diversity in their organizations to hone their edge in a fiercely competitive marketplace.[23]

Aging Population As life spans increase and birthrates decrease, the American population is rapidly aging. Its current median age is 36.8 years, and it's increasing month-by-month. If current trends continue, the nation's elderly population will more than double between 2005 and 2050, and the number of working-age Americans will shrink from 63% to 58% of the population, dramatically increasing the number of people who are depending on each working American. And the United States isn't alone in this trend. The population is aging across the developed world, from Western Europe to Japan. China faces the same issue, magnified by its huge population. Demographers estimate that by the middle of the twenty-first century, China will be home to more than 330 million people age 65 or older, who will comprise a whopping 24% of its total population.[24]

The rapidly aging population brings opportunities and threats for business. Companies in fields that cater to the elderly—such as healthcare, pharmaceuticals, travel, recreation, and financial management—will clearly boom. But creative companies in other fields will capitalize on the trend as well by reimagining their current products to serve older clients. Possibilities include books, movies—maybe even video games—with mature characters, low-impact fitness programs such as water aerobics, and cell phones and PDAs with more readable screens. Again, the potential payoff of age diversity is clear: companies with older employees are more likely to find innovative ways to reach the aging consumer market.

But the larger numbers of retired people also pose significant threats to overall business success. With a smaller labor pool, companies will need to compete even harder for top talent, driving up recruitment and payroll costs. As state and federal governments stretch to serve the aging population, taxes may increase, putting an additional burden on business. And as mid-career workers spend more on elder care, they may find themselves with less to spend on other goods and services, shrinking the size of the consumer market.

Rising Worker Expectations Workers of all ages continue to seek flexibility from their employers. Moreover, following massive corporate layoffs in the early 2000s, employees are much less apt to be loyal to their firms. A recent survey shows that only 59% of employees say they are loyal to their companies, and only 26% believe that their companies are loyal to them. As young people today enter the workforce, they bring higher expectations for their employers in terms of salary, job responsibility, and flexibility—and less willingness to pay dues by working extra-long hours or doing a high volume of "grunt work." Smart firms are responding to the change in worker expectations by forging a new partnership with their employees. The goal is a greater level of mutual respect through open communication, information sharing, and training. And the not-so-hidden agenda, of course, is stronger, long-term performance.[25]

Ethics and Social Responsibility With high-profile ethical meltdowns dominating the headlines in the past few years, workers, consumers, and government alike have begun to hold businesses—and the people who run them—to a higher standard. Recent federal legislation, passed in the wake of the Enron fiasco, demands transparent financial management and more accountability from senior executives. And recognizing their key role in business success, a growing number of consumers and workers have begun to insist that companies play a proactive role in making their communities—and often the world community—better places. Sustainability—doing business today without harming

"There need not be any conflict between the environment and the economy."

—AL GORE, NOBEL PEACE PRIZE WINNER

the ability of future generations to meet their needs—has become a core issue in the marketplace, driving business policies, investment decisions, and consumer purchases on an unprecedented scale.[26]

The Global Environment

The U.S. economy operates within the context of the global environment, interacting continually with other economies. In fact, over the last two decades, technology and free trade have blurred the lines between individual economies around the world. Technology has forged unprecedented

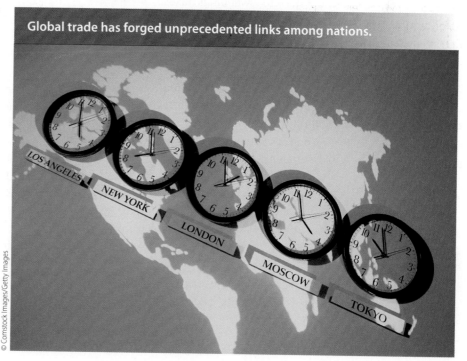

Global trade has forged unprecedented links among nations.

© Comstock Images/Getty Images

© iStockphoto.com/Lasse Kristensen

links among countries, making it cost effective—even efficient—to establish computer help centers in Bombay to service customers in Boston, or to hire programmers in Buenos Aires to make websites for companies in Stockholm. Not surprisingly, jobs have migrated to the lowest bidder with the highest quality—regardless of where that bidder is based.

Often, the lowest bidder is based in China or India. Both economies are growing at breakneck speed, largely because they attract enormous foreign investment. China has been a magnet for manufacturing jobs because of the high population and low wages—an average of 72 cents per hour versus $22.86 per hour in the United States. And India has been especially adept at attracting high-tech jobs, in part because of their world-class, English-speaking university graduates who are willing to work for less than their counterparts around the globe.[27]

The migration of jobs relates closely to the global movement toward **free trade**. In 1995, a re-negotiation of the **General Agreement on Tariffs and Trade (GATT)**—signed by 125 countries—took bold steps to lower tariffs (taxes on imports) and to reduce trade restrictions worldwide. The result: goods move more freely than ever across international boundaries. Individual groups of countries have gone even further, creating blocs of nations with virtually unrestricted trade. Mexico, Canada, and the United States have laid the groundwork for a free-trade mega-market through the North American Free Trade Agreement (NAFTA), and 25 European countries have created a powerful free-trading bloc through the European Union. The free-trade movement has lowered prices and increased quality across virtually every product category, as competition becomes truly global. We'll discuss these issues and their implications in more depth in Chapter 3.

A Multi-Pronged Threat In the past decade alone, war, terrorism, disease, and natural disasters have taken a horrific toll in human lives across the globe. The economic toll has been devastating as well, affecting businesses

In Asia,
the average person's living standards are currently set to rise by 10,000% in one lifetime!

—Newsweek

around the world. The 9/11 terrorist attacks in New York and Washington, D.C., decimated the travel industry and led to multibillion-dollar government outlays for Homeland Security. In 2002 a terrorist bombing at an Indonesian nightclub killed nearly two hundred people, destroying tourism on the holiday island of Bali. The 2003 deadly epidemic of the SARS flu dealt a powerful blow to the economies of Hong Kong, Beijing, and Toronto. Less than two years later, the Indian Ocean tsunami wiped out the fishing industry on long swaths of the Indian and Sri Lankan coastlines and crippled the booming Thai tourism industry. That same year, in 2005, Hurricane Katrina destroyed homes and businesses alike and brought the Gulf Coast oil industry to a virtual standstill. And the war in Iraq—while a boon to the defense industry—has dampened the economic potential of the Middle East. With nationalism on the rise, and growing religious and ethnic tensions around the world, the global economy may continue to suffer collateral damage.[28]

LO6 Business and You: Making It Personal

Whatever your career choice—from video game developer, to real estate agent, to web designer—business will affect your life. Both the broader economy and your own business skills will influence the level of your personal financial success. In light of these factors, making the right career choice can be a bit scary. But the good news is that experts advise graduating students to "Do what you love." And this is a hardheaded strategy, not softhearted puffery. Following your passion makes dollars and sense in today's environment, which values less routine abilities such as creativity, communication, and caring. These abilities tend to be more rewarding for most people than routine, programmable skills that computers can easily emulate. Following your passion doesn't guarantee a fat paycheck, but it does boost your chances of both financial and personal success.[29]

Business today is complex, global, and faster-moving than ever before. Looking forward, the rate of change seems likely to accelerate yet further. While the full impact of the global economic crisis is still unclear, China and India seem poised to gain economic clout, raising worldwide competition to a whole new level. Technology will continue to change the business landscape. And a new focus on ethics and social responsibility will likely transform the role of business in society. This book will focus on the impact of change in every facet of business, from management to marketing to money, with an emphasis on how the elements of business relate to each other, and how business as a whole relates to you.

Business offers a growing range of exciting career opportunities. The possibilities include: accounting, consulting, customer service, entrepreneurship, finance, human resources, marketing, real estate, retail, and sales. The specifics of each job would clearly change, depending on the industry and the company, although the core skills in each area would probably be transferable among industries. Entry-level pay is typically fairly low, but top jobs in business command top dollar. Most positions require at least a college degree, although some demand an advanced degree such as an MBA (Master of Business Administration) or a CPA (Certified Public Accountant). As customers, technology, and the business environment continue to change, your job will likely change considerably over the course of your career, regardless of your specific field. To succeed, you must be a fierce competitor, willing and able to actively embrace change.

CAREERS

What *else?*
RIP & REVIEW CARDS IN THE BACK
and visit www.cengagebrain.com!

2

Economics:
The Framework for Business

LEARNING OBJECTIVES
After studying this chapter, you will be able to...

LO1   Define economics and discuss the evolving global economic crisis

LO2   Analyze the impact of fiscal and monetary policy on the economy

LO3   Explain and evaluate the free market system and supply and demand

LO4   Explain and evaluate planned market systems

LO5   Describe the trend toward mixed market systems

LO6   Discuss key terms and tools to evaluate economic performance

> ## "WE ARE ALL FACED WITH A SERIES OF GREAT OPPORTUNITIES BRILLIANTLY DISGUISED AS IMPOSSIBLE SITUATIONS."
>
> — CHARLES R. SWINDOLL

LO1 Economics: Navigating a Crisis

In September 2008, the United States plunged into a deep economic crisis. The banking system hovered on the edge of collapse. Property values plummeted, and home foreclosure rates soared. Massive layoffs put more than a million Americans out of work. By the end of the year, the stock market had lost more than a third of its value, and financial turmoil in the United States had sparked sequential economic shocks from Europe, to South America, to Asia, and beyond. The outlook was grim.

How did this happen? Why? How could the economy get back on track?

Understanding these issues—and how the government responded to them—requires understanding some basic definitions: The **economy** is essentially a financial and social system. It represents the flow of resources through society, from production, to distribution, to consumption. **Economics** is the study of the choices that people, companies, and governments make in allocating those resources. The field of economics falls into two core categories: macroeconomics and microeconomics. **Macroeconomics** is the study of a country's overall economic dynamics, such as the employment rate, the gross domestic product, and taxation policies. While macroeconomic issues may seem abstract, they directly affect your day-to-day life, influencing key variables such as what jobs will be available for you, how much cash you'll actually take home after taxes,

or how much you can buy with that cash in any given month. **Microeconomics** focuses on smaller economic units such as individual consumers, families, and individual businesses. Both macroeconomics and microeconomics have played an integral role in the global economic crisis.

Global Economic Crisis: How Did This Happen?

The seeds of the crisis were planted more than a decade ago, during a time of prosperity. Through the last half of the 1990s, America enjoyed unprecedented growth. Unemployment was low, productivity was high, inflation was low, and the real standard of living for the average American rose significantly. The American economy grew by more than $2.4 trillion, a jump of nearly 33% in just five years. But the scene changed for the worse when the dot-com bubble burst in 2000, followed by the 9/11 terrorist attacks in 2001. As the stock market dropped and unemployment rose, economic experts feared that the country was hovering on the brink of a full-blown recession.[1]

In an effort to avert recession by increasing the money supply and encouraging investment, the Federal Reserve—the nation's central bank—decreased interest rates from 6.5 % in mid-2000 to 1.25 % by the end of 2002. As a result, the economy was awash with money, but opportunities to invest yielded paltry returns. This is when *subprime mortgage loans* came into play. Most experts define subprime mortgages as loans to borrowers with low credit scores, high debt-to-income ratios, or other signs of a reduced ability to repay the money they borrow.

These subprime mortgage loans were attractive to borrowers and lenders alike. For the borrowers, getting a loan suddenly became a cinch, and for the first time ever, hundreds of thousands of people could afford homes. The lenders were all too willing to give them mortgage loans, sometimes with little or no documentation (such as proof of income), and sometimes with little or no money down. As demand for homes skyrocketed, prices continued to rise year after year. Borrowers took on adjustable-rate loans assuming that when their loans adjusted up—usually sharply up—they could simply refinance their now-more-valuable homes for a new low starter rate and maybe even pull out some cash.

economy A financial and social system of how resources flow through society, from production, to distribution, to consumption.

economics The study of the choices that people, companies, and governments make in allocating society's resources.

macroeconomics The study of a country's overall economic dynamics, such as the employment rate, the gross domestic product, and taxation policies.

microeconomics The study of smaller economic units such as individual consumers, families, and individual businesses.

A *trillion* dollars? Say *what*??

Between stimulating the economy and bailing out the banking system, "a trillion dollars" is a figure you may have heard a lot lately. But getting your mind around what that actually means may be a little tricky, since it's just so much money. To understand the true magnitude of a trillion dollars, consider this:

- ○ If you had started spending a million dollars a day—every day, without fail—at the start of the Roman Empire, you still wouldn't have spent a trillion dollars by 2012; in fact, you'd have more than $250 billion left over

- ○ One trillion dollars, laid end-to-end, would stretch farther than the distance from the earth to the sun. You could also wrap your chain of bills more than 12,000 times around the earth's equator

- ○ If you were to fly a jet at the speed of sound, spooling out a roll of dollar bills behind you, it would take you more than 14 years to release a trillion dollars. But your plane probably couldn't carry the roll, since it would weigh more than one million tons

Turning the economy around may take even more than a trillion dollars, but make no mistake when you hear those numbers thrown around on the news—a trillion dollars is an awful lot of money!

Subprime loans were attractive to lenders because they provided a higher return than many other investments, and—given the growth in housing prices—they seemed relatively low-risk. Banks and investment houses invented a range of stunningly complex financial instruments to slice up and resell the mortgages as specialized securities.

Hedge funds swapped the new securities, convinced that they were virtually risk-free. With a lack of regulation—or any other government oversight—financial institutions did *not* maintain sufficient reserves in case those mortgage-backed funds lost value.

And they did indeed lose value. In 2006, housing prices peaked, and in the months that followed, prices began falling precipitously (see Exhibit 2.1). Increasing numbers of subprime borrowers found themselves "upside down"—they owed their lenders more than the value of their homes. Once this happened, they couldn't refinance to lower their payments. Foreclosure rates climbed at an increasing pace. RealtyTrac, a leading online marketplace for foreclosure properties, reported that foreclosure rates were 33% higher in 2010 than they were in all of 2009. Looking forward, RealtyTrac expects the

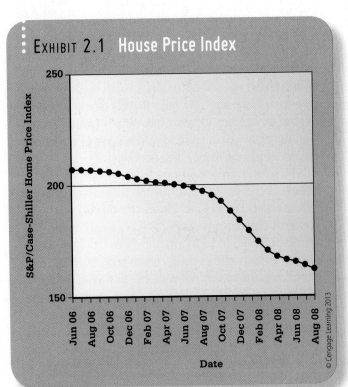

EXHIBIT 2.1 House Price Index

S&P/Case-Shiller Home Price Index (y-axis: 150, 200, 250)

Date (x-axis): Jun 06, Aug 06, Oct 06, Dec 06, Feb 07, Apr 07, Jun 07, Aug 07, Oct 07, Dec 07, Feb 08, Apr 08, Jun 08, Aug 08

© Cengage Learning 2013

A billion here and a billion there, and pretty soon you're talking real

money.

—U.S. Senator Everett Dirksen

trend to continue: "We expect we will top both of those numbers in 2011." The reasons are both continued high unemployment and a backlog of delinquencies working their way through the system.[2]

As mortgage values dropped, financial institutions began to feel the pressure—especially firms such as Bear Stearns that specialized in trading mortgage-backed securities, and firms such as Washington Mutual that focused on selling subprime mortgages. When financial institutions actually began to face collapse, a wave of fear washed over the entire banking industry. Banks became unwilling to lend money to each other or to clients, which meant that funds were not available for businesses to finance either day-to-day operations or longer-term growth. Company after company—from General Motors, to Yahoo!, to American Express, to countless small employers—began to announce layoffs. The December 2008 unemployment rate hit 7.2%. About 2.6 million Americans lost their jobs in 2008, making 2008 the worst year for jobs since 1945. And the unemployment rate continued to rise, hitting 9.3% in 2009, and 9.6% in 2010, leading to total Great Recession job losses of nearly 8 million, many of which will never come back as the economy continues to change, and old skills become obsolete.[3]

Moving in a Better Direction

Although the benefits were not immediately obvious in the face of a downward trend, the Federal Government and the Federal Reserve—known as "the Fed"—intervened in the economy at an unprecedented level to prevent total financial disaster. In March 2008, the Fed staved off bankruptcy at Bear Stearns. In early September 2008, the U.S. Department of the Treasury seized Fannie Mae and Freddie Mac, which owned about half of the U.S. mortgage market. A week later, the Fed bailed out tottering global insurance giant AIG with an $85 billion loan. But the bleeding continued.

The negative spiral spurred Congress to pass a $700 billion economic bailout plan in early October 2008, called TARP (the Troubled Assets Relief Program). By the end of the year, the Treasury had spent the first half of that money investing in banks, although early results were

> # The President
> believes strongly that education is the economic defense budget of the 21st century.
>
> —David Axelrod, Obama's top political strategist

imperceptible for the economy. No sooner had the Treasury begun to release funds to the banks than GM and Chrysler, two of the Big Three U.S. automakers, announced they also desperately needed a bailout. Both firms suggested that bankruptcy was imminent without government assistance. (Ford, the other member of the Big Three, also admitted to financial problems but claimed that it was not in the dire straits faced by its domestic competitors.) Facing the loss of more than 2.5 million auto industry-related jobs, the Treasury agreed to spend a portion of what remained of the $700 billion in a partial auto industry bailout.[4] Although much of the public railed against the expensive government bailout program, by 2010 it appeared likely that that TARP could end up costing taxpayers far less than anticipated, or even nothing, as insurance companies and banks began to break even, or in many cases earn profits, and pay back their government loans.[5]

As the new administration began, President Obama proposed, and Congress passed, an $825 billion economic stimulus package, called the American Recovery and Reinvestment Act, designed to turn the economy around over the next two years. The plan included cutting taxes, building infrastructure, and investing $150 billion in green energy. By early 2011, the economy had begun to turn around at a very slow pace, although unemployment remained high, and economists predicted that the jobless rate would remain painfully high through the middle of the decade.[6]

All of these moves by the federal government and the Federal Reserve are part of fiscal and monetary policy.

LO2 Managing the Economy Through Fiscal and Monetary Policy

While the free market drives performance in the American economy, the federal government and the Federal Reserve can help *shape* performance. During the recent crisis, both the government and the Fed have taken proactive roles to mitigate this economic contraction. The overarching goal is controlled, sustained growth, and both fiscal and monetary policy can help achieve this objective.

Fiscal Policy

fiscal policy Government efforts to influence the economy through taxation and spending.

budget surplus Overage that occurs when revenue is higher than expenses over a given period of time.

budget deficit Shortfall that occurs when expenses are higher than revenue over a given period of time.

federal debt The sum of all the money that the federal government has borrowed over the years and not yet repaid.

Fiscal policy refers to government efforts to influence the economy through taxation and spending decisions that are designed to encourage growth, boost employment, and curb inflation. Clearly, fiscal strategies are closely tied to political philosophy. But regardless of politics, most economists agree that lower taxes can boost the economy by leaving more money in people's pockets for them to spend or invest. Most also agree that government spending can boost the economy in the short term by providing jobs, such as mail carrier, bridge repair, or park ranger, and in the long term by investing in critical public assets, such as a national renewable energy grid. Done well, both taxation and spending can offer economic benefits. The tricky part is finding the right balance between the two approaches.

Every year, the government must create a budget, or a financial plan that outlines expected revenue from taxes and fees, and expected spending. If revenue is higher than spending, the government incurs a **budget surplus** (rare in recent years, but usually quite welcome!). If spending is higher than revenue, the government incurs a **budget deficit** and must borrow money to cover the shortfall. The sum of all the money borrowed over the years and not yet repaid is the total **federal debt**. Exhibit 2.2 shows key sources of revenue and key expenses for the federal government in 2010. Note that spending significantly outstrips receipts, creating a one-year budget deficit of more than a trillion dollars. Clearly, any additional spending without corresponding tax increases could dramatically increase the shortfall.

As of January 2011, the total U.S. federal debt stood at more than $14 trillion, a staggering $45,414 for every U.S.

© Jose Luis Pelaez Inc./Blend Images/Jupiterimages

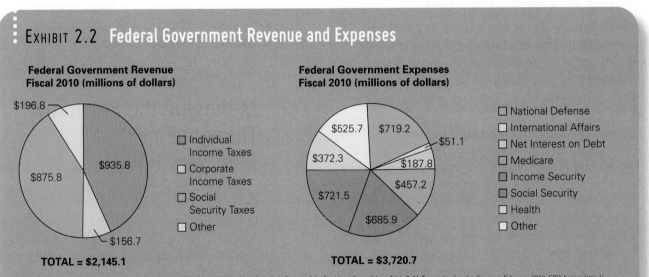

Exhibit 2.2 Federal Government Revenue and Expenses

Federal Government Revenue
Fiscal 2010 (millions of dollars)

$196.8
$935.8
$875.8
$156.7

- ☐ Individual Income Taxes
- ☐ Corporate Income Taxes
- ☐ Social Security Taxes
- ☐ Other

TOTAL = $2,145.1

Federal Government Expenses
Fiscal 2010 (millions of dollars)

$525.7 $719.2
$51.1
$372.3 $187.8
$457.2
$721.5 $685.9

- ☐ National Defense
- ☐ International Affairs
- ☐ Net Interest on Debt
- ☐ Medicare
- ☐ Income Security
- ☐ Social Security
- ☐ Health
- ☐ Other

TOTAL = $3,720.7

Source: Federal receipts, outlays, surplus or deficit, and debt, fiscal years 2006—2011, Economic Report of the President, Spreadsheet Table B-81, Transmitted to the Congress February, 2010, GPO Access. http://www.gpoaccess.gov/eop/tables10.html, accessed January 27, 2011.

The sheer size of the federal debt is tough to grasp for many Americans.

OUR NATIONAL DEBT:
14,524,473,489,013.
YOUR *Family share* 122,921.
THE NATIONAL DEBT CLOCK

© CHIP EAST/Reuters/Landov

citizen (see an online national debt clock at http://brillig.com/debt_clock/ for the latest figures).

The debt has only grown bigger every year since 1957, and the pace of growth will likely increase further in the wake of the economic crisis. This matters to each taxpayer because as the government repays the debt—not to mention paying the skyrocketing interest to finance this debt—less and less money will be available for other uses; services may be eliminated (e.g., student loans, veterans' benefits, housing subsidies), or taxes will soar, or perhaps even both.

Recession Generation: How will the recession affect *your* life?

Evidence abounds that people are deeply affected by cataclysmic events that happened during their youth. In fact, we probably all recognize the thrifty, penny-counting behavior of grandparents or great-grandparents who grew up during the Great Depression. If you were born between 1980 and 1990, you are part of Generation R, the Recession Generation, and the core values, behavior, and psychology of you and your peers has likely been shaped at least in part by the economic downturn. *Newsweek* reports that, "there's an entire body of research to show that recession babies not only invest more conservatively, they tend to make less money, choose safer jobs, and believe in wealth redistribution and more government intervention. Yet paradoxically, they are also more cynical about public institutions and, arguably, about life, embracing the European notion that success is more about luck than effort."

Employment and standard of living will be key issues for the Recession Generation, since the harsh realities of a high unemployment rate are particularly tough for recent graduates with less work experience under their belts. Many members of the Recession Generation will find it difficult, if not impossible, to achieve the same standard of living as their parents. But the Recession Generation will be more geared toward saving rather than spending, and time spent with family and friends, which could ultimately be more satisfying.[7]

© michy/Shutterstock.com

Monetary Policy

Monetary policy refers to actions that shape the economy by influencing interest rates and the supply of money. The Federal Reserve—essentially the central bank of the United States—manages U.S. monetary policy. For the first time in its history, the Fed has also taken an activist role in bailing out and propping up shaky financial firms during the economic crisis. Other Fed functions include banking services for member banks and the federal government.

The Fed is headed by a seven-member Board of Governors. The president appoints each member of the Board to serve a single 14-year term—though a member can also complete a former member's unexpired term and still be appointed to a full term of his or her own. These terms are staggered, with one expiring every two years, so that no single president can appoint all of the members. This structure helps ensure that the Fed can act independently of political pressure.

In addition to setting monetary policy, the Board of Governors oversees the operation of the 12 Federal Reserve Banks that carry out Fed policies and perform banking services for **commercial banks** in their districts. Interestingly, the federal government does not own these Federal Reserve Banks. Instead, they're owned by the member commercial banks in their individual districts.

The President appoints one of the seven members of the Board of Governors to serve as its Chairman—a position so powerful that many consider him the second most powerful person on Earth. For nearly 19 years, the chairman was Alan Greenspan. When Greenspan retired in early 2006, President Bush appointed economist Ben Bernanke to the chairman role. Bernanke has led the Fed's proactive efforts to turn the ailing economy around.

The core purpose of the Fed is to influence the size of the **money supply**—or the total amount of money within the overall economy. Clearly, you know what money is. But the formal definition of **money** is anything generally accepted as a medium of exchange, a measure of value, or a means of payment. The two most commonly used definitions of the money supply are M1 and M2:

- **M1**: All currency—paper bills and metal coins—plus checking accounts and traveler's checks.
- **M2**: All of M1 plus most savings accounts, money market accounts, and certificates of deposit (low-risk savings vehicles with a fixed term, typically less than one year).

As of April 2010, the M1 money supply totaled about $1.7 trillion, and the M2 version of the money supply totaled about $8.5 trillion. In practice, the term "money supply" most often refers to M2. (Note that credit cards are not part of the money supply, although they do have an unmistakable impact on the flow of money through the economy.)[8]

How much money would make you happy?

If you're like most Americans, about $75,000 per year should do the trick. While money does not seem to affect people's changeable day-to-day mood so much, a recent study suggests that those who have a household income of $75,000 or more have a more solid long-term belief that their life is working well, probably because they have more available cash to do things that make them feel good (like going out with friends), so life's daily hassles (e.g., relationship troubles or long commutes) are less grinding. While the study doesn't explain the reason for $75,000, it seems like a plausible number to one of the study's authors, considering that about a third of U.S. households were above that number in 2008. In a global context, the U.S. ranks fifth among 151 nations in happiness, based on surveys of residents, and ninth in the feeling that life is going well, although we all may know plenty of people—both in the U.S. and abroad—who are quite satisfied with their lives on far less than $75,000 per year. So perhaps money isn't quite as connected to happiness as this study suggests.[9]

© Elnur/Shutterstock.com

When the economy contracts, the Fed typically increases the money supply. If more money is available, interest rates usually drop, encouraging businesses to expand and consumers to spend. But when prices begin to rise, the Fed attempts to reduce the money supply. Ideally, if less money is available, interest rates will rise. This will reduce spending, which should bring inflation under control. Specifically, the Fed uses three key tools to expand and contract the money supply: open market operations, discount rate changes, and reserve requirement changes.

Open Market Operations This is the Fed's most frequently used tool. **Open market operations** involve buying and selling government securities, which include treasury bonds, notes, and bills. These securities are the IOUs the government issues to finance its deficit spending.

How do open market operations work? When the economy is weak, the Fed *buys* government securities on the open market. When the Fed pays the sellers of these securities, money previously held by the Fed is put into circulation. This directly stimulates spending. In addition, any of the additional funds supplied by the Fed that are deposited in banks will allow banks to make more loans, making credit more readily available. This encourages even more spending and further stimulates the economy.

When inflation is a concern, the Fed *sells* securities. Buyers of the securities write checks to the Fed to pay for securities they bought, and the Fed withdraws these funds from banks. With fewer funds, banks must cut back on the loans they make, credit becomes tighter, and the money supply shrinks. This reduces spending and cools off the inflationary pressures in the economy.

Open market operations are set by the aptly named Federal Open Market Committee, which consists of the seven members of the Board of Governors and five of the twelve presidents of the Federal Reserve district banks. Each year, the Federal Open Market Committee holds eight regularly scheduled meetings to make decisions about open market operations, although they do hold additional meetings when the need arises. Both businesses and markets closely watch Open Market Committee rate setting and outlook statements in order to guide decision making.

open market operations The Federal Reserve function of buying and selling government securities, which include treasury bonds, notes, and bills.

Federal Deposit Insurance Corporation (FDIC) A federal agency that insures deposits in banks and thrift institutions for up to $250,000 per customer, per bank.

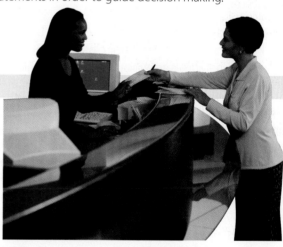

© Keith Brofsky/Photodisc/Getty Images

Looking to Multiply Your Money? Look No Further Than Your Local Bank!

Everyone knows that banks help people save money, but most people don't realize that banks actually create money. While the process is complex, a simplified example illustrates the point: Say you deposit $5,000 in the bank. How much money do you have? Obviously, $5,000. Now imagine that your neighbor Anne goes to the bank for a loan. In line with Federal Reserve requirements, the bank must hold onto about 10% of its funds, so it loans Anne $4,500. She uses the money to buy a used car from your neighbor Jake, who deposits the $4,500 in the bank. How much money does Jake have? Clearly, $4,500. How much money do you have? Still, $5,000. Thanks to the banking system, our "money supply" has increased from $5,000 to $9,500. Multiply this phenomenon times millions of banking transactions, and you can see why cold, hard cash accounts for only about 10% of the total U.S. M2 money supply.[10]

But what happens if everyone goes to the bank at once to withdraw their money? The banking system would clearly collapse. And in fact, in 1930 and 1931, a run on the banks caused wave after wave of devastating bank failures. Panicked customers lost all their savings, ushering in the worst years of the Great Depression. To restore public confidence in the banking system, in 1933 Congress established the **Federal Deposit Insurance Corporation (FDIC)**. The FDIC insures deposits in banks and thrift institutions for up to $100,000 per customer, per bank. In the wake of the banking crisis, the FDIC temporarily increased its coverage to $250,000 per depositor at the end of 2008. Since the FDIC began operations on January 1, 1934, no depositor has lost a single cent of insured funds as a result of a bank failure.[11]

Discount Rate Changes Just as you can borrow money from your bank, your bank can borrow funds from the Fed. And, just as you must pay interest on your loan, your bank must pay interest on loans from the Fed. The **discount rate** is the interest rate the Fed charges on its loans to commercial banks. When the Fed reduces the discount rate, banks can obtain funds at a lower cost and use these funds to make more loans to their own customers. With the cost of acquiring funds from the Fed lower, interest rates on bank loans also tend to fall. The result: businesses and individuals are more likely to borrow money and spend it, which stimulates the economy. Clearly, the Fed is most likely to reduce the discount rate during recessions. In fact, during the early months of the financial crisis, the Fed cut the rate to less than 1%. But in response to inflation—usually a sign of a rapidly expanding economy—the Fed usually increases the discount rate. In response, banks raise the interest rates they charge their customers. Fewer businesses and individuals are willing to take loans, which ultimately slows down the economy and reduces inflation.[12]

Reserve Requirement Changes The Fed requires that all of its member banks hold funds called "reserves," equal to a stated percentage of the deposits held by their customers. This percentage is called the **reserve requirement** (or required reserve ratio). The reserve requirement helps protect depositors who may want to withdraw their money without notice. Currently, the reserve requirement stands at about 10%, depending on the size and type of a bank's deposits. If the Fed increases the reserve requirement, banks must hold more funds, meaning they will have fewer funds available to make loans. This makes credit tighter and causes interest rates to rise. If the Fed decreases the reserve requirement, some of the funds that banks were required to hold become available for loans. This increases the availability of credit and causes interest rates to drop. Since changes in the reserve requirement can have a dramatic impact on both the economy and the financial health of individual banks, the Fed uses this tool quite infrequently.

Other Fed Functions In addition to monetary policy, the Fed has several other core functions, including regulating financial institutions and providing banking services both for the government and for banks. In its role as a regulator, the Fed sets and enforces rules of conduct for

25% of people in the U.S. rarely or never use a bank.

—Time Magazine

banks and oversees mergers and acquisitions to ensure fairness and compliance with government policy. The Fed will likely become even more proactive regarding regulation in the wake of the financial crisis. In its role as a banker for banks, the Fed coordinates the check-clearing process for checks on behalf of any banks that are willing to pay its fees. And as the government's bank, the Fed maintains the federal government's checking account and keeps the U.S. currency supply in good condition.

LO3 Capitalism: The Free Market System

It's a simple fact, more clear now than ever before: no one can get everything they want all of the time. We live in a world of finite resources, which means that societies must determine how to distribute resources among their members. An **economic system** is a structure for allocating limited resources. Over time and around the globe, nations have instituted different economic systems. But a careful analysis suggests that no system is perfect, which may explain why there isn't one standard approach. The next sections of this chapter examine each basic type of economic system and explore the trend toward mixed economies.

The economic system of the United States is called **capitalism**, also known as a "private enterprise system" or a "free market system." Brought to prominence by Adam

Smith in the 1700s, capitalism is based on private ownership, economic freedom, and fair competition. One core capitalist principle is the paramount importance of individuals, innovation, and hard work. In a capitalist economy, individuals, businesses, or nonprofit organizations privately own the vast majority of enterprises. (Only a small fraction are owned by the government.) These private-sector businesses are free to make their own choices regarding everything from what they will produce, to how much they will charge, to whom they will hire and fire. Correspondingly, individuals are free to choose what they will buy, how much they are willing to pay, and where they will work.

To thrive in a free enterprise system, companies must offer value to their customers—otherwise, their customers will choose to go elsewhere. Businesses must also offer value to their employees and suppliers in order to attract top-quality talent and supplies. As companies compete to attract the best resources and offer the best values, quality goes up, prices remain reasonable, and choices proliferate, raising the standard of living in the economy as a whole.

The Fundamental Rights of Capitalism

For capitalism to succeed, the system must ensure some fundamental rights—or freedoms—to all of the people who live within the economy.

- ⊃ *The right to own a business and keep after-tax profits:* Remember that capitalism doesn't guarantee that anyone will actually *earn* profits. Nor does it promise that there won't be taxes. But if you do earn profits, you get to keep your after-tax income and spend it however you see fit (within the limits of the law, of course). This right acts as a powerful motivator for business owners in a capitalist economy; the lower the tax rate, the higher the motivation. The U.S. government strives to maintain low tax rates to preserve the after-tax profit incentive that plays such a pivotal role in the free enterprise system.

- ⊃ *The right to private property:* This means that individuals and private businesses can buy, sell, and use property—which includes land, machines, and buildings—in any way that makes sense to them. This right also includes the right to will property to family members. The only exceptions to private property rights are minimal government restrictions designed to protect the greater good. You can't, for instance, use your home or business to produce cocaine, abuse children, or spew toxic smoke into the air.

- ⊃ *The right to free choice:* Capitalism relies on economic freedom. People and businesses must be free to buy (or not buy) according to their wishes. They must be free to choose where to work (or not work) and where to live (or not live). Freedom of choice directly feeds competition, creating a compelling incentive for business owners to offer the best goods and services at the lowest prices. U.S. government trade policies boost freedom of choice by encouraging a wide array of both domestic and foreign producers to compete freely for our dollars.

- ⊃ *The right to fair competition:* A capitalist system depends on fair competition among businesses to drive higher quality, lower prices, and more choices. Capitalism can't achieve its potential if unfair practices—such as deceptive advertising, predatory pricing, and broken contracts—mar the free competitive environment. The government's role is to create a level playing field by establishing regulations and monitoring the competition to ensure compliance.

Four Degrees of Competition

While competition is essential for the free market system to function, not all competition works the same. Different industries experience different degrees of competition, ranging from pure competition to monopolies.

- ⊃ **Pure competition** is a market structure with many competitors selling virtually identical products. Since customers can't (or won't) distinguish one product from another, no single producer has any control over the price. And new producers can easily enter and leave purely competitive markets. In today's U.S. economy, examples of pure competition have virtually disappeared. Agriculture probably comes closest—corn is basically corn, for example—but with the dramatic growth of huge corporate farms and the success of major cooperatives such as Sunkist, the number of competitors in agriculture has dwindled, and new farmers have trouble entering the market. Not only that, segments of the agriculture market—such as organic farms and hormone-free dairies—have emerged with hit products that command much higher prices than the competition.

- ⊃ **Monopolistic competition** is a market structure with many competitors selling differentiated products. (Caution! Monopolistic competition is quite different from

pure competition A market structure with many competitors selling virtually identical products. Barriers to entry are quite low.

monopolistic competition A market structure with many competitors selling differentiated products. Barriers to entry are low.

a *monopoly,* which we will cover shortly.) Producers have some control over the price of their wares, depending on the value that they offer their customers. And new producers can fairly easily enter categories marked by monopolistic competition. In fact, in monopolistic competition, a successful product usually attracts new suppliers quite quickly. Examples of monopolistic competition include the clothing industry and the restaurant business.

Think about the clothing business, for a moment, in local terms. How many firms do you know that sell tee shirts? You could probably think of at least 50 without too much trouble. And the quality and price are all over the board: designer tee shirts can sell for well over $100, but plenty of options go for less than $10. How hard would it be to start your own tee shirt business? Probably not hard at all. In fact, chances are strong that you know at least one person who sells tee shirts on the side. In terms of product and price variation, number of firms, and ease of entry, the tee shirt business clearly demonstrates the characteristics of monopolistic competition.

◉ **Oligopoly** is a market structure with only a handful of competitors selling products that can be similar or different. The retail gasoline business and the car manufacturing industry, for instance, are both oligopolies, even though gas stations offer very similar products, and car companies offer quite different models and features. Other examples of oligopoly include the soft drink industry, the computer business, and network television. Breaking into a market characterized by oligopoly can be tough because it typically requires a huge upfront investment.

Green Guilt

Since about two-thirds of Americans claim to be active in or sympathetic with the environmental movement, you would think it would be easy to encourage people to engage in eco-friendly behavior such as bringing their own bags to the grocery store in lieu of using plastic bags, or turning on fans during a heat wave rather than just cranking the air conditioning. But changing behavior can tough, and a key tool that the government can use is taxes. In 2010, Washington, D.C., imposed a hefty five-cent tax on every disposable bag, paper or plastic, handed out at any retail outlet in the city that sold food, candy, or liquor. But authorities believe that the magic bullet that caused disposable bag usage to plummet in D.C. was not the tax, but rather the fact that suddenly; "shoppers had to ask for them—right in front of their fellow customers." The same dynamic was at work in a recent study in San Marcos, CA. One group of residents was told that 77% of their neighbors already used fans rather than air conditioning. Those residents reduced their energy consumption by 10% relative to a control group, and they maintained the reduction over the long run. Peer pressure appears to be equally powerful around the world. *The Wall Street Journal* reports that "researchers at Michigan State University found that paying Chinese farmers to adopt environmentally friendly techniques didn't work as well as telling them that their neighbors were already farming that way. And a recent study in India found that publishing a ranked list of the worst-polluting paper factories prodded the biggest offenders to make dramatic improvements." Many of us scoff at the idea that peer pressure motivates us, but the pull of the crowd may be more powerful than we realize.[13]

You could start making tee shirts in your kitchen, for instance, but you'd need a pretty expensive facility to start manufacturing cars. Oligopolies typically avoid intense price competition, since they have nothing to gain— every competitor simply makes less money. When price wars do flare up, the results can be devastating for entire industries.

◉ **Monopoly** is a market structure with just a single producer completely dominating the industry, leaving no room for any significant competitors. Monopolies usually aren't good for anyone but the company that has control, since without competition there isn't any incentive to hold down prices or increase quality and choices. Because monopolies can harm the economy, most are illegal according to federal legislation, such as the Sherman Antitrust Act of 1890 and the Clayton Antitrust Act of 1914. Microsoft is the latest example of an industry giant that ran afoul of antimonopoly laws due to its position and policies in the software business. Even though Microsoft is not an actual monopoly, it was convicted of "monopolistic practices" that undermined fair competition.

However, in a few instances, the government not only allows monopolies, but actually encourages them. This usually occurs when it would be too inefficient for each competitor to build its own infrastructure to serve the public. A **natural monopoly** arises. Cable television offers a clear example. Would it really make sense for even a handful of competitors to wire neighborhoods separately for cable? Clearly, that's not practical. Just imagine the chaos! Instead, the government has granted cable franchises—or monopolies—to individual companies and then regulated them (with mixed results) to ensure that they don't abuse the privilege. In addition to natural monopolies, the government grants patents and copyrights, which create artificial monopoly situations (at least temporarily) in order to encourage innovation.

that commands a higher market price and less of a product that commands a lower price. Think about it in terms of pizza: Assume it costs a local restaurant about $5 to make a pizza. If the market price for pizza hits, say, $20, you can bet that restaurant will start cranking out pizza. But if the price drops to $6, the restaurant has much less incentive to focus on pizza and will probably invest its limited resources in cooking other, more pricy, dishes.

The relationship between price and quantity from a supplier standpoint can be shown on a graph called the **supply curve.** The supply curve maps quantity on the x-axis (or horizontal axis) and price on the y-axis (or vertical axis). In most categories, as the price rises, the quantity produced rises correspondingly, yielding a graph that curves up as it moves to the right. Exhibit 2.3 shows a possible supply curve for pizza.

Demand Demand refers to the quantity of products that consumers are willing to buy at different market prices.

natural monopoly A market structure with one company as the supplier of a product because the nature of that product makes a single supplier more efficient than multiple, competing ones. Most natural monopolies are government sanctioned and regulated.

supply The quantity of products that producers are willing to offer for sale at different market prices.

supply curve The graphed relationship between price and quantity from a supplier standpoint.

demand The quantity of products that consumers are willing to buy at different market prices.

Supply and Demand: Fundamental Principles of a Free Market System

In a free market system, the continual interplay between buyers and sellers determines the selection of products and prices available in the economy. If a business makes something that few people actually want, sales will be low, and the firm will typically yank the product from the market. Similarly, if the price of a product is too high, low sales will dictate a price cut. But if a new good or service becomes a hit, you can bet that similar offerings from other firms will pop up almost immediately (unless barriers—such as government-granted patents—prevent new entrants). The concepts of supply and demand explain how the dynamic interaction between buyers and sellers directly affects the range of products and prices in the free market.

Supply Supply refers to the quantity of products that producers are willing to offer for sale at different market prices. Since businesses seek to make as much profit as possible, they are likely to produce more of a product

EXHIBIT 2.3 Supply Curve

Price per Pizza ($) (y-axis), Quantity of Pizza Supplied per Day (in Thousands) (x-axis)

© Cengage Learning 2013

demand curve The graphed relationship between price and quantity from a customer demand standpoint.

mkt price

equilibrium price The price associated with the point at which the quantity demanded of a product equals the quantity supplied.

socialism An economic system based on the principle that the government should own and operate key enterprises that directly affect public welfare.

Since consumers generally seek to get the products they need (or want) at the lowest possible prices, they tend to buy more products with lower prices and fewer products with higher prices. Pizza and tacos, for instance, are both popular meals. But if pizza costs a lot less than tacos, most people will get pizza more often than tacos. Likewise, if the price of pizza were out of hand, people would probably order tacos (or some other option) more often, reserving their pizza-eating for special occasions.

The relationship between price and quantity from a demand standpoint can be shown on a graph called the **demand curve.** Like the supply curve, the demand curve maps quantity on the *x*-axis and price on the *y*-axis. But different from the supply curve, the demand curve for most goods and services slopes downward as it moves to the right, since the quantity demanded tends to drop as prices rise. Exhibit 2.4 shows how a demand curve for pizza could look.

Equilibrium Price It's important to remember that supply and demand don't operate in a vacuum. The constant interaction between the two forces helps determine the market price in any given category. In theory, market prices adjust toward the point where the supply

EXHIBIT 2.5 Equilibrium

Price per Pizza ($)

Quantity of Pizza per Day (in Thousands)

© Cengage Learning 2013

curve and the demand curve intersect (see Exhibit 2.5). The price associated with this point of intersection—the point where the quantity demanded equals the quantity supplied—is called the **equilibrium price,** and the quantity associated with this point is called the "equilibrium quantity."

LO 4 Planned Economies: Socialism and Communism

In capitalist economies, private ownership is paramount. Individuals own businesses, and their personal fortunes depend on their success in the free market. But in planned economies, the government plays a more heavy-handed role in controlling the economy. The two key categories of planned economies are socialism and communism.

Socialism

Socialism is an economic system based on the principle that the government should own and operate key enterprises that directly affect public welfare, such as utilities, telecommunications, and healthcare. Although

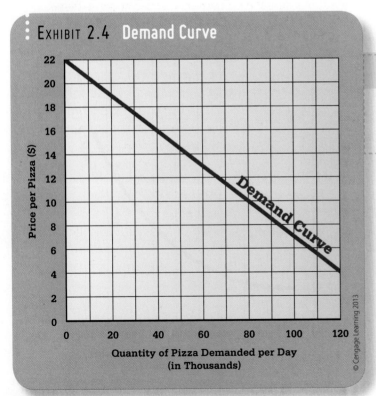

EXHIBIT 2.4 Demand Curve

Price per Pizza ($)

Demand Curve

Quantity of Pizza Demanded per Day (in Thousands)

© Cengage Learning 2013

the official government goal is to run these enterprises in the best interest of the overall public, inefficiencies and corruption often interfere with effectiveness. Socialist economies also tend to have higher taxes, which are designed to distribute wealth more evenly through society. Tax revenues typically fund services that citizens in free enterprise systems would have to pay for themselves in countries with lower tax rates. Examples range from free childcare to free university education to free public healthcare systems. Critics of the recent government intervention in the U.S. economy believe that the new moves have pushed us too far in a socialist direction.

Most Western European countries—from Sweden, to Germany, to the United Kingdom—developed powerful socialist economies in the decades after World War II. But more recently, growth in these countries has languished. Although many factors have contributed to the slowdown, the impact of high taxes on the profit incentive and lavish social programs on the work incentive has clearly played a role. Potential entrepreneurs may migrate to countries that let them keep more of their profits, and workers with abundant benefits may find themselves losing motivation. In late 2010, many of these economies imposed stiff austerity measures to control government spending, eliminating some public benefits many took for granted.

Communism

Communism is an economic and political system that calls for public ownership of virtually all enterprises, under the direction of a strong central government. The communist concept was the brainchild of political philosopher Karl Marx, who outlined its core principles in his 1848 *Communist Manifesto*. The communism that Marx envisioned was supposed to dramatically improve the lot of the worker at the expense of the super-rich.

But countries that adopted communism in the 1900s—most notably the former Soviet Union, China, Cuba, North Korea, and Vietnam—did not thrive. Most imposed authoritarian governments that suspended individual rights and choices. People were unable to make even basic choices such as where to work or what to buy. Without the free market to establish what to produce, crippling shortages and surpluses developed. Corruption infected every level of government. Under enormous pressure from their own people and the rest of the world, communism began to collapse across the Soviet Union

and its satellite nations at the end of the 1980s, replaced with democracy and the free market. Over the past two decades, China has also introduced significant free market reforms across much of the country, fueling its torrid growth rate. And in the 1990s, Vietnam launched free market reforms, stimulating rapid, sustained growth. The remaining communist economic systems— North Korea and Cuba—continue to falter, their people facing drastic shortages and even starvation.

communism An economic and political system that calls for public ownership of virtually all enterprises, under the direction of a strong central government.

mixed economies Economies that embody elements of both planned and market-based economic systems.

privatization The process of converting government-owned businesses to private ownership.

LO5 Mixed Economies: The Story of the Future

In today's world, pure economies—market or planned— are practically nonexistent, since each would fall far short of meeting the needs of its citizens. A pure market economy would make insufficient provision for the old, the young, the sick, and the environment. A pure planned economy would not create enough value to support its people over the long term. Instead, most of today's nations have **mixed economies**, falling somewhere along a spectrum that ranges from pure planned at one extreme to pure market at the other.

Even the United States—one of the most market-oriented economies in the world—does not have a *pure* market economy. The various departments of the government own a number of major enterprises, including the postal service, schools, parks, libraries, entire systems of universities, and the military. In fact, the federal government is the nation's largest employer, providing jobs for more than 4 million Americans. And—although the government does not directly *operate* firms in the financial sector—the federal government has become part owner in a number of financial institutions as part of the recent bailouts. The government also intervenes extensively in the free market by creating regulations that stimulate competition and protect both consumers and workers. Regulations are likely to become stronger in the wake of the economic crisis.[14]

Over the past 30 years, most economies of the world have begun moving toward the market end of the spectrum. Government-owned businesses have converted to private ownership via a process called **privatization**. Socialist governments have reduced red tape, cracked

gross domestic product (GDP) The total value of all final goods and services produced within a nation's physical boundaries over a given period of time.

unemployment rate The percentage of people in the labor force over age 16 who do not have jobs and are actively seeking employment.

down on corruption, and created new laws to protect economic rights. Extravagant human services—from free healthcare to education subsidies—have shrunk. And far-reaching tax reform has created new incentives for both domestic and foreign investment in once-stagnant planned economies.[15]

Unfortunately, the price of economic restructuring has been a fair amount of social turmoil in many nations undergoing market reforms. Countries from France to China have experienced sometimes violent demonstrations in response to social and employment program cutbacks. Change is challenging, especially when it redefines economic winners and losers. But countries that have taken strides toward the market end of the spectrum—from small players like the Czech Republic, to large players like China—have seen the payoff in rejuvenated growth rates that have raised the standard of living for millions of people.

L06 Evaluating Economic Performance: What's Working?

Clearly, economic systems are complex—very complex. So you probably won't be surprised to learn that no single measure captures all the dimensions of economic performance. To get the full picture, you need to understand a range of terms and measures, including gross domestic product, employment level, the business cycle, inflation rate, and productivity.

Gross Domestic Product

Real **gross domestic product**, or GDP, measures the total value of all final goods and services produced within a nation's physical boundaries over a given period of time, adjusted for inflation. (Nominal GDP does not include an inflation adjustment.) All domestic production is included in the GDP, even when the producer is foreign-owned. The U.S. GDP, for instance, includes the value of Toyota pickup trucks built in Texas, even though Toyota is a Japanese firm. Likewise, the Mexican GDP includes the value of Whirlpool appliances built in Mexican factories, even though Whirlpool is an American firm.

GDP is a vital measure of economic health. Business people, economists, and political leaders use GDP to measure the economic performance of individual nations and

Raising a child from birth to age 17 costs about $222,000 (not including college!).

— U.S. DEPARTMENT OF AGRICULTURE

to compare the growth among nations. Interestingly, GDP levels tend to be somewhat understated, since they don't include any illegal activities—such as paying undocumented nannies and gardeners, or selling illegal drugs—which can represent a significant portion of some countries' production. The GDP also ignores legal goods that are not reported to avoid taxation, plus output produced within households. In 2010, the GDP of the United States was just over $14.7 trillion, reflecting a tepid 2.7% growth rate versus 2009.[16] Check out Chapter 3 for a survey of the world's key economies according to total GDP and GDP growth rate.

Employment Level

The overall level of employment is another key element of economic health. When people have jobs, they have money, which allows them to spend and invest, fueling economic growth. Most nations track employment levels largely through the **unemployment rate**, which includes everyone age 16 and older who doesn't have a job and is actively seeking one. The U.S. unemployment rate climbed precipitously through the Great Recession, rising from 5.8% in 2008 to 9.3% in 2009, to 9.4% by December 2010. As the economy began its glacially slow turnaround, competition for new job openings was fierce, since the recession wiped out a staggering 8 million jobs, leaving a record 70 applicants to contend for each open position.[17]

GDP is a vital measure of economic health.

© James Shearman/Atomic Imagery/Digital Vision/Jupiterimages

Interestingly, some unemployment is actually good—it reflects your freedom to change jobs. If you have an awful boss, for instance, you may just quit. If you quit, are you unemployed? Of course you are. Are you glad? You probably are, and in normal times, the chances are good that you'll find another position that's a better fit for you. This type of job loss is called *frictional unemployment*, and it tends to be ultimately positive. *Structural unemployment*, on the other hand, is usually longer-term. This category encompasses people who don't have jobs because the economy no longer needs their skills. In the United States, growing numbers of workers in the past decade have found themselves victims of structural unemployment as manufacturing jobs have moved overseas. Often their only option is expensive retraining. Two other categories of unemployment are *cyclical*, which involves layoffs during recessions, and *seasonal*, which involves job loss related to the time of year. In some areas of the country, construction and agricultural workers are seasonally unemployed, but the best example may be the department store Santa who has a job only during the holiday season!

The Business Cycle

The **business cycle** is the periodic contraction and expansion that occurs over time in virtually every economy. But the word "cycle" may be a little misleading, since it implies that the economy contracts and expands in a predictable pattern. In reality, the phases of the cycle are different each time they happen, and—despite the efforts of countless experts—no one can accurately predict when changes will occur or how long they will last. Those who make the best guesses stand to make fortunes, but bad bets can be financially devastating. The two key phases of the business cycle are contraction and expansion, shown in Exhibit 2.6.

○ **Contraction** is a period of economic downturn, marked by rising unemployment. Businesses cut back on production, and consumers shift their buying patterns to more basic products and fewer luxuries. The economic "feel-good factor" simply disappears. Economists declare an official **recession** when GDP decreases for two consecutive quarters. A **depression** is an especially deep and long-lasting recession. Fortunately, economies seldom spiral into severe depressions, thanks in large part to proactive intervention from the government. The last depression in the United States was the Great Depression of the 1930s. Whether a downturn is mild or severe, the very bottom of the contraction is called the "trough," as shown in Exhibit 2.6.

> It's a recession when your neighbor loses his job; it's a depression when you lose yours.
>
> — HARRY TRUMAN

EXHIBIT 2.6 The Business Cycle

Total National Output (GDP)

Time (Years)

Peak
Recovery
Peak
Contraction
Trough
Expansion

© Cengage Learning 2013

○ **Recovery** is a period of rising economic growth and increasing employment, following a contraction. Businesses begin to expand. Consumers start to regain confidence, and spending begins to rise. The recovery is essentially the transition period between contraction and expansion.

○ **Expansion** is a period of robust economic growth and high employment. Businesses expand to capitalize on emerging opportunities. Consumers are optimistic and confident, which fuels purchasing, which fuels production, which fuels further hiring. As Exhibit 2.6 demonstrates, the height of economic growth is called the peak of the expansion. The U.S. economy had the longest growth spurt on record during the ten-year period from 1991 to 2001. After a relatively mild slowdown in 2001–2002, the U.S. economy again expanded for several years before it plunged into a full-blown recession in 2008.[18]

Price Levels

The rate of price changes across the economy is another basic measure of economic well-being. **Inflation** means that prices, on average, are rising. Similar to unemployment, a low level of inflation is not so bad. It reflects a healthy economy—people have money, and they are willing to spend it. But when the Federal Reserve—the nation's central bank—manages the economy poorly, inflation can spiral out of control, which can lead to **hyperinflation**, when average prices increase more than 50% per month. In Hungary, for example, inflation in its unstable, post–World War II economy climbed so quickly that prices doubled every fifteen hours from 1945 to 1946. More recently, prices in the war-torn former Yugoslavia doubled every sixteen hours between October 1993 and January 1994.

When the rate of price increases slows down, the economy is experiencing **disinflation**, which was the situation in the United States in the mid-1990s and more recently in the second half of 2008. But when prices actually decrease, the economy is experiencing **deflation**, typically a sign of economic trouble that goes hand-in-hand with very high unemployment. People don't have money and simply won't spend unless prices drop. During the Great Depression in the 1930s, the U.S. economy experienced deflation, with prices dropping 9% in 1931 and nearly 10% in 1932. Despite some economic turmoil, inflation in the United States was relatively low from 2000 to 2007, hovering at around 3%. But inflation picked up in the first half of 2008, only to fall during the first months of the economic crisis, remaining low throughout 2009 and 2010.

The government uses two major price indexes to evaluate inflation: the **consumer price index (CPI)** and the **producer price index (PPI)**. The CPI measures the change in weighted-average price over time in a consumer "market basket" of goods and services that the average person buys each month. The U.S. Bureau of Labor Statistics creates the basket—which includes hundreds of items such as housing, transportation, haircuts, wine, and pet care—using data from more than 30,000 consumers. While the market basket is meant to represent the average consumer, keep in mind that the "average" includes a lot of variation, so the CPI may not reflect your personal experience. For example, as a college student, you may be painfully sensitive to increases in tuition and the price of textbooks—a fact the authors of this particular textbook fully realize! But tuition and textbook prices aren't a big part of the "average" consumer's budget, so increases in these prices have a relatively small impact on the CPI.

The PPI measures the change over time in weighted-average wholesale prices, or the prices that businesses pay each other for goods and services. Changes in the PPI can sometimes predict changes in the CPI because producers tend to pass on price increases (and sometimes also price decreases) to consumers within a month or two of the changes.

Productivity

Productivity refers to the relationship between the goods and services that an economy produces and the resources needed to produce them. The amount of output—goods and services—divided by the amount of input (e.g., hours worked) equals productivity. The goal, of course, is to produce more goods and services, using fewer hours and other inputs. A high level of productivity typically correlates with healthy GDP growth, while low productivity tends to correlate with a more stagnant economy.

Over the past couple of decades, the United States has experienced strong productivity growth, due largely to infusions of technology that help workers produce more output, more quickly. But keep in mind that that productivity doesn't measure quality. That's why it's so important to examine multiple measures of economic health rather than relying on simply one or two dimensions.

THE BIG PICTURE

From a business standpoint, one key goal of economics is to guide your decision-making by offering a deeper understanding of the broad forces that affect both your business and your personal life. Knowing even basic economic principles can help you make better business decisions in virtually every area—from production, to marketing, to accounting, to name just a few—regardless of your specific function or level within an organization.

But you won't find an economics department within many (if any) businesses—rather, you'll find people across the organization applying economic theories and trends to their work, even in the face of continual economic flux. As you read through the other chapters in this book, take a moment to consider both the macroeconomic and microeconomic forces that affect each area you study. You're likely to find a surprising number of examples.

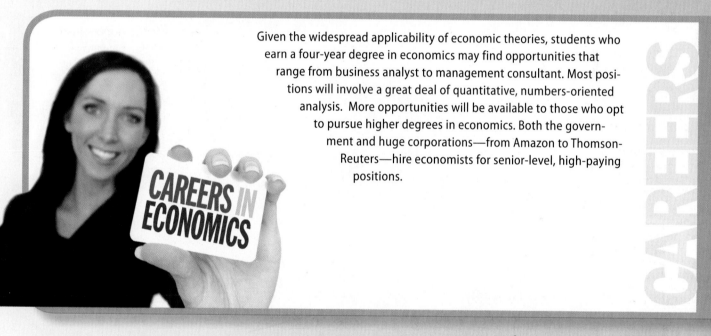

Given the widespread applicability of economic theories, students who earn a four-year degree in economics may find opportunities that range from business analyst to management consultant. Most positions will involve a great deal of quantitative, numbers-oriented analysis. More opportunities will be available to those who opt to pursue higher degrees in economics. Both the government and huge corporations—from Amazon to Thomson-Reuters—hire economists for senior-level, high-paying positions.

CAREERS

Evaluating the economy
Gross Domestic Product
Unemployment Rate
consumer Price Index
Producer Price Index
Productivity

Managing the economy
Fiscal Policy
- taxation
- Govt spending
- controlled by congress/Budget Process
Monetary Policy
- supply & demand of money
- cost of credit
- controlled by the Federal Reserve
  • 7 Member Board
  • Chairman

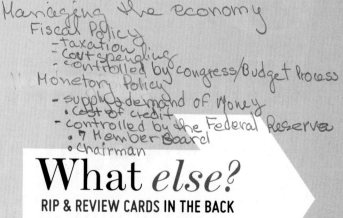

What else?
RIP & REVIEW CARDS IN THE BACK
and visit www.cengagebrain.com!

3

The World Marketplace:
Business Without Borders

LEARNING OBJECTIVES
After studying this chapter, you will be able to...

LO1 Discuss business opportunities in the world economy

LO2 Explain the key reasons for international trade

LO3 Describe the tools for measuring international trade

LO4 Analyze strategies for reaching global markets

LO5 Discuss barriers to international trade and strategies to surmount them

LO6 Describe the free-trade movement and discuss key benefits and criticisms

A COMPANY THAT KEEPS ITS EYE ON TOM, DICK, AND HARRY IS GOING TO MISS PIERRE, HANS, AND YOSHIO.

— AL RIES, MARKETING STRATEGIST AND AUTHOR

LO1 An Unprecedented Opportunity

As access to technology skyrockets and barriers to trade continue to fall, individual economies around the world have become more interdependent than ever before. The result is a tightly woven global economy marked by intense competition and huge, shifting opportunities. The long-term potential for U.S. business is enormous. Although the global economic crisis caused the world GDP to contract in 2009 for the first time since World War II, compared with average increases of about 3.5% per year since 1946, world GDP growth turned positive again in 2010, expanding +4.6% led by lower-income countries, which averaged +6.3% growth, versus higher-income countries, which averaged just +2.8% growth.[1] See Exhibit 3.1 for a sampling of some specific higher- and lower-growth countries.

A quick look at population trends validates the global business opportunity, especially in developing nations. With more than 300 million people, the United States accounts for less than 4.6% of the world's total population. More than 6.4 billion people live beyond our borders, representing more than 95% of potential customers for U.S. firms. But even though the growth rates in many high-population countries are strong, most of these nations remain behind the United States in terms of development and prosperity, posing considerable challenges for foreign firms. (In other words, most of their populations may not have the resources to buy even basic goods and services.) The issue is likely to become even more severe in the wake of the global economic crisis. Exhibit 3.1, a comparison of population, GDP growth rate, and per capita GDP for the world's six largest nations, highlights some of the discrepancies. Note that even though U.S. consumers clearly have money, China and India represent a much bigger opportunity in terms of both sheer size and economic growth.

The growing number of people with cell phones offers an interesting indicator of economic growth. Several

EXHIBIT 3.1 Selected Population and GDP Figures

NATION	POPULATION*	PER CAPITA GDP (U.S. DOLLARS)**	GDP GROWTH RATE***
CHINA	1,330,141,295	$7,400	+10.3%
INDIA	1,173,108,618	$3,400	+8.3%
EUROPEAN UNION	492,387,344	$32,900	+1.7%
UNITED STATES	310,232,863	$47,400	+2.8%
INDONESIA	240,271,522	$4,300	+6.0%
BRAZIL	198,739,269	$10,700	+7.5%

*CIA World Factbook, 2010 Population Estimates, updated February 2010.
**CIA World Factbook, 2010 GDP Estimates, updated February 2010.
***CIA World Factbook, 2010 GDP Growth Estimates, updated February 2010.
Source: Rank Order Estimates, CIA—The World Factbook website: https://www.cia.gov/library/publications/the-world-factbook/rankorder/2004rank.html, accessed February 7, 2010, https://www.cia.gov/library/publications/the-world-factbook/rankorder/2003rank.html, accessed February 7, 2010; https://www.cia.gov/library/publications/the-world-factbook/rankorder/2119rank.html, accessed February 7, 2010.

recent studies have found that if a country increases cell phone penetration by 10 percentage points, GDP will likely increase by anywhere from +.5% to +1.2%. That may seem small, but it equates to somewhere between $49 and $118 billion for an economy the size of China. In other words, when the percentage of the population with cell phones goes up, the entire economy benefits.

Not surprisingly, cell phone penetration in India and China is skyrocketing. China currently boasts the world's largest base of cell phone users—about 766 million—and the growth will likely continue. India's current subscriber base is more than 584 million; it has grown explosively over the last five years and seems likely to follow suit in the next decade. The growth may well continue until China and India hit the 100%+ cell phone penetration rates that characterize a number of developed nations such as Taiwan, Hong Kong, Germany, and Argentina, which have more than one phone per person. In the United States, Europe, and Japan, cell phones followed landlines, but large swaths of developing nations aren't bothering to build conventional phone service. Rather, they're moving directly to cell phone networks. This trend is particularly marked across Africa, where cell phone penetration rates in 2009 were approximately 21% versus 9% for land lines.

The developing world boasts nearly double the cell phone subscriptions in advanced economies.

— THE WASHINGTON POST

In Zimbabwe, for instance, cell phone penetration grew from 4% in 2008 to about 30% in 2009. David Knapp, general director of Motorola Vietnam, points out that many developing nations "can leapfrog technology." And Vietnamese micro-entrepreneur Nguyen Huu Truc says, "It's no longer something that only the rich can afford. Now, it's a basic means of communication." As more people get the chance to get connected, better communication will likely feed economic growth. The upshot is that millions of people worldwide will have a higher standard of living.[2]

Unimpressive Scores

Every three years, the Organization for Economic Cooperation & Development tests 15-year-olds in thirty-four countries. Test results in 2010 showed unequivocally that American students must improve in order to compete effectively in a global economy. U.S. students ranked twenty-fifth among peers from thirty-four countries on a math test and scored in the middle in science and reading. China, Singapore, and South Korea led the pack, outpacing American students by a significant margin. U.S. Education Secretary of Education, Arne Duncan commented "This should be a massive wake-up call to the entire country." But even some of the high-scoring countries face problems with their students. A recent survey of 1,500 South Korean public-school students, for instance, found that 29.3% of them exhibited signs of video game addiction. In response to this growing problem, the South Korean government set a curfew for online play in 2010 and mandated an automated blackout period after midnight for underage players. China has also experienced issues with compulsive gaming among young people. And the United States isn't immune to these issues, either. A global study published in early 2011 found that across cultures, somewhere around 7–11% of gamers are addicted to the point of damaging other areas of their lives (e.g., school, families, social interactions). Specifically, the findings showed addiction levels at: Singapore (9.0%), the United States (8.5%), China (10.3%), Australia (8.0%), Germany (11.9%) and Taiwan (7.5%). Regardless of gaming issues, American students clearly need to up their academic game in order to score successful futures in a fiercely competitive, increasingly globalized world market.[3]

LO2 Key Reasons for International Trade

Companies engage in global trade for a range of reasons beyond the obvious opportunity to tap into huge and growing new markets. The benefits include better access to factors of production, reduced risk, and an inflow of new ideas.

- *Access to factors of production:* International trade offers a valuable opportunity for individual firms to capitalize on factors of production that simply aren't present in the right amount for the right price in each individual country. India, China, and the Philippines, for example, attract multibillion-dollar investments because of their large cohort of technically skilled university graduates who work for about one-fifth the pay of comparable American workers. Russia and the OPEC nations offer a rich supply of oil, and Canada, like other forested nations, boasts an abundant supply of timber. The United States offers plentiful capital, which is less available in other parts of the world. International trade helps even out some of the resource imbalances among nations.

- *Reduced risk:* Global trade reduces dependence on one economy, lowering the economic risk for multinational firms. When the Japanese economy entered a deep, sustained slump in the 1990s, for instance, Sony and Toyota thrived through their focus on other, healthier markets around the world. But a word of caution is key: as national economies continue to integrate, an economic meltdown in one part of the world can have far-reaching impact. Major foreign banks, for example, were badly burned by the U.S. subprime market mess, due to heavy investments in U.S. mortgage markets.

- *Inflow of innovation:* International trade can also offer companies an invaluable source of new ideas. Japan, for instance, is far ahead of the curve regarding cell phone service. Japanese cell phone "extras," including games, ringtones, videos, and stylish new accessories, set the standard for cell service around the world. In Europe, meanwhile, consumers are seeking to bring a top-quality pub experience into their homes

Africa holds 40% of the world's strategic raw materials, including gold, iron ore, and oil.

— TIME MAGAZINE

opportunity cost
The opportunity of giving up the second-best choice when making a decision.

absolute advantage The benefit a country has in a given industry when it can produce more of a product than other nations using the same amount of resources.

comparative advantage The benefit a country has in a given industry if it can make products at a lower opportunity cost than other countries.

balance of trade A basic measure of the difference in value between a nation's exports and imports, including both goods and services.

trade surplus Overage that occurs when the total value of a nation's exports is higher than the total value of its imports.

trade deficit Shortfall that occurs when the total value of a nation's imports is higher than the total value of its exports.

balance of payments A measure of the total flow of money into or out of a country.

balance of payments surplus Overage that occurs when more money flows into a nation than out of that nation.

with professional-quality home beer taps. Companies with a presence in foreign markets experience budding trends like these firsthand, giving them a jump in other markets around the world.[4]

Competitive Advantage

Beyond individual companies, industries tend to succeed on a worldwide basis in countries that enjoy a competitive advantage. But to understand competitive advantage, you need to first understand how **opportunity cost** relates to international trade. When a country produces more of one good, it must produce less of another good (assuming that resources are finite). The value of the second-best choice—the value of the production that a country gives up in order to produce the first product—represents the opportunity cost of producing the first product.

A country has an **absolute advantage** when it can produce more of a good than other nations, using the same amount of resources. China, for example, has an absolute advantage in terms of clothing production, relative to the United States. But having an absolute advantage isn't always enough. Unless they face major trade barriers, the industries in any country tend to produce products for which they have a **comparative advantage**—meaning that they tend to turn out those goods that have the lowest opportunity cost compared to other countries. The United States, for instance, boasts a comparative advantage versus most countries in movie and television program production; Germany has a comparative advantage in the production of high-performance cars; and South Korea enjoys a comparative advantage in electronics.

But keep in mind that comparative advantage seldom remains static. As technology changes and the workforce evolves (through factors such as education and experience), nations may gain or lose comparative advantage in various industries. China and India, for example, are both seeking to build a comparative advantage versus other

nations in technology production by investing in their infrastructure and their institutions of higher education.

L03 Global Trade: Taking Measure

After a decade of robust growth, global trade began slowing in 2007, due largely to turbulence in the worldwide financial markets. In 2008, the rate of growth in world trade slid below 5%, as the global recession tightened its grip. In 2009, global trade plummeted nearly 25% in U.S. dollar terms, and 12% in terms of overall volume from 2008's level, the largest single-year drop since World War II. Global gross fixed investment fell about 4% year-over-year, or by roughly $800 billion. The global trade recover...

rate, although...
omy may dan...
gross fixed in...
global world p...
trade on indivi...
balance of trad...

Balance o...

The **balance of** ...
between a natio...
exports is higher...
has a **trade surplus**...
the total value ...
Balance of trade...
services, and it in...
Although a trade...
that can afford to ...
large deficit can be...
goods and services...
challenge with reg...
United States has ...
and as the American...
the trade deficit has...
over the next few ...
response to the glob...

Balance of Pay...

Balance of payments is a...
into or out of a count...
a central role in dete...
But the balance of pay...
flows such as foreig...
aid payments and re...
A **balance of payments**...

279360 Costco 125
1006 Wabash Ave
Eureka, CA

Member# 111767156156
Invoice #   26899
Date   03/28/13
Time   08:08
Auth #   487717

DB Acct #
XXXXXXXXXXXX3207

Pump   Gallons   Price
  10   10.911 $ 4.079

Product   Amount
Unleaded $ 44.51

Total Sale $ 44.51

SALE - Card Swiped
APPROVED
TranID#308700521829

We appreciate your
Costco membership

40   PART 1: The Business Environment

STRONG DOLLAR VERSUS EURO: WHO BENEFITS? (EXAMPLE: $1.00 · 1.20 EUROS)	WEAK DOLLAR VERSUS EURO: WHO BENEFITS? (EXAMPLE: $1.00 · .60 EUROS)
U.S. travelers to Europe: Their dollars can buy more European goods and services.	*European travelers to the United States:* Their dollars buy more American goods and services.
American firms with European operations: Operating costs—from buying products to paying workers—are lower.	*European firms with American operations:* Operating costs—from buying products to paying workers—are lower.
European exporters: Their products are less expensive in the United States, so Europe exports more, and we import more.	*American exporters:* Their products are less expensive in Europe, so we export more, and Europe imports more.

© Cengage Learning 2013

flows in than out, while a **balance of payments deficit** means that more money flows out than in. Keep in mind that the balance of payments typically corresponds to the balance of trade, since trade is, in general, the largest component.

Exchange Rates

Exchange rates measure the value of one nation's currency relative to the currency of other nations. While the exchange rate does not directly measure global commerce, it certainly has a powerful influence on how global trade affects individual nations and their trading partners. The exchange rate of a given currency must be expressed in terms of another currency. Here are some examples of how the exchange rate can influence the economy, using the dollar and the euro.

Countertrade

A complete evaluation of global trade must also consider exchanges that don't actually involve money. A surprisingly large chunk of international commerce—possibly as much as 25%—involves the barter of products for products rather than for currency. Companies typically engage in **countertrade** to meet the needs of customers that don't have access to hard currency or credit, usually in developing countries. Individual countertrade agreements range from simple barter

to a complex web of exchanges that end up meeting the needs of multiple parties. Done poorly, countertrading can be a confusing nightmare for everyone involved. But done well, countertrading is a powerful tool for gaining customers and products that would not otherwise be available.[6]

L04   Seizing the Opportunity: Strategies for Reaching Global Markets

There is no one "right way" to seize the opportunity in global markets. In fact, the opportunity may not even make sense for every firm. While international trade can offer new profit streams and lower costs, it also introduces a higher level of risk and complexity to running a business. Being ready to take on the challenge can mean the difference between success and failure.

Firms ready to tap the opportunity have a number of options for how to move forward. One way is to seek foreign suppliers through outsourcing and importing. Another possibility is to seek foreign customers through exporting, licensing, franchising, and direct investment. These market development options fall in a spectrum from low cost–low control to high cost–high control, as shown in Exhibit 3.2. In other words, companies that choose to export products to a foreign country spend less to enter that market than companies that choose to build their own factories. But companies that build their own factories have a lot more

Foreign Investment Risk

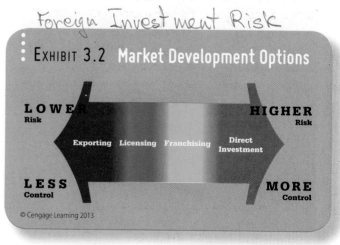

EXHIBIT 3.2 Market Development Options

LOWER Risk — Exporting Licensing Franchising Direct Investment — HIGHER Risk

LESS Control — MORE Control

© Cengage Learning 2013

foreign outsourcing
(also contract manufacturing) Contracting with foreign suppliers to produce products, usually at a fraction of the cost of domestic production.

importing Buying products domestically that have been produced or grown in foreign nations.

exporting Selling products in foreign nations that have been produced or grown domestically.

control than exporters over how their business unfolds. Keep in mind that profit opportunity and risk—which vary along with cost and control—also play a critical role in how firms approach international markets.

Smaller firms tend to begin with exporting and move along the spectrum as the business develops. But larger firms may jump straight to the strategies that give them more control over their operations. Large firms are also likely to use a number of different approaches in different countries, depending on the goals of the firm and the structure of the foreign market. Regardless of the specific strategy, most large companies—such as General Electric, Nike, and Disney—both outsource with foreign suppliers and sell their products to foreign markets.

Foreign Outsourcing and Importing

Foreign outsourcing means contracting with foreign suppliers to produce products, usually at a fraction of the cost of domestic production. Gap, for instance, relies on a network of manufacturers in fifty different countries, mostly in less-developed parts of the world, from Asia, to Africa, to Central America. Apple depends on firms in China and Taiwan to produce the iPhone. And countless small companies contract with foreign manufacturers as well. The key benefit, of course, is dramatically lower wages, which drive down the cost of production.

But while foreign outsourcing lowers costs, it also involves significant risk. Quality control typically requires very detailed specifications to ensure that a company

gets what it actually needs. Another key risk of foreign outsourcing involves social responsibility. A firm that contracts with foreign producers has an obligation to ensure that those factories adhere to ethical standards. Deciding what those standards should be is often quite tricky, given different cultures, expectations, and laws in different countries. And policing the factories on an ongoing basis can be even harder than determining the standards. But companies that don't get it right face the threat of significant consumer backlash in the United States and Europe. This has been a particular issue with products produced in China. In the recent past, for instance, product defects forced U.S. firms to recall a host of Chinese-produced toys, including Thomas the Tank Engine trains that were coated with toxic lead paint, ghoulish fake eyeballs that were filled with kerosene, and Polly Pocket dolls that posed a swallowing hazard.[7]

Many Americans have become personally familiar with the quality/cost tradeoff as a growing number of companies have outsourced customer service to foreign call centers. Research suggests that the approximate cost of offering a live, American-based, customer service agent averages about $7.50 per call, while outsourcing those calls to live agents in another country drops the average cost down to about $3.25 per call. But customers end up paying the difference in terms of satisfaction, reporting high levels of misunderstanding, frustration, and inefficiency. A number of firms – such as jetBlue – have enjoyed the best of both worlds by outsourcing customer service calls to U.S. agents who work from their own homes.[8]

Importing means buying products from overseas that have already been produced, rather than contracting with overseas manufacturers to produce special orders. Imported products, of course, don't carry the brand name of the importer, but they also don't carry as much risk. Pier 1 Imports, a large retail chain, has built a powerful brand around the importing concept, creating stores that give the customer the sense of a global shopping trip without the cost or hassle of actually leaving the country.

Most of the clothing you're wearing right now was probably produced in another country.

© LUCIOPIX/ALAMY

Exporting

Exporting is the most basic level of international market development. It simply means producing products domestically and selling them abroad. Exporting represents an especially strong opportunity for small and mid-sized companies. Ernest Joshua, for instance, developed a thriving Arkansas-based hair care company that specializes in products for African Americans. Recognizing opportunity abroad, his firm now exports products to Africa and the Caribbean.[9]

Foreign Licensing and Foreign Franchising

Foreign licensing and foreign franchising, the next level of commitment to international markets, are quite similar. **Foreign licensing** involves a domestic firm granting a foreign firm the rights to produce and market its product or to use its trademark/patent rights in a defined geographical area. The company that offers the rights, or the *licensor*, receives a fee from the company that buys the rights, or the *licensee*. This approach allows firms to expand into foreign markets with little or no investment, and it also helps circumvent government restrictions on importing in closed markets. But maintaining control of licensees can be a significant challenge. Licensors also run the risk that unethical licensees may become their competitors, using information that they gained from the licensing agreement. Foreign licensing is especially common in the food and beverage industry. The most high-profile examples include Coke and Pepsi, which grant licenses to foreign bottlers all over the world.

© Mystic Arabia/Alamy

Foreign franchising is a specialized type of licensing. A firm that expands through foreign franchising, called a *franchisor*, offers other businesses, or *franchisees*, the right to produce and market its products if the franchisee agrees to specific operating requirements—a complete package of how to do business. Franchisors also often offer their franchisees management guidance, marketing support, and even financing. In return, franchisees pay both a start-up fee and an ongoing percentage of sales to the franchisor. One key difference between franchising and licensing is that franchisees assume the identity of the franchisor. A McDonald's franchise in Paris, for instance, is clearly a McDonald's, not, say, a Pierre's Baguette outlet that also carries McDonald's products.

Foreign Direct Investment

Direct investment in foreign production and marketing facilities represents the deepest level of global involvement. The cost is high, but companies with direct investments have more control over how their business operates in a given country. The high-dollar commitment also represents significant risk if the business doesn't go well. Most direct investment takes the form of either acquiring foreign firms or developing new facilities from the ground up. Another increasingly popular approach is strategic alliances or partnerships that allow multiple firms to share risks and resources for mutual benefit.

Foreign acquisitions enable companies to gain a foothold quickly in new markets. In 2009, for example, Italian carmaker Fiat took over struggling U.S. auto giant Chrysler, with plans to more fully exploit the American market in the wake of the Great Recession. A number of other global giants, such as Microsoft, General Electric, and Nestlé, tend to follow a foreign acquisition strategy.[10]

Developing new facilities from scratch—or "offshoring"—is the most costly form of direct investment. It also involves significant risk. But the benefits include complete control over how the facility develops and the potential for high profits, which makes the approach attractive for corporations that can afford it. Intel, for instance, plans to build a $2.5 billion specialized computer chip manufacturing plant in northeastern China. And foreign car companies, from German Daimler-Benz, to Korean Hyundai, to Japanese Toyota, have built factories in the southern United States.[11]

Joint ventures involve two or more companies joining forces—sharing resources, risks, and profits, but not merging companies—to pursue specific opportunities. A formal, long-term agreement is usually called a **partnership**, while a less formal, less encompassing agreement is usually called a **strategic alliance**. Joint ventures are a popular, though controversial, means of entering foreign markets. Often a foreign company connects with a local firm to ease its way into the market. In fact, some countries, such as Malaysia, require that foreign investors have local partners. But research from Harvard finance professor Mihir Desai finds that joint ventures between multinational firms and

Obstacles are those frightful things you see when you take your eyes off your goal.

— Henry Ford, Founder of Ford Motor Company

domestic partners can be more costly and less rewarding than they initially appear. He and his team suggest that they make sense only in countries that require local political and cultural knowledge as a core element of doing business.[12]

LO5 Barriers to International Trade

Every business faces challenges, but international firms face more hurdles than domestic firms. Understanding and surmounting those hurdles is the key to success in global markets. Most barriers to trade fall into the following categories: sociocultural differences, economic differences, and legal/political differences. As you think about these barriers, keep in mind that each country has a different mix of barriers. Often countries with the highest barriers have the least competition, which can be a real opportunity for the first international firms to break through.

Sociocultural Differences

Sociocultural differences include differences among countries in language, attitudes, and values. Some specific, and perhaps surprising, elements that affect business include nonverbal communication, forms of address, attitudes toward punctuality, religious celebrations and customs, business practices, and expectations regarding meals and gifts. Understanding and responding to sociocultural factors are vital for firms that operate in multiple countries. But since the differences often operate at a subtle level, they can undermine relationships before anyone is aware that it's happening. The best way to jump over sociocultural barriers is to conduct thorough consumer research, cultivate first-hand knowledge, and practice extreme sensitivity. The payoff can be a sharp competitive edge. Hyundai, for instance, enjoys a whopping 17% share of the passenger car market in India. It beat the competition with custom features that reflect Indian culture, such as elevated rooflines to provide more headroom for turban-wearing motorists.[13]

Economic Differences

Before entering a foreign market, it's critical to understand and evaluate the local economic conditions. Key factors to consider include population, per capita income, economic growth rate, currency exchange rate, and stage of economic development. But keep in mind that low scores for any of these measures don't necessarily equal a lack of opportunity. In fact, some of today's biggest opportunities are in countries with low per capita income. For example, the Indian division of global giant Unilever gets 50% of its sales from rural India by selling products to individual consumers in tiny quantities, such as two-cent sachets of shampoo. The rural Indian market has been growing so dramatically that in 2010,

©Nelson Ching/Bloomberg via Getty Images

To Spend or Not to Spend

Both common sense and basic economics suggest that spending more than you earn is a bad idea both for individuals and for countries. In the U.S., we see the results of this reckless policy in a multi-trillion-dollar federal debt that threatens to overwhelm future generations. And over a million Americans file personal bankruptcy each year. China, however, may need to encourage its citizens to save less and spend more. Healthy consumer spending is crucial for long-term economic health; when consumer spending falters, economic growth eventually staggers as well. In line with traditional Confucian thinking, many Chinese save a full third of after-tax income (compared to a personal savings rate of around 5% in the U.S. in 2010), planning for old age, storing up reserves for emergencies, and creating their own social "safety nets." Another factor dampening consumption is that Chinese financial markets for household borrowing – mortgage debt, personal loans, and credit cards are underdeveloped. One startling example is that General Motors reports that 90% of Buicks – a bestseller in China – are purchased with stacks and stacks of cold hard cash, virtually unheard of in the United States, where checks, credit cards, and financing are the norm. Looking forward, China seems likely to encourage greater consumption to maintain its blistering pace of economic growth. One positive result for the U.S. should be a reduction in the huge trade deficit with China, which will bolster the American economy.[14]

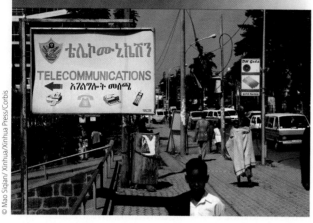

Foreign markets can differ dramatically in terms of infrastructure development.

the Chairman on Hindustan Unilever declared, "What we have done in the last 25 years we want to do it in the next two years," scaling up the reach of its consumer products from about 250,000 rural retail outlets to about 750,000. And Hewlett-Packard has recently joined forces with Unilever to give microdistributors in rural India the ability to check prices and place orders online from "what are now distinctively offline villages and regions." Also capitalizing on the rapid growth and increased demand, Samsung has introduced Guru, a mobile phone that can be charged with solar power, to rural India.[15]

Effectively serving less-developed markets requires innovation and efficiency. Emerging consumers often need different product features, and they almost always need lower costs. C. K. Prahalad, an influential business scholar, believed that forward-thinking companies can make a profit in developing countries if they make advanced technology affordable. Many markets are simply so large that high-volume sales can make up for low-profit margins.

Overall, the profit potential is clear and growing. And as consumers in developing countries continue to gain income—although at a much slower pace in the wake of the economic crisis—companies that established their brands early will have a critical edge over firms that enter the market after them.

Infrastructure should be another key economic consideration when entering a foreign market. Infrastructure refers to a country's physical facilities that support economic activity. It includes basic systems in each of the following areas:

⊙ Transportation (e.g., roads, airports, railroads, and ports)

⊙ Communication (e.g., TV, radio, Internet, and cell phone coverage)

⊙ Energy (e.g., utilities and power plants)

⊙ Finance (e.g., banking, checking, and credit)

The level of infrastructure can vary dramatically among countries. In Africa, for instance, only 11% of the population has Internet access, compared to 77% in North America. In

> **infrastructure** A country's physical facilities that support economic activity.

Veggie Surprise, Anyone?

Travel around the world, and you're likely to see American fast-food franchisees in virtually every city. Although you'll surely recognize the names of these fast-food behemoths, you may not be as familiar with the food that they serve, since many of the dishes have been completely changed in response to local culture.

Some favorites from the Domino's international menus:

⊙ Japan: squid pizza

⊙ England: tuna and sweet corn pizza

⊙ South Korea: broccoli and potato pizza

⊙ Netherlands: grilled lamb pizza

Pizza Hut:

⊙ Japan: crust stuffed with shrimp nuggets and injected with mayonnaise

⊙ South Korea: crust filled with sweet potato mousse

McDonald's:

⊙ India: Paneer Salsa Wrap (cottage cheese with Mexican-Cajun coating)

⊙ Australia: Bacon and Egg Roll ("Rashers of quality bacon and fried egg")

⊙ Kuwait: Veggie Surprise Burger (no detailed description…yikes!)

⊙ United Kingdom: Five "Toasted Deli" sandwich options[16]

Vietnam and Thailand, many consumers buy products directly from vendors in small boats, compared to firmly grounded stores in Europe. While credit card purchases are still relatively low in much of the world, particularly in Asia, recent growth has been explosive and will probably continue for the next few years.[17]

Political and Legal Differences

Political regimes obviously differ around the world, and their policies have a dramatic impact on business. The specific laws and regulations that governments create around business are often less obvious, yet they can still represent a significant barrier to international trade. To compete effectively—and to reduce risk—managers must carefully evaluate these factors and make plans to respond to them both now and as they change.

Laws and Regulations International businesses must comply with international legal standards, the laws of their own countries, and the laws of their host countries. This can be a real challenge, since many developing countries change business regulations with little notice and less publicity. The justice system can pose another key challenge, particularly with regard to legal enforcement of ownership and contract rights. Since 2003, The World Bank has published a "Doing Business" report that ranks the ease of doing business for small and medium-sized companies in 183 different countries. The 2011 "Doing Business" report presented the encouraging news that in the past five years, about 85% of the world's economies have made it easier for local entrepreneurs to operate, through 1,511 improvements to business regulation. For the fifth year running, Singapore leads in the ease of doing business, followed by Hong Kong SAR China, New Zealand, the United Kingdom, and the United States. China and India are among the top 40 most-improved economies. The "Doing Business" project examines the ease of doing business from nine different angles, including the ease of dealing with construction permits to paying taxes to enforcing contracts.[18] The key benefit of an effective legal system is that it reduces risk for both domestic and foreign businesses.

Bribery, the payment of money for favorable treatment, and corruption, the solicitation of money for favorable treatment, are also major issues throughout the world. While bribery and corruption are technically illegal in virtually every major country, they are often accepted as a standard way of doing business. Regardless, U.S. corporations and American citizens are subject to prosecution by U.S. authorities for offering bribes in any nation. See Chapter 4 for more details.

Global Greening: The Ultimate Group Project

Global greening can only happen if every major nation does its share in making it happen. But like any group project, no one will make the grade unless every country participates as significantly as possible. The good news is that global greening seems to be on a roll. According to a 2010 report from the nonprofit Pew Environment Group, overall global investment in clean energy grew 230 percent from 2005 to 2009. And in 2009, in the face of the worldwide economic downturn, investments in clean energy declined only 6.6 percent from 2008. Demonstrating its staying power, the clean energy sector outperformed the oil and gas industry, which experienced investment declines of 19 percent in 2009. The United States leads the world in terms of renewable energy capacity, followed by China, Germany, Spain, and India. In a positive sign for the future, many governments prioritized clean energy within economic recovery funding, devoting more than $184 billion of public stimulus investments to the sector. The bulk of the funds will likely reach innovators, businesses and installers in 2010 and 2011. Looking further forward, students can probably expect that the clean energy sector will offer job opportunities for a number of decades to come as the nations of the world continue to work together to achieve global greening.[19]

Political Climate The political climate of any country deeply influences whether that nation is attractive to foreign business. Stability is crucial. A country subject to strife from civil war, riots, or other violence creates huge additional risk for foreign business. Yet, figuring out how to operate in an unstable environment such as Russia, Bolivia, or the Middle East, can give early movers a real advantage. Grant Winterton, Coca-Cola's regional manager for Russia, commented to *Time* magazine that "the politics do concern us." But having snagged 50% of the $1.9 billion carbonated-soft-drink market, he concludes that "the opportunity far outweighs the risk." Poor enforcement of intellectual property rights across international borders is another tough issue for business. Fortunately, there has been some progress. The Business Software Alliance piracy-tracking study found that worldwide piracy rates increased two percentage points to 43% in 2009 (vs. 2008), which was lower than expected given the economic pressure of the Great Recession; in fact, the rate of PC software piracy dropped in 49% of the 111 economies studied. The highest-piracy countries are Georgia, Zimbabwe, Bangladesh, Moldava, Armenia, and Yemin, all over 90%.[20]

International Trade Restrictions National governments also have the power to erect barriers to international business through a variety of international trade restrictions. The arguments for and against trade restrictions—also called **protectionism**—are summarized below. As you read, note that most economists find the reasons to eliminate trade restrictions much more compelling than the reasons to create them.

Just as trade restrictions have a range of motivations, they can take a number of different forms. The most common trade restrictions are tariffs, quotas, voluntary export restraints, and embargos.

- **Tariffs** are taxes levied against imports. Governments tend to use protective tariffs either to shelter fledgling industries that couldn't compete without help, or to shelter industries that are crucial to the domestic economy. In 2002, for instance, the United States imposed tariffs of 8% to 30% on a variety of imported steel products for a period of three years, in order to give some relief to the large, but ailing, U.S. steel industry.

- **Quotas** are limitations on the amount of specific products that may be imported from certain countries during a given time period. Russia, for instance, has specific quotas for U.S. meat imports.

- **Voluntary Export Restraints (VERs)** are limitations on the amount of specific products that one nation will export to another nation. Although the government of the exporting country typically imposes VERs, they usually do so out of fear that the importing country would impose even more onerous restrictions. As a result, VERs often aren't as "voluntary" as the name suggests. The United States, for instance, insisted on VERs with Japanese auto exports in the early 1980s (which many economists believe ultimately precipitated the decline of the U.S. auto industry).

- An **embargo** is a total ban on the international trade of a certain item, or a total halt in trade with a particular nation. The intention of most embargoes is to pressure the targeted country to change political policies or to protect national security. The U.S. embargo against trade with Cuba offers a high-profile example.

Quotas, VERs, and embargoes are relatively rare compared to tariffs, and tariffs are falling to new lows. But as tariffs decrease, some nations are seeking to control imports through nontariff barriers such as:

- Requiring red-tape-intensive import licenses for certain categories

- Establishing nonstandard packaging requirements for certain products

- Offering less-favorable exchange rates to certain importers

- Establishing standards on how certain products are produced or grown

- Promoting a "buy national" consumer attitude among local people

Nontariff barriers tend to be fairly effective because complaints about them can be hard to prove and easy to counter.[21]

protectionism National policies designed to restrict international trade, usually with the goal of protecting domestic businesses.

tariffs Taxes levied against imports.

quotas Limitations on the amount of specific products that may be imported from certain countries during a given time period.

voluntary export restraints (VERs) Limitations on the amount of specific products that one nation will export to another nation.

embargo A complete ban on international trade of a certain item, or a total halt in trade with a particular nation.

free trade The unrestricted movement of goods and services across international borders.

General Agreement on Tariffs and Trade (GATT) An international trade treaty designed to encourage worldwide trade among its members.

L06 Free Trade: The Movement Gains Momentum

Perhaps the most dramatic change in the world economy has been the global move toward **free trade**—the unrestricted movement of goods and services across international borders. Even though *complete* free trade is not a reality, the emergence of regional trading blocks, common markets, and international trade agreements has moved the world economy much closer to that goal.

GATT and the World Trade Organization

The **General Agreement on Tariffs and Trade (GATT)** is an international trade accord designed to encourage worldwide trade among its members. Established in 1948 by 23 nations, GATT has undergone a number of revisions. The most significant changes stemmed from the 1986–1994 Uruguay Round of negotiations, which took bold steps to slash average tariffs by about 30%

and to reduce other trade barriers among the 125 nations that signed.

The Uruguay Round also created the **World Trade Organization (WTO)**, a permanent global institution to promote international trade and to settle international trade disputes. The WTO monitors provisions of the GATT agreements, promotes further reduction of trade barriers, and mediates disputes among members. The decisions of the WTO are binding, which means that all parties involved in disputes must comply to maintain good standing in the organization. Ministers of the WTO meet every two years to address current world trade issues. As the world economy has shifted toward services rather than goods, the emphasis of WTO meetings has followed suit. Controlling rampant piracy of intellectual property is a key concern for developed countries. For less-developed countries, one central issue is U.S. and European agricultural subsidies, which may unfairly distort agricultural prices worldwide.

In fact, both the broader agenda and the individual decisions of the WTO have become increasingly controversial over the past ten years. Advocates for less-developed nations are deeply concerned that free trade clears the path for major multinational corporations to push local businesses into economic failure. A local food stand, for instance, probably won't have the resources to compete with a global giant such as McDonald's. If the food stand closes, the community has gained inexpensive hamburgers, but the entrepreneur has lost his livelihood, and the community has lost the local flavor that contributes to its unique culture. Other opponents of the WTO worry that the acceleration of global trade encourages developing countries to fight laws that protect the environment and workers' rights, for fear of losing their low-cost advantage on the world market. The concerns have sparked significant protests during the past few meetings of the WTO ministers, and the outcry may well grow louder as developing nations gain economic clout.

The World Bank

Established in the aftermath of World War II, the **World Bank** is an international cooperative of 187 member countries, working together to reduce poverty in the developing world. The World Bank influences the global economy by providing financial and technical advice to the governments of developing countries for projects in a range of areas including infrastructure, communications, health, and education. The financial assistance usually comes in the form of low-interest loans. But to secure a loan, the borrowing nation must often agree to conditions that can involve rather arduous economic reform.

The International Monetary Fund

Like the World Bank, the **International Monetary Fund (IMF)** is an international organization accountable to the governments of its 187 member nations. The basic mission of the IMF is to promote international economic cooperation and

World peace through international trade and commerce.

— HILTON HOTEL'S CORPORATE MOTTO

REASONS TO *CREATE* TRADE RESTRICTIONS	REASONS TO *ELIMINATE* TRADE RESTRICTIONS
Protect domestic industry (e.g., the U.S. steel industry)	Reduce prices and increase choices for consumers by encouraging competition from around the world
Protect domestic jobs in key industries (but perhaps at the cost of domestic jobs in other industries)	Increase domestic jobs in industries with a comparative advantage versus other countries
Protect national security interests	Increase jobs—both at home and abroad—from foreign companies
Retaliate against countries who have engaged in unfair trade practices	Build exporting opportunities through better relationships with other countries
Pressure other countries to change their policies and practices	Use resources more efficiently on a worldwide basis

stable growth. Funding comes from the member nations, with the United States contributing more than twice as much as any other country. To achieve these goals, the IMF:

- ◯ Supports stable exchange rates
- ◯ Facilitates a smooth system of international payments
- ◯ Encourages member nations to adopt sound economic policies
- ◯ Promotes international trade
- ◯ Lends money to member nations to address economic problems.

Although all of its functions are important, the IMF is best known as a lender of last resort to nations in financial trouble. This policy has come under fire in the past few years. Critics accuse the IMF of encouraging poor countries to borrow more money than they can ever hope to repay, which actually cripples their economies over the long term, creating even deeper poverty.

At the end of 2005, the IMF responded to its critics by implementing a historic debt relief program for poor countries. Under this program, which has since been expanded to include other agencies, the IMF and its partners have extended 100% debt forgiveness to 40 poor countries, erasing about $75 billion in debt. The managing director of the IMF pointed out that the canceled debt will allow these countries to increase spending in priority areas to reduce poverty and promote growth (although some experts worry that debt cancellation sets a troubling precedent for future lending). The result should be a higher standard of living for some of the poorest people in the world.[22]

> **Over the** past 40 years, life expectancy in developing countries has risen by 20 years — about as much as was achieved in all of human history prior to the mid-twentieth century.
>
> — World Bank FAQs

International cooperation leads to global economic development.

AP Images/J. Scott Applewhite

Trading Blocs and Common Markets

Another major development in the last decade is the emergence of regional **trading blocs**, or groups of countries that have reduced or even eliminated all tariffs, allowing the free flow of goods among the member nations. A **common market** goes even further than a trading bloc by attempting to harmonize all trading rules. The United States, Mexico, and Canada have formed the largest trading bloc in the world, and the 27 countries of the European Union have formed the largest common market.

NAFTA The **North American Free Trade Agreement (NAFTA)** is the treaty that created the free-trading zone among the United States, Mexico, and Canada. The agreement took effect in 1994, gradually eliminating trade barriers and investment restrictions over a 15-year period. Despite dire predictions of American jobs flowing to Mexico, the U.S. economy has grown significantly since the implementation of NAFTA. The Canadian and Mexican economies have thrived as well (although all three economies have slowed significantly during the global economic crisis).

But NAFTA critics point out that the U.S. trade deficit with both Mexico and Canada has skyrocketed. While exports to both nations have increased, imports have grown far faster; both countries are among the top ten contributors to the total U.S. trade deficit, threatening the long-term health of the American economy. Other criticisms of NAFTA include increased pollution and worker abuse. Companies that move their factories to Mexico to capitalize on lower costs also take advantage of looser environmental and worker-protection laws, creating major ethical concerns. But the full impact of NAFTA—for better or for worse—is tough to evaluate, since so many other variables affect all three economies.[23]

European Union Composed of 27 nations and nearly half a billion people, and boasting a combined GDP of nearly $15 trillion, the **European Union (EU)** is the world's largest common market. Exhibit 3.3 shows a map of the 2011 EU countries plus the three countries that have applied to join.[24]

The overarching goal of the EU is to bolster Europe's trade position and to increase its international political and economic power. To help make this happen, the EU has removed all trade restrictions among member nations and unified internal trade rules, allowing goods and people to move freely among EU countries. The EU has also created standardized policies for import and export between EU countries and the rest of the world, giving the member nations more clout as a bloc than each would have had on its own. Perhaps the EU's most economically significant move was the introduction of a single currency, the euro, in 2002. Of the 15 EU members at the time, 12 adopted the euro (exceptions were the United Kingdom, Sweden, and Denmark). Most economists anticipate that the holdouts plus the 12 newest members of the EU will eventually adopt the euro, creating an even bolder presence on the world market. The EU also affects the global economy with its leading-edge approach to environmental protection, quality production, and human rights.

EXHIBIT 3.3   European Union 2011

© Cengage Learning 2013

JUST BECAUSE THEY CAN...

...DOESN'T MEAN THEY SHOULD.

With 400 million people under the age of 18 and an explosively growing economy, the market for higher education in India has boomed. Since public universities can't keep up with the swelling demand, private colleges have jumped at the chance to fill in the gap, creating opportunities for American institutions to plant their flags in India via joint ventures with Indian colleges and universities (the only option according to Indian law).

A number of top American universities—including Northwestern, Ohio State, Wharton Business School, and Virginia Tech—rushed at the opportunity, eager to boost their enrollment, pump up their bottom line, and enhance their global prestige. But unfortunately, building *quality* programs has been more of a challenge. Only a small portion of private institutions are accredited in India, which means that their graduates are not qualified to take government jobs or pursue most graduate degrees. According to Rahul Choudaha, an associate director at World Education Services, "Across the whole landscape of Indian higher education, at the institutional level, the concept of quality is considered an add-on, not a necessity."[25]

What do YOU think?

- Should top-notch American higher education institutions continue to seek partnerships with Indian institutions?

- Do any differences in quality undermine their brands? Do they have an obligation to inform their other stakeholders (e.g., students, alumni) about any differences in quality?

- What other issues should both parties consider?

THE BIG PICTURE

The last decade has been marked by extraordinary changes in the world economy. The boundaries between individual countries have fallen lower than ever before, creating a new level of economic connectedness. The growing integration has created huge opportunities for visionary companies of every size. But integration also means risk. The dangers became clear in 2008, when the economic crisis in the United States rapidly reverberated around the globe, fueling a deep, worldwide recession.

To succeed abroad—especially in tough economic times—individual firms must make the right choices about how to structure their operations, surmount barriers to trade, meet diverse customer needs, manage a global workforce, and handle complex logistics. Human rights and environmental protection continue to be especially critical for international businesses. Both are vital components of social responsibility and will only gain importance as advocates raise awareness around the world. In the face of economic, political, and social flux, effective global business leaders must master both strategy and implementation at a deeper level than ever before.

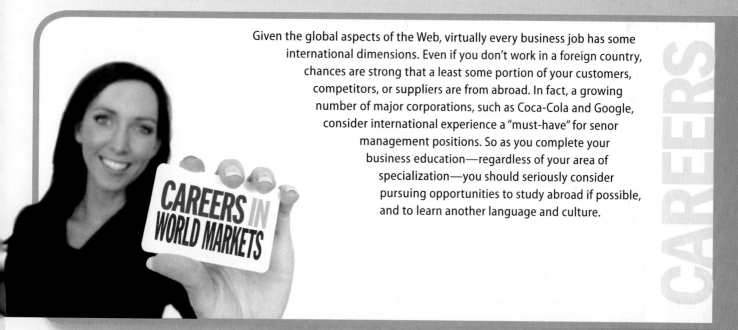

Given the global aspects of the Web, virtually every business job has some international dimensions. Even if you don't work in a foreign country, chances are strong that a least some portion of your customers, competitors, or suppliers are from abroad. In fact, a growing number of major corporations, such as Coca-Cola and Google, consider international experience a "must-have" for senor management positions. So as you complete your business education—regardless of your area of specialization—you should seriously consider pursuing opportunities to study abroad if possible, and to learn another language and culture.

CAREERS

What *else?*
RIP & REVIEW CARDS IN THE BACK
and visit www.cengagebrain.com!

4

Business Ethics and Social Responsibility:
Doing Well by Doing Good

LEARNING OBJECTIVES
After studying this chapter, you will be able to:

LO1   Define ethics and explain the concept of universal ethical standards

LO2   Describe business ethics and ethical dilemmas

LO3   Discuss how ethics relates to both the individual and the organization

LO4   Define social responsibility and examine the impact on stakeholder groups

LO5   Explain the role of social responsibility in the global arena

LO6   Describe how companies evaluate their efforts to be socially responsible

> # "AT THIS MOMENT, AMERICA'S HIGHEST ECONOMIC NEED IS HIGHER *ETHICAL* STANDARDS—STANDARDS ENFORCED BY STRICT LAWS AND UPHELD BY RESPONSIBLE BUSINESS LEADERS."
>
> — George W. Bush

Defining Ethics: Murkier Than You'd Think

In the most general sense, **ethics** are a set of beliefs about right and wrong, good and bad. While your individual ethics stem from who you are as a human being, your family, your social group, and your culture also play a significant role in shaping your ethics. And therein lies the challenge: in the United States, people come from such diverse backgrounds that establishing broad agreement on specific ethical standards can be daunting. The global arena only amplifies the challenge.

A given country's legal system provides a solid starting point for examining ethical standards. The function of laws in the United States (and elsewhere) is to establish and enforce ethical norms that apply to everyone within our society. Laws provide basic standards of behavior. But truly ethical behavior goes beyond the basics. In other words, your actions can be completely legal, yet still unethical. But since the legal system is far from perfect, in rare instances your actions can be illegal, yet still ethical. Exhibit 4.1 shows some examples

> **ethics** A set of beliefs about right and wrong, good and bad.

LO1 Ethics and Social Responsibility: A Close Relationship

Ethics and social responsibility—often discussed in the same breath—are closely related, but they are definitely not the same. Ethics are a set of beliefs about right and wrong, good and bad; business ethics involve the application of these issues in the workplace. Clearly, ethics relate to individuals and their day-to-day decision making. Just as clearly, the decisions of each individual can affect the entire organization.

Social responsibility is the obligation of a business to contribute to society. The most socially responsible firms feature proactive policies that focus on meeting the needs of all their stakeholders—not just investors but also employees, customers, the broader community, and the environment. The stance of a company regarding social responsibility sets the tone for the organization and clearly influences the decisions of individual employees.

While this chapter discusses ethics and social responsibility separately, keep in mind that the two areas have a dynamic, interactive relationship that plays a vital role in building both profitable businesses and a vibrant community.

Exhibit 4.1 Legal-Ethical Matrix

LEGAL AND UNETHICAL	LEGAL AND ETHICAL
Promoting R-rated movies to young teens	Producing high-quality products
Producing products that you know will break before their time	Rewarding integrity
	Leading by example
Paying non-living wages to workers in developing countries	Treating employees fairly
	Contributing to the community
	Respecting the environment

ILLEGAL AND UNETHICAL	ILLEGAL AND ETHICAL
Embezzling money	Providing rock-bottom prices *only* to distributors in underserved areas
Engaging in sexual harassment	Collaborating with other medical clinics to guarantee low prices in low-income countries (collusion)
Practicing collusion with competitors	
Encouraging fraudulent accounting	

© Cengage Learning 2013

universal ethical standards Ethical norms that apply to all people across a broad spectrum of situations.

business ethics The application of right and wrong, good and bad, in a business setting.

ethical dilemma A decision that involves a conflict of values; every potential course of action has some significant negative consequences.

of how business conduct can fall within legal and ethical dimensions. Clearly, legal and ethical actions should be your goal. Legality should be the floor—not the ceiling—for how to behave in business and elsewhere.

Do all actions have ethical implications? Clearly not. Some decisions fall within the realm of free choice with no direct link to right and wrong, good and bad. Examples might include where you buy your morning coffee, what features your company includes on its new MP3 players, or what new machines your gym decides to purchase.

Universal Ethical Standards: A Reasonable Goal or Wishful Thinking?

Too many people view ethics as relative. In other words, their ethical standards shift depending on the situation and how it relates to them. Here are a few examples:

- ⊃ "It's not okay to steal paper clips from the stationery store…*but* it's perfectly fine to 'borrow' supplies from the storage closet at work. Why? The company owes me a bigger salary."

- ⊃ "It's wrong to lie…*but* it's okay to call in sick when I have personal business to take care of. Why? I don't want to burn through my limited vacation days."

- ⊃ "Everyone should have a level playing field…*but* it's fine to give my brother the first shot at my company's contract. Why? I know he really needs the work."

This kind of two-faced thinking is dangerous because it can help people rationalize bigger and bigger ethical deviations. But the problem can be fixed by identifying **universal ethical standards** that apply to everyone across a broad spectrum of situations. Some people argue that we could never find universal standards for a country as diverse as the United States. But the nonprofit, nonpartisan Character Counts organization has worked

© STOCKBYTE/GETTY IMAGES

Exhibit 4.2   Universal Ethical Standards

TRUSTWORTHINESS	Be honest.
	Don't deceive, cheat, or steal.
	Do what you say you'll do.
RESPECT	Treat others how you'd like to be treated.
	Be considerate.
	Be tolerant of differences.
RESPONSIBILITY	Persevere.
	Be self-controlled and self-disciplined.
	Be accountable for your choices.
FAIRNESS	Provide equal opportunity.
	Be open-minded.
	Don't take advantage of others.
CARING	Be kind.
	Be compassionate.
	Express gratitude.
CITIZENSHIP	Contribute to the community.
	Protect the environment.
	Cooperate whenever feasible.

Source: © 2009 Josephson Institute. Reprinted from the Josephson Institute's Report Card on the Ethics of American Youth Summary with permission.

with a diverse group of educators, community leaders, and ethicists to identify six core values, listed in Exhibit 4.2, that transcend political, religious, class, and ethnic divisions.

L02   Business Ethics: Not an Oxymoron

Quite simply, **business ethics** is the application of right and wrong, good and bad in a business setting. But this isn't as straightforward as it may initially seem. The most challenging business decisions seem to arise when values are in conflict…when whatever you do will have negative consequences, forcing you to choose among bad options. These are true **ethical dilemmas.** (Keep in mind that ethical *dilemmas* differ from ethical *lapses*, which involve clear

Bad News Today—Worse News Tomorrow!

© DIGITAL VISION/GETTY IMAGES

In 2010, the Josephson Institute Center for Youth Ethics produced a Report Card on the Ethics of American Youth, based on a survey of 43,000 students in high schools across the United States. The results suggest that students are disturbingly willing to lie, cheat, steal, or intimidate others, despite a sky-high opinion of their own personal character. Some highlights (or perhaps we should call them lowlights):

- ⟳ 59% admitted that they cheated on a test at school within the past 12 months (34% admitted doing so two or more times).

- ⟳ 39% believe that a person has to lie or cheat sometime in order to succeed, even though 84% agree that it's not worth it to lie or cheat because it hurts your character.

- ⟳ 18% admitted that they stole something from a friend within the past twelve months.

- ⟳ 21% admitted that they stole something from their parents within the past twelve months.

- ⟳ 72% agree that it's sometimes OK to hit or threaten a person who makes me very angry.

- ⟳ 28% admitted that they stole something from a store within the past twelve months.

Sadly, the actual rates of bad behavior are probably understated, since more than 25% admitted that they lied on one or two questions, and experts agree that dishonesty on surveys usually reflects an attempt to conceal misconduct.

Despite rampant lying, cheating, and stealing, 98% of respondents agreed that it's important to be a person of good character, and 79% would rate their own character higher than that of their peers. Furthermore, 92% said they were satisfied with their personal character.

A number of analysts find it easy to dismiss the long-term implications of these findings, claiming that as teenagers mature, their judgment and morals will mature as well and their conduct will reflect stronger values. A recent large-scale study by the Josephson Institute of Ethics found unequivocally that high-school attitudes and behaviors and actions are a clear predictor of adult behavior across a range of situations. Cheaters in high school are far more likely as adults to lie to their spouses, customers, bosses, and employers and to cheat on expense reports, taxes, and insurance claims.

Clearly, now is the time for smart companies to clarify their standards and establish safeguards to head off costly ethical meltdowns in their future workforce.[1]

---

misconduct.) Here are a couple of hypothetical examples of ethical dilemmas:

- ⟳ You've just done a great job on a recent project at your company. Your boss has been very vocal about acknowledging your work and the increased revenue that resulted from it. Privately, she said that you clearly earned a bonus of at least 10%, but due to company politics, she was unable to secure the bonus for you. She also implied that if you were to submit inflated expense reports for the next few months, she would look the other way, and you could pocket the extra cash as well-deserved compensation for your contributions.

- ⟳ One of the engineers on your staff has an excellent job offer from another company and asks your advice on whether or not to accept the position. You need him to complete a project that is crucial to your company (and to your own career). You also have been told—in strictest confidence by senior management—that when this project is complete, the company will lay off all internal engineers. If you advise him to stay, he would lose the opportunity (and end up without a job), but if you advise him to go, you would violate the company's trust (and jeopardize your own career).

LO3 Ethics: Multiple Touchpoints

Although each person must make his or her own ethical choices, the organization can have a significant influence on the quality of those decisions. The next two sections discuss the impact of both the individual and the organization on ethical decision making, but as you read them, keep in mind that the interaction between the two is dynamic: sometimes it's hard to tell where one stops and the other starts.

Ethics and the Individual: The Power of One

Ethical choices begin with ethical individuals. Your personal needs, your family, your culture, and your religion all influence your value system. Your personality traits—self-esteem, self-confidence, independence, and sense of humor—play a significant role as well. These factors all come into play as you face ethical dilemmas. The challenge can be overwhelming, which has led a range of experts to develop frameworks for reaching ethical decisions. While the specifics vary, the key principles of most decision guides are very similar:

- Do you fully understand each dimension of the problem?
- Who would benefit? Who would suffer?
- Are the alternative solutions legal? Are they fair?
- Does your decision make you comfortable at a "gut feel" level?
- Could you defend your decision on the nightly TV news?
- Have you considered and reconsidered your responses to each question?

The approach seems simple, but in practice it really isn't. Workers—and managers, too—often face enormous pressure to do what's right for the company or right for their career, rather than simply what's right. And keep in mind that it's completely possible for two people to follow the framework and arrive at completely different decisions, each feeling confident that he or she has made the right choice.

Ethics and the Organization: It Takes a Village

Although each person is clearly responsible for his or her own actions, the organization can influence those actions to a startling degree. Not surprisingly, that influence starts at the top, and actions matter far more than words. The president of the Ethics Resource Center states, "CEOs in particular must communicate their personal commitment to high ethical standards and consistently drive the message down to employees through their actions." Any other approach—even just the *appearance* of shaky ethics—can be deeply damaging to a company's ethical climate. Here are a couple of examples from the news:

- High Flyers: When the CEOs of the Big Three automakers—two of them hovering on the edge of bankruptcy—went to Washington to request a $25 billion bailout package, they flew in three separate corporate jets at an estimated cost of $20,000 per round-trip flight. All three were operating in line with official corporate travel policies, but it just didn't look right. One lawmaker pointedly asked, "Couldn't you all have downgraded to first class or jet-pooled or something to get here? It would have at least sent a message that you do get it." Not surprisingly, the execs left empty-handed.[2]

> You have to do your own growing no matter how tall your grandfather was.
>
> — Abraham Lincoln

- Beach Junket: A few days after the Fed committed $85 billion to keep AIG out of bankruptcy, the insurer spent more than $440,000 on a sales "retreat" at a luxury resort in California. Expenditures included $150,000 for food, $23,000 in spa charges, and $7,000 for golf. Rather than apologizing, CEO Edward Liddy only committed that the company would examine its expenses.[3]

- Retirement Perks: When Jack Welch retired from his post as CEO of General Electric, the Board awarded him a generous financial package and an eye-popping collection of perks. His perks ranged from use of an $80,000 per month apartment, to country club fees, to corporate jet privileges. These perks did not represent an ethical breach—Welch negotiated them in good faith—but when the list surfaced in the press a year after his retirement, he voluntarily gave up his perks to mitigate a public relations problem that could have tarnished his reputation as a tough, ethical, and highly successful CEO.[4]

- Gross Excess: In the mid-1990s, Disney CEO Michael Eisner hired his friend Michael Ovitz as Disney's president. Fourteen months later, Disney fired Ovitz for incompetence, and he walked away with a $140 million settlement. Disgruntled stockholders sued the Disney Board for mismanagement, which led to the release of Ovitz's Disney expense account documents. In 14 months, he spent $4.8 million (that's about $80,000 per week!). Specifics included $54,330 for basketball tickets, a $946 gun for movie director Robert Zemeckis, and $319 for breakfast. Was he stealing? *No*. Was he unethical? You decide.[5] How do you feel about the business decisions described in Exhibit 4.3?

Creating and Maintaining an Ethical Organization

Research from the Ethics Resource Center (ERC) suggests that organizational culture has more influence than any other variable on the ethical conduct of individual employees. According to the ERC, key elements of a strong culture include displays of ethics-related actions at all levels of an organization and accountability for actions. The impact of these elements can be dramatic. Consider, for example, the following research results:

⊙ A 61 percentage-point favorable difference in the level of observed misconduct when employees say they work in a strong ethical culture.

⊙ When employees felt that the great recession negatively impacted the ethical culture of their company, misconduct rose by 16 percentage points.

⊙ If an accountable business is defined as one that confronts misconduct and establishes a rigorous system to prevent a recurrence, nearly 80% of employees said they work in a firm where, in practice, employees at all levels are held accountable to company standards.[6]

Robert Lane, former CEO of Deere, a highly performing, highly ethical corporation, believes in the importance of senior management commitment to ethics, but he points out that the "tone at the top" must be reinforced by the actual behavior observed by suppliers, dealers, customers, and employees. At Deere, this is summed up in highly visible, frequently referenced shorthand known as "the how." Lane declares that to establish an ethical culture, ethical words must be "backed up with documented practices, processes, and procedures, all understood around the globe."[7]

A strong organizational culture works in tandem with formal ethics programs to create and maintain ethical work environments. A written **code of ethics** is the cornerstone of any formal ethics program. The purpose of a written code is to give employees the information they need to make ethical decisions across a range of situations. Clearly, an ethics code becomes even more important for multinational companies, since it lays out unifying values and priorities for divisions that are rooted in different cultures. But a written code is worthless if it doesn't reflect living principles. An effective code of ethics flows directly from ethical corporate values and leads directly to ongoing communication, training, and action.

> **code of ethics** A formal, written document that defines the ethical standards of an organization and gives employees the information they need to make ethical decisions across a range of situations.

Exhibit 4.3   Ethics at Work: How Would You Judge the Actions of These Business Leaders?

Pierre Omidyar eBay creator Omidyar has contributed $100 million to the Tufts University Micro Finance Fund. His goal is to give economic power to poor people around the world through small business loans. Ultimately, he hopes to create entrepreneurial self-sufficiency as eBay has done for so many avid users.

Sherron Watkins Despite intense pressure and high personal stakes, Watkins, a former vice president of Enron, reported the accounting irregularities that led to the discovery of staggering corporate fraud.

Stanley O'Neal As investment house Merrill Lynch began racking up losses that led to its collapse, CEO O'Neal announced his "retirement" and walked away with a compensation package worth more than $160 million.

John A. Thain Thain, the ousted Merrill Lynch executive, under pressure from President Obama, agreed to reimburse Federal bailout recipient Bank of America for an expensive renovation of his office that included an $87,000 area rug and a $35,000 commode.

Bill Gates As Microsoft CEO, Bill Gates made some ethically shaky moves, but he and his wife also established the Bill and Melinda Gates Foundation, by far the largest U.S. charity. Working for the foundation, Gates applies his famous problem-solving skills to global health, global development, and American education.

John Mackey From 1999 until 2006, Whole Foods CEO John Mackey posted thousands of anonymous comments on Yahoo! Finance, hyping his company and occasionally attacking rival Wild Oats, which he hoped to purchase for an advantageous price.

Specific codes of ethics vary greatly among organizations. Perhaps the best-known code is the Johnson & Johnson Credo, which has guided the company profitably—with a soaring reputation—through a number of crises that would have sunk lesser organizations. One of the striking elements of the Credo is the firm focus on fairness. It carefully refrains from overpromising financial rewards, committing instead to a "fair return" for stockholders.

To bring a code of ethics to life, experts advocate a forceful, integrated approach to ethics that virtually always includes the following steps:

1. Get executive buy-in and commitment to follow-through. Top managers need to communicate—even overcommunicate—about the importance of ethics. But talking works only when it's backed up by action: senior management must give priority to keeping promises and leading by example.

2. Establish expectations for ethical behavior at all levels of the organization, from the CEO to the night-time cleaning crew. Be sure that outside parties such as suppliers, distributors, and customers understand the standards.

3. Integrate ethics into mandatory staff training. From new-employee orientation to ongoing training, ethics must play a role. Additional, more specialized training helps for employees who face more temptation (e.g., purchasing agents, overseas sales reps).

4. Ensure that your ethics code is both global and local in scope. Employees in every country should understand both the general principles and the specific applications. Be sure to translate it into as many languages as necessary.

5. Build and maintain a clear, trusted reporting structure for ethical concerns and violations. The structure should allow employees to seek anonymous guidance for ethical concerns and to report ethics violations anonymously.

6. Establish protection for **whistle-blowers**, people who report illegal or unethical behavior. Be sure that no retaliation occurs, in compliance with both ethics and the Sarbanes-Oxley Act (see discussion later in the chapter). Some have even suggested that whistle-blowers should receive a portion of the penalties levied against firms that violate the law.

7. Enforce the code of ethics. When people violate ethical norms, companies must respond immediately and—whenever appropriate—publicly to retain employee trust. Without enforcement, the code of ethics becomes meaningless.

LO4 Defining Social Responsibility: Making the World a Better Place

Social responsibility is the obligation of a business to contribute to society. Similar to ethics, the broad definition is clear, but specific implementation can be complex. Obviously, the number-one goal of any business is long-term profits; without profits, other contributions are impossible. But once a firm achieves a reasonable return, the balancing act begins: how can a company balance the need to contribute against the need to boost profits, especially when the two conflict? The answer depends on the business's values, mission, resources, and management philosophy, which lead in turn to its position on social responsibility. Business approaches fall across the spectrum, from no contribution to proactive contribution, as shown in Exhibit 4.4.

The Stakeholder Approach: Responsibility to Whom?

Stakeholders are any groups that have a stake—or a personal interest—in the performance and actions of an organization. Different stakeholders have different needs, expectations, and levels of interest. The federal government, for instance, is a key stakeholder in pharmaceutical companies but a very minor stakeholder in local art studios. The community at large is a key stakeholder for a coffee shop chain but a minor stakeholder for a web design firm. Enlightened organizations identify key stakeholders for their business and consider stakeholder priorities in their decision making. The goal is to balance their needs and priorities as effectively as possible, with an eye toward building their business over the long term. Core stakeholder groups for most businesses are employees, customers, investors, and the broader community.

Responsibility to Employees: Creating Jobs That Work Jobs alone aren't enough. The starting point for socially responsible employers is to meet legal standards, and the

©Feng Yu/Shutterstock.com

© Cengage Learning 2013

EXHIBIT 4.4 The Spectrum of Social Responsibility

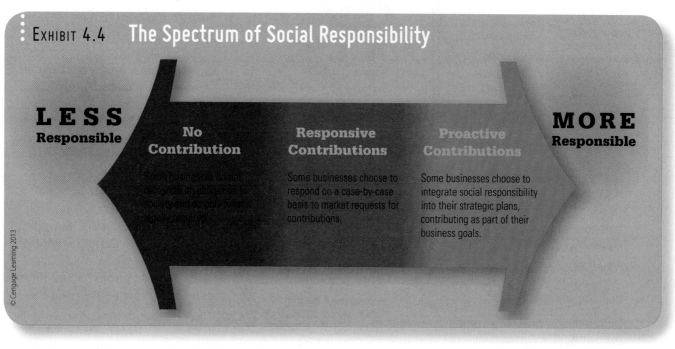

LESS Responsible

No Contribution
Some businesses do not recognize an obligation to society and do only what is legally required.

Responsive Contributions
Some businesses choose to respond on a case-by-case basis to market requests for contributions.

Proactive Contributions
Some businesses choose to integrate social responsibility into their strategic plans, contributing as part of their business goals.

MORE Responsible

---

requirements are significant. How would you judge the social responsibility of the firms listed in Exhibit 4.5? Employers must comply with laws that include equal opportunity, workplace safety, minimum-wage and overtime requirements, protection from sexual harassment, and family and medical unpaid leaves. We will discuss these legal requirements (and others) in Chapter 15 on Human Resource Management.

But socially responsible employers go far beyond the law. They create a workplace environment that respects the dignity and value of each employee. They ensure that hard work, commitment, and talent pay off. They move beyond minimal safety requirements to establish proactive protections, such as ergonomically correct chairs and computer screens that reduce eyestrain. And the best employers respond to the ongoing employee search for a balance between work and personal life. With an increasing number of workers facing challenges such as raising kids and caring for elderly parents, responsible companies are stepping in with programs such as on-site day care, company-sponsored day camp, and referral services for elder care.

Responsibility to Customers: Value, Honesty, and Communication One core responsibility of business is to deliver consumer value by providing quality products at fair prices. Honesty and communication are critical components of this equation. **Consumerism**—a widely accepted social movement—suggests that consumer rights should be the starting point. In the early 1960s, President Kennedy defined these rights, which most businesses respect in response to both consumer expectations and legal requirements:

- The Right to Be Safe: Businesses are legally responsible for injuries and damages caused by their products—even if they have no reason to suspect that their products might cause harm. This makes it easy for consumers to file suits. In some cases, the drive to avert lawsuits has led to absurdities such as the warning on some coffee cups: "Caution! Hot coffee is hot!" (No kidding…)

> **consumerism** A social movement that focuses on four key consumer rights: (1) the right to be safe, (2) the right to be informed, (3) the right to choose, and (4) the right to be heard.

- The Right to Be Informed: The law requires firms in a range of industries—from mutual funds, to groceries, to pharmaceuticals—to provide the public with extensive information. The Food and Drug Administration, for instance, mandates that most grocery foods feature a very specific "Nutrition Facts" label. Beyond legal requirements, many firms use the Web to provide a wealth of extra information about their products. KFC, for example, offers an interactive Nutrition Calculator that works with all of its menu items (and it's fun to use, too).

- The Right to Choose: Freedom of choice is a fundamental element of the capitalist U.S. economy. Our economic system works largely because consumers freely choose to purchase the products that best meet their needs. As businesses compete, consumer value increases. Socially responsible firms support consumer choice by following the laws that prevent anticompetitive behavior such as predatory pricing, collusion, and monopolies.

- The Right to Be Heard: Socially responsible companies make it easy for consumers to express legitimate complaints. They also develop highly trained customer service people to respond to complaints.

In fact, smart businesses view customer complaints as an opportunity to create better products and stronger relationships. Statistics suggest that 1 in 50 dissatisfied customers takes the time to complain. The other 49 quietly switch brands. By soliciting feedback, you're not only being responsible, but also building your business.[8]

Delivering quality products is another key component of social responsibility to consumers. **Planned obsolescence**—deliberately designing products to fail in

> **About one-third** of **Hispanic and African American consumers almost always choose brands because they come from companies that support causes they believe in,** compared to just one in five non-Hispanic Whites.
>
> — Yankelovich Monitor Multicultural Study 2010

order to shorten the time between consumer repurchases—represents a clear violation of social responsibility. In the long term, the market itself weeds out offenders. After all, who would repurchase a product that meets a premature end? But in the short term, planned obsolescence thins consumer wallets and abuses consumer trust.

When businesses do make mistakes, apologizing to consumers won't guarantee renewed sales. But a sincere apology can definitely restore a company's reputation, which can ultimately lead to greater profits. Three recent examples make this point clear:

➲ *Trapped!* Due to a huge snowstorm on Valentine's Day 2007, ten jetBlue planes were stranded on the tarmac at New York's JFK airport, trapping furious passengers—with no information, no

© iStockphoto.com/Lasse Kristensen

How would you judge the actions of these firms?

The Clorox Company In early 2008, Clorox introduced a line of "99% natural" cleaning products called Green Works. This is the first such effort from a major consumer products company, and also the first time that the Sierra Club has endorsed a product line by allowing the use of its logo on the labels. In return, Clorox makes an annual contribution to the Sierra Club, the amount based on total Green Works sales.

Tyson Foods Tyson has been accused of unfair business practices, unsavory labor and environmental practices, and controversial chicken-raising protocols, but in 2009, the factory farmer gave nearly 11% of its profits to charity.

Kraft As obesity among kids spirals out of control, Kraft has taken a brave stand: a pledge to stop advertising unhealthy—yet highly profitable—foods to young children. Kraft also plans to eliminate in-school marketing and drop some unhealthy snacks from school vending machines. As the king of the food business, Kraft has chosen what's right for kids over what's right for its own short-term profits.

Enron/Arthur Andersen (now defunct) Enron, once hailed as a shining example of corporate excellence, collapsed in late 2001 due to massive accounting fraud, which bilked employees and other small investors out of millions of dollars. Arthur Andersen, hired to audit Enron's accountings, participated in the scandal by masking the issues and shredding documents containing potential evidence.

Bank of America After receiving $45 billion in taxpayer bailout funds, Bank of America sponsored a five-day carnival-like event outside the 2009 Super Bowl stadium called the NFL Experience. The high-profile attraction included 850,000 square feet of sports games, plus marketing solicitations for football-themed B of A banking products. The bank defended the event as an effective growth strategy, while critics blasted it as an abuse of taxpayer dollars.

Toyota In 2009 Toyota stonewalled for months before admitting to a defect in some of its most popular cars that appeared to cause fatal accidents due to unintended acceleration. Even after announcing a large-scale recall, Toyota waited five days before halting new sales on models affected by the recall. Some analysts believe that Toyota knew about the defects long before the problems began and opted to do nothing.

© Cengage Learning 2013

Socially responsible employers provide safe workspaces for all of their employees.

© Purestock/ Jupiterimages

power, and limited refreshments—for as long as eight hours. In the wake of the storm, JetBlue canceled more than 1,000 additional flights. JetBlue CEO David Neeleman responded with a profuse apology, reimbursing customers and establishing a customer bill of rights. The airline estimates that the total cost of the crisis was between $20 million and $30 million. But in 2008, JetBlue won its fourth consecutive customer service award from J.D. Power and Associates, clear evidence that the apology worked to regain customer trust.[9]

⊙ *Deleted without Warning*: In mid-2009, Amazon remotely and abruptly deleted some digital editions of books from the Kindle devices of customers who had already purchased them (because Amazon hadn't obtained proper rights to make those sales in the first place). Indignant customers were furious at this violation of their privacy, which many felt was akin to theft, despite an automatic refund of the purchase price from Amazon. Amazon founder and CEO Jeff Bezos issued a characteristically blunt apology, stating that the company's actions were "stupid, thoughtless, and painfully out of line with its principles." But fortunately for Amazon, not too much harm was done, since by the end of 2009, Kindle remained Amazon's best-selling product, and sales of Kindle digital books hit 48 percent of the sales of physical books.[10]

⊙ *Apple Angst:* Apple introduced the iPhone on June 29, 2007, to rave reviews and stellar sales, despite the $599 price tag. But two months later, Apple dropped the price of the phone by $200, in order to expand the user base yet further. Not surprisingly, early adopters were livid—why, they demanded, did Apple repay their trust and support by ripping them off? CEO Steve Jobs quickly apologized and offered every $599 iPhone customer a $100 Apple store credit. The response seemed to work. In 2008, Apple's ranking in the American Customer Satisfaction Index climbed 8%, a full ten percentage points ahead of its nearest competitor in an industry where ratings in general are sinking.[11]

© David Robertson / Alamy

Sarbanes–Oxley Act Federal legislation passed in 2002 that sets higher ethical standards for public corporations and accounting firms. Key provisions limit conflict-of-interest issues and require financial officers and CEOs to certify the validity of their financial statements.

corporate philanthropy All business donations to nonprofit groups, including money, products, and employee time.

Responsibility to Investors: Fair Stewardship and Full Disclosure The primary responsibility of business to investors is clearly to make money—to create an ongoing stream of profits. But companies achieve and maintain long-term earnings in the context of responsibility to *all* stakeholders, which may mean trading short-term profits for long-term success. Responsibility to investors starts by meeting legal requirements, and in the wake of recent corporate scandals, the bar is higher than ever. The 2002 **Sarbanes–Oxley Act** limits conflict-of-interest issues by restricting the consulting services that accounting firms can provide for the companies they audit. Sarbanes-Oxley also requires that financial officers and CEOs personally certify the validity of their financial statements. (See Chapter 8 for more detail on the Sarbanes-Oxley Act.)

But beyond legal requirements, companies have a number of additional responsibilities to investors. Spending money wisely would be near the top of the list. For instance, are executive retreats to the South Pacific on the company tab legal? They probably are. Do they represent a responsible use of corporate dollars? Now that seems unlikely. Honesty is another key responsibility that relates directly to financial predictions. No one can anticipate exactly how a company will perform, and an overly optimistic or pessimistic assessment is perfectly legal. But is it socially responsible? It probably isn't, especially if it departs too far from the objective facts—which is, of course, a subjective call.

Responsibility to the Community: Business and the Greater Good Beyond increasing everyone's standard of living, businesses can contribute to society in two main ways: philanthropy and responsibility. **Corporate philanthropy** includes all

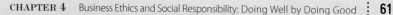

business donations to nonprofit groups, including both money and products. The Giving USA Foundation reported that total corporate donations in 2009 exceeded $14 billion, a somewhat surprising bump of +5.5% versus 2008, in the toughest year of the Great Recession. Experts had anticipated that corporate giving would drop in 2009, since, in the words of one key analyst, "As goes the economy, so goes corporate giving… only more so." At least some of the increased giving appears to come from greater contributions of goods vs. money, since contributions of products seem less vulnerable to economic swings.[12]

Corporate philanthropy also includes donations of employee time; in other words, some companies pay their employees to spend time volunteering at nonprofits. Timberland, an outdoor clothing company, is a leader in corporate philanthropy, not only donating goods but also giving employees paid six-month sabbaticals to work for nonprofits.[13]

Some companies contribute to nonprofits through **cause-related marketing**. This involves a partnership between a business and a nonprofit, designed to spike sales for the company and raise money for the nonprofit. Unlike outright gifts, these dollars are not tax deductible for the company, but they can certainly build the company's brands.

Corporate responsibility relates closely to philanthropy but focuses on the actions of the business itself rather than donations of money and time. The Home Depot, for instance, employs more Olympic hopefuls than any other U.S. company through its Olympic Job Opportunities Program. The firm offers athletes full-time pay and benefits for a flexible 20-hour workweek to accommodate demanding

JUST BECAUSE THEY CAN... ...DOESN'T MEAN THEY SHOULD.

Imagine for a moment that you are a designer of very expensive, fabulous, fashion-forward hats, and every time someone types "hat" into Google, the name of your business pops up first on the list of search results. Clearly, the benefits to your business would be extraordinary; in fact, research shows that about 34% of Google's traffic clicks on the first search result, about twice the percentage that clicks on number two. Because of these benefits, the field of search engine optimization has exploded onto the digital scene in the last decade, with hundreds of consulting firms specializing in helping their clients rise to the top of Google's list. Most of these firms use completely legitimate "white hat" techniques to raise their clients' profiles. But some firms use more controversial "black hat" approaches. These methods involve linking client sites to as many related sites as possible to "fool" Google's search algorithm into thinking that the client sites are extremely popular in their areas of expertise.[14]

Although black hat search optimization is not illegal, Google and other online search experts consider these approaches to be underhanded, deceptive, and equivalent to cheating. Google responds with "corrective action," which basically amounts to punishing offenders by dramatically reducing their ranking in search results, or even temporarily removing offenders altogether from search results.

What do YOU think?

- Do you believe that Google results are usually impartial?
- Do you think that Google overreacts to attempts to manipulate its search results?
- As a business owner, what percentage of your budget (if any) would you invest in search engine optimization? Why?

Singing the Blues about going Green

After several years of avid interest in green marketing and green product development, consumers are beginning to show signs of disinterest, or "green fatigue." Sales of green products have slowed, and sales of less green products (such as bottled water) have grown. In September 2010, a major study showed huge increases between 2008 and 2010 in the number of U.S. consumers who believe that green product alternatives are too expensive, that green products don't work as well, and that green products aren't really better for the environment. According to *Consumer Reports*, it makes sense to be jaded. Their analysis revealed that green dish detergents were neither better for the environment nor less expensive than standard products. Their analysis of laundry detergents showed that green detergents were more expensive and less effective than standard products. All of this doesn't mean that green is dead; it may just mean that we shouldn't expect too much, too soon. According to Eric Ryan, co-founder of Method Home Corporation, "A lot of green choices require a change in behavior, and people are very slow to change…"[15]

training and competition schedules. Taking a different approach to corporate responsibility, Cisco Systems has developed relationships with the different branches of the military to help make recruitment and hiring of disabled veterans a standard part of their hiring practices. Both of these policies ultimately benefit society as a whole.

Responsibility to the Environment Protecting the environment is perhaps the most crucial element of responsibility to the community. Business is a huge consumer of the world's limited resources, from oil, to timber, to fresh water, to minerals. In some cases, the production process decimates the environment and spews pollution into the air, land, and water, sometimes causing irreversible damage. And the products created by business can cause pollution as well, such as the smog generated by cars, and the sometimes-toxic waste caused by junked electronic parts.

The government sets minimum standards for environmental protection at the federal, state, and local levels. But a growing number of companies are going further, developing innovative strategies to build their business while protecting the environment. Many have embraced the idea of **sustainable development**: doing business to meet the needs of this generation without harming the ability

of future generations to meet their needs. This means weaving environmentalism throughout the business decision-making process. Since sustainable development can mean significant long-term cost savings, the economic crisis may even push forward environmentally friendly programs.

The results of sustainability programs have been impressive across a range of industries. McDonald's, for instance, produces mountains of garbage each year, as do virtually all major fast-food chains. But the Golden Arches stands above the others in its attempts to reduce the problem. An article from the Sustainability Institute reports some encouraging statistics:

- "The company used to ship orange juice to its restaurants in ready-to-serve containers. Now it ships frozen concentrate, which reduces orange juice packaging by 75%—4 million pounds less garbage a year."

- "Soft drinks were shipped as syrup in cardboard containers. The local restaurants added the water and the fizz. Now the syrup is delivered by trucks that pump it directly into receiving tanks at the restaurants. No packaging is needed at all. Savings: 68 million pounds of cardboard per year."[16]

Reducing the *amount* of trash is better than recycling, but recycling trash clearly beats dumping it in a landfill. McDonald's participates in this arena as well, through their extensive recycling programs, but more importantly as a big buyer of recycled products.

Taking an even broader perspective, some firms have started to measure their carbon footprint, with an eye toward reducing it. **Carbon footprint** refers to the amount

> **sustainable development** Doing business to meet the needs of the current generation, without harming the ability of future generations to meet their needs.
>
> **carbon footprint** Refers to the amount of harmful greenhouse gases that a firm emits throughout its operations, both directly and indirectly.

Environmental responsibility can boost the bottom line.

© Jamey Ekins/Shutterstock.com

of harmful greenhouse gases that a firm emits throughout its operations, both directly and indirectly. The ultimate goal is to become carbon neutral—either to emit zero harmful gasses or to counteract the impact of emissions by removing a comparable amount from the atmosphere through projects such as planting trees. Dell Inc. became fully carbon neutral in mid-2008, fulfilling its quest to become "the greenest technology on the planet." More recently, PepsiCo calculated the carbon footprint for its Tropicana orange juice brand and was surprised to learn that about a third of its emissions came from applying fertilizer to the orange groves. According to the Conference Board, business leaders have begun to see their carbon footprint—both measurement and reduction—as a burgeoning opportunity.[17] Many large corporations track three different types of emissions. The first, called Scope 1, refers to direct emissions produced by corporate operations. The second, called Scope 2, refers to emissions that result from purchased electricity, heat, and steam. Scope 3 emissions, which are more complex to track, are emissions that occur outside a company's boundary, but over which it has some control. This category includes areas such as employee commutes, supplier emissions, and product-use emissions. Examining Scope 3 emissions has motivated Sony Electronics to make energy efficiency a priority in new product development, and spurred the Coca Cola Corporation to focus on developing more environmentally friendly "cold drink equipment" (e.g., vending machines and fountain drink dispensers). Coke was surprised and dismayed to learn that emissions from their combined cold drink equipment accounted for three times the level of emissions of their total manufacturing.[18]

A growing number of companies use **green marketing** to promote their business. This means marketing environmental products and practices to gain a competitive edge. Patagonia, for example, markets outdoor clothing using 100% organic cotton and natural fibers such as hemp. But green marketing represents a tough challenge: while most people support the idea of green products, the vast majority won't sacrifice price, performance, or convenience to actually buy those products. Sometimes, however, green marketing can be quite consistent with profitability. The Toyota Prius hybrid car offers an interesting example. The Prius costs several thousand dollars more than a standard car, but as gas prices skyrocketed through the summer of 2008, consumers flooded the dealerships, snapping up Prius hybrids faster than Toyota could ship them. Yet, when the economy dropped in late 2008, Toyota sales plummeted along with the rest of the industry, suggesting that the environment may be a fair-weather priority for consumers.[19]

Misconduct declines in turbulent economic times and rises when the pressure's off.

— ETHICS RESOURCE CENTER

LO5 Ethics and Social Responsibility in the Global Arena: A House of Mirrors?

Globalization has made ethics and social responsibility even more complicated for workers at every level. Bribery and corruption are among the most challenging issues faced by companies and individuals that are involved in international business. Transparency International, a leading anticorruption organization, publishes a yearly index of "perceived corruption" across 146 countries. No country scores a completely clean 10 out of 10, and the United States scores a troubling 7.1, which was quite a bit higher than China at 3.5 and India at 3.1, but lower than most of the European countries that dominate the top of the list. Not surprisingly, the world's poorest countries fall largely in the bottom half of the index, suggesting that rampant corruption is part of their business culture.[20]

Corruption wouldn't be possible if companies didn't offer bribes, so Transparency International also researched the likelihood of firms from industrialized countries to pay bribes abroad. The 2008 results indicated that firms from export powers Russia, China, and Mexico rank among the worst, with India following close behind. U.S. corporations, forbidden to offer bribes since 1977 under the Foreign Corrupt Practices Act, show a disturbing inclination to flout the law. The United States scored 8.1 out of a possible 10, falling below many Western European countries.[21]

These statistics raise some thought-provoking questions:

- When does a gift become a bribe? The law is unclear, and perceptions differ from country to country.
- How can corporations monitor corruption and enforce corporate policies in their foreign branches?
- What are other ways to gain a competitive edge in countries where bribes are both accepted and expected?

Other challenging issues revolve around business responsibility to workers abroad. At minimum, businesses should pay a living wage for reasonable hours in a safe

Going Green—It's Not Just Governments

While governments and grassroots groups around the world have led the global push to "go green," make no mistake, multinational businesses have played a leadership role as well, making major contributions to the greening of the planet. Some examples:

- Bank of America reduced paper use by 32% from 2000 to 2005, despite a 24% growth in its customer base. Bank of America also runs an internal recycling program that recycles 30,000 tons of paper each year, good for saving roughly 200,000 trees for each year of the program's operation.

- While no one can argue that bottled water is an environmentally sound business in the developed world, Arrowhead bottled water—owned by Nestle – introduced smaller, "Eco Shape" bottles that helped them save 245 million pounds of plastic resin over the last decade, plus shorter labels that have saved almost ten million pounds of paper per year in the U.S. (versus their previous label), which equates to saving about 30,000 trees per year.

- DuPont, not historically known for earth-friendly practices, successfully reduced greenhouse gas emissions during the '90s by 63%—far ahead of the timetable set forth in the controversial Kyoto Protocol.

- Anheuser-Busch now saves 21 million pounds of metal per year by trimming an eighth of an inch off the diameter of its beer cans without reducing the volume of beer "one bit."

- By opting to use coffee-cup sleeves made of recycled paper, Starbucks has saved roughly 78,000 trees per year since 2006.

- Tesla Motors is developing environmentally friendly sports cars that offer blazing speed and formidable power with virtually no emissions.

- Hewlett-Packard owns gigantic e-waste recycling plants that reclaim not just steel and plastic but also toxic chemicals like mercury. HP takes back any brand of equipment, not just its own 100% recyclable machines. HP also audits its top suppliers for eco-friendliness.[22]

bringing together their own values with the laws of both the United States and their host countries.

The most socially responsible companies establish codes of conduct for their vendors, setting clear policies for human rights, wages, safety, and environmental impact. In 1991, Levi Strauss became the first global company to establish a comprehensive code of conduct for its contractors. Over the years, creative thinking has helped it maintain its high standards, even in the face of cultural clashes. An example from Bangladesh, outlined in the *Harvard Business Review*, illustrates its preference for win-win solutions. In the early 1990s, Levi Strauss "discovered that two of its suppliers in Bangladesh were employing children under the age of 14—a practice that violated the company's principles but was tolerated in Bangladesh. Forcing the suppliers to fire the children would not have ensured that the children received an education, and it would have caused serious hardship for the families depending on the children's wages. In a creative arrangement, the suppliers agreed to pay the children's regular wages while they attended school and to offer each child a job at age 14. Levi Strauss, in turn, agreed to pay the children's tuition and provide books and uniforms." This creative solution allowed the suppliers to maintain their valuable contracts from Levi Strauss, while Levi Strauss upheld its values and improved the quality of life for its most vulnerable workers.[23]

Clearly, codes of conduct work best with monitoring, enforcement, and a commitment to finding solutions that work for all parties involved. Gap Inc. offers an encouraging example. In 1996, Gap published a rigorous Code of Vendor Conduct and required compliance from all of their vendors. Its vendor-compliance officers strive

working environment. But exactly what this means is less clear-cut. Does a living wage mean enough to support an individual or a family? Does "support" mean enough to subsist day to day or enough to live in modest comfort? Should American businesses ban child labor in countries where families depend on their children's wages to survive? Companies must address these questions individually,

> Everyday Americans buy 62 million newspapers and throw out 44 million. That's the equivalent of dumping 500,000 trees into a landfill every week.
>
> —Techsoup

social audit A systematic evaluation of how well a firm is meeting its ethics and social responsibility goals.

to visit each of its 3,000 factories at least once a year. They have uncovered a troubling number of violations, proactively pulling contracts from serious violators and rejecting bids from suppliers who don't meet their standards.

Gap and Levi Strauss seem to be doing their part, but the world clearly needs universal standards and universal enforcement to ensure that the benefits of globalization don't come at the expense of the world's most vulnerable people.[24]

LO6 Monitoring Ethics and Social Responsibility: Who Is Minding the Store?

Actually, many firms are monitoring themselves. The process is called a **social audit**: a systematic evaluation of how well a firm is meeting its ethics and social responsibility objectives. Establishing goals is the starting point for a social audit, but the next step is to determine how to measure the achievement of those goals, and measurement can be a bit tricky. As You Sow, an organization dedicated to promoting corporate social responsibility, recommends that companies measure their success by evaluating a "double bottom line," one that accounts for traditional financial indicators, such as earnings, and one that accounts for social-responsibility indicators, such as community involvement.

Other groups are watching as well, which helps keep businesses on a positive track. Activist customers, investors, unions, environmentalists, and community groups all play a role. In addition, the threat of government legislation keeps some industries motivated to self-regulate. One example would be the entertainment industry, which uses a self-imposed rating system for both movies and TV, largely to fend off regulation. Many people argue that the emergence of salads at fast-food restaurants represents an effort to avoid regulation as well.

Choosing Between a Loaf of Bread and a Packet of Shampoo

© imagebroker / Alamy

Three-quarters of the world's population—nearly 4 billion people—earn less than $2 per day. But C.K. Prahalad, a well-respected consultant and economist, claims that if the "aspirational poor" had a chance to consume, they could add about $13 trillion in annual sales to the global economy. Unilever, a global marketing company headquartered in Europe, has aggressively pursued this market with consumer products. Their customers might not have electricity, running water, or even enough for dinner, but many of them do have packets of Sunsilk shampoo and Omo detergent. Electronics companies have experienced marketing success as well. In Dharavi, for instance—one of the largest urban slums in India—more than 85% of households own a television set.

Critics suggest that the corporate push to reach impoverished consumers will enrich multinationals at the expense of their customers, representing exploitation of the world's poorest people. Ashvin Dayal, East Asia director for the antipoverty group Oxfam UK, expressed concern to *Time* magazine that corporate marketing might unseat locally produced products or encourage overspending by those who truly can't afford it. Citing heavily marketed candy and soda, he points out that "companies have the power to create needs rather than respond to needs."

But Prahalad counters that many people at the bottom of the economic pyramid accept that some of the basics—running water, for instance—are not likely to ever come their way. Instead, they opt to improve their quality of life through affordable "luxuries," such as single-use sachets of fragrant shampoo. He argues that "It's absolutely possible to do very well while doing good." Furthermore, he suggests that corporate marketing may kick-start the poorest economies, triggering entrepreneurial activity and economic growth. Since globalization shows no signs of slowing, let's hope that he's right.[25]

What do you think? Is targeting the poor with consumer goods exploitation or simply smart marketing?

THE BIG PICTURE

Clearly, the primary goal of any business is to earn long-term profits for its investors. But profits alone are not enough. As active participants in society, firms must also promote ethical actions and social responsibility throughout their organizations and their corresponding customer and supplier networks. Although every area matters, a few warrant special mention:

- In tough economic times, effective business leaders focus more than ever on integrity, transparency, and a humane approach to managing the workforce—especially during cutbacks.
- Building or maintaining a presence in foreign markets requires particularly careful attention to human rights and local issues.
- Sustainable development and other environmentally sound practices are not only fiscally prudent and customer-friendly, but also crucial for the health of our planet.

CAREERS

Virtually all organizations seek to hire individuals with a proven track record of ethical behavior, and a strong commitment to integrity in both their personal decision making and actions. But over the past two decades, a number of large corporations—such as BellSouth, Dell, Dow, and Xerox—have established separate offices of ethics and compliance, offering a new career track for professionals eager to work specifically in the field of ethics. Offices of ethics and compliance can focus on a number different areas, but key areas of interest typically include mitigating employee-filed lawsuits, monitoring employee use of the Internet, overseeing corporate compliance with legislation, and taking steps to ensure that the corporate code of ethics moves "off the walls and into the halls." Qualifications for these positions often include education and experience in human resource management, accounting, or law. Many large corporations, such as Disney, Target, and Hasbro, also hire social responsibility professionals, often focused on sustainability and environmental initiatives, or auditing factories—typically foreign factories—to ensure compliance with company standards and local laws. These positions almost always require at least a four-year degree and exceptional communication skills.

CAREERS IN BUSINESS ETHICS AND SOCIAL RESPONSIBILITY

What *else?*
RIP & REVIEW CARDS IN THE BACK and visit www.cengagebrain.com!

5

Business Communication:
Creating and Delivering Messages that Matter

LEARNING OBJECTIVES
After studying this chapter, you will be able to:

LO1 Explain the importance of excellent business communication

LO2 Describe the key elements of nonverbal communication

LO3 Compare, contrast, and choose effective communication channels

LO4 Choose the right words for effective communication

LO5 Write more effective business memos, letters, and emails

LO6 Create and deliver successful verbal presentations

WHAT YOU *DO* SPEAKS SO LOUD THAT I CANNOT HEAR WHAT YOU *SAY*.

— Ralph Waldo Emerson

L01 Excellent Communication Skills: Your Invisible Advantage

Much of your success in business will depend on your ability to influence the people around you. Can you land the right job? Close the deal that makes the difference? Convince the boss to adopt your idea? Motivate people to buy your products? Excellent communicators are not only influential but also well liked, efficient, and effective. Great communication skills can dramatically boost your chance for success, while poor communication skills can bury even the most talented people.

So what exactly are "excellent communication skills"? Many students believe that great business communication equates to a knack for speaking or a flair for writing. But if that's where you stop, you're likely to hit a brick wall again and again as you attempt to achieve your goals. Effective **communication** happens only when you transmit meaning—*relevant* meaning—to your audience.

Communication must be dynamic, fluid, and two-way, which includes listening. Seeking and understanding feedback from your audience—and responding appropriately—form the core of successful business communication. And it isn't as easy as you may think. American novelist Russell Hoban neatly summarized the issue: "When you come right down to it, how many people speak the same language even when they speak the same language?"

Communication Barriers: "That's Not What I Meant!"

Why is effective communication so challenging? The key issue is **noise**: any interference that causes the message you send to be different from the message your audience understands. Some experts define noise in terms of **communication barriers**, which arise in a number of different forms. As you read the definitions, keep in mind that with a bit of extra effort, most are surmountable, and we'll discuss strategies and tips as we move through the chapter.

- **Physical Barriers:** These can range from a document that looks like a wall of type, to a room that's freezing cold, to chairs in your office that force your visitors to sit at a lower level than you.

- **Language Barriers:** Clearly, if you don't speak the language you'll have trouble communicating. But even among people who do share the same language, slang, jargon, and regional accents can interfere with meaning.

- **Body Language Barriers:** Even if your words are inviting, the wrong body language can alienate and distract your audience so completely that they simply won't absorb the content of your message.

- **Perceptual Barriers:** How your audience perceives you and your agenda can create a significant obstacle to effective communication. If possible, explore their perceptions—both positive and negative—in advance!

- **Organizational Barriers:** Some companies have built-in barriers to effective communication, such as an unspoken rule that the people at the top of the organization don't talk to the people at the bottom. These barriers are important to understand but hard to change.

- **Cultural Barriers:** These can include everything from how you greet colleagues and establish eye contact to how you handle disagreement, eat business meals, and make small talk at meetings. As globalization gains speed, **intercultural communication** will become increasingly pivotal to long-term business success.

Identifying and understanding communication barriers is a vital first step toward dismantling them, in order to communicate more effectively with any audience.

communication The transmission of information between a sender and a recipient.

noise Any interference that causes the message you send to be different from the message your audience understands.

communication barriers Obstacles to effective communication, typically defined in terms of physical, language, body language, cultural, perceptual, and organizational barriers.

intercultural communication Communication among people with differing cultural backgrounds.

L02 Nonverbal Communication: Beyond the Words

Most of us focus on what we want to say, but *how* we say it matters even more. In fact, studies cited in *The Wall Street Journal's Career Journal* suggest that during face-to-face communication, only 7% of meaning comes from the verbal content of the message—38% comes from tone of voice, and 55% comes from body language such as facial expressions, gestures, and posture.[1]

The goal of **nonverbal communication** should be to reinforce the meaning of your message. Random facial expressions and disconnected body language—arbitrary arm thrusts, for example—are at best distracting, and at worst clownish. But strong, deliberate nonverbal communication can dramatically magnify the impact of your messages. Here are a few examples of how this can work (but keep in mind that these examples do not necessarily translate from culture to culture):

- **Eye Contact:** Within American culture, sustained eye contact (different from a constant cold stare) indicates integrity, trust, and respectful attention, whether you're communicating with a subordinate, a superior, or a peer.

- **Tone of Voice:** Variation is the key to effectiveness, since paying attention to a monotone takes more concentration than most people are willing to muster. Also, even when you're angry or frustrated, try to keep your voice in a lower pitch to encourage listeners to stay with your message.

- **Facial Expressions:** People vary widely in terms of how much emotion they show on their faces, but virtually everyone communicates, whether or not they know it, through a wide range of expressions that include shy smiles, focused frowns, clenched jaws, squinted eyes, and furrowed brows.

- **Gestures and Posture:** How you handle your body speaks for you. For example, leaning forward can indicate interest, shrugging can suggest a lack of authority, and fidgeting can imply either impatience or nervousness. To increase the power of your message, both your gestures and your posture should be confident, open, and coherent.

As silly as it sounds, one of the easiest, most effective ways to improve your body language is to practice nonverbal communication in front of the mirror. Check out your gestures, notice your facial expressions, and focus on eye contact. If you have the time and ability, it's also helpful (though humbling!) to videotape yourself delivering both a formal and informal message, and ask a trusted friend to dissect the results with you.

Accurately discerning the body language of others is another powerful business communication tool. But keep in mind that you must evaluate others in the context of common sense. When your boss keeps yawning, she may be bored, *or* she may just be tired. When your colleague crosses his arms, he may be indicating defensiveness, *or* he might just normally stand that way.

A New Look at Dressing for Success

Does it ever make sense to go to work looking like THIS? Well, it all depends on your job. If you're a copywriter at an ad agency, or a manager at a record label, or a recruiter for a teen marketing firm, you may even find that a visible tattoo or a pierced tongue can boost your credibility. But if you're a teller at a bank, or a manager at an insurance company, or a salesperson for a pharmaceutical firm, you'll find that a clean-cut, mainstream appearance will work in your favor.

Your appearance is among the most powerful forms of business communication. Some experts believe that more than 50% of another person's perception of you is driven by how you look. Does your appearance always correspond to your performance? Probably not. Perceptions about appearance often aren't fair. But since first impressions and snap judgments are tough to change, don't let how you look get in the way of your success on the job.

Fortunately, first impressions—especially those that stem from your appearance—are easy to manage. Start by observing how others look in your industry. Check out both entry-level workers and people who have made it big. How do you compare? Does the comparison work to your advantage? If not, what can you change? The goal, of course, is to ensure that your appearance sharpens your competitive edge, and the strategy is to tailor your look to reflect the best performers in your type of business.[2]

© Brenda Carson/Shutterstock.com

Same Scene, Different Takes

If you take a stroll across any American college campus, you are likely to see hordes of students with cell phones virtually glued to their ears or dancing under their fingertips from the moment one class ends until the moment the next class begins, and sometimes well into the next class. Social media absorb much of this time and energy. The social media scene has taken hold in China as well, but it has a whole different look and feel. Facebook, Twitter, and YouTube are officially blocked in China, but a raft of homegrown alternatives are thriving in their absence. The average Chinese Internet user is online for a hefty 2.7 hours per day, and social media are particularly popular in part because of rural-to-urban migration that has separated families, the loneliness of the one-child generation, and a distrust of information from government-controlled media. Interestingly, young people in China tend to have even more friends online than offline. The most popular alternative to Twitter in China is Sina Weibo, which—because each character in Chinese represents an entire word—allows for much longer messages within the 140 character limited micro-blogging format. Businesses in China have jumped on the opportunity to use Sina Weibo to deliver relatively long promotional messages, including web links, directly to their target consumers. In today's global environment, businesses must learn to communicate effectively via social media across an array of platforms and countries.[3]

Active Listening: The Great Divider

How we listen (or don't listen) also sends a high-impact, nonverbal message. In fact, an old Chinese proverb asserts that to listen well is as powerful a means of influence as to talk well. Those who do both are unstoppable.

Strong listening skills—**active listening**—play an obvious role in business success. The higher you go in an organization, the more you find that people are listening. Hourly employees may spend 30% of their time listening, while managers often spend 60%, and executives might spend 75% or more. Interestingly, top salespeople also tend to spend about 75% of their communication time listening.[4]

According to the International Listening Association website, 85% of our learning is derived from listening, yet listeners are distracted, forgetful, and preoccupied 75% of the time. If listening is so crucial, why do most of us have such a hard time engaging completely? One reason may be that people *listen* at about 125 to 250 words per minute, but *think* at about 1,000 to 3,000 words per minute—that's a significant gap. Common ways to fill the void include daydreaming, thinking about the past (e.g., last night), and planning for the future (e.g., later in the day).[5]

When you listen, try to use the extra thinking time to make yourself pay closer attention to the speaker. You'll find that people tend to tell more to those who listen better, so if you polish your listening skills, you're also likely to buff up the quality of what you know and when you know it. Exhibit 5.1 highlights some listening do's and don'ts (specific to American culture).[6]

LO3 Choose the Right Channel: A Rich Array of Options

active listening Attentive listening that occurs when the listener focuses his or her complete attention on the speaker.

communication channels The various ways in which a message can be sent, ranging from one-on-one in-person meetings to Internet message boards.

Figuring out the right way to send a message can be a daunting challenge, especially in light of the growing number of choices. The various options are called **communication channels**. Understanding the impact of each channel will help you make the best decision regarding which to use.

Better listening means better results.

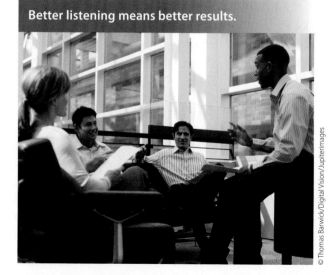

Exhibit 5.1 Tips for Better Listening

LISTENING DO'S	LISTENING DON'TS
Use your extra mental capacity to summarize (to yourself!) what the speaker is saying. Ask yourself: Why does this matter? What's the key point?	Don't even glance at your emails or text messages. You won't fool anyone with those surreptitious peeks.
Take a few notes. It will not only help you concentrate but also communicate to the speaker that his or her thoughts really matter.	Don't begin speaking the moment the person stops talking. Take a brief pause to indicate that you're absorbing the message.
Listen with both your ears and your eyes. Notice any inconsistency between the speaker's words and body language.	Don't get overly comfortable. If your body is too relaxed, your mind may wander more easily.
Use nonverbal communication—nods, smiles, leaning forward—to indicate interest in the speaker.	Don't pick up your phone—or even look at your phone—when you're listening. And whenever it's practical, set your cell phone to vibrate when others are speaking.
Use verbal feedback and questions to indicate understanding and empathy: "So you're saying that…," or "Why do you think that?"	Don't interrupt or finish other people's sentences. There are few better ways to cut off future communication.

© Cengage Learning 2013

Communication channels differ from one another in terms of how much information—or richness—they communicate to the recipient. Exhibit 5.2 provides a brief overview of key channels.

What other channels can you identify? Possibilities include intranet postings, WebEx, Facebook, and text messaging, among others. Where would these additional channels fall on the spectrum? Why?

Consider the Audience: It's Not about You!

Clearly, the needs and expectations of your audience play a crucial role in your choice of communication channel. Even if the recipient's preferences seem absurd—for example, we probably all know someone who refuses to check email or voice mail—remember that your first priority is to communicate your message. If you send it through a channel that the audience doesn't expect or understand or like, you've crippled your chance for successful communication.

Analysis and consideration of your audience should also be a top priority after you choose your communication channel. Meeting the needs of your audience will give you a crucial edge in developing a message that works.

LO4 Pick the Right Words: Is That Car Pre-Loved or Just Plain Used?!

Mark Twain once said, "The difference between the right word and almost the right word is the difference between lightning and the lightning bug." Perhaps that's a little extreme, but it may not be too far from the truth. In the business world, where your messages are competing with so many others for the all-too-limited attention of the recipient, the right words can encourage your audience to stay with you long enough to absorb your message.

Analyze Your Audience

To find the right words, begin with the needs of your audience. Consider:

- **Expectations:** What kind of language do most people use in the organization? Is it formal or informal? Is it direct or roundabout? Should you differ from the norm? Why or why not?
- **Education:** The education level of the audience should drive the level of vocabulary and the complexity of the message.
- **Profession:** Some professions (e.g., website development) are rife with jargon and acronyms. How should this influence your message?

Be Concise

Comedian and sitcom star Jerry Seinfeld, once said, "I will spend an hour editing an eight-word sentence into five." While Jerry might be going a bit too far, it pays to be clear and concise in virtually all business communication. But don't be concise at the expense of completeness; include all information that your audience may need. (It'll save you time down the road.)

Avoid Slang

Unless you're absolutely certain that your audience will understand and appreciate it, do not use slang in either written or verbal communication. The risk of unintentionally alienating yourself from your audience is simply too high.

1 BUSN 8TH EDI

2 6-12 HRS PER WK,

3 STUDENT WILL RECEIVE F ON TWEASSI

4 MON. NIGHT

5 ASSIG CAN BE SUBM UP TO ONE WK LATER PARTIAL CREDIT

6. QUIZZES & EXAMS ARE USUALLY

7. FOR EXAMP: ROWAN S - ASSIG 1

8. MON. MARCH 28

9. MON. MAY 02, @ 10PM

10. MON. MAY 9, @ 10PM

11 *NOT MON. APR. 25 @ 10PM

12. 3

13. 15

14. NO, DISCUSSION FORUMS ARE PART OF YOUR WK REQU & YOU WILL ALSO EARN PARTICIPATION POINTS.

15. BOTH OPTION ARE AVAILABLE

16. FOLLOW THE ADD/DROP,,,

17. ASK CLASSMATES OF YOUR INSTRUCTOR FOR HELP

10. REL UNIFORMITY

11. A WOMAN SURREND OF HER

→ (12) NOT: RESULTED 4PM THE ARRIVAL OF TH
— INCLUDED NO FORM OF RIGHTS
(13) NOT TO EXPAND THEIR EMPIRES
ANSWIS TO AVOID TRADING W/ THE
(14) WOMAN & MEN WERE

1. MEX & PERU

(2) NOT SMALL IN POPULA
       ANSW: LARGE, WEALTHY, & SOP

3. IT CONTAINE A SYST

4 PROBABLY 10,000 - 30,000

5 DEVELOP EFFICIENT

(6) NOT WERE ENTIRELY AGRICUL, ANSW: HAD ELABORATE TRADE

7. REFLECTED THE NATIVE

8 FAM OFTEN CLAIMED

9. NAT AME FAILED

COMMON ENEMY IS THE IGNORANCE OF OUR OWN ENEMY.

1. KNOWLEDGE   TAILOPEZ.COM

2. STRATEGY

3. EXECUTION
   - IMMURSION

QUIZ 3:
*1. NON TARIFF BARRIERZ
2. TO INCREASE DOMESTIC

*3.

4.

5.

6.

7.

8.

9.

10.

Avoid Bias

Intentionally or unintentionally, words can communicate biases that can interfere with your message, alienate your audience, and call your own character into question. As a result, you will be less effective in achieving the immediate goals of your communication (and possibly any future communication as well). Three kinds of **bias** are common:

Gender Bias Gender bias consists of words that suggest stereotypical attitudes toward a specific gender. Avoiding bias becomes tricky when you simply don't know the gender of your audience, which often happens when you apply for a job in writing. The best solution, of course, is to find out the recipient's name, but if you can't do that, do not address your message to "Dear Sir" or "Dear Madam"; rather, use the title of the position (e.g., "Dear Hiring Manager").

> **Companies** that communicate effectively have a 47% higher return to shareholders.
> — BusinessWeek

Another common challenge is to establish agreement in your sentences without creating gender bias. Consider the following example:

The guitarist who loses his instrument must buy a new one.

Technically, this sentence is correct, but it implies that all guitarists are men. A simple solution would be to convert to plural:

Guitarists who lose their instruments must buy new ones.

This approach almost always works to help you sidestep the gender bias issue. In the rare case that it doesn't, you can simply use the "his or her" option.

Age Bias Age bias refers to words that suggest stereotypical attitudes toward people of specific ages. In American culture, older people tend to experience negative age bias much

bias A preconception about members of a particular group. Common forms of bias include gender bias; age bias; and race, ethnicity, or nationality bias.

Exhibit 5.2 Communication Channels

COMMUNICATION CHANNEL	CHANNEL RICHNESS	WHEN SHOULD YOU USE THIS CHANNEL?
MEMOS/REPORTS	Very low: Your audience won't gain any information from your tone or your body language.	When your content is uncontroversial When you must reach a number of people with the same message When you must communicate lengthy or detailed information
EMAIL	Very low: Here, too, your audience learns nothing beyond your words themselves.	When your content is uncontroversial When you must reach a number of people with the same message
INSTANT MESSAGE/TEXTING	Very low: Because so many of us IM or text with as few words as possible, your audience will pick up only the basics.	When your content is uncontroversial When you want a quick response regarding relatively simple issues When you know that your audience won't be annoyed by it
VOICE MAIL	Low: Your audience has the benefit of hearing your tone but not seeing your body language.	When your content is uncontroversial When you don't need a record of your message (but don't forget that the recipient can easily save or forward your voice mail)
TELEPHONE CONVERSATION	Moderate: Your audience benefits from hearing your tone and how it changes through the call.	When you need to either deliver your message or get a response quickly When your content is more personal or controversial When you need or want a spontaneous, dynamic dialogue with the recipient
VIDEOCONFERENCING	High: Especially with state-of-the-art equipment, the channel conveys much of the richness of actually being there.	When you need to reach multiple people with complex or high-priority content When you need or want a spontaneous, dynamic dialogue with an audience that you cannot reach in person
IN-PERSON PRESENTATION	High: Your audience directly experiences every element of your communication, from verbal content, to tone, to body language.	When you need to reach a large audience with an important message When you need or want to experience the immediate response of your audience
FACE-TO-FACE MEETING	Very high: Your audience experiences your full message even more directly.	When your message is personal, emotional, complex, or high-priority (but if the recipient might be volatile, you should consider using a less-immediate channel) When you need or want instant feedback from your audience

© Cengage Learning 2013

Huh?!!

Between the Beijing Olympics in 2008 and the Shanghai World Expo in 2010, China has gained an increasingly high profile on the world stage, and so has Chinglish, a sometimes-bizarre blend of Chinese and mangled English language that seems to pop up on signs, menus, and labels throughout the tourist-heavy cities of China. For example:

○ Plus-sized shoppers at the Scat clothing chain might find themselves needing to buy "fatso" or "lard-bucket" sizes.

○ Before the Beijing Olympics, tourists could visit Racist Park, later rechristened Minorities Park to avoid sending a misleadingly negative message to visitors about Chinese culture.

○ Port-a-potties have sometimes been located in the "urine district."

○ Adventurous eaters can order fried enema at local eateries.

○ In the past, the sick may have sought treatment at the Dongda Anus Hospital, now called the Dongda Proctology Hospital.

Although many of these language goofs are highly amusing, a number of Chinese find the snickers humiliating rather than funny. In fact, as the World Expo approached, the Chinese government established the Shanghai Commission for the Management of Language Use to eradicate by fiat the worst examples of mangled English. One of the chief translators, Jeffrey Yao, underscores that the purpose of signs is communication, not entertainment. "I want to see people nodding that they understand the message on these signs. I don't want to see them laughing."[7]

此段200米,当心
落石,请靠岩壁行走,
快速通过请勿逗留.
Within 200 meters, notice the rockslide, please is run about by cliff.

> *I didn't have time to write a short letter, so I wrote a long one instead.*
> — MARK TWAIN

active voice *Sentence construction in which the subject performs the action expressed by the verb (e.g., My sister wrote the paper). The active voice works better for the vast majority of business communication.*

more often than younger people. This happens despite specific federal legislation outlawing employment discrimination against people over 40 years old. The reason may be that American culture associates youth with highly valued qualities such as creativity, speed, independence, and individualism. This bias will become increasingly detrimental as the workforce ages. Here is an example of age bias:

We need someone young and dynamic in this position!

You could easily eliminate the negative bias by simply deleting the word "young" or by replacing it with the word "energetic." One clear benefit of eliminating bias in this case would be a broader applicant pool that might include an older person who is more dynamic than any of the younger applicants.

Race, Ethnicity, and Nationality Bias Words can also suggest stereotypical attitudes toward specific races, ethnicities, and nationalities. Leaving aside prejudice—which is clearly wrong—the problems in this area are usually unintentional and stem from unarticulated assumptions about a person's attitudes, opinions, and experiences. Your best plan for avoiding bias would be to forgo any references to race, ethnicity, or nationality unless they are directly relevant and clearly necessary. And, of course, never simply assume

that a single person embodies the attitudes, opinions, and experiences of a larger group. If you communicate with each person as an individual, you will not only avoid bias, but also develop deeper, more effective channels of communication.

Use the Active Voice Whenever Possible

Active voice facilitates direct, powerful, concise communication. You have used the **active voice** when the subject of

There's English and then There's English

Most people who have traveled to other English-speaking countries know that speaking the "same" language doesn't guarantee understanding. In the United States, for example, to say that you're full suggests that you've had too much to eat, but to say that you're full in Australia suggests that you're drunk. To table an issue in the United States means to temporarily avoid discussing it, while to table an issue in England means to bring it to the table and discuss it immediately.

The potential for harmful misunderstandings in a business setting should be clear with just these two small examples.

Even just within the United States, regional differences in the meaning of common words abound. According to the *Dictionary of American Regional English*, a sub sandwich is variously known as a sub, a hero, a hoagie, a grinder, a Cuban, or a torpedo, depending on where you live. A Northeasterner might call a dirty bathroom skeevy, while a Californian would simply call it disgusting. Although strangers tend to speak to each other in a somewhat homogenized fashion, business communication will clearly be smoother, and trust will build more quickly, if everyone involved attempts to learn the others' vocabulary, even when they all speak the same language.[8]

© Nayashkova Olga/ Shutterstock.com

---

your sentence *is* doing the action described by the verb. You have used the **passive voice** when the subject of your sentence *is not* doing the action described by the verb.

Here's an example of a sentence that uses the active voice:

Our team made a mistake in the sales forecast.

Our team, the subject of the sentence, did the action described by the verb (making a mistake). The same sentence in the passive voice would read as follows:

A mistake was made in the sales forecast.

In this version, the subject of the sentence is the mistake, which clearly did not do the action. As you can see from these examples, another benefit of active voice is accountability, which can create deeper trust between you and your audience.

LO5 Write High-Impact Messages: Breaking through the Clutter

For many businesspeople, checking email—or even regular mail—is like approaching a fire hose for a sip of water. Goal number one is to crank down the pressure to get what you need without being knocked over by all the rest. To attain this goal, many people simply press the delete button.

Your challenge as a writer is to make your message a must-read, and the starting point should be the needs of your audience. Consider how the audience will respond to your message—think about how they will feel, not what they will

do—and use that information to guide your writing. But keep in mind that it's hard to know for sure how the recipient will respond. For instance, each of the responses in Exhibit 5.3 could be reasonable for different people:

How do you know how your audience will respond? In most cases, you must simply guess based on as much evidence as you can find. The value of making a thoughtful guess is that the chances of achieving your goal will soar if you happen to be correct.

The anticipated audience response should directly affect how you structure your writing.

⊃ If the recipient will feel positive or neutral about your message, the memo or email should begin with your bottom line. What is your request or recommendation or conclusion? Why should the audience care? Once

> **passive voice** Sentence construction in which the subject does not do the action expressed by the verb; rather the subject is acted upon (e.g., *The paper was written by my sister*). The passive voice tends to be less effective for business communication.

EXHIBIT 5.3 Messages and Responses

MESSAGE	POSSIBLE RESPONSES
Please note the new computer password procedures.	Positive: *Great! We've really needed this.* Neutral: *OK, no big deal.* Negative: *Not another change…*
The company plans to restructure your work team when the project is complete	Positive: *I can hardly wait to work with new people!* Neutral: *It's all part of the job…* Negative: *Not another change!*

© Cengage Learning 2013

---

you've clarified those points, follow up with your rationale and explanations (keeping in mind that less is usually more for time-starved businesspeople).

- If the recipient will feel negative about your message, start the memo or email with a couple of lines that present the rationale before you give the bottom line. Follow up with alternatives if there are any, and be sure to end on a positive note (rather than an apology). This structure is less straightforward, but it's a more effective way to communicate your message.

See Exhibit 5.4 for sample emails based on different anticipated responses to messages in an Internet game development firm.

Strike the Right Tone

Good business writing sounds natural—it flows like spoken language and reads like a conversation on paper. To strike the right tone for any given message, remember that you can choose from a wide variety of conversational styles, from formal to chatty. Imagine yourself speaking to the recipient of your message, and you'll find that the right tone emerges naturally. A few guidelines will also help:

- Use common words in most situations (e.g., *use* versus *utilize*).

- Use the active voice (e.g., *We made a mistake* versus *A mistake was made*).

- Use personal pronouns (*I, you*) whenever appropriate.

- Use contractions (*I'll, don't, here's*) as often as you would when speaking.

Don't Make Grammar Goofs

Grammatical errors will distract your reader from your writing and undermine your credibility. Most businesspeople are aware of the more common grammatical errors, so they tend to jump off the page before the content of the message. But if you're uncertain about a particular point, look at how professionally edited publications handle similar issues. Finally, don't be afraid to do a commonsense check on any grammatical question.

Edward P. Bailey, noted professor and business communication author, points out that many writers make grammar mistakes based on phantom knowledge—"mythical" grammar rules that aren't even in grammar handbooks. His research firmly reassures us that:

- It is OK to end a sentence with a preposition when doing so sounds natural and does not involve excess words (e.g., *Where is this book from?* is much better than *From where is this book?*).

- It is OK to begin sentences with "And" or "But" (e.g., *Most teens enjoy videogames with a moderate level of violence. But a small, vocal minority strongly advocates a more clean-cut approach.*).

- It is OK to split infinitives (e.g., *Try to effectively film the next scene* is a perfectly acceptable sentence, even though "effectively" is inserted between "to" and "film.").

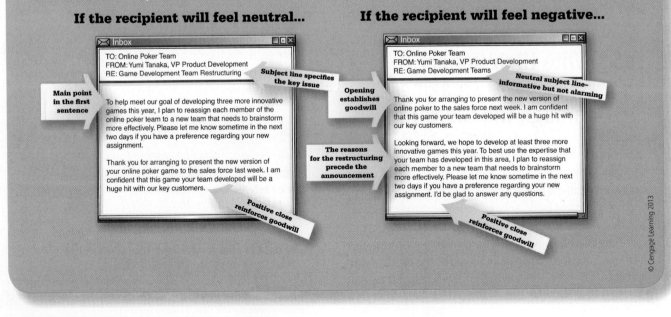

EXHIBIT 5.4 Sample Emails: Same Message, Different Approach

If the recipient will feel neutral...

TO: Online Poker Team
FROM: Yumi Tanaka, VP Product Development
RE: Game Development Team Restructuring

Subject line specifies the key issue

Main point in the first sentence

To help meet our goal of developing three more innovative games this year, I plan to reassign each member of the online poker team to a new team that needs to brainstorm more effectively. Please let me know sometime in the next two days if you have a preference regarding your new assignment.

Thank you for arranging to present the new version of your online poker game to the sales force last week. I am confident that this game your team developed will be a huge hit with our key customers.

Positive close reinforces goodwill

If the recipient will feel negative...

TO: Online Poker Team
FROM: Yumi Tanaka, VP Product Development
RE: Game Development Teams

Neutral subject line—informative but not alarming

Opening establishes goodwill

Thank you for arranging to present the new version of online poker to the sales force next week. I am confident that this game your team developed will be a huge hit with our key customers.

The reasons for the restructuring precede the announcement

Looking forward, we hope to develop at least three more innovative games this year. To best use the expertise that your team has developed in this area, I plan to reassign each member to a new team that needs to brainstorm more effectively. Please let me know sometime in the next two days if you have a preference regarding your new assignment. I'd be glad to answer any questions.

Positive close reinforces goodwill

© Cengage Learning 2013

In 2010, email use by 12-to 17-year olds dropped 59%, due to the increasing popularity of social networking sites.

— Time Magazine

Once you accept these principles, your writing not only will sound more natural but also will flow more easily. Winston Churchill, a renowned writer and speaker, was on-board with this common sense approach decades ago, as we can see from his joking comment that poked fun at tortured writing: "From now on, ending a sentence with a preposition is something up with which I will not put."[9]

Use Block Paragraphs

There are three elements to block paragraphs: (1) use single spacing, (2) double space between paragraphs, and (3) do not indent the first sentence of your paragraphs. This approach has become standard for business writing over the past decade, as writers have begun to include an increasing number of additional elements such as headings and illustrations. The block paragraphs create a more organized look for your page, guiding the reader's eye through the key elements of your structure.

Use Headings and Bulleted Lists Wherever Appropriate

Both headings and bulleted lists will guide your reader more easily through your writing. And the easier it is for your reader, the more likely that he or she will absorb your message, which is, of course, your ultimate goal.

- ◗ **Headings:** A heading is not a title; rather, it is a label for one of several parts. If you have only one part, skip the heading and use a title or a subject line. Consider using informative headings (e.g., "Recruitment has stalled," rather than simply "Recruitment"), or question headings (e.g., "Have we met our recruitment goals for this campaign?"). And remember, headings are just as effective for letters and emails as they are for memos, and they are perfectly OK in one-page documents.

- ◗ **Bulleted Lists:** Bulleted lists are an invaluable tool that you can use to engage your reader's attention whenever you have more than one of anything in your writing (e.g., next steps, similar sections, questions). By formatting your lists with bullets, you are directing your reader's eye through your writing.

Exhibit 5.5 Ten Tips for Excellent Email

1. *Consider both your primary and secondary readers. In other words, never forget that your reader may forward your email without considering the potential impact on you.*

2. Keep it short! Many readers won't scroll down past whatever shows on their screen, so be sure to get your bottom line close to the top of your message.

3. Don't forget to proofread. This is especially important if you're asking someone to do something for you. And remember that your spell checker won't catch every mistake.

4. Use standard writing. Smiley faces, abbreviations, and five exclamation points are all fine if you're emailing your buddies, but in more formal messages they can make you look silly (or like you just don't care).

5. Avoid attachments if possible. They take time and space to open, and they don't always translate well to cell phones and PDAs. Instead, cut and paste relevant sections of the attachment into your email.

6. Don't assume privacy. Think of your emails as postcards that anyone (especially computer system administrators and managers) can read along the way. In that light, try not to use email to communicate negative or critical messages.

7. Respond promptly to emails. If you don't have time to respond to the email itself, consider sending a message such as "Sorry, but I'm swamped right now—will get back to you early next week."

8. Assume the best. Since emails are often brief, they can cause unintentional offense. If you receive an off-key message, don't be afraid to inquire: "I'm not sure what you mean … could you please explain?"

9. Create a compelling subject line. Make your reader want to open your message. Briefly communicate the topic of your message and why your reader should care.

10. Think before you write, and think again before you send! Since it's so easy to send email, too many people send messages in an emotional moment that they later regret. Take time to think and think again.

© Cengage Learning 2013

Be sincere; be brief; be seated.

— Franklin D. Roosevelt

© risteski goce/Shutterstock.com

L06 Create and Deliver Successful Verbal Presentations: Hook 'Em and Reel 'Em In!

What do people fear most? The *Book of Lists* asserts that public speaking ranks number one for the majority of people, high above the fear of death at number four. So, when people say they would rather die than give a speech, they may really mean it! This section is designed to mitigate any fear you might have about public speaking by giving you guidance on how to create and deliver a high-impact verbal presentation.

As with most communication, the needs of the audience are the best place to begin. How does your audience feel about you and your topic? Are they interested? Hostile? Positive? What were they doing before your presentation? Dragging themselves out of bed after a late night at a sales meeting? Eating lunch? Use this information to guide how you develop your presentation. For instance, an eager, educated audience might not need as much background as a more lethargic, less-interested audience.

Giving great presentations may be easier than you think.

© Jon Feingersh/Iconica/Getty Images

Opening

The opening of your presentation gives you a chance to grab the attention of the audience. If your opening hooks them, you've boosted the likelihood that you will hold their attention throughout the presentation. But developing that hook can be a challenge. The following are some suggestions for effective hooks:

- **An Interesting or Startling Statistic:** In a presentation regarding a risk management program, you could open by sharing that "Your odds of being killed in a plane crash are about one in twenty-five million, while your odds of being killed falling out of bed are about one in two million. What does this mean for us?"

- **Audience Involvement:** Pulling the audience into your opening can be very effective. For instance, in a presentation for a clothing company: "Imagine yourself with me at 11 P.M. on a Friday night, standing in line for admission to the hottest club in New York. As we inch forward, we suddenly realize that three other women in line are wearing the exact same dress as you…."

- **A Compelling Story or Anecdote:** This approach works best when it's completely genuine, using specific details that are directly relevant to the audience. For instance, in a presentation about employee benefits, you might want to share the story of a colleague who beat cancer using the company's innovative healthcare program.

- **A Relevant Simile or Metaphor:** Patricia Fripp, an award-winning keynote speaker, shares a simile that worked well to open a presentation for a colleague: "Being a scientist is like doing a jigsaw puzzle in a snowstorm at night… you don't have all the pieces… and you don't have the picture to work from."

- **Engaging Questions:** In a presentation about customer service, you could open by asking: "How many of you have spent far too long waiting on hold for customer service that was finally delivered by a surly agent who clearly knew nothing about your question?"

Body

The most common presentation mistake is to include too many key ideas in the body of your presentation. Audiences simply cannot absorb more than two to four main points, and three are ideal. Specific examples and vivid comparisons will illustrate your points and bring them to life, while trusted sources, specific data, and expert quotations will increase your credibility and persuasiveness. Regardless of the length of your presentation, be sure to use clear transitions as you move from point to point.

Just before launching into the body of your presentation, you should tell the audience your key points, ideally with visual reinforcement. Then as you move to each new point, you can refer to the blueprint that you established upfront. A clear, explicit structure will help the audience track with you as you move through your material.

Close

Ideally, the close of your presentation will summarize your key points. Then circle back to your introduction, so that the beginning and the end serve as "bookends" for the body of your presentation. For instance, if you began by asking questions, end by answering them. If you began with an anecdote, end by referring to the same story. As an alternative (or maybe an addition), consider sharing a quotation or a bit of humor relevant to your content.

Also, keep in mind that you should verbally signal to your audience that you are about to conclude. Once you do so—by saying, "In summary," for instance—be sure that you actually do conclude. Nothing alienates an audience more quickly than launching into another point after you've told them you're finished! Your body language will support your conclusion if you turn off your projector and move toward the audience to answer questions. And even if you aren't so eager to field questions, try to paste a receptive look on your face—it'll increase your credibility and set a positive tone for the Q&A session.

Questions

At the start of your presentation, decide whether you want to handle questions throughout your talk or save them for the end. Tell your audience your preference upfront; most of the time they will respect it. But if you do receive unwanted questions in the middle of your presentation, don't ignore them. Simply remind the questioner that you'll leave plenty of time for questions at the end.

Not surprisingly, the best tip for handling questions is to be prepared. Since it's tough to anticipate questions for your own presentation, you may want to enlist the help of a trusted colleague to brainstorm the possibilities. And don't just come up with the questions—prepare the answers, too!

Visual Aids

Studies suggest that three days after a presentation, people retain 10% of what they heard from an oral presentation, 35% from a visual presentation, and 65% from a combined visual and oral presentation. The numbers are compelling: visual aids matter. Depending on your audience, effective, high-impact visual aids could range from props to charts to mounted boards. But in business communication, PowerPoint slides are the most common option. If you use PowerPoint, consider these suggestions:

- **Showing Works Better Than Simply Telling:** Use pictures and other graphics whenever possible.

- **Less Is More:** Keep this helpful guideline in mind: no more than seven words per line, no more than seven lines per slide.

- **Don't Just Read Your Slides Aloud:** Instead, paraphrase, add examples, and offer analysis and interpretation.

- **Go Easy on the Special Effects:** Too many sounds and too much animation can be painfully distracting.

- **Don't Let Your Slides Upstage You:** Look at your audience, not at the slides. And dim the screen when you're not specifically using it.[10]

Google Presentations

Although Microsoft PowerPoint remains the software option of choice for business presentations, Google Presentations software is swiftly gaining ground. Google Presentations is one of a growing number of applications based in "the cloud." This means that when you buy a new computer, you don't need to spend hundreds of dollars buying PowerPoint. You simply log into your Google account, use the Google Presentations software, and save your finished product on Google's servers. Since your work is stored on the Internet, you can access it from any device with a web connection—you don't need to email it to yourself, or store it on a temperamental local drive, or worry about saving your changes as you move from work to home to school.

But Google Presentations is far from perfect. If you temporarily lose your Internet connection—while on a plane or a bus, for instance—you cannot access your work. Security might be a worry, since web-based data may be vulnerable to hackers. If Google disables your account for any reason, your work is lost. And Google Presentations does not yet include all the features available in PowerPoint, such as chart-making tools and advanced slide animations. The price, though, is pretty attractive: free! And that includes new versions and updates.

From a long-term perspective, another key benefit of Google Presentations—and all other cloud computing applications—is environmental. *Newsweek* writer Brian Braiker points out that "conducting affairs in the cloud is not only convenient, it's also greener: less capital and fewer printouts means less waste." All of which suggests that the forecast for Google Presentations is far from cloudy.[11]

Handling Nerves

Believe it or not, most experts agree that nervousness can be useful before a presentation. A little adrenalin can help you perform better, think faster, and focus more

© Austin Adams/Shutterstock.com

completely. But we all know that out-of-control nerves can interfere with effectiveness. Here are some ideas to mitigate speech anxiety:

- ❍ Send yourself positive messages; visualize success. Examples: "I will be dynamic and engaging." "They will completely support my new product idea."

- ❍ Take ten slow, deep breaths—use the yoga approach of breathing in through your nose and out through your mouth.

- ❍ Take a sip of water to loosen your throat muscles and mitigate a shaking voice. (Water also gives you a way to fill pauses.)

- ❍ Pick a friendly face or two in the audience, and imagine yourself speaking only to those people (but don't stare at them!).

- ❍ Remind yourself that the audience wants you to succeed. Focus on their needs rather than your own nerves.

If possible, have a handful of one-on-one conversations with audience members before your presentation. This will almost certainly reinforce that they want you to succeed, which will likely take the edge off your nerves . . .

Handling Hostility

We've all seen hostile questioners who seem determined to undermine presenters. It can be awful to watch, but it's surprisingly easy to handle. Here are a few tips:

- ❍ Stay calm and professional. Rightly or wrongly, the hostile questioner has won the day if you get defensive or nervous.

- ❍ Don't be afraid to pause before you answer to gather your thoughts and allow the hostility to diffuse. (A sip of water can provide good cover for a thought-gathering moment.)

- ❍ Once you've answered the question, don't reestablish eye contact with the questioner. Doing so would suggest that you are seeking approval for your response, which only invites further hostile follow-up.

- ❍ If the questioner insists on follow-up, you may need to agree to disagree. If so, be decisive: "Sounds like we have two different points of view on this complex issue."

- ❍ Use body language to reinforce that you are done interacting with the questioner. Take a couple of steps away, and ask another part of the group whether they have any questions.

Incorporating Humor

Everyone likes to be funny, but incorporating humor in a business presentation can be risky. Only do it if you're very, very sure that it's funny. Even so, double-check that your jokes are appropriate and relevant. You should never, ever laugh at the expense of any member of your audience. Even laughing at yourself is chancy, since you risk diminishing your credibility. (But a joke at your own expense is always effective if you make a mistake; there's no better way to recover the goodwill of your audience.)

A spot on the back wall?

Many people have heard the old myth that no one will know the difference if you calm your nerves by looking at a spot on the back wall rather than at the audience. Don't do it! While *you* may be more comfortable, your audience will be mystified . . . more often than not, they'll keep turning around to find out what's so interesting back there!

Delivery

Some people are naturals, but for the rest of us, **dynamic delivery** is a learned skill. It begins and ends with preparation, but keep in mind that practice doesn't always make perfect—in fact, practice more often just makes permanent. So be sure that you practice with an eye toward improvement. If possible, you should set up a practice situation that's close to the real thing. If you'll be standing to present, stand while you practice, since standing makes many people feel more vulnerable. Consider practicing in front of a mirror to work on eye contact and gestures. Also, try recording your voice to work on a lively tone.

Finally, practice in front of a trusted friend or two who can give you valuable feedback. See Exhibit 5.6 for Ten Tips for Dynamic Delivery.

EXHIBIT 5.6 Ten Tips for Dynamic Delivery

1. PRACTICE!
2. Know your material, but never memorize it word for word.
3. Look directly at members of your audience at least 50% of the time.
4. Vary your voice, your facial expressions, and your body language.
5. Use selective notes (but keep them inconspicuous).
6. Stick to your allotted time.
7. Slow down and listen to yourself.
8. Don't apologize (unless you really did something wrong!).
9. Remember to use natural gestures.
10. PRACTICE!

© Cengage Learning 2013

THE BIG PICTURE

Effective communication saves time and money—boosting performance and morale—across every area of business. But one vital principle holds true regardless of the more specific nature of your communication: the best way to achieve your goals is to focus on your audience, not on yourself. If you understand the goals, expectations, and needs of your audience, you can tailor your communication to boost your chances (sometimes dramatically) of accomplishing your objectives.

As globalization and technological change continue to accelerate, new communication challenges will likely develop across the spectrum of business. To ensure that your communication continues to be effective, keep an open mind. Pay attention to differences among cultures, to language usage in professional publications, and to new communication technology. And don't be afraid to consult an up-to-date communication website or handbook every so often. When other resources aren't available, rely on courtesy, consideration, and common sense—valuable tools to guide your communication in any situation.

CAREERS IN BUSINESS COMMUNICATION

Clearly, superb communication skills are essential for any career in business, and they become even more important as you climb the ranks of an organization. In fact, even in fields that traditionally have emphasized more analytical skills (such as accounting and finance), recruiters are now seeking candidates with strong writing and speaking skills. These skills have become even more important in the face of increased globalization. But business careers that center almost exclusively on communication are typically in the marketing realm, such as advertising, public relations, sales, and related fields, which we will discuss in more detail later in the text.

What *else?*

RIP & REVIEW CARDS IN THE BACK
and visit www.cengagebrain.com!

6

Business Formation:
Choosing the Form that Fits

LEARNING OBJECTIVES
After studying this chapter, you will be able to...

LO 1 Describe the characteristics of the four basic forms of business ownership

LO 2 Discuss the advantages and disadvantages of a sole proprietorship

LO 3 Evaluate the pros and cons of the partnership as a form of business ownership

LO 4 Explain why corporations have become the dominant form of business ownership

LO 5 Explain why limited liability companies are becoming an increasingly popular form of business ownership

LO 6 Evaluate the advantages and disadvantages of franchising

> # A CORPORATION IS AN *ARTIFICIAL* BEING, INVISIBLE, INTANGIBLE, AND EXISTING ONLY IN THE CONTEMPLATION OF THE *LAW*.
>
> — JOHN MARSHALL, FOURTH CHIEF JUSTICE OF THE UNITED STATES

LO1 Business Ownership Options: The Big Four

One of the most important decisions entrepreneurs must make when they start a new business is the form of ownership they'll use. The form they choose will affect virtually every aspect of establishing and operating their firm, including the initial cost of setting up the business, the way the profits are distributed, the types of taxes (if any) the business itself must pay, and the types of regulations it must obey. Choice of ownership also determines the degree to which each owner has personal liability for the firm's debts and the sources of funds available to the firm to finance future expansion.

The vast majority of businesses in the United States are owned and organized under one of four forms:

1. A **sole proprietorship** is a business that is owned, and usually managed, by a single individual. As far as the law is concerned, a sole proprietorship is simply an extension of the owner. Any earnings of the company are treated as income of the owner; likewise, any debts the company incurs are considered to be the owner's personal debts.

2. A **partnership** is a voluntary agreement under which two or more people act as co-owners of a business for profit. As we'll see later in the chapter, there are several types of partnerships. In its most basic form, known as a **general partnership**, each partner has the right to participate in the company's management and share in profits—but also has unlimited liability for any debts the company incurs.

3. A **corporation** is a business entity created by filing a form (known in most states as the **articles of incorporation**) with the appropriate state agency, paying the state's incorporation fees, and meeting other requirements. (The specifics vary among states.) Unlike a sole proprietorship or a partnership, a corporation is considered to be a legal entity that is separate and distinct from its owners. In many ways, a corporation is like an artificial person. It can legally engage in virtually any business activity a natural person can pursue. For example, a corporation can enter into binding contracts, borrow money, own property, pay taxes, and initiate legal actions (such as lawsuits) in its own name. It can even be a partner in a partnership or an owner of another corporation. Because of a corporation's status as a separate legal entity, the owners of a corporation have **limited liability**—meaning they aren't personally responsible for the debts and obligations of their company.

4. A **limited liability company (LLC)** is a hybrid form of business ownership that is similar in some respects to a corporation while having other characteristics that are similar to a partnership. Like a corporation, a limited liability company is considered a legal entity separate from its owners. Also like a corporation—and as its name implies—an LLC offers its owners limited liability for the debts of their business. But it offers more flexibility than a corporation in terms of tax treatment; in fact, one of the most interesting characteristics of an LLC is that its owners can elect to have their business taxed either as a corporation *or* a partnership. Many states even allow individuals to form single-person LLCs that are taxed as if they were sole proprietorships.

Sole proprietorships, partnerships, and corporations have been around in some form since the beginning of our nation's history, but limited liability companies are a relatively new form of ownership in the United States. In 1977, Wyoming passed the first

sole proprietorship A form of business ownership with a single owner who usually actively manages the company.

partnership A voluntary agreement under which two or more people act as co-owners of a business for profit.

general partnership A partnership in which all partners can take an active role in managing the business and have unlimited liability for any claims against the firm.

corporation A form of business ownership in which the business is considered a legal entity that is separate and distinct from its owners.

articles of incorporation The document filed with a state government to establish the existence of a new corporation.

limited liability When owners are not personally liable for claims against their firm. Owners with limited liability may lose their investment in the company, but their other personal assets are protected.

limited liability company (LLC) A form of business ownership that offers both limited liability to its owners and flexible tax treatment.

state statute allowing LLCs, and Florida became the second state to do so in 1982. But it wasn't until a ruling by the Internal Revenue Service (IRS) in 1988 clarifying the tax treatment of LLCs that most other states followed suit. Today every state has enacted LLC legislation, and the LLC has become a very popular ownership option. In many states, filings to form LLCs now outnumber filings to form corporations.[1]

Exhibits 6.1 and 6.2 provide some interesting insights about the relative importance of each form of ownership. As shown in Exhibit 6.1, the sole proprietorship is by far the most common type of business organization in the United States. In 2007, over 23 million individuals reported operating nonfarm sole proprietorships. This represented more than 72 percent of the total number of business enterprises. As a group, these sole proprietorships reported $1.32 trillion in revenue and almost $281 billion in net income (profit). But while these figures are impressive in the aggregate, most individual sole proprietorships are quite small. According to the U.S. Census Bureau's *2011 Statistical Abstract*, more than two-thirds of all sole proprietorships reported annual revenue of less than $25,000, while only a tiny fraction of 1% reported receipts in excess of $1 million.[2]

As Exhibit 6.2 shows, when it comes to economic impact, the corporate form of ownership rules. Though corporations comprised only 18.3% of all business entities, in 2007 they reported about 66% of all business profits. Corporations like Walmart, ExxonMobil, General Electric, Apple, and Boeing have annual sales revenues measured in the billions (sometimes hundreds of billions) of dollars. But not all corporations are multibillion-dollar enterprises. In 2007, about 24% of all corporations reported total revenues of less than $25,000.[3]

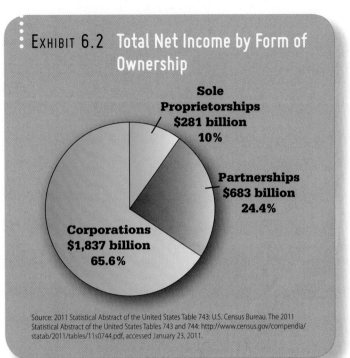

Exhibit 6.2 Total Net Income by Form of Ownership

Sole Proprietorships $281 billion 10%

Partnerships $683 billion 24.4%

Corporations $1,837 billion 65.6%

Source: 2011 Statistical Abstract of the United States Table 743: U.S. Census Bureau. The 2011 Statistical Abstract of the United States Tables 743 and 744: http://www.census.gov/compendia/statab/2011/tables/11s0744.pdf, accessed January 23, 2011.

As you can see from Exhibit 6.1, partnerships are less common than sole proprietorships or corporations. Still, in 2007 over 3 million businesses were classified as partnerships in the United States. And partnerships tend to be both larger and more profitable than sole proprietorships. As Exhibit 6.2 shows, in the aggregate, partnerships earned substantially higher total net income than sole proprietorships, despite the fact that sole proprietorships outnumbered partnerships by a ratio of almost eight to one![4]

You've probably noticed that Exhibits 6.1 and 6.2 don't include specific information about limited liability companies. That's because these exhibits are based on information taken from annual tax returns submitted to the Internal Revenue Service (IRS). The IRS doesn't track LLC information separately. Instead, it classifies each LLC based on the tax treatment the company selects. LLCs that choose to be taxed as partnerships are classified as partnerships, while those choosing to be taxed as corporations are classified as corporations. (The vast majority of LLCs elect to be taxed as partnerships, so most LLC earnings are reported in the partnership category.)

We'll see that each form of ownership has distinct advantages and disadvantages. As a company grows

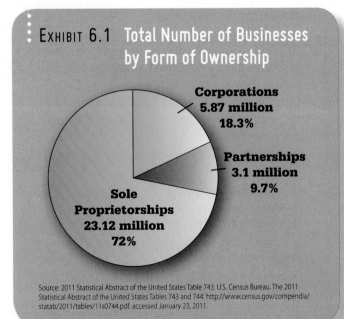

Exhibit 6.1 Total Number of Businesses by Form of Ownership

Corporations 5.87 million 18.3%

Partnerships 3.1 million 9.7%

Sole Proprietorships 23.12 million 72%

Source: 2011 Statistical Abstract of the United States Table 743: U.S. Census Bureau. The 2011 Statistical Abstract of the United States Tables 743 and 744: http://www.census.gov/compendia/statab/2011/tables/11s0744.pdf, accessed January 23, 2011.

Corporation: an ingenious device for obtaining profit without individual responsibility.

— AMBROSE BIERCE, 19TH-CENTURY COMPILER OF *THE DEVIL'S DICTIONARY* and matures, the form of ownership that's best suited to its needs may change. Fortunately, the form of ownership for a business isn't set in stone. For example, it is possible—and in fact quite common—for business owners to convert from a sole proprietorship to a corporation, or from a corporation to a limited liability company.

Advantages and Disadvantages of Sole Proprietorships

Our look at Exhibits 6.1 and 6.2 raises two questions about sole proprietorships. First, why is this form of ownership so popular? Second, why do sole proprietorships usually remain relatively small? A look at the advantages and disadvantages of sole proprietorships can help answer these questions.

Advantages

Sole proprietorships offer some very attractive advantages to people starting a business:

- **Ease of Formation:** Compared to the other forms of ownership we'll discuss, the paperwork and costs involved in forming a sole proprietorship are minimal. No special forms must be filed, and no special fees must be paid. Entrepreneurs who are eager to get a business up and running quickly can find this a compelling advantage.

- **Retention of Control:** As the only owner of a sole proprietorship, you're in control. You have the ability to manage your business the way you want. If you want to "be your own boss," a sole proprietorship might look very attractive.

- **Pride of Ownership:** One of the main reasons many people prefer a sole proprietorship is the feeling of pride and the personal satisfaction they gain from owning and running their own business.

- **Retention of Profits:** If your business is successful, *all* the profits go to you—minus your personal taxes, of course.

- **Possible Tax Advantage:** No taxes are levied directly on the earnings of sole proprietorships as a business. Instead, the earnings are taxed only as income of the proprietor. As we'll see when we discuss corporations, this avoids the undesirable possibility of double taxation of earnings.

Disadvantages

Entrepreneurs thinking about forming sole proprietorships should also be aware of some serious drawbacks:

- **Limited Financial Resources:** Raising money to finance growth can be tough for sole proprietors. With only one owner responsible for a sole proprietorship's debts, banks and other financial institutions are often reluctant to lend it money. Likewise, suppliers may be unwilling to provide supplies on credit. This leaves sole proprietors dependent on their own wealth plus money that their firms generate.

- **Unlimited Liability:** Because the law views a sole proprietorship as an extension of its owner, the debts of the firm become the personal debts of the owner. If someone sues your business and wins, the court could seize your personal possessions—even those that have nothing to do with your business—and sell them to pay the damages. This unlimited personal liability means that operating as a sole proprietorship is a risky endeavor.

- **Limited Ability to Attract and Maintain Talented Employees:** Most sole proprietors are unable to pay the high salaries and offer the perks that highly qualified, experienced employees get when they work for big, well-established companies.

- **Heavy Workload and Responsibilities:** Being your own boss can be very rewarding, but it can also mean very long hours and a lot of stress. Sole proprietors—as the ultimate authority in their business—often must perform tasks or make decisions in areas where they lack expertise.

- **Lack of Permanence:** Because a sole proprietorship is just an extension of the owner, it lacks permanence. If the owner dies, retires, or withdraws from the business for some other reason, the company legally ceases to exist. Even if the company continues to operate under new ownership, in the eyes of the law it becomes a different firm.

Partnerships: Two Heads (and Bankrolls) Can Be Better Than One

There are several types of partnerships, each with its own specific characteristics. We'll focus our discussion mainly on the most basic type, known as a general partnership.

© David Gilder/Shutterstock.com

However, we'll also take a quick look at limited partnerships and limited liability partnerships.

Formation of General Partnerships

There is no specific upper limit on the number of partners who can participate in a general partnership, but most partnerships consist of only a few partners—often just two. The partnership is formed when the partners enter into a voluntary partnership agreement. It is legally possible to start a partnership on the basis of a verbal agreement, but doing so is often a recipe for disaster. It's much safer to get everything in writing and to seek expert legal assistance when drawing up the agreement. A typical partnership agreement spells out such details as the initial financial contributions each partner will make, the specific duties and responsibilities each will assume, how they will share profits (and losses), how they will settle disagreements, and how they will deal with the death or withdrawal of one of the partners. A well-written agreement can prevent a lot of misunderstandings.

Advantages of General Partnerships

Partnerships offer some key advantages relative to both sole proprietorships and corporations:

- **Ability to Pool Financial Resources:** With more owners investing in the company, a partnership is likely to have a stronger financial base than a sole proprietorship.

- **Ability to Share Responsibilities and Capitalize on Complementary Skills:** Partners can share the burden of running the business, which can ease the workload. They can also benefit from complementary skills and interests, splitting up the tasks to use their talents to best advantage.

- **Ease of Formation:** In theory, forming a partnership is easy. As we've already noted, it's possible (but not advisable) to establish a partnership based on a simple verbal agreement. But we shouldn't overemphasize this advantage. Working out all of the details of a partnership agreement can sometimes be a complex and time-consuming process.

- **Possible Tax Advantages:** Similar to a sole proprietorship, the earnings of a partnership "pass through" the business—untouched by the Internal Revenue Service (IRS)—and are taxed only as the partners' personal income. Again, this avoids the potential for double taxation endemic to corporations.

Disadvantages of General Partnerships

General partnerships also have some serious disadvantages. As you read about them, keep in mind that a well-written partnership agreement can mitigate some of the drawbacks:

- **Unlimited Liability:** As a general partner you're not only liable for your own mistakes, but also for those of your partners. In fact, all general partners have unlimited liability for the debts and obligations of their business. So, if the assets they've invested in the business aren't sufficient to meet these claims, the personal assets of the partners are at risk. When someone sues a general partnership, the lawsuit can target *any* individual partner or group of partners. In fact, lawsuits often go after the partners with the deepest pockets, even if they did not personally participate in the act that caused the legal action. In other words, if you have more personal wealth than the other partners, you could lose more than they do even if they were the ones at fault!

- **Potential for Disagreements:** If general partners can't agree on how to run the business, the conflict can complicate and delay decision-making. A well-drafted partnership agreement usually specifies how disputes will be resolved, but disagreements among partners can create friction and hard feelings that harm morale and undermine the cooperation needed to keep the business on track.

- **Lack of Continuity:** If a current partner withdraws from the partnership, the relationship among the

It's very much like a marriage, though I get along better with my wife.

— Zane Carter, General Partner in Carter Cosgrove and Co. on his Relationship with his Partners participants will clearly change, potentially ending the partnership. This creates uncertainty about how long a partnership will remain in business.

- ⊃ **Difficulty in Withdrawing from a Partnership:** A partner who withdraws from a partnership remains personally liable for any debts or obligations the firm had *at the time of withdrawal*—even if those obligations were incurred by the actions of other partners.

Limited Partnerships

The risks associated with unlimited liability make general partnerships unattractive to many individuals who would otherwise be interested in joining a business partnership. Fortunately, two other types of partnerships exist that allow at least some partners to limit their personal liability, though each comes with certain strings attached.

The first of these, known as a **limited partnership,** is a partnership arrangement that includes at least one general partner *and* at least one limited partner. Both types of partners contribute financially to the company and share in its profits. But in other respects they play different roles:

- ⊃ General partners have the right to participate fully in managing their partnership, but they also assume unlimited personal liability for any of its debts—just like the partners in a general partnership.

- ⊃ Limited partners *cannot* actively participate in its management, but they have the protection of limited liability. This means that, as long as they do not actively participate in managing the company, their personal wealth is not at risk.

Limited Liability Partnerships

The **limited liability partnership (LLP)** is another partnership arrangement that is attractive to partners who want to limit their personal risk. It is similar to a limited partnership in some ways, but it has the advantage of allowing *all* partners to take an active role in management, while also offering *all* partners some form of limited liability. In other words, there's no need to distinguish between limited and general partners in an LLP.

limited partnership A partnership that includes at least one general partner who actively manages the company and accepts unlimited liability and one limited partner who gives up the right to actively manage the company in exchange for limited liability.

limited liability partnership (LLP) A form of partnership in which all partners have the right to participate in management and have limited liability for company debts.

The Name Game

One of the first tasks facing entrepreneurs starting a new business is the selection of the company's name. It turns out that the process involved in naming a company depends on the form of ownership the entrepreneur chooses. The specific requirements differ somewhat from state to state. (You can check out the details for any specific state at http://www.business.gov/register/business-name/dba.html.)

Most sole proprietorships and general partnerships operate under the names of their owners. But others use a "fictitious" name to create a more memorable impression. Owners that use a fictitious name must do a name search to make sure that no other company in the area is already using the same name—or one so similar that the two names could be easily confused. Failure to take this precaution could result in being on the losing end of a trademark infringement lawsuit! In many states, companies using fictitious names also must file a document known as a DBA ("Doing Business

© Oliver Suckling/Shutterstock.com

As") certificate with the county clerk where the business is located. This informs the government and the general public that the company is doing business under a fictitious name and identifies the actual owners.

The process for naming corporations and limited liability companies has different requirements. In most states, the name of a corporation or LLC must be registered with the secretary of state where the business is formed. The name also must include specific wording to indicate that the owners are not personally liable for the debts of their company. For example, corporate names typically *must* include one of the following words: "corporation," "incorporated," "company," or "limited" (or a corresponding abbreviation such as "Corp.," "Inc.," "Co.," or "Ltd."). Similarly, the name of a limited liability company typically *must* include either the words "limited liability company" or the abbreviation "LLC." Certain other words, such as "bank" or "cooperative," *cannot* be used in the name of a corporation or limited liability company without approval by an appropriate regulatory agency.[5]

The amount of liability protection offered by LLPs varies among states. In some states, LLPs offer "full-shield" protection, meaning that partners have limited liability for all claims against their company, except those resulting from *their own* negligence or malpractice. In other states, partners in LLPs have a lesser "partial-shield" protection. In these states, each partner has limited liability for the negligence or malpractice of other partners but still has unlimited liability for any other debts. Another drawback is that some states only allow specific types of professional businesses to form limited liability partnerships. For example, California law allows only accountants, lawyers, and architects to form LLPs.

LO4 Corporations: The Advantages and Disadvantages of Being an Artificial Person

There are several types of corporations. The most common is called a **C corporation**; when people use the term "corporation" without specifying which type, they are generally referring to a C corporation. Because it's the most common, we'll devote most of our discussion to C corporations. However, we'll also describe three other types of corporations: S corporations, statutory close (or closed) corporations, and nonprofit corporations.

Forming a C Corporation

As we mentioned earlier, the formation of a corporation requires filing articles of incorporation and paying filing fees. It also requires the adoption of **corporate bylaws**, which are detailed rules that govern the way the corporation is organized and managed. Because of these requirements, forming a corporation tends to be more expensive and complex than forming a sole proprietorship or partnership. But the exact requirements vary among the states. Some states are known for their simple forms, inexpensive fees, low corporate tax rates, and "corporation-friendly" laws and court systems. In these states, forming a corporation is not much harder or more expensive than setting up a sole proprietorship and sometimes can be simpler than forming a partnership. Not surprisingly, many large companies choose

to incorporate in states with such favorable environments—even if they intend to do the majority of their business in other states. Delaware, in particular, has been very successful at attracting corporations. You may not think of Delaware as the home of corporate power, but more than half of all publicly traded corporations—and 63% of the firms listed in the Fortune 500—are incorporated in Delaware.[6]

Ownership of C Corporations

Ownership of C corporations is represented by shares of stock, so owners are called "**stockholders**" (or "shareholders"). Common stock represents the basic ownership interest in a corporation, but some firms also issue preferred stock. One key difference between the two types of stock involves voting rights; common stockholders normally have the right to vote in stockholders' meetings, while preferred stockholders do not. As shown in Exhibit 6.3, many large corporations issue billions of shares of stock and have hundreds of thousands—or even millions—of stockholders.

Stock in large corporations is usually publicly traded, meaning that anyone with the money and inclination to do so can buy shares—and that anyone who owns shares is free to sell them. But many smaller corporations are owned by just a handful of stockholders who don't actively trade their stock. It's even possible for individuals to incorporate their business and be the sole shareholder in their corporation.[7]

Stockholders don't have to be individuals. **Institutional investors,** such as mutual funds, insurance companies, pension funds, and endowment funds, pool money from a large number of individuals and use these funds to buy stocks and other securities. As Exhibit 6.3 illustrates, such institutional investors own the majority of stock in many large corporations.

The Role of the Board of Directors

It's not practical for all of the stockholders of a large corporation to actively participate in the management of their company. Besides, most stockholders don't have the time, management skills, or desire to effectively manage such a complex business enterprise. Thus, in accordance with corporate bylaws, the stockholders elect a **board of directors** and rely on this board to oversee the operation of their company and protect their interests.

The board of directors establishes the corporation's mission and sets its broad objectives. But board members seldom take an active role in the day-to-day management of their company. Instead, again in accordance with corporate bylaws, the board appoints a chief executive officer (CEO) and other corporate officers to manage the company on a daily basis. The board also sets the level of compensation for these officers and monitors their performance to ensure that they act in a manner consistent with stockholder interests. It also provides advice to these officers on broad policy

EXHIBIT 6.3 Stock Ownership in Selected Major U.S. Corporations

CORPORATION	SHARES OF COMMON STOCK OUTSTANDING (BILLIONS)	TOTAL NUMBER OF STOCKHOLDERS	PERCENTAGE OF SHARES OWNED BY INSTITUTIONAL INVESTORS
AT&T	5.91	1,454,030	57.27
COCA-COLA	2.32	268,741	63.50
FORD	3.47	165,026	62.80
GE	10.66	598,000	50.85
MCDONALD'S	1.06	1,198,000	71.90
MICROSOFT	8.56	138,568	61.61
WALMART	3.56	292,983	32.60
WALT DISNEY	1.89	998,373	68.70

Source: Shares outstanding and percentage of institutional ownership is from the Key Statistics for each corporation reported in Yahoo! Finance (http://finance.yahoo.com/); Information about the number of shareholders is found in Item 5 (Market for the Company's Common Equity) of each firm's 2010 10-K annual report filed with the SEC accessed through the Edgar database (http://www.sec.gov/edgar.shtml) accessed January 20, 2011.

issues, approves their major proposals, and ensures that the company adheres to major regulatory requirements.

Advantages of C Corporations

There are several reasons why corporations have become the dominant form of business ownership:

- **Limited Liability:** As we've already explained, stockholders are not personally liable for the debts of their company. If a corporation goes bankrupt, the stockholders might find that their stock is worthless, but their other personal assets are protected.

- **Permanence:** Unless the articles of incorporation specify a limited duration, corporations can continue operating as long as they remain financially viable and the majority of stockholders want the business to continue. Unlike a sole proprietorship or partnership, a general corporation is unaffected by the death or withdrawal of an owner.

- **Ease of Transfer of Ownership:** It's easy for stockholders of publicly traded C corporations to withdraw from ownership—they simply sell their shares of stock.

- **Ability to Raise Large Amounts of Financial Capital:** Corporations can raise large amounts of financial capital by issuing shares of

A New Form of Business Aims for Social Responsibility

In April of 2010, Maryland became the first state to pass a law allowing the formation of an entirely new business entity called a benefit corporation. Formation of a benefit corporation is similar to that of a C corporation, but with the additional requirement that the company's bylaws must include provisions identifying specific social or environmental goals, which the law then holds the board of directors accountable for achieving.

Despite their social orientation, benefit corporations aren't nonprofit organizations. They are allowed—indeed, expected—to earn a satisfactory financial return for their owners. But Maryland's law explicitly allows directors of benefit corporations to give equal or greater priority to other stakeholders such as employees, customers, or environmentalists. This gives a benefit corporation's board legal cover to pursue social and environmental goals without fear of stockholder lawsuits. As Maryland state senator Jamie Raskin, one of the sponsors of the Maryland law, put it, "We are giving companies a way to do good and do well at the same time. The benefit corporations will tie public and private purposes together."

It is too early to tell whether benefit corporations will become a popular type of business entity. But some early developments suggest that it has attracted considerable attention. Many privately held corporations have already expressed interest in converting to this new business entity. And benefit corporation legislation has already been introduced in several other states, with Vermont becoming the second state to allow the formation of benefit corporations in May 2010.[8]

stock or by selling formal IOUs called *corporate bonds*. The ability to raise money by issuing these securities gives corporations a major financial advantage over most other forms of ownership.

- **Ability to Make Use of Specialized Management:** Large corporations often find it easier to hire highly qualified professional managers than proprietorships and partnerships. Major corporations can typically offer attractive salaries and benefits, and their permanence and potential for growth offer managers opportunities for career advancement.

Disadvantages of C Corporations

In addition to their significant benefits, C corporations have a number of drawbacks:

- **Expense and Complexity of Formation and Operation:** As we've already seen, establishing a corporation can be more complex and expensive than forming a sole proprietorship or partnership. Corporations are also subject to more formal operating requirements. For example, they are required to hold regular board meetings and keep accurate minutes.

- **Complications When Operating in More Than One State:** When a business that's incorporated in one state does business in other states, it's called a "*domestic* corporation" in the state where it's incorporated, and a "*foreign* corporation" in the other states. A corporation must register (or "qualify") as a foreign corporation in order to do business in any state other than the one in which it incorporated. This typically requires additional paperwork, fees and taxes. But registration as a foreign corporation is only necessary if the company is involved in substantial business

Think your tax return is complex? If GE's 2009 tax return had been printed, it would have been about 24,000 pages long.

— MSN Moneycentral

activities within the state. Businesses that only engage in minor business activities typically are exempt from the registration requirement. For example, a firm operating a production facility or maintaining a district office in a state other than its corporate home would need to register as a foreign corporation, but a firm that simply held a bank account or solicited sales to customers in that state through the mail would not be required to do so.

- **Double Taxation of Earnings and Additional Taxes:** The IRS considers a C corporation to be a separate legal entity and taxes its earnings accordingly. Then any dividends (earnings the corporation distributes to stockholders) are taxed *again* as the personal income of the stockholders. This double taxation can take a big bite out of the company's earnings that are distributed to shareholders. But note that corporations often reinvest some or all of their profits back into the business. Shareholders don't pay income taxes on these *retained earnings*. Many states also impose separate income taxes on corporations.

EXHIBIT 6.4 **How Double Taxation Reduces Earnings for Stockholders**

Pre-Tax Corporate Earnings · Corporate Taxes · After Tax Corporate Earnings · Personal Income Taxes · Stockholder's After-Tax Income

© Cengage Learning 2013

In addition, most states also impose an annual franchise tax on both domestic and foreign corporations that operate within their borders.

⊃ **More Paperwork, More Regulation, and Less Secrecy:** Corporations are more closely regulated and are required to file more government paperwork than other forms of business. Large, publicly traded corporations are required to send annual statements to all shareholders and to file detailed quarterly and annual reports with the Securities and Exchange Commission (SEC). The annual report filed with the SEC (called a Form 10-K) is often hundreds of pages long and includes a wealth of information about the company's operations and financial condition. Anyone can look at these forms, making it difficult to keep key corporate information secret from competitors.

⊃ **Possible Conflicts of Interest:** The corporate officers appointed by the board are supposed to further the interests of stockholders. But some top executives pursue policies that further their *own* interests (such as prestige, power, job security, high pay, and attractive perks) at the expense of the stockholders. The board of directors has an obligation to protect the interests of stockholders, but in recent years the boards of several major corporations have come under criticism for continuing to approve high compensation packages for top executives even when their companies performed poorly.

Other Types of Corporations: Same but Different

Now that we've described C corporations, let's take a quick look at three other types of corporations: S corporations, statutory close corporations, and nonprofit corporations. Like C corporations, each is created by filing the appropriate paperwork with a government agency. Also like general corporations, these corporations are considered legal entities that stand apart from their owners and can enter into contracts, own property, and take legal action in their own names. But in other key respects they are quite different from C corporations—and from each other. Exhibit 6.5 summarizes the basic features of these corporations.

Corporate Restructuring

Large corporations constantly look for ways to grow and achieve competitive advantages. Some corporations work to achieve these goals, at least in part, through mergers, acquisitions, and divestitures. We'll close our discussion of corporations by taking a quick look at these forms of corporate restructuring.

Mergers and Acquisitions In the news and casual conversation, the terms "merger" and "acquisition" are often used

S corporation A form of corporation that avoids double taxation by having its income taxed as if it were a partnership.

statutory close (or closed) corporation A corporation with a limited number of owners that operates under simpler, less formal rules than a C corporation.

nonprofit corporation A corporation that does not seek to earn a profit and differs in several fundamental respects from C corporations.

EXHIBIT 6.5 Characteristics of S, Statutory Close, and Nonprofit Corporations

TYPE	KEY ADVANTAGES	LIMITATIONS
S CORPORATION	⊃ The IRS does not tax earnings of S corporations separately. Earnings pass through the company and are taxed only as income to stockholders, thus avoiding the problem of double taxation associated with C corporations. ⊃ Stockholders have limited liability.	⊃ It can have no more than 100 stockholders. ⊃ With only rare exceptions, each stockholder must be a U.S. citizen or permanent resident of the United States. (No ownership by foreigners or other corporations.)
STATUTORY CLOSE (OR CLOSED) CORPORATION	⊃ It can operate under simpler arrangements than conventional corporations. For example, it doesn't have to elect a board of directors or hold an annual stockholders' meeting. ⊃ All owners can actively participate in management while still having limited liability.	⊃ The number of stockholders is limited. (The number varies among states but is usually no more than 50.) ⊃ Stockholders normally can't sell their shares to the public without first offering the shares to existing owners. ⊃ Not all states allow formation of this type of corporation.
NONPROFIT (OR NOT-FOR-PROFIT) CORPORATION	⊃ Earnings are exempt from federal and state income taxes. ⊃ Members and directors have limited liability. ⊃ Individuals who contribute money or property to the nonprofit can take a tax deduction, making it easier for these organizations to raise funds from donations.	⊃ It has members (who may pay dues) but cannot have stockholders. ⊃ It cannot distribute dividends to members. ⊃ It cannot contribute funds to a political campaign. ⊃ It must keep accurate records and file paperwork to document tax-exempt status.

interchangeably. However, there's a difference between the two. An **acquisition** occurs when one firm buys another firm. The firm making the purchase is called the "acquiring firm," and the firm being purchased is called the "target firm." After the acquisition, the target firm ceases to exist as an independent entity while the purchasing firm continues in operation, and its stock is still traded. But not all acquisitions are on friendly terms. When the acquiring firm buys the target firm despite the opposition of the target's board and top management, the result is called a "hostile takeover."

In a **merger**, instead of one firm buying the other, the two companies agree to a combination of equals, joining together to form a new company out of the two previously independent firms. Exhibit 6.6 describes the three most common types of corporate combinations.

Divestitures: When Less Is More Sometimes corporations restructure by subtraction rather than by addition. A **divestiture** occurs when a firm transfers total or partial ownership of some of its operations to investors or to another

company. Firms often use divestitures to rid themselves of a part of their company that no longer fits well with their strategic plans. This allows them to streamline their operations and focus on their core businesses. In many (but not all) cases, divestitures involve the sale of assets to outsiders, which raises financial capital for the firm.

One common type of divestiture, called a "spin-off," occurs when a company issues stock in one of its own divisions or operating units and sets it up as a separate company—complete with its own board of directors and corporate officers. It then distributes the stock in the new company to its existing stockholders. After the spin-off, the stockholders end up owning two separate companies rather than one. They can then buy, sell, or hold either (or both) stocks as they see fit. While a spin-off allows a corporation to eliminate a division that no longer fits in its plans, it doesn't actually generate any additional funds for the firm.

A "carve-out" is like a spin-off in that the firm converts a particular unit or division into a separate company and issues stock in the newly created corporation. However, instead of distributing the new stock to its current stockholders, it sells

© Arcady/Shutterstock.com

Financial Reform Gives Stockholders a "Say on Pay"

A corporation's board of directors have an ethical duty to protect the financial interests of the stockholders who elect them. But critics charge that some boards seem to place more emphasis on protecting the financial interests of their company's CEOs than those of its owners. This issue came into sharp focus during the Great Recession of 2008 and 2009 when boards at many major corporations continued to approve high salaries and lavish perks for their CEOs, despite the fact that their companies were laying off workers and reporting huge losses.

Congress responded to the public outcry against this state of affairs by drafting new legislation. The Wall Street Reform and Consumer Protection Act of 2010 (or Dodd-Frank Act) contains a provision that, beginning in 2011, gives stockholders of publicly traded corporations the right to cast an advisory vote on executive compensation. While the vote is non-binding, it finally gives stockholders the opportunity to publicly express their approval or disapproval of board compensation policies.

It's too early to know the long-term impact this provision will have on executive pay, but many experts predict

that it could eventually exert a significant influence on board compensation policies. They reason that few boards will want to risk the embarrassment and negative publicity that would result if shareholders cast a vote against their pay proposals. In fact, a survey by consulting firm Towers Watson in late 2010 found that 48% of the companies had *already* announced adjustments to executive pay practices in anticipation of the new vote.

The Dodd-Frank Act also includes a provision that makes it easier for shareholders to nominate candidates for election to open board positions. This provision is likely to put even more pressure on board members to take stockholder views on compensation seriously. As Stephen Davis, executive director of Yale University's Millstein Center for Corporate Governance, puts it, "If boards fail to persuade shareholders that the compensation plans they are providing to CEOs are sensible then, going forward, directors could lose their seats to shareholder nominees because they are not being responsive." [9]

Corporate mergers involve a combination of equals.

© Tom Merton/OJO Images/Jupiterimages

the stock to outside investors, thus raising additional financial capital. In many cases, the firm sells only a minority of the total shares, so that it maintains majority ownership.

L05 The Limited Liability Company: The New Kid on the Block

As the newest form of business ownership, state laws concerning the legal status and formation of LLCs are still evolving. Several states have recently revised their statutes to make forming LLCs simpler and to make transfer of ownership easier. Other states have kept more restrictive requirements intact. This diversity of state requirements, and the continuing evolution of LLC statutes, makes it difficult to provide meaningful generalizations about this form of ownership.[10]

Forming and Managing an LLC

In many respects, forming an LLC is similar to forming a corporation. As with corporations, LLCs are created by filing a document (which goes by a variety of names, such as *certificate of organization* or *articles of organization*) and paying filing fees in the state where the business is organized. Organizers of most LLCs also draft an operating agreement, which is similar to the bylaws of a corporation. Some states also require LLCs to publish a notice of intent to operate as a limited liability company.

Because LLCs are neither corporations nor partnerships, their owners are called *members* rather than stockholders or partners. Members of LLCs often manage their own company

horizontal merger
A combination of two firms that are in the same industry.

vertical merger A combination of firms at different stages in the production of a good or service.

conglomerate merger A combination of two firms that are in unrelated industries.

© Tim Boyle/Getty Images

EXHIBIT 6.6 Types of Mergers and Acquisitions

TYPE OF MERGER	DEFINITION	COMMON OBJECTIVE	EXAMPLE
HORIZONTAL MERGER	A combination of firms in the same industry.	Increase size and market power within the industry. Improve efficiency by eliminating duplication of facilities and personnel.	United Airlines' acquisition of Continental Airlines in 2010.
VERTICAL MERGER	A combination of firms that are at different stages in the production of a good or service, creating a "buyer-seller" relationship.	It provides tighter integration of production and increased control over the supply of crucial inputs.	Google's announcement in 2011 of its acquisition of Motorola Mobillity, a company that manufactures cell phones using Google's Android operating system.
CONGLOMERATE MERGER	A combination of firms in unrelated industries.	It reduces risk by making the firm less vulnerable to adverse conditions in any single market.	The 2006 acquisition by Berkshire Hathaway (a highly diversified company that holds stock in a wide variety of companies) of Iscar, a privately held company that makes cutting tools.

© Cengage Learning 2013

under an arrangement similar to the relationship among general partners in a partnership. However, some LLCs hire professional managers who have responsibilities much like those of the CEO and other top officers of corporations.

Advantages of LLCs

Why are LLCs becoming so popular? This form of ownership offers significant advantages:

- **Limited Liability:** Similar to a corporation, *all* owners of an LLC have limited liability.

- **Tax Pass-Through:** As we mentioned at the beginning of this chapter, for tax purposes the owners of LLCs may elect to have their companies treated as either a corporation or a partnership—or even as a sole proprietorship if it is owned by a single person. The default tax classification for LLCs with more than one owner—and the one most LLCs choose—is the partnership option. Under this arrangement, there is no separate tax on the earnings of the company. Instead, earnings "pass through" the company and are taxed only as income of the owners. This eliminates the double taxation of profits that is endemic to general corporations. However, there are some cases where it makes sense for LLCs to elect to be taxed as a corporation. For example, the owner of a single-person LLC can avoid paying self-employment taxes by electing to have the LLC treated as a corporation rather than as a sole proprietorship.

- **Simplicity and Flexibility in Management and Operation:** Unlike corporations, LLCs aren't required to hold regular board meetings. Also, LLCs are subject to less paperwork and fewer reporting requirements than corporations.

- **Flexible Ownership:** Unlike S corporations, LLCs can have any number of owners. Also unlike S corporations, the owners of LLCs can include foreign investors and other corporations. However, some states do make it difficult to transfer ownership to outsiders.

Limitations and Disadvantages of LLCs

Despite their increasing popularity, LLCs have some limitations and drawbacks:

- **Complexity of Formation:** Because of the need to file articles of organization and pay filing fees, LLCs can take more time and effort to form than sole proprietorships. In general, forming an LLC is also more difficult than creating a partnership. But as we mentioned earlier, the formation of a partnership requires a "meeting of the minds" of the partners, which isn't always easy to achieve. So in some

GE's "Taxing" Situation: Double or Nothing?

Most textbooks (including this one) cite double taxation as a major drawback of the corporate form of ownership. But corporate tax law is complex and contains provisions that corporations can sometimes take advantage of to minimize their tax liabilities. For example, in 2009 General Electric—one of the largest corporations in the United States—reported a net income (profit) of $10.3 billion, yet its 2009 U.S. tax bill was $0.00. That's right, despite billions in reported earnings GE didn't owe a penny in taxes to Uncle Sam.

How could a huge corporation with multibillion-dollar earnings escape paying any taxes when even a middle-income U.S. household typically owes the IRS thousands of dollars? A key part of the explanation lies in the fact that GE is a global company, and all of its profitable activities were located overseas. (The company reported a loss of over $400 million on its U.S. operations.) U.S. tax law allows American firms to defer taxes on foreign earnings *indefinitely*, so GE was able to escape paying 2009 taxes on these profits.

Before you get too upset about the injustice of a huge corporation paying less in taxes than you did, we should note that GE didn't escape taxes in all other nations–nor in the U.S. in most other years. In fact, in the decade from 2000 to 2009, GE paid over $23 billion in taxes around the globe. Also keep in mind that GE paid its stockholders a significant dividend out of its 2009 earnings—and the stockholders then had to pay taxes on those earnings. And there is another type of "tax burden" that GE didn't escape. In 2009, GE had to complete and file over 7,000 *different tax returns* with government taxing authorities around the globe—and you can bet that it paid a pretty penny to its accounting staff for the preparation of all those tax forms![11]

cases, the formation of a partnership can prove to be every bit as challenging as the formation of an LLC.

- ○ **Annual Franchise Tax:** Even though they may be exempt from corporate income taxes, many states require LLCs to pay an annual franchise tax.

- ○ **Foreign Status in Other States:** Like corporations, LLCs must register or qualify to operate as "foreign" companies when they do business in states other than the state in which they were organized. This results in additional paperwork, fees, and taxes.

- ○ **Limits on Types of Firms That Can Form LLCs:** Most states do not permit banks, insurance companies, and nonprofit organizations to operate as LLCs.

- ○ **Differences in State Laws:** As we've already mentioned, LLC laws are still evolving—and their specific requirements vary considerably among the states. In 2006, the National Conference of Commissioners on Uniform State Laws created a Revised Uniform Limited Liability Company Act that could be used as a model by all states. To date, only a few states have adopted this law. Until there is more uniformity in state laws, operating LLCs in more than one state is likely to remain a complex endeavor.[12]

LO6 Franchising: Proven Methods for a Price

A **franchise** is a licensing arrangement under which one party (the **franchisor**) allows another party (the **franchisee**) to use its name, trademark, patents, copyrights, business methods, and other property in exchange for monetary payments and other considerations. Franchising has become a very popular way to operate a business and an important source of employment and income. A 2011 study conducted by PricewaterhouseCoopers for the International Franchising Association's Education Foundation reported that almost 800,000 franchise establishments operated in the United States, employing over 7.8 million workers. And according to another franchising study published by the Bureau of the Census in 2010, franchise establishments dominate several major markets such as fast food, auto dealerships, convenience stores, and private mail distribution centers.[13]

The two most popular types of franchise arrangements are **distributorships** and **business format franchises**. In a distributorship, the franchisor makes a product and grants distributors a license to sell it. The most common example of this type of franchise is the arrangement between automakers and the dealerships that sell their cars. In a business format franchise, the franchisor grants the franchisee the right to both make *and* sell its good or service. Under this arrangement, the franchisor usually provides a wide range of services to the franchisee, such as help with site selection, training, and help in obtaining financing, but also requires the franchisee to follow very specific guidelines while operating the business. You're no doubt very familiar with business format franchises; examples include Wendy's, Supercuts, Jiffy Lube, and Massage Envy.

Franchising in Today's Economy

Franchising is now a well-established method of operating a business—but that doesn't mean it's static. Let's look at some ways the world of franchising is changing.

One of the biggest trends in franchising for the past several years has been an expansion into foreign markets. Franchisors in a variety of industries have found that opportunities for franchise growth are greater in foreign countries because competition is less intense, and markets are less saturated than in the United States. At the end of 2010, McDonald's had 12,693 franchise outlets in foreign countries (slightly more than it had in the United States), Subway had 7,235, and Curves had 2,868.[14] Of course, operating in foreign countries can pose special challenges. Differences in culture, language, laws, demographics, and economic development mean that franchisors, like other types of business owners, must adjust their business methods—and the specific products they offer—to meet the needs of foreign consumers.

Another notable trend has been the growth in the number of women franchisees. Reliable statistics on women in franchising are difficult to find, but the International Franchising Association (IFA) estimates that women now own about 30% of all franchises, and anecdotal evidence suggests that the trend toward more

franchise A licensing arrangement under which a franchisor allows franchisees to use its name, trademark, products, business methods, and other property in exchange for monetary payments and other considerations.

franchisor The business entity in a franchise relationship that allows others to operate their business using resources it supplies in exchange for money and other considerations.

franchisee The party in a franchise relationship that pays for the right to use resources supplied by the franchisor.

distributorship a type of franchising arrangement in which the franchisor makes a product and licenses the franchisee to sell it.

business format franchise A broad franchise agreement in which the franchisee pays for the right to use the name, trademark, and business and production methods of the franchisor.

women-owned franchisees is continuing. A number of women, such as JoAnne Shaw (founder of the Coffee Beanery), Maxine Clark (founder of Build-A-Bear), and Linda Burzynski (owner and CEO of Liberty Fitness), also have become very successful franchisors. But, despite these highly visible success stories, the number of women franchisors hasn't grown nearly as fast as the number of women franchisees.[15]

Minority participation in franchises, both as franchisees and franchisors, has been relatively low. African Americans, Hispanics, Asian Americans, and Native Americans make up about a third of the population, and that share is expected to steadily grow over the next several decades. Yet, according to C. Everett Wallace, a past chair of the IFA's Minorities in Franchising Committee, fewer than 10% of all franchisees are minorities. One of the main reasons for such low minority involvement in franchising is a lack of awareness of franchising opportunities within minority communities. But many franchisors are now making a strong effort to actively recruit minority franchisees.[16]

Two major initiatives have given the efforts to reach minority franchising a boost in recent years. The first, known as the National Minority Franchising Initiative (NMFI), was founded in 2000. The NMFI's website currently maintains a directory of over 500 franchisors who actively promote minority franchise ownership. The second initiative, called MinorityFran, was established in early 2006 by the IFA. This initiative has the cooperation of a variety of organizations interested in promoting minority business ownership, including the National Urban League, the Association of Small Business Development Centers, the U.S. Pan Asian American Chamber of Commerce, and the Minority Business Development Agency. Franchisors participating in the program receive information and marketing materials designed to help them reach potential minority franchisees more effectively. As of late 2010, MinorityFran had over 100 participating franchisors, including such major players as ExxonMobil, McDonald's and YUM! Brands (which owns KFC, Taco Bell and Pizza Hut), all pledging to actively recruit minority franchisees.[17]

Advantages of Franchising

Both the franchisee and the franchisor must believe they'll benefit from the franchise arrangement; otherwise they wouldn't participate. The advantages of franchising for the franchisor are fairly obvious. It allows the franchisor to expand the business and bring in additional revenue (in the form of franchising fees and royalties) without investing its own capital. Also, franchisees—business owners who are motivated to earn a profit—may have a greater incentive than salaried managers to do whatever it takes to maximize the success of their outlets.

From the franchisee's perspective, franchising offers several advantages:

- **Less Risk:** Franchises offer access to a proven business system and product. The systems and methods offered by franchisors have an established track record. People who are interested in buying a franchise can do research to see how stores in the franchise have performed and can talk to existing franchisees before investing.

- **Training and Support:** The franchisor normally provides the franchisee with extensive training and support. For example, Subway offers two weeks of training at its headquarters and additional training at meetings. The franchisor also sends out newsletters, provides Internet support, maintains a toll-free number for phone support, and provides on-site evaluations.[18]

- **Brand Recognition:** Operating a franchise gives the franchisee instant brand-name recognition, which can be a big help in attracting customers.

- **Easier Access to Funding:** Bankers and other lenders may be more willing to lend you money if your business is part of an established franchise than if it is a new, unproven business.

Disadvantages of Franchising

Franchising also has some drawbacks. From the franchisor's perspective, operating a business with perhaps thousands of semi-independent owner–operators can be complex and challenging. With such a large number of owners, it can be difficult to keep all of the franchisees satisfied, and disappointed franchisees sometimes go public with their complaints, damaging the reputation of the franchisor. In fact, it isn't unusual for disgruntled fran-. chisees to sue their franchisors.

Franchisees are also likely to find some disadvantages:

○ **Costs:** The typical franchise agreement requires franchisees to pay an initial franchise fee when they enter into the franchise agreement and an ongoing royalty (usually a percentage of monthly sales revenues) to the franchisor. In addition, the franchisor may assess other fees to support national advertising campaigns or for other purposes. These costs vary considerably, but for high-profile franchises, they can be substantial. Exhibit 6.7 compares the franchise fees, royalties, and minimum total investment for several well-established franchises. (Total investment reflects the fact that the cost of starting a franchise generally requires the franchisee to invest in property, equipment, and inventory in addition to paying the franchise fee. The actual total investment that franchisees make is often substantially higher than the estimated minimum investment cited in the Exhibit 6.7.)

○ **Lack of Control:** The franchise agreement usually requires the franchisee to follow the franchisor's procedures to the letter. People who want the freedom and flexibility to be their own boss can find these restrictions frustrating.

○ **Negative Halo Effect:** The irresponsible or incompetent behavior of a few franchisees can create a negative perception that adversely affects not only the franchise as a whole but also the success of other franchisees.

○ **Growth Challenges:** While growth and expansion are definitely possible in franchising (many franchisees own multiple outlets), strings are attached. Franchise agreements usually limit the franchisee's territory and require franchisor approval before expanding into other areas.

○ **Restrictions on Sale:** Franchise agreements normally prevent franchisees from selling their franchises to other investors without prior approval from the franchisor.

○ **Poor Execution:** Not all franchisors live up to their promises. Sometimes the training and support are of poor quality, and sometimes the company does a poor job of screening franchisees, leading to the negative halo effect we mentioned previously.

These considerations suggest that before buying a franchise, potential owners should carefully research the franchise opportunity.

franchise agreement
The contractual arrangement between a franchisor and franchisee that spells out the duties and responsibilities of both parties.

Entering into a Franchise Agreement

To obtain a franchise, the franchisee must sign a **franchise agreement**. This agreement is a legally binding contract that specifies the relationship between the franchisor and the franchisee in great detail. There's no standard form for the contract, but some of the key items normally covered include:

○ **Terms and Conditions:** The franchisee's rights to use the franchisor's trademarks, patents, and signage, and any restrictions on those rights. It also covers how long the agreement will last and under what terms (and at what cost) it can be renewed.

○ **Fees and Other Payments:** The fees the franchisee must pay for the right to use the franchisor's products and methods, and when these payments are due.

○ **Training and Support:** The types of training and support the franchisor will provide to the franchisee.

EXHIBIT 6.7 Franchisee Costs for Selected Franchises

FRANCHISE	TYPE OF BUSINESS	FRANCHISE FEE	ROYALTY*	ESTIMATED MINIMUM TOTAL INVESTMENT
COFFEE NEWS	Local newsletters	$8,000	$80/wk.	$8,925
MERLE NORMAN	Cosmetics and skin care	$0	0%	$33,300
ANYTIME FITNESS	Health club	$19,999	$419/mo.	$44,074
SUBWAY	Fast food	$15,000	8%	$84,300
PAPA JOHN'S	Pizza delivery	$25,000	5%	$98,823
SUPERCUTS	Hair styling	$22,500	6%	$112,500
JENNY CRAIG	Weight loss	$25,000	7%	$169,600
JIFFY LUBE	Automobile maintenance	$35,000	4%	$194,000

*Royalty is expressed as a percentage of gross revenues unless otherwise specified.

Source: Individual franchise opportunity pages for each listed franchise on the Entrepreneur.com website, http://www.entrepreneur.com/franchiseopportunities/index.html, accessed January 22, 2011.

Franchise Disclosure Document (FDD) A detailed description of all aspects of a franchise that the franchisor must provide to the franchisee at least fourteen calendar days before the franchise agreement is signed.

○ **Specific Operational Requirements:** The methods and standards established by the franchisor that the franchisee is required to follow.

○ **Conflict Resolution:** How the franchisor and franchisee will handle disputes.

○ **Assigned Territory:** The geographic area in which the franchisee will operate and whether the franchisee has exclusive rights in that area.

It's vital for anyone thinking about entering into a franchise agreement to know all the facts before signing on the dotted line. Fortunately, the Federal Trade Commission (FTC) requires franchisors to provide potential franchisees with a document known as a **Franchise Disclosure Document (FDD)**. This long, complex document (covering 23 separate major topics and sometimes running well over 100 pages) can be an invaluable source of information about virtually every aspect of the franchise arrangement. For example, the FDD must provide

It's not hard to meet expenses. They're everywhere.

— Anonymous Franchisee

contact information for at least 100 current franchisees. (If the franchisor has fewer than 100 current franchisees, it must list all of them.) This gives a potential franchisee the ability to contact other franchisees and ask them about their experiences with the franchisor. As an added bonus, the FTC requires the FDD to be written in "plain English" rather than in the complex legal jargon that often characterizes such documents. This rule means you actually have a chance to understand what you're reading![19]

Under FTC rules, the franchisor must give the franchisee at least 14 calendar days to review the FDD before the franchise agreement can be signed. A careful study of the FDD can go a long way toward ensuring that the franchisee makes an informed decision. Even though the FDD is written in "plain English," it's a good idea to have a lawyer who is knowledgeable about franchise law review it. You'll have to pay for any legal advice, but entering into a bad franchise agreement can be a lot more expensive (and stressful) than a lawyer's fees.

© David Lee/Alamy

Some Franchisees Are Quite Happy When They Don't Earn a Profit

While most franchisees are out to make a profit, a small but growing number of nonprofit organizations, such as Center-Force (a provider of services to people with developmental disabilities), Common Ground (a provider of shelter for the homeless), and the Chicago Children's Choir have turned to franchising as a new way to raise funds. Everybody seems to win from this arrangement:

○ Many customers like doing business with nonprofit franchisees; they get a well-known product while supporting a worthy cause.

○ Franchisors view their arrangements with nonprofit franchisees as a good way to meet their social responsibilities and build goodwill within local communities.

○ The nonprofits gain access to a business with proven products and methods. This can boost their fundraising efforts at a time when funds from more traditional

sources are no longer growing quickly enough to keep up with needs.
In addition, some nonprofit youth organizations have found that operating a franchise allows them to offer employment opportunities to the teenagers they serve.

Several well-known franchisors, including Krispy Kreme, ServiceMaster, Maggie Moo's, AIM Mail Centers, and Popeye's, have entered into arrangements with nonprofit franchisees in recent years. But Ben & Jerry's has taken the most proactive approach, establishing a special program called PartnerShops to help nonprofits get started in franchising. The company has even taken its efforts global, opening up a Ben & Jerry's PartnerShop with the Cresco Trust (an organization serving disadvantaged youth) in Northern Ireland.[20]

THE BIG PICTURE

This chapter discusses the four major forms of business ownership. Each form of ownership has both advantages and limitations, so no single form of ownership is the best in all situations.

Sole proprietorships are appealing to entrepreneurs who want to start a business quickly, with few formalities or fees, and who want to be their own boss. But sole proprietorships aren't well suited for raising financing from external sources, so growth opportunities are limited. And sole proprietors have unlimited liability for their company's debts and obligations.

General partnerships allow two or more owners to pool financial resources and take advantage of complementary skills. But each owner must assume the risk of unlimited liability, and disagreements among partners can complicate and delay important decisions.

Corporations are more complex and expensive to create than other forms of business. Another potentially serious drawback is the double taxation of earnings. But corporations have the greatest potential for raising financial capital and provide owners with the protection of limited liability.

The limited liability company (LLC) is a relatively new form of business ownership that offers many of the advantages of corporations without as many regulations. One major advantage of LLCs compared to corporations is that its earnings can be taxed as if the company is a partnership, thus avoiding double taxation. But the laws governing limited liability companies vary considerably among states, making it a challenge to operate an LLC in multiple states.

Many Americans view business ownership as a means of achieving both personal satisfaction and financial success. In fact, millions of Americans each year choose to pursue those goals by starting (or buying) and operating their own small business. Between 1990 and 2007, the number of nonfarm sole proprietorships in the United States grew from 14.8 million to over 23.1 million, the number of partnerships increased from 1.6 million to 3.1 million, and the number of corporations from 3.7 million to 5.9 million. Even during the depths of the recent recession, business formation boomed, in part because many unemployed workers who were unable to find jobs with existing firms viewed starting their own business as the key to economic survival. In 2008, in the face of the deepening recession, American adults started new businesses at the rate of 530,000 per month.[21]

Individuals who want to own and operate a business, but don't want to build their organization from the ground up, often find franchising to be an attractive alternative. Today, there are almost 800,000 franchise establishments in the United States, and current projections suggest that franchise opportunities will continue to grow.[22] One notable trend is that many franchisors are seeking to grow by reaching out to minorities and women.

Starting and running a business requires an entrepreneurial mindset that not everyone possesses. Another way to participate in business ownership and pursue financial goals is to buy stock in publicly traded corporations. Corporate stock has proven a popular investment for many people. And historically, stock ownership has yielded attractive financial returns over the long run. But as the ups and downs in stock prices over the past few years indicate, investing in the stock market isn't for the faint of heart!

CAREERS IN BUSINESS

CAREERS

What *else?*
RIP & REVIEW CARDS IN THE BACK
and visit www.cengagebrain.com!

7

Small Business and Entrepreneurship:
Economic Rocket Fuel

LEARNING OBJECTIVES
After studying this chapter, you will be able to…

LO1 Explain the key reasons to launch a small business

LO2 Describe the typical entrepreneurial mindset and characteristics

LO3 Discuss funding options for small business

LO4 Analyze the opportunities and threats that small businesses face

LO5 Discuss ways to become a new business owner and tools to facilitate success

LO6 Explain the size, scope, and economic contributions of small business

> DO WHAT YOU *LOVE*. THIS WAY, WHETHER YOU MAKE MONEY AT IT OR NOT, AT LEAST YOU'RE *ENJOYING* YOURSELF.
>
> — GUY KAWASAKI, VENTURE CAPITALIST

LO1 Launching a New Venture: What's in It for Me?

Over time, the entrepreneurship rate has played a powerful, positive role in the U.S. economy. Despite the raging recession, new business creation increased steadily from 2007 to 2009. Among teenagers, interest in someday launching their own business has remained at about 40% throughout the Great Recession (from 2007 – 2010), a critically important element to long-term economic recovery.[1] In 2010, overall U.S. entrepreneurship rates reached their highest level in 15 years, driven in part by unemployed workers looking to stay afloat as they seek new jobs, representing a hopeful sign for the future of our economy, as job seekers become potential job creators.[2]

Make no mistake: starting a new business can be tough—very tough. Yet for the right person, the advantages of business ownership far outweigh the risk and hard work. Although people start their own ventures for a variety of reasons, most are seeking some combination of greater financial success, independence, flexibility, and challenge. Others are simply seeking survival.[3]

Greater Financial Success

Although you can make a pretty good living working for someone else, your chances of getting really rich may be higher if you start your own business. The *Forbes* magazine annual list of the 400 richest Americans is dominated by

entrepreneurs, such as Bill Gates and Paul Allen (founders of Microsoft), Phil Knight (founder of Nike), Michael Dell (founder of Dell Inc.), and Sergey Brin and Larry Page (founders of Google). And many people feel that their chances of even moderate financial success are higher if they're working for themselves rather than someone else. The opportunity to make more money is a primary motivator for many entrepreneurs, although other factors clearly play a role as well.[4]

> **entrepreneurs** People who risk their time, money, and other resources to start and manage a business.

Independence

Being your own boss is a huge benefit of starting your own business. You answer to no one other than yourself and any investors whom you invite to participate in your business. Bottom line: you are the only one who is ultimately responsible for your success or failure. This setup is especially compelling for people who have trouble being subordinates because of their personalities (and we probably all know someone who fits that description!). But while independence is nice, it's important to keep in mind that every business depends on meeting the needs of its customers, who can be even more demanding than the toughest boss.

Flexibility

The ability to set your own hours and control your own schedule is a hugely appealing benefit for many business owners, especially parents seeking more time with their kids or retirees looking for extra income. Given current technological tools—from email to eBay—it's easy for small business owners to manage their firms on the go or after hours. Of course, there's often a correlation between hours worked and dollars earned. (It's rare to work less and earn more.) But when more money isn't the primary goal, the need for flexibility can be enough to motivate many entrepreneurs to launch their own enterprise.

Challenge

Running your own business provides a level of challenge unmatched by many other endeavors. Most business owners—especially new business owners—never find themselves bored! Starting a business also offers endless opportunities for learning that can provide more profound satisfaction for many people than grinding out the hours as an employee.

Survival

Although most entrepreneurs launch their business in response to an opportunity with hopes of improving their lives, some entrepreneurs—called "necessity entrepreneurs"—launch their business because they believe it is their *only* economic option. Necessity entrepreneurs range from middle-aged workers laid off from corporate jobs, to new immigrants with limited English and heavy accents, to those who experience discrimination in the standard workplace. For each of these types of people, small business ownership can be the right choice in the face of few other alternatives.

Business opportunities are like buses... there's always another one coming.

—Richard Branson, founder, Virgin Enterprise

of Amazon—aims to change the world through blockbuster goods or services. That isn't the case for all small-business owners. Most people who launch new firms expect to better themselves, but they don't expect huge, transformative growth; in fact, nearly 70% of small business owners say they don't want to grow any larger.[5]

However, classic entrepreneurs who deliver on the promise of their best ideas can dramatically change the economic and social landscape worldwide. Examples of business owners who thought and delivered big include Henry Ford, founder of the Ford Motor Company and originator of assembly line production; Walt Disney, founder of The Walt Disney Company and creator of Mickey Mouse; Mary Kay Ash, founder of a cosmetics powerhouse; Martha Stewart, lifestyle innovator for the masses; George Lucas, creator of the *Star Wars* empire; and Mark Zuckerberg, founder of Facebook.

L02 The Entrepreneur: A Distinctive Profile

Successful entrepreneurs tend to stand out from the crowd in terms of both their mindset and their personal characteristics. As you read this section, consider whether you fit the entrepreneurial profile.

The Entrepreneurial Mindset: A Matter of Attitude

Almost every entrepreneur starts as a small businessperson—either launching a firm or buying a firm—but not every small businessperson starts as an entrepreneur. The difference is a matter of attitude. From day one, a true entrepreneur—such as Sam Walton of Walmart, Steve Jobs of Apple, or Jeff Bezos

Entrepreneurial Characteristics

While experts sometimes disagree about the specific characteristics of successful entrepreneurs, virtually all include vision, self-reliance, energy, confidence, tolerance of uncertainty, and tolerance of failure. (See Exhibit 7.1.) Most successful entrepreneurs have all of these qualities and more, but they come in a huge variety of combinations that highlight the complexity of personality: there is no one successful entrepreneurial profile.

Opportunity Lost

While launching a new business can provide a number of benefits, it also—like most worthwhile endeavors—involves trade-offs. Before launching a business, you need to make sure that you're willing to give up the perks of corporate life. One of the biggies is paid vacation time. As a new business owner, if you don't work, you don't get paid, and you may even need to hire someone to replace yourself when you take time off. You give up other high-value benefits that you might currently take for granted, such as paid health insurance and life insurance (although if you do well, you may eventually afford much better insurance than a standard employee package). Perhaps the biggest loss is the stability that comes from a regular paycheck as an employee. No "regular" job lasts forever—many people are laid off at the whim of a bad boss—but while you're employed, you can usually count on a stable income. Although it may not be for everyone, the possibility of making it big makes the trade-offs worthwhile for a growing number of entrepreneurs.

Oprah Winfrey is the most inspirational entrepreneur to American women, and Donald Trump is the most inspirational entrepreneur to American men.

— USA TODAY

Vision Most entrepreneurs are wildly excited about their own new ideas, which many seem to draw from a bottomless well. Entrepreneurs find new solutions to old problems, and they develop new products that we didn't even know we needed until we had them. And entrepreneurs stay excited about their ideas, even when friends and relatives threaten to call the loony bin. For instance, Fred Smith, founder of the FedEx empire, traces the concept for his business to a term paper he wrote at Yale, which supposedly received a C from a skeptical professor. But that didn't stop him from creating a business logistics system that transformed the industry, and along with UPS, enabled e-commerce to flourish.

Self-Reliance As an entrepreneur, the buck stops with you. New business owners typically need to do everything themselves, from getting permits, to motivating employees, to keeping the books—all in addition to producing the product or service that made them start the business in the first place. Self-reliance seems to come with an **internal locus of control**, or a deep-seated sense that the

individual is personally responsible for what happens in his or her life. When things go well, people with an internal locus of control feel that their efforts have been validated, and when things go poorly, those same people feel that they need to do better next time. This sense of responsibility encourages positive action. In contrast, people with an **external locus of control** rely less on their own efforts, feeling buffeted by forces such as random luck and the actions of others, which they believe will ultimately control their fate.

Energy Entrepreneurs simply can't succeed without an enormous amount of energy. Six or seven 12-hour workdays are not atypical in the start-up phase of running a business. A survey by the Wells Fargo/Gallup Small Business Index found that today's small-business owner works an average of 52 hours per week, with 57% working at least six days a week, and more than 20% working all seven. Even a day off isn't *really* off—Discover Financial Services learned that only 36% of small business owners describe a day off as completely work free, versus 58% of the rest of working Americans. But small business owners seem to find the grind worthwhile: 47% of small business owners said that if they won $10 million in the lottery, they would still work in their current job. Only 9% would stop working, and 8% would combine work, volunteering, and other areas of interest.[6]

Confidence Successful entrepreneurs typically have confidence in their own ability to achieve, and their confidence encourages them to act boldly. But too much confidence has a downside. Entrepreneurs must take care not to confuse likelihood with reality. In fact, many could benefit from the old adage "Hope for the best and plan for the worst." A study for the Small Business Administration Office of Advocacy confirmed that entrepreneurs are typically overconfident regarding their own abilities. As a result they're sometimes willing to plunge into a new business, but they don't always have the skills to succeed.[7]

> **internal locus of control** A deep-seated sense that the individual is personally responsible for what happens in his or her life.
>
> **external locus of control** A deep-seated sense that forces other than the individual are responsible for what happens in his or her life.

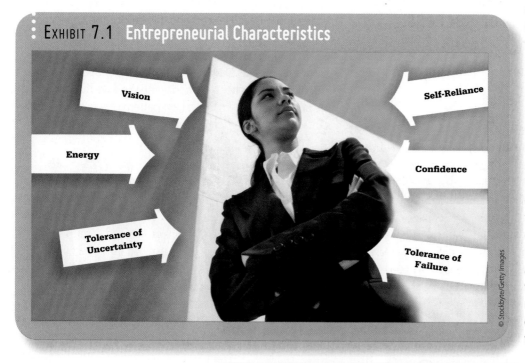

EXHIBIT 7.1 Entrepreneurial Characteristics

Vision

Energy

Tolerance of Uncertainty

Self-Reliance

Confidence

Tolerance of Failure

© Stockbyte/Getty Images

Entrepreneurship: Do you have what it takes?

How about YOU? Are YOU ready to start your own business? Successful entrepreneurs clearly have a wide range of personalities and characteristics. But these four questions, posed by Andy Swan on Small Biz Survival website, may help separate those who *want* to launch a business from those who actually *can*.[8]

1. "Do you enjoy working? No... not thinking... not ideating... working. Executing. You have to execute. A mediocre idea well-executed is worth 100 times as much as a great idea that isn't carried out. Yes, having your own business is WORK, that dirty four-letter word that some have the misguided impression does not apply when you are the boss."

2. "Do you gamble? I really think that there is something deep inside of some people that makes them CRAVE risk, thrive on it. This one is hard—if not impossible—to fake, since entrepreneurs face risk every day of the week. The ones who are good at it typically flourish, the ones who are not, usually fail in business."

3. "Can you fake it? A lot of entrepreneurship is promotion. You can't wear your emotions on your sleeve, or you're DEAD. Why? Because 90–95% of the time, your company is in trouble, and you have major doubts. But guess what... investors, customers, partners... everyone... they DO NOT want to hear it, see it or sense it. They want confidence. Yes.... later you HAVE to deliver quality.... but today, you have to deliver confidence."

   How true is that statement? The ability to roll with the punches and come up smiling can get a new business owner a long way. How's your duck n' dodge?

4. "Are you good on your feet? Things change. ALL the time... Poof... the business plan you spent 6 months perfecting is gone. A lot of people can't stand it when plans change at the last minute. Others expect it and stay up late."

You work eight hours per day for survival; everything over eight hours per day is for success.

— Brian Tracy, Bestselling Author and Life Coach

Tolerance of Uncertainty

More often than others, entrepreneurs see the world in shades of gray, rather than simply black and white. They tend to embrace uncertainty in the business environment, turning it to their advantage rather than shying away. Uncertainty also relates to risk, and successful entrepreneurs tend to more willingly accept risk—financial risk, for instance, such as mortgaging their home for the business, and professional risk, such as staking their reputation on the success of an unproven product.

Tolerance of Failure Even when they fail, entrepreneurs seldom label themselves losers. They tend to view failure as a chance to learn, rather than as a sign that they just can't do it (whatever "it" may be for them at any given moment). Interestingly, Isaac Fleischmann, director of the U.S. Patent Office for 36 years, pointed out that "During times of economic decline when unemployment increases, so does the number of patents. Dark days often force us to become more ingenious, to monitor and modify the ways we reached failure and reshape them into a new pattern of success." Failure can actually be an effective springboard for achievement.[9]

Entrepreneurs are a diverse group of people who tend to share some similar personal characteristics.

Roach Coaches Minus the Roaches

When most people think of lunch trucks, unappetizing images, such as limp French fries, greasy mystery meat, and scuttling cockroaches, may jump to mind. But the roach coaches of yesterday may soon go the way of rotary phones and VHS tapes. Lunch trucks today have gone way upscale, a good number featuring high end ethnic fusion food, such as Korean/Mexican tacos, or gourmet desserts, such as crème brulée, or even green options, such as "sustainably harvested" fish tacos and locally grown pizza toppings. Today's big city food truck owners tend to be tech-savvy entrepreneurs, building loyal customers via social media and alerting followers about their whereabouts via Twitter. The famed Kogi BBQ truck in Los Angeles, for instance, has 28,000 active Twitter followers and attributes 70% of its sales directly to social media. Building a successful lunch truck business is no easy task, but high-end food trucks are transforming the restaurant business, particularly in large cities.[10]

A surprising number of twentieth-century entrepreneurial stars experienced significant failure in their careers yet bounced back to create wildly successful ventures. Early in his career, for instance, Walt Disney was fired from an ad agency (in hindsight, a rather foolish ad agency) for a "singular lack of drawing ability." Ray Kroc, the man who made McDonald's into a fast-food empire, couldn't make a go of real estate, so he sold milkshake machines for much of his life. He was 52 years old, and in failing health, when he discovered the McDonald brothers' hamburger stand and transformed it into a fast food empire. And Steve Jobs, founder of Apple computer, found himself unceremoniously dumped by his board of directors less than ten years after introducing the world's first personal computer. After another decade, he returned in triumph, restoring Apple's polish with blockbuster new products such as the iPod and the iPhone. So next time you fail, keep your eyes open for opportunity—your failure may be the first step of the next big thing.[11]

LO3 Finding the Money: Funding Options for Small Businesses

For many entrepreneurs, finding the money to fund their business is the top challenge of their start-up year. The vast majority of new firms are funded with the personal resources of their founder. In fact, 94% of companies on the "Inc. 500 List" of fastest-growing firms raised start-up funds from personal accounts, family, and friends. Other key funding sources include bank loans, angel investors, and venture capital firms.[12]

Personal Resources

While the idea of using just your own money to open a business sounds great, the financial requirements of most new firms typically force entrepreneurs to also tap personal resources such as family, friends, and credit cards. According to *Consumer Reports*, 68% of total start-up financing comes from personal resources.[13] If you do borrow from family or friends, virtually every small business expert recommends that you keep the relationship as professional as possible. If the business fails, a professional agreement can preserve personal ties. And if the business succeeds, you'll need top-quality documentation of financing from family and friends to get larger-scale backing from outside sources.

Personal credit cards can be an especially handy—though highly risky—financing resource. In fact, a recent survey found that nearly half of all start-ups are funded with plastic. (It's no wonder, given that those solicitations just keep on coming.) Credit cards do provide fast, flexible money, but watch out—if you don't pay back your card company fast, you'll find yourself socked with financing fees that can take years to pay off.[14]

Loans

Getting commercial loans for a new venture can be tough. Banks and other lenders are understandably hesitant to fund a business that doesn't have a track record. And when they do, they require a lot of paperwork and often a fairly long waiting period. Given these hurdles, only 20% of new business owners launch with commercial loans. And virtually no conventional lending source—private or government—will lend 100% of the start-up dollars for a new business. Most require that the entrepreneur provide a minimum of

25 to 30% of total start-up costs from personal resources.[15]

Another source for loans may be the U.S. Small Business Administration (SBA). The SBA doesn't give free money to start-up businesses—neither grants nor interest-free loans—but it does partially guarantee loans from local commercial lenders. This reduces risk for the lenders, who are, in turn, more likely to lend money to a new business owner. The SBA also has a microloan program that lends small amounts of money—$13,000 on average—to start-up businesses through community nonprofit organizations.[16]

Peer-to-peer lending offers yet another potential funding source for new business start-ups. Websites such as Prosper.com and LendingClub.com bring together borrowers and investors so that both can benefit financially. Many entrepreneurs have found this is an easier way to get money, at more favorable terms, than through more-established sources.

Angel Investors

Angel investors aren't as saintly—or as flighty—as they sound. They are wealthy individuals who invest in promising start-up companies for one basic reason: to make money for themselves. According to Jeffrey Sohl, director of the Center for Venture Research, angels look for companies that seem likely to grow at 30 to 40% per year and will then either be bought or go public. He estimates that 10 to 15% of private companies fit that description, but points out that finding those firms isn't easy. It doesn't help, he says, that "80% of entrepreneurs think they're in that 10 to 15%." In the first half of 2010, the number of firms that received angel funding increased 3% versus 2009, despite the economic crisis. But unfortunately, total angel investments in the first half of 2010 dropped by 6.5 percent compared to the same period in 2009, and a smaller total number of angels are investing. Furthermore, today's angels are focusing on later-stage companies, largely ignoring the need for seed and start-up capital, which could have long-term negative implications for the economic recovery.[17]

Venture Capital

Venture capital firms fund high-potential new companies in exchange for a share of ownership, which can sometimes be as high as 60%. These deals tend to be quite visible, but keep in mind that only a tiny fraction of new businesses receive any venture capital money. The advice and guidance that come with the dollars can also be quite significant. David Barger, chief executive officer of JetBlue Airways, remembers that he and JetBlue's founder, David Neeleman, originally planned to call the airline Taxi and to fly bright yellow planes. But an influential venture capitalist changed their minds. He called them into his office and said, "If you call this airline Taxi, we're not going to invest." The name changed, and the venture capitalist stayed.[18]

Although the economic crisis drastically reduced venture capital spending, 2010 saw a 19% increase in deal flow versus 2009, and a 12% increase in the number of deals. The environment continued to be a bright spot: Investments in clean technology firms grew 76% in terms of total dollars and 37% in the number of deals compared with 2009. Five of the top ten venture deals in the last quarter of 2010 were in the clean tech sector. The flow of money suggests that the clean tech sector would be a ripe segment for new business start-ups.[19]

LO4 Opportunities and Threats for Small Business: A Two-Sided Coin

Most small businesses enjoy a number of advantages as they compete for customers. But they also must defuse a range of daunting potential threats in order to succeed over the long term.

Small Business Opportunities Small businesses enjoy a real competitive edge across a range of different areas. Because of their size, many small firms can exploit narrow but profitable market niches, offer personal customer service, and maintain lower overhead costs. And due to advances in technology, small firms can compete more effectively than ever in both global and domestic markets.

Market Niches Many small firms are uniquely positioned to exploit small, but profitable, **market niches**. These sparsely

Angel investors and venture capitalists actively seek to invest in high growth potential start-up firms.

© Colin Anderson/Blend Images/Jupiterimages

> # More than 50% of Americans trust small business owners to guide the economy compared with less than 15% who trust members of Congress.
>
> — Washington Post

occupied spaces in the market tend to have fewer competitors because they simply aren't big enough—or high-profile enough—for large firms. They nonetheless offer more than enough potential for small, specialized companies. For example, Kazoo & Company, a relatively small toy store, competes effectively with Walmart, Target, and Kmart by stocking different—and complementary—products, deliberately zigging when the big players zag.[20]

Personal Customer Service With a smaller customer base, small firms can develop much more personal relationships with individual customers. Shel Weinstein, for instance, former owner of a Los Angeles corner pharmacy, knew his customers so well that they would call him at home in the middle of the night for help with medical emergencies. The personal touch can be especially beneficial in some foreign markets, where clients prize the chance to deal directly with top management.

Lower Overhead Costs With entrepreneurs wearing so many hats, from CEO to customer service rep, many small firms have lower overhead costs. They can hire fewer managers and fewer specialized employees. Perhaps more importantly, smaller firms—due to a lack of resources—tend to work around costs with tactics such as establishing headquarters in the owner's garage or offering employees flexible schedules instead of costly healthcare benefits.

Technology The Internet has played a powerful role in opening new opportunities for small businesses. Using a wealth of online tools, from eBay to eMachineshop, companies-of-one can create, sell, publish, and even manufacture goods and services more easily than ever before. The Internet has also created international opportunities, transforming small businesses into global marketers. The

Small Business Sustainability

Sustainable, eco-friendly business practices may seem like a relatively low priority for a small business struggling simply to get off the ground and to stay in the black. But sustainable business practices can add up to significant savings, and can lead to distribution with a growing number of huge corporations such as Walmart, Procter & Gamble, and Kaiser Permanente that are assessing and selecting their suppliers based on environmental benchmarks. So, how to begin the process? *Small Business Trends* website offers some tips on sustainability planning:[21]

1. *Establish a benchmark:* You can't improve sustainability without knowing where you stand at the outset. This involves a thorough examination of your business's environment footprint, including both obvious issues, such as how much trash you produce each year, and more subtle issues, such as how many miles your employees commute each day.
2. *Identify best opportunities:* Once you have thoroughly analyzed your business, opportunities for improvement should be clear. Would a recycling program make sense? Should you upgrade your building for more energy efficiency?
3. *Develop implementation plans:* The more specific your steps, the more likely you will follow them. Remember that it's often easier and more effective to start with baby steps and slowly work up to bigger changes.
4. *Set deadlines*: Attach a specific deadline to every step in your implementation plan, and assign a person by name to accomplish each step. The more accountability you build into your planning, the more likely you will accomplish your goals.
5. *Keep the plan alive*: You should keep the plan handy, monitor progress, and revise as needed. An evolving plan is a relevant plan that will achieve meaningful results.

Effective sustainability planning can pay off for a small business both financially and ecologically.

London-based Anything Left-Handed retail store, for instance, evolved into an award-winning global wholesaler of left-handed items within a year of launching its website. Founder Keith Milsom comments that "our website has allowed us to communicate with potential customers and market our business worldwide at very little cost, making international development possible."[22]

Small Business Threats While small businesses do enjoy some advantages, they also face intimidating obstacles, from a high risk of failure to too much regulation.

High Risk of Failure Starting a new business involves risk—a lot of risk—but the odds improve significantly if you make it past the crucial four-year mark. Check out the seven-year survival rate in Exhibit 7.2. Notice that it declines much more slowly after Year 4.

Even though these numbers may look daunting, it's important to remember that owners shut down their businesses for many reasons other than the failure of the firm itself. The possibilities include poor health, divorce, better opportunities elsewhere, and interestingly, an unwillingness to make the enormous time commitment of running a business. Small business expert David Birch jokingly calls this last reason—which is remarkably common—the "I had no idea!" syndrome. It highlights the importance of anticipating what you're in for *before* you open your doors.[23]

Lack of Knowledge and Experience People typically launch businesses because they either have expertise in a particular area—like designing websites or cooking Vietnamese food—or because they have a breakthrough idea—like a new way to develop computer chips or run an airline. But in-depth knowledge in a specific area doesn't necessarily mean expertise in running a business. Successful business owners must know everything from finance to human resources to marketing.

Too Little Money The media is filled with stories of business owners who made it on a shoestring, but lack of start-up money is a major issue for most new firms. Ongoing profits don't usually begin for a while, which means that entrepreneurs must plan on some lean months—or even years—as the business develops momentum. That means a real need to manage money wisely and to resist the temptation to invest in fixed assets, such as fancy offices and advanced electronics, before sufficient regular income warrants it. It also requires the nerve to stay the course despite initial losses.[24]

Bigger Regulatory Burden Complying with federal regulations can be challenging for any business, but it can be downright overwhelming for small firms. A study sponsored by the federal government shows that firms with fewer than 20 employees spend an average of $7,647 per employee abiding by federal regulations, compared with $5,282 spent by firms with more than 500 employees. The overall burden is 45% greater for small business than for its larger business counterparts. But relief may be on the way: in mid-2008, Congress began to examine ways to reduce the growing regulatory burden on small businesses—an urgent need in the face of the struggling economy.[25]

Higher Health Insurance Costs Administrative costs for small health plans are much higher than for large businesses, making it even tougher for small firms to offer coverage to their employees. Given skyrocketing healthcare costs in general, the best employees are likely to demand a great insurance plan, putting small business at a real disadvantage in terms of building a competitive workforce.[26] But this may change as healthcare reform goes into effect over the next decade.

LO5 Launch Options: Reviewing the Pros and Cons

When you imagine starting a new business, the first thought that comes to mind would probably be the process of developing your own big idea from an abstract concept to a thriving enterprise. But that's not the only option. In fact, it may make more sense to purchase an established business, or even buy a franchise such as a Pizza Hut or Subway restaurant. Each choice, of course, involves pros and cons. The trick is finding the best fit for you: the combination that offers you the least harmful downsides and the most meaningful upsides. Broadly speaking, it's less risky to buy an established business or franchise, but it can be more satisfying to start from scratch. Exhibit 7.3 offers a more detailed overview of the pros and cons.

Making It Happen: Tools for Business Success

Whatever way you choose to become a small business owner, several strategies can help you succeed over the long term: gain experience in your field, learn from others, educate yourself, access **Small Business Administration (SBA)** resources, and develop a business plan.

EXHIBIT 7.2 New Business Survival Rates

YEAR IN BUSINESS	SURVIVAL RATE	CHANGE VS. PRIOR YEAR (PERCENTAGE POINTS)
YEAR 1	81%	−19
YEAR 2	66%	−15
YEAR 3	54%	−12
YEAR 4	44%	−10
YEAR 5	38%	−6
YEAR 6	34%	−4
YEAR 7	31%	−3

Source: Business Employment Dynamics data: survival and longevity, II, by Amy E. Knaup and Merissa C. Piazza, September 2007, Monthly Labor Review, Bureau of Labor Statistics website, http://www.bls.gov/opub/mlr/2007/09/art1full.pdf, accessed February 15, 2009.

Gain Experience Getting roughly three years of experience working for someone else in the field that interests you is a good rule of thumb. That way, you can learn what does and doesn't fly in your industry with relatively low personal risk (and you'd be making any mistakes on someone else's dime). You can also start developing a vibrant, relevant network before you need to ask for favors. But if you stay much longer than three years, you may get too comfortable to take the plunge and launch your own venture.

Learn from Others You should actively seek opportunities to learn from people who've succeeded in your field. If you don't know anyone personally, use your network to get introductions. And don't forget industry associations, local events, and other opportunities to build relationships. Also, remember that people who failed in your field may be able to give you valuable insights (why make the same mistakes they did?). As a bonus, they may be more willing to share their ideas and their gaffes if they're no longer struggling to develop a business of their own.

Educate Yourself The opportunities for entrepreneurial learning have exploded in the past decade. Many colleges and universities now offer full-blown entrepreneurship programs that help students both develop their plans and secure their initial funding. But education shouldn't stop there. Seek out relevant press articles, workshops, websites, and blogs so that your ongoing education will continue to boost your career.

Access SBA Resources The SBA offers a number of resources beyond money (which we'll discuss in the next section). The SBA website, www.sba.gov, provides a wealth of information from industry-specific statistics, to general trends, to updates on small business regulations. The SBA also works hand in hand with individual states to fund local **Small Business Development Centers (SBDCs)**. SBDCs provide a range of free services for small businesses from developing your concept,

EXHIBIT 7.3   Pros and Cons of Starting a Business from Scratch versus Buying an Established Business

STARTING YOUR BUSINESS FROM SCRATCH

Key Pros	Key Cons
It's all *you:* Your concept, your decisions, your structure, and so on. You don't have to deal with the prior owner's bad decisions.	It's all *you*. That's a lot of pressure. It takes time, money, and sheer sweat equity to build a customer base. Without a track record, it's harder to get credit from both lenders and suppliers. From securing permits to hiring employees, the logistics of starting a business can be challenging.

BUYING AN ESTABLISHED BUSINESS

Key Pros	Key Cons
The concept, organizational structure, and operating practices are already in place. Relationships with customers, suppliers, and other stakeholders are established. Getting financing and credit is less challenging.	Working with someone else's idea can be a lot less fun for some entrepreneurs. You may inherit old mistakes that can range from poor employee relations to pending lawsuits.

BUYING A FRANCHISE

Key Pros	Key Cons
In most cases, you're buying your own piece of a well-known brand and proven way of doing business. Typically, management expertise and consulting come with the franchise package. Franchisers occasionally offer not just advice but also the financing that can make the purchase possible. These advantages add up to a very low 5% first-year failure rate.	You have less opportunity for creativity since most agreements tie you to franchise requirements. If something goes wrong with the national brand (e.g., *E. coli* at a burger joint), your business will suffer, too. The initial purchase price can be steep, and that doesn't include the ongoing percent-of-sales royalty fee.

Source: Five Reasons Why Franchises Flop, by Steve Strauss, February 28, 2005, *USA Today* Money website, http://www.usatoday.com/money/smallbusiness/columnist/strauss/2005-02-28-franchise_x.htm.

to consulting on your business plan, to helping with your loan applications. And the SBA supports **SCORE**, the Service Corps of Retired Executives at www.score.org. They provide free, comprehensive counseling for small businesses from qualified volunteers.

Develop a Business Plan Can a business succeed without a plan? Of course. Many do just fine by simply seizing opportunity as it arises, and changing direction as needed. Some achieve significant growth without a plan. But a **business plan** does provide an invaluable way to keep you and your team focused on success. And it's absolutely crucial for obtaining outside funding, which is why many entrepreneurs write a business plan after they've used personal funding sources (such as savings, credit cards, and money from family and friends) to get themselves up and running. Even then, the plan may be continually in flux if the industry is rapidly changing.

An effective business plan, which is usually 25 to 50 pages long, takes about six months to write. While the specifics may change by industry, the basic elements of any business plan answer these core questions:

- What service or product does your business provide, and what needs does it fill?
- Who are the potential customers for your product or service, and why will they purchase it from you?
- How will you reach your potential customers?
- Where will you get the financial resources to start your business?
- When can you expect to achieve profitability?

The final document should include all of the following information:

- Executive summary (two to three pages)
- Description of business (include both risks and opportunities)

© RAGMA IMAGES/Shutterstock.com

Bill Gates, Steve Jobs, Michael Dell, and Mark Zuckerberg built blockbuster firms without a college degree, but 57% of those who start a business in high-income countries do have a college degree.
— GLOBAL ENTREPRENEURSHIP MONITOR

© Alex Staroseltsev/Shutterstock.com

- Marketing
- Competition (don't underestimate the challenge)
- Operating procedures
- Personnel
- Complete financial data and plan, including sources of start-up money (be realistic!)
- Appendix (be sure to include all your research on your industry)[27]

Check out the SBA business-planning site for more information on how to write your own business plan and for samples of actual business plans (http://www.sba.gov/smallbusinessplanner/index.html). Other excellent resources (among many) on the Internet include the sample business plan resource center (www.bplans.com/) and the business plan pages of AllBusiness.com (www.allbusiness.com/).

L06 Small Business and the Economy: An Outsized Impact

The most successful entrepreneurs create goods and services that change the way people live. Many build blockbuster corporations that power the stock market and dominate pop culture through ubiquitous promotion. But small businesses—despite their lower profile—also play a vital role in the U.S. economy. Here are a few statistics from the U.S. Small Business Administration:

- In 2008, 99.9% of the 29,600,000 businesses in the United States had fewer than 500 employees.
- About three-quarters of those business owners—21,700,000 people, totaling about 7% of the population—ran their businesses without any employees.

Accidental Inventions

Every new business begins with a great idea, but not all great ideas begin with careful planning—a number of hugely successful businesses have been built on inventions that simply happened by accident. But that doesn't mean that you shouldn't be prepared; first-century philosopher Seneca said, "Luck is what happens when preparation meets opportunity." Here is a sampling of "accidental inventions":[28]

© haveseen/Shutterstock.com

- *Penicillin*: When scientist Alexander Fleming left for vacation in 1928, he supposedly didn't clean up his workstation. When he returned, he found a strange fungus growing on some of his cultures. Oddly, bacteria seemed adverse to the fungus, which led him to do further testing, thus uncovering penicillin, the "wonder drug" of the twentieth century.

- *Coca-Cola*: Atlanta pharmacist John Pemberton was mixing ingredients to create a new headache remedy when he discovered, instead, a tasty beverage, Coca-Cola, which was sold from his pharmacy for eight years before it was popular enough to be sold in bottles.

- *Saccharin*: One of the most popular artificial sweeteners in the world was discovered in 1879 when chemist Constantin Fahlberg didn't wash his hands after a day of working with coal tar. He ate some bread rolls with his meal and noticed that they tasted curiously sweet. Wondering why, he tasted the chemicals that had been on his hand, and discovered the formula that eventually became saccharin.

- Yet, these small businesses generate about half of the U.S. gross domestic product.

- Over the last 15 years, small businesses created 64% of the net new jobs in the United States.

- In total, small business provides jobs for about half of the nation's private workforce.[29]

The statistics, of course, depend on the definition of small business. For research purposes, the SBA defines small business as companies with up to 500 employees, including the self-employed. But the SBA also points out that the meaning of small business differs across industries. To officially count as "small," the number of employees can range from fewer than 100 to 1,500, and the average revenue can range from $0.75 million to $28.5 million, depending on the type of business. But regardless of the specific definition, the fact is clear: small business is a big player in the U.S. economy.

Beyond the sheer value of the goods and services they generate, small businesses make a powerful contribution to the U.S. economy in terms of creating new jobs, fueling innovation, and vitalizing inner cities.

- Creating New Jobs: Small businesses with employees start up at a rate of more than 600,000 per year. Four years after they launch, 44% of those businesses—and many of the jobs they create—remain viable. In 2005 (the most recent year with data), small firms created 79% of the net new jobs in the economy, while large firms created only 21%. But while small businesses are quick to add new jobs, they're often the first to contract when times are tough; instability comes with the territory.[30]

- Fueling Innovation: Small businesses are much more likely to develop revolutionary new ideas. Small patenting firms produce about 13% more patents per employee than their large-firm counterparts, and those patents are twice as likely to be found among the top 1% of highest-impact patents. Small firms tend to be effective innovators for a number of reasons. Perhaps most importantly, their very reason for being often ties to a brand new idea. In the early years, they need innovation in order to simply survive. And they often display a refreshing lack of bureaucracy that allows new thinking to take hold.[31]

- Vitalizing Inner Cities: New research shows that small businesses are the backbone of urban economies, finding opportunity in niches that may not be worthwhile for larger firms. Small business comprises more than 99 of inner-city business establishments. In addition to creating new jobs, these small businesses generate 80% of total employment in American inner cities, providing a springboard for economic development.[32]

Entrepreneurship Around the World

Research suggests that entrepreneurship has an economic impact in countries around the world. Societies need entrepreneurs to ensure that new ideas actualize and to ensure that people are able to self-employ when their economy

© BSH Stock/Image Source

does not provide for their basic needs. For the past 12 years, the Global Entrepreneurship Monitor (GEM) has measured the annual rate of new business start-ups across a range of countries across the globe, adding new nations each year. The twelfth annual GEM study included 59 countries. The research for this study was conducted mostly in 2010—incorporating learning from the global economic crisis. Surprisingly, despite improving economic conditions, the results showed that 60% of entrepreneurs evaluated conditions for starting a new business in 2010 as worse than the prior year, versus 50% in 2009. Earlier GEM studies showed that intentions to launch a business in the next three years do not decline as sharply as perceived opportunities. Possible reasons: 1) People who are afraid of losing their jobs might consider entrepreneurship more seriously. 2) Potential entrepreneurs may be highly optimistic about their own ability to cope. ("This crisis may be a problem for everyone else, but not for me.") 3) Potential entrepreneurs may simply plan to delay their launches until the end of the three-year period, assuming the economy will get back on a better track.

The current entrepreneurship rate varies dramatically from country to country, ranging from a high of 31.2% in Vanuatu to a low of 1.3% in Italy. (See Exhibit 7.4 for the ten nations with the highest and lowest entrepreneurship rates.) The differences among countries seem to depend largely on several key factors: What is the national per-capita income? What will the entrepreneur need to give up (i.e., the opportunity costs)? How high is the risk of failure? How strongly do the national culture and political environment support business start-ups?

Per-Capita Income In low-income countries, such as Bolivia and Vanuatu, a high percentage of entrepreneurs start their own businesses because they simply have no other options. This contributes heavily to the startlingly high overall level of entrepreneurship. The rate of such "necessity entrepreneurship" declines in higher-income countries, such as the United States and Japan, where entrepreneurs are more likely to strike out on their own in response to an opportunity that they spot in the marketplace.

In 15,000 single room factories, local entrepreneurs handle at least 80% of plastic recycling in

Mumbai, India's
largest city.

—TIME

Opportunity Costs Entrepreneurship rates are significantly lower in countries that provide a high level of employment protection (it's hard to get fired) and strong unemployment insurance (financial support if you do get fired). With these benefits in place, the sense of urgency regarding entrepreneurship tends to fall, in part because fear of failure is much lower. The European Union provides a number of clear examples.

Cultural/Political Environment Extensive, complex regulations can hinder entrepreneurship by raising daunting barriers. And a lack of cultural support only compounds the problem. These factors certainly contribute to the relatively low entrepreneurship rates in much of the European Union and Japan. Entrepreneurs in more supportive nations such as the United States and New Zealand get a boost from limited regulation and strong governmental support. A thriving "cowboy culture" helps, too—standout individuals who break free of old ways attract attention and admiration in many of the countries with higher entrepreneurship rates.[33]

EXHIBIT 7.4 Entrepreneurship Rates

TOP TEN ENTREPRENEURSHIP RATES		BOTTOM TEN ENTREPRENEURSHIP RATES	
COUNTRY	ENTREPRENEUR-SHIP RATE	COUNTRY	ENTREPRE-NEURSHIP RATE
VANUATU	31.2%	Italy	1.3%
BOLIVIA	28.8%	Malaysia	1.4%
PERU	22.1%	Japan	1.5%
ZAMBIA	17.3%	Tunisia	2.7%
ANGOLA	13.6%	Denmark	1.8%
MONTENEGRO	12.0%	Korea	1.8%
CHILE	11.1%	Portugal	1.8%
GHANA	10.7%	Greece	2.0%
UGANDA	10.6%	Switzerland	2.0%
COSTA RICA	10.4%	Slovenia	2.2%

Source: Global Entrepreneurship Monitor 2010 Report, by Donna J. Kelley, Niels Bosma, José Ernesto Amorós, College and London School of Economics, file:///C:/Users/Marce/AppData/Local/Temp/GEM%20GLOBAL%20REPORT%202010rev.pdf, published March 2011, accessed March 21, 2011 Global Entrepreneurship Monitor, 2008 Executive Report, by Niels Bosma, Zoltan J. Acs, Erkko Autio, Alicia Coduras, and Jonathan Levie, Babson College and London School of Economics, http://www.gemconsortium.org/article.aspx?id=76, published January 15, 2009, accessed February 17, 2009.

THE BIG PICTURE

Successful entrepreneurs need more than simply a great idea. Bringing that idea to market—and earning a profit in the process—requires deep knowledge of every area of business. Finding money, attracting customers, and absorbing risk are only some of the challenges. But for the right person, the payoff can be huge in terms of everything from financial success to scheduling flexibility. The key is finding something you love to do that offers value to others. While that doesn't guarantee success, building on a passion suggests that you'll at least enjoy the journey. Looking forward from the global economic crisis, entrepreneurship seems likely to become a way of life, either part-time or full-time, for a growing swath of the population. The ideal result would be a higher standard of living—and a higher quality of life—for business owners and their customers worldwide.

CAREERS

If your personality fits the entrepreneurial profile, you may want to consider launching your own business as a means of achieving your financial and your lifestyle goals in an uncertain and rapidly changing economic environment. And no need to wait until you've earned your degree to realized your dreams. A recent large scale survey by the Young Entrepreneurs Council found that 36 of college students are sidepreneurs–they have started their own businesses in addition to getting their degrees.[34] If you do decide to pursue entrepreneurship, be sure to seek as much information and support as possible from your local Small Business Development Center.

CAREERS IN ENTERPRENEURSHIP

What else?
RIP & REVIEW CARDS IN THE BACK
and visit www.cengagebrain.com!

8

Accounting:
Decision Making by the Numbers

© iStockphoto.com/a-wrangler

> "I HAVE NO USE FOR BODYGUARDS, BUT I HAVE VERY SPECIFIC USE FOR TWO HIGHLY TRAINED, CERTIFIED PUBLIC *ACCOUNTANTS*."
>
> — ELVIS PRESLEY

multiple times—layoffs might be in the offing, so many employees might decide to polish their résumés!

○ Creditors: The late, great comedian Bob Hope once defined a bank as a place that would only lend you money if you could prove you didn't really need it. That's a bit of an exaggeration, but it is true that before granting a loan, responsible bankers and other lenders will want to assess a firm's creditworthiness by looking at its financial statements.

○ Suppliers: Like bankers, companies that provide supplies want to know that the company can pay for the orders it places.

○ Government agencies: Accurate accounting information is critical for meeting the reporting requirements of the Internal Revenue Service (IRS), the Securities and Exchange Commission (SEC), and other federal and state agencies.

A number of other groups—including the news media, competitors, and unions—might also have a real interest in a firm's accounting information—whether the firm wants them to have it or not! If you have any interest in managing, investing in, or working for a business, the ability to understand accounting information is extremely valuable.

> **accounting** A system for recognizing, organizing, analyzing, and reporting information about the financial transactions that affect an organization.

LO1 Accounting: Who Needs It—and Who Does It?

Accounting is a system for recognizing, organizing, analyzing, and reporting information about the financial transactions that affect an organization. The goal of this system is to provide its users with relevant, timely information that helps them make better economic decisions.

Who uses the information that accounting provides? It's a long list; after all, everyone wants to make good decisions! In fact, a variety of business stakeholders rely so heavily on accounting information that it's sometimes called the "language of business."

Accounting: Who Uses It?

Key users of accounting information include:

○ Managers: Marketing managers, for instance, need information about sales in various regions and for various product lines. Financial managers need up-to-date facts about debt, cash, inventory, and capital.

○ Stockholders: As owners of the company, most stockholders have a keen interest in its financial performance, especially as indicated by the firm's financial statements. Has management generated a strong enough return on their investment?

○ Employees: Strong financial performance would help employees make their case for nice pay raises and hefty bonuses. But if earnings drop—especially

Accounting: Who Does It?

Accountants work in a variety of positions to provide all of this information. Let's take a quick look at some of the roles accountants play:

○ **Public accountants** provide services such as tax preparation, external auditing (a process we'll describe later in this chapter), or management consulting to clients on a fee basis.

○ **Management accountants** work within a company and provide analysis, prepare reports and financial

© Digital Vision/Jupiterimages

8

statements, and assist managers in their own organization. *Internal auditors* also work within their organizations to detect internal problems such as waste, mismanagement, embezzlement, and employee theft.

- ⊙ **Government accountants** perform a variety of accounting functions for local, state, or federal government agencies. Some ensure that the government's own tax revenues and expenditures are recorded and reported in accordance with regulations and requirements. Others work for the IRS to audit tax returns or for other government agencies, such as the SEC or FDIC, to help ensure that our nation's banks and other financial institutions comply with the rules and regulations governing their behavior.

Many jobs performed by accountants require expertise in complex subject areas. For this reason, accountants who want to move up in their profession often seek certification in a particular field. But achieving such recognition isn't easy. For example, in order to be recognized as a *certified public accountant* in most states, a candidate must complete the equivalent of 150-semester hours (five years) of college education with a heavy emphasis in accounting and other business-related courses, must pass a rigorous two-day, four-part exam (very few candidates pass all four parts on their first try), and must complete at least one year of direct work experience in the field of accounting. Individuals seeking to become *certified management accountants* or *certified fraud examiners* must satisfy similarly challenging requirements.

LO2 Financial Accounting: Intended for Those on the Outside Looking In

Financial accounting is the branch of accounting that addresses the needs of external stakeholders, including stockholders, creditors, and government regulators. These stakeholders are seldom interested in poring over detailed accounting information about the individual departments or divisions within

Before becoming the most famous of ancient Chinese philosophers, Confucius worked as an accountant.

—ChinaCulture.org

a company. Instead, they're interested in the financial performance of the firm as a whole. They often want to know how a firm's financial condition has changed over a period of several years, or to compare its results to those of other firms in the same industry. The major output of financial accounting is a set of financial statements designed to provide this broad type of information. We'll describe these statements in the next section.

© iStockphoto.com/Lasse Kristensen

Role of the Financial Standards Accounting Board

Imagine how confused and frustrated investors, creditors, and regulators would become if every firm could just make up its own financial accounting rules as it went along and change them whenever it wanted! To reduce confusion and provide external stakeholders with consistent and accurate financial statements, the accounting profession has adopted a set of **generally accepted accounting principles (GAAP)** that guide the practice of financial accounting. In the United States, the Securities and Exchange Commission (SEC) has the ultimate legal authority to set and enforce accounting standards. In practice, however, the SEC has delegated the responsibility for developing these rules to a private organization known as the **Financial Accounting Standards Board (FASB)**. This board consists of five members appointed by the Financial Accounting Foundation. Each member serves a five-year term and can be reappointed to serve one additional term. In order to preserve independence and impartiality, the members are required to sever all ties with any firms or institutions they served prior to joining the Board.

Through GAAP, the FASB aims to ensure that financial statements are:

- ⊙ Relevant: They must contain information that helps the user understand the firm's financial performance and condition.

- ⊙ Reliable: They must provide information that is objective, accurate, and verifiable.

- ⊙ Consistent: They must provide financial statements based on the same core assumptions and procedures over time; if a firm introduces any significant changes in how it prepares its financial statements, GAAP requires it to clearly identify and describe these changes.

- ⊙ Comparable: They must present accounting statements in a reasonably standardized way, allowing users to track the firm's financial performance over a period of years and compare its results with those for other firms.

He Madoff With How Much?

On March 12, 2009, Bernie Madoff was sentenced to 150 years in prison for perpetrating the biggest investment fraud in U.S. history. Madoff's scheme devastated thousands of individual and institutional investors. Many charitable foundations and pension funds took huge hits, as did the personal portfolios of many rich and famous individuals who trusted Madoff with their savings.

How could billions of dollars seemingly vanish? Where had the money gone? Could any of it be recovered? Even before Madoff was formally sentenced, the courts appointed Irving Picard as a trustee for the liquidation of Madoff's estate and assigned him the task of finding answers to these questions. In his quest to do so, Picard relied heavily on the expertise of financial sleuths known as *forensic accountants*.

How do forensic accountants help in cases like the one Picard is pursuing? "I liken it to CSI or Law and Order," says Terry McCarthy, audit partner at Green & Seifter, in Syracuse, New York. "But instead of figuring out the trajectory of a bullet, you're trying to find out how a transaction occurred." Like the forensic scientists on the television series CSI, forensic accountants often have impressive credentials. Many are Certified Public Accountants or Certified Fraud Examiners who also hold additional degrees in fields like law enforcement and criminal justice. They are mystery solvers who use their skills to analyze financial transactions that often are intended to be misleading. "Forensic accountants untangle events and details that are tangled by design," says Barry Mukamal of Rachlin Cohen & Holtz, a forensic accounting practice in Miami.

Using the findings of forensic accountants and an aggressive (and somewhat controversial) collection strategy, Picard had already recovered over $10 billion by late 2010. And he appeared on the way to recovering many billions more. But as this text was going to press, many of the individuals and institutions Picard targeted in pursuit of more money claimed that they, too, were innocent victims of Madoff's schemes and vowed to fight Picard's collection efforts in court. The legal maneuverings are likely to continue for years and to rival anything seen on a television crime drama, so stay tuned.[1]

The FASB is constantly modifying, clarifying, and expanding GAAP as business practices evolve and new issues arise. Perhaps the most important focus in recent years has been a move by the FASB and its international counterpart, the International Accounting Standards Board (IASB), to find ways to make U.S. accounting practices more consistent with those in other nations. This effort is likely to have far-reaching consequences.

Ethics in Accounting

Even clear and well-established accounting principles won't result in accurate and reliable information if managers and accountants flaunt them. A series of accounting scandals rocked the American business world during the late 1990s and the first few years of the twenty-first century. Between October 2001 and July 2002, several large corporations—Enron, Tyco, WorldCom, and Adelphia, to name only a few—were implicated in major accounting scandals. In many cases, these firms overstated earnings by billions of dollars or hid billions of dollars in debts. Once their accounting improprieties became known, most of these firms suffered severe financial difficulties. Some of the companies went bankrupt, leaving stockholders with worthless stock, and employees without jobs or pension plans. Many of the CEOs and top financial officers for these companies ended up in prison.[2]

These scandals served as a wake-up call to the accounting profession that their ethical training and standards need major improvement. In the wake of the scandals, many state accounting boards passed new ethics-related requirements.

LO3 Financial Statements: Read All About Us

One of the major responsibilities of financial accounting is the preparation of three basic financial statements: the balance sheet, income statement, and statement of cash flows. Taken together, these financial statements provide external stakeholders with a broad picture of an organization's financial condition and its recent financial performance. Large corporations with publicly traded stock must provide an annual report containing all three statements to all stockholders. They also must file quarterly and annual reports, including financial statements, with the SEC. Let's take a look at the information each statement provides.

The Balance Sheet: What We Own and How We Got It

The **balance sheet** summarizes a firm's financial position at a specific point in time. Though the balance sheets of different firms vary in specifics, all of them are organized to reflect the most famous equation in all of accounting—so famous that it is usually referred to simply as the **accounting equation**:

$$\text{Assets} = \text{Liabilities} + \text{Owners' Equity}$$

Exhibit 8.1 shows a simplified balance sheet for Bigbux, a hypothetical company we'll use to illustrate the information provided by financial statements. As you look over this exhibit, keep in mind that real-world balance sheets may include

additional accounts and that different firms sometimes use different names for the same type of account. Despite these differences, Exhibit 8.1 should help you understand the basic structure common to all balance sheets. Notice that the three major sectors of this statement reflect the key terms in the accounting equation. Once we've defined each of these terms, we'll explain the logic behind the accounting equation and how the balance sheet illustrates this logic.

⊃ **Assets** are things of value that the firm owns. Balance sheets usually classify assets into at least two major categories. The first category, called *current assets,* consists of cash and other assets that the firm expects to use up or convert into cash within a year. For example, in Bigbux's balance sheet, the value for *accounts receivable* refers to money owed to Bigbux by customers who bought its goods on credit. (These receivables are converted into cash when customers pay their bills.) *Inventory* is the other current asset listed on Bigbux's balance sheet. For a wholesale or retail company, inventory consists of the stock of goods it has available for sale. For a manufacturing firm, inventory includes not only

Accounting Fraud: As American as Wiener Schnitzel?

As if the embarrassment from the accounting scandals among major U.S. corporations in the early days of the twenty-first century weren't bad enough, American business leaders had to endure a smug condescension from their European counterparts. Many European observers suggested the scandals were the result of a uniquely American combination of corporate greed and lax regulatory standards, and implied that such episodes could never happen in Europe.

Even before the dust had settled on the Enron case European regulators were stung by accounting shenanigans at major firms that were every bit as appalling as those in America. Two of the most high- profile cases involved Parmalat (Italy's largest producer of dairy products) and Royal Ahold (a Dutch-owned retail grocer with over 9,000 stores in 27 countries). In Parmalat's case, the company claimed to have $10 billion in assets located in foreign accounts. The problem was that these assets simply didn't exist! In Royal

Ahold's case, regulators found that the company had used "creative" accounting techniques to overstate its total profits by half a billion dollars in both 2001 and 2002. As investigators dug into the details of these (and several other) scandals, it became clear that unethical accounting practices had been a problem in Europe for years.

How did these firms get away with these practices for so long? One factor was that European regulators were even less diligent than their American counterparts. For example, at the beginning of the twenty-first century, Britain's Financial Reporting Review Panel—that nation's regulatory equivalent to the U.S. Securities and Exchange Commission—had only one full-time accountant on staff to investigate accounting irregularities. With its limited staff, the British panel didn't—and in fact couldn't— take a proactive role in upholding accounting standards. [3]

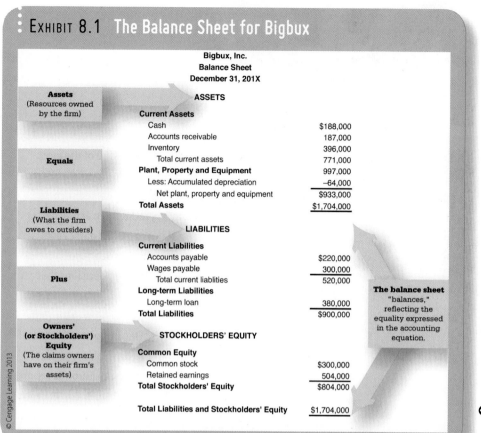

EXHIBIT 8.1 The Balance Sheet for Bigbux

Assets
(Resources owned by the firm)

Equals

Liabilities
(What the firm owes to outsiders)

Plus

Owners'
(or Stockholders')
Equity
(The claims owners have on their firm's assets)

Bigbux, Inc.
Balance Sheet
December 31, 201X

ASSETS

Current Assets	
Cash	$188,000
Accounts receivable	187,000
Inventory	396,000
Total current assets	771,000
Plant, Property and Equipment	997,000
Less: Accumulated depreciation	−64,000
Net plant, property and equipment	$933,000
Total Assets	$1,704,000

LIABILITIES

Current Liabilities	
Accounts payable	$220,000
Wages payable	300,000
Total current liablities	520,000
Long-term Liabilities	
Long-term loan	380,000
Total Liabilities	$900,000

STOCKHOLDERS' EQUITY

Common Equity	
Common stock	$300,000
Retained earnings	504,000
Total Stockholders' Equity	$804,000
Total Liabilities and Stockholders' Equity	$1,704,000

The balance sheet "balances," reflecting the equality expressed in the accounting equation.

© Cengage Learning 2013

liabilities Claims that outsiders have against a firm's assets.

owners' equity The claims a firm's owners have against their company's assets (often called "stockholders' equity" on balance sheets of corporations).

owes to workers for work they have already performed, is another example. *Long-term liabilities* are debts that don't come due until more than a year after the date on the balance sheet. The only long-term liability that Bigbux lists is a long-term loan, which is a formal written IOU with a due date more than a year after the date on the balance sheet.

○ **Owners' (or Stockholders') equity** refers to the claims the owners have against their firm's assets. The specific accounts listed in the owners' equity section of a balance sheet depend on the form of business ownership. As Exhibit 8.1 shows, common stock is a key owners' equity account for corporations. So, for corporations such as Bigbux, the owners' equity section is usually titled *stockholders' equity*. Also notice that retained earnings, which are the accumulated earnings reinvested in the company (rather than paid to owners), is another major component of the owners' equity section.

The logic behind the accounting equation is based on the fact that firms must finance the purchase of their assets, and owners and non-owners are the only two sources of funding. The accounting equation tells us that the value of a firm's assets must equal the amount of financing provided by owners (as measured by owners' equity) plus the amount

finished goods but also materials and parts used in the production process as well as any unfinished goods.

The other major category of assets on Bigbux's balance sheets is *Property, plant, and equipment*. It lists the value of the company's land, buildings, machinery, equipment, and other long-term assets. With the exception of land, these assets have a limited useful life, so accountants subtract *accumulated depreciation* from the original value of these assets to reflect the fact that these assets are being used up over time.

Though Bigbux doesn't do so, some companies list a third category of assets, called *intangible assets*. These are assets that have no physical existence—you can't see or touch them—but they still have value. Examples include patents, copyrights, trademarks, and even the goodwill a company develops with its stakeholders.

○ **Liabilities** indicate what the firm owes to non-owners—in other words, the claims non-owners have against the firm's assets. Balance sheets usually organize liabilities into two broad categories: current liabilities and long-term liabilities. *Current liabilities* are debts that come due within a year of the date on the balance sheet. Accounts payable—what the firm owes suppliers when it buys supplies on credit—is a common example of a current liability. Wages payable, which indicate what the firm

It sounds extraordinary, but it's a fact that balance sheets can make fascinating reading.

— BARONESS MARY ARCHER, CAMBRIDGE UNIVERSITY LECTURER AND CHAIRWOMAN OF THE NATIONAL ENERGY FOUNDATION

JUST BECAUSE THEY CAN...

...DOESN'T MEAN THEY SHOULD.

Firms often create special purpose entities (SPEs) to help them achieve their financial objectives. An SPE is a trust, partnership, or subsidiary corporation set up for a limited and well-defined purpose, such as obtaining money for a special project on more favourable terms. The use of SPEs can be a legitimate part of a firm's financial strategy, but in recent years some firms have used them to hide financial problems from stakeholders.

In the late 1990s, Enron appeared to be one of the most successful (and fastest growing) corporations in the U.S. Unfortunately, most of the company's reported success was due to "creative" accounting rather than actual performance. In reality, during the late 1990s and early 2000s, Enron was saddled with extremely high debt and suffered from a string of questionable investment decisions that were gradually pushing it toward bankruptcy.

Enron financed most of its apparent growth through the creation of hundreds of SPEs. One important feature of these SPEs was that they qualified as off-balance sheet financing, meaning that GAAP didn't require Enron to report their assets and liabilities on its own balance sheet. Enron's top management took advantage of this loophole to hide the company's growing debt burden and underperforming assets from regulators, investors, and employees. Thus, stakeholders were unaware that Enron was in trouble until its collapse was imminent—a collapse that cost thousands of workers their jobs (and pensions) and wiped out the investments of Enron's stockholders.

The FASB responded to the Enron scandal by revising GAAP to require disclosure of the assets and debts of SPEs on their parent company's consolidated balance sheet under certain circumstances. But new types of SPEs and other forms of off-balance sheet financing designed to circumvent these requirements surfaced during the financial meltdown in 2008–09, suggesting that the temptation to hide debt remains a problem.[4]

What do YOU think?

- What steps could the FASB take to minimize the adverse effects of off-balance sheet financing?
- What responsibility did Enron's board of directors have to oversee—and rein in—their company's aggressive use of SPEs?
- Suppose you owned stock in a major corporation. What steps would you take to find out whether the company used off-balance sheet financing?

provided by creditors (as indicated by the firm's liabilities) to purchase those assets. Because a balance sheet is based on this logic, it must *always* be in balance. In other words, the dollar value of the assets *must* equal the dollar value of the liabilities plus owners' equity. This is true for *all* firms, from the smallest sole proprietorship to the largest multinational corporation. Notice in Exhibit 8.1 that the $1,704,000 in total assets listed on Bigbux's balance sheet matches the $1,704,000 in liabilities plus owners' equity.

The Income Statement: So, How Did We Do?

The **income statement** summarizes the financial results of a firm's operations over a given period of time. The figure that attracts the most attention on the income statement is net income, which measures the company's profit or loss. In fact, another name for the income statement is the *profit and loss statement* (or, informally, the *P&L*). Just as with the balance sheet, we can use a simple equation to illustrate the logic behind the organization of the income statement:

$$\text{Revenue} - \text{Expenses} = \text{Net Income}$$

In this equation:

- **Revenue** represents the increase in the amount of cash and other assets (such as accounts receivable) the firm earns in a given time period as the result of its business activities. A firm normally earns revenue by selling goods or by charging fees for providing services (or both). Accountants use **accrual-basis accounting** when recognizing revenues. Under the accrual approach, revenues are recorded when they are earned, and payment is reasonably assured. It's important to realize that this is not always when the firm receives cash from its sales. For example, if a firm sells goods on credit, it reports revenue before it receives cash. (The revenue would show up initially as an increase in accounts receivable rather than as an increase in cash.)

- **Expenses** indicate the cash a firm spends, or other assets it uses up, to carry out the business activities necessary to generate its revenue. Under accrual-basis accounting, expenses aren't necessarily recorded when cash is paid. Instead, expenses are matched to the revenue they help generate. The specific titles given to the costs and expenses listed on an income statement vary among firms—as do the details provided. But the general approach remains the same: costs are deducted from revenue in several stages to show how net income is determined. The first step in this process is to deduct *costs of goods sold*, which are costs directly related to buying, manufacturing, or providing the goods and services the company sells. (Manufacturing companies often use the term *cost of goods manufactured* for these costs.) The difference between the firm's revenue and its cost of goods sold is its *gross profit*. The next step is to deduct *operating expenses* from gross profit. Operating expenses are costs the firm incurs in the regular operation of its business. Most income statements divide operating expenses into *selling expenses* (such as salaries and commissions to salespeople and advertising

expenses) and *general* (or *administrative*) *expenses* (such as rent, insurance, utilities, and office supplies). The difference between gross profit and operating expenses is *net operating income*. Finally, interest expense and taxes are deducted from net operating income to determine the firm's net income.

- **Net income** is the profit or loss the firm earns in the time period covered by the income statement. If net income is positive, the firm has earned a profit. If it's negative, the firm has suffered a loss. Net income is called the "bottom line" of the income statement because it is such an important measure of the firm's operating success. But income statements usually include additional information below the net income, so it isn't literally the bottom line. For example, the income statement for Bigbux indicates how much of the net income was retained and how much was distributed to stockholders in the form of dividends.

Take a look at Exhibit 8.2 to see how the income statement for Bigbux is organized. See if you can identify the

EXHIBIT 8.2 Income Statement for Bigbux

Bigbux, Inc.
Income Statement
For Year Ending December 31, 201X

Revenue: (What the firm earns)	
Minus	
Costs and Expenses (Cash spent and other resources used up)	
Equals	
Net Income (Profit if positive or loss if negative)	

Sales Revenue	890,000.00
Cost of goods sold	550,000.00
Gross Profit	340,000.00
Operating Expenses	
Selling expenses	79,000.00
Administrative expenses	86,000.00
Total Operating Expenses	165,000.00
Net Operating Income	175,000.00
Interest expense	12,000.00
Taxable Income	163,000.00
Taxes	62,000.00
Net Income	101,000.00
Dividends	55,000.00
Transfer to Retained Earnings	46,000.00

© Cengage Learning 2013

statement of cash flows The financial statement that identifies a firm's sources and uses of cash in a given accounting period.

accounts that represent the revenue, expense, and income concepts we've just described.

The Statement of Cash Flows: Show Me the Money

The last major financial statement is the **statement of cash flows**. Cash is the lifeblood of any business organization. A firm must have enough cash to pay what it owes to workers, creditors, suppliers, and taxing authorities—hopefully, with enough left to pay a dividend to its owners! So it's not surprising that a firm's stakeholders are very interested in how and why a company's cash balance changed over the past year. The statement of cash flows provides this information by identifying the amount of cash that flowed into and out of the firm from three types of activities:

1. Cash flows from *operating activities* show the amount of cash that flowed into the company from the sale of goods or services, as well as cash from dividends and interest received from ownership of the financial securities of other firms. It also shows the amount of cash used to cover expenses resulting from operations and any cash payments to purchase securities held for short-term trading purposes. Remember that under the accrual method not all revenues and expenses on the income statement represent cash flows, so operating cash flows may differ substantially

Remind people that profit is the difference between revenue and expense. This makes you look smart.

—Scott Adams, creator of Dilbert

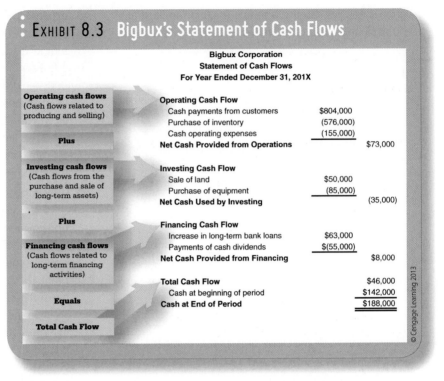

EXHIBIT 8.3 Bigbux's Statement of Cash Flows

Bigbux Corporation
Statement of Cash Flows
For Year Ended December 31, 201X

Operating Cash Flow		
Cash payments from customers	$804,000	
Purchase of inventory	(576,000)	
Cash operating expenses	(155,000)	
Net Cash Provided from Operations		$73,000
Investing Cash Flow		
Sale of land	$50,000	
Purchase of equipment	(85,000)	
Net Cash Used by Investing		(35,000)
Financing Cash Flow		
Increase in long-term bank loans	$63,000	
Payments of cash dividends	$(55,000)	
Net Cash Provided from Financing		$8,000
Total Cash Flow		$46,000
Cash at beginning of period		$142,000
Cash at End of Period		$188,000

Left side flow diagram:
- Operating cash flows (Cash flows related to producing and selling)
- Plus
- Investing cash flows (Cash flows from the purchase and sale of long-term assets)
- Plus
- Financing cash flows (Cash flows related to long-term financing activities)
- Equals
- Total Cash Flow

from the revenues and expenses shown on the income statement.

2. Cash flows from *investing activities* show the amount of cash received from the sale of fixed assets (such as land and buildings) and financial assets bought as long-term investments. It also shows any cash used to buy fixed assets and long-term financial investments.

3. Cash flows from *financing activities* show the cash the firm received from issuing additional shares of its own stock or from taking out long-term loans. It also shows cash outflows from payment of dividends to shareholders and to repay principal on loans.

Exhibit 8.3 shows the Statement of Cash Flows for Bigbux. You can see that Bigbux experienced a substantial increase in its total cash balance. You can also see that this increase in cash was primarily due to two factors. First, a look at operating cash flows shows that the cash Bigbux collected from customer payments exceeded its cash payments for inventory and operating expenses by a significant margin. Second, the section on financing activities shows that Bigbux took out a large long-term loan. The net increases in cash from these sources more than offset the net cash outflow from investing due to the purchase of new equipment. Note that the cash balance at the end of the period matches the amount of cash reported in the current balance sheet (see Exhibit 8.1 again)—as it always should.

Other Statements: What Happened to the Owners' Stake?

In addition to the three major statements we've just described, firms usually prepare either a statement of retained earnings or a stockholders' equity statement. Let's take a quick look at each of these statements.

The *statement of retained earnings* is a simple statement that shows how retained earnings have changed from one accounting period to the next. The change in retained earnings is found by subtracting dividends paid to shareholders from net income.

Firms that have more complex changes in the owners' equity section sometimes report these changes in notes to the financial statements in the annual report. But they often disclose these changes by providing a *stockholders' equity statement*. Like the statement of retained earnings, this statement shows how net income and dividends affect retained earnings. But it also shows other changes in stockholders' equity, such as those that arise from the issuance of additional shares of stock.

LO4 Interpreting Financial Statements: Digging Beneath the Surface

The financial statements we've just described contain a lot of important information. But they don't necessarily tell the whole story. In fact, the numbers they report can be misleading if they aren't put into proper context. Thus, in addition to looking at the statements, it's also important to check out the independent auditor's report and read the management discussion and footnotes that accompany these statements. It's also a good idea to compare the figures reported in current statements with those from earlier statements to see how key account values have changed.

The Independent Auditor's Report: Getting a Stamp of Approval

U.S. securities laws require publicly traded corporations in the United States to have an independent CPA firm (an accounting firm that specializes in providing public accounting services) perform an annual *external audit* of their financial statements. And many companies that aren't publicly traded also obtain external audits even though they aren't legally required to do so.

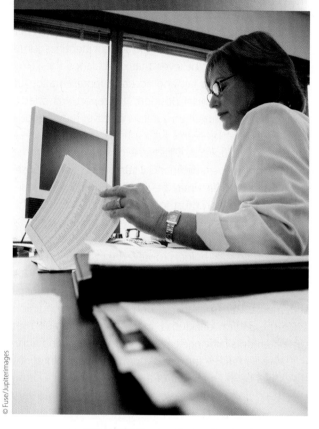

External auditors carefully examine a company's financial records before rendering their opinion.

© Fuse/Jupiterimages

The purpose of an audit is to verify that the company's financial statements were properly prepared in accordance with generally accepted accounting principles and fairly present the financial condition of the firm. So external auditors don't just check the figures; they also examine the accounting *methods* the company used to *obtain* those figures. For example, auditors interview the company's accounting and bookkeeping staff to verify that they understand and properly implement procedures that are consistent with GAAP. They also examine a sample of specific source documents (such as a sales receipts or invoices) and verify that the transactions they represent were properly posted to the correct accounts. Auditors also look for signs of fraud or falsified records. They often conduct an actual physical count of goods or supplies in inventory to determine the accuracy of the figures reported in the company's inventory records and contact the company's banker to verify its account balances. The audit process is rigorous, but it's important to realize that in large, public companies it would be impossible for auditors to check the accuracy of every transaction.

The results of the audit are presented in an *independent auditor's report*, which is included in the annual report the firm sends to its stockholders. If the auditor doesn't find any problems with the way a firm's financial statements were prepared and presented, the report will offer an *unqualified* (or *"clean"*) *opinion*—which is by far the most common outcome. If the auditor identifies some minor concerns but believes that on balance the firm's statements remain a fair and accurate representation of the company's financial position, the report will offer a *qualified opinion*. But when auditors discover more serious and widespread problems with a firm's statements, they offer an *adverse opinion*. An adverse opinion indicates that the auditor believes the financial statements are seriously flawed and that they may be misleading and unreliable. (An adverse opinion must include an explanation of the specific reasons for the opinion.) Adverse opinions are very rare, so when an auditor renders one it should set off alarm bells, warning stakeholders to view the information in the firm's financial statements with real skepticism. Exhibit 8.4 shows the auditor's opinion for Google's 2010 financial statements. This is clearly an unqualified (clean) opinion since the auditor concludes in the third paragraph that the statements fairly present Google's financial condition.

In order for CPA firms to perform audits with integrity, they must be independent of the firms they audit. During the 1990s, many of the major CPA firms entered into very lucrative consulting contracts with some of the businesses they were auditing. It became increasingly difficult for these CPA firms to risk losing these high-paying contracts by raising issues about accounting practices when they audited the books of their clients. In other words, the auditors ceased to be truly independent and objective. The lack of rigorous oversight by external auditors contributed to the accounting scandals we mentioned earlier in this chapter.

In the aftermath of the scandals, Congress passed the Sarbanes-Oxley Act of 2002 (commonly referred to as "SOX" or "Sarbox"). This law banned business relationships that might create conflicts of interest between CPA firms and the companies they audit. It also established a private-sector nonprofit corporation known as the Public Company Accounting Oversight Board (PCAOB). The PCAOB defines its mission as "to protect the interests of investors and further the public interest in the preparation of informative, fair, and independent audit reports."[5]

Checking Out the Notes to Financial Statements: What's in the Fine Print?

Some types of information can't be adequately conveyed by numbers alone. Annual reports include notes (often *many* pages of notes) that disclose additional information about the firm's operations, accounting practices, and special circumstances that clarify and supplement

---

EXHIBIT 8.4 An External Auditor's Opinion

THE BOARD OF DIRECTORS AND STOCKHOLDERS OF GOOGLE INC.

We have audited the accompanying consolidated balance sheets of Google Inc. as of December 31, 2009 and 2010, and the related consolidated statements of income, stockholders' equity, and cash flows for each of the three years in the period ended December 31, 2010. Our audits also included the financial statement schedule listed in the Index at Item 15(a)2. These financial statements and schedule are the responsibility of the company's management. Our responsibility is to express an opinion on these financial statements and schedule based on our audits.

We conducted our audits in accordance with the standards of the Public Company Accounting Oversight Board (United States). Those standards require that we plan and perform the audit to obtain reasonable assurance about whether the financial statements are free of material misstatement. An audit includes examining, on a test basis, evidence supporting the amounts and disclosures in the financial statements. An audit also includes assessing the accounting principles used and significant estimates made by management, as well as evaluating the overall financial statement presentation. We believe that our audits provide a reasonable basis for our opinion.

In our opinion, the financial statements referred to above present fairly, in all material respects, the consolidated financial position of Google Inc. at December 31, 2009 and 2010, and the consolidated results of its operations and its cash flows for each of the three years in the period ended December 31, 2010, in conformity with U.S. generally accepted accounting principles. Also, in our opinion, the related financial statement schedule, when considered in relation to the basic financial statements taken as a whole, presents fairly in all material respects the information set forth therein.

We also have audited, in accordance with the standards of the Public Company Accounting Oversight Board (United States), Google Inc.'s internal control over financial reporting as of December 31, 2010, based on criteria established in *Internal Control—Integrated Framework* issued by the Committee of Sponsoring Organizations of the Treadway Commission and our report dated February 11, 2011 expressed an unqualified opinion thereon.

/s/   ERNST & YOUNG LLP

San Jose, California
February 11, 2011

© Cengage Learning 2013

GAAP ♥ IFRS?

Accounting practices in the United States are based on GAAP, but a different set of principles governs accounting in most other nations, including key U.S. economic partners in Europe, Asia, and South America. Called the International Financial Reporting Standards (or IFRS), these standards differ from GAAP in several important respects. For example, they specify different rules for when revenue can be recognized and for how leases are treated, how benefits to retired employees are reported, and even how the financial statements themselves are presented.

The presence of different accounting rules greatly complicates matters for U.S. firms that have foreign subsidiaries or deal in international financial transactions—and for foreign firms that have U.S. subsidiaries or deal in U.S. financial transactions. It also means that financial statements prepared under these different rules aren't directly comparable, making analysis difficult for investors, creditors, and other stakeholders.

In recent years, the FASB has been working with its international counterpart, the International Accounting Standards Board (IASB), to reduce the differences between U.S. GAAP and IFRS. The negotiation process has been long, complex, and controversial, requiring compromises on both sides. But progress is definitely being made—and both the FASB and IASB have publicly stated that they are confident that the end result will be an improved and more consistent set of accounting principles for everyone involved.

Though much work remains to be done, you can expect to see some significant changes in U.S. accounting practices over the next few years as the convergence of GAAP and IFRS moves from the drawing board to the real world. It is even possible that the process will go beyond the goal of having the standards "play nice" with each other; the two standards could eventually merge into one consistent set of rules that the U.S. shares with everyone else.[6]

the numbers reported on the financial statements. These notes can be *very* revealing. For example, GAAP often allows firms to choose among several options when it comes to certain accounting procedures—and the choices the firm makes can affect the value of assets, liabilities, and owners' equity on the balance sheet and the revenues, costs, and net income on the income statement. The notes to financial statements explain the specific accounting methods used to recognize revenue, value inventory, and depreciate fixed assets. They might also provide details about the way the firm funds its pension plan or health insurance for its employees. They must also disclose *changes* in accounting methods that could affect the comparability of the current financial statements to those of previous years. Even more interesting, the notes might disclose important facts about the status of a lawsuit against the firm or other risks the firm faces. Stakeholders who ignore these notes are likely to miss out on important information.

Another important source of information is the section of the annual report usually titled "Management's Discussion and Analysis." As its name implies, this is where the top management team provides its take on the financial condition of the company. SEC guidelines require top management to disclose any trends, events, or risks likely to have a significant impact on the firm's financial condition in this section of the report.

Looking for Trends in Comparative Statements

The SEC requires publicly traded corporations to provide *comparative financial statements*. This simply means that

In 2004 a horse named "Read The Footnotes" ran in the Kentucky Derby.

— SECURITIES AND EXCHANGE COMMISSION

the balance sheet, income statement, and statement of cash flows must list two or more years of figures side by side, making it possible to see how account values have changed over a period of time. Many firms that aren't publicly traded also present comparative statements, even though they are not required to do so by GAAP.

Comparative balance sheets allow users to trace what has happened to key assets and liabilities over the past two or three years, and whether its owners' equity had increased. Comparative income statements show whether the firm's net income increased or decreased and what has happened to revenues and expenses over recent years. Using comparative statements to identify changes in key account values over time is called **horizontal analysis**.

LO5 Inside Intelligence: The Role of Managerial Accounting

Now that we've looked at financial accounting, let's turn our attention to the other major branch of accounting, **managerial (or management) accounting**. As its name implies, this branch of accounting is designed to meet the needs of a company's managers, though in recent years many firms have empowered other employees and given them access to some of this information as well. Exhibit 8.5 identifies several ways that managerial accounting differs from financial accounting.

Managers throughout an organization rely on information created by managerial accountants to make important decisions. The accuracy and reliability of this information can make a huge difference in the performance of a firm. In fact, many firms view their management accounting systems as a source of competitive advantage and regard the specifics of these systems as highly valuable company secrets.[7]

It's impossible to describe all the functions performed by managerial accountants in a single chapter. So we'll be selective and focus on only two of them—but the two we'll discuss often play a crucial role in managerial decision making: measuring and assigning costs and developing budgets.

Cost Concepts: A Cost for All Reasons

Without good information on costs, managers would be operating in the dark as they try to set prices, determine the most desirable mix of products, and locate areas where efficiency is lagging. A firm's management accounting system helps managers throughout an organization measure costs and assign them to products, activities, and even whole divisions.

Accountants define **cost** as the value of what is given up in exchange for something else. Depending on the type of problem they are analyzing, managerial

Exhibit 8.5 Comparison of Financial and Managerial Accounting

	FINANCIAL ACCOUNTING	MANAGERIAL ACCOUNTING
PURPOSE	Primarily intended to provide information to external stakeholders, such as stockholders, creditors, and government regulators. Information provided by financial accounting is available to the general public.	Primarily intended to provide information to internal stakeholders, such as the managers of specific divisions or departments. This information is proprietary—meaning that it isn't available to the general public.
TYPE OF INFORMATION PRESENTED	Focuses almost exclusively on financial information.	Provides both financial and nonfinancial information.
NATURE OF REPORTS	Prepares a standard set of financial statements.	Prepares customized reports to deal with specific problems or issues.
TIMING OF REPORTS	Presents financial statements on a predetermined schedule (usually quarterly and annually).	Creates reports upon request by management rather than according to a predetermined schedule.
ADHERENCE TO ACCOUNTING STANDARDS?	Governed by a set of generally accepted accounting principles (GAAP).	Uses procedures developed internally that are not required to follow GAAP.
TIME PERIOD FOCUS	Summarizes past performance and its impact on the firm's present condition.	Provides reports dealing with past performance, but also involves making projections about the future when dealing with planning issues.

© Cengage Learning 2013

A payment made for office rent is an out-of-pocket (or explicit) cost.

accountants actually measure and evaluate several different types of costs. We'll begin our discussion by describing some of the cost concepts commonly used by managerial accountants.

At the most basic level, accountants distinguish between out-of-pocket costs and opportunity costs. **Out-of-pocket costs** (also called *explicit costs*) are usually easy to measure because they involve actual expenditures of money or other resources. The wages a company pays to its workers, the payments it makes to suppliers for raw materials, and the rent it pays for office space are examples.

But accountants realize that not all costs involve a monetary payment; sometimes what is given up is the *opportunity* to use an asset in some alternative way. Such costs are often referred to as **implicit costs**. For example, suppose a couple of lawyers form a partnership and set up their office in a building one of the partners already owns. They feel good about their decision because they don't have to make any out-of-pocket payments for rent. But a good managerial accountant would point out to the partners that they still incur an implicit cost, because by using the building themselves they forgo the opportunity to earn income by renting the office space to someone else.

Managerial accountants also distinguish between fixed costs and variable costs. As the name implies, **fixed costs** don't change when the firm changes its level of production. Examples of fixed costs include interest on a bank loan, property insurance premiums, rent on office space and other payments that are set by a contract or by legal requirements. Many fixed costs are really only fixed for some "relevant range" of output. For example, if a company sees a dramatic rise in sales it might have to move into bigger facilities, thus incurring a higher rent.

Variable costs are costs that rise (vary) when the firm produces more of its goods and services. As a company ramps up its production it is likely to need more labor and materials and to use more electrical power. Thus payments for many types of labor, supplies and utilities are variable costs.

Assigning Costs to Products: As (Not So) Simple as ABC?

Finally, accountants often want to assign costs to specific *cost objects*, such as one of the goods or services their firm produces. When they assign costs to specific cost objects, accountants distinguish between *direct costs* and *indirect costs*. **Direct costs** are those that can be directly traced to the production of the product. For example, the wage payments made to workers directly involved in producing a good or service would be a direct cost for that product. On the other hand, the costs a firm incurs for plant maintenance, quality control, or depreciation on office equipment are usually classified as **indirect costs** since they tend to be the result of the firm's general operation rather than the production of any specific product.

Direct costs for labor and materials are usually easy to measure and assign, since they have an easily identifiable link to the object. Unfortunately, indirect costs aren't tied in such a simple and direct way to the production of a specific product. In the past, managerial accountants usually relied on simple rules to assign indirect costs to different products—and in some cases they still do. One such approach is to allocate indirect costs in proportion to the number of direct labor hours involved in the production of each product. Under this method, products that require the most labor to produce are assigned the most indirect costs. But, while this approach is simple, it can provide very misleading information. There is simply no logical reason for many types of indirect costs to be related to the amount of direct labor used to produce a product.

In recent years, managerial accountants have developed more sophisticated ways to allocate costs. One relatively new method is called **activity-based costing (ABC)**.

out-of-pocket cost A cost that involves the payment of money or other resources.

implicit cost The opportunity cost that arises when a firm uses owner-supplied resources.

fixed costs Costs that remain the same when the level of production changes within some relevant range.

variable costs Costs that vary directly with the level of production.

direct cost Costs that are incurred directly as the result of some specific cost object.

indirect costs Costs that are the result of a firm's general operations and are not directly tied to any specific cost object.

activity-based costing (ABC) A technique to assign product costs based on links between activities that drive costs and the production of specific products.

This approach is more complex and difficult to implement than the direct labor method. Basically, it involves a two-stage process. The first stage is to identify specific activities that create indirect costs and determine the factors that "drive" the costs of these activities. The second stage is to tie these cost drivers to the production of specific goods (or other cost objects). Once the relationships between cost drivers and specific products are identified, they can be used to determine how much of each indirect cost is assigned to each product.

Clearly, ABC is much more complex to implement than a system that assigns costs based on a simple "one size fits all" rule, such as the direct labor method. However, it's likely to provide more meaningful results because it is based on a systematic examination of how indirect costs are related to individual goods.

LO6 Budgeting: Planning for Accountability

Management accountants also play an important role in the development of budgets. **Budgeting** is a management tool that explicitly shows how a firm will acquire and allocate the resources it needs to achieve its goals over a specific time period. The budgetary process facilitates planning by requiring managers to translate goals into measurable quantities and identify the specific resources needed to achieve these goals. But budgeting offers other advantages as well. If done well, budgeting:

- ⊙ Helps managers clearly specify how they intend to achieve the goals they set during the planning process. This should lead to a better understanding of how the organization's limited resources will be allocated.

- ⊙ Encourages communication and coordination among managers and employees in various departments within the organization. For example, the budget process can give middle and first-line managers and employees an opportunity to provide top managers with important insights about the challenges facing their specialized areas—and the resources they need to meet those challenges. But, as we will explain in the next session, the extent to which this advantage is realized depends on the specific approach used in the budgeting process.

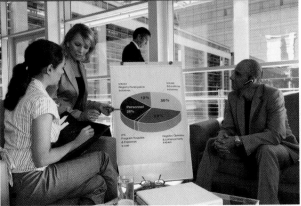

Budgeting encourages communication and coordination among managers and employees.

- ⊙ Serves as a motivational tool. Good budgets clearly identify goals *and* demonstrate a plan of action for acquiring the resources needed to achieve them. Employees tend to be more highly motivated when they understand the goals their managers expect them to accomplish and when they view these goals as ambitious but achievable.

- ⊙ Helps managers evaluate progress and performance. Managers can compare actual performance to budgeted figures to determine whether various departments and functional areas are making adequate progress toward achieving their organization's goals. If actual performance falls short of budgetary goals, managers can look for reasons and, if necessary, take corrective action.

Preparing the Budget: Top-Down or Bottom-Up?

There are two broad approaches to budget preparation. In some organizations, top management prepares the budget with little or no input from middle and supervisory managers—a process known as *top-down budgeting*. Supporters of this approach point out that top management knows the long-term strategic needs of the company and is in a better position to see the big picture when making budget decisions.

The other approach to budgeting is called *bottom-up (or participatory) budgeting*. Organizations that use a participatory process allow middle and supervisory managers to participate actively in the creation of the budget. Proponents of this approach maintain that it has two major advantages. First, middle and supervisory managers are likely to know more about the

New Accounting Trend: Stretching a Single into a Triple

Accounting has always focused on measures of the *financial* performance of an organization. But many of today's leading accounting firms are heeding a call to develop a much broader set of performance measures called the triple bottom line (TBL). The TBL approach evaluates the company's performance in three key areas:

- ○ Profits: how well the company satisfies the traditional goal of providing a fair financial return for stockholders
- ○ People: how well the company meets the needs of other stakeholders such as employees, customers, and community
- ○ Planet: the extent to which the company pursues environmentally sound and sustainable practices.

The TBL concept was first described by social responsibility guru John Elkington in 1994. But in the 1990s most accounting firms were reluctant to devote the time and effort needed to develop measures of TBL performance. So for several years TBL was more a catchphrase than a real-world approach to evaluating corporate performance. That began to change soon after the turn of the century, as a wave of corporate accounting scandals, growing concerns about global warming, and a devastating financial crash convinced many in the accounting and finance professions that a narrow focus on financial performance was distorting corporate incentives.

Gradually, a consensus emerged that broader measures of corporate performance were needed. As Rodger Hill, Head of Financial Management Advisory for accounting giant KPMG, observed, "The days of purely measuring business performance by financial result may well be numbered. In its place, I believe that discerning investors will look for something broader to measure an entity's real contribution and performance." And according to Hill, that broader approach should be the triple bottom line.

Today virtually most major accounting firms, including all of the "Big 4" accounting firms that perform the vast majority of external audits of public companies, have developed their own versions of triple bottom line accounting.[8]

issues and challenges facing their departments—and the resources it will take to address them—than top management. Second, middle and first-line managers are likely to be more highly motivated to achieve budgetary goals when they have a say in how those goals are developed. On the negative side, the bottom-up approach is more time consuming and resource intensive to carry out than the top-down approach. Also, some middle managers may be tempted to overstate their needs or set low budget goals in order to make their jobs easier—an outcome known as *budgetary slack*.[9] Despite these drawbacks, the participatory approach currently is more common than the top-down process.

operating budgets
Budgets that communicate an organization's sales and production goals and the resources needed to achieve these goals.

Developing the Key Budget Components: One Step at a Time

The budgeting process actually requires the preparation of several different types of budgets. But all of these individual budgets can be classified into two broad categories: operating budgets and financial budgets.

Operating budgets are budgets that identify projected sales and production goals and the various costs the firm will incur to meet these goals. These budgets are developed in a specific order, with the information from earlier budgets used in the preparation of later budgets.

The preparation of operating budgets begins with the development of a *sales budget* that provides quarterly estimates of the number of units of each product the firm expects to sell, the selling price, and the total dollar value of expected sales. The sales budget *must* be created first because many of the production and cost figures that go into other operating budgets depend on the level of sales. Once the sales budget is complete, the budgeted sales level can be used to develop the production budget, the administrative expenses and the selling expenses budgets. And once the production budget is completed, the information it contains is used to prepare budgets for direct labor costs, direct materials costs, and manufacturing overhead. The final stage in the preparation of operating budgets is the creation of a *budgeted income statement*. This budget looks much like the income statement we described earlier, but instead of describing the actual results of the firm's past operations, it combines the revenue projections from the sales budget and the cost projections from the other operating budgets to present a forecast of *expected* net income.

Financial budgets focus on the firm's financial goals and identify the resources needed to achieve these goals. The two main financial budget documents are the *cash budget* and the *capital expenditure budget*. The cash budget identifies short-term fluctuations in cash flows, helping managers identify times when the firm might face cash flow problems—or when it might have a temporary surplus of cash that it could invest. The capital expenditure budget identifies the firm's planned investments in major fixed assets and long-term projects. The information from these two financial budgets and the budgeted income statement are combined to construct the *budgeted balance sheet*. This is the last financial budget; it shows how the firm's operations, investing, and financing activities are expected to affect all of the asset, liability, and owners' equity accounts.

The firm's **master budget** organizes the operating and financial budgets into a unified whole, representing the firm's overall plan of action for a specified time period. In other words, the master budget shows how all of the pieces fit together to form a complete picture. Exhibit 8.6 shows all of the budget documents that are included in a typical master budget. The arrows indicate the order in which the budgets are developed, starting with the sales budget and ending with the budgeted balance sheet.

Being Flexible: Clearing Up Problems with Static

The budget process, as we've described it so far, results in a *static* budget, meaning that it is based on a single assumed level of sales. Static budgets are excellent tools for planning, but they have weaknesses when they are used to measure progress, evaluate performance, and identify problem areas that need correcting.

The problem with a static budget is that real-world sales can (and often do) vary considerably from their forecasted value—often for reasons that aren't under the control of the firm's management. For example, the collapse of the U.S. economy into a deep recession, beginning in late 2007, caused sales to drop sharply and unexpectedly even at many well-managed companies.

As we mentioned earlier, many cost figures in budgets are based on the level of sales specified in the sales budget. When actual sales differ significantly from the sales volume assumed in a static budget all of these related budget figures will be erroneous. Using these inaccurate figures to evaluate real-world performance is likely to result in very poor assessments!

One common way managerial accountants avoid this problem is to develop a *flexible budget* for control purposes. A flexible budget is one that isn't based on a single assumed level of sales. Instead, it is developed over a *range* of possible sales levels, and is designed to show the appropriate budgeted level of costs for each different level of sales. This flexibility enables managers to make more meaningful comparisons between actual costs and budgeted costs.

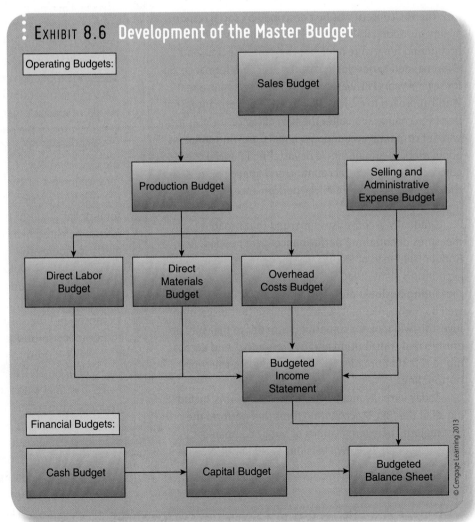

EXHIBIT 8.6 Development of the Master Budget

Operating Budgets:

Sales Budget → Production Budget, Selling and Administrative Expense Budget

Production Budget → Direct Labor Budget, Direct Materials Budget, Overhead Costs Budget → Budgeted Income Statement

Financial Budgets:

Cash Budget → Capital Budget → Budgeted Balance Sheet

© Cengage Learning 2013

Accounting provides vital information to both the internal and external stakeholders of a firm. The balance sheet, income statement, and statement of cash flows that are the main output of financial accounting help external stakeholders, such as owners and creditors, evaluate the financial performance of a firm. And managerial accounting helps managers throughout an organization make better decisions by providing them with relevant and timely information about the costs and benefits of the choices they have to make. Clearly, a basic knowledge of accounting concepts will help you succeed in just about any career path you choose.

Over 1.3 million jobs in the United States are in the accounting profession. And the most recent forecast by the Bureau of Labor Statistics predicts that employment in accounting will grow much faster than for most other occupations over the next five years.[10] One reason for this rapid growth: the new regulations enacted in the aftermath of the recent financial meltdown will require many firms to keep more records and file more financial reports—and this extra workload will require more accountants. Another reason is that several recent high-profile cases of accounting and investment fraud have increased the demand for skilled internal auditors and forensic accountants to detect illegal behavior and trace the resulting money trails. On a more positive note, the desire of businesses to meet their environmental responsibilities has led to the development of new accounting techniques to measure the costs and benefits of "green" business practices—and a demand for accountants who know how to use and interpret them. Finally, the SEC's push to overhaul GAAP and make U.S. accounting practices more consistent with those in other nations may open up opportunities for a new breed of accountants who are well-versed in the application of these new principles.

CAREERS IN ACCOUNTING

CAREERS

What *else?*
RIP & REVIEW CARDS IN THE BACK
and visit www.cengagebrain.com!

9

Finance:
Acquiring and Using Funds to Maximize Value

> ## "THE *WASTE* OF MONEY CURES ITSELF, FOR SOON THERE IS NO *MONEY* TO WASTE."
>
> — M. W. Harrison

ethical obligation (called a *fiduciary duty*) to make decisions consistent with the financial interests of their firm's owners. After all, the stockholders are the ones with their money at risk. The managers who work for the company have a fiduciary responsibility to act in the best interests of the stockholders, and that means increasing the value of their investment in the company.

> **financial capital** The funds a firm uses to acquire its assets and finance its operations.
>
> **finance** The functional area of business that is concerned with finding the best sources and uses of financial capital.

Another reason for emphasizing shareholder wealth is more pragmatic. Firms that fail to create shareholder wealth are unlikely to be viewed as attractive investments. Thus, in order to continue attracting the financial capital needed to achieve its other goals, a firm must provide value to its existing stockholders.

But finding the mix of sources and uses of funds that maximize shareholder value isn't a simple process. Let's look at two major issues that confront financial managers as they seek to achieve their primary goal.

LO1 What Motivates Financial Decisions?

Financial capital refers to the funds a firm uses to acquire its assets and finance its operations. Firms use some of their capital to meet short-term obligations, such as paying bills from suppliers, meeting payroll, repaying loans from banks, and paying taxes owed to the government. Other funds are used to finance major long-term investments, such as the purchase of plant and equipment or the launch of a new product line. And, of course, firms need some funds to pay a return to the owners for their investment in the company.

Companies also have a variety of ways to acquire the financial capital they need: direct contributions by owners, reinvestment of earnings, loans from banks, credit provided by suppliers, and (for corporations) newly issued stocks or bonds. This isn't a complete list by any means—in fact, we'll discuss additional sources later in the chapter—but you get the idea: firms often have several ways to raise money.

In a nutshell, **finance** is the functional area of business that is responsible for finding, among all these alternatives, the best sources of funds and the best way to use them. But which sources and uses are "best" depends on the goals of the financial managers. Historically, the most widely accepted goal of financial management has been to *maximize the value of the firm to its owners*. For corporations with publicly traded stock, this translates into finding the sources and uses of financial capital that will maximize the market price of the company's common stock.

Financial managers emphasize the goal of maximizing the market price of stock because they have a legal and

Shareholder Value and Social Responsibility: Does Good Behavior Pay Off?

The emphasis that financial managers place on maximizing shareholder value may seem to conflict with the modern view that a socially responsible firm has an obligation to respect the needs of *all* stakeholders—not just its owners, but also its employees, customers, creditors, suppliers, and even society as a whole. The good news is that being socially responsible *can* be (and often is) a good strategy for also achieving the goal of shareholder wealth maximization—especially if managers take a *long-term* perspective.

When a company respects the needs of customers by providing high-quality goods and services at competitive prices, and when it listens and responds fairly to their concerns, those customers are more likely to keep coming back—and to recommend the company to friends and relatives. Similarly, when a firm provides its employees with a good work environment, those employees are likely to have better morale and greater loyalty, resulting in higher productivity and lower employee turnover. And when a company supports its local community through corporate philanthropy or cause-related marketing, the resulting goodwill may boost sales and create a more favorable business climate. All of these outcomes suggest that a commitment to meeting social responsibilities can contribute to a more profitable company and an increase in shareholder value.[1]

But things aren't always that simple. Being socially responsible requires a long-term commitment to the needs of many different stakeholders. Unfortunately, the incentives of top executives (in the form of raises, bonuses and other perks) are often tied to their firm's *short-term* performance. In such cases, some managers focus on policies that make their firm's stock price rise in the short run, but which are unsustainable over the long haul. And when managers fix their attention on raising the market price of the company's stock in the next year (or next quarter) concerns about social responsibility sometimes get lost in the shuffle.

It is also worth noting that responding to the needs of all stakeholders isn't always a simple and straightforward task. Diverse stakeholder groups can have very different goals, and finding the right balance among the competing interests of these groups can be difficult. For example, a firm's managers might believe they can increase its profits (and the value of its stock) by shutting down its existing plant in the United States and outsourcing the work to China. While this might benefit shareholders, it would clearly be devastating to its existing U.S. workforce and the community in which its current plant is located. When conflicts arise between the long-term interests of owners and those of other stakeholders, financial managers generally adopt the policies they believe are most consistent with the interests of ownership.

Risk and Return: A Fundamental Tradeoff in Financial Management

One of the most important lessons in financial management is that there is a tradeoff between risk and return. In financial management **risk** refers to the degree of uncertainty about the actual outcome of a decision. The **risk-return tradeoff** suggests that sources and uses of funds that offer the potential for high rates of return tend to be more risky than sources and uses of funds that offer lower returns.

Financial managers want to earn an attractive rate of return for shareholders. But they also must realize that the higher the expected return they seek, the more they expose their company to risk. Our nation's recent economic history illustrates this point. In the years just prior to the Great Recession,

> **In a 2010** survey of 2,000 executives and investors, over 75% agreed that socially responsible policies create corporate value over the long run.
>
> —Harvard Business Review

many firms in the financial sector invested heavily in the housing market—a strategy that offered the potential for high returns but was very risky. Many of these same firms chose to finance most of their investments by increasing their own debt, which made the risk even greater.

When the housing market faltered, and prices dropped, these firms found themselves in serious trouble; their debts were coming due at the same time the value of their investments was falling.

Many of the companies who engaged in these risky strategies went belly-up during the early stages of the financial meltdown. The list of failures included some major banks and Wall Street firms that had been considered icons of free-market capitalism. In fact, firms with almost $1.2 trillion in assets filed for bankruptcy in 2008. To put that in perspective, the total asset value of all of the firms that went bankrupt in the post-9/11 recession of 2001–2002 (a downturn that included the bankruptcies of Enron, WorldCom and several other huge corporations) was less than $500 billion. And it could have been worse; without massive assistance (what some critics called a "bailout") by the federal government, many other major corporations might have suffered the same fate.[2]

LO2 Identifying Financial Needs: Evaluation and Planning

Before financial managers can determine the best financial strategies for their firm, they must identify its existing strengths and weaknesses. Then they must devise financial plans that provide a roadmap the firm can use to improve its financial performance and acquire the resources it needs to achieve both its short-term and long-term objectives.

Using Ratio Analysis to Identify Current Strengths and Weaknesses

One way financial managers evaluate the firm's current strengths and weaknesses is by computing ratios that compare values of key accounts listed on their firm's financial statements—mainly its balance sheet and income statement. This technique is called **financial ratio analysis.** Over the years, financial managers have developed an impressive array of specific ratios. Most of the key ratios fall into one of four basic categories:

1. **Liquidity ratios**: In finance a **liquid asset** is one that can be quickly converted into cash with little risk of loss. **Liquidity ratios** measure the ability of an organization to convert assets into the cash it needs to pay off liabilities that come due in the next year. Liquidity concerns became a major issue for many companies in 2008, when declining sales cut into operating cash flows and credit markets dried up with the onset of the recession.

One of the simplest and most commonly used liquidity ratios is the *current ratio*, which is computed by dividing a firm's current assets by its current liabilities. Current assets include cash and other assets expected to be converted

liquid asset An asset that can quickly be converted into cash with little risk of loss.

liquidity ratios Financial ratios that measure the ability of a firm to obtain the cash it needs to pay its short-term debt obligations as they come due.

JUST BECAUSE THEY CAN...

...DOESN'T MEAN THEY SHOULD.

The housing boom between 2003 and 2007 seemed like a win-win situation for everyone. The surge in housing construction created jobs and stimulated economic growth. Millions of Americans who had never owned a home found themselves moving into their dream house. Even Americans who already owned homes saw the value of their houses soar. And lenders in the mortgage market made huge profits.

But in reality, these gains were the result of an unsustainable bubble, due in part to the shortsighted—and sometimes unethical—behavior of mortgage brokers who arranged housing loans and the lenders who provided the funds. These brokers and lenders increasingly tapped the subprime mortgage market, consisting of borrowers who lacked the financial capacity to qualify for conventional loans. To make these loans *appear* affordable, brokers pushed variable rate mortgages with very low initial rates. They knew that subprime borrowers would be unable to make the higher payments if interest rates rose, but often neglected to explain this fact to the borrowers. They also pushed many unsophisticated borrowers into mortgage agreements that generated high fees, which they folded into the mortgage. The result: more income for the brokers and lenders and higher payments for the borrower.

While such policies increased the profits of brokers and lenders at first, in the long run they were unsustainable. When interest rates on variable rate mortgages increased a huge number of subprime borrowers defaulted on their loans. In many areas, the surge in foreclosures contributed to a steep decline in housing prices. Mortgage lending collapsed, and many of the most aggressive firms in the subprime market were wiped out.

Many observers believe more ethical mortgage lending practices could have resulted in a better outcome. As Nobel Prize winning economist Joseph Stiglitz put it, "Had the designers of these mortgages focused on the ends—what we actually wanted from our mortgage market—rather than how to maximize *their* revenues, then they might have devised products that *permanently* increased homeownership. They could have 'done well by doing good.'"[3]

What do YOU think?

- What ethical responsibilities do mortgage brokers and lenders have to their borrowers?
- What responsibility did subprime borrowers have to "read the fine print" in their loan agreements?
- How do the lessons of the mortgage crisis illustrate the need to focus on the long-term consequences of financial decisions?

into cash in the next year, while current liabilities are the debts that must be repaid in the next year. The larger the current ratio, the easier it should be for a firm to obtain the cash needed to pay its short-term debts. But, as we'll explain when we discuss how a firm manages its cash and other liquid assets, it is also possible to have too much liquidity.

2. **Asset management ratios**: Asset management ratios (also sometimes called *activity ratios*) provide measures of how effectively an organization is using its assets to generate net income. For example, the *inventory turnover ratio*—computed by dividing the firm's cost of goods sold by average inventory—measures how many times a firm's inventory is sold and replaced each year. Up to a point, a high turnover ratio is good because it indicates that the firm's products are moving quickly. On the other hand, a low inventory turnover indicates that goods may be sitting on the firm's shelves or stored in its warehouses for long periods of time—usually not a positive sign. However, it is possible for an inventory turnover ratio to be *too* high. For instance, a high ratio could mean that the company isn't keeping enough goods in stock, causing frequent stockouts. This can frustrate customers and result in lost sales if they take their business elsewhere.

For firms that sell a lot of goods on credit, the *average collection period* is another important asset management ratio. This ratio is computed by dividing accounts receivable by average daily credit sales. A value of 45 for this ratio means that customers take 45 days (on average) to pay for their credit purchases. In general, the smaller the ratio the better, since a lower value indicates that the firm's customers are paying for their purchases more quickly. But we'll see in our discussion of working capital management that low collection periods can also have drawbacks.

3. **Leverage ratios**: **Financial leverage** is the use of debt to meet a firm's financing needs; a *highly leveraged* firm is one that relies heavily on debt. While the use of leverage can benefit a firm when times are good, a high degree of leverage is very risky. As we mentioned earlier, the extensive use of debt financing by big banks and major Wall Street firms played a major role in the financial meltdown that began during the latter part of the last decade.

Leverage ratios measure the extent to which a firm uses financial leverage. One common measure of leverage is the *debt-to-asset ratio* (which is sometimes just called the *debt ratio*), which is computed by dividing a firm's total liabilities by its total assets. If a firm financed half its assets with debt and half with owners' equity, its debt ratio would be .5 (or 50%). The higher the debt-to-asset ratio, the more heavily leveraged the firm is.

4. **Profitability ratios**: Firms are in business to earn a profit, and **profitability ratios** provide measures of how successful they are at achieving this goal. There are many different profitability ratios, but we'll look at just a couple of examples. *Return-on-equity* (ROE), calculated by dividing net income (profit) by owners' equity, measures the income earned per dollar invested by the stockholders. If a firm issues both common and preferred stock, the computation of this ratio typically measures only the return to the common stockholders, since they are considered to be the true owners of the company. Thus, dividends paid to preferred stockholders are subtracted from net income in the numerator when computing ROE because these dividends aren't available to common stockholders. Similarly, the denominator of this ratio includes only equity provided by common stockholders and retained earnings.

Another profitability ratio, called *earnings per share* (EPS), indicates how much net income a firm earned per share of common stock outstanding. It is calculated by dividing net income minus preferred dividends by the average number of shares of common stock outstanding.

Exhibit 9.1 defines each of the ratios we've just described and shows how it is computed. As you look at the exhibit, keep in mind that it represents only a sample; financial managers have developed many more ratios than we can describe.

Planning Tools: Creating a Road Map to the Future

Ratio analysis helps managers identify their firm's current financial strengths and weaknesses. The next step is to develop plans that build on the firm's strengths and correct its weaknesses. Financial planning is an important part of the firm's overall planning process. Assuming that the overall planning process has established appropriate goals and objectives for the firm, financial planning must answer the following questions:

⊙ What specific assets must the firm obtain in order to achieve its goals?

- How much additional financing will the firm need to acquire these assets?

- How much financing will the firm be able to generate internally (through additional earnings), and how much must it obtain from external sources?

- When will the firm need to acquire external financing?

- What is the best way to raise these funds?

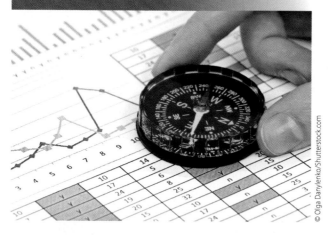

Financial planning points managers in the right direction.

© Olga Danylenko/Shutterstock.com

The planning process involves input from a variety of areas. In addition to seeking input from managers in various functional areas of their business, financial managers usually work closely with the firm's accountants during the planning process.

Basic Planning Tools: Budgeted Financial Statements and the Cash Budget

The budgeting process provides financial managers with much of the information they need for financial planning. In fact, the **budgeted income statement** and **budgeted balance sheet** are two key financial planning tools. Also called *pro forma financial statements*, they provide a framework for analyzing the impact of the firm's plans on the financing needs of the company.

- The budgeted income statement uses information from the sales budget and various cost budgets (as well as other assumptions) to develop a forecast of

budgeted income statement A projection showing how a firm's budgeted sales and costs will affect expected net income. (Also called a *pro forma* income statement.)

budgeted balance sheet A projected financial statement that forecasts the types and amounts of assets a firm will need to implement its future plans and how the firm will finance those assets. (Also called a *pro forma* balance sheet.)

EXHIBIT 9.1 Key Financial Ratios

RATIO NAME	TYPE	WHAT IT MEASURES	HOW IT IS COMPUTED
CURRENT	Liquidity: measures ability to pay short-term liabilities as they come due.	Compares current assets (assets that will provide cash in the next year) to current liabilities (debts that will come due in the next year).	$\dfrac{Current\ Assets}{Current\ Liabilities}$
INVENTORY TURNOVER	Asset management: measures how effectively a firm is using its assets to generate revenue.	How quickly a firm sells its inventory to generate revenue.	$\dfrac{Cost\ of\ Goods\ Sold}{Average\ Inventory}$
AVERAGE COLLECTION PERIOD	Asset management: measures how effectively a firm is using its assets to generate revenue.	How long it takes for a firm to collect from customers who buy on credit.	$\dfrac{Accounts\ Receivable}{\left(\dfrac{Annual\ Credit\ Sales}{365}\right)}$
DEBT-TO-ASSETS	Leverage: measures the extent to which a firm relies on debt to meet its financing needs.	Similar to debt-to-equity, but compares debt to assets rather than equity. This is another way of measuring the degree of financial leverage, or debt, the firm is using.	$\dfrac{Total\ Debt}{Total\ Assets}$
RETURN ON EQUITY	Profitability: compares the amount of profit to some measure of resources invested.	Indicates earnings per dollar invested by the owners of the company. Since common stockholders are the true owners, preferred stockholders' dividends are deducted from net income before computing this ratio.	$\dfrac{Net\ Income - Preferred\ Dividend}{Average\ Common\ Stockholders\ Equity}$
EARNINGS PER SHARE	Profitability: compares the amount of profit to some measure of resources invested.	Measures the net income per share of common stock outstanding.	$\dfrac{Net\ Income - Preferred\ Dividend}{Average\ Number\ of\ Common\ Share\ Outstanding}$

© Cengage Learning 2013

net income for the planning period. This can help the firm evaluate how much internal financing (funds generated by earnings) will be available.

⊙ The budgeted balance sheet forecasts the types and amounts of assets a firm will need to implement its future plans. It also helps financial managers determine the amount of additional financing (liabilities and owners' equity) the firm must arrange in order to acquire those assets.

© iStockphoto.com/Henrik Jonsson

The **cash budget** is another important financial planning tool. Cash budgets normally cover a one-year period and show projected cash inflows and outflows for each month. Financial managers use cash budgets to get a better understanding of the *timing* of cash flows within the planning period. This is important because most firms experience uneven inflows and outflows of cash over the course of a year, which can lead to cash shortages and cash surpluses. Projecting cash flows helps financial managers determine when the firm is likely to need additional

funds to meet short-term cash shortages, and when surpluses of cash will be available to pay off loans or to invest in other assets.

Even firms with growing sales can experience cash flow problems, especially if many of their customers buy on credit. To meet increasing sales levels, a growing firm must hire more labor and buy more supplies. These workers and suppliers may expect to be paid well before the company's credit customers pay their bills, leading to a temporary cash crunch.

Exhibit 9.2 illustrates this type of situation by presenting a partial cash budget for a hypothetical firm called Oze-Moore. The cash budget shows that, despite its increasing sales, Oze-Moore will have cash shortages in March and April. Knowing this in advance gives financial managers time to find the best sources of short-term financing to cover these shortages. The cash budget also shows that Oze-Moore will experience a big cash surplus in May as the credit customers start paying for the purchases they made in March and April. Knowing this ahead of time helps managers forecast when they will be able to repay the loans they took out to cover their previous cash shortages. It also gives them time to evaluate short-term interest-earning investments they could make to temporarily "park" their surplus cash.

EXHIBIT 9.2 Cash Budget for Oze-Moore

Cash Budget for Oze-Moore

	February	March	April	May
Sales	$75,000	$110,000	$125,000	$90,000
Cash balance at beginning of month		$10,000	$10,000	$10,000
Receipts of Cash				
Cash sales		$16,500	$18,750	$13,500
Collection of accounts receivable from last month's sales		$63,750	$93,500	$106,250
Total Cash Available		$90,250	$122,250	$129,750
Disbursements of Cash				
Payment of accounts payable		$60,500	$68,750	$49,500
Wages and salaries		$27,500	$31,250	$22,500
Fixed costs (rent, interest on debt, etc.)		$8,000	$8,000	$8,000
Purchase of new computers			$6,500	
Total Cash Payments		$96,000	$114,500	$80,000
Excess or Deficit of Cash for Month		-$5,750	$7,750	$49,750
Loans needed to maintain cash balance of $10,000		$15,750	$2,250	$0
Amount of cash available to repay short-term loans		$0	$0	$39,750
Cash balance at end of month		$10,000	$10,000	$31,750
Cumulative loans		$15,750	$18,000	$0

Sales increase in both March and April. But since most of Oze-Moore's customers buy on credit, its receipt of cash lags behind these sales increases.

While receipts of cash lag behind sales, Oze-Moore's payments of wages and accounts payable are due in the same month as sales.

Despite big increases in sales in March and April, Oze-Moore suffers a shortfall of cash because of the difference in *timing* between cash receipts and cash payments.

Financial managers want to have at least $10,000 in the cash balance at the beginning of each month. When cash falls below this amount they take out a short-term loans.

In May, Oze-Moore has a surplus in cash. This gives it enough cash to pay off the loans from earlier months.

© Cengage Learning 2013

L03 Finding Funds: What Are the Options?

Once financial managers have identified the amount of financial capital needed to carry out their firm's plans, the next step is to determine which sources of funds to tap. The most appropriate sources of funds for a business depend on several factors. One of the most important considerations is the firm's stage of development. Start-up firms face different challenges and have different needs than more established firms. Another factor is the reason the funds are needed. Funds used to meet short-term needs, such as meeting payroll, paying suppliers, or paying taxes typically come from different sources than funds used to finance major investments in plant, property, and equipment.

The financing options available to new firms are generally much more limited than those available to more mature firms with an established track record. In fact, for start-up firms the main source of funds is likely to be the personal wealth of the owner (or owners), supplemented by loans from relatives and friends. Given how risky new business ventures are banks and other established lenders are likely to be hesitant to make loans to an unproven new company. (In some cases, the Small Business Administration may help overcome this reluctance by guaranteeing loans for startups and other small businesses that satisfy its criteria.) As the firm grows and becomes more established, it may be able to obtain financing from other sources.

Some start-ups with the potential for generating rapid growth may be able to attract funds from wealthy individuals, called *angel investors*, or from venture capital firms. Both angel investors and venture capitalists typically invest in risky opportunities that offer the possibility of high rates of return. Both also typically provide funds in exchange for a share of ownership.

Sources of Short-Term Financing: Meeting Needs for Cash

Firms that have survived the start-up phase of the business life cycle often have several sources of short term financing. Let's take a look at some of the most common options.

Trade credit One of the most important sources of short term financing for many firms is **trade credit**, which arises when suppliers ship materials, parts, or goods to a firm without requiring payment at the time of delivery. By allowing the firms to "buy now, pay later," they help the firm conserve its existing cash, thus avoiding the need to acquire funds from other sources.

For a Socially Responsible Firm in Need of Funds, There's No Need to Fear...

Venture capital (VC) firms have long been an important source of financing for hot new companies offering the potential for rapid growth. VCs are limited partnerships or limited liability companies that pool funds from wealthy individuals and institutional investors (such as pension funds and college endowments) and invest those funds in firms with high profit potential. Many of today's best-known corporations, including Staples, Google, Apple, and Starbucks, got their first major funding from venture capitalists.

Traditional venture capital firms focus almost exclusively on the bottom line. They are willing to invest in "green" companies (and often do), but only if the firms offer potentially high (and quick) returns. But beginning around the turn of the new century, a new breed of "green" VC firm emerged. These new firms still seek a solid financial return, but that isn't their *only* goal. They exist to fund firms that pursue worthy social and environmental goals—and do so even if the expected financial return is a bit lower and they have to wait longer to receive it.

Consider Underdog Ventures, a VC firm whose managing partner, David Berge, was listed in *Inc. Magazine* in 2009 as one of 30 entrepreneurs who were "saving the world." Underdog invests *only* in firms that exhibit socially responsible business practices. And it is more patient with its investments, putting less pressure on the firms to create a quick return. Another difference between Underdog and traditional VC firms is that it allows investors to specify the type of firm they want to fund and to target certain demographic or geographic opportunities, such as businesses owned and operated by women or minorities, or those located in depressed areas. Finally, it has set up its own philanthropic organization, called the Underdog Foundation, to support socially responsible projects that cannot be satisfied by profit-seeking investments. Even more impressive: *every* investor in Underdog Ventures and *every* firm that has received funds from Underdog has contributed to the foundation.[4]

spontaneous financing
Financing that arises during the natural course of business without the need for special arrangements.

factor A company that provides short-term financing to firms by purchasing their accounts receivables at a discount.

line of credit A financial arrangement between a firm and a bank in which the bank pre-approves credit up to a specified limit, provided that the firm maintains an acceptable credit rating.

revolving credit agreement A guaranteed line of credit in which a bank makes a binding commitment to provide a business with funds up to a specified credit limit at any time during the term of the agreement.

commercial paper Short-term (and usually unsecured) promissory notes issued by large corporations.

In most cases, the terms of trade credit are presented on the invoice the supplier includes with the shipment. For example, the invoice might list the terms as 2/10 net 30. The "net 30" indicates that the supplier allows the buyer 30 days before payment is due. But the "2/10" tells the buyer that the supplier is offering a 2% discount off the invoice price if it pays within 10 days.

At first glance, the 2% discount in our example may not seem like a big deal. But failing to take the discount can be very costly. Consider the terms we mentioned above: 2/10, net 30. If the firm fails to pay within 10 days, it loses the discount and must pay the full amount 20 days later. Paying 2% more for the use of funds for only 20 days is equivalent to an *annual* finance charge of over 37%![5]

Suppliers will grant trade credit only after they've evaluated the creditworthiness of the firm. But once they've granted this credit to a company, they generally continue offering it as long as the firm satisfies the terms of the credit arrangements. Trade credit is sometimes called **spontaneous financing** because it is granted when the company places its orders without requiring any additional paperwork or special arrangements. The level of trade credit automatically adjusts as business conditions change and the company places larger or smaller orders with its suppliers.

Although firms of all sizes use this type of financing, trade credit is a particularly important source of financing for small businesses. The Federal Reserve Board's *Survey of Small Business Finances* indicates that about 60% of all small firms rely on trade credit as a major source of short-term financial capital.[6]

Factoring The money that customers owe a firm when they buy on credit shows up in the accounts receivable account on the company's balance sheet. A **factor** is a company that buys the accounts receivables of other firms. The factor makes a profit by purchasing the receivables at a discount from the firm and collecting the full amount from the credit customer.

Although firms that use factors don't receive the full amount their customers owe, factoring offers some definite advantages. Instead of having to wait for credit customers to pay, the firm gets its money almost immediately. Also, since the factor is responsible for collection efforts, the firm using the factor may be able to save money by eliminating its own collection department. Finally, the factor typically assumes the risk for bad debts on any receivables it buys. (However, factors typically perform a careful evaluation of the quality of accounts receivable before they buy them and may refuse to buy receivables that are highly risky.) According to the Commercial Finance Association, factoring has typically provided more than $130 billion dollars in short-term funds to American businesses in recent years.[7]

Short-Term Bank Loans Banks are another common source of short-term business financing. Short-term bank loans are usually due in 30 to 90 days, though they can be up to a year in length. When a firm negotiates a loan with a bank, it signs a *promissory note*, which specifies the length of the loan, the rate of interest the firm must pay, and other terms and conditions of the loan. Banks sometimes require firms to pledge collateral, such as inventories or accounts receivable, to back the loan. That way, if the borrower fails to make the required payments, the bank has a claim on specific assets that can be used to pay off the amount due.

Rather than going through the hassle of negotiating a separate loan each time they need more funds, many firms work out arrangements with their bankers to obtain pre-approval so that they can draw on funds as needed. One way they do this is by establishing a **line of credit**. Under this arrangement, a bank agrees to provide the firm with funds up to some specified limit, as long as the borrower's credit situation doesn't deteriorate, and the bank has sufficient funds—conditions that aren't always met, as the recent financial meltdown clearly illustrated.

A **revolving credit agreement** is similar to a line of credit, except that the bank makes a formal, legally binding commitment to provide the agreed-upon funds. In essence, a revolving credit agreement is a *guaranteed* line of credit. In exchange for the binding commitment to provide the funds, the bank requires the borrowing firm to pay a commitment fee based on the *unused* amount of funds. Thus, under the terms of a revolving credit agreement, the firm will pay interest on any funds it borrows, and a commitment fee on any funds it does not borrow. The commitment fee is lower than the interest on the borrowed funds, but it can amount to a fairly hefty charge if the firm has a large unused balance.

Commercial paper Well-established corporations have some additional sources of short-term financial capital. For instance, many large corporations with strong credit ratings issue **commercial paper**, which consists of short-term promissory notes (IOUs). Historically, commercial paper issued by corporations has been unsecured—meaning it isn't backed by a pledge of collateral. Because it is normally unsecured, commercial paper is only offered by firms with excellent credit ratings; firms with less-than-stellar financial reputations that tried to issue unsecured commercial paper would be unlikely to find buyers. In recent years, a new class of commercial paper has emerged, called *asset-backed commercial paper,* which, as its name implies, is backed by some form of collateral.

Commercial paper can be issued for up to 270 days, but most firms typically issue it for much shorter periods—sometimes for as little as two days. One key reason commercial paper is popular with companies is that it typically carries a lower interest rate than commercial banks charge on short-term loans. By far the biggest issuers of commercial paper are financial institutions, but other large corporations also use this form of financing.

The market for commercial paper normally is huge—often close to $2 trillion—but it can fluctuate dramatically as economic conditions change. Because most commercial paper is unsecured, investors tend to view it as risky when business conditions deteriorate. In fact, when the economy spiraled into the Great Recession of 2008–2009 the market for commercial paper essentially dried up. This put a tremendous strain on many struggling financial institutions that relied on commercial paper to meet their short-term cash needs. The situation became so grim that in October of 2008 the Fed established the Commercial Paper Funding Facility, a limited liability company funded by the Federal Reserve Bank of New York. This facility, which the Fed operated until February 1, 2010, ultimately purchased several hundred billion dollars of commercial paper, providing a crucial infusion of cash into this stressed market.[8]

Sources of Long-term Funds: Providing a Strong Financial Base

The sources of financial capital we've looked at so far have been appropriate for dealing with cash needs that arise from short-term fluctuations in cash flows. But financial managers typically seek more permanent funding to finance major investments and provide a secure financial base for their company. Let's take a look at some of the more common sources of long-term funds.

Direct Investments from Owners One key source of long-term funds for a firm is the money the owners themselves invest in their company. For corporations, this occurs when it sells *newly issued* stock—and it's important to realize that the *only* time the corporation receives financial capital from the sale of its stock is when it is initially issued. If Google issued some new shares of stock which you bought, the funds would go to Google. But once you own Google's stock, if you decide to sell your shares to another investor Google would get nothing. The money from the sale is all yours—less, of course, the commission you pay to your broker and taxes on any gains you make on the sale.

Another way firms can meet long-term financial needs is by reinvesting their earnings. The profits that a firm reinvests are called **retained earnings**. This source isn't a pool of cash; it simply reflects the share of the firm's earnings that has been used to finance the purchase of assets and pay off liabilities. If you want to find the amount of cash the firm has, check the figure in the cash account at the top of its balance sheet. You'll typically find that the value in the firm's cash account is quite different from the amount listed in the retained earnings!

retained earnings The part of a firm's net income it reinvests.

Retained earnings are a major source of long-term capital for many corporations, but the extent to which they are used depends on the state of the economy. When the economy is booming and profits are high, retained earnings tend to soar. But when the economy slides into a recession, most corporations find they have few earnings to reinvest. For instance, in 2006 (the last real "boom" year prior to the Great Recession) corporate retained earnings exceeded $430 billion, while in the recession year of 2008 the figure fell to $157 billion—a drop of well over 60%.[9]

The decision to retain earnings involves a tradeoff, because firms have another way to use their earnings: they can pay out some or all of their profits to their owners by declaring a dividend. You might think that stockholders would be unhappy with a firm that retained most of its earnings, since that would mean they would receive a smaller dividend. But many stockholders actually prefer their companies to reinvest earnings—at least if management invests them wisely—because doing so can help finance their firm's growth. And a growing, more profitable firm usually translates into an increase in the market price of the firm's stock.

Apple historically has paid *no* dividends, choosing instead to reinvest *all* of its substantial profits. This strategy has paid off handsomely for stockholders. During the ten-year period between March 1, 2001, and February 18, 2011, the value of Apple's stock soared from $9.38 to $353.21 per share.[10] Despite the fact that Apple paid them no dividend, you can bet that most of Apple's shareholders were pleased with the capital gains that resulted from this strategy!

Long Term Debt In addition to contributions from owners, firms can also raise long term funds by borrowing from banks and other lenders or by issuing bonds.

Term Loans There are many different types of long-term loans, but the most typical arrangement—sometimes simply called a *term loan*—calls for a regular schedule of fixed payments sufficient to ensure that all interest and principal (the amount initially borrowed) are repaid by the end of the loan's term.

Lenders often impose requirements on long-term loans to ensure repayment. Most lenders require that the loans to be

CHAPTER 9   Finance: Acquiring and Using Funds to Maximize Value   **141** backed by the pledge of some type of collateral. Banks and other lenders also often include *covenants* in their loan agreements. A **covenant** is a requirement a lender imposes on the borrower as a condition of the loan. One common covenant requires the borrower to carry a specified level of liability insurance. Another requires the borrower to agree not to borrow any *additional* funds until the current loan is paid off. Covenants sometimes even restrict the size of bonuses or pay raises the firm can grant to employees. The purpose of covenants is to protect creditors by preventing the borrower from pursuing policies that might undermine its ability to repay the loan. While covenants are great for the lender, borrowers often view them as highly restrictive.[11]

Corporate bonds Rather than borrow from banks or other lenders, corporations sometimes issue their own formal IOUs, called *corporate bonds*, which they sell to investors. Bonds often have due dates (maturities) of ten or more years after issuance. Like corporate stock, bonds are marketable, meaning that bondholders can sell them to other investors before they mature. But it is important to realize that unlike shares of stock, which represent ownership in a corporation, bonds are certificates of debt.

LO4 Leverage and Capital Structure: How Much Debt Is Too Much Debt?

Most firms use a combination of **equity** and **debt financing** to acquire needed assets and to finance their operations. Owners provide equity financing, while creditors (lenders) provide debt

Decisions about capital structure require managers to weigh the risks and rewards of financial leverage.

financing. Thus, when a company issues and sells new stock or uses retained earnings to meet its financial needs, it is using equity financing. But when it takes out a bank loan or issues or issues and sells corporate bonds, it is relying on debt financing.

Both equity and debt financing have advantages and drawbacks. The extent to which a firm relies on various forms of debt and equity to satisfy its financing needs is called that firm's **capital structure**. To simplify our discussion, we'll focus mainly on the capital structure of corporations, but many of the basic principles apply to other forms of ownership.

Pros and Cons of Debt Financing

When a firm borrows funds, it enters into a contractual agreement with the lenders. This arrangement creates a *legally binding* requirement to repay the money borrowed (called the principal) *plus interest*. These payments take precedence over any payments to owners. In fact, lenders often require the firm to pledge collateral, such as real estate, financial securities, or equipment, to back the loan. Should the firm be unable to make the required payments, the lenders can use this collateral to recover what they are owed.

Debt financing offers some advantages to firms. For instance, the interest payments a firm makes on debt are a tax-deductible expense. So Uncle Sam (in the form of the IRS) subsidizes the interest payments. For example, if the corporation's tax rate is 30%, then each dollar of interest expense reduces the firm's taxes by $.30—meaning the true cost to the firm of each dollar of interest is only $.70.

Another advantage of debt is that it enables the firm to acquire additional funds without requiring existing stockholders to invest more of their own money or the sale of stock to new investors (which would dilute the ownership of existing owners). Moreover, if the firm invests the borrowed funds profitably, the use of debt can substantially improve the return on equity to the shareholders. We'll illustrate this result in our discussion of financial leverage.

One obvious disadvantage of debt is the requirement to make fixed payments. This can create real problems when the firm finds itself in an unexpectedly tight financial situation. In bad times, required interest payments can eat up most (or all) of the earnings, leaving little or no return to the firm's owners. And if the firm is unable to meet these payments, its creditors can force it into bankruptcy.

As we mentioned earlier, another disadvantage of debt financing is that creditors often impose covenants on the borrower. These covenants can hamper the firm's flexibility and might result in unintended problems. For example, a covenant that restricts bonuses and pay raises to employees might undermine the morale of key workers and tempt them to seek employment elsewhere. Similarly, restrictions on dividends or on the ability of the firm to borrow additional funds may make it difficult for the firm to raise more money.

Pros and Cons of Equity Financing

For corporations, equity financing comes from two major sources: retained earnings and money directly invested by stockholders who purchase newly issued stock. Equity financing is more flexible and less risky than debt financing. Unlike debt, equity imposes no required payments. A firm can skip dividend payments to stockholders without having to worry that it will be pushed into bankruptcy. And a firm doesn't have to agree to burdensome covenants to acquire equity funds.

On the other hand, equity financing doesn't yield the same tax benefits as debt financing. In addition, existing owners might not want a firm to issue more stock, since doing so might dilute their share of ownership. Finally, a company that relies mainly on equity financing forgoes the opportunity to use financial leverage. But as we've already noted, leverage can be a two-edged sword. We'll illustrate the risks and rewards of leverage in our next section.

Financial Leverage: Using Debt to Magnify Gains (And Losses)

As mentioned in our discussion of ratios, firms that rely on a lot of debt in their capital structure are said to be *highly leveraged*. The main advantage of financial leverage is that it magnifies the return on the stockholders' investment when times are good. Its main disadvantage is that it also reduces the financial return to stockholders when times are bad.

Let's illustrate both the advantages and disadvantages of financial leverage with a simple example. Exhibit 9.3 shows the revenues, expenses, and earnings that two firms—Eck-Witty Corporation and Oze-Moore International—would experience for two different levels of sales, one representing a strong year and the other a weak year. To make the impact of leverage easy to see, we'll assume that Eck-Witty and Oze-Moore are *identical* in all respects *except* their capital structure. In particular, our example assumes that the two companies have the same amount of assets and experienced exactly the same *earnings before interest and taxes* (abbreviated as EBIT). Thus, any differences in the net income of these firms results from differences in their use of debt and equity financing. We'll use return on equity (ROE) to measure the financial return each firm offers its stockholders. (See Exhibit 9.1 if you need a reminder about how to interpret or compute this ratio.)

Note that *both* firms have a total of $1 million of assets, but they've financed the purchase of their assets in very different ways. Eck-Witty used only common stock and retained earnings in its capital structure, so it has $1 million in equity financing and no debt. Oze-Moore's capital structure consists of $200,000 in owners' equity and $800,000 in debt, so it is highly leveraged. The interest rate on its debt is 10%, so Oze-Moore has to make required interest payments of $80,000 per year to its lenders. Both companies must pay taxes equal to 25% of their earnings, but Oze-Moore's total tax bill will be lower than Eck-Witty's because its interest payments are tax deductible.

As Exhibit 9.3 shows, when sales are strong Oze-Moore's use of leverage really pays off. Eck-Witty's ROE of 12% under

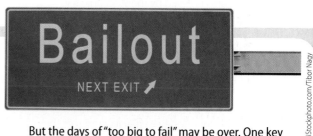

© iStockphoto.com/Tibor Nagy

Is Too Big to Fail a Thing of the Past?

At the onset of the Great Recession, government officials quickly concluded that they couldn't allow financial giants such as Citigroup, Goldman Sachs, AIG and Bank of America to go under. They reasoned that these firms were so huge and so interdependent that the collapse of one of them could bring down the entire U.S. financial system, plunging the already fragile economy into a full-fledged depression. In other words, these firms were deemed "too big to fail." This line of reasoning led the government to hastily create a huge bailout program for the financial sector.

While most experts agreed that the government's bailout was necessary, they also agreed that it sent the wrong message for the future. As long as financial institutions are too big to fail, they will continue to make excessively risky decisions, believing that the government will protect them from any negative consequences of these risks. In other words, "Heads we win, tails the taxpayers lose."

But the days of "too big to fail" may be over. One key goal of the Dodd-Frank Act was to eliminate the problem of "too big to fail." Among the law's key provisions:

- ☉ **Establishment of a Financial Stability Oversight Council (FSOC):** One goal of this council will be to track the risks associated with big financial firms and propose restrictions that may limit their growth and complexity.

- ☉ **Tighter restrictions on financial leverage:** The FSOC will establish rules requiring larger financial institutions to hold larger amounts of capital against their debts, effectively limiting their use of risky financial leverage.

- ☉ **Requirement for funeral plans:** Large financial institutions are required to develop and periodically update plans for their rapid and orderly shutdown should they go under.

- ☉ **Prohibition of government bailouts for individual banks:** While the Fed can still engage in broad-based emergency lending during a future crisis, bailouts that target specific companies are now prohibited.[12]

EXHIBIT 9.3 How Financial Leverage Affects the Return on Equity

Eck-Witty (Capital structure is all only equity)

				Strong Sales	Weak Sales
Equity (Funds supplied by owners)				$1,000,000	
Debt (Funds obtained by borrowing)				$0	
EBIT				$160,000	$80,000
Interest				0	0
Taxable income				160,000	80,000
Taxes				40,000	20,000
After Tax Earnings				120,000	60,000
ROE				12.0%	6%

Eck-Witty's use of only equity financing results in a lower ROE than Oze-Moore's when sales are strong. But it enjoys better ROE than Oze-Moore when sales are weak.

Oze-Moore (Capital structure is 20% equity and 80% debt)

				Strong Sales	Weak Sales
Equity (Funds supplied by owners)				$200,000	
Debt (Funds obtained by borrowing)				$800,000	
EBIT				$160,000	$80,000
Interest				80,000	80,000
Taxable income				80,000	0
Taxes				20,000	0
After Tax Earnings				60,000	0
ROE				30.0%	0.0%

Oze-Moore's use of leverage magnifies ROE when sales are strong. But the required interest payments of $80,000 completely wipe out the return owners when sales are weak.

© Cengage Learning 2013

the strong sales scenario isn't bad, but it pales in comparison to the 30% return Oze-Moore generates for its owners under the same scenario. Oze-Moore's higher ROE occurs because its interest payments are *fixed*. It pays its creditors $80,000—no more, no less—whether EBIT is high or low. When Oze-Moore can borrow funds at an interest rate of 10% and invest them in assets that earn *more* than 10% (as it does in the strong sales scenario), the extra return goes to the *owners* even though creditors provided the funds. This clearly adds a significant boost to the returns enjoyed by the stockholders!

But in the weak sales scenario, the results are quite different. In this case, the $80,000 of *required* interest payments eats up all of Oze-Moore's earnings, leaving it with no net income for its owners, so its ROE is zero. If EBIT had been anything less than $80,000, Oze-Moore wouldn't have had enough earnings to cover the interest—and if it failed to come up with the money to pay its creditors they could force it into bankruptcy. This illustrates the risk associated with financial leverage. In comparison, notice that Eck-Witty still earns a positive ROE for its owners in the weak sales scenario; granted an ROE of 6% isn't spectacular, but it sure beats the 0% return Oze-Moore experienced!

Our leverage example contains important lessons for the real world—lessons that recent financial history clearly illustrates. During the economic boom between 2003 and early 2007, many companies found that the use of leverage magnified their ROEs. When the economy slowed, the required interest and principal payments on their debt became a heavy burden on highly leveraged firms. As we mentioned at the beginning of this chapter, many of these firms ended up in bankruptcy.

By late 2008, many of the highly leveraged firms that survived the initial carnage were frantically looking for ways to replace much of the debt in their capital structure with more equity—a strategy known as *deleveraging*.

In 2007 Citigroup held $48 in debt for every $1 in equity, making it the most highly leveraged major U.S. financial institution.

— FINANCIAL CRISIS INQUIRY REPORT

Unfortunately, most companies found deleveraging to be a slow and painful process. Their poor financial performance during the financial meltdown meant their earnings were low (or even negative), so they couldn't use retained earnings to build their equity capital. And the plummeting stock market and lack of investor confidence made it difficult to sell new stock. The moral of the story: if the financial returns of leverage seem too good to be true, over the long run they probably are. Sound financial management requires keeping a level head and considering the riskiness of financial decisions as well as their return.[13]

In the wake of the financial crisis, the federal government enacted new legislation designed to reduce the likelihood of similar meltdowns in the future. The **Dodd-Frank Act** included requirements for large firms in the financial sector to hold more equity and less debt in their capital structures and established a Financial Stability Oversight Council to monitor financial markets and to identify and respond to emerging risks. If also created a Consumer Financial Protection Bureau to protect consumers from predatory lending practices by financial institutions.[14]

LO5 Acquiring and Managing Current Assets

Let's turn our attention to how a firm determines the amount and type of current assets to hold. As we'll see, holding current assets involves trade-offs; either too much or too little of these assets can spell trouble.

Managing Cash: Is It Possible to Have *Too Much Money?*

A company must have cash to pay its workers, suppliers, creditors, and taxes. Many firms also need cash to pay dividends. And most firms also want to hold enough cash to meet unexpected contingencies. But cash has one serious shortcoming compared to other assets: it earns little or no return. If a firm holds a lot more cash than necessary to meet its required payments, stockholders are likely to ask why the excess cash isn't being invested in more profitable assets. And if the firm can't find a profitable way to invest the money, the stockholders are likely to ask management why it doesn't use the excess cash to pay them a higher dividend—most shareholders can think of plenty of ways *they'd* like to use the cash!

In the narrowest sense, a firm's cash refers to its holdings of currency (paper money and coins issued by the government) plus demand deposits (the balance in its checking account). However, when most firms report their cash holdings on their balance sheet, they take a broader view, including **cash equivalents** along with their actual cash. Cash equivalents are very safe and highly liquid assets that can be converted into cash quickly and easily. Commercial paper, U.S. Treasury Bills (T-bills), and money market mutual funds are among the most popular cash equivalents. The advantage of these cash equivalents is that they offer a better financial return (in the form of interest) than currency or demand deposits.

As we explained in our discussion of short-term sources of funds, major corporations with strong credit ratings often *sell* commercial paper to raise needed short-term funds. On the other side of such transactions are firms that *buy* commercial paper as part of their portfolio of cash equivalents because—at least under normal economic conditions—it is a safe and liquid way to earn some interest. But during economic downturns the appeal of commercial paper as a cash equivalent plummets due to increased risk.

U.S. Treasury bills, or "T-bills," are short-term IOUs issued by the U.S. government. Most T-bills mature (come due) in 4, 13, or 26 weeks. There is a very active secondary market for T-bills, meaning that their owners can sell them to other investors before they mature. Thus, T-bills are highly liquid. And, unlike commercial paper, T-bills are backed by the U.S. government, so they are essentially risk-free. The safety and liquidity of T-bills make them very attractive cash equivalents even in times of economic distress.

Money market mutual funds raise money by selling shares to large numbers of investors. They then pool these funds to purchase a portfolio of short-term, liquid securities. (In fact, money market mutual funds often include large holdings of commercial paper and T-bills.) Money market mutual funds are an affordable way for small investors to get into the market for securities, which would otherwise be beyond their means. This affordability also makes these funds a particularly attractive cash equivalent for smaller firms.

Managing Accounts Receivable: Pay Me Now or Pay Me Later

Accounts receivable represents what customers who buy on credit owe the firm. Allowing customers to buy on credit can significantly increase sales. However, as our discussion of the cash budget showed, credit sales can create cash flow problems because they delay the receipt of cash the firm needs to meet its financial obligations. Credit customers who pay late or don't pay at all only exacerbate the problem. So it's important for firms to have a well-thought-out policy that balances the advantages of offering credit with the costs. The key elements of this policy should include:

- Setting credit terms: For how long should the firm extend credit? What type of cash discount should the firm offer to encourage early payments?
- Establishing credit standards: How should the firm decide which customers qualify for credit? What type of

Dodd–Frank Act A law enacted in the aftermath of the financial crisis of 2008–2009 that strengthened government oversight of financial markets and placed limitations on risky financial strategies such as heavy reliance on leverage.

cash equivalents Safe and highly liquid assets that many firms list with their cash holdings on their balance sheet.

U.S. Treasury bills (T-bills) Short-term marketable IOUs issued by the U.S. federal government.

money market mutual funds A mutual fund that pools funds from many investors and uses these funds to purchase very safe, highly liquid securities.

The Dodd-Frank Act was 2,319 pages in length. Apparently there was a lot about our financial system in 2010 that Congress wanted to change!

— David Skeel, The New Financial Deal

© Picsfive/Shutterstock.com

credit information should it require? How strict should its standards be?

- Deciding on an appropriate collection policy: How aggressive should the firm be at collecting past-due accounts? At what point does it make sense to take (or at least threaten to take) legal action against late-paying customers, or to turn over the accounts to collection agencies? When does it make sense to work out compromises?

In each area, financial managers face trade-offs. For example, a firm that extends credit for only 30 days will receive its payments sooner than a firm that allows customers 90 days. But setting short credit periods may also result in lost sales. Similarly, setting high credit standards reduces the likelihood a firm will have problems with customers who pay late (or not at all). However, strict standards may prevent many good customers from getting credit, resulting in lower sales. Finally, an aggressive collection policy may help the firm collect payments that it would otherwise lose. But an aggressive policy is costly, and it might alienate customers who make honest mistakes, causing them to take future business to competitors.

Some small businesses have found that being flexible and creative about the form of payment can help them get at least some of what they are owed. Barter arrangements sometimes work better than demanding cash—especially in troubled times such as the recent recession. For example, a health spa took payments from one of its customers in the form of hundreds of granola bars. Similarly, the owner of a bookkeeping firm agreed to accept payment from a veterinarian in the form of emergency surgery on her pet cat![16]

Managing Inventories: Taking Stock of the Situation

Inventories are stocks of finished goods, work-in-process, parts and materials that firms hold as a part of doing business. Clearly, businesses must hold inventories to operate. For example, you'd probably be disappointed if you visited a Best Buy store and were confronted with empty shelves rather than with a wide array of electronic gadgets to compare and try out. Similarly, a manufacturing firm wouldn't be able to assemble its products without an inventory of parts and materials.

But for many firms, the costs of storing, handling, and insuring inventory items are significant expenses. In recent years, many manufacturing firms have become very aggressive about keeping inventories as low as possible in an attempt to reduce costs and improve efficiency. Such "lean" inventory policies can be very effective, but they leave the firm vulnerable to supply disruptions. For instance, both General Motors and Mazda had to shut down some of their assembly lines in early 2011 soon after a fire at one of their key suppliers delayed shipments of dashboard assemblies for their cars. Had the two automakers held larger inventories, they might have been able to continue operating their assembly lines until the supplier could resume its shipments.[17]

T-Bills: Why Lots of Investor Interest Meant Earning Zero Interest

When most people lend money, they expect to get back that money plus interest, right? But in late 2008, investors actually paid the federal government for the privilege of lending them money!

First, some background: Each week the U.S. Treasury "sells" newly issued T-bills via competitive auction. When investors "buy" T-bills, they essentially lend the government the amount of money determined by the auction. When the bills come due, the Treasury pays the investor an amount called the par value. The spread between what investors pay and par value represents the interest on the T-bill. Thus, in order to receive interest on their T-bills investors must bid less than the par value.

But on December 8, 2008, investors bid the price of 4-week T-bills all the way up to par value, meaning that those who bought these bonds were essentially making a loan to the Treasury at zero interest! The outcome in the secondary market for 13-week T-bills during the same week was even stranger—the price of these bills briefly rose above their par value resulting in a *negative* rate of interest. Standard & Poor's chief economist, David Wyss, declared the bidding behavior of investors in these markets to be "totally insane." While the negative rates soon vanished, T-bill interest rates remained extremely low through late 2008 and into 2009.

On the bright side, taxpayers had to be pleased by these results. T-bills are government debt, and it is taxpayers who ultimately stand behind this debt. Low-interest rates on T-bills have the effect of reducing the interest burden on the money the federal government borrowed to deal with the economic downturn.[15]

LO6 Capital Budgeting: In It for the Long Haul

We'll conclude the chapter with a look at how firms evaluate proposals to invest in long-term assets or undertake major new projects. **Capital budgeting** refers to the procedure a firm uses to plan for investments in assets or projects that it expects will yield benefits for more than a year. The capital budgeting process evaluates proposals such as:

- Replacing old machinery and equipment with new models to reduce cost and improve the efficiency of current operations;
- Buying additional plant, machinery and equipment to expand production capacity in *existing* markets;
- Investing in plant, property and equipment needed to expand into *new* markets
- Installing new, or modifying existing, plant and equipment to achieve goals not directly related to expanding production, such as reducing pollution or improving worker safety

The number of capital budgeting proposals a firm considers each year can be quite large. But it's unlikely that all proposals will be worth pursuing. How do financial managers decide whether or not to accept a proposal?

Evaluating Capital Budgeting Proposals

Financial managers measure the benefits and costs of long-term investment proposals in terms of the cash flows they generate. These cash flows are likely to be negative at the start of a project because money must be spent to get a long-term investment project up and running before it begins generating positive cash flows. But a project must eventually generate enough positive cash flows to more than offset these negative initial cash outflows if it is to benefit the company.

Accounting for the Time Value of Money

One of the most challenging aspects of the evaluation of a long-term project's cash flows is that they are spread out over a number of years. When financial managers compare cash flows that occur at different times, they must take the **time value of money** into account. The time value of money reflects the fact that, from a financial manager's perspective, a dollar received today is worth *more* than a dollar received in the future because the sooner you receive a sum of money, the sooner you can put that money to work to earn even *more* money.

Suppose, for example, that you were given the choice of receiving $1,000 either today or the same amount one year from

today. If you think like a financial manager, this choice is a no-brainer! Let's be conservative and say that if you receive the money today you can deposit it in an insured one-year **certificate of deposit (CD)** at your local bank that pays 4% interest. (A CD is similar to a savings account, except that it requires the funds to remain on deposit for a fixed term; in our example the term is one year.) You would incur a penalty if you withdrew your funds early.) Investing in your 4% CD means that a year from today you would have $1,040 (the $1,000 you deposited plus $40 in interest). But if you wait until next year to receive the $1,000, you'll lose the opportunity to earn that $40 in interest. Clearly, receiving the cash today is the better option.

Because money has a time value, a cash flow's value depends not only on the *amount* of cash received, but also on *when* it is received. Financial managers compare cash flows occurring at different times by converting them to their present values. The **present value** of a cash flow received in a future time period is the amount of money that, if invested *today* at an assumed rate of interest (called the *discount rate*), would grow to become that future amount of money. For example, take a look at Exhibit 9.4. It shows that $1,000 invested today at 6% grows to a future value of $1,262.48 in four years. Thus, $1,000 is the present value of $1,262.48 received in four years.

The Risk-Return Tradeoff Revisited

Unfortunately, financial managers don't have crystal balls, so they don't know the *actual* cash flows a proposed project will generate. Instead, they base their analysis on the cash flows the proposal is *expected* to generate. Once a company actually invests in a project, it may find that the *actual* cash flows are quite different than these estimated flows. This uncertainty means that capital budgeting decisions must consider risk.

In general, projects with the potential for highs return are also the projects with a high degree of uncertainty and risk. This is another example of the risk-return tradeoff we introduced at the beginning of this chapter. Clearly, financial managers must take this tradeoff into account when they compare different capital budgeting proposals; they must determine whether riskier proposals generate a high enough expected return to justify their greater risk.

© iStockphoto.com/VikZa

capital budgeting The process a firm uses to evaluate long-term investment proposals.

time value of money The principle that a dollar received today is worth more than a dollar received in the future.

certificate of deposit (CD) An interest-earning deposit that requires the funds to remain deposited for a fixed term. Withdrawal of the funds before the term expires results in a financial penalty.

present value The amount of money that, if invested today at a given rate of interest (called the discount rate), would grow to become some future amount in a specified number of time periods.

net present value (NPV) The sum of the present values of expected future cash flows from an investment, minus the cost of that investment.

One common way financial managers try to do this is to use a higher discount rate when they compute the present values of cash flows for risky projects than when they compute present values for less risky projects. This reflects the idea that a higher return is required to compensate for the greater risk.

Net Present Value: A Decision Rule for Capital Budgeting

The most common method financial managers use to evaluate capital budgeting proposals is to compute their **net present value (NPV)**. The NPV of an investment proposal is found by adding the present values of *all* of its estimated future cash flows and subtracting the initial cost of the investment from the sum. A positive NPV means that the present value of the expected cash flows from the project is greater than the cost of the project. In other words, the benefits from the project exceed its cost even after accounting for the time value of money. Financial managers approve projects with positive NPVs. A negative NPV means that the present value of the expected future cash flows from the project is less than the cost of the investment. This would indicate that the cost of the project outweighs its cash flow benefits. Financial managers would reject proposals with negative NPVs. (See Exhibit 9.5.)

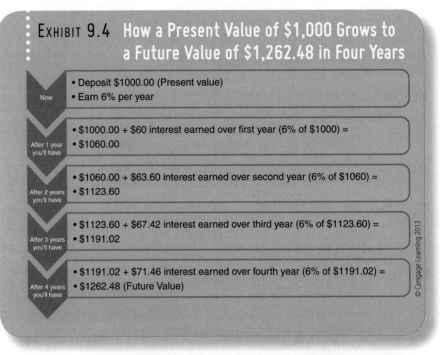

EXHIBIT 9.4 How a Present Value of $1,000 Grows to a Future Value of $1,262.48 in Four Years

Now
- Deposit $1000.00 (Present value)
- Earn 6% per year

After 1 year you'll have
- $1000.00 + $60 interest earned over first year (6% of $1000) =
- $1060.00

After 2 years you'll have
- $1060.00 + $63.60 interest earned over second year (6% of $1060) =
- $1123.60

After 3 years you'll have
- $1123.60 + $67.42 interest earned over third year (6% of $1123.60) =
- $1191.02

After 4 years you'll have
- $1191.02 + $71.46 interest earned over fourth year (6% of $1191.02) =
- $1262.48 (Future Value)

© Cengage Learning 2013

EXHIBIT 9.5 Decision Rule for Capital Budgeting

RESULT OF NPV CALCULATION	DECISION
NPV ≥ 0	Accept proposal ✓
NPV < 0	Reject proposal ✗

© Cengage Learning 2013

Are "Minsky Moments" Inevitable?

As the U.S. economy began to slow in late 2007, a small but influential group of economists began voicing concerns that the U.S. economy was about to experience a "Minsky Moment." Their fears were based on a theory first developed in the 1970s by Washington University economics professor Hyman Minsky (1919–1996), who suggested that free market economies would periodically experience financial meltdowns that would lead to severe and prolonged recessions. Minsky laid the blame for these crises squarely on the decisions made by financial managers.

Minsky's theory was based on the notion that as an economic boom continues, financial managers become less worried about risk. This overconfidence, coupled with the desire to "cash in" on the good times, encourages them to engage in overly aggressive and risky financial strategies. Eventually, a combination of speculative investment decisions combined with extensive use of leverage makes the financial system vulnerable to even minor disruptions. Minsky believed that once these vulnerabilities became apparent, panic would set in, leading to behavior that would make the problems even worse. With 20-20 hindsight, the events leading to the Great Recession certainly seem to be consistent with Minsky's views.

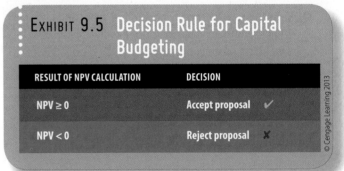

One of the most controversial implications of Minsky's theory is that the recent financial meltdown wasn't an isolated event, but rather the result of a fundamental characteristic of a free market economy. If Minsky and his followers are right—and not all economists believe that they are—then we should recognize the possibility of another crisis soon after the next boom tempts financial managers to once again ignore risk.[18]

©iStockphoto.com/Viktor Georgiev

THE BIG PICTURE

In this chapter, we described the tasks financial managers perform as they attempt to find the "best" sources and uses of financial resources—meaning those that will maximize the value of the firm to its owners. We saw that in their attempt to achieve this goal financial managers face two challenges. The first is to balance the needs of owners against those of the other stakeholders; the second is to balance the potential rewards of their decisions against the risks.

Recent history illustrates how important sound financial management is to the success of a firm—and how devastating poor financial decisions can be. Indeed, the recent decline and fall of some of the biggest and best-known U.S. corporations can be traced in large measure to poor financial decisions—especially decisions that failed to adequately take risk into account, resulting in the use of too much leverage.

These lessons from the recent past will probably result in a different approach to financial management over the next several years. While memories of the Great Recession are still relatively fresh, firms may be more conservative in their view of what constitutes the best sources and uses of funds. In particular, they are likely to shy away from excessive debt and put more emphasis on equity financing. They also are less likely to use their funds to invest in highly risky or speculative assets. These more conservative tendencies are likely to be reinforced by the major regulatory reforms designed to curb aggressive (and risky) behavior introduced by the Dodd-Frank Act.

Financial managers are employed by firms in every sector of the economy, but the greatest numbers are in the insurance, banking, and financial services sectors. About 550,000 financial managers were employed in the United States in 2010. Financial managers need strong computer and analytical skills. The work often involves long hours, can be mentally challenging, and is sometimes stressful. But salaries and other compensation tend to be attractive. The median salary in 2008 was $99,330—a figure that doesn't include bonuses or stock options, which, for many financial managers, have been a significant source of additional income.[19] However, bonuses may be less generous in the wake of the financial crisis.

The Bureau of Labor Statistics (BLS) projects that job growth in financial management will grow by 8% between 2008 and 2018, which is about as fast as the average rate of growth for all occupations. However, the BLS also projects that the competition for these jobs is likely to be intense, because the number of applicants may increase even faster than the number of jobs. Thus, even though the minimum requirements for most financial management positions is a bachelor's degree in finance, economics, or business administration, an advanced degree in one of these fields, such as a masters in business administration (MBA), may be necessary to be considered for the more desirable jobs.[20]

CAREERS

What *else?*

RIP & REVIEW CARDS **IN THE BACK**
and visit **www.cengagebrain.com!**

10
Financial Markets:
Allocating Financial Resources

LEARNING OBJECTIVES
After studying this chapter, you will be able to...

LO 1 Explain the role of financial markets in the U.S. economy and identify the key players in these markets

LO 2 Identify the key laws that govern the way financial markets operate and explain the impact of each law

LO 3 Describe and compare the major types of securities that are traded in securities markets

LO 4 Explain how securities are issued in the primary market and traded on secondary markets

LO 5 Compare several strategies that investors use to invest in securities

LO 6 Interpret the information provided in the stock quotes available on financial websites

> # "ANYONE WHO THINKS THERE IS SAFETY IN *NUMBERS* HASN'T LOOKED AT THE STOCK MARKET PAGES."
>
> — IRENE PETER, AMERICAN WRITER

LO1 The Role of Financial Markets and Their Key Players

Financial markets perform a vital function: they transfer funds from savers (individuals and organizations willing to defer the use of some of their income in order to earn a financial return and build their wealth) to borrowers (individuals, and organizations that need additional funds to achieve their financial goals in the current time period). Without these markets, companies would find it difficult to obtain the financial resources they need to meet their payrolls, invest in new facilities, develop new products, and compete effectively in global markets.

But it's not just businesses that benefit from these markets. You'll almost certainly participate on both sides of financial markets. In fact, you already participate in these markets as a borrower when you use a credit card to finance daily purchases or when you take out a loan to pay college tuition. And you'll participate as a saver when you put money into a savings account to accumulate the money you'll need for a down payment on your first house, or when you invest in financial securities to build up a nest egg for your retirement years.

In the U.S. and other well-developed market economies, the vast majority of financing occurs indirectly, with *financial intermediaries* coming between the ultimate savers and borrowers. We'll see that they perform a variety of functions, but what they all have in common is that they help channel funds from savers to borrowers.

Depository Institutions

Depository institutions are financial intermediaries that obtain funds by accepting checking or savings deposits (or both) from individuals, businesses, and other institutions and then lend these funds to borrowers.

⊙ Commercial banks are the most common depository institutions. When you make a deposit into a checking or savings account at your bank, you are providing funds that the bank can use for making loans to businesses, governments, or other individuals.

At the end of 2010, almost half (47%) of total bank assets were in the form loans, including over $3.6 trillion in real estate and mortgage loans, more than $1 trillion in consumer, loans and over $1.7 trillion in commercial and other loans. And compared to historical trends, this was a low percentage; in the immediate aftermath of the Great Recession, banks were still quite conservative in their loan-making decisions. For comparison, in 2007 loans comprised 57% of all bank assets.[1]

⊙ **Credit unions** are cooperatives, meaning that they are not-for-profit organizations that are owned by their depositors. As not-for-profit organizations, they strive to pay higher interest rates on member deposits and charge lower interest rates on loans.

Credit unions are open to individuals who belong to a specific "field of membership." For example, membership in some credit unions is limited to the employees who work for a specific employer and their family members; other credit unions base membership on church or union affiliation or are open to people living in a certain geographic area.[2]

Credit unions are a much smaller player in financial markets than commercial banks, but at the end of 2010 they held more than $319 billion in mortgage financing and $226 billion in consumer credit on their books.[3]

⊙ **Savings and loan associations** (also called "S&Ls" or "thrifts") traditionally accepted only savings account deposits and used them to make mortgage loans. During the early 1980s, regulations on S&Ls were relaxed, allowing them to accept checking account deposits and make a broader range of loans. Still, the major focus of the savings and loan industry remains mortgage loans.

financial markets Markets that transfer funds from savers to borrowers.

depository institution A financial intermediary that obtains funds by accepting checking or savings deposits (or both) and uses these funds to make loans to borrowers.

credit union A depository institution that is organized as a cooperative, meaning that it is owned by its depositors.

savings and loan association A depository institution that has traditionally obtained most of its funds by accepting savings deposits, which have been used primarily to make mortgage loans.

At the end of 2010, S&Ls held about $620 billion in mortgage financing on their books—not a trivial sum by any means, but a big drop from 2006 when the figure was almost $1.1 trillion.[4] In large part, this reflected the collapse of the housing market at the end of the last decade. But S&Ls began declining in importance well before the Great Recession.[5]

Nondepository Financial Institutions

In addition to banks and other depository institutions, a number of other financial intermediaries play important roles in financial markets.

- **Institutional Investors** don't accept deposits but amass huge pools of financial capital from other sources and use these funds to acquire a portfolio of many different assets. Mutual funds obtain money by selling shares to investors; insurance companies obtain money by collecting premiums from policyholders; and pension funds obtain money by collecting funds

employers and their employees contribute for the employees' retirement. These institutions invest heavily in corporate stock; the majority of shares in most major U.S. corporations are held by institutional investors. They are also major holders of corporate bonds and government securities.

- **Securities brokers** act as agents for investors who want to buy or sell financial securities, such as corporate stocks or bonds. In addition to handling the trades, many brokers provide their clients with additional services such as financial planning and market research. Brokers are compensated by charging fees and commissions for the services they provide.

- **Securities dealers** participate directly in securities markets, buying and selling stocks and bonds for their own account. They earn a profit by selling securities for higher prices than they paid to purchase them. (The difference between the prices at which they buy and sell a security is called the *spread*.)

- **Investment banks** are financial intermediaries that help firms issue new securities to raise financial capital. Sometimes investment banks actually buy the newly issued securities themselves; in other cases they simply help arrange for their sale. Today's investment

Congress Decides It's Time to Trim the Hedges

Hedge funds are basically mutual funds that limit the number of investors they accept, and require that all investors meet certain standards for wealth. There are different classes of hedge funds, but even the least restrictive type requires that all investors have a net worth of at least $1 million excluding their home.

Until recently, hedge funds were not subject to strict federal regulation. As hedge fund manager Clifford Asness put it in 2007, hedge funds "Are relatively unregulated (for now), charge very high fees, will not necessarily give you your money back when you want it, and will generally not tell you what they do."

Some hedge funds took advantage of the lack of regulatory oversight to pursue extremely risky investment strategies. This approach often paid off quite spectacularly but also resulted in some devastating failures. In 1998, Long-Term Capital Management—a fund with assets worth $80 billion in its portfolio—was on the verge of collapse until the Federal Reserve Bank of New York organized a rescue plan. Fed officials justified the rescue by saying the fund was too big to fail—a rationale that presaged the justification given for the government bailouts of several major financial institutions a decade later.

The lack of oversight also enabled unethical and illegal behavior by some fund managers. For example, in 2004 the Securities and Exchange Commission noted a "troubling growth in the number of hedge fund fraud enforcement cases." And during the first decade of the twenty-first century, a number of hedge fund advisors were involved in high-profile insider trading scandals.

These issues created pressure to put hedge funds under federal regulatory scrutiny. With the passage of the Dodd-Frank Act in 2010, these calls for regulation were realized. Under the new law, hedge fund managers must register with the SEC as investment advisers and must provide information about their trades and their investment portfolios that will allow regulators to assess their systemic risk.[6]

banks aren't actually independent companies. Instead, they are typically divisions of huge bank holding companies which also own commercial banks.

L02 # Regulating Financial Markets to Protect Investors and Improve Stability

Financial markets only work well when savers and borrowers have confidence in the soundness of key financial institutions and in the fairness of the market outcomes. When depositors lose confidence in their banks, or when investors discover that financial markets are rigged by practices such as insider trading or unethical and deceptive accounting, the financial system breaks down.

The financial crisis of 2008 is only the latest example of the disruptions that result when financial markets malfunction. From the early twentieth century to the present day, the U.S. economy has experienced several other major financial crises. The economy experienced massive bank failures in 1907 and in the early 1930s. It also weathered a savings and loan crisis in the late 1980s which brought the failure of over 1,000 S&Ls and required a federal bailout that cost over $120 billion.[7] And a variety of scandals involving ethical lapses (and in many cases outright fraud) roiled financial markets at the turn of the century.

Financial Regulation: Early Efforts

During most of the twentieth century, the federal government responded to financial upheavals by introducing new laws and regulations. This trend first emerged in the wake of the banking panic of 1907, which created pressure for Congress to find a way to stabilize the nation's banking system. The result was the **Federal Reserve Act of 1913**. As its name implies, this act created the Federal Reserve System (the Fed) to serve as the central bank in the United States. The law gave the Fed the primary responsibility for overseeing our nation's banking system.

Unfortunately, the creation of the Fed didn't solve all of the nation's banking problems. Another wave of bank failures occurred in the early 1930s as the economy sank into the Great Depression. Congress responded by passing the **Banking Act of 1933**, also known as the *Glass-Steagall Act*. This law established the Federal Deposit Insurance Corporation, which insured depositors against financial losses when a bank failed. The insurance initially covered only $2,500 of deposits—but $2,500 bought a lot more in the 1930s than it does today! Over the years, coverage has been increased several times. Today, the FDIC insures up to $250,000 in deposits.

Another major provision of the Glass-Steagall Act banned commercial banks from dealing in securities markets, selling insurance, or otherwise competing with nondepository institutions such as insurance companies and investment banks. The rationale for these restrictions was that involvement in such activities exposed banks and their depositors to higher levels of risk.

Congress responded to the stock market crash that occurred in 1929 with two laws that are still the foundation of U.S. securities markets regulation. The first of these was the **Securities Act of 1933,** which dealt mainly with the process of issuing new securities. It prohibited misrepresentation or other forms of fraud in the sale of newly issued stocks and bonds. It also required firms issuing new stock in a public offering to file a registration statement with the SEC. The next year, Congress passed the **Securities Exchange Act of 1934**, which regulated the trading of previously issued securities. This law created the **Securities and Exchange Commission** (SEC) and gave it broad powers to oversee the securities industry. The law required that all publicly traded firms with at least 500 shareholders and $10 million in assets file quarterly and annual financial reports with the SEC, and that brokers and dealers register with the SEC.

The Securities Exchange Act also gave the SEC the power to prosecute individuals and companies that engaged in fraudulent securities market activities. For example, the SEC has the authority to go after individuals who engage in illegal *insider trading*, which is the practice of using inside information (important information about a company that isn't available to the general investing public) to profit unfairly from trading in a company's securities.

Deregulation During the 1980s and 1990s: Temporarily Reversing Course

The passage of these laws ushered in a period of more stable financial markets. But critics argued that the laws—especially the Glass-Steagall Act—represented an onerous government intrusion into the financial sector that stifled competition and impeded financial innovation. During the 1980s and 1990s Congress responded to these criticisms by easing restrictions on banks and other depository

Federal Reserve Act of 1913 The law that established the Federal Reserve System as the central bank of the United States.

Banking Act of 1933 The law that established the Federal Deposit Insurance Corporation (FDIC) to insure bank deposits. It also prohibited commercial banks from selling insurance or acting as investment banks.

Securities Act of 1933 The first major federal law regulating the securities industry. It requires firms issuing new stock in a public offering to file a registration statement with the SEC.

Securities and Exchange Act of 1934 A federal law dealing with securities regulation that established the Securities and Exchange Commission to regulate and oversee the securities industry.

Securities and Exchange Commission The federal agency with primary responsibility for regulating the securities industry.

institutions. For instance, the **Financial Services Modernization Act of 1999**, also known as the *Gramm-Bliley-Leach Act*, reversed the Glass-Steagall Act's prohibition of banks selling insurance or acting as investment banks.

The financial sector initially seemed to prosper under its less regulated environment. It responded to its increased freedom with a variety of new services. And new technologies such as ATMs and online banking made financial transactions easier and more convenient.

Recent Developments: Re-regulation in the Aftermath of Financial Turmoil

But the wave of deregulation didn't last. A series of accounting scandals at the beginning of the twenty-first century, followed by a near collapse of the financial system in 2008, created pressure for new laws.

Congress reacted to the accounting scandals in the first years of the new century by passing the Sarbanes-Oxley Act in 2002. This law included provisions to ensure that external auditors offered fair, unbiased opinions when they examined a company's financial statements. It also increased the SEC's authority to regulate financial markets and investigate charges of fraud and unethical behavior.[8]

In the wake of the financial crisis of 2008–09 Congress passed the Dodd-Frank Act of 2010. This far-reaching law expanded the Fed's regulatory authority over nondepository financial institutions, such as hedge funds and mortgage brokers, that had previously operated with little regulatory oversight or accountability. It also created the Financial Stability Oversight Council to identify emerging risks in the financial sector so that action could be taken to rein in risky practices *before* they led to a crisis. The council was given the authority to recommend new rules to the Federal Reserve that would limit risky practices of the nation's largest, most complex financial institutions.[9]

LO3 Investing in Financial Securities: What Are the Options?

Financial securities markets are critical to corporations that rely on them to obtain much of their long-term financial capital. They also provide one of the most important venues

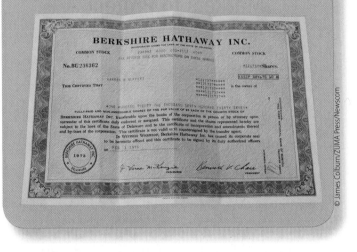

EXHIBIT 10.1 Stock certificates represent shares of ownership in a corporation.

Common stock is the basic form of ownership in a corporation.

that individuals can use to build their long-term wealth and earn significant financial returns.

Common Stock: Back to Basics

Common stock is the basic form of ownership in a corporation. Exhibit 10.1 shows a stock certificate for Berkshire Hathaway, Inc. As owners of corporations, common stockholders have certain basic rights:

⊙ **Voting Rights:** Owners of common stock have the right to vote on important issues in the annual stockholders' meeting. Under the most common arrangement, stockholders can cast one vote for each share of stock they own. One of the key issues that stockholders vote on is the selection of members to the corporation's board of directors, but they also may vote on other major issues, such as the approval of a merger with another firm or a change in the corporation's by-laws. A provision of the Dodd-Frank Act of 2010 gives stockholders the right to cast a vote on their company's executive compensation policies. While non-binding, this "say on pay" vote gives shareholders a way to make their feelings about executive compensation known.[10]

⊙ **Right to Dividends:** Dividends are a distribution of earnings to the corporation's stockholders. All common stockholders have the right to receive a dividend *if* their corporation's board of directors declares one. The "catch" is that the board has no legal obligation to declare a dividend. In fact, many rapidly growing

Some companies have a long history of paying dividends. For example, on April 14, 2011, the Dow Chemical Company announced its 399th consecutive quarterly dividend, a string going all the way back to 1912.

— YAHOO! FINANCE WEBSITE

companies routinely choose to skip dividends and reinvest most or all of their earnings to finance growth.

- **Capital Gains:** Stockholders receive another type of return on their investment, called a **capital gain**, *if* the price of the stock rises above the amount they paid for it. Capital gains can create very attractive financial returns for stockholders. Of course, there is no guarantee the stock's price will rise. If it falls, stockholders would experience a capital loss rather than a capital gain.

- **Preemptive Right:** If a corporation issues new stock, existing stockholders sometimes have a preemptive right to purchase new shares in proportion to their existing holdings before the stock is offered to the other investors. For example, if you own 5% of the existing shares of stock, then the preemptive right gives you the right to purchase 5% of the new shares. This could be important for large stockholders who want to maintain their share of ownership. However, the conditions under which existing stockholders have preemptive rights vary among the states. In several states, a preemptive right is only available if it is specifically identified in the corporation's charter.

- **Right to a Residual Claim on Assets:** The final stockholder right is a residual claim on assets. If the corporation goes out of business and liquidates its assets, stockholders have a right to share in the proceeds in proportion to their ownership. But note that this is a *residual* claim—it comes *after all other claims* have been satisfied. In other words, the firm must pay any back taxes, legal expenses, wages owed to workers, and debts owed to creditors before the owners get anything. By the time all of these other claims have been paid, nothing may be left for the owners.

Preferred Stock: Getting Preferential Treatment

Common stock is the basic form of corporate ownership, but some companies also issue **preferred stock**, so named because it offers its holders preferential treatment in two respects:

- **Claim on Assets:** Holders of preferred stock have a claim on assets that comes before common stockholders if the company goes out of business. This gives preferred stockholders a better chance than common stockholders of recovering their investment if the company goes bankrupt.

- **Payment of Dividends:** Unlike dividends on common stock, dividends on preferred stock are usually a stated amount. And a corporation can't pay *any* dividend to its common stockholders unless it pays the full stated dividend on its preferred stock. Still, it is important to note that a corporation has no *legal* obligation to pay a dividend to *any* stockholders, not even those who hold preferred stock.

  Preferred stock sometimes includes a *cumulative feature.* This means that if the firm skips a preferred dividend in one period, the amount it must pay the next period is equal to the dividend for that period *plus* the amount of the dividend it skipped in the previous period. Additional skipped dividends continue to accumulate, and the firm can't pay *any* dividends to common stockholders until *all* accumulated dividends are paid to preferred stockholders.

  Preferred stock isn't necessarily "preferred" to common stock in all respects. For instance, preferred stockholders normally don't have voting rights, so they can't vote on issues that come up during stockholders meetings. And even though preferred stockholders are more likely to receive a dividend, they aren't guaranteed a *better* dividend; the board can declare a dividend to common stockholders that offers a higher return.[11] Finally, when a company experiences strong earnings, the market price of its common stock can—and often does—appreciate more in value than the price of its preferred shares, thus offering common shareholders a greater capital gain.

Bonds: Earning Your Interest

A **bond** is a formal IOU issued by a corporation or government entity. Bonds come in many different varieties. Our discussion will focus on the basic characteristics of long-term bonds issued by corporations.

capital gain The return on an asset that results when its market price rises above the price the investor paid for it.

preferred stock A type of stock that gives its holder preference over common stockholders in terms of dividends and claims on assets.

bond A formal debt instrument issued by a corporation or government entity.

The date a bond comes due is called its **maturity date,** and the amount the issuer owes the bondholder at maturity is called the bond's **par value** (or face value). Long-term bonds issued by corporations usually mature ten to thirty years after issuance, but longer maturities are possible. During the 1990s, several major corporations, including Disney and Coca-Cola, issued *century bonds* that matured 100 years after they were issued.[12]

Bondholders can sell their bonds to other investors before they mature, but the price they receive might not correspond to the bond's par value because bond prices fluctuate with conditions in the bond market. When a bond's market price is above its par value, it is selling at a *premium*; when its price is below par value, it is selling at a *discount*.

Most bonds require their issuers to pay a stated amount of interest to bondholders each year until the bond matures. The **coupon rate** on the bond expresses the annual interest payment as a percentage of the bond's par value. For example, investors who own a bond with a par value of $1,000 and a coupon rate of 7.5% receive $75 in interest (7.5% of $1,000) each year until the bond reaches

maturity—or until they sell their bonds to someone else. But since bonds can sell at a premium or a discount, the coupon rate doesn't necessarily represent the rate of return that investors earn on the amount they actually *paid* for the bond. The **current yield** expresses a bond's interest payment as a percentage of the bond's *current market price* rather than its par value. If the market price of the bond in our example was $833.33, then the current yield would be 9% (found by dividing the $75 interest payment by $833.33).

Unlike dividends on stock, a firm has a *legal obligation* to pay interest on bonds—and to pay the bondholder the par value of the bond when it matures. Thus, bondholders are more likely to receive a financial return than stockholders. But that doesn't mean that bonds are without risk. Corporations that get into serious financial difficulties sometimes *default* on their bonds, meaning that they are unable to make required payments. When that happens, bankruptcy proceedings usually allow bondholders to recover some (but not all) of what they are owed; historically, the average amount recovered has been about 72 cents on the dollar. While that is better than what stockholders can expect, it is far short of being risk free![13]

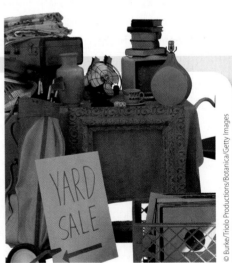

© Burke/Triolo Productions/Botanica/Getty Images

Could Your Best Investment Be a Piece of Junk?

Bonds are generally considered to be safer investments than common stocks. However, there are definitely some exceptions to this rule. Junk bonds are bonds issued by companies with poor credit ratings. Investors who hold such bonds face the real possibility that the issuer will be unable to make the required payments of interest and principal. And the risk increases when the economy weakens. In 2007, only 22 companies in the world defaulted on their bonds. But with the deepening recession, that number soared to 126 companies in 2008.

Given this risk, why would anyone invest in junk bonds? The answer is that with high risk comes the possibility of attractive returns. Firms with poor credit ratings must offer higher returns to entice investors to buy their riskier bonds. Thus, junk bonds pay higher rates of interest—sometimes much higher rates—than safer "investment grade" bonds. And these bonds generally sell at a deep discount, making their current yields even higher than their coupon rates. Toward the end of 2008, yields on many junk bonds exceeded 20%—more than double the yield earned on safer "investment grade" bonds.

By late 2008, many investors concluded that the high yield on these bonds made the risks of investing in junk bonds worth taking—especially given the poor performance of stocks during the same period. Investing in junk became a hot strategy. But most investors who bought junk bonds did so in moderation, limiting their holdings of junk bonds to only a small part of a broadly diversified portfolio of securities.[14]

Convertible Securities: The Big Switch

Corporations sometimes issue **convertible securities**, which are bonds or shares of preferred stock that investors can exchange for a given number of shares of the issuing corporation's common stock. A *conversion ratio* indicates the number of shares of common stock exchanged for each convertible security. For example, if the conversion ratio is 20, then each convertible security can be exchanged for 20 shares of common stock. The ratio is set at the time the convertible securities are issued so that it is only financially desirable to convert the securities if the price of the common stock increases.

Owning a convertible security allows investors to gain from an increase in the price of common stock, while limiting their risk if the price of the stock falls. If the price of the common stock increases, the holders of convertible securities can convert them into the now more valuable stock. But if the price of the company's common stock falls, investors can continue to hold their convertible securities and collect their interest or preferred dividends.

The firm also can benefit from issuing convertible bonds because the popularity of this feature with investors allows it to offer a lower coupon rate on convertible bonds (or a lower dividend on preferred stock), thus reducing its fixed payments. And if investors convert to common stock, the firm no longer has to make these fixed payments at all. But there is one important group that may be unhappy with this arrangement; the corporation's existing stockholders may be displeased if the new stock issued to holders of convertible securities dilutes their share of ownership—and their share of any profits!

Mutual Funds and ETFs: Diversification Made Easy

Financial **diversification**—the practice of holding many different securities in many different sectors—is generally considered a desirable strategy because it helps reduce (but not completely eliminate) risk. If you hold many different securities in different sectors of the economy, then losses on some securities may be offset by gains on others.

Many investors who want to hold diversified portfolios find that investing in large numbers of individual stocks and bonds is prohibitively expensive. And even if they could afford to do so, investors often lack the time and expertise to select a large number of individual securities. Faced with these limitations, many investors find that **mutual funds** and exchange traded funds are attractive options.

Mutual Funds: Portfolios Made Easy

There are two ways mutual funds can be structured. A c*losed-end fund* issues a fixed number of shares and invests the money received from selling these shares in a portfolio of assets. Shares of closed-end funds can be traded among investors much like stocks. An *open-end mutual fund* doesn't have a fixed number of shares, nor are its shares traded like stocks. Instead, the fund issues additional shares when demand increases, and redeems (buys back) old shares when investors want to cash in.

The price at which shares of an open-end mutual fund are issued and redeemed is based on the fund's **net asset value per share** (NAVPS), which is computed by dividing the total value of the fund's cash, securities, and other assets (less any liabilities) by the number of fund shares outstanding. Though the NAVPS is the basis for the price of a fund's shares, investors often also pay commissions and purchase fees.

Several features make mutual funds a popular choice for investors:

- **Diversification at Relatively Low Cost:** By pooling the funds of thousands of investors, mutual funds have the financial resources to invest in a broader portfolio of securities than individual investors could afford. This high level of diversification can help reduce risk.

- **Professional Management:** Most mutual funds are managed by a professional fund manager who selects the assets in the fund's portfolio. This can be appealing to investors who lack the time and expertise to make complex investment decisions.

---

convertible security A bond or share of preferred stock that gives its holder the right to exchange it for a stated number of shares of common stock.

financial diversification A strategy of investing in a wide variety of securities in order to reduce risk.

mutual fund An institutional investor that raises funds by selling shares to investors and uses the accumulated funds to buy a portfolio of many different securities.

Net Asset Value Per Share The value of a mutual fund's securities and cash holdings minus any liabilities, divided by the number of shares of the fund outstanding.

With today's technology investors can track the assets in their portfolios at any time and from just about any place.

© iStockphoto.com/Skip Odonnell

"Does Green Investing Earn Green Returns?"

Is it possible to meet your personal financial goals while also satisfying your desire to invest in companies that pursue environment-friendly policies? Several so-called "green" mutual funds claim to help you do just that. The New Alternatives Fund, established in 1982, was the first fund that selected stocks based primarily on environmental considerations. In recent years the fund's portfolio has emphasized firms that develop alternative energy sources, recycle waste, and produce pollution abatement equipment.

Green funds vary in terms of the criteria they use for selecting their stocks. For instance, the Winslow Green Growth Fund invests aggressively in small-growth firms that meet their environmental responsibilities. The more conservative Portfolio 21 selects large, well-established companies that emphasize environmental sustainability. Its portfolio of over 100 stocks typically includes such well-known corporations as Nike, Staples, Google, and Johnson & Johnson.

An obvious question is whether these *environmentally* green funds provide investors with the other type of "green" investors seek—namely, an attractive *financial* return. Over the long haul, the answer appears to be yes. The Winslow Green Growth Fund had an average annual return of 12.27% from its inception in 1994 through March 2011. That significantly outperformed the average return on stock indices such as the S&P 500 over the same time period. Likewise, the Portfolio 21 Fund also performed much better than the S&P 500 over the five-year period ending on March 31, 2011. The New Alternative Fund hasn't performed quite as well, but its returns over the same five-year period have come close to matching the S&P performance.

These average returns concealed big fluctuations over shorter time periods. The Winslow fund earned an eye-popping total return of 92% in 2003, but saw returns drop by 60% in 2008—and then rise again by 43.7% in 2009. The returns reported by New Alternatives and Portfolio 21's returns fluctuated by similar amounts over the same time period.[15]

○ **Variety:** Whatever your investment goals and philosophy, you can probably find a fund that's a good match. There are many different types of funds; some invest only in certain types of securities (such as municipal bonds or stocks of large corporations), others invest in specific sectors of the economy (such as energy, technology or health care), and yet others seek more balanced and broad-based portfolios. Some funds simply invest in a portfolio of stocks that matches those in a specific stock index, such as the Standard & Poor 500 or the Wilshire 5000. These *index funds* have become very popular in recent years.

○ **Liquidity:** It's easy to withdraw funds from a mutual fund. For a closed-end fund, you simply sell your shares. For an open-end fund, you redeem your shares from the fund itself. However, regardless of when you initiate your withdrawal, redemptions of an open-end fund are not carried out until its NAVPS is determined after the *next* trading session is completed.

Mutual funds do have some drawbacks. Perhaps the most serious is that the professional management touted by many funds doesn't come cheap. Investors in mutual funds pay a variety of fees that typically range from 1% to 3% of the amount invested. The fees charged by mutual funds can make a serious dent in the overall return received by the fund's investors. And funds assess these fees even when they perform poorly. One reason for the popularity of index funds is that they don't require professional management, so their fees are lower.

Another drawback of actively managed funds is that when their professional managers engage in a lot of trading, any financial gains can have significant tax consequences. It is also important to realize that some of the specialized mutual funds that invest in only one sector of the economy or only one type of security may not provide enough diversification to reduce risk significantly.

Exchange Traded Funds: Real Basket Cases (and We Mean That in a Good Way)

An **exchange traded fund (ETF)** is similar to a mutual fund in some respects but differs in how it is created and how its shares are initially distributed. ETFs allow investors to buy ownership in what is called a *market basket* of many different securities. In fact, the market basket for most ETFs reflects the composition of a broad-based stock index, much like an index mutual fund. But in recent years more specialized ETFs that focus on narrower market baskets of assets have appeared on the market. Like closed-end mutual funds—but unlike the more common open-end funds—ETFs are traded just like stocks. Thus, you can buy and sell ETFs any time of the day.

Compared to most actively managed mutual funds, ETFs usually have lower costs and fees. However, since ETFs are bought and sold like stocks, you do have to pay brokerage commissions every time you buy or sell shares.

There are approximately 8,000 mutual funds now in the United States—far more than the total number of actively traded individual stocks in the United States.

—Investment Company Institute

LO4 Issuing and Trading Securities: The Primary and Secondary Markets

There are two distinct types of securities markets: the primary securities market and the secondary securities market. The **primary securities market** is where corporations raise additional financial capital by selling *newly issued* securities. The **secondary securities market** is where *previously issued* securities are traded.

The Primary Securities Market: Where Securities Are Issued

There are two methods of issuing securities in the primary market:

- In a **public offering**, securities are sold (in concept, at least) to anyone in the investing public who is willing and financially able to buy them.

- In a **private placement**, securities are sold to one or more private investors (who may be individuals or institutions) under terms negotiated between the issuing firm and the private investors.

Public Offerings Many corporations are initially owned by a small number of people who don't sell the stock to outsiders. But growing corporations often need to obtain more financial capital than such a small group can provide. Such firms may *go public* by issuing additional stock and offering it to investors outside their group. The first time a corporation sells its stock in a public offering, the sale is called an **initial public offering (IPO)**.

Going public is a complicated and high-stakes process; obtaining sufficient funds in an IPO is often critical to the firm's success. So, almost all firms that go public enlist the help and advice of an investment bank that specializes in helping firms issue new securities. The investment bank assists the firm at every step of the IPO, from the planning and market assessment phase until the actual securities are distributed to investors after the offering is conducted.

One of the key responsibilities of the investment bank is to arrange for the actual sale of the securities. The investment bank uses either a *best efforts* or a *firm commitment* approach. Under the best efforts approach the bank provides advice about pricing and marketing the securities and assists in finding potential buyers. But it doesn't guarantee that the firm will sell all of its securities at a high enough price to meet its financial goals. The investment bank earns a commission on all of the shares sold under a best efforts approach.

Under a *firm-commitment* arrangement, the investment bank **underwrites** the issue. This means that the investment bank itself purchases *all* of the shares at a specified price, thus guaranteeing that the firm issuing the stock will receive a known amount of new funds. The investment bank that underwrites the offer seeks to earn a profit by reselling the stock to investors at a higher price. For large public offerings a group of investment banks, called an *underwriting syndicate*, may temporarily work together to underwrite the securities.

Before going public, a firm must file a **registration statement** with the Securities and Exchange Commission (SEC). This long, complex document must include the firm's key financial statements plus additional information about the company's management, its properties, its competition, and the intended uses for the funds it plans to obtain from the offering. The corporation cannot legally offer its new securities for sale until the SEC has examined this statement and declared it effective.

Private Placements In a private placement, the issuing firm negotiates the terms of the offer directly with a

exchange traded fund (ETF) Shares traded on securities markets that represent the legal right of ownership over part of a basket of individual stock certificates or other securities.

primary securities market The market where newly issued securities are traded. The primary market is where the firms that issue securities raise additional financial capital.

secondary securities market The market where previously issued securities are traded.

public offering A primary market issue in which new securities are offered to any investors who are willing and able to purchase them.

private placement A primary market issue that is negotiated between the issuing corporation and a small group of accredited investors.

initial public offering (IPO) The first time a company issues stock that may be bought by the general public.

underwriting An arrangement under which an investment banker agrees to purchase all shares of a public offering at an agreed-upon price.

registration statement A long, complex document that firms must file with the SEC when they sell securities through a public offering.

small number of **accredited investors**. These are individuals, businesses, or other organizations that meet specific financial requirements set by the SEC. Private placements are usually quicker, simpler, and less expensive than public offerings. The investment bank often helps the firm identify and contact accredited investors and assists the firm as it negotiates the terms of the private placement.

The main reason private placements are simpler and less expensive than public offerings is that privately placed securities are exempt from the requirement to register with the SEC. The ability to obtain financing without having to prepare complex registration documents can be a real attraction. But because the pool of potential investors is limited to accredited investors, private placements normally don't have the potential to raise as much money as public offerings. Another drawback is that securities that haven't been registered with the SEC can't be sold to anyone except other accredited investors.

Secondary Securities Markets: Let's Make a Deal

The firms that issue stocks and bonds don't receive any additional funds when their securities are traded in the secondary markets. But few investors would want to buy securities issued in the primary markets without the liquidity and possibility of earning capital gains provided by the opportunity to sell these securities in the secondary markets.

Stock (Securities) Exchanges The stocks of most large publicly traded corporations are listed and traded on a **stock (or securities) exchange**. A securities exchange provides an organized venue for stockbrokers and securities dealers to trade listed stocks and other securities. Each exchange establishes its own requirements for the securities it lists. The requirements vary among the exchanges, but they're typically based on the earnings of the company, the number of shares of stock outstanding, and the number of shareholders. In addition to meeting listing requirements, exchanges require firms to pay an initial fee at the time their securities are first listed, and an annual listing fee to remain listed on the exchange.

For the past several decades, the largest exchanges in the U.S. were the New York Stock Exchange (part of a holding company called NYSE Euronext) and the NASDAQ market. However, as this book went to print, it appeared likely that NYSE Euronext would be acquired by a German exchange called Deutsche Boerse. Such a consolidation

The federal Office of Management and Budget estimates that on average the standard registration statement for newly issued securities takes 972 hours to complete.

— Securities and Exchange Commission

might have significant consequences for the organization and operation of the surviving exchanges.

Trading on early stock exchanges occurred at physical locations where brokers met on trading floors to buy and sell securities for their clients. Some exchanges still maintain actual trading floors, but most trading on today's exchanges is done electronically. The participants in these markets carry out their trades mainly via computer networks.

The trend toward electronic trading began in 1971 with the establishment of NASDAQ, which initially was just a system used to report stock prices electronically. But over the years, it evolved into a complete market with formal listing requirements and fees. The stocks of many of today's high-profile technology companies, such as Apple, Google, and Microsoft, are traded on the NASDAQ market.

The key players in the NASDAQ market are known as **market makers**. These are securities dealers that make a

Many of the biggest players in our nation's financial markets have their headquarters on New York's Wall Street.

© Songquan Deng/Shutterstock.com

commitment to continuously offer to buy and sell (make a market in) specific NASDAQ-listed stocks. Each NASDAQ stock has several market makers who compete against each other by posting two prices for each stock: the *bid price* indicates how much the market maker will pay per share to buy a stated quantity of the stock, while the *ask price* indicates the price per share at which it will sell the same stock. The ask price is higher than the bid price; the difference is called the *bid/ask spread* (or just the *spread*) and is the source of the market maker's profit.

The Over-the-Counter Market Many corporations with publicly traded stock don't meet the requirements to have their shares listed on an organized exchange; others choose not to list on exchanges because they don't want to pay the listing fees. The **over-the-counter market (OTC)** is where the stocks of such companies are traded. OTC stocks are traded through a system of market makers much like stocks are traded on the NASDAQ exchange. However, the market for most OTC stocks is much less active than for stocks listed on the major exchanges. Because of this, most stocks listed on the OTC have only a few market makers. The lack of competition often leads to much higher spreads between bid and ask prices for stocks traded in the OTC than normally exist for stocks traded on the NASDAQ exchange.

Electronic Communications Networks The newest development in stock market technology involves the rise of **electronic communications networks** (ECNs). The SEC classifies ECNs as alternative trading systems because they represent an alternative to established stock exchanges as a venue for buying and selling securities. ECNs are entirely automated and computerized trading systems that allow traders to bypass the market makers used in the NASDAQ and OTC markets. However, individuals can only take advantage of this venue by opening an account with a broker-dealer that subscribes to an ECN.

If you place an order to buy a security on an ECN, the computer system checks to see if there is a matching order from another trader to sell the same security. If so, it immediately and automatically executes the transaction in a process that typically takes less than a second to complete. ECNs obviously speed up transactions. They also make it possible for investors to trade securities "after hours" when the U.S. exchanges are closed.

over-the-counter (OTC) market The market where securities that are not listed on exchanges are traded.

electronic communications network (ECN) An automated, computerized securities trading system that automatically matches buyers and sellers, executing trades quickly and allowing trading when securities exchanges are closed.

LO5 Personal Investing

Would investing in stocks, bonds, and other securities make sense for you? If so, how could you get started? What are the potential risks and rewards of various investment strategies?

Symbolic Logic: Do You LUV this HOG's DNA?

Every publicly traded corporation is identified by a unique combination of letters known as its stock symbol. The use of symbols began in the mid-1800s when people began sending information about stock prices via telegraph. The symbols allowed telegraph operators to tap out a few letters rather than having to spell out a company's entire name.

Although we no longer rely on the telegraph for stock quotes, the symbols are still used today. For example, symbols are used to quote stock prices on those scrolling tickers at the bottom of many financial news channels on cable TV. And many financial websites ask you to enter a company's symbol when you request the latest quotes and statistics for its stock.

The combination of letters used in a symbol is usually tied to the company's business, but the connection can be a bit subtle. See if you can identify the well-known corporation that uses each of the symbols listed in the table below. (Answers are given below.)[16]

GOOG	HOG
MMM	DNA
JAVA	LUV

Answers: Google, 3M, Sun Microsystems (JAVA is its best-known programming language), Harley-Davidson (Hog is the nickname for its motorcycles), Genentech (the company specializes in genetic research), Southwest Airlines (its first major hub of operations was Love Field in Dallas, TX).

Investing in securities requires you to think carefully about your specific situation, your personal goals, and your attitudes:

- What are your short-term and long-term goals?

- Given your budget, how much are you able to invest?

- How long can you leave your money invested?

- How concerned are you about the tax implications of your investments?

- How much tolerance do you have for risk?

Notice that the last question deals with your attitudes toward risk. Most people are not comfortable with high levels of risk. But no investment strategy completely avoids risk. And in general, the riskier the approach, the greater the *potential* rewards. To achieve your goals, you'll need to find the balance between risk and return that works for you.

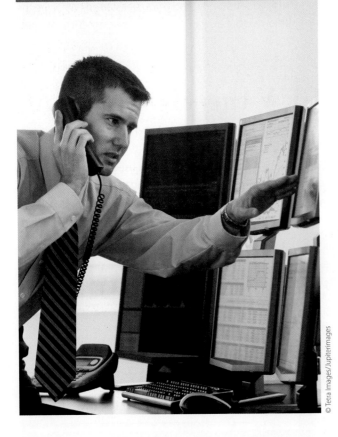

Stockbrokers place orders to buy and sell stocks and other securities for their clients.

© Tetra Images/Jupiterimages

Choosing a Broker: Gaining Access to the Markets

Members of the general public cannot directly trade stocks and other securities on the exchanges, the over-the-counter market, or ECNs we described earlier in the chapter. Thus, most investors enlist the services of a brokerage firm to carry out their trades. Choosing the right broker is the first step in implementing your investment plans.

A *full service broker* provides a wide range of services—such as market research, investment advice, and tax planning—in addition to carrying out your trades. *Discount brokers* provide the basic services needed to buy and sell securities, but offer fewer additional services. They may also restrict your ability to trade certain types of securities. For example, some discount brokers don't offer the ability to buy and sell foreign securities. Discount brokers tend to charge significantly lower commissions than full service brokers. In fact, many discount brokers charge flat fees of only a few dollars per trade for basic transactions. But brokerage firms also charge a variety of fees—sometimes including "inactivity fees" if you don't place enough orders! Once these fees are considered brokerage firms that offer low commissions may not be as inexpensive as they first appear!

In recent years, competition among brokerage firms has blurred the distinction between full service and discount brokers. To stop clients from defecting to discount brokers, many full-service firms have lowered their commissions. At the same time, many discount brokers have begun to offer a broader range of services to attract more clients. Now many brokerage firms offer investors the choice of discount or full-service accounts.

Once you've decided on a broker you need to open an account. This is a fairly simple process; it requires filling out some forms (usually available online) and making an initial investment. The minimum initial investment varies, but $1,000 to $3,000 is fairly typical.

Buying Securities: Let's Make a Deal

Once you've set up your account, you can trade securities by contacting your broker and indicating the security you want to trade and the quantity you want to buy or sell. You can also specify the type of order you want to place. The most common types of orders are market orders and limit orders:

- **Market orders** instruct the broker to buy or sell a security at the current market price. Placing a market

JUST BECAUSE THEY CAN...

...DOESN'T MEAN THEY SHOULD.

Normally, the way to make money in the stock market is to "buy low, sell high." This is a logical strategy, but it only works if the price of the stock increases. Investors who believe the price of a company's stock will fall sometimes turn to a different strategy called "short selling." This approach simply reverses the standard procedure: the investor sells high *then* buys low. Short sellers do this by borrowing shares of stock and selling them. (They usually borrow the shares from their broker.) Then they wait for the price to fall, buy the stock at the lower price, and replace the shares they borrowed. They profit from the difference between the high price at which they sold the borrowed shares and the lower price they paid for the replacement shares.

Short selling is legal—and even desirable. As certified financial analyst Alex Dumortier puts it, "Short selling is an integral part of a well-functioning market, since it allows market participants to voice their view that a stock is overpriced. Without short sellers, the market would be inherently positively biased, and stocks would be priced less efficiently."

But short selling sometimes tempts investors to behave in unethical ways. One questionable tactic is called naked "short selling." This occurs when a short seller sells shares without first borrowing them—meaning that the seller actually has no stock to sell. The sale isn't actually completed until the seller furnishes the shares, but it is still recorded. This can put downward pressure on the price of the stock. The short seller benefits from the lower price, but other investors find the value of their stock declining because of transactions that haven't occurred.

An even more appalling tactic is called "short and distort." This involves selling borrowed stock and then spreading negative (and unfounded) rumors about the company to put downward pressure on its stock. As with naked short selling, the lower stock prices that result from these distortions benefit the short seller, but can cause significant harm to the company and losses to investors who aren't part of the scam.

What do YOU think?

- What are the risks involved in short selling?
- Why are short-and-distort tactics likely to be more successful in recessions?
- How can abusive naked short selling be controlled?[17]

OCTOBER

October. This is one of the peculiarly dangerous months to speculate in stocks. The others are July, January, September, April, November, May, March, June, December, August and February.

— MARK TWAIN IN PUDD'NHEAD WILSON

© iStockphoto.com/kyoshino

order virtually guarantees that your order will be executed. The downside is that you may end up buying at a higher price than you expected to pay (or selling your stock for less than you expected to receive).

- **Limit orders** place limits on the prices at which orders are executed. A buy limit order tells a broker to buy a stock *only* if its price is at or below a specified value. You'd use this approach if you wanted to make sure you didn't pay more for the stock than you thsought it was worth. A sell limit order tells your broker to sell the shares only if the price is at or above a specified value. This prevents your broker from selling your stock at a price you believe is too low.

Strategies for Investing in Securities

There are several strategies you can use to guide your investment decisions. We'll provide an overview of the more common approaches, but none of these approaches is foolproof—alas, there is no known strategy that is guaranteed to earn you millions.

Investing for Income Some investors focus on buying bonds and preferred stocks in order to generate a steady, predictable flow of income. This approach is popular with retirees who want to supplement their retirement income. But the return on such low-risk securities is relatively low, and their market value seldom increases much over time. Thus, it probably isn't the best strategy for younger investors who are trying to grow their wealth.

Market Timing Investors who rely on *market timing* use a variety of analytical techniques to try to predict when prices of specific stocks are likely to rise and fall. Market timers try to make quick gains by buying low and selling high over a relatively short time horizon.

The problem with market timing is that so many factors can influence stock prices—some of them random in nature—that it's tough to consistently identify the timing and direction of changes in stock prices. Market timing also requires investors to make frequent trades. Given the commissions paid on trades and the taxes incurred on short-term capital gains, this approach may do a better job of enriching the broker than enriching the trader!

Value Investing Investors who favor *value investing* try to find stocks that are undervalued in the market. They believe that the market price will rise over time to reflect its true value, thus generating a capital gain. This approach requires a lot of research to identify discrepancies between a company's true (or intrinsic) value and its current market price.

The drawback with value investing is that you are one of thousands of investors all trying to do the same thing, so the competition to locate undervalued stocks is intense. Unless you're among the first to discover a good value, the investors who beat you to it will rush to buy up the stock, increasing demand and driving up the stock's price so that it is no longer undervalued.

Investing for Growth Investors who focus on growth look for companies that have the potential to grow much faster than average for a sustained period of time, which they believe will lead to a steady (and sometimes spectacular) rise in the stock's price. Investors using this strategy often invest in stocks of relatively new companies with innovative products in a hot sector of the economy.

Investing for growth entails a lot of risk. Small new companies don't have an established track record. And rapidly expanding industries tend to attract a lot of start-up companies, so competition can be intense. Finally, given the rapid pace of technological change, today's hot prospects may soon be dethroned by the next big thing. It's hard to predict which firms will be winners; even experts often make the wrong choice.

Buying and Holding If you're a patient person with steady nerves, a buy-and-hold approach might appeal to you. This strategy involves purchasing a diversified set of securities and holding them for a long period of time. Buy-and-hold investors put their faith in the ability of the *overall market* to continue the long-run upward trend it has exhibited throughout its history. One way that many buy-and-hold investors do this is by investing in index mutual funds and ETFs. The buy-and-hold strategy seldom allows investors to "get rich quick," but it usually results in a solid financial return over the long haul.

Obviously, the buy-and-hold strategy will work only if you can afford to leave your money invested for a long time. When the stock market takes a dive, it can sometimes take years for stocks to recover and start to show solid returns. Some people who think they're comfortable with a buy-and-hold strategy end up getting "happy feet" after a few weeks of declining stock prices. They panic and sell off their stocks at exactly the wrong time, locking in big losses. For the buy-and-hold strategy to work, you've got to have the patience—and mental toughness—to ride out short-term downturns in the market.

LO6 Keeping Tabs on the Market

Once you've begun to invest in securities, you'll want to keep track of how your investments are doing. Using the Internet, you can easily find information about both general market trends and the performance of specific securities.

Stock Indices: Tracking the Trends

One of the most common ways to track general market conditions and trends is to follow what's happening to various stock indices. A **stock index** tracks the prices of a large group of stocks that meet certain defined criteria. Many investors like to compare how the stocks in their own portfolio compare to the performance of these broad indices. Two of the best-known indices are the Dow Jones Industrial Average and the S&P 500.

- The **Dow Jones Industrial Average (DJIA)**: Often called just "the Dow," this is the most widely followed stock index. The Dow is based on the adjusted average price of 30 stocks picked by the editors of *The Wall Street Journal*. All of the Dow firms are large, well-established corporations, such as American Express, General Electric, Coca-Cola, Hewlett-Packard, and Disney.

- The **Standard & Poor's 500**: With 500 stocks instead of just 30, the S&P 500 is a much broader index than the DJIA. Still, like the Dow, all of the companies included in the S&P 500 are large, well-established American corporations.

Exhibit 10.2 identifies several other well-known indices, including some that track prices of stocks in foreign securities markets.

Tracking the Performance of Specific Securities

Many financial websites offer detailed stock quotes that provide the current price of a company's stock and a wealth of related information. To check out a specific stock, you simply type its *stock symbol*—a short combination of letters that uniquely identifies a corporate security—into a "Get Quote" box. (Most sites have a lookup feature that finds the symbol if you type in the company's name.)

Exhibit 10.3 illustrates the information a popular financial website, Yahoo! Finance (http://finance.yahoo.com/), provides about Harley-Davidson's common stock. Some of the key figures reported for Harley-Davidson include:

- *Last trade*: The price of Harley-Davidson's common stock for the most recent trade was $39.52.

- *Change*: The last trade of Harley-Davidson's stock was $1.03 lower than the closing price for the stock on the previous day.

- *Bid and Ask*: The highest price currently offered (bid) to buy Harley-Davidson stock is $39.51 for 100 shares. The lowest price currently offered (asked) to sell the stock is $39.52 for 800 shares.

- *Day's range*: The highest price for the stock during the day was $40.28, and the lowest price was $39.03.

- *52-Week range*: The highest price for Harley-Davidson stock over the previous 52 weeks was $43.15, while its lowest price was $21.26.

- *Volume*: 1,922,025 shares of the stock have been traded up to this point in the current trading session.

- *Market Cap*: The total market value of all shares of Harley-Davidson common stock outstanding was $9.31 billion. This is found by multiplying the price per share times the number of shares of common stock outstanding.

stock index A statistic that tracks how the prices of a specific set of stocks have changed.

Dow Jones Industrial Average An index that tracks stock prices of thirty large, well-known U.S. corporations.

Standard & Poor's 500 A stock index based on prices of 500 major U.S. corporations in a variety of industries and market sectors.

EXHIBIT 10.2 Major Stock Price Indices

INDEX	WHAT IT TRACKS
NASDAQ COMPOSITE	All of the domestic and foreign common stocks traded on the NASDAQ exchange
WILSHIRE 5000	Stock prices of all U.S. corporations with actively traded stock. Despite the 5000 in its name, this index actually includes well over 6000 stocks. (The exact number changes frequently.)
RUSSELL 2000	Stock prices of 2000 relatively small but actively traded U.S. corporations.
FTSE 100	Stock prices of 100 of the largest and most actively traded companies listed on the London Stock Exchange.
NIKKEI 225	Stock prices of 225 of the largest and most actively traded companies listed on the Tokyo Stock Exchange.
SSE COMPOSITE	Stock prices of all stocks listed on the Shanghai Stock Exchange.

© Cengage Learning 2013

Exhibit 10.3   Yahoo! Finance Quote for a Stock

Harley–Davidson, Inc. Common St (NYSE: HOG)
Real-time 39.57 ↓ 0.99 (−2.43%) 3:04 PM EDT

Last Trade:	39.52	Day's Range:	39.03–40.28
Trade Time:	2:49 PM EDT	52wk Range:	21.26–43.15
Change:	↓ 1.03 (2.54%)	Volume:	1,922,025
Prev Close:	40.55	Avg Vol (3m):	2,274,240
Open:	40.09	Market Cap:	9.31B
Bid:	39.51 x 100	P/E (ttm):	62.93
Ask:	39.52 x 800	EPS (ttm):	0.63
1y Target Est:	44.58	Div & Yield:	0.40 (1.00%)

Source: Yahoo! Finance stock quote accessed April 18, 2011. Reproduced with permission of Yahoo! Inc. YAHOO! and the YAHOO! logo are registered trademarks of Yahoo! Inc.

- **P/E:** The price-to-earnings ratio is found by dividing the stock's price per share by its earnings per share. In general, a higher P/E ratio means investors expect a greater growth in earnings over time.

- **EPS (earnings per share):** Harley-Davidson earned $0.63 per share of common stock outstanding. EPS is computed by dividing the net income available to common stockholders by the number of shares of common stock outstanding.

- **Div & Yield:** The sum of dividends paid by Harley-Davidson over the past 12 months was $0.40 per share. Yield is found by dividing the dividend per share by the previous day's price per share. It tells us that at that price the dividend paid by Harley-Davidson represented a 1.4% return to the investor. (But since the total return to stockholders may also include a capital gain or loss this yield doesn't tell us the whole story.)

Financial websites also provide information about other types of securities such as mutual funds, ETFs, and bonds.

THE BIG PICTURE

Many different organizations participate in financial markets, including banks, finance companies, securities brokers and dealers, investment banks and institutional investors such as mutual funds, insurance companies and pension funds. While they differ in their functions, each of these participants helps financial markets achieve their primary purpose of channeling funds from savers to borrowers.

In this chapter, we focused on one particular type of financial market, namely the market for financial securities. The financial capital that corporations raise when they issue stocks and bonds in these markets is critical to every functional area of their operations. Without these funds, the marketing department would lack the resources needed to develop new products, information technology professionals would be unable to update hardware and software, and operations managers would be unable to acquire the machinery and equipment needed to produce the goods and services the company sells to earn its profits.

On the other side of these markets, investors who buy corporate securities do so to acquire assets that they believe will help them achieve their own financial goals. But investing in securities involves risk. Over any short-run time period, there is simply no guarantee that stocks and bonds will provide investors with the returns they expect. The good news—at least if you plan to invest—is that history shows that, over the long run, the return on these securities is positive. Given enough time and patience, investing in stocks and other securities is likely to result in a substantial increase in wealth.

Financial markets offer employment opportunities in a wide range of occupations.

Securities brokers advise clients on appropriate investments based on their needs and financial ability. When a client makes an investment decision, the broker electronically sends the order to the floor of the securities exchange to complete the transaction.

Brokerage firms normally require brokers to have a minimum of a bachelor's degree in business, finance, accounting, or economics. In addition, brokers must register with the Financial Industry Regulatory Authority (FINRA). Before they can register, they must be an employee of a registered brokerage firm for at least four months and pass a rigorous exam administered by FINRA.

Brokers earn most of their income in the form of commissions based on the amount of stocks, bonds, and other securities they trade for their clients. The average annual income of brokers in 2008 was $66,680. The BLS projects that, over the next several years, job opportunities for brokers will grow about as fast as the average for all occupations.

Financial analysts assess the performance of stocks, bonds, commodities, and other types of investments and make recommendations about investments. They normally work for banks, pension funds, insurance companies, mutual funds, and securities firms.

Most firms require financial analysts to have a bachelor's degree in finance, economics, or statistics; large firms strongly prefer a master's degree in one of these fields. Licensure is sometimes required, but the type of license (if any) depends on the specific job.

Financial analysts are well paid; their average income in 2008 was $73,150 (a figure that doesn't include bonuses). The BLS projects that job growth for this profession will be faster than average for the next several years. However, the BLS also projects that competition for these jobs will be intense.[18]

CAREERS IN FINANCIAL MARKETS

What else?
RIP & REVIEW CARDS IN THE BACK
and visit www.cengagebrain.com!

11

Marketing:
Building Profitable Customer
Connections

> # YOU NEED TO GIVE CUSTOMERS WHAT THEY WANT—NOT WHAT YOU *THINK* THEY WANT.
>
> — John Ilhan, Australian Entrepreneur

LO1 Marketing: Getting Value by Giving Value

What comes to mind when you hear the term **marketing**? Most people think of the radio ad they heard this morning, or the billboard they saw while driving to school. But advertising is only a small part of marketing; the whole story is much bigger. The American Marketing Association defines marketing as *the activity, set of institutions, and processes for creating, communicating, delivering, and exchanging offerings that have value for customers, clients, partners, and society at large.*

The ultimate benefit that most businesses seek from marketing is long-term profitability. But attaining this benefit is impossible without first delivering value to customers and other stakeholders. A successful marketer delivers value by filling customer needs in ways that exceed their expectations. As a result, you get sales today and sales tomorrow and sales the next day, which—across the days and months and years—can translate into long-term profitability. Alice Foote MacDougall, a successful entrepreneur in the 1920s, understood this thinking early on: "In business you get what you want by giving other people what they want." **Utility** is the ability of goods and services to satisfy these wants. And since there is a wide range of wants, products can provide utility in a number of different ways:

- *Form utility* satisfies wants by converting inputs into a finished form. Clearly, the vast majority of products provide some kind of form utility. For example, Jamba Juice pulverizes fruit, juices, and yogurt into yummy smoothies, and UGG Australia stretches, treats, and sews sheepskins into comfortable, stylish boots.

- *Time utility* satisfies wants by providing goods and services at a convenient time for customers. For example, FedEx delivers some parcels on Sunday, LensCrafters makes eyeglasses within about an hour, 7-Eleven opens early and closes late, and e-commerce, of course, provides the ultimate 24-7 convenience.

- *Place utility* satisfies wants by providing goods and services at a convenient place for customers. For example, ATMs offer banking services in many large supermarkets, Motel 6 lodges tired travelers at the bottom of highway off-ramps, and vending machines refuel tired students on virtually every college campus.

- *Ownership utility* satisfies wants by smoothly transferring ownership of goods and services from seller to buyer. Virtually every product provides some degree of ownership utility, but some offer more than others. Apple, for example, has created a hassle-free purchase process that customers can follow by phone, by computer, and in person.

Satisfying customer wants—in a way that exceeds expectations—is a job that never ends. Jay Levinson, a recognized expert in breakthrough marketing, comments, "Marketing is … a process. You improve it, perfect it, change it, even pause it. But you never stop it completely."

The Scope of Marketing: It's Everywhere!

For many years, businesspeople have actively applied the principles of marketing to goods and services that range from cars, to fast food, to liquor, to computers, to movies. But within the last decade or two, other organizations have successfully adopted marketing strategies and tactics to further their goals.

Nonprofit organizations—in both the private and public sectors—play a significant role in our economy, employing more people than the federal government and all 50 state governments combined (not to mention an army of volunteers!). These organizations use marketing, sometimes quite assertively, to achieve their

> **marketing** An organizational function and a set of processes for creating, communicating, and delivering value to customers and for managing customer relationships in ways that benefit the organization and its stakeholders.
>
> **utility** The ability of goods and services to satisfy consumer "wants."

objectives. The U.S. Army's advertising budget, for example, sometimes hits as much as $300 million per year, which ranks on the list of top U.S. advertisers. Your own college probably markets itself to both prospective students and potential alumni donors. Private-sector nonprofit organizations also use marketing strategies for everything from marshalling AYSO soccer coaches for kids, to boosting attendance at the local zoo, to planning cultural events.[1]

Nonprofit organizations play a pivotal role in the expansion of marketing across our economy to include people,

Avon helps breast cancer organizations market the idea of hope for a cure.

© Kevin Mazur/WireImage/ Getty Images

places, events, and ideas. But for-profit enterprises have also begun to apply marketing strategies and tactics beyond simply goods and services.

- **People Marketing:** Sports, politics, and art dominate this category, but even some businesspeople merit mentioning. Top banking executives, for instance, took a beating from a marketing standpoint during the financial meltdown at the end of 2008. Also in 2008, President Barack Obama was named Ad Age Marketer of the Year, edging out powerhouse consumer brands that were also on the short list, such as Apple, Nike, and Coors. He became a living symbol of change in the minds of the electorate. Countless entertainers and athletes have used people marketing to their advantage as well. Consider, for example, Paris Hilton, who appeared to build her career on promotion alone. In fact, as you pursue your personal goals—whether you seek a new job or a Friday night date—people marketing principles can help you achieve your objective. Start by figuring out what your "customer" needs, and then ensure that your "product" (you!) delivers above and beyond expectations.[2]

- **Place Marketing:** This category involves drawing people to a particular place. Cities and states use place marketing to attract businesses. Delaware, for instance, the second-smallest state in the Union, is

home to more than half of the Fortune 500 firms because it deliberately developed a range of advantages for corporations. But more visibly, cities, states, and nations use place marketing to attract tourists. Thanks to powerful place marketing, most people have probably heard that "What happens in Vegas stays in Vegas." But in late 2008, Las Vegas shelved the high-rolling campaign in favor of a more recession-proof strategy: the "Take a Break USA" campaign. While the campaign features traditional television and newspaper advertising, it also includes a YouTube component meant to involve consumers at a more personal level.[3]

- **Event Marketing:** This category includes marketing—or sponsoring—athletic, cultural, or charitable events. Partnerships between the public and private sectors are increasingly common. Examples include the Olympics, the Super Bowl, and the Lady Gaga/MTV Video Music Aid Japan concert to benefit victims of the 2011 Japanese earthquake and tsunami.

- **Idea Marketing:** A whole range of public and private organizations market ideas that are meant to change how people think or act. Recycle, don't pollute, buckle your seatbelt, support our political party, donate blood, don't smoke; all are examples of popular causes. Often, idea marketing and event marketing are combined, as we see in the annual Avon

Walk for Breast Cancer. The planners actively market the idea of annual mammograms, as they solicit contributions for breast cancer research and participation in the event itself.

The Evolution of Marketing: From the Product to the Customer

The current approach to marketing evolved through a number of overlapping stages, as you'll see in Exhibit 11.1. But as you read about these eras, keep in mind that some businesses have remained lodged—with varying degrees of success—in the thinking of a past era.

Production Era Marketing didn't always begin with the customer. In fact, in the early 1900s, the customer was practically a joke. Henry Ford summed up the prevailing mindset when he reportedly said "You can have your Model T in any color you want as long as it's black." This attitude made sense from a historical perspective, since consumers didn't have the overwhelming number of choices that are currently available; most products were purchased as soon as they were produced and distributed to consumers. In this context, the top business priority was to produce large quantities of goods as efficiently as possible.

Selling Era By the 1920s, production capacity had increased dramatically. For the first time, supply in many categories exceeded demand, which caused the emergence of the hard sell. The selling focus gained momentum in the 1930s and 1940s, when the Depression and World War II made consumers even more reluctant to part with their limited money.

Marketing Era The landscape changed dramatically in the 1950s. Many factories that had churned out military supplies converted to consumer production, flooding the market with choices in virtually every product category. An era of relative peace and prosperity emerged, and—as soldiers returned from World War II—marriage and birthrates soared. To compete for the consumer's dollar, marketers attempted to provide goods and services that met customer needs better than anything else on the market. As a result, the marketing concept materialized in the 1950s. The **marketing concept** is a philosophy that makes customer satisfaction—now and in the future—the central focus of the entire organization. Companies that embrace this philosophy strive to delight customers, integrating this goal into all business activities. The marketing concept holds that delivering unmatched value to customers is the only effective way to achieve long-term profitability.

Relationship Era The marketing concept has gathered momentum across the economy, leading to the current era, unfolding over the last decade, which zeros in on long-term customer relationships. Acquiring a new customer can cost five times more than keeping an existing customer. Retaining your current customers—and getting them to spend additional dollars—is clearly cost-effective. Moreover, satisfied customers can develop into advocates for your business, becoming powerful generators of positive "word-of-mouth."

> **marketing concept** A business philosophy that makes customer satisfaction—now and in the future—the central focus of the entire organization.

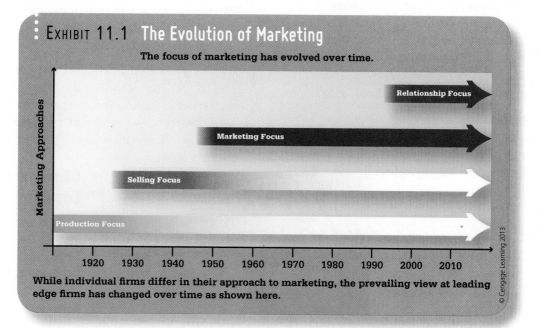

Exhibit 11.1   The Evolution of Marketing

The focus of marketing has evolved over time.

Marketing Approaches (vertical axis)

Relationship Focus

Marketing Focus

Selling Focus

Production Focus

1920 1930 1940 1950 1960 1970 1980 1990 2000 2010

© Cengage Learning 2013

While individual firms differ in their approach to marketing, the prevailing view at leading edge firms has changed over time as shown here.

LO2 The Customer: Front and Center

Customer Relationship Management (CRM)

Customer relationship management (CRM) is the centerpiece of successful, twenty-first-century marketing. Broadly defined, CRM is the ongoing process of acquiring, maintaining, and growing profitable customer relationships by delivering unmatched value. CRM works best when marketers combine marketing communication with one-on-one personalization. Amazon is a champion player at CRM, greeting customers by name, recommending specific products, and providing streamlined checkout. Clearly, information is an integral part of this process—you simply can't do CRM without collecting, managing, and applying the right data at the right time for the right person (and every repeat customer is the "right person"!).

Limited Relationships Clearly, the scope of your relationships will depend not just on the data you gather but also on your industry. Colgate-Palmolive, for example, can't forge a close personal bond with every person who buys a bar of Irish Spring soap. However, they do invite customers to call their toll-free line with questions or comments, and they maintain a vibrant website with music, an e-newsletter, special offers, and an invitation to contact the company. You can bet that they actively gather data and pursue a connection with customers who do initiate contact.

Full Partnerships If you have a high-ticket product and a smaller customer base, you're much more likely to pursue a full partnership with each of your key clients. Colgate-Palmolive, for instance, has dedicated customer service teams working with key accounts such as Walmart and Costco. With a full partnership, the marketer gathers and leverages extensive information about each customer and often includes the customer in key aspects of the product development process.

Value You know you've delivered **value** when your customers believe that your product has a better relationship between the cost and the benefits than any competitor. By this definition, low cost does not always mean high value. In fact, a recent survey suggests that loyal customers are often willing to pay *more* for their products rather than switch to lower-cost competitors. Apple provides a clear example. We probably all know at least a handful of Apple fanatics who gladly pay far more for their PowerBooks (or iPhones or iPads) than they would pay for a competing product.

Perceived Value Versus Actual Value

The operative idea here is *perceived*. Simply creating value isn't enough; you also must help customers believe that your product is uniquely qualified to meet their needs. This becomes a particular challenge when you're a new business competing against a market leader with disproportionately strong perceived value.

Customer Satisfaction

You know you've satisfied your customers when you deliver perceived value above and beyond their expectations. But achieving **customer satisfaction** can be tricky. Less savvy marketers frequently fall into one of two traps:

- The first trap is overpromising. Even if you deliver more value than anyone else, your customers will be disappointed if your product falls short of overly high expectations. The messages that you send regarding your product influence expectations—keep them real!

- The second trap is underpromising. If you don't set expectations high enough, too few customers will be willing to try your product. The result will be a tiny base of highly satisfied customers, which usually isn't enough to sustain a business.

Finding the right balance is tricky, but clearly not impossible. Judging by their high scores on the American Customer Satisfaction Index, the following companies come close to mastering the art of customer satisfaction: Costco, State Farm, Clorox Company, Nordstrom, Amazon, H.J. Heinz, and FedEx.[4]

Customer Loyalty

Customer loyalty is the payoff for delivering value and generating satisfaction. Loyal customers purchase from you again and

© Tim Boyle/Getty Images

again—and they sometimes even pay more for your product. They forgive your mistakes. They provide valuable feedback. They may require less service. They refer their friends (and sometimes even strangers). Moreover, studying your loyal customers can give you a competitive edge for acquiring new ones, since people with a similar profile would likely be a great fit for your products.[5]

LO3 Marketing Strategy: Where Are You Going, and How Will You Get There?

In marketing terms, the questions become: Who is your target audience, and how will you reach them? Many successful firms answer this question by developing a formal **marketing plan**, updated on a yearly basis; other firms handle their planning on a more informal basis. But regardless of the specific approach, the first step in planning your marketing strategy should be to determine where to target your efforts. Who are those people who are most likely to buy your products? The first step is **market segmentation**—dividing your marketing into groups of people, or segments, that are similar to one another and different from everyone else. One or more of these segments will be your target market. Once you've identified your target market, your next step is to determine how you can best use marketing tools to reach them. And finally, you need to anticipate and respond to changes in the external environment. This section will define target market, explain market segmentation, introduce the marketing mix, and review the key factors in the marketing environment. Taken together, these elements will shape an effective marketing strategy, as shown in Exhibit 11.2.

The marketer creates the marketing mix but responds to the marketing environment with a single-minded focus on the target market.

Target Market

Your **target market** is the group of people who are most likely to buy your product. This is where you should concentrate your marketing efforts. But why not target your efforts toward everyone? After all, even if most middle-aged moms wouldn't buy purple polka-dotted miniskirts, an adventurous few just might do it. Well, you can always hope for the adventurous few, but virtually every business has limited resources, and marketing toward the people who are most likely to buy your flamboyant minis—say,

teenage girls—will maximize the impact of each dollar you spend. A well-chosen target market embodies the following characteristics:

- ◗ Size: There must be enough people in your target group to support a business.

- ◗ Profitability: The people must be willing and able to spend more than the cost of producing and marketing your product.

- ◗ Accessibility: Your target must be reachable through channels that your business can afford.

- ◗ Limited competition: Look for markets with limited competition; a crowded market is much tougher to crack.

Consumer Markets Versus Business Markets

Consumer marketers (B2C) direct their efforts to people who are buying products for personal consumption (e.g., candy bars, shampoo, and clothing), whereas **business marketers (B2B)** direct their efforts to customers who are

EXHIBIT 11.2 Marketing Strategy

Competitive
Social/Cultural
Economic
Product Strategy
Pricing Strategy
Promotion Strategy
Distribution Strategy
TARGET MARKET
Technological
Political/Legal

© Cengage Learning 2013

demographic segmentation Dividing the market into smaller groups based on measurable characteristics about people, such as age, income, ethnicity, and gender.

geographic segmentation Dividing the market into smaller groups based on where consumers live. This process can incorporate countries, cities, or population density as key factors.

psychographic segmentation Dividing the market into smaller groups based on consumer attitudes, interests, values, and lifestyles.

behavioral segmentation Dividing the market based on how people behave toward various products. This category includes both the benefits that consumers seek from products and how consumers use the products.

buying products to use either directly or indirectly to produce other products (e.g., tractors, steel, and cash registers). But keep in mind that the distinction between the market categories is not in the products themselves; rather, it lies in how the buyer will use the product. For instance, shampoo that you buy for yourself is clearly a consumer product, but shampoo that a hair stylist buys for a salon is a business product. Similarly, a computer that you buy for yourself is a consumer product, but a computer that your school buys for the computer lab is a business product. Both B2C and B2B marketers need to choose the best target, but they tend to follow slightly different approaches.

Consumer Market Segmentation

Choosing the best target market (or markets) for your product begins with dividing your market into segments, or groups of people who have similar characteristics. But people can be similar in a number of different ways, so, not surprisingly, marketers have several options for segmenting potential consumers.

Demographic B2C **demographic segmentation** refers to dividing the market based on measurable characteristics about people such as age, income, ethnicity, and gender. Demographics are a vital starting point for most marketers. Rockstar, for example, targets young women with its Rockstar Pink energy drink, and Jaguar targets the wealthy. Sometimes the demographic makeup of a given market is tough to discern; African American artists, for instance, create the bulk of rap music, yet Caucasian suburban males form the bulk of the rap music market.

Geographic B2C **geographic segmentation** refers to dividing the market based on where consumers live. This process can incorporate countries, or cities, or population density as key factors. For instance, Toyota Sequoia does not concentrate on European markets, where tiny, winding streets and nonexistent parking are common in many cities. Cosmetic surgeons tend to market their services more heavily in urban rather than rural areas. And finding a great surfboard is easy in California but more challenging in South Dakota.

Tony Hsieh, CEO of Zappos.com has tapped into the stylish, fun-loving mind-set of his target customers.

Psychographic B2C **psychographic segmentation** refers to dividing the market based on consumer attitudes, interests, values, and lifestyles. Porsche Cayenne, for instance, targets consumers who seek the thrill of driving. A number of companies have found a highly profitable niche providing upscale wilderness experiences for people who seek all the pleasure with none of the pain (you enjoy the great outdoors, while someone else lugs your gear, pours your wine, slices your goat cheese, and inflates your extra-comfy air mattress). Both magazine racks and the Internet are filled with products geared toward psychographic segments, including celebrity gossip blog PerezHilton.com, shoe-selling mega site Zappos.com, and business and financial powerhouse WallStreetJournal.com. NOTE: Marketers typically use psychographics to complement other segmentation approaches rather than to provide the core definition.

Behavioral B2C **behavioral segmentation** refers to dividing the market based on how people behave toward various products. This category includes both the benefits that consumers seek from products and how consumers use the product. The Neutrogena Corporation, for example, built a multimillion-dollar hair care business by targeting consumers who wanted an occasional break from their favorite shampoo. Countless products such as Miller Lite actively target the low-carbohydrate consumer. But perhaps the most common type of behavioral segmentation is based on usage patterns. Fast-food restaurants, for instance, actively target heavy users (who, ironically, tend to be slender): young men in their 20s and 30s. This group consumes about 17% of their total calories from fast food, compared to 12% for adults in general. Understanding the usage patterns of your customer base gives you the option of either focusing on your core users or trying to pull light users into your core market.

Business Market Segmentation

B2B marketers typically follow a similar process in segmenting their markets, but they use slightly different categories:

Geographic B2B geographic segmentation refers to dividing the market based on the concentration of customers. Many industries tend to be highly clustered in certain areas, such as technology in California, and auto suppliers in the "auto corridor" that stretches south from Michigan to Tennessee. Geographic segmentation, of course, is especially common on an international basis, where variables such as language, culture, income, and regulatory differences can play crucial roles.

Customer-based B2B customer-based segmentation refers to dividing the market based on the characteristics of customers. This approach includes a range of possibilities. Some B2B marketers segment based on customer size. Others segment based on customer type. Johnson & Johnson, for example, has a group of salespeople dedicated exclusively to retail accounts such as Target and Publix, while other salespeople focus solely on motivating doctors to recommend their products. Other potential B2B markets include institutions—schools and hospitals, for instance, are key segments for Heinz Ketchup—and the government.

Product-use–based B2B product-use–based segmentation refers to dividing the market based on how customers will use the product. Small and midsized companies find this strategy especially helpful in narrowing their target markets. Possibilities include the ability to support certain software packages or production systems or the desire to serve certain customer groups, such as long-distance

Color me... hungry?!

Have you ever noticed that fast-food restaurants typically feature vivid shades of red, yellow, and orange in both their logos and their décor? Think McDonald's, KFC, Burger King, and Pizza Hut. The color choice is no coincidence.

Marketing researchers have learned that consumers in the United States associate red with energy, passion, and speed. Yellow suggests happiness and warmth, while orange suggests playfulness, affordability, and fun. A simulated cocktail party study found that partygoers in red rooms reported feeling hungrier and thirstier than others, and guests in yellow rooms ate twice as much as others. The implication? Surrounding customers with red, yellow, and orange encourages them to eat a lot quickly and leave, which aligns nicely with the goals of most fast-food chains.

Color psychology is a powerful—though often overlooked—marketing tool. Colors evoke emotions and trigger specific behaviors, which can dramatically influence how people buy your product. Here is a list of common colors and some of their associations in U.S. mainstream culture:

Keep in mind that while some color associations are universal, others can differ significantly among cultures. White, for instance, signifies death and mourning in Chinese culture, while purple represents death in Brazil.

As a marketer, your goal should be to align your color choice with the perceptions of your target market and the features of your product. The result should be more green for your bottom line![6]

© David P. Smith/Shutterstock.com

RED - Love, passion, warmth, food, excitement, action, danger, need to stop

BLUE - Power, trustworthiness, calm, success, seriousness, boredom

GREEN - Money, nature, health, healing, decay, illness

ORANGE - Playfulness, affordability, youth, fun, low quality, cheap

PURPLE - Royalty, luxury, dignity, spirituality, nightmares, craziness

WHITE - Purity, innocence, simplicity, mildness

BLACK - Sophistication, elegance, seriousness, sexuality, mystery, evil truckers or restaurants that deliver food.

The Marketing Mix

Once you've clearly defined your target market, your next challenge is to develop compelling strategies for product, price, distribution, and promotion. The blending of these elements becomes your **marketing mix,** as shown below in Exhibit 11.3.

- **Product Strategy:** Your product involves far more than simply a tangible good or a specific service. Product strategy decisions range from brand name, to product image, to package design, to customer service, to guarantees, to new product development, and more. Designing the best product clearly begins with understanding the needs of your target market.

- **Pricing Strategy:** Pricing is a challenging area of the marketing mix. To deliver customer value, your prices must be fair, relative to the benefits of your product. Other factors include competition, regulation, and public opinion. Your product category plays a critical role as well. A low-cost desk, for instance, might be appealing, but who would want discount-priced knee surgery?

- **Distribution Strategy:** The goal is to deliver your product to the right people, in the right quantities, at the right time, in the right place. The key decisions include shipping, warehousing, and selling outlets (e.g., the

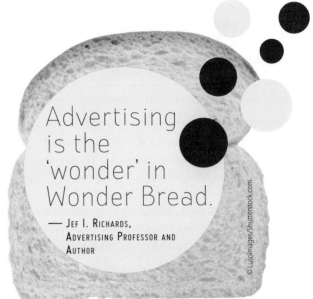

Advertising is the 'wonder' in Wonder Bread.

— Jef I. Richards, Advertising Professor and Author

Web versus network marketing versus brick-and-mortar stores). The implications of these decisions for product image and customer satisfaction can be significant.

- **Promotion Strategy:** Promotion includes all of the ways that marketers communicate about their products. The list of possibilities is long and growing, especially as the Internet continues to evolve at breakneck speed. Key elements today include advertising, personal selling, sales promotion, public relations, word-of-mouth, and product placement. Successful promotional strategies typically evolve in response to both customer needs and competition. A number of innovative companies are even inviting their customers to participate in creating their advertising through venues such as YouTube. Check out Exhibit 11.4 to see how easily you can analyze promotional strategies.

The Global Marketing Mix

As you decide to enter foreign markets, you'll need to reevaluate your marketing mix for each new country. Should it change? If so, how should it change? Many business goods simply don't require much change in the marketing mix, since their success isn't dependent on culture. Examples include heavy machinery, cement, and farming equipment. Consumer products, however, often require completely new marketing mixes to effectively reach their consumers.

Nike's approach to marketing in China offers an interesting example of how one firm managed the complex process of building a successful business in a foreign market. When Nike first entered China in the 1990s, the

EXHIBIT 11.3 Marketing Mix

Product Strategy

Pricing Strategy

Promotion Strategy

Distribution Strategy

company seemed to face an insurmountable challenge: not only did a pair of Nike sneakers cost twice the Chinese average monthly salary, but most Chinese just didn't play sports, according to Terry Rhoads, then director of Nike sports marketing. So he boldly set out to change that. Rhoads created a Nike high-school basketball league, which has since spread to 17 cities. To loosen up fans, he blasted canned cheering during games and arranged for national TV coverage of the finals. He even leveraged connections with the NBA to bring Michael Jordan for visits.

The gamble quickly paid off, as the Chinese middle class emerged—along with more individualistic values, which are a strong fit with the Nike ethos. By 2001, Nike had dubbed its marketing approach "hip hoop," which they described as an effort to "connect Nike with a creative lifestyle." Sales in 2008 exceeded $1 billion, about a year ahead of when Nike had anticipated. In 2010, sales were still growing at a blistering pace of +23%, driven largely by basketball shoes. And a recent survey suggests that Chinese youth rank Nike as their favorite sports brand. Winning over young buyers is especially important, according to researcher Mary Bergstrom, because young people are China's "most influential" consumers, often affecting what the whole household buys.[7]

The Marketing Environment

While marketers actively influence the elements of the marketing mix, they must anticipate and respond to the elements of the external environment, which they typically cannot control. **Environmental scanning** is a key tool; the goal is simply to continually collect information from sources that range from informal networks, to industry newsletters, to the general press, to customers, to suppliers, to the competition, among others. The key elements of the external environment include the following components:

Competitive The dynamic competitive environment probably affects marketers on a day-to-day basis more than any other element. Understanding the competitive environment often begins with analysis of **market share,** or the percentage of the marketplace that each firm controls. To avoid ambushes—and to uncover new opportunities—you must continually monitor how both dominant and emerging competitors handle each element of their marketing mix. And don't forget indirect competitors, who meet the same consumer needs as you but with a completely different product (e.g., cable TV and Internet games).

Economic The only certainty in the economic environment is change, but the timing of expansions and contractions is virtually impossible to predict. Your goal as a marketer is to identify and respond to changes as soon as possible, keeping in mind that a sharp eye sees opportunity even in economic downturns. For instance, affordable luxuries and do-it-yourself enterprises can thrive during recessions.

Social/Cultural The social/cultural element covers a vast array of factors, including lifestyle, customs, language, attitudes, interests, and population shifts. Trends can change rapidly, with a dramatic impact on marketing

environmental scanning The process of continually collecting information from the external marketing environment.

market share The percentage of a market controlled by a given marketer.

:::: EXHIBIT 11.4 *Analyzing Promotional Strategies*

Who is the target audience for each of these ads? How does each ad position the product relative to the competition? Which strategy is most effective? Why?

JUST BECAUSE THEY CAN...

...DOESN'T MEAN THEY SHOULD.

It's not your imagination—the food you buy at the market really does disappear faster, even though you may not have realized that the package was smaller. In 2008, about 30% of all packaged goods got smaller, most of them unnoticed by consumers. Skippy peanut butter jars, for instance, got about 10% smaller, but the jar looks just the same—it's the dimple in the bottom that's more indented. PepsiCo reduced the size of its orange juice jugs by 7 ounces but touted the container's "new ergonomic design" and "easy-pour lid." The agenda, some say, was to distract consumers from the *de facto* price increase. And cereal makers have reduced the depth of their packages—much less noticeable than reducing the height or width. When commodities prices spiked in 2011, a number of producers used the same strategy again to keep their costs in line. The Mars Company, for instance, split their "King Size" Snickers bar in half "so that it could be more easily shared between two people," and at the same time, they reduced the amount of candy in each package by 11%.

Food manufacturers assert that these size reductions—and the associated cost cuts—are crucial in the face of skyrocketing food and fuel costs. Some analysts also point out that the reductions are ultimately good for the environment, because less packaging eliminates waste. But others see deception. "It's become a game," said Susan Broniarczyk, a professor of marketing at the University of Texas at Austin. "How far can you go in reducing the size of a package while flying under the consumers' radar screen?" Consumer advocate Ben Popken takes an even harder line: "This is the packaging equivalent of three-card monte. By changing several factors at the same time, food companies disguise the fact that you're getting less for the same price."

What do YOU think?

- Are food firms playing fair? Or are they going too far in an attempt to deliberately mislead customers? Whatever your conclusions, it clearly makes sense to shop carefully, looking at both the price tag and the cost per unit.[8]

decisions. Anticipating and responding to trends can be especially important in industries such as entertainment, fashion, and technology. In late 2009, for instance, Facebook removed some key privacy controls from its News Feed. The social media giant did not anticipate the black eye it received from outraged consumers who believed that Facebook had violated their privacy. Facebook was also surprised that the privacy controls it implemented in May 2010, which required consumers to opt out of sharing, would not be enough to appease privacy advocates.[9]

Technological Changes in technology can be very visible to consumers (e.g., the introduction of the iPhone). However, technology often affects marketers in ways that are less directly visible. For example, technology allows mass customization of Levi's blue jeans at a reasonable price and

facilitates just-in-time inventory management for countless companies that see the results in their bottom lines.

Political/Legal The political/legal area includes laws, regulations, and political climate. Most U.S. laws and regulations are clear (e.g., those declaring dry counties in certain states), but others are complex and evolving (e.g., qualifications for certain tax breaks). Political climate includes changing levels of governmental support for various business categories. Clearly, the political/legal issues affect heavily regulated sectors (e.g., telecommunications and pharmaceuticals) more than others.

The Global Marketing Environment

As the Internet has grown, the world market has become accessible to virtually every business. This boosts the importance of understanding each element of the marketing

consumer behavior Description of how people act when they are buying, using, and discarding goods and services for their own personal consumption. Consumer behavior also explores the reasons behind people's actions.

environment—competitive, economic, social/cultural, technological, and political/legal—in each of your key markets. Among the biggest global challenges are researching opportunities in other countries and delivering your product to customers in other countries.

LO4 Customer Behavior: Decisions, Decisions, Decisions!

If successful marketing begins with the customer, then understanding the customer is critical. Why do people buy one product but not another? How do they use the products they buy? When do they get rid of them? Knowing the answers to these questions will clearly help you better meet customer needs.

Consumer Behavior

Consumer behavior refers specifically to how people act when they are buying products for their own personal consumption. The decisions they make often seem spontaneous (after all, how much thought do you give to buying a pack of gum?), but they often result from a complex set of influences, as shown in Exhibit 11.5.

Marketers, of course, add their own influence through the marketing mix. For instance, after smelling pretzels in the mall and tasting pretzel morsels from the sample tray, many of us would at least be tempted to cough up the cash for a hot, buttery pretzel of our own . . .

EXHIBIT 11.5 Elements That Influence the Consumer Decision-Making Process

INFLUENCE	DESCRIPTION
CULTURAL	*Culture:* The values, attitudes, and customs shared by members of a society *Subculture:* A smaller division of the broader culture *Social Class:* Societal position driven largely by income and occupation
SOCIAL	*Family:* A powerful force in consumption choices *Friends:* Another powerful force, especially for high-profile purchases *Reference Groups:* Groups that give consumers a point of comparison
PERSONAL	*Demographics:* Measurable characteristics such as age, gender, or income *Personality:* The mix of traits that determine who you are
PSYCHOLOGICAL	*Motivation:* Pressing needs that tend to generate action *Attitudes:* Lasting evaluations of (or feelings about) objects or ideas *Perceptions:* How people select, organize, and interpret information *Learning:* Changes in behavior based on experience

© Cengage Learning 2013

cognitive dissonance Consumer discomfort with a purchase decision, typically for a higher-priced item.

business buyer behavior Describes how people act when they are buying products to use either directly or indirectly to produce other products.

marketing research The process of gathering, interpreting, and applying information to uncover marketing opportunities and challenges, and to make better marketing decisions.

secondary data Existing data that marketers gather or purchase for a research project.

primary data New data that marketers compile for a specific research project.

regardless of any other factors! Similarly, changes in the external environment—for example, a series of hurricanes in Florida—dramatically affect consumer decisions about items such as flashlights, batteries, and plywood.

All these forces shape consumer behavior in each step of the process regarding purchase decisions. Exhibit 11.6 shows how the consumer decision process works.

Clearly, marketing can influence the purchase decision every step of the way, from helping consumers identify needs (or problems), to resolving that awful feeling of **cognitive dissonance** (or kicking oneself) after a major purchase. Some marketers attempt to avoid cognitive dissonance altogether by developing specific programs to help customers validate their purchase choices. One example might be postpurchase mailings that highlight the accolades received by an expensive product.

But does every consumer go through every step of the process all the time? That's clearly not the case! People make low-involvement decisions (such as buying that pack of gum) according to habit … or even just on a whim. But when the stakes are high—either financially or socially—most people move through the five steps of the classic decision-making process. For example, most of us wouldn't think of buying a car, a computer, or the "right" pair of blue jeans without stepping through the decision-making process.

Business Buyer Behavior

Business buyer behavior refers to how people act when they're buying products to use either directly or indirectly to produce other products (e.g., chemicals, copy paper, computer servers). Business buyers typically have purchasing training and apply rational criteria to their decision-making process. They usually buy according to purchase specifications and objective standards, with a minimum of personal judgment or whim. Often, business buyers are integrating input from a number of internal sources, based on a relatively formal process. And finally, business buyers tend to seek (and often secure) highly customized goods, services, and prices.

LO5 Marketing Research: So What Do They REALLY Think?

If marketing begins with the customer, marketing research is the foundation of success. **Marketing research** involves gathering, interpreting, and applying information to uncover opportunities and challenges. The goal, of course, is better marketing decisions: more value for consumers and more profits for businesses that deliver. Companies use marketing research to:

⊃ Identify external opportunities and threats (from social trends to competition).

⊃ Monitor and predict customer behavior.

⊃ Evaluate and improve each area of the marketing mix.

Types of Data

There are two main categories of marketing research data—**secondary data** and **primary data**—each with its own set of benefits and drawbacks, as shown in Exhibit 11.7.

EXHIBIT 11.6   Consumer Decision Process

Need Recognition
Your best friend suddenly notices that she is the only person she knows who still wears high-rise blue jeans to class...problem alert!

Information Search
Horrified, your friend not only checks out your style, but also notices what the cool girls on campus are wearing. AND she snitches your copy of *Cosmo* to leaf through the ads.

Evaluation of Alternatives
Your friend compares the prices and styles of the various brands of blue jeans that she identifies.

Purchase Decision
After a number of conversations, your friend finally decides to buy True Religion jeans for $215.

Postpurchase Behavior
Three days later, she begins to kick herself for spending so much money on jeans, because she can no longer afford her daily Starbucks habit.

© Cengage Learning 2013

Ooops! What were they thinking?

"If you can't be a good example, then you'll just have to serve as a horrible warning."

Even the heavy-hitters make marketing gaffes. Their biggest mistakes are often entertaining, but they also serve as a powerful warning to consult with the customer *before* taking action. A few amusing examples:

- ⊃ In mid-2009, Microsoft showed a photo on its U.S. website of three office workers—white, Asian American, and African American—and then changed the photo on the Polish version of the website to replace the head of the African American man with the head of a white man, while leaving the original hand of the African American man clearly visible. Although Microsoft quickly apologized and pulled the photo from its Polish site, they didn't clearly explain why they thought it made sense to mask the diversity of the photo in the first place.

- ⊃ In 2007, Hershey's introduced Ice Breakers Pacs, nickel-sized dissolvable pouches with a powdered sweetener inside. But they discontinued production in early 2008, in response to concerns from police narcotics officers and other community leaders that the mints too closely resembled tiny heat-sealed bags used to sell powdered street drugs. Announcing that the candy would be discontinued, Hershey's CEO commented that the company was "sensitive to these concerns." Apparently they weren't sensitive soon enough.

- ⊃ In 2009, Tropicana introduced a new package for its premium orange juice. The redesign supplanted the longtime Tropicana brand symbol—an orange from which a straw protrudes—with a picture of a glass of orange juice. Consumers were outraged. They described the package as "ugly," "stupid," and "generic." One even asked, "Do any of these package design people actually shop for orange juice?" Deluged with negative feedback, the company scrapped the new packaging less than two months after they introduced it.

- ⊃ In early 2010, the Denny's restaurant menu invited diners to join in the Denny's conversation at twitter.com/dennys. That Twitter account, however, is owned by a Taiwanese man named Dennys Hsieh. The Denny's restaurant account can actually be found on Twitter at twitter.com/dennysallnightr and twitter.com/dennysgrandslam.

These fiascos only highlight the importance of *marketing research*. But sometimes, of course, even research isn't enough to identify marketing issues before they hit. At that point, the priority should shift to dealing with the mistake openly, honestly, and quickly, which can help a company win the game, despite the gaffe.[10]

Clearly, it makes sense to gather secondary data before you invest in primary research. Look at your company's internal information. What does previous research say? What does the press say? What can you find on the Web? Once you've looked at the secondary research, you may find that primary research is unnecessary. But if not, your secondary research will guide your primary research and make it more focused and relevant, which ends up saving time and money.

Exhibit 11.7 Research Data Comparison

SECONDARY DATA:	PRIMARY DATA:
EXISTING DATA THAT MARKETERS GATHER OR PURCHASE	New data that marketers compile for the first time
TENDS TO BE LOWER COST	Tends to be more expensive
MAY NOT MEET YOUR SPECIFIC NEEDS	Customized to meet your needs
FREQUENTLY OUTDATED	Fresh, new data
AVAILABLE TO YOUR COMPETITORS	Proprietary—no one else has it
EXAMPLES: U.S. CENSUS, *THE WALL STREET JOURNAL*, *TIME* MAGAZINE, YOUR PRODUCT SALES HISTORY	Examples: Your own surveys, focus groups, customer comments, mall interviews

© Cengage Learning 2013

observation research Marketing research that *does not* require the researcher to interact with the research subject.

survey research Marketing research that requires the researcher to interact with the research subject.

Primary Research Tools

There are two basic categories of primary research: observation and survey. **Observation research** happens when the researcher *does not* directly interact with the research subject. The key advantage of watching versus asking is that what people actually *do* often differs from what they *say*—sometimes quite innocently. For instance, if an amusement park employee stands outside an attraction and records which way people turn when they exit, he may be conducting observation research to determine where to place a new lemonade stand. Watching would be better than asking because many people could not honestly say which way they'd likely turn. Examples of observation research include:

- Scanner data from retail sales.
- Traffic counters to determine where to place billboards.
- Garbage analysis to measure recycling compliance.

Observation research can be both cheap and amazingly effective. A car dealership, for instance, can survey the preset radio stations on every car that comes in for service. That information helps them choose which stations to use for advertising. But the biggest downside of observation research is that it doesn't yield any information on consumer motivation—the reasons behind consumer decisions. The preset radio stations wouldn't matter, for example, if the bulk of drivers listen only to CDs in the car.

Survey research happens when the researcher *does* interact with research subjects. The key advantage is that you can secure information about what people are thinking and feeling, beyond what you can observe. For example, a carmaker might observe that the majority of its purchasers are men. They could use this information to tailor their advertising to men, or they could do survey research and possibly learn that even though men do the actual purchasing, women often make the purchase decision . . . a very different scenario! But the key downside of survey research is that many people aren't honest or accurate about their experiences, opinions, and motivations, which can make survey research quite misleading. Examples of survey research include:

- Telephone and online questionnaires
- Door-to-door interviews

- Mall-intercept interviews
- Focus groups
- Mail-in questionnaires

An International Perspective

Doing marketing research across multiple countries can be an overwhelming challenge. In parts of Latin America, for instance, many homes don't have telephone

"It ain't easy being green"

Despite financial concerns, consumers around the world plan to spend more on green products, particularly in China, India, and Brazil. Although interest in sustainability and the environment is on the rise globally, the specific issues of interest vary from market to market. While reduction in use of toxic substances is important across the board, deforestation is the top priority issue in Brazil and India, water conservation is the top issue in Australia, and energy use is the top issue in the U.S. According to the 2010 ImagePower Green Brands survey, U.S. consumers rank the following brands "greenest":

1. Burt's Bees
2. Whole Foods
3. Tom's of Maine
4. Trader Joe's
5. Google
6. Aveeno
7. SC Johnson
8. Publix
9. Microsoft
10. IKEA

It's not surprising that each of these brands touts green credentials *and* performance in a simple, compelling message. Successful green marketers know that if a product doesn't perform, you won't buy it twice. They also know that green activists won't let them rest if their green claims are bogus. Delivering on both fronts—without a wallet-busting price—is a tough challenge that more marketers are racing to meet. Analysts have also noticed a trend toward "helper brands" that make going green easier for them through online communication. Worldwide, intellectuals and activists are the most credible spokespeople about green products, and to achieve success, marketers must reach them in a way that creates a groundswell of positive "buzz."[11]

connections, so the results from telephone surveys could be very misleading. Door-to-door tends to be a better approach. But in parts of the Middle East, researchers could be arrested for knocking on a stranger's door, especially if they aren't dressed according to local standards. Because of these kinds of issues, many companies hire research firms with a strong local presence (often based in-country) to handle their international marketing research projects.

On average, consumer spending on goods and services accounts for around 60% of world GDP.

—WORLD BUSINESS COUNCIL FOR SUSTAINABLE DEVELOPMENT

LO6 Social Responsibility and Technology: A Major Marketing Shift

Two key factors have had a dramatic impact on marketing in the last couple of decades: a surge in the social responsibility movement, and the dramatic emergence of the Internet and digital technology. This section will cover how each factor has influenced marketing.

Marketing and Society: It's Not Just About You!

Over the past couple of decades, the social responsibility movement has accelerated in the United States, demanding that marketers actively contribute to the needs of the broader community. Leading-edge marketers have responded by setting a higher standard in key areas such as environmentalism, abolishment of sweatshops, and involvement in the local community. Starbucks, Target, and General Electric, for instance, all publish corporate responsibility reports that evaluate the social impact of how the companies run their businesses, and all highlight their programs on their corporate websites.

Innovation: Unleashed!

In today's hyper-competitive marketplace, businesses must differentiate their products from an astonishing array of alternatives. While life-changing innovation is rare, many successful products simply provide a new twist on an existing product. Examples include Go-Gurt's portable yogurt in a tube, Arrowhead's Sport Top water bottles, and Colgate's pump toothpaste dispenser.

To help you make those kinds of jumps, the game in this box uses rebus puzzles to stretch your creativity. Rebus puzzles present common words and phrases in novel orientation to each other. The goal is to determine the meaning. The puzzles are below, and the answers are at the bottom of the box.

ARREST YOU'RE	HISTORY HISTORY HISTORY	Chimadena	print	BAN ANA
funny funny words words words words	ST4ANCE	herring	MEREPEAT	BPULSEIANSEUSRSE

Answers: You're under arrest, too funny for words, history repeats itself, for instance, made in China, red herring , small print, repeat after me, banana split, mixing business with pleasure

green marketing The development and promotion of products with ecological benefits.

mass customization The creation of products tailored for individual consumers on a mass basis.

Green Marketing Companies employ **green marketing** when they actively promote the ecological benefits of their products. Toyota has been especially successful promoting the green benefits of its Prius (although like all carmakers, Toyota has struggled during the global financial crisis and more recently, during the Japanese earthquake and tsunami). Its strategy highlights fuel economy and performance, implying that consumers can "go green" without making any real sacrifices. Environmentally friendly fashion offers another emerging example of green marketing. Over the past few years, a number of designers have rolled out their versions of upscale ecofashion. In addition to clothing made of organic cotton, recent entries include vegan stilettos with four-inch heels, bamboo dresses, biodegradable umbrellas, and solar-powered jackets, (These jackets feature solar cells, integrated into the collar, that collect solar energy and route it to charge devices.) Green marketing items are aimed at a growing number of consumers who make purchase decisions based (at least in part) on their convictions. But reaching these consumers may be an increasing challenge in tough economic times, when low prices trump all other considerations for a growing swath of the population.[12]

Technology and Marketing: Power to the People!

The emergence of the digital age has revolutionized every element of marketing. Perhaps the most dramatic change has been a shift in power from producers to customers. The Internet gives customers 24/7 access to information and product choices from all over the world. In response, competition has intensified as marketers strive to meet an increasingly high standard of value.

Just over 20% of people say they think most creatively in their cars, while 5% say they think most creatively in the shower, and—surprisingly—only 1% say they think most creatively while listening to music.

—M.I.T. Invention Index

But technology has also created opportunities for marketers. The Internet has opened the door for **mass customization:** creating products tailored for individual consumers on a mass basis. Using sophisticated data collection and management systems, marketers can now collect detailed information about each customer, which allows them to develop one-on-one relationships and to identify high-potential new customers. Through the Web, marketers can tap into (or even create) communities of users that yield valuable information about their goods and services. Technology also helps marketers lower costs, so they can deliver greater value to their customers.

The digital boom has also created an abundance of promotional opportunities as marketers reach out to consumers via new tools, such as interactive advertising, virtual reality displays, text messaging, and video kiosks. We'll discuss these tools in more detail in Chapter 12.

THE BIG PICTURE

Since the ultimate goal of most marketing is long-term profitability, a core marketing principle must infuse every facet of a successful organization: the need to deliver products that exceed customer expectations. The customer must come first for *every* department—including finance, accounting, engineering, manufacturing, and human resources—although the specifics of how that plays out will clearly differ for each organizational function. Competition in the future will only intensify. Customer choices will continue to multiply as globalization and technology march forward. While these forces will weed out the weaker players, firms with a deeply engrained marketing orientation and a strong customer focus will continue to flourish—delivering value to their stakeholders, and dollars to their bottom line.

CAREERS

Since the marketing concept permeates every aspect of successful organizations, you won't be surprised to learn that virtually every position in business requires an understanding of basic marketing principles. Furthermore, the spectrum of marketing positions is very wide, ranging from sales, to advertising, to public relations, to brand management, to marketing research, and increasingly, social media marketing. Entry-level positions will have titles such as assistant, analyst, and coordinator, moving up to manager and director slots, and top-level positions are typically at the vice-presidential or corporate officer level. Most positions require a college degree, and many also demand an MBA. In 2010 and 2011, the starting median salary for undergraduate marketing majors was $38,600, and the median mid-career salary was $77,300. According to the Bureau of Labor Statistics, marketing management jobs are likely to increase about 13% by 2018.[13]

What *else?*

RIP & REVIEW CARDS IN THE BACK
and visit www.cengagebrain.com!

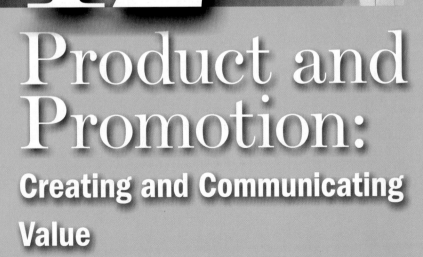

12

Product and Promotion:

Creating and Communicating

Value

LEARNING OBJECTIVES

After studying this chapter, you will be able to…

LO1 Explain "product" and identify product classifications

LO2 Describe product differentiation and the key elements of product planning

LO3 Discuss innovation and the product life cycle

LO4 Analyze and explain promotion and integrated marketing communications

LO5 Discuss development of the promotional message

LO6 Discuss the promotional mix and the various promotional tools

> CUSTOMERS
> BUY FOR
> *THEIR*
> REASONS, NOT
> YOURS.
>
> — ORVEL RAY WILSON, CONSULTANT

Product and promotional strategy are the two most visible elements of the promotional mix: what benefits are you offering consumers, and how are you communicating those benefits? This chapter covers product and promotional strategies separately, but as you read, keep in mind that effective marketers carefully interweave all the elements of the marketing mix—including distribution and pricing strategies—to create a coherent whole that's even stronger than the sum of the parts.

LO1 Product: It's Probably More Than You Thought

When most people hear the term "product," they immediately think of the material things that we buy and use and consume every day: for example, an Android cell phone or a pair of 7 jeans. But from a marketing standpoint, product means much more. A **product** can be anything that a company offers to satisfy consumer needs and wants; the possibilities include not only physical goods but also services and ideas. A car wash, laser eye surgery, and a cooking lesson all qualify as products.

When you buy a product, you also "buy" all of the attributes associated with the product. These encompass a broad range of qualities, such as the brand name, the image, the packaging, the reputation, and the guarantee. From a consumer standpoint, these attributes (or the lack of these attributes) are part of the product purchase, even if they don't add to its value. As a marketer, it's worth your while to carefully consider each element of your product

to ensure that you're maximizing value without sacrificing profitability. With the introduction of the translucent, multicolored iMac computers in 1998, Apple established its reputation for creating value through product design—an attribute that other PC manufacturers completely overlooked as they churned out their inventories of boring, beige boxes. Over the years, Apple has continued to polish its reputation by introducing sleek, elegantly designed products such as its iPad tablet computers and its iPhones.

product Anything that an organization offers to satisfy consumer needs and wants, including both goods and services.

Services: A Product by Any Other Name...

If a "product" includes anything that satisfies consumer needs, services clearly fit the bill. But services have some obvious differences from tangible goods. You often cannot see, hear, smell, taste, or touch a service, and you can virtually never "own" it. After a haircut, for example, you might possess great-looking hair, but you don't own the haircutting experience (at least not literally). Most services embody these qualities:

- **Intangibility:** You typically cannot see, smell, taste, or touch a service before you buy it. Clearly, this creates a lot of uncertainty. Will the purchase really be worthwhile? Smart marketers mitigate the uncertainty by giving clues that suggest value. For example, the Formosa Café, a funky, old-time Hollywood bar and restaurant, plasters the walls with signed pictures of movie stars, providing "evidence" of its movie biz credentials.

- **Inseparability:** Try as you might, you simply can't separate the buyer of a service from the person who renders it. Delivery requires interaction between the buyer and the provider, and the customer directly contributes to the quality of the service. Consider a trip to the doctor. If you accurately describe your symptoms, you're likely to get a correct diagnosis. But if you simply say, "I just don't feel normal," the outcome will likely be different.

- **Variability:** This one ties closely to inseparability. A talented masseuse would probably help you relax, whereas a mediocre one might actually create tension. And even the talented masseuse might give better service at the end of the day than at the beginning, or worse service on the day she breaks up with her boyfriend. Variability also applies to the difference among providers. A massage at a top-notch spa is likely to be better than a massage at your local gym.

○ **Perishability:** Marketers cannot store services for delivery at peak periods. A restaurant, for instance, only has so many seats; they can't (reasonably) tell their 8 p.m. dinner customers to come back the next day at 5 p.m. Similarly, major tourist destinations, such as Las Vegas, can't store an inventory of room service deliveries or performances of Cirque du Soleil. This creates obvious cost issues; is it worthwhile to prepare for a peak crowd but lose money when it's slow? The answer depends on the economics of your business.

Goods Versus Services: A Mixed Bag

Identifying whether a product is a good or a service can pose a considerable challenge, since many products contain elements of both. A meal at your local Italian restaurant obviously includes tangible goods: You definitely own that calzone. But someone else took your order, brought it to the table, and (perhaps most importantly) did the dishes! Service was clearly a crucial part of the package.

A goods and services spectrum can provide a valuable tool for analyzing the relationship between the two. (See Exhibit 12.1.) At one extreme, **pure goods** don't include any services. Examples include a bottle of shampoo or a package of pasta. At the other extreme, **pure services** don't include any goods. Examples include financial consulting or math tutoring. Other products—such as a meal at Pizza Hut—fall somewhere between the poles.

Product Layers: Peeling the Onion

When customers buy products, they actually purchase more than just the good or service itself. They buy a complete product package that includes a core benefit, the actual product, and product augmentations. Understanding these layers is valuable, since the most successful products delight consumers at each one of them.

Core Benefit At the most fundamental level, consumers buy a *core benefit* that satisfies their needs. When you go to a concert, the core benefit is entertainment. When you buy a motorcycle, the core benefit is transportation. And when you go to the gym, the core benefit is fitness. Most products also provide secondary benefits that help distinguish them from other goods and services that meet the same customer needs. A secondary benefit of a motorcycle might include the thrill of the ride.

Actual Product

This *actual product* layer, of course, is the product itself: the physical good or the delivered service that provides the core benefit. A U2 concert is the actual "service" that provides a live music experience. A Kawasaki Ninja is the actual product that provides a thrilling ride. Sports Club LA is the actual gym that provides fitness. Identifying the actual product is sometimes tough when the product is a service. For example, the core benefit of personal training might be weight loss, but the actual product may be some very fit person haranguing you to do ten more sit-ups. Keep in mind that the actual product includes all of the attributes that make it unique, such as the brand name, the features, and the packaging.

Augmented Product Most marketers wrap their actual products in additional goods and services, called the *augmented product*, that sharpen their competitive edge. Augmentations come in a range of different forms, such as warranties, free service, and customer help lines. A U2 concert might give fans a chance to win backstage passes. The Kawasaki Ninja usually comes with a two-year warranty and free dealer prep. And Sports Club LA offers valet parking, overnight laundry service, and delicious smoothies.

Product Classification: It's a Bird, It's a Plane...

Products fall into two broad categories—consumer products and business products—depending on the reason for the purchase. **Consumer products** are purchased for personal use or consumption, while

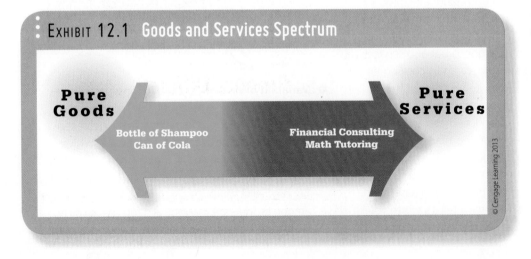

EXHIBIT 12.1 Goods and Services Spectrum

Pure Goods — Bottle of Shampoo, Can of Cola — Financial Consulting, Math Tutoring — Pure Services

© Cengage Learning 2013

business products are purchased to use either directly or indirectly in the production of another product. The bag of chips that you buy to eat is a consumer product, while the bag of chips that a Subway owner buys to sell is a business product.

Consumer Product Categories Marketers further divide consumer products into several different subcategories, as shown below. Understanding the characteristics of the subcategories can help marketers develop better strategies.

- ☉ *Convenience products* are the inexpensive goods and services that consumers buy frequently with limited consideration and analysis. Distribution tends to be widespread, with promotion by the producers. Examples include staples such as milk and toothpaste, impulse items such as candy bars and magazines, and emergency products such as headache tablets and plumbing services.

- ☉ *Shopping products* are the more expensive products that consumers buy less frequently. Typically, as consumers shop, they search for the best value and learn more about features and benefits through the shopping process. Distribution is widespread but more selective than for convenience products. Both producers and retailers tend to promote shopping products. Examples include computers, appliances, and maid services.

- ☉ *Specialty products* are those much more expensive products that consumers seldom purchase. Most people perceive specialty products as being so important that they are unwilling to accept substitutes. Because of this, distribution tends to be highly selective. (Consumers are willing to go far out of their way for the "right" brand.) Both producers and retailers are apt to promote specialty products, but to a highly targeted audience. Some specialty product examples are Lamborghini sports cars, Tiffany jewelry, and Rolex watches.

- ☉ *Unsought products* are the goods and services that hold little interest (or even negative interest) for consumers. Price and distribution vary wildly, but promotion tends to be aggressive to drum up consumer interest. Home warranties, prepaid legal services, and blood donations are some examples.

Business Product Categories Marketers also divide business products into subcategories. Here, too, understanding the subcategories can lead to better marketing strategies.

- ☉ *Installations* are large capital purchases designed for a long productive life. The marketing of installations emphasizes personal selling and customization. Examples include industrial robots, new buildings, and railroad cars.

- ☉ *Accessory equipment* includes smaller, movable capital purchases, designed for a shorter productive life than installations. Marketing focuses on personal selling but includes less customization than installations. Examples include personal computers, copy machines, and furniture.

- ☉ The *maintenance, repair, and operating products* category consists of small-ticket items that businesses consume on an ongoing basis, but don't become part of the final product. Marketing tactics emphasize efficiency. Examples include brooms, nails, and lubricants.

- ☉ *Raw materials* include the farm and natural products used in producing other products. Marketing emphasizes price and service rather than product differentiation. Examples include cotton, turkeys, and oil.

- ☉ *Component parts and processed materials* include finished (or partially finished) products used in producing other products. Marketing emphasizes product quality as well as price and service. Examples include batteries for cars and aluminum ingots for soda cans.

- ☉ *Business services* are those services that businesses purchase to facilitate operations. Marketing focuses on quality and relationships; the role of price can vary. Examples include payroll services, marketing research, and legal services.

> **business products**
> Products purchased to use either directly or indirectly in the production of other products.
>
> **product differentiation**
> The attributes that make a good or service different from other products that compete to meet the same or similar customer needs.

L02 Product Differentiation and Planning: A Meaningful Difference

While some products have succeeded with little or no forethought, you'll dramatically boost your chance of a hit with careful planning. **Product differentiation** should be a key consideration. Winning products must embody a real or

© Simon Lord/Alamy

perceived difference versus the glut of goods and services that compete in virtually every corner of the market. But different alone isn't enough; different from, and better than, the competition are both critical in order to create form the shortest path to success. A quick look at some high-profile product failures illustrates the point.

⊙ **Nehru suits:** In the 1960s, fashion experts predicted that Nehru suits—with their oddly tailored collars—would be a major hit. Few were disappointed when that trend fizzled.

⊙ **Clear Beer:** In the 1990s, several companies introduced clear beers, reflecting an ill-fated obsession with clear products, including shampoo, soap, and the short-lived, clear Crystal Pepsi.

⊙ **Funky French Fries:** In 2002, Ore-Ida introduced Funky Fries. The flavors included cinnamon-sugar, chocolate, and "radical blue." Not surprisingly, they were off the market in less than a year.

Product Quality

Product quality relates directly to product value, which comes from understanding your customer. Peter Drucker, a noted business thinker, writer, and educator, declared:

Quality in a product or service is not what the supplier puts in. It's what the customer gets out and is willing to pay for. A product is not quality because it is hard to make and costs a lot of money ... this is incompetence. Customers pay only for what is of use to them and gives them value. Nothing else constitutes quality.

In other words, a high-quality product does a great job meeting customer needs. Seimans, a huge electronics conglomerate, embodies this thinking in its approach to quality: "Quality is when our customers come back and our products don't."

But the specific definition of quality—and the attributes that indicate quality—changes across product categories. Here are a few examples:

Regardless of product category, the two key aspects of quality are level and consistency. **Quality level** refers to how well a product performs its core functions. You might think that smart companies deliver the highest possible level of performance, but this is seldom profitable, or even desirable. For instance, only a tiny group of consumers would pay for a speed boat to go 200 mph, when 80 mph offers a sufficient thrill (at least for most of us!). The right level of product performance is the level that meets the needs of your consumers, and those needs include price. Decisions about quality level must also consider the competition. The goal is to outperform the other players in your category while maintaining profitability.

The second dimension of quality is **product consistency**. How consistently does your product actually deliver the promised level of quality? With a positive relationship between price and performance, consistent delivery can offer a competitive edge at almost any quality level.

Honda offers an excellent example. When most people consider the Accord, the Civic, and the CRV, all Honda-owned models, quality quickly comes to mind. And all three dominate their markets. But clearly, the quality *levels* (and price) are is different for each. The Accord serves the upper, more conservative end of the market; the Civic tends to appeal to younger, hipper, more budget-minded consumers; the CRV tends to appeal to middle-of-the-road shoppers seeking a reliable, small SUV. In short, Honda succeeds at delivering product consistency at several markedly different quality levels.

Features and Benefits

Product features are the characteristics of the product you offer. If a product is well designed, each feature corresponds to a meaningful **customer benefit**. The marketer's challenge is to design a package of features that offers the highest level of value for an acceptable price. And the equation must also account for profitability goals.

One winning formula may be to offer at least some low-cost features that correspond to high-value benefits. Creating an "open kitchen" restaurant, for instance, has limited impact on costs, but gives patrons an exciting, up-close view of the drama and hustle of professional food preparation. Exhibit 12.3 lists some other examples of product features and their corresponding customer benefits.

Exhibit 12.2 Product Quality Indicators

PRODUCT CATEGORY	SOME QUALITY INDICATORS
INTERNET SEARCH ENGINES	Fast, relevant, and far-reaching results
STYLISH BLUE JEANS	High-profile designer, high price, and celebrity customers
TV EDITING EQUIPMENT	Reliability, flexibility, and customer service
ROLLER COASTERS	Thrill factor, design, and setting
CHAIN SAWS	Effectiveness, safety, and reliability

© Cengage Learning 2013

Quality is remembered long after the price is forgotten.

— GUCCI FAMILY SLOGAN

Product Lines and the Product Mix

Some companies focus all of their efforts on one product, but most offer a number of different products to enhance their revenue and profits. A **product line** is a group of products that are closely related to each other, in terms of either how they work or the customers they serve. Amazon's first product line was books. To meet the needs of as many book lovers as possible, Amazon carries well over a million different titles in its product line. A **product mix** is the total number of product lines and individual items sold by a single firm. Amazon's product mix includes a wide range of product lines, from books, to electronics, to toys (to name just a few!).

Decisions regarding how many items to include in each product line and in the overall product mix can have a huge impact on a firm's profits. With too few items in each line, the company may be leaving money on the table. With too many items, the company may be spending unnecessarily to support its weakest links.

One reason that firms add new product lines is to reach completely new customers. Gap, for instance, added Old Navy to reach younger, lower-income customers, and Banana Republic to reach older, higher-income customers. Each line includes a range of different products designed to meet the needs of their specific customers. But one risk of adding new lines—especially lower-priced lines—is **cannibalization**, which happens when a new entry "eats" the sales of an existing line.

This is especially dangerous when the new products are lower-priced than the current ones. You could see the problem, for instance, if a $20 blue jean purchase from Old Navy replaces a $50 blue jean purchase from Gap; the company has lost more than half its revenue on the sale. Like other companies with multiple lines, Gap carefully monitors the cannibalization issue and works to differentiate its lines as fully as possible.

Branding

At the most basic level, a **brand** is a product's identity that sets it apart from other players in the same category. Typically, brands represent the combination of elements such as product name, symbol, design, reputation, and image. But today's most powerful emerging brands go far beyond the sum of their attributes. They project a compelling group identity that creates brand fanatics: loyal customers who advocate for the brand better than any advertising a marketer could buy. The overall value of a brand to an organization—the extra money that consumers will spend to buy that brand—is called **brand equity**.

Since 2001, *BusinessWeek* and Interbrand, a leading brand consultancy, have teamed up to publish a ranking of the 100 Best Global Brands by dollar value. The top ten brands are listed in Exhibit 12.4, but you can find the complete list at Interbrand's website.

> **product line** A group of products that are closely related to each other, either in terms of how they work, or the customers they serve.
>
> **product mix** The total number of product lines and individual items sold by a single firm.
>
> **cannibalization** When a producer offers a new product that takes sales away from its existing products.
>
> **brand** A product's identity—including product name, symbol, design, reputation, and image—that sets it apart from other players in the same category.
>
> **brand equity** The overall value of a brand to an organization.

Exhibit 12.3 Product Features and Customer Benefits

PRODUCT	PRODUCT FEATURE	CUSTOMER BENEFIT
SUBWAY SANDWICHES	Lower fat	Looser pants
GROUPON	Great deals on valuable products and services	More cash for other needs
WHOLE FOODS MARKET	Organic produce	A healthier planet
GPS SYSTEM	Gives you accurate directions with little or no hassle	You don't get lost/arrive late
TRIPLE LATTE	Caffeine, caffeine, caffeine	More time to, uh, study

© Cengage Learning 2013

Exhibit 12.4 *BusinessWeek*/Interbrand Top Ten Global Brands

BRAND	COUNTRY OF OWNERSHIP
COCA-COLA	United States
IBM	United States
MICROSOFT	United States
GOOGLE	United States
GE	United States
MCDONALD'S	United States
INTEL	United States
NOKIA	Finland
DISNEY	United States
HP	United States

Source: *BusinessWeek* "100 Best Global Brands," http://bwnt.businessweek.com/interactive_reports/best_global_brands_2009/, accessed December 14, 2009.

Brand Name A catchy, memorable name is among the most powerful elements of your brand. While the right name will never save a bad business, it can launch a good business to new heights. But finding the right name can be tough. According to the respected Brighter Naming consulting group, the following characteristics can help:

1. Short, sweet, and easy to pronounce and spell: Examples include Dell, Gap, Dove, Tide, and Kool-Aid.

2. Unique within the industry: Think Apple, Monster, jetBlue, and Victoria's Secret.

3. Good alliteration, especially for long names: The words should roll off your tongue. Some examples are Coca-Cola, BlackBerry, and Minute Maid.[1]

Brand names typically fall into four categories, as described in Exhibit 12.5.

Line Extensions versus Brand Extensions

As companies grow, marketers look for opportunities to grow their businesses. **Line extensions** are similar products offered under the same brand name. Possibilities include new flavors, sizes, colors, ingredients, and forms. One example is Coca-Cola, which offers versions with lemon, lime, vanilla; with caffeine, without caffeine, with sugar, and without sugar. The marketing challenge is to ensure that line extensions steal market share from competitors rather than from the core brand.

Brand extensions, on the other hand, involve launching a product in a new category under an existing brand name. The Bic brand, for instance, is quite elastic, stretching nicely to include diverse products such as pens, glue, cigarette lighters, and disposable razors. The Virgin brand demonstrates similar elasticity, covering more than 350 companies that range from airlines, to cell phones, to soft drinks, to cars. But the concept of brand extension becomes most clear (and most entertaining) through examining brand extension failures. Examples include Bic perfume, Budweiser Dry, and Harley-Davidson Cologne.[2]

Licensing Some companies opt to license their brands from other businesses. **Licensing** means purchasing—often for a substantial fee—the right to use another company's brand name or symbol. The benefits, of course, are instant name recognition, an established reputation, and a proven track record. On a worldwide basis, the best-known licensing arrangements are probably character names, which range from Bart Simpson to Sponge Bob and appear on everything from cereal, to toys, to underwear. Many movie producers also do high-profile licensing, turning out truckloads of merchandise that features movie properties such as Harry Potter and *Twilight*.

Another fast-growing area is the licensing of corporate names. Coca-Cola, for instance, claims to have more than 300 licensees who sell over a billion dollars of licensed merchandise each year. The potential benefits for Coca-Cola are clear: more promotion, increased exposure, and enhanced image. But the risk is significant. If licensed products are of poor quality or overpriced, the consumer backlash hits the core brand rather than the producer of the licensed product.

Cobranding Cobranding is when established brands from different companies join forces to market the same product. This cooperative approach has a long history but is currently enjoying a new popularity. Examples include:

- Ford Explorer markets an Eddie Bauer model.
- Kohl's markets Vera Wang's fashions under the name Simply Vera.
- Kmart markets Martha Stewart housewares.

Cobranding can offer huge advantages to both partners, by leveraging their strengths to enter new markets and gain more exposure. Through the Kohl's–Wang agreement, Vera Wang gained exposure to a mass audience (and their shopping dollars), while Kohl's bolstered its image by gaining exclusive rights to trendy fashions. But cobranding can be risky. If one partner makes a major goof (think Martha Stewart), the fallout can damage the reputation of the other partner as well.

National Brands Versus Store Brands National brands, also called *manufacturers' brands*, are brands that the

Exhibit 12.5 Brand Name Categories

CATEGORY	DESCRIPTION	EXAMPLES
LOCATION-BASED	Refers to either the area served or the place of origin	Southwest Airlines, Bank of America, Best Western Hotels
FOUNDER'S NAME	Can include first name, last name, or both	McDonald's, Suzy's Sub Sandwiches, Ford, Disney, Hewlett-Packard
DESCRIPTIVE OR FUNCTIONAL	Describes what the product is or how it works	eBay, U.S. News and World Report, Weight Watchers, Krispy Kreme
EVOCATIVE	Communicates an engaging image that resonates with consumers	Yahoo!, Craftsman, Virgin, Intel, Lunchables, Cosmopolitan, Starbucks

© Cengage Learning 2013

producer owns and markets. Many are well-known and widely available, such as Pantene shampoo, Tide detergent, and 7-Up. Although most retailers carry lots of national brands, an increasing number have opted to also carry their own versions of the same products, called **store brands**, or *private label*. Deep discounters, such as Walmart and Costco, have had particular success with their private-label brands (e.g., Sam's Choice and Kirkland). *Private labels* play a growing role in grocery stores as well. In the United States, about one out of four grocery purchases is private label, and the numbers are even higher in Europe—hitting half of all grocery sales in a number of markets. As the global recession deepened in 2008 and 2009, private-label sales increased by more than 7%. But by 2011, as the economic recovery gained traction, fewer consumers traded down to private-label options. The growing influence and increasing quality of low-end private-label brands increase the pressure on national brands to continually innovate while holding down prices.[3]

© s70/ZUMA Press/Newscom

At the upper end of the market—especially in the clothing business—key retailers specialize in private brands to create and protect a consistent, upscale image. Examples include Neiman Marcus, Coldwater Creek, and Saks Fifth Avenue. Private-label clothing accounts for more than 40% of all U.S. apparel sales.[4]

Packaging

Great packaging does more than just hold the product. It can protect the product, provide information, facilitate storage, suggest product uses, promote the product brand, and attract buyer attention. Great packaging is especially important in the crowded world of grocery stores and mass merchandisers. In the average supermarket, the typical shopper passes about 300 items per minute and makes anywhere from 20% to 70% of purchases on sheer impulse. In this environment, your package must call out to your target customers and differentiate your product from all

Ooops! What were they thinking?

Oops! If You Drive a Yugo, Maybe You Will Go and Maybe You Won't Go...

The tiny Yugo hatchback hit the U.S. market with great fanfare in the summer of 1985. Billed as the cheapest new car in the United States, the Yugoslavian import captured the imagination of the consumer market. Eager buyers stormed the dealerships before the first cars were off the boat. The price was an unimaginably low $3,990.

But low price wasn't enough. As buyers began to actually drive their cars, they uncovered flaw after flaw, including major issues such as premature engine failure and poor dealer service. Reviewers described the Yugo as more of a toy than a car. Not surprisingly, sales plummeted, leading to bankruptcy in 1989.

The short life of the Yugo was long enough to establish its place as a cultural icon of cheap. Countless disillusioned owners competed to coin the best description of their Yugo. Sample comments from the CarTalk website (which featured the Yugo as the worst car of the millennium):

"The Yugo's first stop after the showroom was the service department; 'Fill 'er up and replace the engine!'"
"At least it had heated rear windows—so your hands would stay warm while you pushed."

But despite its problems (or perhaps because of them!) the Yugo also spawned a remarkable artistic effort. A professor at the NYC School of Visual Arts challenged his students several years ago to turn discarded Yugos into something useful. The results, displayed for a time in New York City's Union Station, included a toaster, a Port-o-Potty, a confessional, a diner, and a submarine.[5]

the others lined up beside it. Yet, in attracting consumer attention, a good package cannot sacrifice the basics such as protecting the product.[6]

Bottom line: great packaging stems from consumer needs, but it usually includes at least a smidge of creative brilliance. Examples include yogurt in a pouch that doesn't need a spoon, soup-to-go that can be microwaved in the can, and single-serving baby carrot packets that moms can toss into kids' lunches.

LO3 Innovation and the Product Life Cycle: Nuts, Bolts, and a Spark of Brilliance

For a business to thrive long term, effective new product development is vital. And the process works only if it happens quickly. As technological advances hit the market at breakneck speed, current products are becoming obsolete faster than ever before. The need for speed compounds as hungry competitors crowd every niche of the market. But the rush is risky, since new product development costs can be in the millions, and the success rate is less than a third. Marketers who succeed in this challenging arena devote painstaking effort to understanding their customers, but they also nurture the creativity they need to generate new ideas. An example of how this can work: The 3M Corporation—makers of Post-it notes and Scotch Tape—introduces about 500 new products per year by pushing its employees to "relentlessly ask, "What if?" 3M also encourages workers to spend 15% of their work time (paid work time!) on projects of personal interest.[7]

Types of Innovation

Clearly, the first personal computer represented a higher degree of newness than the first personal computer with a color screen. And the computer with a color screen represented a higher degree of newness than the first low-cost knockoff. Levels of innovation fall along a spectrum, as shown in Exhibit 12.6.

Discontinuous Innovation *Discontinuous innovations* are brand-new ideas that radically change how people live. Examples include the first car, the first television, and the first computer. These dramatic innovations require extensive customer learning, which should guide the marketing process.

Dynamically Continuous Innovation *Dynamically continuous innovations* are characterized by marked changes to existing products. Examples include cell phones, MP3 players, and digital cameras. These types of innovations require a moderate level of consumer learning in exchange for significant benefits.

Continuous Innovation A slight modification of an existing product is called a *continuous innovation*. Examples include new sizes, flavors, shapes, packaging, and design. The goal of continuous innovation is to distinguish a product from the competition. The goal of a knockoff is simply to copy a competitor and offer a lower price.

The New Product Development Process

An efficient, focused development process will boost your chances of new product success. The standard model includes six stages:

Each stage requires management to "green light" ideas before moving forward, to ensure that the company doesn't waste resources on marginal concepts.

- **Idea Generation:** Some experts estimate that it takes 50 ideas for each new product that makes it to market, so you should definitely cast a wide net. Ideas can come from almost anywhere, including customer research, customer complaints, salespeople, engineers, suppliers, and competitors.

- **Idea Screening:** The purpose of this stage is to weed out ideas that don't fit with the company's objectives and ideas that would clearly be too expensive to develop. the Walt Disney Company, for instance, would

EXHIBIT 12.6
Levels of Innovation

© Cengage Learning 2013

Discontinuous Innovation

Dynamically Continuous Innovation

Continuous Innovation

> ## If you're not failing every now and again, it's a sign you're not doing anything very innovative.
>
> — Woody Allen, FILM DIRECTOR

certainly eliminate the idea of a XXX cable channel because it just doesn't fit their mission.

- **Analysis:** The purpose of the analysis stage is to estimate costs and forecast sales for each idea to get a sense of the potential profit and of how the product might fit within the company's resources. Each idea must meet rigorous standards to remain a contender.

- **Development:** The development process leads to detailed descriptions of each concept with specific product features. New product teams sometimes also make prototypes, or samples, that consumers can actually test. The results help fully refine the concept.

- **Testing:** This stage involves the formal process of soliciting feedback from consumers by testing the product concept. Do they like the features? Are the benefits meaningful? What price makes sense? Some companies also test-market their products or sell them in a limited area to evaluate the consumer response.

- **Commercialization:** This stage entails introducing the product to the general market. Two key success

factors are gaining distribution and launching promotion. But a product that tested well doesn't always mean instant success. The VW Beetle, for example, sold only 330 cars during its first year in the United States, but it later became a hit.

New Product Adoption and Diffusion

In order to become a commercial success, new products must spread throughout a market after they are introduced. That process is called *diffusion*. But diffusion clearly happens at different speeds, depending on the individual consumer and on the product itself.

Product Adoption Categories Some consumers like to try new things; others seem terrified of change. These attitudes clearly affect the rate at which individual people are willing to adopt (or begin buying and using) new products. The first adopters, about 2.5% of the total, are adventurous risk takers. The laggards, about 16% of the total, sometimes adopt products so late that earlier adopters have already moved to the next new thing. The rest of the population falls somewhere in between. Keep in mind that individuals tend to adopt new products at different rates. For instance, we probably all know someone who is an innovator in technology but a laggard in fashion, or vice-versa.

Product Diffusion Rates Some new products diffuse into the population much more quickly than others. For example, Apple iPods and Segway Human Transporters appeared on the market around the same time; iPods have become a pop culture icon, while Segways remain on the fringe. What accounts for the difference? Researchers have identified five product characteristics that affect the rate of adoption and diffusion. The

Wacky Labels

As product lawsuits take on a life of their own, manufacturers are responding with warning labels that seem increasingly wacky. To call attention to this trend, a Michigan anti-lawsuit group called M-LAW sponsors the annual Wacky Warning Label Contest. Top finishers over the past few years have included the following gems:

- A toilet brush tag that says "Do not use for personal hygiene."

- A bag of livestock castration rings warns, "For animal use only."

- A "drive 'n talk" speakerphone labeled, "Never operate your speakerphone while driving."

- A Bluetooth headset that warns, "Use of a headset that covers both ears will impair your ability to hear other sounds."

- A disappearing ink marker that cautions "The Vanishing Fabric Marker should not be used as a writing instrument for signing checks or any legal documents."[8]

!
WARNING
For animal use only

©Login/Shutterstock.com

more characteristics a product has, the faster it will diffuse into the population.

- **Observability:** How visible is the product to other potential consumers? Some product categories are easier to observe than others. If you adopt a new kind of car, the whole neighborhood will know, plus anyone else who sees you on the streets and highways.

- **Trialability:** How easily can potential consumers sample the new product? Trial can be a powerful way to create new consumers, which is why many markets fill their aisles with sample tables during popular shopping hours. Other examples of trial-boosting strategies include test-driving cars, sampling music, and testing new fragrances.

- **Complexity:** Can potential consumers easily understand what your product is and how it works? If your product confuses people—or if they find it hard to explain to others—adoption rates will slow. For example, many people who test-ride Segway Human Transporters love the experience, but they have trouble explaining to others how it works or why it beats other transportation options.

- **Compatibility:** How consistent is your product with the existing way of doing things? Cordless phones,

for example, caught on almost instantly, since they were completely consistent with people's prior experiences—only better!

- **Relative Advantage:** How much better are the benefits of your new product compared to existing products? When gas prices climb, for example, the benefits of a hybrid car take on a much higher value relative to standard cars. As a result, demand skyrockets.

The Product Life Cycle: Maximizing Results over Time

When marketers introduce a new product, they hope it will last forever, generating sales and profits for years to come. But they also realize that all products go through a **product life cycle**: a pattern of sales and profits that typically changes over time. The life cycle can be dramatically different across individual products and product categories, and predicting the exact shape and length of the life cycle is virtually impossible. But most product categories do move through the four distinct stages shown in Exhibit 12.7.

- **Introduction:** This is a time of low sales and nonexistent profits as companies invest in raising awareness about the product and the product category. Some categories, such as the microwave, languish in this phase for years, while other categories, such as computer memory sticks, zoom through this phase. And some categories never get beyond introduction. (Think clear beers.)

- **Growth:** During the growth period, sales continue to rise, although profits usually peak. Typically, competitors begin to notice emerging categories in the growth phase. They enter the market—often with new variations of existing products—which further fuels the growth. Portable MP3 players are

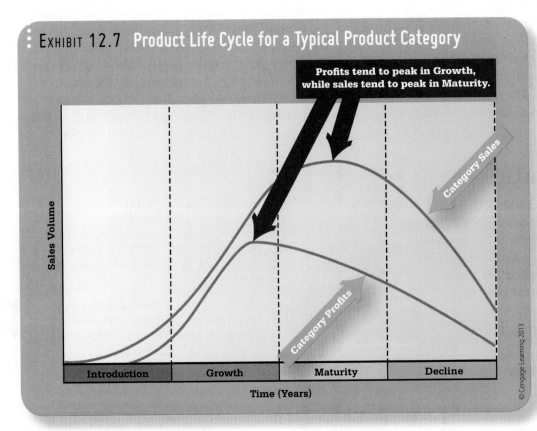

EXHIBIT 12.7 Product Life Cycle for a Typical Product Category

Profits tend to peak in Growth, while sales tend to peak in Maturity.

Category Sales

Category Profits

Sales Volume

Introduction | Growth | Maturity | Decline

Time (Years)

© Cengage Learning 2013

currently in the growth phase, and a number of competitors are challenging Apple's hold on the market.

- ⊙ **Maturity:** During maturity, sales usually peak. Profits continue to decline as competition intensifies. Once a market is mature, the only way to gain more users is to steal them from competitors, rather than to bring new users into the category. Weaker players begin to drop out of the category. Gasoline-powered cars and network TV are in maturity in the United States.

- ⊙ **Decline:** During this period, sales and profits begin to decline, sometimes quite rapidly. The reasons usually relate to either technological change or change in consumer needs. For instance, the introduction of word processing pushed typewriters into decline, and a change in consumer taste and habits pushed hot cereal into decline. Competitors continue to drop out of the category.

Familiarity with the product life cycle helps marketers plan effective strategies for existing products and identify profitable categories for new products. Exhibit 12.8 summarizes typical marketing strategies and offers examples for each phase.

Individual products also have life cycles that usually follow the category growth pattern but sometimes vary dramatically. Clearly, it's in the marketer's best interest to extend the profitable run of an individual brand as long as possible. There are several ways to make this happen: finding new uses for the product, changing the product, and changing the marketing mix. For example, *American Idol* renewed interested in their franchise by introducing new celebrity judges.

promotion Marketing communication designed to influence consumer purchase decisions through information, persuasion, and reminders.

LO4 Promotion: Influencing Consumer Decisions

Promotion is the power to influence consumers—to remind them, to inform them, to persuade them. The best promotion goes one step further, building powerful consumer bonds that draw your customers back to your product again and again. But don't forget that great promotion only works with a great product. Bill Bernbach, an ad industry legend, captures this concept by noting that "A great ad campaign will make a bad product fail faster. It will get more people to know it's bad."

Marketers can directly control most promotional tools. From TV advertising to telephone sales, the marketer creates the message and communicates it directly to the target audience. But, ironically, marketers *cannot* directly control the most powerful promotional tools: publicity, such as a comment on *The View*, or a review in *Consumer Reports*, and word-of-mouth such as a recommendation from a close friend or even a casual acquaintance. Marketers can only influence these areas through creative promotional strategies.

Promotion in Chaos: Danger or Opportunity?

Not coincidentally, the Chinese symbol for crisis resembles the symbols for danger and opportunity—a perfect description of promotion in today's market. The pace of change is staggering. Technology has empowered consumers to choose how and when they interact with media, and they are grabbing control with dizzying speed. Cable-based on-demand video continues to soar, and digital movie downloads are poised for explosive growth. In 2010, Internet users spent an average of 32 hours per week surfing the Web, compared to about 30 hours per week watching TV. Meanwhile, more passive forms of entertainment, such as network television, are slowly losing their audience. And those people who do still watch TV are gleefully changing the schedules and zapping the ads with TiVo or similar devices. As media splinters across an array of entertainment options, usage patterns have changed as well: tech-savvy viewers are more prone to consume media in on-the-fly snacks rather than sit-down meals. Rising

Exhibit 12.8 The Product Life Cycle and Marketing Strategies

PHASE	EXAMPLES	SALES/ PROFITS	KEY MARKETING STRATEGIES
Introduction	Virtual reality games, fuel cell technology	Low sales, low profits	Build awareness, trial, and distribution
Growth	Hybrid cars, flat-screen TVs, electronic book readers, Internet gambling	Rapidly increasing sales and profits	Reinforce brand positioning, often through heavy advertising
Maturity	Airlines, DVD players, personal computers, online stock trading, energy drinks	Flat sales and declining profits	Target competitors, while defending franchise with new product features, competitive advertising, promotion, and price cuts
Decline	Pagers, videocassettes	Declining sales and profits	Reduce spending and consider terminating the product

© Cengage Learning 2013

consumer power and the breakneck pace of technology have created a growing need—and a stunning opportunity—for marketers to zero in on the right customers, at the right time, with the right message.[9]

Integrated Marketing Communication: Consistency and Focus

How many marketing messages have you gotten in the past 24 hours? Did you flip on the TV or radio? Surf the Web? Notice a billboard? Glance at the logo on a T-shirt or cap? Chat with a friend about some product he likes? Marketing exposure quickly snowballs: the typical consumer receives about 3,000 advertising messages each day. Some of those messages are hard to avoid as marketers find new, increasingly creative ways to promote their products to a captive audience. The venues include elevators, taxicabs, golf carts, and other surprising settings.[10] Given the confounding level of clutter, smart companies use **integrated marketing communication** to coordinate their messages through every promotional vehicle—including their advertising, website, and salespeople—creating a coherent impression in the minds of their customers. Why bother coordinating all of these elements? The answer is clear. Consumers don't think about the specific source of the communication; instead, they combine—or integrate—the messages from *all* the sources to form a unified impression about your product. If the messages are out of sync or confusing, busy consumers won't bother to crack the code. They'll simply move on to the next best option.

Can you really control every message that every consumer sees or hears about your product? It's not likely. But if you accurately identify the key points of contact between your product and your target market, you can focus on those areas with remarkable effectiveness. For instance, the most common points of contact for McDonald's are probably advertising and the in-store experience. From upbeat commercials, to smiling employees, to brightly striped uniforms, McDonald's spends millions of dollars to support its core message of fast, tasty food in a clean, friendly environment—heavily concentrated in the areas that are key to its brand.

Other companies are likely to encounter the bulk of their customers through different channels. You'd probably learn about Dell computers, for example, through either its website or word-of-mouth. Dell has invested heavily in both areas. The company maintains an innovative, user-friendly website that allows even novice users to create customized systems. And Dell delivers award-winning customer service and technical support, which gets its customers to recommend its products to family and friends.

Coordinating the Communication

Even after you've identified the key points of contact, coordinating the messages remains a challenge. In many companies, completely different teams develop the different promotional areas. Salespeople and brand managers often have separate agendas, even when the same executive manages both departments. Frequently, disconnected outside agencies handle advertising, Web development, and sales promotion programs. Coordinating the messages will happen only with solid teamwork, which must begin at the top of the organization.

Information also plays a crucial role. To coordinate marketing messages, everyone who creates and manages them must have free access to knowledge about the customer, the product, the competition, the market, and the strategy of the organization. Some of this information, such as strategic goals, will come from the top down, but a fair amount, such as information about the customer, should come from the bottom up. Information must also flow laterally, across departments and agencies. The marketing research department, for instance, might have critical information about product performance, which might help the Web management agency create a feature page that might respond to competitive threats identified by the sales force. When all parties have access to the same data, they are much more likely to remain on the same page.

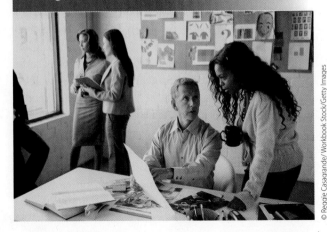

Coordinating marketing messages throughout an organization can be a huge challenge.

© Reggie Casagrande/Workbook Stock/Getty Images

L05 A Meaningful Message: Finding the Big Idea

Your promotional message begins with understanding how your product is different from and better than the competition. But your **positioning statement**—a brief statement that articulates how you want your target market to envision your product relative to the competition—seldom translates directly into the promotional message. Instead, it marks the beginning of the creative development process, often spearheaded by ad agency creative professionals. When it works, the creative development process yields a *big idea*—a meaningful, believable, and distinctive concept that cuts through the clutter. Big ideas are typically based on either a rational or an emotional premise. Here are a few examples from the last decade:

RATIONAL:	Price:	Walmart: "Always low prices. Always."
	Engineering:	BMW: "The ultimate driving machine."
	Ingredients:	Subway: "Eat Fresh"
EMOTIONAL:	Sex:	Axe: "Bom Chicka Wah Wah"
	Humor:	Virgin Atlantic: "More experience than our name suggests"
	Happiness:	Coca Cola: "Open Happiness"

© Cengage Learning 2013

Not surprisingly, funny ads are a consumer favorite, although humor can be risky. For a record ten years in a row, from 1998 through 2008, Budweiser—known for using humor effectively—nabbed the top spot in *USA Today's* annual Ad Meter consumer ranking of Super Bowl ads. But in 2009, a very funny "Free Doritos" ad—created by talented amateurs in an online contest sponsored by Frito-Lay—knocked Budweiser off its pedestal. Budweiser regained the top spot in 2011, sharing the honor with Doritos, which, once again, took the top prize with a hilarious customer-created ad.[11]

The best big ideas have entrenched themselves in popular culture, spawning both imitators and parodies. A small sampling includes:

- The Energizer Bunny
- "Got Milk?"
- Budweiser: "Whasssssuuup?!?!
- GE: "We bring good things to life"
- Motel 6: "We'll leave the light on for you."

An International Perspective

Some big ideas translate well across cultures. The Marlboro Man now promotes rugged individualism across the globe. But other big ideas don't travel as smoothly. DeBeers tried running ads in Japan using their proven strategy in the West: fabulously dressed women smiling and kissing their husbands who have just given them glittering diamonds. The ads failed in Japan because a Japanese woman would be more likely to shed a few tears and feign anger that her husband would spend so much money. The revised DeBeers campaign featured a hardworking husband and wife in their tiny apartment. Receiving a diamond, the wife chides her extravagant husband: "Oh, you stupid!" The campaign was a wild success. Taking a big idea to a foreign market can mean big money and a powerful brand, but careful research should still be your first step.[12]

promotional channels Specific marketing communication vehicles, including traditional tools, such as advertising, sales promotion, direct marketing, and personal selling, and newer tools such as product placement, advergaming, and Internet minimovies.

LO6 The Promotional Mix: Communicating the BIG IDEA

Once you've nailed your message, you need to communicate the big idea to your target market. The traditional communication tools—or **promotional channels**—include advertising, sales promotion, direct marketing, and personal selling. But more recently, a number of new tools have emerged, ranging from advergaming to Internet minimovies. The combination of communication tools that you choose to promote your product is called your "promotional mix."

Emerging Promotional Tools: The Leading Edge

In the last decade, the promotional landscape has changed dramatically. Consumer expectations and empowerment have skyrocketed. Consumer tolerance for impersonal corporate communication has fallen. And digital technology has surged forward at breakneck speed. As a result, new promotional tools have emerged, and previously minor tools have burst into the mainstream. This section covers several leading-edge promotional tactics, but keep in mind that other tools—such as mobile phone promotion, social media marketing (e.g., Facebook) and widget-based marketing—are growing explosively, too.

Internet Advertising Internet advertising has been highly visible for more than a decade. But the industry has moved far beyond simple banner ads and annoying pop-up ads. The highest growth areas include paid search advertising, search engine optimization, and online video advertising.

Paid search advertising includes both sponsored links on Google that relate to the topic you've searched and targeted Google text ads on a number of different websites—both of which are at the heart of Google's outsized financial success. Industry expert *eMarketer* estimates that paid search advertising, including both Google and other similar services, surpassed $12 billion in 2010 and may surpass $18 billion by 2014. Paid search seems to be an especially attractive tactic during tough economic times, since it offers high accountability—marketers can tell exactly how well their limited advertising dollars are working.[13]

Search engine optimization (SEO) also demonstrated strong growth as the economy weakened. SEO involves taking specific steps to ensure that your website appears high on the list when customers look for your product or service via an Internet search engine such as Google or Yahoo!. Typically, the higher a firm appears, the more traffic that site will receive from potential customers. Predictions from *eMarketer* suggest that U.S. spending on search-engine marketing will nearly double from $12.2 billion in 2008 to $23.4 billion by 2013.[14]

Online video advertising represents another high-growth area. This includes the increasingly popular "pre-roll" ads, the 15- to 30-second spots that viewers often sit through before watching an online video on YouTube, Hulu, or many other sites. Online video advertising more than tripled in the first half of 2008 (although the base was miniscule compared to search advertising). According to *eMarketer* estimates, the growth will increase—even in the face of the global recession—from $1.42 billion in 2010 to $5.71 billion in 2014, representing an extraordinary increase.[15]

Social Media Clearly, social media – including Facebook, Twitter, Blogger, Tumblr, Foursquare, and many others – is not a fad, but rather, a paradigm shift in how successful businesses market themselves. According to advertising heavyweight Alex Bogusky, "You can't buy attention anymore. Having a huge budget doesn't mean anything in social media…The old media paradigm was PAY to play. Now you get back what you authentically put in." And the evidence is building that social media offers a truly impressive return on investment, especially compared to traditional media. A few examples compiled by social media expert Erik Qualman underscore the potential return on investment:

- Wetpaint/Altimeter Study found companies that are both deeply and widely engaged in social media

Our head of social media is the
customer.

— McDonald's

significantly surpass their peers in both revenues and profits. The study also found the company sales with the highest levels of social media activity grew on average by +18%, while those companies with the least amount of social activity saw their sales decline −6%.

- BlendTec increased its sales 5x by running the often humorous "Will It Blend" videos on YouTube, blending everything from an iPhone to a sneaker.

- Dell sold $3,000,000 worth of computers on Twitter.

- Ford Motor Company gave away 100 Fiestas to influential bloggers, resulting in 37% of Generation Y learning of the Ford Fiesta before it was launched in the United States.

- Software company Genius.com reports that 24% of its social media leads convert to sales opportunities.

- Web host provider Moonfruit more than recouped its $15,000 social media investment as its website traffic soared +300% while sales increased +20%.

Looking ahead, smart marketers of both large and small businesses are investing their limited resources in social marketing, and reaping an unprecedented return, forging the future of marketing promotion.[16]

Product Placement Product placement—the paid integration of branded products into movies and TV—exploded into big-screen prominence in 1982, when Reese's Pieces played a highly visible role in Steven Spielberg's blockbuster film *E.T.* Reese's Pieces sales shot up 65% (a major embarrassment for the marketers of M&Ms, who had passed on the opportunity). Over the years, product placement in movies has moved rapidly into the limelight. A few notable examples are:

- *Risky Business* (1983): This movie launched Tom Cruise and fueled a run on Ray-Ban sunglasses. The shades got another boost in 1997 with *Men in Black*.

- *You've Got Mail* (1998): AOL scored big in this Tom Hanks–Meg Ryan romance that etched the AOL signature mail call onto the national consciousness.

- James Bond: This longstanding movie icon hawked so many products in recent movies (e.g., Omega watches, Heineken beer, and British Airways) that it triggered a backlash from annoyed moviegoers and critics.[17]

Overall, Apple takes top honors in the movie product placement sweepstakes. In 2010, Apple products appeared in 30% of all films that were number one in the U.S. box office. That performance actually represents a decline from 2008, when Apple products appeared in 50% of all number one films. The decline happened because other electronics firms stepped up their product placement efforts in response to

Apple. In fact Sony Studios, pursuing corporate synergy, actually banned Apple products from all their films, replacing them with Sony VAIO products wherever possible.[18]

In an interesting combination of promotional tactics, product placement and online video have begun to merge. In 2010, Lady Gaga's, YouTube smash hit video *Telephone* featured no fewer than ten product placements. Some of the placements, for instance, Miracle Whip, were paid, while others, such as Virgin Mobile and Polaroid, were extensions of existing partnerships with Gaga. Given its efficacy in reaching younger consumers this approach seems sure to grow in the future.

Product placement on TV has catapulted into the mainstream in response to the growing prominence of digital video recorders (DVRs) such as TiVo. Nielsen estimates that 35.7% of U.S. households had at least one DVR in 2010, 39.7% in 2011, up from fewer than 10% in 2005. DVRs allow consumers not only to watch on their own schedule, but also to zap ads. Worried marketers see product placement as a chance to "TiVo-proof" their messages by integrating them into the programming. Media experts anticipate that product placement will soar from a $3.6 billion business in 2009 to a $6.1 billion market by 2014.[19]

Product placement works best for marketers if the product seamlessly integrates into the show as a player rather than simply a prop. For instance, it's hard to miss Coke in *American Idol*. The judges are seldom without their Coca-Cola–emblazoned cups, and the contestants sit on a Coca-Cola couch in a Coca-Cola room as they wait to hear their fate. The price tag for this exposure—including commercial time and online content—is about $35 million. Media buyers often negotiate product placement deals as part of a package that includes

© Luba V Nel/Shutterstock.com

Raising your F-Factor

For years, the implications of getting an F have been anything but positive. But in today's social media world, smart brands are doing everything they can to raise their F-Factor. F is for friends, fans, followers, who influence purchasing decisions in more sophisticated ways. A few examples, cited by Trendwatching website:

- ⊃ The daily deal site Groupon has used referrals from friends to drive sales of over 40 million deals in the two and a half years since its email launch
- ⊃ Incipio Technologies, a gadget accessory retailer, found that referrals from Facebook had a conversion rate double the average
- ⊃ Juicy Couture found that their product purchase conversion rate increased by 160% after installing social sharing features

According to Trendingwatching, there are several different ways that the F-Factor can work:

1. **F-Discovery:** Consumers rely on their social networks to *discover* new products and services. An increasing number of sites allow consumers to compile sets of merchandise that they "like" and share them with their friends.

2. **F-Rated:** A growing number social network sites automatically serve up *ratings, recommendations, and reviews* from friends next to products that they are researching.

3. **F-Feedback:** Consumers ask their friends and followers to *improve and validate* their buying decisions. Product recommendations from family (63%) and friends (31%) are the most trusted. However 81% of U.S. consumers now go online to do additional research, with 55% looking for user reviews, and 10% soliciting advice from their social networks. However amongst people aged 25-34, this figure rises to 23%. 90% of people trust the recommendations of their Facebook friends.

4. **F-Together:** Shopping is becoming increasingly *social*, even when consumers and their peers are not physically together. 83% of consumers say they tell friends if they get a good deal. In April 2011, Facebook announced that every time a user posts about buying a ticket from Ticketmaster, the company estimates they receive an extra $5.30.

5. **F-Me:** Consumers' social networks are literally turned into products and services. A couple of examples: 1)*Twournal* enables users of Twitter to transform their tweets and pictures into a real-life published journal. In addition to creating their own 'books', users can also buy and sell publications from other users and 2) *CrowdedInk* offers an app that allows users to generate mugs filled with pictures of their Facebook friends or Twitter followers.

As the F-Factor gains momentum, customer satisfaction becomes more important than ever. Only brands that consistently deliver on their promises will fully capitalize on the benefits that the F-factor can offer.[20]

regular ads, which reinforce the product that appeared in the program (unless, of course, the ads are zapped).[21]

Whether in TV or movies, product placement offers marketers huge sales potential in a credible environment, which may account for its huge growth rate. But product placement is risky—if your show is a dud, your placement is worthless. And the cost is high and growing, which only increases the financial risk. The benefits of product placement are tough to measure as well, especially for existing brands. But in the end, the only measure that really counts is consumer acceptance, which may disappear if product placement intrudes too much on the entertainment value of movies and TV.

Advergaming Interactive games have exploded into pop culture, with about 72% of U.S. consumers playing some kind of videogame. Not surprisingly, marketers have followed closely behind, developing a new promotional channel: **advergaming**. Market analysts expect that spending in the advergame industry, which surpassed a billion dollars in 2007, will surpass $1.9 billion by 2011.[22]

According to Massive, an advertising network that specializes in video games, advergaming works for marketers. Gamers exposed to embedded ads show a 64% increase in brand familiarity, a 37% increase in brand rating, and a 41% increase in purchase consideration; furthermore, rather than despising the ads, 55% of gamers said they "look cool." But Massive isn't the only game in town. In early 2007, Google purchased AdScape, a nimble video game advertising company, and independent agency Double Fusion also provides fierce competition. Despite the strong research results, analysts anticipate that advergaming will move in a new direction over the next few years, with deals that link brands with tangible rewards for players. Dr. Pepper, for instance, seeded 500 million bottles and fountain drink cups in 2010

© MARIO ANZUONI/Reuters/ Landov

with special codes that allowed gamers to download content such as virtual weapons for EA game. This approach still leaves room for purely promotional in-games ads to support the out-of-game campaigns. Given the effectiveness of advergaming and the explosive growth, gamers may soon see a cyberworld filled with as much promotion as the real world.[23]

Buzz Marketing A recent study defined "buzz" as the transfer of information from someone who is in the know to someone who isn't. Buzz is essentially word-of-mouth, which now influences two-thirds of all consumer product purchases. And it makes sense. In a world that's increasingly complex, people turn to people they know and trust to help sort the garbage from the good stuff. Other popular terms for **buzz marketing** are "guerrilla marketing" and "viral marketing."

Not surprisingly, marketers have actively pursued buzz for their brands, especially with the rising cost and diminishing effectiveness of more traditional media channels. Innovative buzz campaigns are typically custom-designed to meet their objectives, and they often cost significantly less than more traditional approaches. Here are some notable examples:

- Whopper Sacrifice: Burger King has been among the most successful buzz marketers, using the Internet to develop quirky and creative campaigns that have quickly gone viral. In late 2009, Burger King invited customers to download their Whopper Sacrifice Facebook application and use it to drop ten Facebook friends in exchange for a free Angry Whopper coupon worth $3.69. The application then bluntly notified each friend that he or she had been dumped in exchange for about $.37 worth of burger. Consumers responded in droves, apparently thankful for the excuse to purge their friend lists. Burger King terminated the campaign when Facebook requested that they terminate the "de-friending" notification. But Burger King could still loudly proclaim "Your love for the Whopper sandwich proved to be stronger than 233,906 friendships"

- **Tremor:** Procter & Gamble, known for its traditional marketing, has mobilized buzz marketing on an unprecedented scale. Its Tremor marketing group, launched in 2001, recruited about 200,000 sociable kids, ages 13 to 19, to talk up products to their peers. These teens talk for free—or if not for free, for the chance to influence companies and get the early inside scoop on new products. In addition to P&G brands, Tremorites have worked on heavy-hitters such as Sony Electronics, DreamWorks SKG, and Coca-Cola. The results have been impressive. A dairy foods firm, for instance, introduced a new chocolate malt milk in Phoenix and Tucson with the same marketing mix and the same spending level. One exception: they used Tremor teens in Phoenix. After six months, sales in Phoenix were 18% higher than in Tucson. That kind of success tells its own story.[24]

Sponsorships Sponsorships certainly aren't new, but they are among the fastest-growing categories of promotional spending, hitting nearly $17.2 billion in 2010, and forecast to grow faster than other advertising and promotional spending over the next decade. Sponsorships provide a deep association between a marketer and a partner (usually a cultural or sporting event). Even though sponsors can't usually provide more than simply their logo or slogan, consumers tend to view them in a positive light, since they are clearly connected to events that matter to the target audience. The best sponsorship investments, of course, occur when the target audience for the marketer completely overlaps the target audience for the event. The high level of integration between the sponsors and events can provide millions of dollars in valuable media coverage, justifying the hefty price.[25]

Traditional Promotional Tools: A Marketing Mainstay

Although new tools are gaining prominence, traditional promotional tools—advertising, sales promotion, public relations, and personal selling—remain powerful. In fact, many marketers use the new tools in conjunction with the traditional to create a balanced, far-reaching promotional mix.

Advertising The formal definition of **advertising** is paid, nonpersonal communication, designed to influence a

> Doing business without advertising is like winking at a girl in the dark. You know what you are doing, but nobody else does.

— Steuart Henderson Britt, psychologist and marketing expert

> **Dealing with** unwanted mail not only wastes our time—eight months over the average lifespan—but also bears environmental costs, killing about 100 million trees each year, with 44% of junk mail ending up—unopened—in landfills.
>
> —Time Magazine

target audience with regard to a product, service, organization, or idea. Most major brands use advertising not only to drive sales, but also to build their reputation, especially with a broad target market. Television (network broadcasts and cable combined) remains the number-one advertising media, with magazines and newspapers following. As mass media prices increase and audiences fragment, fringe media is roaring toward the mainstream.

But measurement is tough, since alternative media tactics are buried in other categories, including magazines, outdoor, and Internet. The overall media spending patterns for 2009 are shown in Exhibit 12.9. As you review the table, note that Internet spending does not include search advertising or online video advertising, which are typically tracked separately. Also note that overall media spending has dropped significantly in response to the recession.

Each type of media offers advantages and drawbacks, as summarized in Exhibit 12.10. Your goal as a marketer should be to determine which media options reach your target

sponsorship A deep association between a marketer and a partner (usually a cultural or sporting event), which involves promotion of the sponsor in exchange for either payment or the provision of goods.

advertising Paid, nonpersonal communication, designed to influence a target audience with regard to a product, service, organization, or idea.

EXHIBIT 12.9	**2010 Measured Media Spending (billions)**	

MEASURED MEDIA	2009 SPENDING	PERCENTAGE OF TOTAL
BROADCAST TV	$23,600	18.9%
CABLE TV	$19,300	15.4%
SPOT TV	$13,200	10.5%
SYNDICATED TV	$4,200	3.4%
NEWSPAPERS	$20,600	16.5%
RADIO	$7,600	6.0%
MAGAZINES	$23,500	18.8%
OUTDOOR	$3,400	2.7%
INTERNET*	$9,800	7.8%
TOTAL	$125,300	100%

Source: Top 100 Outlays Plunge 10% but Defying Spend Trend Can Pay Off, by Bradley Johnson and Matthew Carmichael, *Advertising Age*, June 21, 2010, Vol. 81 Issue 25, pp. 1–24, 10p, * Internet figures are based on display advertising. They do not include paid search or broadband video advertising.

Exhibit 12.10 Major Media Categories

MAJOR MEDIA	ADVANTAGES	DISADVANTAGES
BROADCAST TV	*Mass audience:* Season finales for top-rated shows garnered up to 20 million viewers in 2008. *High impact:* TV lends itself to vivid, complex messages that use sight, sound, and motion.	*Disappearing viewers:* The 20 million viewers for top-rated shows in 2008 are dwarfed by the 1983 record of 105 million viewers for the finale of M*A*S*H. *Jaded viewers:* Consumers who aren't zapping ads with TiVo are prone to simply tuning them out. *High cost:* A 30-second ad during Super Bowl 2009 cost a record $3 million, and a typical primetime ad cost $200,000 to $400,000, depending on the show.
CABLE TV	*Targeted programming:* Cable helps advertisers target highly specialized markets (Zhong Tian Channel, anyone?). *Efficient:* The cost per contact is relatively low, especially for local buys. *High impact:* Cable offers the same sight, sound, and motion benefits as broadcast.	*DVRs:* As with broadcast TV, many viewers simply aren't watching ads. *Uneven quality:* Many cable ads are worse than mediocre, providing a seedy setting for quality products.
NEWSPAPERS	*Localized:* Advertisers can tailor their messages to meet local needs. *Flexible:* Turnaround time for placing and pulling ads is very short. *Consumer acceptance:* Readers expect, and even seek, newspaper ads.	*Short life span:* Readers quickly discard their papers. *Clutter:* It takes two or three hours to read the average metro paper from cover to cover. Almost no one does it. *Quality:* Even top-notch color newsprint leaves a lot to be desired.
DIRECT MAIL	*Highly targeted:* Direct mail can reach very specific markets. *International opportunity:* Less jaded foreign customers respond well to direct mail. *Email option:* Opt-in email can lower direct mail costs.	*Wastes resources:* Direct mail uses a staggering amount of paper. And most recipients don't even read it before they toss it. *High cost:* Cost per contact can be high, although advertisers can limit the size of the campaign. *Spam:* Unsolicited email ads have undermined consumer tolerance for all email ads.
RADIO	*Highly targeted:* In L.A., for example, the dial ranges from Vietnamese talk radio, to urban dance music, each station with dramatically different listeners. *Low cost:* Advertisers can control the cost by limiting the size of the buy. *Very flexible:* Changing the message is quick and easy.	*Low impact:* Radio relies only on listening. *Jaded listeners:* Many of us flip stations when the ads begin.
MAGAZINES	*Highly targeted:* From Cosmo to Computerworld, magazines reach very specialized markets. *Quality:* Glossy print sends a high-quality message. *Long life:* Magazines tend to stick around homes and offices.	*High cost:* A full-page, four-color ad in People can cost more than $300,000. *Inflexible:* Advertisers must submit artwork months before publication.
OUTDOOR	*High visibility:* Billboards and building sides are hard to miss. *Repeat exposure:* Popular locations garner daily viewers. *Breakthrough ideas:* Innovative approaches include cars and buses "wrapped" in ads, video billboards, and blimps.	*Simplistic messages:* More than an image and a few words will get lost. *Visual pollution:* Many consumers object to outdoor ads. *Limited targeting:* It's hard to ensure that the right people see your ad.
INTERNET	*24/7 global coverage:* Offers a remarkable level of exposure. *Highly targeted:* Search engines are especially strong at delivering the right ad to the right person at the right time. *Interactive:* Internet ads can empower consumers.	*Intrusive:* The annoyance factor from tough-to-close pop-ups alienates consumers, infuriating many. *Limited readership:* Web surfers simply ignore the vast majority of ads.

© Cengage Learning 2013

market efficiently and effectively, within the limits of your budget.

Sales Promotion Sales promotion stimulates immediate sales activity through specific short-term programs aimed at either consumers or distributors. Traditionally, sales promotion has been subordinate to other promotional tools, but spending has accelerated in the past decade. Sales promotion falls into two categories: consumer and trade.

Consumer promotion is designed to generate immediate sales. Consumer promotion tools include premiums, promotional products, samples, coupons, rebates, and displays.

- **Premiums** are items that consumers receive free of charge—or for a lower than normal cost—in return for making a purchase. Upscale cosmetics companies use the gift-with-purchase approach on a regular basis. Successful premiums create a sense of urgency—"Buy me now!"—while building the value of the brand.

- **Promotional** products are also essentially gifts to consumers of merchandise that advertise a brand name. Or pizza delivery places give away refrigerator magnets with their logo and phone number. Promotional products work best when the merchandise relates to the brand, and it's so useful or fun that consumers will opt to keep it around.

- **Samples** reduce the risk of purchasing something new by allowing consumers to try a product before committing their cash. Starbucks, invited customers into local stores to sample its new flavored VIA coffees in late 2010. Sampling also drives immediate purchases. At one time or another, most of us have probably bought food we didn't need after tasting a delicious morsel in the supermarket aisle. Costco and Trader Joe's do especially well with this angle on sampling.

- **Coupons** offer immediate price reductions to consumers. Instant coupons require even less effort, since they are attached to the package right there in the store. The goal is to entice consumers to try new products. But the downside is huge. Marketers who depend on coupons encourage consumers to focus on price rather than value, which makes it harder to differentiate brands and build loyalty. In categories with frequent coupons (such as soap and cereal), too many consumers wait for the coupon in order to buy. They end up getting great deals, but marketers pay the price in reduced profits.

- **Rebates,** common in the car industry and the electronics business, entice consumers with cash-back offers. This is a powerful tactic for higher-priced items, since rebates offer an appealing purchase motivator. And rebates provide an incentive for marketers as well: breakage. Most people who buy a product because of the rebate don't actually follow through and do the paperwork to get the money (some estimates suggest that breakage rates are as high as 90 to 95%). This means that marketers can offer hefty discounts without actually coughing up the cash, so it isn't surprising that rebates are a popular promotional tool!

- **Displays** generate purchases in-store. Most experts agree that consumers make a hefty chunk of their purchase decisions as they shop, which means that displays can play a crucial role in sales success. Marketers of consumer products often give prefabricated display materials to grocery stores and mass merchandisers to encourage promotion.

Trade Promotion is designed to stimulate wholesalers and retailers to push specific products more aggressively. Special deals and allowances are the most common form of trade promotion, especially for consumer products. The idea is that if you give your distributors a temporary price cut, they will pass the savings on to consumers via a short-term "special."

Trade shows are another popular form of trade promotion. Usually organized by industry trade associations, trade shows give exhibitors a chance to display and promote

sales promotion
Marketing activities designed to stimulate immediate sales activity through specific short-term programs aimed at either consumers or distributors.

consumer promotion
Marketing activities designed to generate immediate consumer sales, using tools such as premiums, promotional products, samples, coupons, rebates, and displays.

trade promotion
Marketing activities designed to stimulate wholesalers and retailers to push specific products more aggressively over the short term.

© Scott Olson/Getty Images

their products to their distributors. They typically attract hundreds of exhibitors and thousands of attendees. Trade shows are especially common in rapidly changing industries such as toys and consumer electronics. Every year the Consumer Electronics Association hosts "The world's largest annual trade show for consumer electronics!" in Las Vegas.

Other forms of trade promotion include contests, sweepstakes, and special events for distributors. A soda company might sponsor a contest to see which grocery store can build the most creative summer display for its soda brands. Or a cable TV programmer might take a group of system managers to Key West to "learn more about their programming" (really an excuse for a great party that makes the system managers more open to the programmer's pitch).

Public Relations In the broadest sense, **public relations (or PR)** involves the ongoing effort to create positive relationships with all of a firm's different "publics," including customers, employees, suppliers, the community, the general public, and the government. But in a more focused sense, PR aims to generate positive **publicity**, or unpaid stories in the media that create a favorable impression about a company or its products. The endgame, of course, is to boost demand.

For the most part, the media covers companies or products that they perceive as newsworthy. To get coverage, smart firms continually scan their own companies for potential news—a hot product or a major corporate achievement—and present that news to the media. But finding news on a regular basis can be tough. To fill the gaps, innovative PR people sometimes simply create "news." PR guru Bill Stoller offers some interesting ideas for how to invent stories that will grab media attention:

- ○ **Launch a Hall of Fame:** Induct some luminaries from your industry, create a simple website, and send your press release to the media. Repeat each year, building your reputation along the way.

- ○ **Make a List:** The best, the worst, the top ten, the bottom ten—the media loves lists, and the possible topics are endless! Just make sure that your list is relevant to your business.

- ○ **Create a Petition:** The Web makes this tactic easy. Harness a growing trend or identify a need in your industry, and launch your petition. The more signatures you get, the better your chances for publicity.[26]

The biggest advantage of publicity is that it is usually credible. Think about it: Are you more likely to buy a product featured on the news or a product featured in a 30-second ad?

Are you more likely to read a book reviewed by *The New York Times* or featured on a billboard? Publicity is credible because most people believe that information presented by the media is based on legitimate opinions and facts rather than on the drive to make money. And it also helps that publicity is close to free (excluding any fees for a PR firm).

But publicity has a major downside: the marketer has no control over how the media presents the company or its products. For example, in an effort to protect customers from a growing tide of solicitors in front of its stores, Target banned Salvation Army bell ringers in front of all its stores in 2004. The press cried foul, focusing not on the service to consumers, but rather on the disrespect to a venerable charity. Target's archrival Walmart, spotting an opportunity for itself at Target's expense, announced that it would match customer donations to the Salvation Army at all of its locations.

Personal Selling Personal selling—the world's oldest form of promotion—is person-to-person presentation of products to potential buyers. But successful selling typically begins long before the actual presentation and ends long afterward. In today's competitive environment, selling means building relationships on a long-term basis.

Creating and maintaining a quality sales force are expensive. Experts estimate that each business-to-business sales call costs nearly $400. So why are more than 10% of Americans

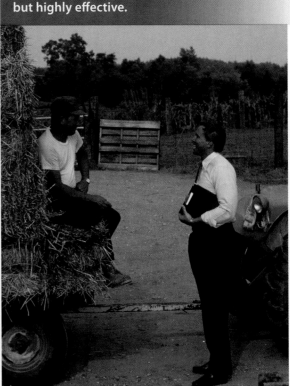

Individual sales calls can be very expensive, but highly effective.

employed in sales?[27] Because nothing works better than personal selling for high-ticket items, complex products, and high-volume customers. In some companies, the sales team works directly with customers; in other firms, the sales force works with distributors who buy large volumes of products for resale.

Salespeople fall along a spectrum that ranges from order takers who simply process sales to order seekers who use creative selling to persuade customers. Most department stores hire order takers who stand behind the counter and ring up sales. But Nordstrom hires creative order seekers who actively garner sales by offering extra services such as tasteful accessory recommendations for a clothing shopper.

A separate category of salespeople focuses on *missionary selling*, which means promoting goodwill for a company by providing information and assistance to customers. The pharmaceutical industry hires a small army of missionary salespeople who call on doctors to explain and promote its products, even though the actual sales move through pharmacies.

The sales process typically follows six key stages. Keep in mind that well before the process begins, effective salespeople seek a complete understanding of their products, their industry, and their competition. A high level of knowledge permeates the entire selling process.

1. **Prospect and Qualify:** Prospecting means identifying potential customers. Qualifying means choosing those who are most likely to buy your product. Choosing the right prospects makes salespeople more efficient, since it helps them focus their limited time in areas that will yield results. Companies find prospects in a number of different ways, from trade shows, to direct mail, to cold calling. In a retail environment, everyone who walks in the door is a prospect, so salespeople either ask questions or look for visual cues to qualify customers.

2. **Prepare:** Before making a sales call, research is critical, especially in a business-to-business environ-ment. What are your prospect's wants and needs? What are his or her current product lines? Who are the key competitors? What are the biggest internal and external challenges? How much time is your prospect willing to give you? The answers to these questions will help you customize your presentation for maximum effectiveness.

3. **Present:** You've probably heard that you don't get a second chance to make a good first impression, and that's especially true in sales. With so many options and so little time, buyers often look for reasons to eliminate choices; a weak first impression provides an easy reason to eliminate you. Your presentation itself should match the features of your product to the benefits that your customer seeks (a chance to use all that preparation). Testimonials, letters of praise from satisfied current customers, can push forward the sale by reducing risk for your prospect. A demonstration can be the clincher. When test driving cars, a demonstration is a no-brainer. But in other categories, technology can help demonstrate products that are too big to move.

4. **Handle Objections:** The key to success here is to view objections as opportunities rather than criticism. Objections give you a chance to learn more about the needs of your prospects and to elaborate on the benefits of your product. You should definitely anticipate as many objections as possible and prepare responses. One response may be connecting prospects with others in your company who can better handle their concerns. This approach offers the additional benefit of deepening ties between your prospect and your company.

© Richard Levine/Alamy

Too Much of a Good Thing

Months after Kentucky Fried Chicken changed its name to KFC, consumers remembered that the "F" stands for "Fried." So KFC grilled chicken was a bit of a "disconnect" for many consumers. But undaunted, KFC pushed ahead with an Oprah Winfrey promotion, offering two free pieces of grilled chicken, two sides, and a biscuit to anyone who downloaded a coupon within a two-day period. But the offer went awry when KFC failed to execute effectively. KFC claimed that it prepared for a huge response, but it failed to account for consumers photocopying the coupon, and the response—magnified by Twitter—utterly swamped its stores. As a result of the overwhelming response, KFC canceled the promotion, forcing disappointed consumers to go back to KFC, fill out a form, and wait for another coupon to arrive in the mail to award them with a free Pepsi in lieu of their free chicken meal. Although the promotional concept certainly generated a lot of consumer buzz, it ultimately did more harm than good, since the fast-fooder was ultimately unable to deliver.[28]

5. **Close Sale:** Closing the sale—or asking the prospect to buy—is at the heart of the selling process. The close should flow naturally from the prior steps, but often it doesn't—sealing the deal can be surprisingly tough. One approach may be a trial close: "Would you like the 15-inch screen or the 17-inch screen?" If your prospect is still reluctant to buy, you may want to offer another alternative, or a special financial incentive. Even if the prospect doesn't actually make the purchase, remember that he or she may be willing in the future, so keep the door open.

6. **Follow-up:** The sales process doesn't end when the customer pays. The quality of service and support plays a crucial role in future sales from the same customer, and getting those sales is much easier than finding brand new prospects. Great relationships with current customers also lead to testimonials and referrals that build momentum for long-term sales success.

Two personal selling trends are gathering momentum in a number of organizations: consultative selling and team selling. *Consultative selling* involves shifting the focus from the products to the customers. On a day-to-day basis, the practice involves a deep understanding of customer needs. Through lots and lots of active listening, consultative salespeople offer practical solutions to customer problems—solutions that use their products. While consultative selling generates powerful customer loyalty, it involves a significant—and expensive—time investment from the sales force.

Team selling tends to be especially effective for large, complex accounts. The approach includes a group of specialists from key functional areas of the company—not just sales, but also engineering, finance, customer service, and others. The goal is to uncover opportunities and respond to needs that would be beyond the capacity of a single salesperson. In these situations, a key part of the salesperson's role is to connect and coordinate the right network of contacts.

Choosing the Right Promotional Mix: Not Just a Science

There are no fail-safe rules for choosing the right combination of promotional tools. The mix varies dramatically among various industries, but also within specific industry segments. The best approach may simply be to consider the following questions in developing the mix that works best for your products.

⊙ **Product Characteristics:** How can you best communicate the features of your product? Is it simple or complex? Is it high-priced or inexpensive? A specialized, high-priced item, for example, might require an investment in personal selling, whereas a simple, low-cost product might lend itself to billboard advertising.

⊙ **Product Life Cycle:** Where does your product stand in its life cycle? Are you developing awareness? Are you generating desire? What about driving purchases? And building loyalty? The answers will clearly affect your promotional focus. For instance, if you're developing awareness, you might focus more on advertising, but if you're aiming to drive immediate sales, you'll probably emphasize sales promotion.

⊙ **Target Audience:** How big is your target audience? Where do they live and work? A small target audience—especially if it's geographically dispersed—would lend itself to personal selling or direct mail. A sizable target audience might suggest advertising as an effective way to reach large numbers. Audience expectations should also play a role in your promotional mix decisions.

⊙ **Push Versus Pull:** Does your industry emphasize push or pull strategies? A **push strategy** involves motivating distributors to "push" your product to the final consumers, usually through heavy trade promotion and personal selling. A **pull strategy** involves creating demand from your final consumers so that they "pull" your products through the distribution channels. Many successful brands use a combination of push and pull strategies to achieve their goals. P&G recently launched a consumer marketing campaign for Crest toothpaste featuring an "Irresistibility IQ" quiz for club-goers, but it also promotes heavily to dentists, hoping that those dentists will recommend Crest to their patients.

⊙ **Competitive Environment:** How are your key competitors handling their promotional strategies? Would it make more sense for you to follow their lead or to forge your own promotional path? If all your competitors offer coupons, for instance, your customers may expect you to offer them as well. Or if the environment is cluttered, you might want to focus on emerging promotional approaches such as advergaming.

⊙ **Budget:** What are your promotional goals? How much money will it take to achieve them? (Answering this question is tough, but it's clearly important.) How much are your competitors spending in each area of the mix? And how much money do you have for promotion? Even though available budget shouldn't drive the promotional mix, it plays a crucial role, especially for smaller businesses.

The possibilities in both product development and promotional strategy have rapidly multiplied in the last few years alone. But companies can't deliver on the potential without well-oiled teamwork throughout the organization. For instance, the operations group must focus on quality, the accounting group must focus on cost, and the finance group must focus on funding—but from a big picture standpoint, all groups must work toward the same overarching goal: maximizing customer value. Promotion also requires coordination within the organization and among the outside suppliers who provide promotional services. Finally, the best ideas for both product and promotion can come from any department. Marketers who stay ahead of the curve will only sharpen their competitive edge in the decade to come.

Product development decisions are often the bailiwick of the most senior managers who may work quite closely with engineering departments to bring their product development visions to life. The senior management team at Apple is famous for meticulously (some say relentlessly) guiding Apple's blockbuster product development process. In this scenario, a key role of marketers, whose titles may be product manager or brand manager is typically to provide input and feedback from consumers and distributers.

Jobs in promotion are highly varied. Most medium and large firms use a sales force, but in small organizations, everyone typically participates in sales to varying degrees, helping to land clients and keep them happy. Marketing promotion is handled both within companies and within agencies that specialize in everything from website development to advertising. Given the growing role of the Internet in marketing promotion, creativity and technological savvy are critical success factors.

CAREERS IN PRODUCT AND PROMOTION

CAREERS

What *else?*
RIP & REVIEW CARDS IN THE BACK
and visit www.cengagebrain.com!

© Thomas Barwick/Digital Vision/Jupiterimages

13

Distribution and Pricing:

Right Product, Right Person, Right Place, Right Price

LEARNING OBJECTIVES

After studying this chapter, you will be able to...

LO1   Define distribution and differentiate between channels of distribution and physical distribution

LO2   Describe the various types of wholesale distributors

LO3   Discuss strategies and trends in store and nonstore retailing

LO4   Explain the key factors in physical distribution

LO5   Outline core pricing objectives and strategies

LO6   Discuss pricing in practice, including the role of consumer perceptions

> MAKE YOUR PRODUCT *EASIER* TO BUY THAN YOUR COMPETITION, OR YOU WILL FIND CUSTOMERS BUYING FROM THEM, NOT YOU.
>
> — MARK CUBAN, ENTREPRENEUR

to sell their products directly to their customers through a **direct channel**. No one stands between the producer and the customer. Examples range from Dell computers, to local farmers markets, to factory outlet stores. But most producers use **channel intermediaries** to help their products move more efficiently and effectively from their factories to their consumers. Hershey's, for example, sells chocolate bars to Costco—a channel intermediary—which may, in turn, sell them to you.

The Role of Distributors: Adding Value

You might be asking yourself why we need distributors. Wouldn't it be a lot less expensive to buy directly from the producers? The answer, surprisingly, is no. Distributors add value—additional benefits—to products. They charge for adding that value, but typically they charge less than it would cost for consumers or producers to add that value on their own. When distributors add to the cost of a product without providing comparable benefits, the middlemen don't stay in business. Fifteen years ago, for instance, most people bought plane tickets from travel agents. But when the Internet reduced the cost and inconvenience of buying tickets directly from airlines, thousands of travel agencies lost their customers.

One core role of distributors is to reduce the number of transactions—and the associated costs—for goods to flow from producers to consumers. As you'll see in Exhibit 13.1, even one marketing intermediary in the distribution channel can funnel goods from producers to consumers with far fewer costly transactions.

Distributors add value, or utility, in a number of different ways: form, time, place, ownership, information, and service. Sometimes the distributors deliver the value (rather than adding it themselves), but often they add new utility that wouldn't otherwise be present. As you read through the various types of utility, keep in mind that they are often interrelated, building on each other to maximize value.

Form utility provides customer satisfaction by converting inputs into finished products. Clearly, form utility is primarily a part of manufacturing. Nabisco provides form utility by transforming flour and sugar into cookies. But retailers

distribution strategy A plan for delivering the right product to the right person at the right place at the right time.

channel of distribution The network of organizations and processes that links producers to consumers.

physical distribution The actual, physical movement of products along the distribution pathway.

direct channel A distribution process that links the producer and the customer with no intermediaries.

channel intermediaries Distribution organizations—informally called "middlemen"—that facilitate the movement of products from the producer to the consumer.

Distribution and pricing are not the most glamorous elements of the marketing mix, but managed effectively, they can provide a powerful competitive advantage. While this chapter will cover distribution and pricing strategies separately, keep in mind that the two are linked both with each other, and with the product and promotional strategies of any successful brand.

LO1 Distribution: Getting Your Product to Your Customer

Next time you go to the grocery store, look around—the average U.S. supermarket carries about 50,000 different products.[1] Is your favorite brand of soda part of the mix? Why? How did it get from the factory to your neighborhood store? Where else could you find that soda? How far would you be willing to go to get it? These are marketing distribution questions that contribute directly to the **distribution strategy**: getting the right product to the right person at the right place, at the right time.

The distribution strategy has two elements: channels of distribution and physical distribution. A **channel of distribution** is the path that a product takes from the producer to the consumer, while **physical distribution** is the actual movement of products along that path. Some producers choose

retailers Distributors that sell products directly to the ultimate users, typically in small quantities, that are stored and merchandised on the premises.

wholesalers Distributors that buy products from producers and sell them to other businesses or nonfinal users such as hospitals, nonprofits, and the government.

independent wholesaling businesses Independent distributors that buy products from a range of different businesses and sell those products to a range of different customers.

merchant wholesalers Independent distributors who take legal possession, or title, of the goods they distribute.

agents/brokers Independent distributors who do not take title of the goods they distribute (even though they may take physical possession on a temporary basis before distribution).

can add form utility as well. Starbucks, for example, converts coffee beans into iced coffees and espressos.

Time utility adds value by making products available at a convenient time for consumers. In our 24/7 society, consumers feel entitled to instant gratification, a benefit that distributors can provide more easily than most producers. Consider one-hour dry cleaning, or even vending machines. These distributors provide options for filling your needs at a time that works for you.

Place utility satisfies customer needs by providing the right products in the right place. Gas stations and fast food, for instance, often cluster conveniently at the bottom of freeway ramps. ATMs—essentially electronic distributors—are readily available in locations that range from grocery stores to college cafeterias.

Ownership utility adds value by making it easier for customers to actually possess the goods and services that they purchase. Providing credit, cashing checks, and delivering

ATMs provide time and place utility, offering their customers 24/7 access to cash in a variety of convenient locations.

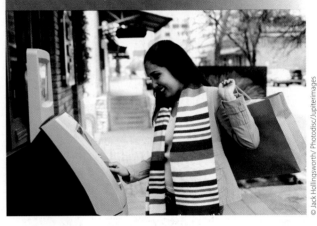

© Jack Hollingsworth/ Photodisc/Jupiterimages

products are all examples of how distributors make it easier for customers to own their products.

Information utility boosts customer satisfaction by providing helpful information. EB Games, for instance, hires gaming experts to guide its customers to the latest games and systems. Similarly, most skateboard stores hire skater salespeople who gladly help customers find the best board for them.

Service utility adds value by providing fast, friendly, personalized service. Examples include placing a special order for that part you need to customize your computer, or picking out outfits that work for your body type in your local clothing boutique. Distributors that provide service utility typically create a loyal base of customers.

The Members of the Channel: Retailers Versus Wholesalers Many producers sell their goods through multiple channels of distribution. Some channels have many members, while others have only a few. The main distinction among channel members is whether they are retailers or wholesalers. **Retailers** are the distributors that most of us know and use on a daily basis. They sell products directly to final consumers. Examples include 7-Eleven markets, Starbucks, and Urban Outfitters. **Wholesalers**, on the other hand, buy products from the producer and sell them to businesses (or other nonfinal users, such as hospitals, nonprofits, and the government). The businesses that buy from wholesalers can be retailers, other wholesalers, or business users. To complicate this fairly simple concept, some distributors act as both wholesalers and retailers. Sam's Club, for example, sells directly to businesses *and* to consumers.

EXHIBIT 13.1 Reducing transactions through marketing intermediaries

Manufacturer	Manufacturer	Manufacturer	Manufacturer

Customer	Customer	Customer	Customer

Manufacturer	Manufacturer	Manufacturer	Manufacturer

Marketing Intermediary

Customer	Customer	Customer	Customer

© Cengage Learning 2013

LO2 Wholesalers: Sorting Out the Options

Some wholesalers are owned by producers, while others are owned by retailers, but the vast majority—accounting for about two-thirds of all the wholesale trade—are **independent wholesaling businesses**. These companies represent a number of different producers, distributing their goods to a range of customers. Independent wholesalers fall into two categories: (1) **merchant wholesalers**, who take legal possession, or title, of the goods they distribute, and (2) **agents/brokers**, who don't take title of the goods.

Merchant Wholesalers

Merchant wholesalers comprise about 80% of all wholesalers. By taking legal title to the goods they distribute, merchant wholesalers reduce the risk of producers' products being damaged or stolen—or even that they just won't sell. Taking title also allows merchant wholesalers to develop their own marketing strategies, including pricing.

- Full-service merchant wholesalers provide a complete array of services to the retailers or business users who typically purchase their goods. This includes warehousing, shipping, promotional assistance, product repairs, and credit.

- Limited-service merchant wholesalers provide fewer services to their customers. For example, some might warehouse products but not deliver them. Others might warehouse and deliver but not provide credit or marketing assistance. The specific categories of limited-service merchant wholesalers include the following:

  - *Drop Shippers:* Drop shippers take legal title of the merchandise, but they never physically process it. They simply organize and facilitate product shipments directly from the producer to their customers. Drop shippers are common in industries with bulky products, such as coal or timber. Amazon, however, successfully

AP Images/Ross D. Franklin

Go Green, Go Local!

Not long ago, summer fruit meant exactly that – but no longer. Thanks to modern agribusiness, technology, and transportation, summer fruit is available throughout the year (sometimes for a hefty price), across the U.S. A few statistics:

- 17% of petroleum demand in the U.S. comes from the food-production industry.
- The food on your plate has traveled an average of 1,500 miles to get there.
- 91 cents of each dollar spent at traditional food markets (e.g., commercial) goes to suppliers, processors, middlemen, and marketers; only 9 cents of each dollar actually goes to the farmer.

If you find these statistics disturbing, one solution lies with local farmers' markets. As of 2010, more than 6,000 farmers' markets were operating in communities in the U.S., selling fresh, locally grown food and developing the businesses of small and medium-sized farmers.

But locally grown does not mean environmentally friendly—harmful pesticides can be used in any location. We do know that industrial food production is entirely dependent on fossil fuels, which create greenhouse gases that are significant contributors to climate change. The biggest part of fossil fuel use in industrial farming is not transporting food or fueling machinery, it's chemicals. As much as forty percent of the energy used in the food system goes towards the production of chemical fertilizers and pesticides.

By adding transportation, processing and packaging to the food system equation, the fossil fuel and energy use of our current food system puts stress on the environment. Food processors use a large amount of packaging to keep fresh food from spoiling as it is transported and stored for long periods of time. This packaging is difficult to reuse or recycle. Industrial farms are also major sources of air and water pollution. So going greener could be as easy as going shopping at your local farmers' market.[2]

pioneered the use of drop shipping in e-commerce, where it has become a standard shipping method for a number of major websites.

- *Cash and Carry Wholesalers:* These distributors service customers who are too small to merit in-person sales calls from wholesaler reps. Customers must make the trip to the wholesaler themselves and cart their own products back to their stores. Costco and Staples are both examples.

multichannel retailing
Providing multiple distribution channels for consumers to buy a product.

○ *Truck Jobbers:* Typically working with perishable goods such as bread, truck jobbers drive their products to their customers, who are usually smaller grocery stores. Their responsibilities often include checking the stock, suggesting reorder quantities, and removing out-of-date goods.

Agents and Brokers

Agents and brokers connect buyers and sellers and facilitate transactions in exchange for commissions. But they do not take legal ownership of the goods they distribute. Many insurance companies, for instance, distribute via agents, while brokers often handle real estate and seasonal products such as fruits and vegetables.

LO3 Retailers: the Consumer Connection

Retailers represent the last stop on the distribution path, since they sell goods and services directly to final consumers. Given their tight consumer connection, retailers must keep in especially close touch with rapidly changing consumer needs and wants.

Smart retailers gain a competitive edge by providing more utility, or added value, than their counterparts. Low prices are only part of the equation. Other elements clearly include customer service, product selection, advertising, and location. The look and feel of the retailer—whether online or on-ground—is another critical element.

Retailing falls into two main categories: store and nonstore. But as we discuss each type, keep in mind that the lines between them are not always clear. In fact, **multichannel retailing**—or encouraging consumers to buy through different venues—is an emerging phenomenon. Some marketers have sold their products through multiple channels for many years. For example, on any given day, you could purchase a Coke from a grocery store, a restaurant, or a vending machine. But the emergence of the Internet has provided a host of new opportunities for firms that hadn't previously considered a multichannel approach. An active relationship between on-ground and online outlets has become pivotal for many retailers.

Store Retailers

While other retail channels are growing, traditional stores remain the 800-pound gorilla of the retail industry, accounting for well over 90% of total retail. Stores range in size from tiny mom-and-pop groceries to multi-acre superstores dwarfed only by their parking lots. Exhibit 13.2 highlights examples of different store types.

Both retailers and the producers who distribute through them must carefully consider their distribution strategy. The three key strategic options are intensive, selective, and exclusive.

EXHIBIT 13.2 Retail Store Categories

STORE TYPE	STORE DESCRIPTION	EXAMPLES
CATEGORY KILLER	Dominates its category by offering a huge variety of one type of product.	OfficeMax, Best Buy, Staples
CONVENIENCE STORE	Sells a small range of everyday and impulse products at easy-to-access locations with long hours and quick checkout.	7-Eleven, AM/PM markets, Famima, and a wide range of local stores
DEPARTMENT STORE	Offers a wide variety of merchandise (e.g., clothes, furniture, cosmetics), plus (usually) a high level of service.	Nordstrom, Macy's, JCPenney
DISCOUNT STORE	Offers a wide array of merchandise at significantly lower prices and with less service than most department stores.	Target, Walmart, Kmart
OUTLET STORE	Producer-owned store sells directly to the public at a huge discount. May include discontinued, flawed, or overrun items.	Nike, Versace, Quicksilver, Calvin Klein, Converse, GUESS
SPECIALTY STORE	Sells a wide selection of merchandise within a narrow category, such as auto parts.	Barnes & Noble, Victoria's Secret, Claire's, AutoZone
SUPERMARKET	Offers a wide range of food products, plus limited nonfood items (e.g., toilet paper).	Kroger, Safeway, Albertson's, Whole Foods, Trader Joe's
SUPERCENTER	Sells a complete selection of food and general merchandise at a steep discount in a single enormous location.	Walmart Supercenters, Super Target
WAREHOUSE CLUB	Sells discounted food and general merchandise to club members in a large warehouse format.	Costco, Sam's Club

© Cengage Learning 2013

Reed Hastings created Netflix—which revolutionized video distribution—partly out of anger that Blockbuster charged him $40 in late fees on his overdue rental of *Apollo 13.*

— NEWSWEEK

Intensive Distribution Intensive distribution involves placing your products in as many stores as possible (or placing your stores themselves in as many locations as possible). This strategy makes the most sense for low-cost convenience goods that consumers won't travel too far to find. Marketers have chosen this strategy for McDonald's, Crest toothpaste, and *US* magazine, among thousands of other examples.

Selective Distribution Selective distribution means placing your products only with preferred retailers (or establishing your stores only in limited locations). This approach tends to work best for medium- and higher-priced products or stores that consumers don't expect to find on every street corner. Marketers have chosen this strategy for Nordstrom, Grand Lux Cafe, and most brands of paintball equipment, for instance.

Exclusive Distribution Exclusive distribution means establishing only one retail outlet in a given area. Typically, that one retailer has exclusive distribution rights and provides exceptional service and selection. This strategy tends to work for luxury-good providers with a customer base that actively seeks their products. Examples include top-end cars such as Lamborghini, and fashion trendsetters such as Gucci.

The **wheel of retailing** offers another key strategic consideration. The wheel is a classic theory that suggests that retail firms—sometimes even entire retail categories—become more upscale as they go through their life cycles. For instance, it's easiest to enter a business on a shoestring, gaining customers by offering low prices. But eventually businesses trade up their selection, service, and facilities to maintain and build their customer base. Higher prices then follow, creating vulnerability to new, lower-priced competitors. And thus the wheel keeps rolling.

Although the wheel of retailing theory does describe many basic retail patterns, it doesn't account for stores that launch at the high end of the market (e.g., Whole Foods) and those that retain their niche as deep discounters (e.g., Big Lots! or Taco Bell). But the wheel theory does underscore the core principle that retailers must meet changing consumer needs in a relentlessly competitive environment.

wheel of retailing A classic distribution theory that suggests that retail firms and retail categories become more upscale as they go through their life cycles.

Nonstore Retailers

While most retail dollars flow through brick-and-mortar stores, a growing number of sales go through other channels, or nonstore retailers. The key players represent online retailing, direct-response retailing, direct selling, and vending.

Online retailing Also known as "e-tailing," online retailing grew at the astonishing rate of nearly 25% per year for most of the early 2000s. But the torrid pace began to slow in 2008 with the onset of the recession. Online retailing grew only 1.6% in 2009, but growth bounced back to over 14.8% in 2010. Looking forward, experts predict that annual growth will remain robust. Much of the growth will likely come at the expense of on-ground retail, as consumers continue to shift to online channels. The bigger name brands—including online-only brands, such as Amazon, and on-ground brands with a strong Web presence, such as Best Buy—seem poised to benefit most, since cautious consumers are most familiar with them.[3]

Online retailers, like their on-ground counterparts, have learned that great customer service can be a powerful differentiator. Simply "getting eyeballs" isn't enough, since—depending on the industry—fewer than 5% of the people visiting a typical website convert into paying customers. Overstock.com, for instance, has been a pioneer in online customer service, hiring and training 60 specialists who engage customers in live chats, available 24/7. When a customer has a live chat with one of its specialists, the average purchase amount doubles. In fact, according to the National Retail Federation (NRF), shoppers have increasingly identified Internet-only retailers among those who offered the best customer service. In 2011, Zappos.com took top honors in the annual NRF/American Express Customers' Choice survey, and two other online retailers—Overstock.com and Amazon.com—placed in its top five positions for the third year in a row for retailers that offer the best customer service in any retail format.[4]

Despite the advantages, online retailers face two major hurdles. The first is that products must be delivered, and even the fastest deliery services typically take at least a couple of days. But the truly daunting hurdle is the lack of security on the Web. As online retailers and software developers create increasingly secure systems, hackers develop more sophisticated tools to crack their new codes.

Direct Response Retailing This category includes catalogs, tele-marketing, and advertising (such as infomercials) meant to elicit direct consumer sales. While many traditional catalog retailers have also established successful websites, the catalog side of the business continues to thrive. Victoria's Secret, for instance, sends a mind-boggling 395 million catalogs each year—that's four catalogs for every American woman between the ages of 15 and 64. Telemarketing, both inbound and outbound, also remains a potent distribution channel, despite the popular National Do Not Call list established in 2003.

Direct Selling This channel includes all methods of selling directly to customers in their homes or workplaces. Door-to-door sales has enjoyed a resurgence in the wake of the National Do Not Call list, but the real strength of direct selling lies in **multilevel marketing**, or **MLM**. Multilevel marketing involves hiring independent contractors to sell products to their personal network of friends and colleagues and to recruit new salespeople in return for a percentage of their commissions. Mary Kay Cosmetics and The Pampered Chef have both enjoyed enormous success in this arena, along with pioneering companies such as Tupperware.

©o44/ZUMA Press/Newscom

Vending Until about a decade ago, vending machines in the United States sold mostly soft drinks and snacks. But more recently, the selection has expanded (and the machines have gone more upscale) as marketers recognize the value of providing their products as conveniently as possible to their target consumers. Banana Boat, for example, has placed sunscreen vending units in high-traffic spots across sunny southern Florida. But other countries are far ahead of the United States in the vending arena. In Japan, for instance, people buy everything from blue jeans to beef from vending machines. As technology continues to roll forward, U.S. consumers are likely to see a growing number of vending machines for products as diverse as fresh-cooked french fries, digital cameras, and specialty coffee drinks.

We own the relationship with the customer and we subcontract to others.

— Kevin Rollins, Dell CEO

LO4 Physical Distribution: Planes, Trains, and Much, Much More

Determining the best distribution channels for your product is only the first half of your distribution strategy. The second half is physical distribution strategy: determining how your product will flow through the channel from the producer to the consumer.

The **supply chain** for a product includes not only its distribution channels but also the string of suppliers who deliver products to the producers. (See Exhibit 13.3.) Planning and coordinating the movement of products along the supply chain—from the raw materials to the final consumers—is called **supply chain management** or **SCM**. **Logistics** is a subset of SCM that focuses more on tactics (the actual movement of products) than on strategy.

At one time, relationships among the members of the supply chain were contentious. But these days, companies that foster collaboration, rather than competition, have typically experienced more success. Vendor-managed inventory is an emerging strategy—pioneered by Walmart—that allows suppliers to determine buyer needs and automatically ship product. This strategy saves time and money but also requires an extraordinary level of trust and information-sharing among members of the supply chain.

In our turbocharged 24/7 society, supply chain management has become increasingly complex. Gap, for instance, contracts with more than 3,000 factories in more than 50 different countries, and distributes its products to

Exhibit 13.3 Elements of the Supply Chain

The supply chain highlights the links among the various organizations in the production and distribution process.

Raw Materials

Logistics (transportation, coordination, etc.)

Warehouse/Storage

Production

Warehouse/Storage

Logistics (transportation, coordination, etc.)

Distributors—Marketing and Sales

© Cengage Learning 2013

- **Order Processing:** How should we manage incoming and outgoing orders? What would be most efficient for our customers and suppliers?

- **Customer Service:** How can we serve our customers most effectively? How can we reduce waiting times and facilitate interactions?

- **Transportation:** How can we move products most efficiently through the supply chain? What are the key tradeoffs?

- **Security:** How can we keep products safe from vandals, theft, and accidents every step of the way?

And fragile or perishable products, of course, require even more considerations.

modes of transportation The various transportation options—such as planes, trains, and railroads—for moving products through the supply chain.

---

about 3,000 stores in five different countries. The coordination requirements are mind-boggling. Key management decisions include the following considerations:

- **Warehousing:** How many warehouses do we need? Where should we locate our warehouses?

- **Materials Handling:** How should we move products within our facilities? How can we best balance efficiency with effectiveness?

- **Inventory Control:** How much inventory should we keep on hand? How should we store and distribute it? What about costs such as taxes and insurance?

Transportation Decisions

Moving products through the supply chain is so important that it deserves its own section. The various options—trains, planes, and railroads, for instance—are called **modes of transportation**. To make smart decisions, marketers must consider what each mode offers in terms of cost, speed, dependability, flexibility, availability, and frequency of shipments. The right choice, of course, depends on the needs of the business and on the product itself. See Exhibit 13.4 for a description of the transportation options.

Depending on factors such as warehousing, docking facilities, and accessibility, some distributors use several different

Exhibit 13.4 Modes of Transportation

MODE	PERCENTAGE OF U.S. VOLUME BASED ON 2007 TON-MILES	COST	SPEED	ON-TIME DEPENDABILITY	FLEXIBILITY IN HANDLING	FREQUENCY OF SHIPMENTS	AVAILABILITY
RAIL	39.5%	Medium	Slow	Medium	Medium	Low	Extensive
TRUCK	28.6%	High	Fast	High	Medium	High	Most extensive
SHIP	12.0%	Lowest	Slowest	Lowest	Highest	Lowest	Limited
PLANE	0.3%	Highest	Fastest	Medium	Low	Medium	Medium
PIPELINE	19.6%	Low	Slow	Highest	Lowest	Highest	Most limited

Source: Table 1-46b: U.S. Ton-Miles of Freight (BTS Special Tabulation), 2007 data, Bureau of Transportation website, http://www.bts.gov/publications/national_transportation_statistics/html/table_01_46b.html (accessed June 30, 2010).

penetration pricing
A new product pricing strategy that aims to capture as much of the market as possible through rock-bottom prices.

everyday-low-pricing (EDLP) Long-term discount pricing, designed to achieve profitability through high sales volume.

modes of transportation. If you owned a clothing boutique in Las Vegas, for example, chances are that much of your merchandise would travel by boat from China to Long Beach, California, and then by truck from Long Beach to Las Vegas.

Proactive Supply Chain Management

A growing number of marketers have turned to supply chain management to build a competitive edge through greater efficiency. But given the complexity of the field, many firms choose to outsource this challenge to experts rather than handling it internally. Companies that specialize in helping other companies manage the supply chain—such as UPS—have done particularly well in today's market.

L05 Pricing Objectives and Strategies: A High-Stakes Game

Pricing strategy clearly has a significant impact on the success of any organization. Price plays a key role in determining demand for your products, which directly influences a company's profitability. Most people, after all, have a limited amount of money and a practically infinite number of ways they could spend it. Price affects their spending choices at a more fundamental level than most other variables.

But ironically, price is perhaps the toughest variable for marketers to control. Both legal constraints and marketing intermediaries (distributors) play roles in determining the final price of most products. Marketers must also consider costs, competitors, investors, taxes, and product strategies.

In today's frenetic environment, stable pricing is no longer the norm. Smart marketers continually evaluate and refine their pricing strategies to ensure that they meet their goals. Even the goals themselves may shift in response to the changing market. Common objectives and strategies include building profitability, boosting volume, matching the competition, and creating prestige.

Building Profitability

Since long-term profitability is a fundamental goal of most businesses, profitability targets are often the starting point for pricing strategies. Many firms express these goals in terms of either return on investment (ROI) or return on sales (ROS). Keep in mind that profitability is the positive difference between revenue (or total sales) and costs. Firms can

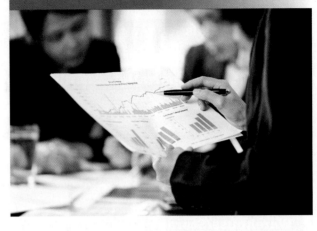

Many firms express long term profitability goals in terms of either return on investment or return on sales.

boost profits by increasing prices or decreasing costs, since either strategy will lead to a greater spread between the two. Doing both, of course, is tricky, but companies that succeed—such as Apple—typically dominate their markets.

Boosting Volume

Companies usually express volume goals in terms of market share—the percentage of a market controlled by a company or a product. Amazon.com, for example, launched with volume objectives. Its goal was to capture as many "eyeballs" as possible, in hopes of later achieving profitability through programs that depend on volume, such as advertising on its site. A volume objective usually leads to one of the following strategies:

Penetration Pricing Penetration pricing, a strategy for pricing new products, aims to capture as much of the market as possible through rock-bottom prices. Each individual sale typically yields a tiny profit; the real money comes from the sheer volume of sales. One key benefit of this strategy is that it tends to discourage competitors, who may be scared off by the slim margins. But penetration pricing makes sense only in categories that don't have a significant group of consumers who would be willing to pay a premium (otherwise, the marketer would be leaving money on the table). For obvious reasons, companies that use penetration pricing are usually focused on controlling costs. JetBlue is a key example. Its prices are often unbeatable, but it strictly controls costs by using a single kind of jet, optimizing turnaround times at the gate, and using many non-major airports.

Everyday-low pricing Also known as "sustained discount pricing," everyday-low pricing (EDLP) aims to achieve long-term profitability through volume. Walmart is clearly the king of EDLP with "Always low prices. *Always!*" But Costco uses the same strategy to attract a much more upscale audience. The difference between the two customer groups quickly becomes apparent by glancing at the cars, while strolling through the two parking lots. Costco customers are typically seeking everyday discounts because they want to, not because they need to. The product mix—eclectic and upscale—reflects the customer base. (Costco sells discounted fine wine, low-priced rotisserie chickens, fresh king crab legs, and high-end electronics.) While Costco posted years of healthy, sustained growth, the firm ran into trouble at the end of 2008. As the recession tightened its grip, sales began to soften, especially in non-food categories, suggesting that EDLP may be most effective for less-upscale products.[5] By 2010, Costco had recovered and returned to its historical growth trajectory.

High/Low Pricing The high/low pricing strategy tries to increase traffic in retail stores by special sales on a limited number of products, and higher everyday prices on others. Often used—and overused—in grocery stores, drug stores, and department stores, this strategy can alienate customers who feel cheated when a product they bought for full price goes on sale soon afterward. High/low pricing can also train consumers to buy only when products are on sale.

Loss-Leader Pricing Closely related to high/low pricing, loss-leader pricing means pricing a handful of items—or loss leaders—temporarily below cost to drive traffic. The retailer loses money on the loss leaders but aims to make up the difference (and then some) on other purchases. To encourage other purchases, retailers typically place loss leaders at the back of the store, forcing customers to navigate past a tempting array of more profitable items. The loss-leader strategy has been used effectively by producers, as well. Gillette, for instance, gives away some shavers practically for free but reaps handsome profits as consumers buy replacement blades. Similarly, Microsoft has sold its Xbox systems at a loss in order to increase potential profits from high-margin video games. But the loss-leader strategy can't be used everywhere, since a number of states have made loss leaders illegal for anticompetitive reasons.[6]

Matching the Competition

The key goal is to set prices based on what everyone else is doing. Usually, the idea is to wipe out price as a point of comparison, forcing customers to choose their product based on other factors. Examples include Coke and Pepsi, Honda and Toyota, Chevron and Mobil, Delta and United. But sometimes one or two competitors emerge that drive pricing for entire industries. Marlboro, for instance, leads the pack in terms of cigarette pricing, with other brands falling into place behind.

> **If automobiles** had followed the same development cycle as the computer, a Rolls-Royce would today cost $100, get a million miles per gallon, and explode once a year, killing everyone inside.
>
> — Robert Cringely, technology journalist

high/low pricing A pricing strategy designed to drive traffic to retail stores by special sales on a limited number of products, and higher everyday prices on others.

loss-leader pricing Closely related to high/low pricing, loss leader pricing means pricing a handful of items—or loss leaders—temporarily below cost to drive traffic.

Right Is Always Right, But Sometimes Left Is Wrong

© Stephen Chernin/Getty Images

Confused? This twisted bit of wisdom comes from UPS, whose drivers worldwide log about 2 billion miles a year. In a determined effort to go green and reduce costs, UPS company leaders determined that eliminating left-hand turns from delivery routes—and the sitting in traffic that accompanies them—could dramatically improve gas mileage, so they implemented computer-generated delivery routes that eliminate as many left turns as possible. According to UPS, the new system "shaved nearly 30 million miles off UPS's delivery routes, saved 3 million gallons of gas, and reduced emissions by 32,000 metric tons of CO_2—the equivalent of removing 5,300 passenger cars off the road for an entire year." The resulting publicity has drawn attention to relatively minor driving changes that even small businesses and individuals can make to waste less gas and create less pollution. Other high-impact driving "tweaks" include driving under 60 mph, maintaining recommended air pressure in tires, and replacing clogged air filters. UPS vividly demonstrated that small, positive changes can pay huge dividends for business and the environment alike.[7]

Ooops! What were they thinking?

"Slippery Finger" Pricing Goofs

If a price seems too good to be true, it probably is. But seeking an incredible bargain can still make sense—dollars and cents. Due to "slippery finger" typos, frequent price changes, and programming glitches, online retailers are especially vulnerable to pricing mistakes. Without human cashier confirmation, it's tough to catch the goofs. And to magnify the problem, quick communication on the Web almost ensures a flood of customers placing orders as soon as the wrong price goes live.

A sampling of recent online "deals":

⟳ **Free flights from Los Angeles to Fiji**

⟳ **Round-trip tickets from San Jose, CA, to Paris for $27.98**

⟳ **$1,049 televisions wrongly listed for $99.99 on Amazon**

⟳ **$588 Hitachi monitors mistakenly marked down to $164**

⟳ **$379 Axim X3i PDAs wrongly priced at $79 on Dell's site**

⟳ **Five watches, worth $11,332, briefly sale-priced at $0.0 (with free shipping) on Ashford.com**

After the first few high-profile pricing disasters, online retailers have taken steps to protect themselves through specific disclaimers in their terms of use. And the courts have generally ruled that a company need not honor an offer if a reasonable person would recognize that it was a mistake.

But disclaimers and legal protections won't protect a retailer from customers who feel cheated. So companies that post pricing mistakes must choose between losing money by honoring offers or losing customer goodwill by canceling them—there simply isn't a winning option. But Travelocity—home of those unintended free tickets from Los Angeles to Fiji—has at least found a way to handle snafus with grace. Its Travelocity Guarantee program notes "If, say, we inadvertently advertise a fare that's just 'too good to be true,' like a free trip to Fiji, we'll work with you and our travel partners to make it up to you and find a solution that puts a smile on your face." So—happy shopping!

Creating Prestige

The core goal is to use price to send consumers a message about the high quality and exclusivity of a product—the higher the price, the better the product. Of course, this strategy works only if the product actually delivers top quality; otherwise, nobody would buy more than once (and those who do so would clearly spread the word). Rolex watches, Mont Blanc pens, and Bentley cars all use prestige pricing to reinforce their image.

Skimming Pricing This new product pricing strategy is a subset of prestige pricing. **Skimming pricing** involves offering new products at a premium price. The idea is to entice price-insensitive consumers—music fanatics, for example—to buy high when a product first enters the market. Once these customers have made their purchases, marketers will often introduce lower-priced versions of the same product to capture the bottom of the market. Apple used this strategy with its iPod, introducing its premium version for a hefty price tag. Once it had secured the big spenders, Apple introduced the lower-priced iPod Nanos and Shuffles with a powerful market response. But keep in mind that skimming works only when a product is tough to copy in terms of design, brand image, technology, or some other attribute. Otherwise, the fat margins will attract a host of competitors.

LO6 Pricing in Practice: A Real-World Approach

At this point, you may be wondering about economic theory. How do concepts such as supply and demand and price elasticity affect pricing decisions?

Even though most marketers are familiar with economics, they often don't have the information they need to apply the theories to their specific pricing strategies. Collecting data for supply and demand curves is expensive and time consuming, which may be unrealistic for rapidly changing markets. From a real-world standpoint, most marketers consider market-based factors—especially customer expectations and competitive prices—but they rely on cost-based pricing. The key question is: what price levels will allow me to cover my costs and achieve my objectives?

Breakeven Analysis

Breakeven analysis is a relatively simple process that determines the number of units a firm must sell to cover all costs. Sales above the breakeven point will generate a profit; sales below the breakeven point will lead to a loss. The actual equation looks like this:

$$\text{Breakeven Point (BP)} = \frac{\text{Total fixed costs (FC)}}{\text{Price/Unit (P)} - \text{Variable cost/unit (VC)}}$$

If you were selling pizza, for example, your fixed costs might be $300,000 per year. Fixed costs stay the same regardless of how many pizzas you sell. Specific fixed costs might include the mortgage, equipment payments, advertising, insurance, and taxes. Suppose your variable cost per pizza—the cost of the ingredients and the cost of wages for the baker—were $4 per pizza. If your customers would pay $10 per pizza, you could use the breakeven equation to determine how many pizzas you'd need to sell in a year so that your total sales were equal to your total expenses. Remember: a company that is breaking even is not making a profit.

Here's how the break-even analysis would work for our pizza business:

$$\text{BP} = \frac{\text{FC}}{\text{P} - \text{VC}} = \frac{\$300,000}{\$10 - \$4} = \frac{\$300,000}{\$6} = 50,000 \text{ pizzas}$$

Over a one-year horizon, 50,000 pizzas would translate to about 303 pizzas per day. Is that reasonable? Could you do better? If so, fire up those ovens! If not, you have several choices, each with its own set of considerations:

- **Raise Prices:** How much do other pizzas in your neighborhood cost? Are your pizzas better in some way? Would potential customers be willing to pay more?

- **Decrease Variable Costs:** Could you use less-expensive ingredients? Is it possible to hire less-expensive help? How would these changes affect quality and sales?

- **Decrease Fixed Costs:** Should you choose a different location? Can you lease cheaper equipment? Would

it make sense to advertise less often? How would these changes affect your business?

Clearly, there isn't one best strategy, but a break-even analysis helps marketers get a sense of where they stand and the hurdles they need to clear before actually introducing a product.

Fixed Margin Pricing

Many firms determine upfront how much money they need to make for each item they sell. The **profit margin**—which is the gap between the cost and the price on a per product basis—can be expressed as a dollar amount but more often is expressed as a percent. There are two key ways to determine margins.

1. **Cost-Based Pricing:** The most popular method of establishing a fixed margin starts with determining the actual cost of each product. The process is more complex than it may initially seem, since fixed costs must be allocated on a per-product basis, and some variable costs fluctuate dramatically on a daily or weekly basis. But once the per-product cost is set, the next step is to layer the margin on the cost to determine the price. Costco, for instance, has a strict policy that no branded item can be marked up by more than 14%, and no private-label item by more than 15%. Supermarkets, on the other hand, often mark up merchandise by 25%, and department stores by 50% or more. Margins in other industries can be much thinner.[8]

© pixelbully /Alamy

Putting iTunes on the Spot

The Apple iTunes store has enjoyed fantastic success since its introduction in 2001. The iTunes pay-99-cents-per-track pricing format revitalized a music industry badly battered by the wild popularity of music pirating sites such as Napster. Over the years, iTunes has had little or no meaningful competition, garnering 200 million accounts by 2011. But music fans in Europe may be just as likely to get their music from Swedish music subscription service, Spotify.com, which has a free, ad-supported option available to customers, as well as a premium service for unlimited access to the tracks on mobile phones and offline for about $16.50 per month. In mid-2011, Spotify announced a major service update, allowing people to sync the songs in their Spotify playlists with the iPod Classic, iPod Nano, and iPod Shuffle. According to the company, people will need only to plug their iPods into their computers via USB, and they will see the player pop up in the Spotify app's "Devices" section. From there, they can sync all the MP3s in their playlists in a single step. Spotify's service upgrade, plus its active pursuit of licensing deals with major music labels, may pave the way for Spotify to enter the U.S. market and offer some real competition to Apple iTunes.[9]

odd pricing The practice of ending prices in numbers below even dollars and cents in order to create a perception of greater value.

2. **Demand-Based Pricing:** This approach begins by determining what price consumers would be willing to pay. With that as a starting point, marketers subtract their desired margin, which yields their target costs. This method is more market-focused than cost-based pricing, but it's also more risky, since profits depend on achieving those target costs. A number of Japanese companies, such as Sony, have been very successful with this approach, achieving extraordinarily efficient production.

Consumer Pricing Perceptions: The Strategic Wild Card

You just don't know if you've found the right price until you figure out how consumers perceive it. And those perceptions can sometimes defy the straightforward logic of dollars and cents. Two key considerations are price–quality relationships and odd pricing.

The link between price and perceived quality can be powerful. Picture yourself walking into a local sporting goods store, looking for a new snowboard. They have several models of your favorite brand, most priced at around $450. But then you notice another option—same brand, same style—marked down to $79. Would you buy it? If you were like most consumers, you'd probably assume that something were wrong with a board that cheap. Would you be right? It's hard to know. Sometimes the relationship between price and quality is clear and direct, but that is not always the case. Regardless, consumers will use price as an indicator of quality unless they have additional information to guide their decision. Savvy marketers factor this tendency into their pricing strategies.

Marketers also must weigh the pros and cons of **odd pricing**, or ending prices in numbers below even dollars and

> There are two kinds of fools in any market. One doesn't charge enough. The other charges too much.

— RUSSIAN PROVERB

cents. A micro stereo system at Target, for instance, costs $99.99. Gasoline, of course, uses odd pricing to 99/100ths of a cent. But wouldn't round numbers be easier? Does that extra penny really make a difference? While the research is inconclusive, many marketers believe that jumping up to the "next" round number sends a message that prices have hit a whole new level. In other words, they believe that the *perceived* gap between $99.99 and $100.00 is much greater than the *actual* gap of 1%. And it certainly makes sense from an intuitive standpoint.

Odd prices have also come to signal a bargain, which is often—but not always—a benefit for the marketer. For instance, a big-screen TV for $999.99 might seem like a great deal, while knee surgery for $4,999.99 sounds kind of scary—you'd probably rather that your doctor charge $5,000. Likewise, a fast-food joint might charge $3.99 for its value meal, while fine restaurants almost always end their prices in zeros. Marketers can determine whether odd pricing would work for them by evaluating the strategy in light of the messages it sends to the target market.

Go Figure!!

Classic economics – plus common sense – says that as consumers we will research and weigh our options and make the best choice. But in the real world, consumers are not so rational. Our emotions can trump our minds. In fact, recent research shows that money can act like a drug on our brains. Even just counting your money can literally raise your pain threshold. Pricing hot buttons, such as "FREE!," "99 cents!," and "limited time!" can play games with our minds, too, luring us to purchase and consume products that we don't really even want! But the good news for marketers is that consumers are irrational in somewhat predictable ways – go figure!

Mere exposure to a high price makes a lower price seem reasonable, even if it isn't. So smart marketers often keep overpriced items in their line simply to promote sales of other items. For instance, if the most expensive necklace in a jewelry store is $100, and no one wants to buy it, the owner might add a $200 necklace to boost sales of the $100 necklace. Economists call this effect anchoring. And research shows that anchors are tough to shake. One key takeaway that goes beyond consumer goods: "be first to name a price in a negotiation – especially a salary negotiation – and don't worry about being overly reasonable."[10]

Distribution and pricing are two fundamental elements of the marketing mix. In today's frenzied global economy, marketers are seeking a competitive edge through distribution management. Creating a profitable presence in multiple retail venues requires constant focus throughout the organization. And managing the supply chain—how products move along the path from raw materials to the final consumer—plays a crucial role in controlling costs and providing great customer service. Integrating effective technology during the entire process can separate the winners from the losers.

Pricing objectives and strategies are also pivotal since they directly impact both profitability and product image. As the market changes, successful companies continually re-evaluate and modify their approach, working hand in hand with their accountants.

Looking ahead, a growing number of companies will probably move toward collaboration, rather than competition, as they manage their supply chains. And pricing will likely become even more dynamic in response to the changing market.

As the economy globalized, the process of distributing countless numbers of goods and services around the world as efficiently as possible led to the rise of the field of logistics, which encompasses transportation, warehousing, inventory management, and inspection. Specific jobs include truck driver, freight agent, warehouse manager, inspector, purchase agent, and scheduler. Some positions do not require higher education, but virtually all demand superior organizational skills and an entrenched detail orientation, plus a deep understanding of the complex web of rules, regulations, and laws that govern many aspects of logistics in our increasingly globalized world economy. In 2011, the median salary for logistics professionals was $90,000, with job growth anticipated in the south and southeast regions of the United States, plus significant opportunities abroad.[11]

In most companies, pricing is an integral part of the marketing manager's job – rather than a separate position – typically handled with support from cost accountants. Determining effective, profitable pricing strategies requires strong analytical skills and a broad strategic perspective with a focus on the long term.

CAREERS IN DISTRIBUTION AND PRICING

CAREERS

What *else?*
RIP & REVIEW CARDS IN THE BACK
and visit www.cengagebrain.com!

14

Management, Motivation, and Leadership:

Bringing Business to Life

© Ben Bloom/Stone/Getty Images

> IT'S OKAY TO TRY *BIG* THINGS.
>
> — Mark Zuckerberg, Founder and CEO, Facebook

L01 Bringing Resources to Life

To grow and thrive, every business needs resources—money, technology, materials—and an economic system that helps enterprise flourish. But those resources, or factors of production, are nothing without **management** to bring them to life. Managers provide vision and direction for their organizations, they decide how to use resources to achieve goals, and they inspire others—both inside and outside their companies—to follow their lead. By formal definition, managers achieve the goals of an organization through planning, organizing, leading, and controlling organizational resources, including people, money, and time.

In simple terms, **planning** means figuring out where to go and how to get there. **Organizing** means determining a structure for both individual jobs and the overall organization. **Leading** means directing and motivating people to achieve organizational goals. And **controlling** means checking performance and making adjustments as needed. In today's chaotic, hyper-competitive business environment, managers face daunting challenges. But for the right people, management positions can provide an exhilarating—though sometimes exhausting—career.

As the business pace accelerates and the environment continues to morph—especially in the wake of economic turmoil—the role of management has radically transformed. The successful manager has changed from boss to coach, from disciplinarian to motivator, from dictator to team builder. But the bottom-line goal has remained the same: to create value for the organization.

Management Hierarchy: Levels of Responsibility

Most medium-sized and large companies have three basic levels of management: **top management**, **middle management**, and **first-line (or supervisory) management**. The levels typically fall into a pyramid of sorts, with a small number of top managers and a larger number of supervisory managers. Responsibilities shift as managers move up the hierarchy, and the skills that they use must shift accordingly. Here are the differences between three key levels:

- **Top management** sets the overall direction of the firm. Top managers must articulate a vision, establish priorities, and allocate time, money, and other resources. Typical titles include chief executive officer (CEO), president, and vice president.

- **Middle management** manages the managers. (Say that three times!) Middle managers must communicate up and down the pyramid, and their primary contribution often involves coordinating teams and special projects with their peers from other departments. Typical titles include director, division head, and branch manager.

- **First-line management** manages the people who do the work. First-line managers must train, motivate, and evaluate nonmanagement employees, so they are heavily involved in day-to-day production issues. Typical titles include supervisor, foreman, and section leader.

Smaller companies usually don't have a hierarchy of management. Often the owner must act as the top, middle, and first-line manager, all rolled into one. This clearly requires enormous flexibility and well-developed management skills.

Management Skills: Having What It Takes to Get the Job Done

Given the turbulence of today's business world, managers must draw on a staggering range of skills to do their jobs efficiently and effectively. Most of these abilities cluster into three broad categories: technical skills, human skills, and conceptual skills.

- **Technical Skills: Technical skills** refer to expertise in a specific functional area or department. Keep in mind

---

management Achieving the goals of an organization through planning, organizing, leading, and controlling organizational resources including people, money, and time.

planning Determining organizational goals and action plans for how to achieve those goals.

organizing Determining a structure for both individual jobs and the overall organization.

leading Directing and motivating people to achieve organizational goals.

controlling Checking performance and making adjustments as needed.

top management Managers who set the overall direction of the firm, articulating a vision, establishing priorities, and allocating time, money, and other resources.

middle management Managers who supervise lower-level managers and report to a higher-level manager.

first-line management Managers who directly supervise nonmanagement employees.

technical skills Expertise in a specific functional area or department.

human skills The ability to work effectively with and through other people in a range of different relationships.

conceptual skills The ability to grasp a big-picture view of the overall organization, the relationships among its various parts, and its fit in the broader competitive environment.

Maslow's hierarchy of needs theory A motivation theory that suggests that human needs fall into a hierarchy and that as each need is met, people become motivated to meet the next-highest need in the pyramid.

that technical skills don't necessarily relate to technology. People can have technical skills—or specific expertise—in virtually any field, from sales, to copywriting, to accounting, to airplane repair, to computer programming.

◗ **Human Skills: Human skills** refer to the ability to work with and through other people in a range of different relationships. Human skills include communication, leadership, coaching, empathy, and team building. A manager with strong human skills can typically mobilize support for initiatives and find win–win solutions for conflicts.

◗ **Conceptual Skills: Conceptual skills** refer to the ability to grasp a big-picture view of the overall organization and the relationship between its various parts. Conceptual skills also help managers understand how their company fits into the broader competitive environment. Managers with strong conceptual skills typically excel at strategic planning.

All three categories of skill are essential for management success. But their importance varies according to the level of the manager. Front-line managers must have a high degree of technical skills, which help them hire, train, and evaluate employees; avoid mistakes; and ensure high-quality production. Middle-level managers need an especially high level of human skills. They typically act as the bridge between departments, coordinating people and projects that sometimes have mismatched priorities. Top-level managers must demonstrate excellent conceptual skills in order to formulate a vision, interpret marketplace trends, and plan for the future. To move up in an organization, managers must constantly learn and grow, nurturing skills that reflect their new tasks.

Across all three skill sets, critical thinking and decision-making abilities have become increasingly important. Critical thinking helps managers find value even in an overload of information, while decision-making skills help them respond wisely and rapidly, with an unwavering focus on customer satisfaction.

Managers who expect to grow in the company hierarchy must expect to foster new skills. Too often, workers get promotions because of great technical skills—e.g., the top salesperson lands the sales manager slot—but they struggle to move further because they don't fully develop their human and conceptual skills.

The Power of One

Some people seem compelled to succeed no matter what . . . and those are the folks who tend to drive the economy. A quick survey of some well-known super-achievers suggests that a high level of motivation was part of their personalities from the very beginning:

◗ *Tiger Woods, golf star:* At the age of six, Tiger practiced his golf swing in the mirror while listening to motivational tapes (sample: "I will make my own destiny.")

◗ *Martha Stewart, lifestyle mogul:* Still in elementary school, Martha catered local birthday parties for other kids, because the going rate for babysitting "wasn't quite enough money."

◗ *Sean "Diddy" Combs, music mogul:* Diddy learned by doing at Howard University, raking in money by selling term papers and dance party tickets to his peers.

◗ *Richard Branson, Virgin Group CEO:* Branson attributes at least some of his motivation to his mom: when he was six, she would shove him out of the car and tell him to find his own way home.

◗ *Condoleeza Rice, former Secretary of State:* A competitive ice skater as a child, Rice got up at 4:30 A.M. every morning to spend two hours at the rink practicing her skating before a full day at school.

But keep in mind that some high achievers don't gear up until well after childhood. True motivation requires clear goals, which people can develop at any point in their lives. When meaningful goals merge with energy and determination, anything becomes possible.[1]

Ooops! What were they thinking?

Bad Decisions, Big Impacts

Every day, managers around the globe make high-stakes decisions, from expanding overseas, to introducing new products, to closing factories. The great decisions have become the stuff of legends, shaping the business world as we know it today. Bad choices also abound. Consider these five business decisions that made history for their silliness:

○ Faced with the opportunity to buy rights to the telephone in 1876, Western Union, the telegraph behemoth, rejected the newfangled device: "This 'telephone' has too many shortcomings to be seriously considered as a means of communication. The device is inherently of no value to us."

○ In 1899, two young attorneys approached Asa Chandler—owner of the briskly selling new fountain drink Coca-Cola—with an innovative proposal to bottle the beverage. Chandler sold them exclusive rights to bottle Coke across most of the United States for the grand sum of $1. Oops.

○ Reviewing technology at the dawn of the television age, *The New York Times*—a bellwether for key trends in business and otherwise—decided that TV just wasn't happening: "The problem with television is that people must keep their eyes glued to a screen; the average American family hasn't time for it." Imagine their surprise a few short years later....

○ Former presidential candidate and self-made Texas tech tycoon Ross Perot blew a chance to buy out Microsoft in 1979 because he wasn't willing to meet their relatively low asking price; he now calls the decision "one of the biggest business mistakes I've ever made."

○ Mike Smith, one of the executives in charge of evaluating new talent for the London office of Decca Records, rejected the Beatles in 1962 with the now infamous line: "Groups are out; four-piece groups with guitars particularly are finished." Not so much....

With the help of hindsight, momentous decisions may seem almost inevitable. But these bloopers clearly show that in the fog of the moment, the right choice can be anything but clear.

LO2 Motivation: Lighting the Fire

Standout managers motivate others to reach for their best selves—to accomplish more than they ever thought possible. Motivated workers tend to feel great about their jobs, and workers who feel great tend to produce more. But the thinking about *how* to motivate workers has changed dramatically over time. In the early 1900s, key management thinkers focused on efficiency and productivity, dictating precisely how workers should do each element of their jobs. But more recent research suggests that people's thoughts and feelings play a vital role in motivation, which leads to a range of new theories.

Theories of Motivation

Maslow's Hierarchy of Needs Theory Noted psychologist Abraham Maslow theorized that people are motivated to satisfy only unmet needs. He proposed a hierarchy of human needs—from basic to abstract—suggesting that as each need is met, people become motivated to meet the next highest need in the pyramid. Maslow's five specific needs are shown in Exhibit 14.1. While he didn't develop his theory based on the workplace, Maslow's ideas can illuminate the needs behind motivation at work.

EXHIBIT 14.1 Maslow's Hierarchy of Needs and the Workplace

MASLOW'S NEED	DESCRIPTION	WORKPLACE EXAMPLES
PHYSIOLOGICAL	Need for basic survival—food, water, clothing, and shelter	A job with enough pay to buy the basics
SAFETY	Need to feel secure—free of harm and free of fear	Safety equipment, healthcare plans, life insurance, retirement plans, job security
SOCIAL (BELONGING)	Need to feel connected to others—accepted by family and friends	Teamwork, positive corporate culture, company lunchroom, department outings
ESTEEM	Need for self-respect and respect from others—recognition and status	Acknowledgment, feedback, promotions, perks
SELF-ACTUALIZATION	Need for fulfillment, the need to realize one's fullest potential	Challenging, creative jobs; meaningful work that ties to a greater good

© Cengage Learning 2013

Theory X and Theory Y A motivation theory that suggests that management attitudes toward workers fall into two opposing categories based on management assumptions about worker capabilities and values.

job enrichment The creation of jobs with more meaningful content, under the assumption that challenging, creative work will motivate employees.

From a workplace perspective, the idea that people are motivated only by unmet needs clearly holds true for the first two levels of the hierarchy. Finding a job that pays the bills, for instance, is the primary motivator for most people who don't have any job at all. People who have a job, but no healthcare, would find health insurance much more motivating than, say, a company picnic geared toward meeting social needs.

But once physiological and safety needs are met, the other needs are motivating to different degrees in different people. An employee with strong social connections outside work might be more motivated by a promotion that meets esteem needs than by a company outing that meets social needs. A number of firms actually use self-actualization needs as a starting point for motivating employees, by creating a mission statement that communicates the importance of the work. Google inspires employees through its lofty purpose: to organize the world's information and make it universally accessible and useful.

Theory X and Theory Y

Psychologist Douglas McGregor, one of Maslow's students, studied workplace motivation from a different angle. He proposed that management attitudes toward workers would directly affect worker motivation. His research suggested that management attitudes fall into two opposing categories, which he called **Theory X and Theory Y**, described in Exhibit 14.2.

McGregor proposed that managers should employ Theory Y assumptions in order to capitalize on the imagination and intelligence of every worker. In American business today, some organizations use a Theory X approach, but a growing number have begun to at least experiment with Theory Y, tapping into a rich pool of employee input.

> ## Leaders don't create followers, they create more leaders.
> — Tom Peters

Job Enrichment A number of researchers have focused on creating jobs with more meaningful content, under the assumption that challenging, creative work will motivate employees to give their best effort. **Job enrichment** typically includes the following factors:

1. **Skill Variety:** Workers can use a range of different skills.
2. **Task Identity:** Workers do complete tasks with clear beginnings and endings.
3. **Task Significance:** Workers understand the impact of the task on others.
4. **Autonomy:** Workers have freedom and authority regarding their jobs.
5. **Feedback:** Workers receive clear, frequent information about their performance.

Richard Branson, maverick founder of the Virgin Group, relies on job enrichment, especially autonomy and feedback, to keep people motivated at his 350-company empire (which includes a startling range of firms, such as Virgin Atlantic Airlines, Virgin Music, Virgin mobile phones, and Virgin Galactic space travel). Branson gives his managers a stake in their companies and then tells them "to run it as if it's their own." He says, "I intervene as little as possible. Give them that, and they will give everything back." According to Virgin's website,

---

EXHIBIT 14.2 Theory X and Theory Y

THEORY X ASSUMPTIONS ABOUT WORKERS	THEORY Y ASSUMPTIONS ABOUT WORKERS
• Workers dislike work and will do everything they can to avoid it.	• Work is as natural as play or rest—workers do not inherently dislike it.
• Fear is motivating—coercion and threats are vital to get people to work toward company goals.	• Different rewards can be motivating—people can exercise self-direction and self-control to meet company goals.
• People prefer to be directed, avoiding responsibility and seeking security.	• People can accept and even seek responsibility. • The capacity for imagination, creativity, and ingenuity is widely distributed in the population. • The intellectual capacity of the average worker is underutilized in the workplace.

© Cengage Learning 2013

"we pretty much practice a collaborative and supportive style of custodianship." Due in large part to Branson's motivational approach, the Virgin workforce is fully engaged with the company, contributing to its remarkable long-term success.[2]

Expectancy Theory Usually attributed to researcher Victor Vroom, **expectancy theory** deals with the relationship among individual effort, individual performance, and individual reward. The key concept is that a worker will be motivated if he or she believes that effort will lead to performance, and performance will lead to a meaningful reward.

Effort → Performance → Reward

The theory suggests that if any link in the chain is broken, the employee will not be motivated.

Imagine if your professor announced on the first day of class that he or she had never given any student an A, as a matter of principle. Would you be motivated to perform in class? Not likely—the link between performance and reward would be broken. Retailer Hot Topic has done a particularly strong job implementing the link between effort and performance. A Hot Topic employee describes the connection, saying, "I've worked for HT for five years, and the best thing I've learned is that if you work hard enough and dedicate enough of yourself to something, you can achieve your goals!" Hot Topic has also established strong links between performance and rewards. Perhaps it's no coincidence that Hot Topic was one of the few retail chains that continued to perform well, even as the recession tightened its grip in late 2008 and early 2009.[3]

Equity Theory Pioneered by J. Stacy Adams, **equity theory** proposes that perceptions of fairness directly affect worker motivation. The key idea is that people won't be motivated if they believe that the relationship between what they contribute and what they earn is different from the relationship between what others contribute and what others earn. For example, if you worked ten-hour days, and earned less than the guy in the next cube who works seven-hour days, you'd

Motivated employees have played a central role in Hot Topic's strong performance.

© Richard Levine/Alamy

probably think it was pretty unfair. To restore a sense of balance, you might:

- ➋ Demand a raise
- ➋ Start coming in late, leaving early, and taking extra long lunch hours
- ➋ Convince yourself that the other guy is about to be fired (or try to get him fired)
- ➋ Look for another job

The response to perceived inequity almost always involves trying to change the system, changing your own work habits, distorting your perceptions, or leaving the company.

But keep in mind that equity theory is based on perceptions, which are not always on the mark. People are all too prone to overestimate their own contributions, which throws perceived equity out of balance. The best way to combat equity issues is through clear, open communication from management.[4]

Motivation Today

Companies today use a range of approaches to motivation, although several key themes have emerged. Most firms no longer seek to make their employees happy; instead, they want their workers to be productive and engaged. Yet, for employees, work is about more than just productivity. University of Michigan business school professor David Ulrich points out that even in today's hyper-competitive environment, "people still want to find meaning in their work and in the institutions that employ them."[5]

A growing emphasis on corporate culture has captured the best of both worlds for companies that do it right. A look at *Fortune* magazine's 100 Best Companies to Work for in 2011 demonstrates that a distinctive, positive culture tends to create productive employees who are deeply attached to their work and their companies. The winners tend to emphasize the health and well-being of their employees, and to offer strong commitments to make to world a better place. Software giant SAS, for instance, which earned the number-one slot for the second year in a row, offers employees unlimited sick days, a medical center staffed by four physicians and ten nurse practitioners (at no cost to employees), a free 66,000-square-foot fitness center and natatorium, and a 35-hour work week. Not surprisingly, turnover at SAS is the industry's lowest at 2.6%, vs. 22% for the info tech industry overall, and the firm is highly profitable.

Boston Consulting Group (BCG), in the number 2 slot, provides generous pay and strong job security, but the firm also offers a chance to work with the U.N. World Food Program and Save the Children; following the devastating 2010 Haitian earthquake, BCG pulled its consultants off client projects to

expectancy theory A motivation theory that concerns the relationship among individual effort, individual performance, and individual reward.

equity theory A motivation theory that proposes that perceptions of fairness directly affect worker motivation.

strategic planning High-level, long-term planning that establishes a vision for the company, defines long-term objectives and priorities, determines broad action steps, and allocates resources.

tactical planning More specific, shorter-term planning that applies strategic plans to specific functional areas.

operational planning Very specific, short-term planning that applies tactical plans to daily, weekly, and monthly operations.

provide on-the-ground support in Haiti. Zappos.com, which leaped from #15 to #6 in 2011, enjoys a happy, quirky culture that includes no-charge vending machines, plus the services of a full-time life coach. After 15 years of service, employees at Recreational Equipment Inc (REI) are entitled to a four-week paid sabbatical; after that, they can take one every five years. Employee-owned Building contractor DPR Construction has a wine bar at each of its 17 locations. Whole Foods employees who meet the goals of a healthy-living challenge get up to 30% off all products sold in the stores. Employees at Umpqua Bank get 40 hours of paid time off every year to do volunteer work.[6]

Finally, a growing number of businesses have expanded their range of employee incentives beyond just cash. While money certainly matters, *Fortune* magazine points out that "telling employees they're doing a great job costs nothing but counts big." Employee training is a noncash motivational tactic gaining momentum across the economy in response to the growing array of complex skills needed by the workforce. The emphasis on training and education is especially motivating given that more and more employees identify themselves based on their field of expertise rather than their organization.[7]

Successful businesses ensure that their workforce has up-to-date training in an array of skills.

©iStockphoto.com/TommL

planning as their most valuable management tool. But even though planning is critical, it's also highly risky in light of cutthroat competition, rapid change, and economic uncertainty. The best plans keep the organization on track without sacrificing flexibility and responsiveness; they incorporate ways to respond to change both inside and outside the organization.[8]

Although all managers engage in planning, the scope of the process changes according to the manager's position as shown in Exhibit 14.3. Top-level managers focus on **strategic planning**. They establish a vision for the company, define long-term objectives and priorities, determine broad action steps, and allocate resources. Middle managers focus on **tactical planning**, or applying the strategic plan to their specific areas of responsibility. And first-line managers focus on **operational planning**, or applying the tactical plans to daily, weekly, and monthly operations. Successful firms often encourage a flow of feedback up and down the organization to ensure that all key plans are sound and that all key players "buy in." Some typical planning decisions and timeframes are shown in Exhibit 14.3.

LO3 Planning: Figuring Out Where to Go and How to Get There

The planning function—figuring out where to go and how to get there—is the core of effective management. A survey in The *Wall Street Journal* found that 80% of executives identify

EXHIBIT 14.3 Managerial Planning

TYPE OF PLANNING	MANAGEMENT LEVEL	SCOPE OF PLANNING	EXAMPLES OF PLANNING QUESTIONS AND CONCERNS
STRATEGIC PLANNING	Senior management	Typically five-year timeframe	Should we acquire a new company? Should we begin manufacturing in China? Should we expand to overseas markets? Should we take our company public?
TACTICAL PLANNING	Middle management	Typically one-year timeframe	Should we spend more time servicing each customer? Should we hire a public relations agency to handle PR? Should we spend fewer ad dollars on TV and more on the Web?
OPERATIONAL PLANNING	First-line management	Daily, weekly, and monthly timeframe	How should we schedule employees this week? When should we schedule delivery for each batch of product? How should customer service people answer the phones?

© Cengage Learning 2013

A fourth category of planning has gained new prominence in the last decade: **contingency planning**, or planning for unexpected events. Senior management usually spearheads contingency planning, but with input from the other levels of management. Contingency plans consider what might go wrong—both inside the business and with the outside environment—and develop responses. Potential issues include:

- ⊙ How should we respond if our competitors knock off our best-selling product?
- ⊙ What should we do if the government regulates our industry?
- ⊙ How should we respond if our data management/computer system fails?
- ⊙ How can we restart our business if a natural disaster destroys our plant or supply channels?
- ⊙ How will we evacuate employees if terrorists strike our headquarters?

Clearly, anticipating every potential problem is impossible (and impractical!). Instead, effective contingency plans tend to focus only on the issues that are most probable, most potentially harmful, or both (see Exhibit 14.4). For example, a southern California warehouse store (e.g., Costco) might concentrate its contingency plans on earthquake response, while an online brokerage firm might focus its plans on responding to a computer hacker attack.

Strategic Planning: Setting the Agenda

Strategic planning is the most fundamental part of the planning process, since all other plans—and most major management decisions—stem from the strategic plan. The strategic planning process typically includes these steps:

1. Define the mission of the organization.
2. Evaluate the organization's competitive position.
3. Set goals for the organization.
4. Create strategies for competitive differentiation.
5. Implement strategies.
6. Evaluate results, and incorporate lessons learned.

Defining Your Mission The mission of an organization articulates its essential reason for being. The **mission** defines the organization's purpose, values, and core goals, providing the framework for all other plans (see Exhibit 14.5). Most large companies present their mission as a simple, vivid, compelling statement that everyone involved with the company—from the janitor to the CEO, from customers to investors—can easily understand. Mission statements tend to vary in their length, their language, and even their names, but they share a common goal: to provide a clear, long-term focus for the organization.

Evaluating Your Competitive Position Strategy means nothing in a vacuum—every firm must plan in the context of the marketplace. Many companies use a **SWOT analysis** (strengths, weaknesses, opportunities, and threats) to evaluate where they stand relative to the competition. Strengths and weaknesses are internal to the organization, and they include factors that would either build up or drag down the firm's performance. Opportunities and threats are external,

contingency planning Planning for unexpected events, usually involving a range of scenarios and assumptions that differ from the assumptions behind the core plans.

mission The definition of an organization's purpose, values, and core goals, which provides the framework for all other plans.

SWOT analysis A strategic planning tool that helps management evaluate an organization in terms of internal strengths and weakness, and external opportunities and threats.

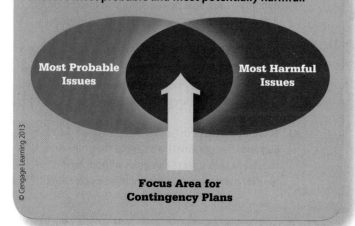

Exhibit 14.4 Contingency Planning Paradigm

Businesses tend to focus their contingency plans on issues that are most probable *and* most potentially harmful.

Most Probable Issues — Most Harmful Issues

Focus Area for Contingency Plans

© Cengage Learning 2013

Exhibit 14.5 Examples of Mission Statements

COMPANY	MISSION STATEMENT
AMAZON	To be earth's most customer-centric company; to build a place where people can come to find and discover anything they might want to buy online.
STARBUCKS	To inspire and nurture the human spirit—one person, one cup and one neighborhood at a time.
GOOGLE	To organize the world's information and make it universally accessible and useful.
CHILI'S BAR AND GRILL	To spice up everyday life.

© Cengage Learning 2013

and they include factors that would affect the company's performance, but are typically out of the company's control. Exhibit 14.6 offers some examples.

Initial information about internal strengths and weaknesses usually comes from careful analysis of internal reports on topics such as budget and profitability. But to better understand strengths and weaknesses, executives should actively seek firsthand information—on a personal basis—from key people throughout the company, from front-line workers to the board of directors.

Gathering information about external opportunities and threats can be more complex, since these areas include both current and potential issues (which can be tough to predict). Information about external factors can come from many different sources, including the news, government reports, customers, and competitors.

Exhibit 14.6 SWOT Analysis

POTENTIAL INTERNAL STRENGTHS:	POTENTIAL EXTERNAL OPPORTUNITIES:
• Premium brand name • Proven management team • Lower costs/higher margins	• Higher consumer demand • Complacent competitors • Growth in foreign markets
POTENTIAL INTERNAL WEAKNESSES:	**POTENTIAL EXTERNAL THREATS:**
• Low employee satisfaction • Inadequate financial resources • Poor location	• A powerful new competitor • A deep recession • New government regulations

© Cengage Learning 2013

© Yuri Arcurs/Shutterstock.com

Slackers? Not so much…

Generation Y—which includes the 76 million kids born between 1978 and 1998—is changing the face of the workforce. These self-confident, outspoken young people have posed a new set of challenges for managers across the economy. A quick profile of Generation Y—also known as "millennials," "echo-boomers," and "Gen F" (for Facebook)—highlights their key characteristics. Keep in mind that no general overview can clearly describe each member of Generation Y. Yet, chances are strong that you recognize at least parts of yourself in this profile. Companies that understand you and your peers—and figure out how to harness your talents—will find themselves with a sharp competitive edge in the years to come.

Unfortunately, not all employers "get" Gen Y. According to a 2009 Pew Research Center study, three out of four Americans believe that today's youth are less virtuous and industrious than their elders. But the facts suggest otherwise. Volunteerism among young people has exploded. Between 1989 and 2006, the share of teenagers doing volunteer work doubled. Furthermore, millennials are more willing to accept that their work will bleed into evenings and weekends. Some experts also believe that millennials are better at switching quickly from one activity to another, a real plus in today's fast-paced work environment.[9] More Gen Y characteristics:

- **Goal Driven:** Gen Yers expect to perform for their rewards. But they tend to find smaller, short-term goals much more motivating than long-term goals. The reason: a week in their fast-paced world is more like a year was for their parents.
- **NOW Focused:** Gen Yers often look for instant gratification. They typically expect to make an impact in their companies right away, and they are less willing to "pay dues" or "suck up" to people they don't respect in order to make it happen.
- **Change Oriented:** Gen Yers actively embrace change and excitement. Many anticipate—even hope—to change jobs frequently. They don't share the expectation of long-term employment that disillusioned so many of their parents.
- **Tech Savvy:** Gen Yers are masters of the Internet and the iPhone. They often expect top technology in the workplace, and they use virtually all of it (often at the same time!) to boost their performance.
- **Diverse:** Gen Y is among the most diverse demographic groups in America—one in three is a minority—and most don't believe that their ethnicity defines their character. Many were born in other countries and speak multiple languages fluently.
- **Idealistic:** Gen Yers grew up in a scary world, marked by violence in their own backyards. Yet, they remain convinced that they can make a positive difference, seeking solutions through a refreshing commitment to volunteerism.
- **Fulfillment Focused:** Gen Yers tend to value their families and their personal lives deeply. They fully expect to achieve their lofty career goals without sacrificing time for themselves and the people they care about.[10]

Setting Your Goals Strategic goals represent concrete benchmarks that managers can use to measure performance in each key area of the organization. They must fit the firm's mission and tie directly to its competitive position. The three most effective goals are:

1. **Specific and Measurable:** Whenever possible, managers should define goals in clear numerical terms that everyone understands.

2. **Tied to a Timeframe:** To create meaning and urgency, goals should be linked to a specific deadline.

3. **Realistic but Challenging:** Goals that make people stretch can motivate exceptional performance.

Exhibit 14.7 offers examples of how weak goals can transform into powerful goals.

Creating Your Strategies Strategies are action plans that help the organization achieve its goals by forging the best fit between the firm and the environment. The underlying aim, of course, is to create a significant advantage versus the competition. Sources of competitive advantage vary, ranging from better product quality, to better technology, to more motivated employees. The most successful companies build their advantage across several fronts. Southwest Airlines, for example, has a more motivated workforce and a lower cost structure. H&M has lower prices and more fashionable clothing choices. And Procter & Gamble has more innovative new products and strong core brands.

The specifics of strategy differ by industry and by company, but all strategies represent a roadmap. The SWOT analysis determines the starting point, and the objectives signify the immediate destination. Since speed matters, you must begin mapping the next leg of the journey even before you arrive. For added complexity, you never know—given the turbulent environment—when you might hit roadblocks. This means that strategies must be dynamic and flexible. Top managers have responded to this challenge by encouraging front-line managers to participate in the process more than ever before.

Exhibit 14.7 Goal Setting: Getting It Right

WEAK GOAL	POWERFUL GOAL
BECOME MORE INNOVATIVE	Introduce one new product each quarter for the next three years.
REDUCE DELINQUENT ACCOUNTS.	Reduce delinquent accounts to no more than 1% of the total by the next quarter.
INCREASE MARKET SHARE.	Become the #1 or #2 brand in each market where we compete by the end of 2012.

Implementing Your Strategies Implementation should happen largely through tactical planning. Middle managers in each key area of the company must develop plans to carry out core strategies in their area. If the strategic plan, for example, calls for more new products, marketing would need to generate ideas, finance would need to find funding, and sales would need to prepare key accounts. And all of these steps would require tactical planning.

Evaluating Your Results and Incorporating Lessons Learned Evaluation of results should be a continual process, handled by managers at every level as part of their controlling function, covered further in this chapter. But for evaluation to be meaningful, the lessons learned must be analyzed objectively and factored back into the next planning cycle.

strategic goals Concrete benchmarks that managers can use to measure performance in each key area of the organization.

strategies Action plans that help the organization achieve its goals by forging the best fit between the firm and the environment.

LO4 Organizing: Fitting Together the Puzzle Pieces

The organizing function of management means creating a logical structure for people, their jobs, and their patterns of interaction. And clearly, the pieces can fit together in a number of different ways. In choosing the right structure for a specific company, management typically considers many factors, including the goals and strategies of the firm, its products, its use of technology, its size, and the structure of its competitors. Given the potential for rapid change in each of these factors, smart companies continually re-examine their structure and make changes whenever necessary. Microsoft, for instance, restructures its organization every couple of years as new challenges emerge.

But to be effective, reorganizations—and their purpose—must be clear to employees throughout the company. Xerox CEO Anne Mulcahy learned the hard way. Her comments: "During the 1990s, we had lots of consultants on organizational effectiveness. We sliced and diced the business into industries, product lines, and geographies ... you name it. It looked good on paper, but fell apart in implementation. I found myself in a job where I couldn't look anybody in the eye and feel clear accountability for anything ... I'll trade off organizational design for clarity and accountability any day of the week!"[11]

To be effective, reorganizations—and their purpose—must be clear to employees throughout the company. In order to help employees understand how they and their

organization chart A visual representation of the company's formal structure.

degree of centralization The extent to which decision-making power is held by a small number of people at the top of the organization.

span of control Span of management; refers to the number of people a manager supervises.

departmentalization The division of workers into logical groups.

jobs fit within the broader organization, most firms issue an **organization chart**, or a visual representation of the company's formal structure, as shown in Exhibit 14.8.

Looking at the company represented by Exhibit 14.8, you would probably assume that the vice president of production has more power than a regular employee in the marketing department. And in terms of formal power, you'd be absolutely right. But if the marketing employee babysits on the weekend for the president's granddaughter, the balance of power may actually be a bit different than it seems. Make no mistake: the formal structure matters. But knowing how power flows on an informal basis could dramatically increase your effectiveness as well, by helping you target your ideas to the right managers and marshal the support of the most influential employees.

Key Organizing Considerations

In developing the organizational structure, management must make decisions about the degree of centralization, the span of management control, and the type of departmentalization that makes the most sense at any given time.

Centralization The **degree of centralization** relates directly to the source of power and control. In centralized companies, a small number of people at the top of the organization have the power to make decisions. This approach is

Laughing All the Way

Most of us who regularly watch hundreds of dollars evaporate each month at the gas station would scoff at the notion that soaring oil prices are the "best thing that has happened to this world." This statement is all the more surprising from Richard Branson, CEO of Virgin Enterprises, which has earned millions of dollars from oil-guzzling enterprises such as planes, trains, and automobiles. In fact, Virgin's fuel bill has risen by millions as oil prices have skyrocketed. From Branson's perspective, this represents an unprecedented opportunity for business and governments to reduce their destructive dependence on oil. Branson has put his money where his mouth is, investing heavily in earth-friendly, alternative fuels. Perhaps his greenest venture to date is Virgin Galactic, his commercial space travel firm. The launch system for Virgin spaceships will rely on an efficient fuel compound derived from laughing gas and rubber. The spaceships are much greener than NASA's equivalent, which can go further into space, but use the equivalent of two weeks' worth of New York state's total electric supply.[12]

simple and efficient, and the result tends to be a strong corporate image and a uniform customer approach across the front lines. But the downside is that centralized companies typically respond more slowly to customer needs and have lower employee morale. The trade-off may be worthwhile in steady, stable markets, but those are rare.

Faced with today's turbulent environment, most firms are moving toward greater decentralization, pushing power to the lower levels of the organization. Employees with the power to make decisions can respond to customer needs more quickly and effectively. They can also capitalize on opportunities that would likely vaporize in the time it would take to get permission to act. But for decentralization to work, every employee must fully understand the firm's mission, goals, and strategy; otherwise, the company could develop a fragmented image, which would

Exhibit 14.8 Sample Organization Chart

President

Vice President, Marketing

Vice President, Production

Employee   Employee   Employee   Employee

Employee   Employee

© Cengage Learning 2013

undermine its long-term strength. Also, active communication across departments is essential so that all employees can benefit from innovations in other parts of the organization.

Span of Control The **span of control, or span of management**, refers to the number of people a manager supervises. There is no ideal number for every manager. The "right" span of control varies based on the abilities of both the manager and the subordinates, the nature of the work being done, the location of the employees, and the need for planning and coordination. Across industries, the general trend has moved toward wider spans of control as a growing number of companies have pruned layers of middle management to the bare minimum.

Departmentalization **Departmentalization** means breaking workers into logical groups. A number of different options make sense, depending on the organization.

©iStockphoto.com/studiovision

- ⊙ **Functional:** Dividing employees into groups based on area of expertise, such as marketing, finance, and engineering, tends to be efficient and easy to coordinate. For those reasons, it works especially well for small to medium-sized firms.

- ⊙ **Product:** Dividing employees into groups based on the products that a company offers helps workers develop expertise about products that often results in especially strong customer relations.

- ⊙ **Customer:** Dividing employees into groups based on the customers that a company serves helps companies focus on the needs of specific customer groups. Many companies have separate departments for meeting the needs of business and consumer users. This approach is related to product departmentalization.

- ⊙ **Geographical:** Dividing employees into groups based on where customers are located can help different departments better serve specific regions within one country. Similarly, many international firms create a separate department for each different country they serve.

- ⊙ **Process:** Dividing into groups based on what type of work employees do is common in manufacturing, where management may divide departments by processes such as cutting, dyeing, and sewing.

As companies get larger, they usually adopt several different types of departmentalization at different levels of the organization. This approach, shown in Exhibit 14.9 on the following page, is called "hybrid departmentalization."

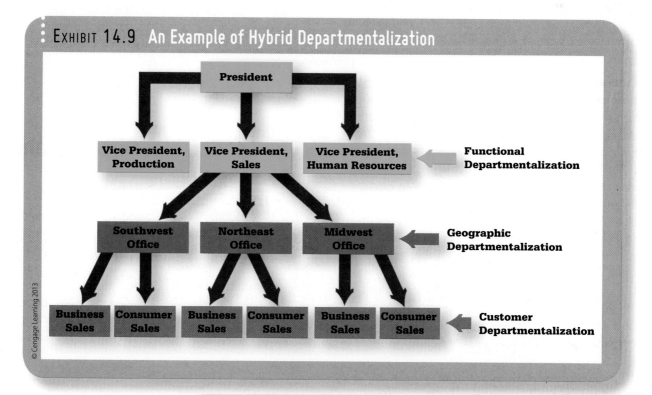

EXHIBIT 14.9   An Example of Hybrid Departmentalization

President

Vice President, Production — Vice President, Sales — Vice President, Human Resources ← **Functional Departmentalization**

Southwest Office — Northeast Office — Midwest Office ← **Geographic Departmentalization**

Business Sales — Consumer Sales — Business Sales — Consumer Sales — Business Sales — Consumer Sales ← **Customer Departmentalization**

© Cengage Learning 2013

Organization Models

Company structures tend to follow one of three different patterns: line organizations, line-and-staff organizations, and matrix organizations. But these organizationa models are not mutually exclusive. In fact, many management teams build their structure using elements of each model at different levels of the organization.

Line Organizations A line organization typically has a clear, simple chain of command from top to bottom. Each person is directly accountable to the person immediately above, which means quick decision making and no fuzziness about who is responsible for what. The downside is a lack of specialists to provide advice or support for line managers. This approach tends to work well for small businesses, but for medium-sized and large companies the result can be inflexibility, too much paperwork, and even incompetence, since experts aren't available to give their input on key decisions.

Line-and-Staff Organizations A line-and-staff organization incorporates the benefits of a line organization without all the drawbacks. **Line managers** supervise the functions that contribute directly to profitability: production and marketing. **Staff managers**, on the other hand, supervise the functions that provide advice and assistance to the line departments. Examples include legal, accounting, and human resources. In a line-and-staff organization, the line managers form the primary chain of authority in the company. Staff departments work alongside line departments, but there is no direct reporting relationship (except at the top of the company). Since staff people don't report to line people, their authority comes from their know-how. This approach, which overlays fast decision making with additional expertise, tends to work well for

Management
is doing things right; leadership is doing the right things.

— Peter Drucker, Management Researcher, Writer, and Speaker

medium-sized and large companies. But in some firms, the staff departments gain so much power that they become dictatorial, imposing unreasonable limitations on the rest of the company.

Matrix Organizations Matrix organizations build on the line-and-staff approach by adding a lot more flexibility. A matrix structure brings together specialists from different areas of the company to work on individual projects on a temporary basis. A new-product-development team, for instance, might include representatives from sales, engineering, finance, purchasing, and advertising. For the course of the project, each specialist reports to the project manager and to the head of his or her own department (e.g., the vice president of marketing). The matrix approach has been particularly popular in the high-tech and aerospace industries.

The matrix structure offers several key advantages. It encourages teamwork and communication across the organization. It offers flexibility in deploying key people. It lends itself to innovative solutions. And not surprisingly—when managed well—the matrix structure creates a higher level of motivation and satisfaction for employees. But these advantages have a clear flip side. The need for constant communication can bog down a company in too many meetings. The steady state of flux can be overwhelming for both managers and employees. And having two bosses can cause conflict and stress for everyone.

LO5 Leadership: Directing and Inspiring

While most people easily recognize a great leader, defining the qualities of leaders can be more complex, since successful leaders have a staggering range of personalities, characteristics, and backgrounds. Most researchers agree that true leaders are trustworthy, visionary, and inspiring. After all, we don't follow people who don't know where they're going, and we definitely don't follow people we don't trust. Other key leadership traits include empathy, courage, creativity, intelligence, and fairness.

Leadership Style

How a leader uses power defines his or her leadership style. While the range of specific styles is huge, most seem to cluster into three broad categories: autocratic, democratic, and free-rein. The categories fall along a continuum of power, with the manager at one end and the employees at the other, as shown in Exhibit 14.10.

Exhibit 14.10 The Continuum of Leadership and Power

Employee Power

Management Power

Free-Rein Leadership

Democratic Leadership

Autocratic Leadership

© Cengage Learning 2013

Autocratic leaders hoard decision-making power for themselves, and they typically issue orders without consulting their followers. **Democratic leaders** share power with their followers. Even though they still make final decisions, they typically solicit and incorporate input from their followers. **Free-rein leaders** set objectives for their followers but give them freedom to choose how they accomplish those goals.

Interestingly, the most effective leaders don't use just one approach. They tend to shift their leadership style, depending on the followers and the situation. When a quick decision is paramount, autocratic leadership may make the most sense. An army officer, for example, probably shouldn't take a vote on whether to storm a hill in the middle of a firefight. But when creativity is the top priority—during new product brainstorming, for instance—free-rein management would probably work best. Likewise, a brand-new worker might benefit from autocratic (but friendly)

management, while a talented, experienced employee would probably work best under free-rein leadership.

Another vital consideration is the customer. When the customer seeks consistency in the delivery of the product—in fast food, for instance—the autocratic leadership style may be appropriate. But when the customer needs flexibility and problem-solving assistance—a consulting client, for example—the free-rein leadership style may be most effective. The democratic leadership style typically provides customers with a balance of consistency and flexibility, which works across a wide range of industries.

L06 Controlling: Making Sure It All Works

Controlling may be the least glamorous of the management functions, but don't be fooled: it's critically important. Controlling means monitoring performance of the firm—or individuals within the firm—and making improvements when necessary. As the environment changes, plans change. And as plans change, the control process must change as well, to ensure that the company achieves its goals. The control process includes three key steps:

1. Establish clear performance standards.
2. Measure actual performance against standards.
3. Take corrective action if necessary.

Establishing clear standards—or performance goals—begins with planning. At every level of planning, objectives should emerge that are consistent

90% of managers believe that they're in the top 10% of performers.
— BusinessWeek

Successful Psychopaths and Productive Narcissists

Watch out! That good-looking guy on the corporate fast track may be a psychopath…

Check out the profile: Psychopaths demonstrate hypnotic charm, coupled with a fundamental lack of empathy and conscience. They can perceive your feelings—often with spooky accuracy—but they just don't care. Canadian researcher Robert Hare describes them as "callous, cold-blooded individuals… They have no sense of guilt or remorse." And they take real pleasure from leveraging their power.

While not every psychopath is a budding Charles Manson, Hare has found that the psychopaths in the workplace share a basic personality profile with their more violent counterparts. Corporate psychopaths, however, score higher in the "selfish, callous, remorseless use of others" category, and much lower in the "unstable, antisocial, and socially deviant lifestyle" category that lands people in jail for more brutal crimes.

The headlines are filled with stories of corporate psychopaths gone way wrong for crimes that range from creative accounting to stock manipulation. CEOs such as Enron's Bernie Ebbers and Bernie Madoff have plundered their companies at the expense of thousands of people losing their jobs or their savings or both. But countless corporate psychopaths have stayed on the right side of the law, delivering bottom-line results at a staggering personal cost to the colleagues they betray and demoralize on a daily basis.

Another unpleasant personality in the corner office is the productive narcissist. These characters don't have much empathy either, but they often have a powerful vision, a flair for innovation, and a knack for attracting committed followers. While their goal may be helping humanity in the abstract, they're often insensitive to the real people around them. Bill Gates, widely respected for his razor-sharp mind, his visionary strategic management, and his world-changing philanthropic generosity—has been known to deflate eager subordinates with comments such as "That's the stupidest thing I've ever heard." And when engineers asked Steve Jobs why they were creating the iMac, he replied, "Because I'm the CEO, and I think it can be done." But despite their abrasive approach, productive narcissists are much less scary than psychopaths, since they're committed to their vision for the company rather than simply to themselves.

Today's chaotic, results-driven business environment may be a magnet for corporate psychopaths and productive narcissists, since both personalities thrive on constant, chaotic change. And the broader culture doesn't help. Americans idealize the idea of the corporate cowboy—the charismatic maverick who delivers against all odds, regardless of the cost. You can protect yourself by learning to recognize and steer clear of unhealthy personalities, no matter how charming they may initially seem.[13]

with the company's mission and strategic plan. The objectives must be (1) specific and measurable, (2) realistic but challenging, and (3) tied to a timeframe. Individual managers may need to break these goals into smaller parts for specific employees, but the subgoals should retain the same three qualities as the original objective.

Measuring performance against standards should happen well before the end of the timeframe attached to the goal. A strong information tracking system is probably management's best tool in this phase of the control process.

If the company or individual is not on track to meet the goals, management's first response should be communication. Employees with full information are far more likely to improve their performance than employees who never learn that they're falling behind. But sometimes workers need more than information—they may need additional resources or coaching in order to meet their goals. Apple's Steve Jobs was often accused of being a tyrannical boss—especially in the employee-evaluation process—but he defended himself by saying, "My job is not to be easy on people. My job is to make them better." If they still don't succeed, perhaps the goals themselves need re-examination as part of a dynamic planning process. Given the expense in both human and financial terms, disciplining employees for poor performance should come only after exploring the reasons for not meeting goals and making changes if necessary.

THE BIG PICTURE

In the past decade, management has become more complex and demanding than ever before. Managers in every area of the business must carry out their roles—planning, organizing, leading, and controlling—in a relentlessly fast-paced world, seething with constant change. While management isn't for everyone, it's often a fit for people with vision, courage, integrity, energy, and a passionate commitment to their companies.

Looking forward, the role of management will continue to evolve in response to the environment. Regardless of how the changes unfold, several key factors will be absolutely vital for successful managers in the twenty-first century: a constant focus on the customer, a commitment to globalization, excellent judgment, and the right mix of talented, motivated employees.

CAREERS

Every business field, from information technology to accounting, includes management jobs and virtually all of those positions require experience in the field before promotion to management. If you are interested in pursuing a management track, your best strategy from a career development perspective would be to deliberately cultivate the skills required at the level above you, without neglecting the skills you need to excel at your current level. Managers typically have more accountability than employees—which often requires more work hours—and therefore have higher salary structures.

What *else?*
RIP & REVIEW CARDS IN THE BACK
and visit www.cengagebrain.com!

15
Human Resource Management:
Building a Top-Quality
Workforce

LEARNING OBJECTIVES
After studying this chapter, you will be able to...

LO1   Explain the importance of human resources to business success

LO2   Discuss key human resource issues in today's economy

LO3   Outline challenges and opportunities that the human resources function faces

LO4   Discuss human resource planning and core human resources responsibilities

LO5   Explain the key federal legislation that affects human resources

> IF YOU HIRE GOOD PEOPLE, GIVE THEM GOOD JOBS, AND PAY THEM GOOD WAGES, SOMETHING *GOOD* IS GOING TO HAPPEN.
>
> — JIM SINEGAL, FOUNDER OF COSTCO

Companies that get the most from their people often consider their human resources their biggest investment. They view the core goal of **human resource (HR) management** in a similar light: to nurture their human investment so that it yields the highest possible return. HR can achieve that goal by recruiting world-class talent, promoting career development, and boosting organizational effectiveness. But clearly, this can happen only in partnership with key managers throughout the company, especially senior executives. (In smaller companies, of course, the owners usually handle HR management in addition to their other responsibilities.)

> **human resource management** The management function focused on maximizing the effectiveness of the workforce by recruiting world-class talent, promoting career development, and determining workforce strategies to boost organizational effectiveness.

LO1 Human Resource Management: Bringing Business to Life

As competition accelerates across the globe, leading firms in every business category have recognized that a quality workforce can vault them over the competition. Southwest Airlines was early to recognize the untapped potential of its people. Executive Chairman Herb Kelleher declared, "We value our employees first. They're the most important, and if you treat them right, then they treat the customers right, and if you treat the customers right, then they keep coming back and shareholders are happy." His attitude has more than paid off. Southwest Airlines has posted profits for 38 consecutive years, even as other airlines have spiraled into decline.

As the Great Recession constricted the economy in 2009, managing human resources remained a top priority for Southwest CEO Gary Kelly. "We've never had a layoff. We've never had a pay cut. And we're going to strive mightily, especially this year, to avoid them once again . . ." Instead, he says, "We're being more creative about encouraging employees to move about the company. We are not threatening people with their jobs." He points out, "We're known for being the greatest company to work for and at the top of the customer service rankings." He maintains, "There is a devotion to the people and a commitment to our people, once we hire them, that we have lived up to. We have proven many times that we're going to be there for our employees in the bad times."[1]

LO2 Human Resource Management Challenges: Major Hurdles

Building a top-quality workforce can be tougher than it may initially seem. Human resource managers—and their counterparts throughout the company—face huge challenges. The best strategies still aren't clear, but forward-thinking firms tend to experiment with new approaches.

Layoffs and Outsourcing

As high-tech, high-end jobs follow low-tech, low-end jobs out of the country—or even just to local contractors—human resources find themselves in turmoil. Many jobs have disappeared altogether as companies have contracted in response to the Great Recession. By mid-2011, many economists were concerned about a "jobless recovery," as labor markets faltered and unemployment rates began to rise again. How can businesses boost the morale and the motivation level of the employees who are left behind? Does less job security translate to less worker loyalty? How can human resources continue to add value as the ground shifts beneath them—and as they wonder how long their own jobs will last?[2]

Wage Gap

Comparing CEO pay to worker pay demonstrates a startling wage gap, bigger in the United States than in any other developed country. In 2007, the average CEO earned 275 times the average worker. As a point of comparison,

Humble Beginnings

Everyone starts somewhere. Not even the rich and famous always had glamour jobs. In today's challenging economy, getting any job at all can be tough for young people, but whatever work you do get, consider that it might be the first step on the road to the next big thing. Some early job examples of the rich and famous:

- Steve Jobs (Apple founder): assembly line worker at HP. At age 13, Jobs put in screws on an HP assembly line. The young computer geek later described the first day of work as "bliss."

- Rachel Ray (celebrity chief): dishwashing machine operator at Howard Johnson. "It was the most degrading job to have. Everyone you go to school with comes in and they see you covered with sweat and old rotten food and you smell."

- Quentin Tarantino (writer and film director): usher at an adult movie theatre. "I could care less about the movies and was totally bored by them."

- Mark Burnett (producer of Survivor and The Apprentice): childcare worker. "The only position I could get was childcare. I thought I'd do it for two weeks. It was two years later before I moved on from nanny."

---

30 years ago, chief executives averaged only 30 to 40 times the average American worker's paycheck. In 2009, median CEO salaries at 200 large, publicly held U.S. firms fell by 0.9%, while net income decreased by 5%. In 2010, the gap widened again, with the average CEO earning 343 times the average worker. Most observers don't object to the pay gap when top CEO pay is tied to top performance. But as the value of formerly high-flying corporations began to evaporate in 2008 and 2009, public rage over senior management salaries and bonuses hit new highs. This issue regained momentum in mid-2011, when data for 2010 revealed that the median pay raise for CEOs of 23% far exceeded the 16% median gain in shareholders' total return. The discrepancy—and the public response—clearly represents a strategic challenge for HR management.[3]

Older Workers

As the oversized Baby Boomer generation begins turning 60, their employers—which include virtually every major American company—face a potential crisis: the loss of key talent and experience through massive retirements. Beginning January 1, 2011 every single day more than 10,000 baby boomers reached the age of 65, and that will continue to happen every single day until 2030.[4] Enlightened companies have responded with programs to retain their best employees through flexible schedules, training opportunities, and creative pay schedules. But as companies aggressively trimmed their payrolls in 2008 and 2009, the

priority of these kinds of programs plummeted, which may leave some firms with a critical dearth of highly experienced workers when the economy revs back up.

Younger Workers

As twenty-somethings enter the workforce, they often bring optimism, open minds, technological know-how, a team orientation, a proven ability to multitask, and a multicultural perspective. But a number of them also bring an unprecedented sense of entitlement. This can translate into startlingly high expectations for their pay, their responsibilities, and their job flexibility, but little willingness to "pay dues." Many have no expectation that their employers will be loyal to them, and they don't feel that they owe their

With a supportive work environment, people feel less stress and become more productive. Organizations can minimize stress by supporting work–life balance.

— Monica Belcourt,
Professor of Human
Resource Management, NYU

companies strong loyalty. Managing this group can sometimes be a challenge, but companies that do it well stand to deliver results for years to come.[5]

Women Workers

Over the last few decades, women have made enormous strides in terms of workplace equality. But several large-scale studies confirm that women continue to face daunting discrimination in terms of both pay and promotions. While unfair treatment has been an issue for many years, recent legal changes have made it easier for women to sue, costing companies millions of dollars in the last decade alone. And the flood of lawsuits shows no signs of slowing. Many women have responded to the unfriendly business environment by leaving the workforce; 37% of highly qualified, professional women step out of the workforce early, versus 24% of men—usually to raise children, start their own companies, or pursue other interests. As a result, we are experiencing a harmful, ongoing brain drain. Human resource managers can help mitigate this issue by implementing specific retention plans for valued women workers and by taking proactive steps to reintegrate returning women back into the workforce.[6]

Work-Life Balance

Over the last decade, workers across all ages and both genders have actively pursued more flexibility and work–life balance in their jobs. But as the recession deepened in 2009, companies began to cut back on these initiatives, describing them as "nice to have" programs in a time when "need to have" goals—such as meeting payroll each month—are tough to attain. Middle-level managers are also apt to demonstrate bias against worker flexibility, even when top management actively supports work–life balance programs. In spite of these issues, insightful HR managers try hard to offer enough flexibility to keep their best workers without jeopardizing their company's business goals.[7]

Lawsuits

The United States has become a wildly litigious society, with employees, customers, and shareholders levying lawsuit after lawsuit against firms of all sizes. Even though many of the lawsuits are legitimate—some profoundly important—a good number are just plain silly. But even if a lawsuit is frivolous, and even if it's thrown out of court, it can still cost a company millions of dollars. Even more importantly, a frivolous lawsuit can cost a business its reputation. Avoiding employee lawsuits by knowing the law and encouraging legal practices is a growing human resources challenge.

LO3 Human Resources Managers: Corporate Black Sheep?

The Problem

The human resource management function is clearly critical, but human resources departments—and the people who work in them—face major challenges. Leading-edge firms expect every department to offer "big picture," strategic contributions that boost company value. But a report in *Fast Company* suggests that most HR professionals lack sufficient strategic skills. Among other data, the report quotes a respected executive at a top U.S. company: "Business acumen is the single biggest factor that HR professionals in the U.S. lack today."[8]

But even highly qualified, strategically focused HR managers face daunting perception problems. A management professor at a leading school comments that "The best and the brightest just don't go into HR." Once in the workforce, many employees see the human resources department as irrelevant—or even worse, as the enemy. This perception clearly undermines their effectiveness.

The Solution

To gain respect from both senior management and their peers, human resources executives must earn a seat at the table. The first step is to know the company. What are the strategic goals? Who is the core customer? Who is the competition? Respected HR departments typically figure out ways to quantify their impact on the company in dollars and cents. They determine how to raise the value of the firm's human capital, which in turn increases the value of the firm itself. Effective HR people also remain open to exceptions even as they enforce broad company policies.

> HR matters enormously in good times. It defines you in the **bad.**
>
> — JACK AND SUZY WELCH

job analysis The examination of specific tasks that are assigned to each position, independent of who might be holding the job at any specific time.

job description An explanation of the responsibilities for a specific position.

job specifications The specific qualifications necessary to hold a particular position.

But clearly, these solutions will work only if senior management recognizes the potential value of effective human resource management. One simple test of senior management commitment is the reporting relationship. If the HR department reports to the CFO, it may be on the fast track to outsourcing. But if the HR department reports to the CEO, the strategic possibilities are unlimited.

LO4 Human Resource Planning: Drawing the Map

Great human resource management begins with great planning: Where should you go? And how should you get there? Your objectives should flow from the company's master plan, and your strategies must reflect company priorities.

One of the first steps in the HR planning process should be to figure out where the company stands in terms of human resources. What skills does the workforce already have? What skills does it need? A company-wide **job analysis** often goes hand in hand with evaluating the current workforce. Job analysis examines what exactly needs to be done in each position to maximize the effectiveness of the organization—independent of who might be holding each job at any specific time. Smaller companies often handle job analysis on an informal basis, but larger companies typically specify a formal **job description** and **job specifications** (or "specs").

A job description defines the jobholder's responsibilities, and job specs define the qualifications for doing the job. Consider the job of band manager. The job description might include finding engagements for the band, and

settling disputes among band members. The job specs might include the type of education and experience required. Taken together, the two might look something like Exhibit 15.1.

The next step is to forecast future human resource requirements. The forecasting function requires a deep understanding of the company's goals and strategies. HR managers must also assess the future supply of workers. Assessing supply can be a real challenge, since the size and quality of the workforce shift continually. But key considerations should include retirement rates, graduation rates in relevant fields, and the pros and cons of the international labor market.

A complete HR plan—which falls under the company's strategic planning umbrella—must cover each core area of human resource management (see Exhibit 15.2):

- ⊘ Recruitment
- ⊘ Selection
- ⊘ Training
- ⊘ Evaluation
- ⊘ Compensation
- ⊘ Benefits
- ⊘ Separation

Recruitment: Finding the Right People

Finding people to hire is easy—especially as the unemployment rate hit new highs in 2009 and spiked up in 2010 and 2011—but finding *qualified* employees can still be a daunting challenge. The U.S. Census Bureau points out that a college degree typically doubles earning power, and the U.S. Bureau of Labor Statistics attests that most of the fastest-growing fields in the next five years will require college graduates. But only 30% of adults in America over the age of 25 have a college degree. And as highly trained, highly educated Baby Boomers hit retirement, HR recruiters may face a hiring crunch. In addition to finding qualified hires, recruiters also must find new employees who fit with the company culture in terms of both personality and style.[9]

EXHIBIT 15.1 Job Description and Job Specifications: Band Manager

JOB DESCRIPTION	JOB SPECIFICATIONS
Work with the music group to help make major decisions regarding the creative and business direction of the band	A bachelor's degree in music management
Negotiate recording contracts and engagement fees	A minimum of three years' experience managing a high-profile band
Help band members understand their rights and responsibilities	Excellent communication and networking skills

© Cengage Learning 2013

EXHIBIT 15.2 Human Resource Management

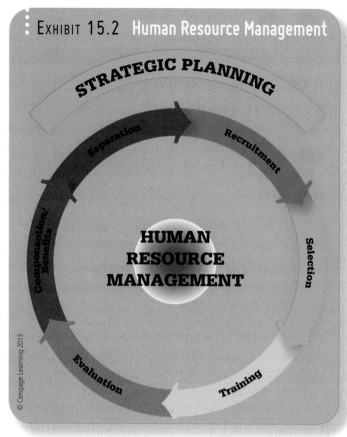

STRATEGIC PLANNING

HUMAN RESOURCE MANAGEMENT

Separation · Recruitment · Selection · Training · Evaluation · Compensation/Benefits

© Cengage Learning 2013

New employees come from two basic sources: internal and external. **Internal recruitment** involves transferring or promoting employees from other positions within the company. This approach offers several advantages:

- ➲ Boosts employee morale by reinforcing the value of experience within the firm
- ➲ Reduces risk for the firm, since current employees have a proven track record
- ➲ Lowers costs of both recruitment and training

Job fairs and professional conferences provide opportunities for external recruitment.

© Kevork Djansezian/Getty Images

But companies often find that they don't have the right person within their organization. The firm may be too small, or perhaps no one has the right set of skills to fill the immediate needs. Or maybe the firm needs the fresh thinking and energy that can come only from outside. When this is the case, companies turn to **external recruitment**.

External recruitment, or looking for employees outside the firm, usually means tapping into a range of different resources. The possibilities include employment websites, newspaper ads, trade associations, college and university employment centers, and employment agencies. But the most promising source of new hires may be referrals from current employees. A growing number of organizations offer their current employees a cash bonus—typically $1,000 to $2,000—for each person they refer to the company who makes it past a probationary period. As an added benefit, employees who come through referrals have an excellent chance at success, since the person who recommended them has a stake in their progress. Employee-referral programs also represent a real bargain for employers, compared to the average cost per new hire of more than $4,000. Not surprisingly, a higher level of employee referrals correlates to a higher level of shareholder returns, although lack of diversity may become a long-term problem with relying on employee referrals.[10]

Selection: Making the Right Choice

Once you have a pool of qualified candidates, your next step is to choose the best person for the job. This, too, is more easily said than done, yet making the right selection is crucial. The costs of a bad hire—both the direct costs such as placing ads, and the intangibles such as lost productivity and morale—can drain company resources. A typical selection process includes accepting applications, interviewing, testing, checking references and background, and making the job offer. Keep in mind that small businesses often follow a more streamlined process.

Applications Many companies use written applications simply as an initial screening mechanism. Questions about education and experience will determine whether a candidate gets any further consideration. In other words, the application is primarily a tool to reject unqualified candidates, rather than to actually choose qualified candidates.

Interviews Virtually every company uses interviews as a central part of the selection process. In larger companies, the HR department does initial interviews and then sends qualified candidates to the hiring manager for the actual selection. The hiring manager usually recruits co-workers to participate in the process.

internal recruitment
The process of seeking employees who are currently within the firm to fill open positions.

external recruitment
The process of seeking new employees from outside the firm.

Although employers frequently give interviews heavy weight in hiring decisions, interviews often say surprisingly little about whether a candidate will perform on the job. Too many managers use the interview as a get-to-know-you session rather than focusing on the needs of the position. To help ensure that interviews better predict performance, experts recommend a **structured interview** process: developing a list of questions beforehand and asking the same questions to each candidate. The most effective questions are typically behavioral: they ask the candidate to describe a situation that he or she faced at a previous job—or a hypothetical situation at the new job—and to explain the resolution. Interviewers should gear the specific questions toward behaviors and experiences that are key for the new position. Consider the following examples of how these questions could be worded:

- Describe a time when you had to think "outside the box" to find a solution to a pressing problem.
- Describe a situation that required you to do a number of things at the same time. How did you handle it? What was the outcome?
- If you realized that a co-worker was cheating on his expense report, how would you handle the situation?
- What would you do if your boss asked you to complete a key project within an unreasonable timeframe?

Cultural differences also affect interview performance. As the U.S. labor pool becomes more diverse, even domestic companies must be aware of cultural differences. And it isn't simply a matter of legality or ethics. Firms that hire the best people regardless of cultural background will gain a critical edge in our increasingly competitive world.

Most colleges and universities offer comprehensive career services. Especially in today's competitive labor market, you would be wise to visit your career center early in your college career and use those services to prepare yourself for a smooth transition into the workforce.

Testing Either before or after the interview process (and sometimes at both points), a growing number of companies have instituted employment testing of various sorts. The main categories include skills testing, personality testing, drug testing, and physical exams. Skills testing and personality testing carry a fair amount of legal risk, since these tests must measure skills and aptitudes that relate directly to the job itself. Virtually 100% of Fortune 500 companies conduct pre-employment drug testing, as do most other companies. Physical exams are also standard

A company is known by the people it keeps.
— Meehan & Meehan

but are highly regulated by state and federal law to ensure that firms don't use them just to screen out certain individuals.

References and Background Checks Even if you feel absolutely certain that a candidate is right for the job, don't skip the reference check before you make an offer. Research from the Society for Human Resource Managers suggests that more than 50% of job candidates lie on their résumé in some way. Although it may be tough to verify contributions and accomplishments at former jobs, it's pretty easy to uncover lies about education, job titles, and compensation. And it's quite worthwhile, given that the costs of bringing an unethical employee on board can be staggering. Furthermore, if you happen to hire a truly dangerous employee, you can open the door to negligent-hiring lawsuits for not taking "reasonable care." But surprisingly—despite the high risk—employment expert John Challenger estimates that only about 15% of candidates are thoroughly vetted by the companies that consider them.[11]

Job Offers After a company finds the right person, the next hurdle is to design the right job offer and getting your candidate to accept it. To hook an especially hot contender, you may need to get creative. A phone call from top management, the royal treatment, and special perks go a long way, but most superb candidates also want to know in very specific terms how their contributions would affect the business. And no matter how excited you are about your candidate, be certain to establish a **probationary period** upfront. This means a specific timeframe (typically three to six months) during which a new hire can prove his or her worth on the job. If everything works out, the employee will move from conditional to permanent status; if not, the company can fire the employee fairly easily.

Contingent Workers Companies that experience a fluctuating need for workers sometimes opt to hire **contingent workers**—or employees who don't expect regular, full-time jobs—rather than permanent, full-time workers. Specifically, contingent employees include temporary full-time workers, independent contractors, on-call workers, and temporary agency or contract agency workers. As a group, these contingent workers account for more than 10% of U.S. employment.[12]

Employers appreciate contingent workers because they offer flexibility, which can lead to much lower costs. But the hidden downside can be workers who are less committed and less experienced. Too much reliance on contingent workers could unwittingly sabotage company productivity and the customer experience.

Training and Development: Honing the Competitive Edge

For successful companies in virtually every field, training and development have become an ongoing process rather than a one-time activity. Even in a recession, training and development must gather speed for companies and individuals to maintain their competitive edge. Experts offer five key reasons that relate directly to a healthy bottom line:

1. Increased innovation in strategies and products
2. Increased ability to adopt new technologies
3. Increased efficiency and productivity
4. Increased employee motivation and lower employee turnover
5. Decreased liability (e.g., sexual harassment lawsuits)

Training programs take a number of different forms, from orientation to skills training, to management development, depending on the specific employee and the needs of the organization.

orientation The first step in the training and development process, designed to introduce employees to the company culture and provide key administrative information.

Orientation Once you hire new employees, **orientation** should be the first step in the training and development process. Effective orientation programs typically focus on introducing employees to the company culture (but without sacrificing need-to-know administrative information). Research consistently shows that strong orientation programs significantly reduce employee turnover, which lowers costs.

The Boeing aerospace company has mastered the art of employee orientation. Boeing Military Aircraft and Missile Systems revamped its orientation process to include mentoring, meetings with senior executives, and an after-work social program. One highlight of the orientation—meant to crystallize the "wow" factor of working at Boeing—is the chance to take the controls of an F/A-18 fighter plane flight simulator. Management rightfully sees the program as a chance to develop "future leaders…the ones who will

Ooops! What were they thinking?

Interview Gaffes: The Top Ten Things NOT to Do

As you get ready to interview for your dream job, you'll almost certainly find yourself awash in a torrent of advice from family and friends, and flooded with tips found on the Web and elsewhere. "Don't be late, don't be early… Don't ask too many questions, don't ask too few… Don't look too casual, don't look too stuffy…. And whatever you do, never let anyone see that you're nervous!" But however you actually feel—and whatever you actually say—take heart from knowing that you probably won't top these "real-life" interview-question blunders:

1. Question: "What five or six adjectives best describe you?"
   Answer: "Really, really, really, really, really cool!"

2. Question: "Were you late because you got lost?"
   Answer: "No. It was such a nice day that I didn't mind driving slowly."

3. Question: "Why should I hire you?"
   Answer: "Because they say you should always hire people better than yourself."

4. Question: "What do you find interesting about this job? Answer: "The money. I don't really care what your company does."

5. Question: "Is it important to you to get benefits right away?"
   Answer: "I don't believe in healthcare. If I broke my leg, I'd just live with it."

6. Question: "What is your greatest strength?"
   Answer: "I'm a quick learner if I'm in the mood to pay attention."

7. Question: "What can you tell me about your creative ability?"
   Answer: "My answers to most of your questions are pretty good indicators."

8. Question: "Would you be willing to take a drug test?"
   Answer: "Sure. What kind of drugs do I get to test?"

9. Question: "What would your boss say about you?"
   Answer: "That I'm insubordinate."

10. Question: "How would you define a 'problem person'?"
    Answer: "Anyone who disagrees with me."[13]

make sure that Boeing continues to be a great place to work."[14]

On-the-Job Training On-the-job training is popular because it's very low-cost. Employees simply begin their jobs—sometimes under the guidance of more experienced employees—and learn as they go. For simple jobs, this can make sense, but simple jobs are disappearing from the U.S. market due to the combined impact of offshoring and technology. On-the-job training can also compromise the customer experience. Have you ever waited much too long in a short line at the grocery store because the clerk couldn't figure out how to use the cash register? Multiplied across hundreds of customers, this kind of experience undermines the value of a company's brand.

Formal apprenticeship programs tend to be a more effective way of handling on-the-job training. **Apprenticeship** programs mandate that each beginner serve as an assistant to a fully trained worker for a specified period of time before gaining full credentials to work in the field. In the United States, apprenticeships are fairly common in trades such as plumbing and bricklaying. But in Europe, apprenticeships

On-the-job training often works best for relatively simple jobs.

© Digital Vision/Jupiterimages

are much more common across a wide range of professionals, from bankers to opticians.

Off-the-Job Training Classroom training happens away from the job setting but typically during work hours. Employers use classroom training—either on- or off-site—to teach a wide variety of topics from new computer programming languages, to negotiation skills, to stress management, and more. Going one step further than classroom training, some employers train workers off-site on "real" equipment (e.g., robots) similar to what they would actually use on the job. This approach is called "vestibule training." Police academies often use vestibule training for firearms. Job simulation goes even further than vestibule training, by attempting to duplicate the exact conditions that the trainee will face on the job. This approach makes sense for complex, high-risk positions such as astronaut or airline pilot.

Computer-Based Training Computer-based training—mostly delivered via the Web—now plays a crucial role in off-the-job training. Broadband technology has turbocharged audio and visual capabilities, which support engaging and interactive online training programs. Online training also standardizes the presentation of the material, since it doesn't depend on the quality of the individual instructor. And the Web helps employers train employees wherever they may be in the world, at their own pace and convenience. But there is a key drawback: it takes a lot of discipline to complete an online program, and some people simply learn better through direct human interaction.

Management Development As the bulk of top-level U.S. executives move toward retirement (or lose their jobs in the recession), developing new leaders has become a priority in many organizations. **Management development** programs help current and potential executives develop the skills they need to move into leadership positions. These programs typically cover specific issues that the business faces, but also less-tangible—yet equally important—topics, such as communication, planning, business-analysis, change-management, coaching, and team-building skills.

Evaluation: Assessing Employee Performance

Straightforward, frequent feedback is a powerful tool to improve employee performance. The best managers provide informal feedback on a constant basis so that employees always know where they stand. But most companies also require that managers give formal feedback through periodic **performance appraisals**, usually every six months or once a year. Typically, managers conduct the appraisals by sitting down with each employee on a one-to-one basis and comparing actual results to expected results. The performance appraisal affects decisions regarding compensation, promotions, training, transfers, and terminations.

The HR role in performance appraisals begins with the strategic process of creating evaluation tools that tie directly into the company's big-picture objectives. Then, on a day-to-day basis, HR coordinates the actual appraisal process, which typically involves volumes of paperwork. HR must also ensure that managers are trained in providing relevant, honest, objective feedback, and that workers at every level know how to respond if they believe their appraisal is not fair.

Both giving and receiving evaluations tend to be awkward for everyone involved, and unfortunately, uncomfortable people tend to make mistakes. As you read the following list, you'll probably find that you've been on the receiving end of at least a couple of the most common appraisal goofs.

1. **Gotcha!** Too many managers use the performance appraisal as a chance to catch employees doing something wrong, rather than doing something right.

2. **The Once-a-Year Wonder** Many companies mandate annual reviews, but some managers use that as an excuse to give feedback only once a year.

3. **Straight from the Gut** Although "gut feel" can have real value, it's no substitute for honest, relevant documentation of both expectations and accomplishments.

4. **What Have You Done for Me Lately?** Many managers give far too much weight to recent accomplishments, discounting the early part of the review period.

5. **The "Me Filter"** While appraisals are a bit subjective by their very nature, some managers filter every comment through their personal biases. Here are some examples:

   - **Positive Leniency:** "I'm a nice guy, so I give everyone great scores."

   - **Negative Leniency:** "I have high expectations, so I give everyone low scores."

   - **Halo Effect:** "I like this employee so I'll give her top scores across the board."

For a performance appraisal to be effective, the manager must focus on fairness, relevance, objectivity, and balance. Equally important, the manager should give feedback on a continual basis to eliminate surprises and maximize performance.

Compensation: Show Me the Money

The term **compensation** covers both pay and benefits, but when most people think about compensation, they think about cash. Yet your paycheck is only part of the picture. Many companies also offer noncash benefits such as healthcare, which can be worth up to 30% of each employee's pay. Researching, designing, and managing effective compensation systems are core HR functions.

From a company perspective, compensation—both cash and noncash—represents a big chunk of product costs, especially in labor-intensive businesses such as banks, restaurants, and airlines. Although many firms opt to cut labor costs as far as possible, others boost compensation above the norm to find and keep the best workers. In fact, research suggests that companies that offer higher-than-average compensation generally outperform their competitors in terms of total return to shareholders—both stock price and dividend payouts.[15]

Regarding specific individuals and positions, companies typically base compensation on a balance of the following factors:

- **Competition:** How much do competing firms offer for similar positions?

- **Contribution:** How much does a specific person contribute to the bottom line?

- **Ability to Pay:** How much can the company afford?

- **Cost of Living:** What would be reasonable in light of the broader local economy?

- **Legislation:** What does the government mandate?

The most common compensation systems in the United States are wages and salaries. **Wages** refer to pay in exchange for the number of hours or days that an employee works. Variations can be huge, starting

performance appraisal
A formal feedback process that requires managers to give their subordinates feedback on a one-to-one basis, typically by comparing actual results to expected results.

compensation The combination of pay and benefits that employees receive in exchange for their work.

wages The pay that employees receive in exchange for the number of hours or days that they work.

at the federal minimum wage of $7.25 per hour (as of mid-2011) and ranging up to more than $50 per hour. Jobs that require less education—such as flipping burgers—typically pay hourly wages. Federal law requires companies to pay non-exempt wage earners overtime, 50% more than their standard wage, for every hour worked over 40 hours per week.

Salaries, on the other hand, cover a fixed period, most often weekly or monthly. Most professional, administrative, and managerial jobs pay salaries. While salaries are usually higher than wages, salaried workers do not qualify for overtime, which means that sometimes a low-level manager's overall pay may be less than the pay of wage-based employees who work for that manager.

SALARY

© Arkady/Shutterstock.com

Pay for Performance In addition to wages and salaries, many organizations link some amount of worker pay directly to performance. The idea, of course, is to motivate employees to excel. Exhibit 15.3 lists some common approaches.

As you look over the range of variable pay options, which would you find most motivating? Why? What type of business might use each form of variable pay? Why?

Benefits: From Birthday Cakes to Death Benefits

Benefits represent a significant chunk of money for employers, but for many years workers took benefits for granted. No longer. As the unemployment rate skyrocketed in 2009, employees began to appreciate their benefits more than ever, recognizing that health care, dental care, paid sick days, retirement plans, and other perks add enormous value to their paychecks—and can be yanked at the discretion of their employer.[16]

Exhibit 15.3 Performance Pay Options

VARIABLE PAY SYSTEM	DESCRIPTION
COMMISSION	Commission involves payment as a percentage of sales. Usually, larger commissions go with smaller base pay.
BONUSES	Bonuses are lump-sum payments, typically to reward strong performance from individual employees.
PROFIT SHARING	Profit-sharing plans reward employees with a share of company profits above and beyond predetermined goals.
STOCK OPTIONS	Stock options are the right to buy shares of company stock at some future date for the price of the shares on the day that the company awarded the options.
PAY FOR KNOWLEDGE	This approach involves awarding bonuses and pay increases in exchange for increases in knowledge such as earning an MBA.

© Cengage Learning 2013

In fact, a number of budget-minded employers already stick to the legally mandated basics: Social Security and Medicare contributions, payments to state unemployment and workers' compensation programs, and job protection per the Federal Family and Medical Leave Act. However, socially responsible employers—and companies that seek a competitive advantage through a top-notch workforce—tend to offer far more. Optional benefits usually include some or all of the following:

- Paid vacation days and holidays
- Paid sick days
- Health insurance
- Retirement programs
- Product discounts

A smaller number of companies also offer less traditional benefits such as backup childcare options, free massage, subsidized concierge services, tuition reimbursement, and paid time off for volunteering. During the recession of 2009, companies that offered "extras" focused extra attention on perks that would boost morale without an outrageous price tag.[17]

In the past decade, a growing number of companies have begun to offer **cafeteria-style benefits**. This approach involves giving their employees a set dollar amount per person that they must spend on company benefits. The key to these plans is choice, which allows employees to tailor their benefits to their individual needs.

Over the past couple of decades, employees across the U.S. economy have demanded more flexibility from their employers, and companies have responded. Flexible scheduling options include flextime, telecommuting, and job-sharing plans, discussed in detail below. But unfortunately, as massive, widespread layoffs swept across the economy in 2009, workers began to give up flexible schedules—or to stop even asking about them in the first place—out of fear that they would appear less committed to their jobs.[18]

Flextime A **flextime** plan gives workers some degree of freedom in terms of when they start and finish their workday, as long as they complete the required number of hours. Typically, companies with flextime scheduling oblige their employees to start work between mandated hours in the morning—say, anytime between 7 A.M. and 10 A.M.—to take lunch between certain hours in the middle of the day, and to complete work at the end of eight hours. This approach ensures that everyone is present during core hours for communication and coordination, but it provides choice outside those parameters. Flextime tends to increase employee morale and retention, but it makes less sense in jobs that entail extensive teamwork and customer interaction. It also requires careful management to avoid abuse.

The **compressed workweek**, another version of flextime scheduling, allows employees to work a full-time number of hours in less than the standard workweek. The most popular option is to work four ten-hour days rather than five eight-hour days. Major companies, such as Intel, have developed successful compressed workweek programs at a number of their facilities.

Telecommuting Working remotely—most often from home—is a growing phenomenon on a global scale. Booming technological advances allow employees to "commute" to the office via phones, fax machines, and broadband networks. More than 60% of companies allow **telecommuting**, and about a third of Americans telecommute at least occasionally. The bottom-line benefits for companies that embrace the approach can be significant. Over two-thirds of employers report increased productivity among their telecommuters. Telecommuting employees are 35%–40% more productive than their office-bound colleagues. And direct savings from decreased costs add up fast, as well. By establishing telecommuting programs, employers can realize annual cost savings of $5,000 per employee, which

Wacky Benefits

While most benefits are optional, you would not be unreasonable to expect your firm to offer standard perks, such as paid vacation days or sick time, but a handful of creative companies have developed a package of perks to create a unique, compelling corporate culture.[19] Some examples:

© Poulsons Photography/Shutterstock.com

- ⊘ **Zappos.com:** Offers a full-time, on-site life coach who helps employees achieve work/life balance and discover a "higher purpose/higher self."

- ⊘ **Chesapeake Energy:** Offers an on-site medical center with a full range of services, including Botox injections—and the company's fitness center has seven tanning beds as well as spray tanning capabilities.

- ⊘ **NetApp:** Actively supports employee volunteer work. Allowed one employee to take five straight weeks to get the required 200 hours of training to be a volunteer fire fighter. That employee says, "Now I'm a hero to my three children because I'm a fireman."

- ⊘ **DPR Construction:** Features a wine bar in 17 of its offices, where employees can pop a bottle to toast major accomplishments or a project's completion. The construction company's Texas branch features an in-house saloon instead.

"Commuting at Zero Gallons per Mile"

Countless studies confirm that telecommuting can offer real benefits for both employers and employees. But it can also make a world of difference for our planet.

More telecommuters mean fewer vehicles spewing pollution on the roads. In fact, the 3.9 million workers who telecommuted in 2007 reduced CO2 emissions at a level roughly equal to removing 2 million vehicles from the road for the entire year. According to the National Technology Readiness Survey, we could save about 1.35 billion gallons of fuel per year if everyone who was able to telecommute were to do just 1.6 days per week.

Telecommuting can also go a long way toward reducing the overall carbon footprint of many businesses. Sun Microsystems, which boasts a robust telecommuting program, found that its 24,000 telecommuting U.S. employees *avoided* producing 32,000 metric tons of CO_2 by driving to and from work less often.

But the environmental benefits don't stop there. Sun also found that employees used less energy at home than they did at the office. "Office equipment energy consumption rate at a Sun office was two times that of home office equipment energy consumption, from approximately 64 watts per hour at home to 130 watts per hour at a Sun office." One key reason: laptops—used by most telecommuting employees—require less power than traditional desktop PC/monitor combos.

Factoring in the environmental benefits, we might conclude that the overall cost of telecommuting is even less than zero.[20]

adds up to hundreds of millions of dollars each year for big players, such as IBM, Sun Microsystems, and AT&T.[21]

While telecommuting sounds great at first glance, it offers benefits and drawbacks for organizations and employees alike, as you'll see in Exhibit 15.4.

Job Sharing Job sharing allows two or more employees to share a single full-time job. Typically, job-share participants split the salary equally, but they often need to allocate full benefits to just one of the partners. On a nationwide basis, fewer than 20% of employers (e.g., American Express and PricewaterhouseCoopers) offer job-sharing programs and reap the benefits such as higher morale and better retention.[22]

Separation: Breaking Up Is Hard to Do

Employees leave jobs for a number of different reasons. Experiencing success, they may be promoted or lured to another firm. Experiencing failure, they may be fired. Or in response to changing business needs, their employer might transfer them or lay them off. And employees also leave jobs for completely personal reasons such as family needs, retirement, or a change in career aspirations.

When companies terminate employees, they must proceed very carefully to avoid wrongful-termination lawsuits. The best protection is honesty and documentation. Employers should always document sound business reasons for termination and share those reasons with the employee.

But employees can still lose their jobs for reasons that have little or nothing to do with their individual performance. In response to the recession, employers eliminated 5.1 million jobs between December 2007 and March 2009. And while the recession eased in 2010 and 2011, employment has not returned to pre-recession levels, and many experts anticipate that it will not fully rebound for many years. As companies have become leaner, the remaining workers have experienced enormous stress. Managers can mitigate the trauma most effectively by showing empathy and concern for employees who remain, and by treating the laid-off employees with visible compassion.[23]

LO5 Legal Issues: HR and the Long Arm of the Law

Even when the company is right—even when the company wins—employment lawsuits can cost millions of dollars and deeply damage the reputation of an organization, as we briefly discussed earlier in this chapter. To avoid employment lawsuits, most firms rely on HR to digest the complex, evolving web of employment legislation and court decisions, and to ensure that management understands the key issues.

The bottom-line goal of most employment legislation is to protect employees from unfair treatment by employers. Some would argue that the legislation goes so far that it hinders the ability of companies to grow. But regardless of your personal perspective, the obligation of an ethical employer is to understand and abide by the law as it stands—even if you're working within the system to change it.

The most influential piece of employment law may be the **Civil Rights Act of 1964**. **Title VII** of this act—which applies only to employers with 15 or more workers—outlaws discrimination in hiring, firing, compensation, apprenticeships, training, terms, conditions, or privileges of employment based on race, color, religion, sex, or national origin. Over time, Congress has supplemented Title VII with legislation that prohibits discrimination based on pregnancy, age (40+), and disability.

Title VII also created the **Equal Employment Opportunity Commission (EEOC)** to enforce its provisions. And in 1972, Congress beefed up the EEOC with additional powers to regulate and to enforce its mandates, making the EEOC a powerful force in the human resources realm.

Here are some additional key pieces of employment legislation:

- **Fair Labor Standards Act of 1938:** Established a minimum wage and overtime pay for employees working more than 40 hours a week.

- **Equal Pay Act of 1963:** Mandated that men and women doing equal jobs receive equal pay.

> ## Even a small
> layoff shocks and demoralizes survivors so much that voluntary quit rates rise an average of 31% above previous levels.
>
> — **The Wall Street Journal**

- **Occupational Safety and Health Act of 1970:** Required safety equipment for employees and established maximum exposure limits for hazardous substances.

- **Immigration Reform and Control Act of 1986:** Required employers to verify employment eligibility for all new hires.

- **Americans with Disabilities Act of 1990:** Prohibited discrimination in hiring, promotion, and compensation against people with disabilities and required employers to make "reasonable" accommodations for them.

- **Family and Medical Leave Act of 1993:** Required firms with 50 or more employees to provide up to 12 weeks of job-secure, unpaid leave on the birth or adoption of a child or the serious illness of a spouse, child, or parent.

Civil Rights Act of 1964 Federal legislation that prohibits discrimination in hiring, firing, compensation, apprenticeships, training, terms, conditions, or privileges of employment based on race, color, religion, sex, or national origin.

Title VII A portion of the Civil Rights Act of 1964 that prohibits discrimination in hiring, firing, compensation, apprenticeships, training, terms, conditions, or privileges of employment based on race, color, religion, sex, or national origin for employers with 15 or more workers.

Equal Employment Opportunity Commission (EEOC) A federal agency designed to regulate and enforce the provisions of Title VII.

Exhibit 15.4 An Analysis of Telecommuting

	BENEFITS	DRAWBACKS
ORGANIZATION	• Lower costs for office space, equipment, and upkeep • Higher employee productivity due to better morale, fewer sick days, and more focused performance • Access to a broader talent pool (not everyone needs to be local)	• Greater challenges maintaining a cohesive company culture • Greater challenges fostering teamwork • Greater challenges monitoring and managing far-flung employees
EMPLOYEE	• Much more flexibility • Zero commute time (less gas money) • Better work-family balance • Every day is casual Friday (or even pajama day!) • Fewer office politics and other distractions	• Less fast-track career potential • Less influence within the organization • Weaker connection to the company culture • Isolation from the social structure at work

Source: Flexible Hours and Telecommuting—Not the Ticket to the Top of Corporate America, Five Questions for Susan DePhillips, Workforce Management, September 2005, http://www.workforce.com/section/02/article/24/14/66.html

Affirmative Action: The Active Pursuit of Equal Opportunity

The term **affirmative action** refers to policies meant to increase employment and educational opportunities for minority groups—especially groups defined by race, ethnicity, or gender. Emerging during the American civil rights movement in the 1960s, affirmative action seeks to make up for the systematic discrimination of the past by creating more opportunities in the present.

Over the past couple of decades, affirmative action has become increasingly controversial. Opponents have raised concerns that giving preferential treatment to some groups amounts to "reverse discrimination" against groups who do not get the same benefits. They claim that affirmative action violates the principle that all individuals are equal under the law. But supporters counter that everyone who benefits from affirmative action must—by law—have relevant and valid qualifications. They argue that proactive measures are the only workable way to right past wrongs and to ensure truly equal opportunity.

Recent U.S. Supreme Court decisions have supported affirmative action, pointing out that government has a "compelling interest" in ensuring racial diversity. But the Court has rejected "mechanistic" affirmative action programs that amount to quota systems based on race, ethnicity, or gender.

The long-term fate of affirmative action remains unclear, but achieving the underlying goal—a diverse workplace with equal opportunity for all—stands to benefit both business and society as a whole.

Sexual Harassment: Eliminating Hostility

Sexual harassment—which violates Title VII of the Civil Rights Act of 1964—involves discrimination against a person based on his or her gender. According to the EEOC, sexual harassment can range from requests for sexual favors to the presence of a hostile work environment. The EEOC also points out that a sexual harasser may be either a woman or a man, and the harasser doesn't need to be the victim's supervisor. The victim could be anyone affected—either directly or indirectly—by the offensive conduct. And clearly, to qualify as sexual harassment, the conduct must be unwelcome. The total number of sexual harassment charges filed with the EEOC in the last decade dropped 11% from 1998 to 2008, but the number of charges filed by men rose from 12.9% to 15.9%.[24]

Not just the perpetrator is liable for sexual harassment; employers may share accountability if they did not take "reasonable care" to prevent and correct sexually harassing behavior, or if they did not provide a workable system for employee complaints. Simply adopting a written policy against sexual harassment is not enough. Taking "reasonable care" also means taking proactive steps—such as comprehensive training—to ensure that everyone in the organization understands 1) that the firm does not tolerate sexual harassment, and 2) that the firm has a system in place for complaints and will not tolerate retaliation against those who complain.[25]

Odd Jobs

As you contemplate your post-college career, chances are good that you are mostly considering the more typical fields, where people you know have built successful careers. Although there are many satisfying options, a number of folks have built rewarding careers in fields that initially appear somewhat odd. A few examples:[26]

- ◐ **Resort Biologist:** Four Seasons Resort in Jackson Hole Wyoming staffs a resort biologist to take guests on four-hour animal-scouting expeditions, where they typically spot wolves and grizzlies.

- ◐ **Crash Designer:** One of Mattel's engineers has spent the last 27 years coming up with new, inventive ways to flip tiny cars around plastic tracks as a designer for Mattel's Hot Wheels brand. "If your toy is hurting, add loops and crashing. Crashing inside loops, even better," he says.

- ◐ **Vacation facilitator:** In today's hyper-competitive travel market, a wide range of offbeat positions are available, designed to create the "wow factor" that differentiates each service provider. Some examples: a "tanning butler" who applies sunscreen to pool-goers, "bath sommeliers" who fill your tub, or "bibliotherapists" who choose your reading material.

Effective human resource management can create an unbeatable competitive edge—a fair, productive, empowering workplace pays off in bottom-line results. In good times, one core HRM goal is to find, hire, and develop the best talent. While that function remains crucial in tough economic times, the focus changes to managing HR costs while maintaining morale. Looking forward, a growing number of firms will most likely outsource traditional HR tasks such as payroll and benefits administration to companies that specialize in these areas. HR departments could then focus on their core mission: working with senior management to achieve business goals by cultivating the firm's investment in human resources.

The Bureau of Labor Statistics projects that jobs in human resources will experience much faster growth than average through 2018.[27] But attaining one of these positions will require much more than simply liking people. Human resources jobs include analysts, benefits administrators, negotiators, recruiters, trainers, managers, and more. Most positions require at least a four-year degree in business or human resources, several years of related experience, and excellent interpersonal skills.

What *else?*
RIP & REVIEW CARDS IN THE BACK
and visit **www.cengagebrain.com!**

16

Managing Information and Technology:
Finding New Ways to Learn and Link

LEARNING OBJECTIVES

After studying this chapter, you will be able to…

LO1 Explain the basic elements of computer technology—including hardware, software, and networks—and describe key trends in each area

LO2 Discuss the reasons for the increasing popularity of cloud computing

LO3 Describe how data becomes information and how decision support systems can provide high-quality information that helps managers make better decisions

LO4 Explain how Internet-based technologies have changed business-to-consumer and business-to-business commerce

LO5 Describe the problems posed by the rapid changes in Internet-based technologies, and explain ways to address these problems

> ## ANY SUFFICIENTLY ADVANCED TECHNOLOGY IS INDISTINGUISHABLE FROM *MAGIC*.
>
> — Arthur C. Clarke, Science Fiction Author

LO1 Information Technology: Explosive Change

Over the past few decades, computer and communications hardware and software have changed dramatically. The capabilities of hardware have increased by orders of magnitude. In the late 1950s, for example, you would have needed 50 24-inch disks—costing tens of thousands of dollars—to store five megabytes of data. Today you can buy a flash memory device, about the same size as a postage stamp, that stores 16 gigabytes of data—over 3,000 times more than that whole 1950s disk array—for under $25. And in terms of processing power, Apple's iPad2 tablet computer, introduced in 2011 with a base price under $500, can complete more than 1.5 *billion* mathematical operations *per second*—making it faster than many multimillion-dollar supercomputers from the early 1990s.[1] While more difficult to quantify with specific statistics, it's also clear that software has become more powerful and more flexible and easier to use.

Perhaps an even more important development than the increased power of hardware and sophistication of software is the degree to which today's technology is linked by networks. These networks allow businesses to coordinate their internal functions, reach their customers, and collaborate with their suppliers and partners in ways that could not have been envisioned a quarter of a century ago. Networks have not only improved the efficiency and effectiveness of existing businesses, they've also opened up entirely new business opportunities. Of course, these new linkages pose challenges and threats as well as benefits and opportunities; a quarter of a century ago, people hadn't heard of computer viruses, spyware, phishing, or spam (except for the Hormel meat product variety). Over the course of this chapter, we'll take a look at both sides of this rapidly changing story.

Hardware and Software

Hardware refers to the physical components used to collect, input, store, and process data, and to display and distribute information. This hardware includes the various components of a computer system as well as communications and network equipment. Examples include barcode scanners, hard drives, printers, routers, and smartphones.

Software refers to the programs that provide instructions to a computer so that it can perform a desired task. There are two broad categories of software: system software and application software. Both types of software have taken advantage of the tremendous increase hardware capabilities to become both more powerful and easier to use.

System software performs the critical functions necessary to operate a computer at the most basic level. The fundamental form of system software is the operating system, which controls the overall operation of the computer. It implements vital tasks, such as managing the file system, reading programs and data into main memory, and allocating system memory among various tasks to avoid conflicts.

Operating system software also provides the interface that enables users to interact with their computers. Early operating systems required users to type complex commands with very precise syntax in order to carry out tasks such as running programs or opening, saving, or deleting files. If you made an error while typing a command, your monitor would just sit there until you typed the correct command. Today's operating systems are much simpler and more intuitive. Most use a *graphical user interface* (or GUI—pronounced "gooey") that allows users to enter commands by mouse-clicking on images on the computer screen called icons—or by tapping or swiping them if you're using a device with a touch screen.

Utility programs supplement operating system software in ways that increase the security or abilities of the computer system. Examples include firewalls, antivirus software and antispyware programs. Over the years, operating systems have incorporated many features that were originally provided by such utility programs.

Applications software is software that helps users perform a desired task. Horizontal applications software, such as word processing, spreadsheet, and personal information management

hardware The physical tools and equipment used to collect, input, store, organize, and process data and to distribute information.

software Programs that provide instructions to a computer so that it can perform a desired task.

system software Software that performs the critical functions necessary to operate the computer at the most basic level.

applications software Software that helps a user perform a desired task.

software, is used by many different businesses and occupations. Vertical applications software is designed for a specific industry or profession. For example, brokerage firms have special software that allows them to transact business on the stock exchanges, and product designers have computer-aided design (CAD) software that enables them to produce technical drawings in three dimensions.

Networks

Today, most firms (and households) use networks that allow users to communicate with each other and share both files and hardware resources. A network links computer resources using either a wired or wireless connection. Firms usually want to prevent outsiders from obtaining access to their networks for privacy and security reasons, but they sometimes allow customers or suppliers partial access to their private networks to strengthen their relationships with these important stakeholders.

The Internet and the World Wide Web
The development and growth of the **Internet** is one of the great networking stories of the last two decades. The Internet is often referred to as the world's largest computer network. It's actually a network of networks, consisting of hundreds of thousands of smaller networks operating under a common set of protocols (rules) so that they can communicate with each other.

One common way to experience the Internet is through the World Wide Web. But while the Internet supports the Web and provides access to it, only about a quarter of the traffic on the Internet involves the Web. (Other traffic includes, but isn't limited to, email, VoIP phone calls, Internet chat, online gaming, and machine-to-machine communications.)[2] Still, the Web is an incredibly rich environment; it consists of billions of documents—the number grows every day—written and linked together using Hypertext Markup Language (HTML).

The increased availability of broadband Internet connections has fueled the popularity of Internet applications. A **broadband Internet connection** has the capacity to transmit large amounts of data very quickly, allowing users to quickly download large files such as music, games, and movies. A survey by the Pew Internet and American Life Project, summarized in Exhibit 16.1, found that access to broadband Internet connections grew rapidly for much of the last decade. As the exhibit

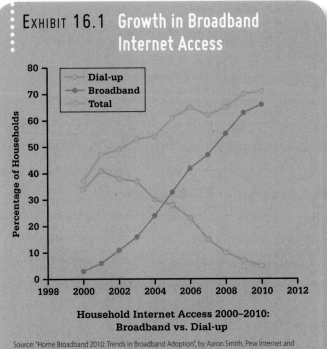

EXHIBIT 16.1   Growth in Broadband Internet Access

Household Internet Access 2000–2010: Broadband vs. Dial-up

Source: "Home Broadband 2010: Trends in Broadband Adoption", by Aaron Smith, Pew Internet and American Life Project: http://www.pewinternet.org/Reports/2010/Home-Broadband-2010/Part-1/Little-change-in-home-broadband-in-2010.aspx accessed May 16, 2011.

shows, only 3% of American adults had access to high-speed Internet at home in 2000, but by 2010 that figure had climbed to 66%.[3] From a business perspective, the growth in broadband penetration allows companies to offer richer, more interactive experiences to customers who visit their websites or use their apps.

But even today's broadband connections are too slow and inefficient for many business and scientific applications. Such projects often require high-definition video and audio files to be shared among multiple sites at the same time. Beginning in 1996, several leading research universities, corporations, and other organizations formed a coalition to create a new generation of Internet technology in the United States based on fiber-optic cable. The resulting network became known as **Internet2** (or "I2").

Access to I2 is was initially limited to dues-paying members of the Internet2 consortium, which today consists of over 200 major universities as well as 70 leading high-tech corporations, 45 government agencies, and about 50 international organizations.[4] But under an initiative begun in 2001, members of the I2 consortium can sponsor access to the network for other research and educational organizations that otherwise would be unable to qualify for membership. This initiative has given many elementary schools, high schools, community colleges, libraries, and museums access to I2 resources.[5]

© iStockphoto.com/Alex Slobodkin

Internet2 isn't simply a faster way to surf the Web or send email. In fact, such routine uses of the current Internet aren't even allowed. Instead, it is a noncommercial network that uses high-speed connectivity to improve education, research, and collaboration. Member organizations see Internet2 as a way to bring together their researchers, scientists, and engineers at various locations in a way that allows real-time collaboration on complex and important topics. It also allows corporations to collaborate with other companies, universities, and organizations located thousands of miles apart. One of the missions of the Internet2 consortium is to "facilitate the development, deployment and use of revolutionary Internet technologies."[6] So, the benefits of Internet2 will eventually become commonplace on the Internet that the rest of us use.

Intranets and extranets An **intranet** is a private network that has the same look and feel as the Web and uses the same Web browser software to display documents, but limits access to the employees of a single firm (or members of a single organization). When properly implemented, intranets enhance communication and collaboration among employees and provide an effective way to distribute information and applications throughout the organization. Employees can usually log onto their company's intranet from remote locations using password-protected Internet access, allowing them to use company resources when working on the road or from home.

> **At current** speeds, Internet2 is capable of transmitting five feature-length DVD movies from one location to another in less than one second.
>
> — Socaltech.com

Firms sometimes also create **extranets** by giving key stakeholders, such as suppliers or customers, limited access to certain areas of their intranet. Extranets enable firms to provide additional services and information to their external stakeholders. For example, the firm might allow customers to check on the status of their order, or suppliers to check on the state of the firm's inventory to plan shipments of parts and materials.

intranet A private network that has the look and feel of the Internet and is navigated using a Web browser, but which limits access to a single firm's employees (or a single organization's members.

extranet An intranet that allows limited access to a selected group of stakeholders, such as suppliers or customers.

The Role of the IT Department

Many business organizations have an information technology (IT) department to manage their information resources. But the role of this department varies significantly from one company to another. In some firms, the IT department plays a strategic role, making and implementing key decisions about the technologies the firm will use. In other organizations, the role of IT is largely operational; managers in functional departments make the key decisions about

© iStockphoto.com/pearleye

The Web Is Dead, You Say? That's App-surd!

For the past two decades, the World Wide Web was the main portal to Internet based content for ordinary users. But in recent years, the Web's pre-eminence has eroded. As access to broadband Internet connections became common, users began desiring access to more interactive content. The version of HTML used to create websites prior to 2010 wasn't capable of providing direct support for this content. Users had to install special plug-ins, such as Flash or Silverlight, to view videos and experience other multimedia content. The rapid rise of smartphones and tablet computers only exacerbated this problem. While these mobile devices could display web content, the results often weren't optimized for their smaller screens. And Apple refused to support the Flash plug-in needed to play many videos on its iPhones, iPods, and iPads.

The solution for mobile devices was to bypass the Web and use specialized "apps" to provide content and services via the Internet. Soon, owners of smartphones and other mobile devices were able to use apps to access Facebook, listen to music, view videos, or do just about anything else they'd previously done on the Web. In late 2010, *Wired Magazine* noted this trend in a cover story titled "The Web is Dead. Long Live the Internet."

But some experts believe the Web is far from dead, and point out that Web-based applications have some distinct advantages over apps. For example, the Web still provides the best way to reach a broad audience. And most Web-based content can be displayed on any browser, while apps have to be rewritten for different mobile platforms. But perhaps the greatest argument in favor of a Web renaissance is the advent of HTML5, a long-anticipated new version of HTML that makes it much easier to incorporate rich content into websites. By 2011, new versions of all popular Web browsers offered support for at least some of the advanced HTML5 features.[7]

the computer and information resources their areas need, and the IT department simply maintains these resources and provides technical support to employees.

L02 Cloud Computing: The Sky's the Limit!

In most companies, employees use applications and access data stored on their own computers or their companies' servers. But a relatively new trend called "cloud computing" is challenging that approach. **Cloud computing** means using Internet-based storage capacity, applications and processing power to supplement or replace internally owned computer resources.

You're already familiar with consumer-focused cloud computing services if you share photos on Shutterfly, store your music on Apple's iCloud storage services, or use a service like Dropbox to access and share documents and files. These services clearly offer significant benefits, such as the ability to store large files without taking up valuable space on your computer's hard drive and the convenience of being able to access your documents, music, or photos from any computer (and many mobile devices) with an Internet connection.

Until recently, most businesses were reluctant to embrace cloud computing, citing concerns about security and reliability. These issues remain, fuelled by some high-profile failures of cloud computing services from major providers such as Amazon and Google in recent years.[8] If these issues aren't resolved, the use of cloud computing by businesses may be limited. But the rapid increase in the number of firms using cloud-based services suggests that more and more businesses are becoming convinced that the advantages of cloud computing outweigh its risks. More specifically, the cloud offers to its users the ability to:

⊃ Access a vast array of computing resources without the need to invest heavily in expensive new hardware, software, and IT personnel;

⊃ Quickly adjust the amount of computer resources to meet their needs—and pay only for the resources that are actually used. This lowers costs and eliminates the problem of excess capacity. In fact, the cost reductions are often so great that even small firms can afford to take advantage of sophisticated and powerful cloud computing resources;

⊃ Encourage collaboration among employees and business partners. Cloud resources aren't confined to a specific platform or operating system, so it is easy for people using different computer systems to share files and programs. In addition, many cloud-based applications include tools specifically designed to facilitate collaboration;

⊃ Take advantage of incredible gains in processing speed. Not only does cloud computing give users access to more resources, but also it enables them to use those resources more efficiently by taking advantage of a technique called *massively parallel computing*, which can combine the processing power of hundreds (or even thousands) of computers to work on different elements of a problem simultaneously. The result is that data processing projects that used to take weeks to complete on a firm's internal computer resources can be completed in less than a day using cloud resources.[9]

If cloud computing can overcome its issues with security and reliability, it may usher in a fundamental change in the way most firms acquire and use information resources. This could result in big changes to the way IT departments operate. In fact, some analysts believe the very survival of internal IT departments—at least the ones that maintain and support only a firm's internal computer resources—is in doubt. Nicholas Carr, author of *The Big Switch: Rewiring the World from Edison to Google*, puts it this way: "In the long run, the IT department is unlikely to survive, at least not in its familiar form. It will have little left to do once the bulk of business computing shifts out of private data centers and into 'the cloud.'"[10]

Cloud computing may revolutionize the role of IT departments.

© iStockphoto.com/Luca di Filippo

L03 Information Technology and Decision Making: A Crucial Aid

One of the vital functions of information technology—at least in relationship to business—is to transform data into useful information for decision makers. In order to make decisions, managers must have information about the current state of their business, their competitive environment, and the trends and market conditions that offer new opportunities. Where does this information come from? How can it be made more useful? How can managers process the information to make better decisions?

Data and Information

Let's start by distinguishing between data and information. **Data** are the facts and figures a firm collects. Data in their raw form have limited usefulness because they lack the context needed to give them meaning. Data become **information** when they are processed, organized, and presented in a way that makes them useful to a decision maker. Sometimes firms can obtain useful information from external sources, but sometimes they must create information by processing their own data. Given today's competitive environment, the speed with which managers obtain good-quality information can be a crucial competitive advantage.

Internally, every department of an organization generates facts and figures that the firm must store and track. Every time a financial transaction is completed, for example, the firm's accounting system must record the specific accounts affected. Similarly, a firm's human resources department must enter new data every time an employee is hired, fired, or promoted or changes jobs or retires. Firms must also keep track of the names, addresses, and credit information of each customer. This is hardly a complete list, but you get the picture; firms must store mountains of data and convert them into useful information.

Typically, today's businesses store their data in **databases**, which are files of related data organized according to a logical system and stored on hard drives or some other computer-accessible storage media. It isn't unusual for a company to have many different databases, each maintained by a different department or functional area to meet its specific needs. For example, the human resources department might have a database of employee pay rates, and the marketing department may have another database of customer history.

Once all these data are stored, the firm must convert them into information. One common method is to query a database. A query is a request for the database management software to search the database for data that match criteria specified by the user. Suppose, for instance, that a marketing manager plans to introduce a product

It used to be the big eat the small, but today the fast run over the slow.

— Bob Helms, The Former CEO of International Sematech

upgrade. She can enter a query that asks for the email addresses of all customers who have purchased the product in the past year. She can use this information to send a targeted email message, promoting the upgrade to the customers who are most likely to buy it.

Characteristics of Good Information

We've seen that businesses have many sources of information. But not all information is of good quality. High-quality information is:

- ⊃ Accurate: It should be free of errors and biases.

- ⊃ Relevant: It should focus on issues that are important to decision-makers.

- ⊃ Timely: It should be available in time to make a difference.

- ⊃ Understandable: It must help the user grasp its meaning.

- ⊃ Secure: Confidential information must be secure from hackers and competitors.

Using Information Technology to Improve Decision Making

A company's information technology (IT) department frequently works closely with managers throughout the organization to support decision making. In fact, many companies develop **decision support systems** (DSS) that give managers access to large amounts of data and the processing power to convert the data into high-quality information quickly and efficiently.

Over the past two decades, a new class of decision support system has evolved to take advantage of the dramatic increase in data storage and processing capabilities. Called **business intelligence systems**, these systems help businesses discover subtle and complex relationships hidden in their data. Such systems can be a source of competitive advantage for the businesses that develop them.

One of the most common approaches to implementing a business intelligence system is to create a data warehouse and use data mining to discover unknown relationships. A **data warehouse** is a very large, organization-wide database that provides a centralized location for storing

data Raw, unprocessed facts and figures.

information Data that have been processed in a way that make them meaningful to their user.

database A file consisting of related data organized according to a logical system and stored on a hard drive or some other computer-accessible media.

decision support system (DSS) A system that gives managers access to large amounts of data and the processing power to convert these data into high-quality information, thus improving the decision-making process.

business intelligence system A sophisticated form of decision support system that helps decision makers discover information that was previously hidden.

data warehouse A large, organization-wide database that stores data in a centralized location.

data from both the organization's own databases and external sources.

Data mining uses powerful statistical and mathematical techniques to analyze vast amounts of data to identify useful information that had been hidden. In recent years, data mining has had considerable success in areas as diverse as fraud and crime detection, quality control, scientific research, and even professional sports. For example, several NBA basketball teams have used data-mining techniques to discover the best combinations of players to put on the courts under various game situations.[11]

Expert Systems

Managers who use decision-support systems usually already know quite a bit about the problem and how they want to solve it. They just need access to the right data and a system to "crunch the numbers" in a way that provides relevant, accurate, and timely information to help them make their decisions. But what happens when the problem is beyond the expertise of the manager? One way to deal with this problem is to set up an **expert system** (ES) to guide the manager through the decision-making process.

To develop expert systems, programmers ask experts in the relevant area to explain how they solve problems. They then devise a program to mimic the expert's approach, incorporating various rules or guidelines that the human

expert uses. The finished program will ask a user a series of questions, basing each question on the response to the previous question. The program continues to ask questions until it has enough information to reach a decision and make a recommendation.

Expert systems routinely solve problems in areas as diverse as medical diagnoses, fraud detection, and consumer credit evaluation. The troubleshooting systems that many companies have on the customer-support pages of their websites are another type of expert system. If your product doesn't work, the troubleshooter will ask a series of questions designed to diagnose the problem and suggest solutions. Based on your responses to each question, the system selects the next question as it starts narrowing down the possible reasons for the problem until it identifies the cause and offers a solution. Often you can solve your problem without waiting on hold to talk to a human expert over the phone.[12]

Despite impressive results in many fields, expert systems have their limitations. Programming all of the decision rules into the system can be time-consuming, complicated, and expensive. In fact, it's sometimes impossible because the experts themselves can't clearly explain how they make their decisions—they just "know" the answer based on their years of experience. If the experts can't clearly explain how they reach their conclusions, then programmers can't include the appropriate decision rules in the system. Finally, an expert system has little flexibility and no common sense. It probably won't be able to find a solution to a problem that deviates in any significant way from the specific type of problem it was programmed to solve.[13]

L04 Information Technology and the World of E-Commerce

Over the past 20 years, advances in information technology have had a dramatic and widespread effect on how companies conduct their business. But in this chapter, we'll just concentrate on one key area: the growth and development of e-commerce.

E-commerce refers to marketing, buying, selling, and servicing of products over a network (usually the Internet). You're probably most familiar with **business-to-consumer (B2C) e-commerce**. You participate in this form of e-commerce when you purchase songs from iTunes, use Expedia to make travel arrangements, or buy stocks through an online broker such as Charles Schwab. However, **business-to-business (B2B) e-commerce**, which consists

Data mining can help firms discover information previously hidden in vast amounts of data.

© Amy Walters/Shutterstock.com

of markets where businesses sell supplies, components, machinery, equipment, or services to other businesses, actually accounts for a much larger volume of business.

While both B2C and B2B involve exchanging goods over the Internet, they differ in some important ways, as shown in Exhibit 16.2. Given these structural differences, it isn't surprising that the two markets operate so differently.

While B2B and B2C are the most obvious forms of e-commerce, they aren't the *only* forms. For example, in C2C (consumer-to-consumer) e-commerce consumers buy from and sell to other consumers—think e-Bay and Craigslist. And in B2G (business-to-government) e-commerce businesses sell information, goods and services to government agencies.

Using Information Technology in the B2C Market

Firms in the B2C market use information technology in a variety of ways. In this section, we'll describe how firms use technology in general (and the Internet in particular) to attract new customers and strengthen the loyalty of existing customers.

Web 2.0 One major goal for most firms today is to develop stronger relationships with their customers. The Internet has proven to be an excellent tool for fostering such relationships—though it took a while for businesses to discover the best way to do so. In the early days of e-commerce, most companies tried to maintain tight control over all of the content presented on their websites. These websites presented information about products and allowed customers to place orders for goods and services, but offered little opportunity for user participation or involvement. However, by the early years of the twenty-first

century, innovative businesses were developing ways to make e-commerce more interactive and collaborative. In doing so, they not only forged stronger relationships with the customers who posted this content, they also created a richer, more interesting, and more useful experience for *others* who visited the site. This new approach became known as **Web 2.0**.

Many Web 2.0 sites rely on users (or members) to provide most of their content. For instance, the online encyclopedia Wikipedia uses wiki software to allow users to comment on and contribute to its articles. And social networking sites such as Facebook and Twitter wouldn't exist without user-created material. The more users who participate on these sites, the more useful (and entertaining) they become—and the easier it is for them to attract even more visitors and contributors.

Interestingly, many companies have found that techniques used to encourage collaboration among their customers can be used to accomplish the same result with their employees. Major corporations such as HP, Wells Fargo, and Procter & Gamble now use Web 2.0 techniques to help their own employees work more effectively together. The use of Web 2.0 technologies within organizations is called Enterprise 2.0.[14]

Advertising on the Internet Many B2C companies have large target markets, so advertising is an important part of their marketing strategy. Internet advertising revenue grew rapidly in the early twenty-first century, increasing almost fourfold from 2002 to 2008. It dropped slightly in early 2009 (as did most types of advertising expenditures during the onset of the recession) but began rising again later that year.

> **Web 2.0** Websites that incorporate interactive and collaborative features in order to create a richer, more interesting, and more useful experience for their users.

Exhibit 16.2 Key Differences Between B2C and B2B e-Commerce

	B2C	B2B
TYPE OF CUSTOMERS	Individual final consumers	Other businesses
NUMBER OF CUSTOMERS IN TARGET MARKET	Very large	Often limited to a few major business customers
SIZE OF TYPICAL INDIVIDUAL TRANSACTION	Relatively small (usually a few dollars to a few hundred dollars)	Potentially very large (often several thousand dollars, sometimes several million dollars)
CUSTOMER BEHAVIOR	May do some research, but many purchases may be based on impulse.	Usually does careful multiple research and compares vendors. May take bids.
COMPLEXITY OF NEGOTIATIONS	Purchase typically involves little or no negotiation. Customer usually buys a standard product and pays the listed price.	Often involves extensive negotiation over specifications, delivery, installation, support, and other issues
NATURE OF RELATIONSHIP WITH CUSTOMERS	Firm wants to develop customer loyalty and repeat business but seldom develops a close working relationship with individual customers.	Buyers and sellers often eventually develop close and long-lasting relationships that allow them to coordinate their activities.

© Cengage Learning 2013

"Want to Go Green? There Are Apps for That!"

Looking for ways to be more environmentally responsible? If you own a smartphone or tablet computer a good strategy is to check out the "green" apps available for your device. Literally hundreds of such apps are available. Some help you find places to recycle, others help you identify "green" businesses, and yet others provide tips to improve your fuel economy while driving. These apps not only allow you to be "green," they also allow you to save some "green" (as in money). Most green apps are priced under $5—in fact, several of them are free. Even the ones that cost a few bucks often quickly pay for themselves by helping you save on gasoline consumption or utility bills.

The greatest numbers of green apps are available for the iPhone and Android phones, but several are also available for other types of smartphones and for tablet computers. Here's an "apps sampler" to illustrate some of the possibilities:

iRecycle: helps you find convenient locations for recycling over 240 categories of waste materials, including paper, plastics, electronics and paint.

Good Guide: provides ratings for over thousands of products to help you pick the ones that are good for both you and the environment.

Green Genie: provides lifestyle tips that help the environment while saving you money. This app also suggests green projects you can try and provides links to additional green resources.

Find Green: uses your smartphone's GPS to determine your location and suggests nearby businesses that are environmentally friendly.

Green Gas Saver: monitors your driving habits and offers tips and suggestions on ways to get better gas mileage—an outcome that both helps the environment and saves you money at the pump.

Avego: dynamically matches drivers and riders who want to share rides. The app includes built-in safety and security measures. It uses GPS technology to measure the length of the shared ride, and electronically transfers micropayments from the rider to the driver.

Keep in mind that this is far from a complete list. There are hundreds of additional apps that can help you in your quest to be green—and more are being developed all the time. So be sure to check for new green apps on a regular basis.[15]

By the end of 2009, it surpassed magazine advertising revenue for the first time, and in 2010 it increased another 15% to over $26 billion. If current trends continue, it will soon surpass newspaper advertising—perhaps doing so by the time you read this. Ads placed on pages containing search results (such as those you see on Google or Bing) accounted for 46% of all Internet advertising revenues.[16]

Firms in B2C markets also use opt-in email as an advertising medium. Opt-in emails are messages that the receiver has explicitly chosen to receive. Customers often opt in when they register their products online and click to indicate that they would like to receive product information from the company. Since the customer has agreed to receive the message, opt-in emails tend to reach interested consumers. And, because email requires no envelopes, paper, or postage, it's much less expensive than direct mail.

Viral Marketing The Internet has also proven to be an effective medium for **viral marketing**, which attempts to get customers to communicate a firm's message to friends, family, and colleagues. Despite its name, legitimate viral marketing doesn't use computer viruses. Effective viral marketing campaigns can generate a substantial increase in consumer awareness of a product. As a strategy, viral marketing isn't unique to the Internet; even before the World Wide Web, marketers were adept at buzz marketing, the use of unconventional (and usually low-cost) tactics to stimulate word-of-mouth product promotion. But the Internet has made it possible to implement such strategies in clever ways and reach large numbers of people very quickly. Many viral marketing campaigns in recent years have used social media such as Facebook, Twitter, and YouTube.

Handling Payments Electronically B2C e-commerce normally requires customers to pay at the time the purchase is made. Clearly, the use of cash and paper checks isn't practical. In the United States, most payments in the B2C market are made by credit cards. To ensure that such transactions are secure, most sites transmit payment information using a secure socket layer (SSL) protocol. You can tell if a site on which you're doing business is using SSL in two fairly subtle ways. First, the URL will begin with

In 2011, users spent over 700 billion minutes each month on **Facebook.**

— USA Today

https:// instead of simply http://. (Note the "s" after http in the address.) Also, a small closed lock icon will appear near the bottom of your web browser (the exact location depends on the specific browser you are using). 🔒

Another common method of payment is to use a **cybermediary**—an Internet-based company that specializes in the secure electronic transfer of funds. By far the best-known cybermediary is PayPal. According to figures on its website, PayPal (which is owned by eBay) had over 98 million active accounts worldwide as of mid-2011.[17]

A final way of making electronic payments is **electronic bill presentment and payment**. This is a relatively new method in which bills are sent to customers via email. The bill includes a simple mechanism (such as clicking on a button-shaped icon) that allows the customer to make a payment once the amount of the bill has been verified. Many banks now offer this payment method, as do services such as Quicken and Fiserv.

Using Information Technology in the B2B Market

B2B e-commerce generally requires a very different approach than B2C e-commerce. Not only do B2B transactions often involve much larger sums of money and require much more negotiation than B2C transactions, they also often result in long-term supply chain relationships that require close collaboration between buyer and seller. A *supply chain* is the network of organizations and activities needed to obtain materials and other resources, produce final products, and get those products to their final users. Forging tight and efficient supply chain relationships can be a key competitive advantage for firms.

An effective supply chain requires close coordination between a company and its suppliers. Information technology can provide the tools needed to foster this coordination. For example, the extranets we mentioned earlier can allow suppliers to keep tabs on their customers' inventories, thus anticipating when to make shipments of parts or materials.

Many firms involved in B2B business also make use of specialized Internet sites, called **e-marketplaces**, which provide a platform for businesses in specific B2B markets to interact. These platforms generally allow buyers in the market to solicit bids by posting requests for proposals (RFPs) on the site. Suppliers can then respond by bidding on RFPs that interest them.

E-marketplaces provide a number of advantages to their participants:

- ⊙ Compared to older methods, they reduce time, effort, and cost of doing business for both buyers and sellers.

© Tatiana Popova/Shutterstock.com

- ⊙ Because they are Internet-based, they don't require expensive dedicated connections between firms, so even smaller firms can afford to participate.

- ⊙ They enable sellers and buyers to contact and negotiate with a large number of market participants on the other side of the market, thus maximizing the chances of finding good matches.

- ⊙ They often provide additional services—beyond simple trade—that allow firms to exchange information and collaborate, thus forging tighter supply chain relationships.

In recent years, many firms have begun using another information technology known as **radio frequency identification (RFID)** to improve the efficiency of their supply chains. This technology stores information on a microchip and transmits it to a reader when it's within range—which is usually limited to a few feet. The chips can be extremely small— some are difficult to see with the naked eye—and can be embedded in most types of tangible products. The chips are usually powered by the energy in the radio signal sent by the reader so they don't need batteries.

RFID chips can store and transmit all sorts of information, but most commonly they transmit a serial number that uniquely identifies a product, vehicle, or piece of equipment. This type of information can be used to help track goods and

viral marketing An Internet marketing strategy that tries to involve customers and others not employed by the seller in activities that help promote the product.

cybermediary An Internet-based firm that specializes in the secure electronic transfer of funds.

electronic bill presentment and payment A method of bill payment that makes it easy for the customer to make a payment, often by simply clicking on a payment option contained in an email.

e-marketplace A specialized Internet site where buyers and sellers engaged in business-to-business e-commerce can communicate and conduct business.

radio frequency identification (RFID) A technology that stores information on small microchips that can transmit the information when they are within range of a special reader.

Some Las Vegas casinos now include RFID chips in their poker chips, allowing them to calculate the average bet and win/ loss rate of individual players.

— CNET

other resources as they move through a supply chain. Deliveries can be recorded automatically and electronically without the need to make manual records. The chips also can make taking inventory much quicker and simpler, since the items in stock identify themselves to readers. And the chips can be used to reduce the chances of pilferage. The results of these advantages are lower costs and a more efficient supply chain.

Walmart was one of the earliest proponents of RFID technology. In 2003, it announced that it would require all of its major suppliers to include RFID chips on *all* of their suppliers' shipments by 2006. (Its original plan was to place RFID chips on pallets, crates and other containers, but *not* on individual items.) But some suppliers balked at the plan because they believed the cost of adopting the new technology was too high. Because of this resistance, Walmart wasn't able to achieve its goal of 100% supplier participation for its RFID initiative. But the suppliers that did adopt the technology have generally reported very positive results. And in July of 2010, Walmart announced that it was so pleased with its initial results that it would expand its program to include tagging individual units of certain items.[18]

LO5 # Challenges and Concerns Arising from New Technologies

So far, we've concentrated on the benefits of advances in information technology—and it's clear that these benefits are enormous. But rapid technological advances also pose challenges and create opportunities for abuse. These problems affect businesses, their customers, and their employees, as well as the general public. In this section, we'll look at annoyances, security concerns, and legal and ethical issues.

Malware

The Internet—for all its advantages—creates the possibility that unwanted files and programs may land on your computer. In many cases, this happens without your knowledge, much less your permission. Some of these files and programs are relatively benign (even useful), but others can create major problems. Software that is created

© iStockphoto.com/Pgiam

A Crowd Pleasing Approach to Finance

Small businesses often face long odds when it comes to raising money. But the Internet is changing that by providing new ways for entrepreneurs to reach potential backers.

One new approach is called peer-to-peer (P2P) lending. P2P websites such as Prosper.com and LendingClub.com bring together individual lenders (investors) and borrowers. These sites process online applications for small loans and evaluate the creditworthiness of the borrower. Then they channel individual investors' funds to finance projects they approve.

P2P sites usually offer borrowers lower rates than those charged by banks while yielding higher returns to investors than they could earn on CDs or savings accounts. But note that they reject more loan applications than they accept. And before you get too excited about the high returns you could earn if you were to invest with a P2P site, remember that high returns aren't guaranteed. If you make loans to unsuccessful projects, you could suffer losses. And, unlike money you put into a CD or savings account at your bank, the money you invest in P2P sites is not protected by deposit insurance!

Crowdfunding is another new source of funds for entrepreneurs and uses the Internet to connect people who need funds with those who are willing to provide them. One key difference is that backers of crowdfunded projects generally don't expect to be paid back. Their motivation is not to earn a financial return but rather to support a project that they believe is important or exciting. The funding they provide is more like a donation than a loan. (Project creators often do provide a "reward" to their backers, but it's more likely to be a tee shirt or DVD than a financial return.)

Crowdfunding websites such as Kickstarter.com and Indiegogo.com provide platforms for project creators to describe their ideas to potential supporters. And when a project proves popular, the amount of money raised can be impressive. For example, Scott Wilson garnered contributions totaling over $940,000 from over 13,500 backers to successfully finance his idea to develop a wristband he claimed would transform the iPad Nano into the world's coolest digital wristwatch.[19]

and distributed with malicious intent is called **malware** (short for "malicious software"). Spyware, computer viruses and worms are all examples of malware.

Spyware is software that installs itself on your computer without permission and then tracks your computer behavior in some way. It might track which Internet sites you visit to learn more about your interests and habits in order to send you targeted ads. Or, more alarmingly, it might log every keystroke (thus capturing passwords, account numbers, and user names to accounts as you enter them), allowing someone to steal your identity. Some spyware even goes beyond passive watching and takes control of your computer, perhaps sending you to websites you didn't want to visit.

Computer viruses are programs that install themselves on computers without the users' knowledge or permission and spread—sometimes very rapidly—by attaching themselves to other files that are transferred from computer to computer. Viruses are often attached to emails, instant messages, or files downloaded from the Internet. Some viruses are little more than pranks, but others can cause great harm. They can erase or modify data on your hard drive, prevent your computer from booting up, or find and send personal information you've stored on your computer to people who want to use it for identity theft. **Worms** are similar to viruses, except that they are independent programs that can spread across computer networks without being attached to other files.

How can you protect yourself from spyware, viruses, and worms? Take these common-sense steps:

- ⊙ Perform regular backups. This can come in handy should a virus tamper with (or erase) the data on your hard drive. Store the backed-up data in a separate place.

- ⊙ Install high-quality antivirus and antispyware software, and keep it updated. (Today's Internet security software usually has the ability to download and install updates automatically, but they may need to be configured to do so.)

- ⊙ Update your operating system regularly so that any security holes it contains are patched as soon as possible.

- ⊙ Don't open email messages or attachments if you don't know and trust the sender.

- ⊙ Don't download files from websites unless you are sure they are legitimate. And be sure to read the licensing agreement of any programs you install—especially those of freeware you download from the Internet. The wording of these agreements will often indicate if other programs (such as spyware) will be installed along with your free program.

> **Technology** is so much fun, but we can drown in our technology. The fog of information can drive out knowledge.
>
> — Daniel Boorstin, historian and former Librarian of Congress

Spam, Phishing, and Pharming

Spam refers to unsolicited commercial emails, usually sent to huge numbers of people with little regard for whether they are interested in the product or not. It's hard to get exact measures of the amount of spam that is sent each year, but experts agree that it now comprises the vast majority of all email in the United States. It clogs email inboxes and makes it tough for people to find legitimate messages among all the junk. Spam filters exist that help detect and eliminate spam, but spammers are very good at eventually finding ways to fool these filters.[20]

The U.S. Congress enacted the Controlling the Assault of Non-Solicited Pornography and Marketing Act (usually called the CAN-SPAM Act) in 2003. This act requires senders of unsolicited commercial email to label their messages as ads and to tell the recipient how to decline further messages. It also prohibits the use of false or deceptive subject lines in email messages. But the rapid increase in the amount of spam in recent years suggests this law hasn't been an effective deterrent.

Phishing is another common use of spam. Phishers send email messages that appear to come from a legitimate business, such as a bank, credit card company, or retailer. The email attempts to get recipients to disclose personal information, such as their social security or credit card numbers, by claiming that there is a problem with their account—or sometimes simply that the account information needs to be verified or updated. The messages appear authentic; in addition to official-sounding language, they often include official-looking corporate logos. The email also usually provides a link to a website where the recipient is supposed to log in and enter the desired information. When the victims of the scam click on this link, they go to a website that can look amazingly like the site for the real company—but it's not. It's a clever spoof of the site where the phishers collect personal information and use it to steal identities.

malware A general term for malicious software, such as spyware, computer viruses, and worms.

spyware Software that is installed on a computer without the user's knowledge or permission for the purpose of tracking the user's behavior.

computer virus Computer software that can be spread from one computer to another without the knowledge or permission of the computer users by attaching itself to emails or other files.

worm Malicious computer software that, unlike viruses, can spread on its own without being attached to other files.

spam Unsolicited email advertisements usually sent to very large numbers of recipients, many of whom may have no interest in the message.

phishing A scam in which official-looking emails are sent to individuals in an attempt to get them to divulge private information such as passwords, usernames, and account numbers.

One of the best ways to avoid such scams is to be skeptical of email requests for personal information; reputable businesses almost *never* ask you to divulge such information via email. Also, never click on a link in an email message to go to a website where you have financial accounts—if the message is from a phisher, that link is used to direct you to the fake site. Instead, use a link to the site that you've bookmarked, or type in the link to the real site yourself.

Not content with phishing expeditions, some scam artists have now taken to **pharming**. Like phishing, pharming uses fake websites to trick people into divulging personal information. But pharming is more sophisticated and difficult to detect than phishing because it doesn't require the intended victim to click on a bogus email link. Instead, it uses techniques to redirect Internet traffic to the fake sites. Thus, even if you type in the *correct* URL for a website you want to visit, you still might find yourself on a very realistic-looking pharming site. One way to check the validity of the site is to look for the indications that the site is secure, such as the https:// in the URL and the small closed lock icon mentioned earlier.[21]

Computers aren't the only devices plagued by these threats and annoyances. Cell phone users are facing increasing problems with spam delivered via text messaging. Even more alarming, some scammers have found ways to take their phishing expeditions to cell phones—a practice known as "smishing." One typical smishing ploy is to use text messaging to entice cell phone users to visit the scammer's fake website.[22]

Hackers: Break-Ins in Cyberspace

Hackers are skilled computer users who have the expertise to gain unauthorized access to other people's computers. Not all hackers intend to do harm, but some—called "black hat hackers" (or "crackers")—definitely have malicious intent. They may attempt to break into a computer system to steal identities or to disrupt a business.

Protecting against hackers requires individuals and businesses to be security conscious. Some of the precautions used against hackers, such as making frequent backups, are similar to those used to protect against viruses. Another key to protecting against hackers is to make sure that all data transmitted over a network are encrypted, or sent in encoded form that can only be read by those who have access to a key. Security experts also suggest that organizations restrict access to computer resources by requiring users to have strong passwords. According to Microsoft,

Hackers use their computer expertise to gain unauthorized access to other people's computers, often for malicious purposes.

© Photosani/ Shutterstock.com

strong passwords are at least 14 characters in length; include a mix of letters, numbers and special characters; and don't contain any common words or personal information.[23]

But strong passwords not only make it difficult for hackers to gain unauthorized access to a system, they also pose a challenge to legitimate users—it's tough to remember long, random strings of letters, numbers, and characters—especially when you're supposed to use different passwords for different accounts and change them frequently. One security expert found that many people have such a hard time keeping up with their passwords that they simply write them down and hide them under their mouse pads—hardly a secure location![24]

Firewalls are another important tool to guard against hackers and other security threats. A firewall uses hardware or software (or sometimes both) to create a barrier that prevents unwanted messages or instructions from entering a computer system. As threats from spyware, hackers, and other sources have developed, the use of firewalls has become commonplace.

Ethical and Legal Issues

Information technology raises a number of legal and ethical challenges, such as the need to deal with privacy issues and to protect intellectual property rights. These issues are controversial and don't have simple solutions.

Personal Privacy Firms now have the ability to track customer behavior in ways that were never before possible. This has advantages for you because it allows firms to offer better, more personalized service. But all this extra information comes at the expense of your privacy. Does the fact that firms know so much about your preferences and behavior make you a bit nervous?

Does it bother you that your email messages lack confidentiality? When you send an email, it could be stored on at several computers: your personal computer, the server of your email provider, the server of your recipient's provider, and your recipient's own computer. If you send the email from your company's system, it's also likely to be stored when the company backs up its information. If you thought that deleting an email message from your own computer erased it permanently and completely, you need to think again.

The list of other ways in which information technology can erode your personal privacy is long and getting longer. For example, RFID chips are now embedded in U.S. passports and in many states' driver's licenses. Some privacy experts are concerned that such chips will make it easy for government organizations to track individuals. One reason government officials gave for embedding RFID chips in passports and driver's licenses was to make it harder for criminals and terrorists to forge IDs. But in 2009, a hacker publicly demonstrated the ability to read the information in these chips from a distance of several yards, leading to fears that identity thieves could use similar techniques to obtain personal information and perhaps even create convincing copies of these important identification documents. The U.S. government responded to these concerns by issuing assurances that passports and driver's licenses include additional security features that minimize such risks, but skeptics remain unconvinced.[25]

The bottom line is that there's no simple way to solve privacy concerns. Privacy is an elusive concept, and there is no strong consensus about how much privacy is enough.

Protecting Intellectual Property Rights Intellectual property refers to products that result from creative and intellectual efforts. There are many types of intellectual property, but we'll focus on forms of intellectual property that are protected by copyright law, such as books, musical works, computer programs, video games, and movies. Copyright law gives the creators of this property the exclusive right to produce, record, perform, and sell their work for a specified time period.

Piracy of intellectual property occurs when someone reproduces and distributes copyrighted work without obtaining permission from—or providing compensation to—the owner of the copyrighted material. When piracy becomes widespread, creators of intellectual property receive much less income for their efforts. This can substantially reduce their incentive to continue developing creative material.

The Business Software Alliance estimates that globally 42% of all business software installed on personal computers in 2010 was pirated, resulting in the loss of over $59 billion in revenue to software companies. In several smaller

> **intellectual property**
> Property that is the result of creative or intellectual effort, such as books, musical works, inventions, and computer software.

Information Overload: Too Much of a Good Thing?

From email to cell phones (and text messaging) to Twitter updates to blogs on the Web, many of today's workers (and students) are connected to what seems to be an endless flow of information. But while the diversity and volume of the information generated by the communications technologies of the twenty-first century can be gratifying, they're also often distracting—and sometimes even intimidating.

How serious is information overload? One study, conducted by University of London psychiatrist Glenn Wilson, suggested that when workers were constantly bombarded with new information, their ability to remain focused and to complete tasks was disrupted. In fact, he found that information overload could actually temporarily reduce the worker's decision-making IQ by up to ten points! The problem is so common that there is even an organization—the Information Overload Research Group—dedicated to exploring its causes and cures.

Dealing with information overload requires discipline. If you find yourself swamped by too much information, try to set aside a few times a day when you will check and respond to emails and voicemails, read blogs, and surf the Web and leave other times free to concentrate on getting work done without these interruptions. Prioritize your work, and don't let yourself get distracted by irrelevant (though often interesting) topics. Finally, resist the urge to subscribe to information sources just because they are available and might be interesting—they won't help you if you never have time to read them.[26]

JUST BECAUSE THEY CAN...

...DOESN'T MEAN THEY SHOULD.

In early May of 2011 Burson-Marsteller, a high-powered public relations firm, contacted several newspaper reporters and technology bloggers claiming that Google was using an initiative called Social Circle to collect, mine, and share the personal information of millions of people without their knowledge or consent. The firm implied that Google's tactics were unethical—perhaps even illegal—and urged the reporters and bloggers to write stories about Google's misdeeds. In fact, it even offered to help at least one of the bloggers actually write his anti-Google piece.

Some bloggers and newspapers looked into the claims made by the PR firm—but the results weren't what Burson-Marsteller was hoping for. The reporters all concluded that the allegations were either overblown or misrepresented how Social Circle worked. One of the reporters even characterized Burson-Marsteller's efforts as a "smear campaign" against Google.

It was clear that Burson-Marsteller wasn't making the allegations on its own but was rather working under the direction of a client. But the firm refused to identify who had hired it. The mystery was solved when Facebook issued a press release admitting that it was the client behind the efforts. It justified its actions by claiming that it had legitimate concerns about Google's tactics and was just trying to get its concerns investigated by the independent press.

Even if Facebook had legitimate concerns, launching an anonymous PR campaign that contained misleading information about a rival firm went against its core value of transparency. Facebook admitted that "The issues are serious, and we should have presented them in a serious and transparent way."

Burson-Marsteller also expressed embarrassment for its role in the incident. In a prepared statement, the PR firm concluded that "Whatever the rationale, this was not at all standard operating procedure and is against our policies, and the assignment on those terms should have been declined. When talking to the media, we need to adhere to strict standards of transparency about clients, and this incident underscores the absolute importance of that principle."[27]

What do YOU think?

- How concerned are you that your personal information on social networking sites might be used without your permission?
- What should Burson-Marsteller have done when Facebook approached them for this assignment?
- How does this incident affect your perception of Google, Facebook, and Burson-Marsteller?

countries, including Georgia, Zimbabwe and Yemen, the rate of piracy was over 90%. Among larger nations, the piracy rate in China exceeded 78%, while in India it was 64%. The good news is that the piracy rate was much lower in the United States at 20%. But given the huge size of the U.S. software market, even this relatively low rate of piracy still resulted in losses of over $9.5 billion in revenue for software companies. Faced with such a widespread problem, many software publishers have become very aggressive at prosecuting firms and individuals engaged in software piracy.[28]

Music studios, video game developers, and motion picture producers also face significant problems with piracy. For instance, Japan's Computer Entertainment Suppliers Association estimated that video game piracy cost game developers for the Nintendo DS and PlayStation Portable $41.5 billion in sales between 2004 and 2009.[29]

Given how lucrative piracy can be, it's unlikely that this problem will go away anytime soon. You can expect the companies hurt by these practices to continue aggressively prosecuting pirates and to work on new technologies that make pirating digital media more difficult.

THE BIG PICTURE

Information technology plays a vital role in virtually every aspect of business operations. For instance, marketing managers use information technology to learn more about customers, reach them in novel ways, and forge stronger relationships with them—as we showed in our discussion of Web 2.0. Operations managers use RFID technologies to coordinate the movement of goods within supply chains and to keep more accurate inventory records. And financial managers use IT to track financial conditions and identify investment opportunities. Managers in all areas of a business can use decision-support systems to improve their decision making. They also can apply techniques such as data mining to obtain interesting new insights hidden in the vast streams of data that flow into their companies.

Cloud computing represents the newest and one of the most exciting new approaches to how companies acquire and utilize IT resources. The use of cloud-based resources not only has the potential to lower costs and increase flexibility, but it also offers the ability to significantly magnify computation power. If cloud computing can overcome concerns about security and stability, it is likely to continue growing in popularity, which could result in significant changes to the role IT departments play within their organizations.

The rapid changes in IT in recent years—especially those related to the rise of Internet as a business venue—have opened up exciting new commercial opportunities. But these changes have also created a host of legal and ethical challenges and security. One thing is certain: business organizations that find ways to leverage the advantages of new IT developments while minimizing the accompanying risks are most likely to enjoy competitive success.

The rapidly changing nature of information technology and the increasing importance this technology plays in the success of modern businesses suggest that careers in this field are likely to see significant growth over the next several years. Let's take a look at two common occupations in information technology.

Computer support specialists provide technical assistance and advice to the users of their organization's information technology resources—which in today's business world is just about everyone in the organization! They diagnose and resolve computer- and network-related problems. They also may write training manuals and participate in sessions to train other workers in the proper use of new hardware and software. Finally, these workers often oversee the daily performance of their company's computer systems.

Requirements for employment as a computer support specialist vary. Some employers strongly prefer candidates with a bachelor's degree in computer science, computer engineering, or information technology. Other employers accept individuals with an associate's degree in a computer-related field. Still other firms will hire applicants with college degrees in any field as long as they possess strong technical and communications skills. The Bureau of Labor Statistics projects that employment opportunities for computer support specialists will be quite good for the next several years, with employment expected to grow faster than average. In May of 2009, the average salary for this occupation was $47,360.

Computer systems analysts design, maintain, and upgrade computer systems and select, install, and configure the hardware and software needed to implement their designs. They also devise ways to apply existing resources to meet new challenges. This work generally requires a high degree of technical competence, so most employers require systems analysts to have at least a bachelor's degree in a technical field such as computer science, information technology, or computer or software engineering. Many prefer candidates with advanced degrees in these fields. The Bureau of Labor Statistics forecasts that employment opportunities for computer system analysts will grow very rapidly for the next several years. In May of 2009, the average salary for systems analysts was $80,430.[30]

CAREERS IN INFORMATION TECHNOLOGY

What *else?*
RIP & REVIEW CARDS IN THE BACK
and visit www.cengagebrain.com!

17

Operations Management:
Putting It All Together

SUCCESS IS SIMPLE. DO WHAT'S *RIGHT*, THE RIGHT WAY, AT THE RIGHT TIME.

— ARNOLD H. GLASGOW, AMERICAN PSYCHOLOGIST

LO1 Operations Management: Producing Value in a Changing Environment

Operations management is concerned with managing all of the activities involved in creating value by producing goods and services and distributing them to customers. When operations managers do their job well, their firms produce the *right* goods and services in the *right* quantities and distribute these to the *right* customers at the *right* time—all the while keeping quality high and costs low. Obviously, the decisions of operations managers can have a major impact on a firm's revenues and its costs, and thus on its overall profitability.

Responding to a Changing Environment

The practice of operations management has changed dramatically over the past half century. New technologies, shifts in the structure of the economy, challenges posed by global competition and concerns about the impact of production on the environment have fueled this revolution. Let's begin by identifying the key changes that have characterized the practice of operations management over the past fifty years.

From a Focus on Efficiency to a Focus on Effectiveness:
To operations managers, **efficiency** means producing a product at the *lowest cost*. **Effectiveness** means producing products that *create value* by providing customers with goods and services that offer a better relationship between price and perceived benefits. In other words, effectiveness means finding ways to give customers more for their money—while still making a profit.

In the 1960s the focus of operations management was mainly on efficiency. The goal was to keep costs low so the firm could make a profit while keeping its prices competitive. In today's highly competitive global markets, efficiency remains important. But operations managers now realize that keeping costs (and prices) low are only part of the equation. Customers usually buy goods that offer the best value—and these aren't always the same as the goods that sell for the lowest price. A product that offers better features, more attractive styling and higher quality may provide more value—and attract more customers—than a product with a lower price. Thus, today's operations managers have broadened their focus to look at benefits as well as costs.

From Goods to Services
Goods are tangible products that you can see and touch. *Durable goods* are expected to last three years or longer; examples include furniture, cars and appliances. *Nondurable goods*, such as toothpaste, apples, and paper towels, are used up more quickly and are often perishable. **Services** are activities that yield benefits but don't directly result in a physical product. Examples include legal advice, entertainment, and medical care. Goods are consumed, while services are experienced.

In the 1960s, the U.S. economy was a manufacturing powerhouse, with more than a third of its labor force employed in the goods-producing sector. But over the past fifty years, the American economy has experienced a fundamental shift away from the production of goods and toward the provision of services. By 2010, less than 15% of the nonfarm labor force worked in the goods-producing sector. By contrast, employment in the service sector had risen to well over 80% of the labor force.[1]

From Mass Production to Mass Customization
Fifty years ago, one common production strategy was to keep costs low by producing large quantities of standardized products. The goal of this *mass production* strategy was to achieve reductions in average cost by taking advantage of specialization and the efficient use of capital. But today's technologies allow many firms to pursue *mass customization*—the production of small quantities of customized goods and services that more precisely meet

operations management Managing all of the activities involved in creating value by producing goods and services and distributing them to customers.

efficiency Producing output or achieving a goal at the lowest cost.

effectiveness Using resources to create value by providing customers with goods and services that offer a better relationship between price and perceived benefits.

goods Tangible products.

services Intangible products.

the needs of specific customers—with very little increase in costs.

From Local Competition to Global Competition For the first twenty-five years after World War II, American firms dominated key markets. This strength was based partly on the fact that the United States possessed a rich base of natural resources, a growing and increasingly well-educated labor force, excellent infrastructure, and the strong incentive system inherent in a market economy. But it also reflected the fact that the production facilities and infrastructure in many European and Asian nations had been severely damaged during the war.

By the early 1970s, the economies of Japan, Germany, and other war-ravaged nations had been rebuilt, with many of their major companies boasting efficient new production facilities with state-of-the-art technology. In addition, many Japanese firms had adopted new techniques that greatly improved the quality of their products. With lower labor costs, impressive technology and world-class quality, these foreign producers quickly began to take market share from American firms. In more recent years, firms in Korea, India, and China have also become formidable competitors.

From Simple Supply Chains to Complex Value Chains Over the past fifty years, the increasingly competitive and global nature of markets has brought about major changes in how firms produce and distribute their goods and services. Many supply chains today span multiple organizations located in many different countries. The shift from a cost perspective to a value perspective has led operations managers to extend their view beyond the traditional supply chain to encompass a broader range of processes and organizations known as a *value chain*.

From Exploiting the Environment to Protecting the Environment In the 1960s, many operations managers viewed the natural environment as something to exploit. The emphasis on keeping costs low made it tempting to dispose of wastes as cheaply as possible—often by dumping them into rivers, lakes, or the atmosphere. But the serious consequences of environmental pollution have become increasingly apparent. Operations managers at socially responsible companies have responded by adopting a variety of green practices to produce goods and services in more environmentally responsible ways.

Exhibit 17.1 summarizes the discussion of the key ways in which operations management has changed over the past fifty years. We'll look at these changes in greater detail as we move through this chapter. But first let's take a look at the some of the key tasks operations managers perform.

> **Efficiency** is concerned with doing things right; effectiveness is doing the right thing.
>
> —Peter F. Drucker

© iStockphoto.com/Lasse Kristensen

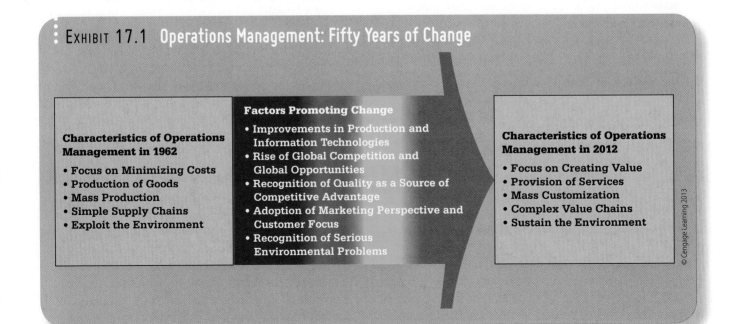

Exhibit 17.1 Operations Management: Fifty Years of Change

Characteristics of Operations Management in 1962

- Focus on Minimizing Costs
- Production of Goods
- Mass Production
- Simple Supply Chains
- Exploit the Environment

Factors Promoting Change

- Improvements in Production and Information Technologies
- Rise of Global Competition and Global Opportunities
- Recognition of Quality as a Source of Competitive Advantage
- Adoption of Marketing Perspective and Customer Focus
- Recognition of Serious Environmental Problems

Characteristics of Operations Management in 2012

- Focus on Creating Value
- Provision of Services
- Mass Customization
- Complex Value Chains
- Sustain the Environment

© Cengage Learning 2013

LO2 What Do Operations Managers Do?

Understanding the marketing definition of *product* plays a pivotal role in understanding what operations managers do. A product consists of all of the tangible and intangible features (sometimes called the *customer benefit package*) that create value for consumers by satisfying their needs and wants. For example, when you purchase a car made by General Motors, you not only get the physical automobile, you also get (among other things) a warranty and (for many models) a year of OnStar services.

Marketing research typically determines which features a product should include to appeal to its target customers. Although operations managers don't normally have the primary responsibility for designing these goods and services, they provide essential information and advice during the product-design process, especially regarding the challenges and constraints involved in creating actual products on time and within budget.

Once the actual goods and services are designed, operations managers must determine the processes needed to produce them and get them to the customer. A **process** is a set of related activities that transform inputs into outputs, thus adding value. Once these processes are designed, operations managers also play a key role in determining where they will be performed, what organizations will perform them, and how the processes will be organized and coordinated.

The most obvious processes are those directly involved in the production of goods and services. But there are many other processes that play necessary "supporting roles." For example, purchasing and inventory management processes ensure that the firm has an adequate supply of high-quality materials, parts, and components needed to produce the goods without delays or disruptions.

Let's take a closer look at some of the functions that operations managers perform to move goods and services from the drawing board to the final user.

Process Selection and Facility Layout

Once a product is designed, operations managers must determine the best way to produce it. This involves determining the most efficient processes, deciding the best sequence in which to arrange those processes, and designing the appropriate layout of production and distribution facilities. Well-designed processes and facility layouts enable a firm to produce high-quality products effectively and efficiently, giving it a competitive advantage. Poorly designed processes can result in production delays, quality problems, and high costs.

There are several ways to organize processes. The best approach depends on considerations such as the volume of production and the degree of standardization of the product.

process A set of related activities that transform inputs into outputs, thus adding value.

- ➲ Firms often use a *product layout* when they produce goods that are relatively standardized and produced in large volumes. This type of layout organizes machinery, equipment, and other resources according to the specific sequence of operations that must performed. The machinery used in this type of layout is often highly specialized, designed to perform one specific task *very* efficiently. One classic example of a product layout is an assembly line, where the product being produced moves from one station to another in a fixed sequence, with the machinery and workers at each station performing specialized tasks. Services that provide a high volume of relatively standardized products also use flow-shop processes. For example, fast food restaurants often use a simple product layout to prepare sandwiches, pizzas, or tacos in a standard sequence of steps.

- ➲ A *process layout* is used by many firms that need to produce small batches of goods that require a degree of customization. This approach arranges equipment according to the type of task performed. For example, in a machine shop all of the drills may be located in one area, all of the lathes in another area, and all

© LYSTSEVA MARINA/ITAR-TASS/Landov

The Bureau of Labor Statistics forecasts the U.S. service sector will generate 14.5 million new jobs between 2008 and 2018, while employment in the goods producing sector will remain unchanged over the same period.

— Bureau of Labor Statistics

of the grinders in yet another. Unlike assembly lines and other product layouts, a process layout doesn't require work to be performed in a specific sequence; instead, the product can be moved from one type of machinery to another in whatever sequence is necessary. Thus, process layouts can be used to produce a variety of products without the need for expensive retooling. But this flexibility sometimes comes at the cost of longer processing times and more complex planning and control systems. Also, because the machinery and equipment used in a process layout is usually more general-purpose in nature and may be used to produce a greater variety of goods, the process layout requires workers to be more versatile than those employed in a product layout.

⊃ A *cellular layout* falls between the product layout and the process layout. It groups different types of machinery and equipment into self-contained cells. A production facility might have several cells, each designed to efficiently produce a family of parts (or entire products) that have similar processing requirements. Like an assembly line, the product moves from one station in the cell to the next in a specific sequence. However, unlike most assembly lines, cells are relatively small and are designed to be operated by a few workers who perform a wider array of tasks than assembly line workers.

⊃ A fixed position layout is used for goods that must be produced at a specific site (such as a building or a dam) or that are so large and bulky that it isn't feasible to move them from station to station (such as a ship or commercial airplane). Even some services, such as concerts or sporting events that are performed at a specific location use this approach. In a fixed position layout, the good or service stays in one place, and the employees, machinery, and equipment are brought to the fixed site when needed during various stages of the production process.

Facility Location

There is an old saying in real estate that the three most important factors determining the value of a property are "location, location, and location." There is no doubt that the location is also important to operations managers. The location of facilities can have an important influence on the efficiency and effectiveness of an organization's processes.

For some types of facilities, the location decision is dominated by one key consideration. A coalmine, for instance, must be located where there's coal. But for many other types of facilities, the decision is more complex. Exhibit 17.2 identifies some key factors that operations managers evaluate when they decide where to locate a facility, but importance of each factor varies depending on the specific industry. For instance, many service firms place primary interest on locating close to their markets, while manufacturing firms are often more concerned about the cost and availability of land and labor and access to highways, railways, and port facilities.

Exhibit 17.2 Factors That Affect Location Decisions

GENERAL LOCATION FACTORS	EXAMPLES OF SPECIFIC CONSIDERATIONS
ADEQUACY OF UTILITIES	Is the supply of electricity reliable? Is clean water available?
LAND	Is adequate land available for a facility? How much does the land cost?
LABOR MARKET CONDITIONS	Are workers with the right skills available? How expensive is labor?
TRANSPORTATION FACTORS	Is the location near customers and suppliers? Is appropriate transportation nearby?
QUALITY OF LIFE FACTORS	What is the climate like? Are adequate healthcare facilities available?
LEGAL AND POLITICAL ENVIRONMENT	Does the local government support new businesses? What are the local taxes, fees, and regulations?

© Cengage Learning 2013

Inventory Control: Knowing When to Hold'em

Inventories are stocks of goods or other items held by an organization. Manufacturing firms usually hold inventories of raw materials, components and parts, work in process, and finished goods. Retail firms don't normally hold work in process or raw materials, but they do hold inventories of the finished goods they sell as well as basic supplies that they need.

Deciding how much inventory to hold can be a real challenge for operations managers because increasing (or decreasing) the amount of inventory involves both benefits and costs. For example, benefits of holding larger inventories include:

- **Smoother Production Schedules:** A candy maker might produce more candy than it needs in August and September and hold the excess in inventory so that it can meet the surge in demand for Halloween treats without investing in more production capacity.

- **Protection Against Stock-Outs and Lost Sales:** Holding larger inventories reduces the chance of stock-outs and lost sales due to supply disruptions or unexpected surges in demand.

- **Reduced Ordering Costs:** Every time a company orders supplies, it incurs paperwork and handling costs. Holding a larger average inventory reduces the number of orders the firm must make and thus reduces ordering costs.

But holding larger inventories involves costs as well as benefits:

- **Tied-Up Funds:** Items in inventory don't generate revenue until they're sold, so holding large inventories can tie up funds that could be better used elsewhere within the organization.

- **Additional Holding Costs:** Bigger inventories require more storage space, which can mean extra costs for heating, cooling, taxes, insurance, and more.

- **Increased Risk:** Holding large inventories exposes the firm to the risk of losses due to spoilage, depreciation, and obsolescence.

Operations managers determine the optimal amount of inventory by comparing the costs and benefits associated with different levels of inventory. In our discussion of lean manufacturing, we'll see that one recent trend has been toward finding ways to reduce inventory levels at every stage of the supply chain.

Project Scheduling

Projects such as constructing a new production facility, developing a new commercial airliner or filming a movie are complex and expensive endeavors. It's vital to monitor them carefully to avoid major delays or cost overruns. The **critical path method (CPM)** is one of the most important tools that operations managers use to manage such projects. We can illustrate the basic idea behind this tool by looking at a simple example in which a theater company wants to stage a play. Exhibit 17.3 presents the steps involved in this project.

Notice that Exhibit 17.3 identifies **immediate predecessors** for all of the activities except activity A. *Immediate predecessors* are activities that must be completed before another activity can begin. For example, it is clear that the cast for the play cannot be determined until the play has been selected, so activity A (selecting the play) is an immediate predecessor to activity B (selecting the cast). Similarly, since sets can't be built without lumber, paint, and other materials, activity E (buying materials for the sets) is an immediate predecessor for activity G (building the sets).

Using the Critical Path Method to Focus Efforts Now look at Exhibit 17.4, which is a CPM network for the theater project. This network shows how all of the activities in the theater project are related to each other. The direction of the arrows shows the immediate predecessors for each activity. Notice that arrows go from activities B (selecting the cast) *and* F (purchasing material for the costumes) to activity H (making the costumes). This indicates that *both* of these activities are immediate predecessors for activity H—the costumes can't be made without material, and they must be made in the correct sizes to fit the actors. But also notice that no arrow links activities B and C. This shows that these are independent activities; in other words, the theater company doesn't have to select the cast before it designs the sets (or vice versa).

We can use Exhibit 17.4 to illustrate some basic concepts used in CPM analysis. A *path* is a sequence of activities that *must be completed in the order specified by the arrows* for the overall project to be completed. You can trace several paths in our example by following a series of arrows from start to finish. For example, one path is A → B → I → J → K, and another path is A → C → E → G → J → K.

The **critical path** consists of the sequence of activities that takes the longest to complete. A *delay in any activity on a critical path is likely to delay the completion of the entire project.* Thus, operations managers watch activities on the

inventory Stocks of goods or other items held by organizations.

critical path method (CPM) A project-management tool that illustrates the relationships among all the activities involved in completing a project and identifies the sequence of activities likely to take the longest to complete.

immediate predecessors Activities in a project that must be completed before some other specified activity can begin.

critical path The sequence of activities in a project that is expected to take the longest to complete.

EXHIBIT 17.3 Activities Involved in Presenting a Play

ACTIVITY	DESCRIPTION	IMMEDIATE PREDECESSOR(S)	ESTIMATED COMPLETION TIME (WEEKS)
A	Select Play	None	2
B	Select Cast	A (must know play to know what roles are available)	4
C	Design Sets	A (must know play before sets be designed)	4
D	Design Costumes	A (must know play to determine what costumes are needed)	5
E	Buy Materials for Sets	C (set must be designed to determine types and quantities of materials needed to build it)	2
F	Buy Materials for Costumes	D (costumes must be designed before materials for costumes are determined)	2
G	Build Sets	E (must have materials in order to build the sets)	4
H	Make Costumes	B, F (must have materials in order to make the costumes, and must know actors' sizes to ensure that costumes fit)	6
I	Initial Rehearsals	B (actors must be selected for each role before they can rehearse their parts)	2
J	Final (Dress) Rehearsal	G, H, I (costumes and sets must be completed, and initial rehearsals performed, before the final rehearsal can occur)	1
K	Perform Play (end of project)	J	N/A

© Cengage Learning 2013

critical path very carefully and take actions to help ensure that they remain on schedule. We've shown the critical path for the theater project (A → D → F → H → J → K) with red arrows on our diagram.

Distinguishing between the critical path and other paths can help operations managers allocate resources more efficiently. Activities that aren't on the critical path can be delayed without causing a delay in the overall completion of the project—as long as the delay isn't too great. In CPM termi-

nology, these activities have *slack*. When operations managers see delays in critical path activities, they may be able to keep the project on track by diverting manpower and other resources from activities with slack to activities on the critical path.

Designing and Managing Value Chains

Perhaps the most important function of operations management is the design and management of value chains. A **value chain** is the network of relationships that channels the flow of inputs, information, and financial resources through all of the processes directly or indirectly involved in producing goods and services and distributing them to customers.

An organization's value chain clearly includes its supply chain, which consists of the organizations, activities, and processes involved in the physical flow of goods, from the raw materials stage

EXHIBIT 17.4 A CPM Network for Staging a Play

© Cengage Learning 2013

to the final consumer. In fact, some organizations use the terms *value chain* and *supply chain* interchangeably. But a value chain is a broader concept; in addition to the supply chain, it includes activities and processes involved in *acquiring customers*—such as contract negotiations and customer financing—as well as activities and processes involved in *keeping customers* by providing services after the sale, such as performing warranty repairs, offering call center assistance, and helping customers recycle used goods. In a value chain, the main focus is on the customer; in contrast, the supply chain is more oriented toward traditional production relationships.[2]

One of the most important issues that operations managers examine when they design value chains is the trade-off between vertical integration and outsourcing. **Vertical integration** occurs when a firm attempts to gain more control over its value chain by either developing the ability to perform processes previously performed by other organizations in the chain or by acquiring those organizations. **Outsourcing** is essentially the opposite of vertical integration; it involves arranging for other organizations to perform value chain functions that were previously performed internally.

In recent years, the trend in value chain design has been to rely more on outsourcing and less on vertical integration. Outsourcing allows a firm to shed functions it doesn't perform well in order to focus on its areas of strength. It also frees people, money, and other resources that had been tied up in the outsourced activities, allowing these resources to be employed in more profitable ways.

Even when a firm decides to perform processes itself, it still faces a choice: should it perform these functions domestically, or should it offshore these activities? **Offshoring** means moving processes previously performed domestically to a foreign location. It is important to realize that offshoring is *not* the same thing as outsourcing processes to other organizations. Offshoring doesn't require outsourcing; a firm often offshores processes by directly investing in its *own* foreign facilities. Similarly, outsourcing doesn't require a firm to go offshore; activities can be outsourced to other *domestic* firms. Despite this distinction, many firms have combined these approaches by hiring organizations in other countries to perform some of the processes that they previously performed at their own domestic facilities.

It is also worth noting that offshoring can go in both directions. Just as American firms offshore processes to other countries, some foreign companies offshore some of their processes to the U.S. For example, several Japanese, European, and Korean automakers now have extensive design and production facilities in the U.S.

One common reason for offshoring by U.S. firms is to take advantage of less expensive labor. But other factors can also play a role. Land and other resources also may be less expensive in developing nations than in the United States. And some foreign governments, eager to attract American investments, may offer financial incentives or other inducements. In addition, many foreign markets are growing much more rapidly than the relatively mature U.S. market. Firms often find it advantageous to locate production facilities close to these rapidly growing markets.

While foreign outsourcing can often reduce costs, it also can complicate value chains and create coordination problems. And it can expose the firm to certain types of risks. When a firm outsources important functions, it may have to entrust others in its value chain with confidential information and intellectual property, such as copyrighted material or patented designs. These strategic assets have less legal protection in some countries than in the United States, so providing access to foreign firms may increase the risk that the firm's intellectual property will be pirated or counterfeited. This issue has been of greatest concern when firms have outsourced some of their supply chain functions to organizations in China.[3]

Given the trend toward offshoring and outsourcing, value chains (and the supply chains at their core) have become increasingly complex, often involving many

Offshoring involves moving activities previously performed domestically to a foreign location.

© Mark Elias/Bloomberg via Getty Images

different organizations and processes located in many different countries. Modern operations managers rely on sophisticated *supply chain management software* to streamline the communications among supply chain participants and to help them plan and coordinate their efforts.

The newest versions of **enterprise resource planning (ERP)** software take supply chain management to its highest level. ERP initially focused on integrating the flow of information among *all* aspects of a single organization's operations—accounting, finance, sales and marketing, production, and human resources. But the newest versions go beyond a single organization to help manage activities along an entire supply chain or value chain. The common information system makes it easier for organizations throughout the chain to communicate and coordinate their activities.

ERP systems do have some drawbacks. They are complex, expensive, and difficult to implement, and they require users to learn new ways to enter and access data. Productivity can actually fall until users become accustomed to these new methods. But despite these challenges, ERP systems have become very popular. And they continue to evolve and take advantage of new technologies. One of the newest developments is the arrival of Web-based ERP systems that can be "rented" from online providers—a strategy that reduces the need to invest in new hardware and software. The use of Web-based ERP services is an example of a relatively new trend in information technology known as *cloud computing*.[4]

LO3 Implications of a Service-Based Economy: Responding to Different Challenges

Exhibit 17.5 illustrates how services differ from tangible goods. These differences present a number of challenges to service providers. One key challenge arises because customers often participate in the provision of services, which means that service providers have less control over how the process is carried out, how long it takes to complete, and whether the result is satisfactory. For instance, the accuracy of a doctor's diagnosis depends on how honestly

EXHIBIT 17.5 Differences Between Goods and Services

GOODS	SERVICES
Are tangible: They have a physical form and can be seen, touched, handled, etc.	Are intangible: They can be "experienced," but they don't have a physical form.
Can be stored in an inventory.	Must be consumed *when* they are produced.
Can be shipped.	Must be consumed *where* they are provided.
Are produced independently of the consumer.	Often require the customer to be actively involved in their production.
Can have at least *some* aspects of their quality determined objectively by measuring defects or deviations from desired values.	Intangible nature means quality is based mainly on customer perceptions.

© Cengage Learning 2013

and completely the patient answers the doctor's questions. And the amount of time the doctor spends with each patient will depend on the seriousness of the problem and the complexity of the diagnosis and treatment.

Designing the Servicescape

Because of the interaction between customers and service providers, the design of service facilities often must take the experiences of the participants into account. A **servicescape** is the environment in which the customer and service provider interact. A well-designed servicescape can have a positive influence on the attitudes and perceptions of both the customer and those who provide the service. A poor servicescape can have the opposite effect.[5]

The design of servicescapes centers on three types of factors: ambience; functionality; and signs, symbols, and artifacts.

- ⊙ *Ambience* refers to factors such as decor, background music, lighting, noise levels, and even scents. For example, massage therapists often use low light, soothing background music, and pleasant scents to create a relaxing atmosphere for a massage.

- ⊙ *Functionality* involves how easy is it for the customer to move through the facility and find what they are looking for.

- ⊙ *Signs, symbols,* and *artifacts* convey information to customers and create impressions. Obviously, signs like

"Place Your Order Here" and "Pick Up Your Order Here" provide useful information that helps consumers maneuver through the service encounter. But other signs and symbols can be used to create favorable impressions. For instance, lawyers and accountants often prominently display their diplomas, professional certifications and awards in their offices to communicate their qualifications and accomplishments to their clients.

How Big Is Big Enough?

Because services are intangible and often must be experienced at the time they are created, service providers can't produce the service in advance and store it to meet temporary surges in demand. This can create challenges for operations managers because the demand for many types of services varies significantly, depending on the season, the day of the week, or the time of day. During peak lunch and dinner hours, popular restaurants tend to be very busy—often with crowds waiting to get a table. The same restaurants may be nearly empty during the mid-afternoon or late at night. Given such fluctuations in demand, the selection of *capacity*—the number of customers the service facility can accommodate per time period—becomes a crucial consideration.

If the capacity of a service facility is too small, customers facing long waits during periods of peak demand may well take their business elsewhere. But a facility large enough to handle peak capacity is more expensive to build; costs more to heat, cool, and insure; and may have substantial excess capacity during off—peak periods. Operations managers must weigh these drawbacks against the ability to handle a larger number of customers during peak hours.

Many service firms try to minimize this tradeoff by finding ways to spread out demand so that big surges don't occur. One way to do this is to give customers an incentive to use the service at off-peak times. Many bars and restaurants have "happy hours" or "early-bird specials." Similarly, movie theaters have lower prices for matinée showings, and resort hotels offer reduced rates during their off seasons.

LO4 The Technology of Operations

Now let's take a close look at how technology has revolutionized operations management. Some of the new technologies involve the increasing sophistication of machinery and equipment. Others involve advances in software and information technology. The impact of these technological advances is greatest when the automated machinery is directly linked to the new software running on powerful new computers.

Automation: The Rise of the Machine

For the past half century, one of the biggest trends in operations management has been increased **automation** of many processes. Automation means replacing human operation and control of machinery and equipment with some form of programmed control. The use of automated systems has become increasingly common—and increasingly sophisticated.

Automation began in the early 1950s with primitive programmed machines. But in recent decades, **robots** have taken automation to a whole new level. Robots are reprogrammable machines that can manipulate materials, tools, parts, and specialized devices in order to perform a variety of tasks. Some robots have special sensors that allow them to "see," "hear," or "feel" their environment. Many robots are mobile and can even be guided over rugged terrain.

Robots offer many advantages to firms:

- They often perform jobs that most human workers find tedious, dirty, dangerous, or physically demanding.

- They don't get tired, so they can work very long hours while maintaining a consistently high level of performance.

- They are flexible; unlike old dogs, robots *can* be taught new tricks because they are reprogrammable.

automation Replacing human operation and control of machinery and equipment with some form of programmed control.

robot A reprogrammable machine that is capable of manipulating materials, tools, parts, and specialized devices in order to perform a variety of tasks.

Automation involves programming machines and equipment to carry out tasks previously performed by humans.

© iStockphoto.com/Jonathan Heger

Robots are most commonly used for tasks such as welding, spray painting, and assembling products, but they can do many other things ranging from packaging frozen pizza to disposing of hazardous waste.

Software Technologies

Several types of software have become common in operations management, and as the processing power of computers has improved, the capabilities of these applications have become increasingly sophisticated. Some of the most common examples include:

⊙ **computer-aided design (CAD)** software provides powerful drawing and drafting tools that enable users to create and edit blueprints and design drawings quickly and easily. Current CAD programs allow users to create 3-D drawings.

> You seldom improve quality by cutting costs, but you can often cut costs by improving **quality.**
>
> — Karl Albrecht, Author and Futurist

⊙ **computer-aided engineering (CAE)** software enables users to test, analyze, and optimize their designs through computer simulations. CAE software can help engineers find and correct design flaws *before* production.

⊙ **computer-aided manufacturing (CAM)** software takes the electronic design for a product and creates the programmed instructions that robots and other automated equipment must follow to produce that product as efficiently as possible.

Photo by 3D Systems Corp. via Getty Images

A New Dimension in Production Technology

A technology known as *3D printing* is poised to take the concept of mass customization to a whole new level—and it could revolutionize operations management in the process. Unlike traditional manufacturing, 3D printing creates products by downloading computer specifications to a special "printer," which then prints and deposits layer upon layer of material to build up the product.

3D printing was developed in the mid-1980s, but like many technologies it was initially too expensive and crude to see widespread use. But in recent years, the cost of 3D printers has dropped dramatically, and their speed and quality have improved. Leading-edge firms are now using this technology to produce everything from intricate jewelry to complex aircraft parts.

The increasing popularity of 3D production stems from its many advantages over traditional manufacturing methods. It is more energy-efficient, results in less waste, and can be faster. Most importantly, it is ideal for mass customization, since the printer can switch quickly and seamlessly from producing one product to another with virtually no retooling costs. Given these advantages, analysts predict that 3D printing will become a mainstream technology by 2020.

Some 3D enthusiasts even see a not-too-distant future when we all will have our own personal 3D printers. In this scenario, when you needed a personalized product, you'd simply download its basic design from the Internet, tweak it to meet your own specific preferences, load the appropriate "printing materials" into the printer's hopper, and press the start button. In minutes, you'd have a new cover for your iPod, a pair of running shoes that precisely fit your feet, or new designer eyeglasses complete with the correct prescription lenses.[6]

Today, **computer-aided design and computer-aided manufacturing** software are often combined into a single system, called **CAD/CAM**. This enables CAD designs to flow directly to CAM programs, which then send instructions directly to the automated equipment on the factory floor to guide the production process.

When a CAD/CAM software system is integrated with robots and other high-tech equipment, the result is **computer-integrated manufacturing (CIM),** in which the whole design and production process is highly automated. The speed of computers, the ability to reprogram computers rapidly, and the integration of all these functions make it possible to switch from the design and production of one good to another quickly and efficiently. CIM allows firms to produce custom-designed products for individual customers quickly and at costs almost as low as those associated with mass-production techniques, thus allowing firms to pursue the strategy of mass customization mentioned at the beginning of this chapter.

LO5 Focus on Quality

Almost everyone agrees that quality is important. But the concept of quality is tough to define—even expert opinions differ. For our purposes, we'll adopt the view that quality is defined in terms of how well a good or service satisfies customer preferences.

Why is quality so important? First, better quality clearly improves effectiveness (creates value) since consumers perceive high-quality goods as having greater value than low-quality goods. But finding ways to increase quality can also can lead to greater efficiency because the cost of poor quality can be very high. When a firm detects defective products, it must scrap, rework, or repair them. And the costs of poor quality can be even higher when a firm *doesn't* catch defects before shipping products to consumers. These costs include handling customer complaints, warranty repair work, loss of goodwill, and the possibility of bad publicity or lawsuits. In the long run, firms often find that improving quality reduces these costs by more than enough to make up for their investment.

These ideas aren't especially new. W. Edwards Deming, viewed by many as the father of the quality movement, first proposed the relationship between quality and business success in the early 1950s. His ideas, which came to be known as the *Deming Chain Reaction*, are summarized in Exhibit 17.6.

Waking Up to the Need for Quality

In the years immediately after World War II, most Japanese goods had a reputation for being cheap and shoddy. But during the 1950s, many Japanese firms sought advice from Deming and other U.S. quality gurus. They learned to view quality improvement as a *continuous* process that was the responsibility of all employees in the organization. During the 1950s and 1960s, the quality of Japanese goods slowly but steadily improved.

By the early 1970s, many Japanese firms had achieved a remarkable turnaround, with quality levels that exceeded those of companies in most other countries (including the U.S.) by a wide margin. This improved quality was a major reason why Japanese firms rapidly gained global market share, often at the expense of American firms that had faced little competition in years immediately following World War II.

computer-integrated manufacturing (CIM) A combination of CAD/CAM software with flexible manufacturing systems to automate almost all steps involved in designing, testing, and producing a product.

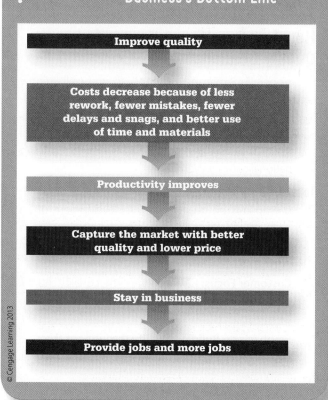

Exhibit 17.6 The Deming Chain Reaction: Improved Quality Helps the Business's Bottom Line

Improve quality

Costs decrease because of less rework, fewer mistakes, fewer delays and snags, and better use of time and materials

Productivity improves

Capture the market with better quality and lower price

Stay in business

Provide jobs and more jobs

© Cengage Learning 2013

Ooops! What were they thinking?

Toyota Learns That Bigger Isn't Always Better

From the 1980s to the beginning of the 21st century, the name Toyota was synonymous with safe, dependable, high-quality automobiles. During this period, the company's glowing reputation for quality contributed to a spectacular rise in sales and market share. In 2009 Toyota passed General Motors to become the world's largest automaker.

But instead of being able to celebrate, the company soon found itself embarrassed by events that raised serious doubts about its commitment to quality and safety. The percentage of its models recommended by *Consumer Reports* dropped from 85% in 2007 to 47% in 2009. Then, in late 2009 and early 2010, the company had to recall more than 8.4 million cars because of serious safety concerns. Toyota exacerbated its troubles by being slow to react, seeming to believe the problems couldn't possibly be its own fault. This created a perception that the company was arrogant and unconcerned about consumer safety. Professor Paul Argenti

of Dartmouth's Tuck School of Business summarized this decline in Toyota's image when he remarked, "I would give Toyota an F in my class for their social responsibility."

What led to Toyota's problems? Many outside analysts—and key Toyota executives—now suggest that the decline in quality reflected a change in priorities. As the company's leadership became obsessed with becoming the biggest, they lost focus on their core value: putting quality first. The rapid growth began stretching its engineers too thin, leading to design errors and lapses in quality control. The ramped-up production schedules also created stresses—and hence more mistakes—on the company's production lines.

Faced with a major drop in sales and increasing criticism in the press and government, Toyota executives vowed to restore their reputation for quality. But just as it was beginning to get its focus back, Japan was devastated by a major earthquake and tsunami. It will be interesting to see how the company adapts to these challenges in coming years.[7]

How American Firms Responded to the Quality Challenge

When operations managers at American firms realized how far they trailed the Japanese in quality, they made a real effort to change their ways. Like the Japanese a few decades earlier, American business leaders began to view improving the quality of their goods and services as a key to regaining international competitiveness.

Total Quality Management The first result of this newfound emphasis on quality was the development of an approach called **total quality management**, better known as TQM. There are several variations, but all versions of TQM share the following characteristics:

- **Customer Focus:** TQM recognizes that quality should be defined by the preferences and perceptions of customers.

- **Emphasis on Building Quality throughout the Organization:** TQM views quality as the concern of every department and every employee.

- **Empowerment of Employees:** Most TQM programs give teams of workers the responsibility and authority to make and implement decisions to improve quality.

- **Focus on Prevention Rather Than Correction:** The TQM philosophy agrees with the old adage that an "ounce of prevention is worth a pound of cure." Thus, TQM pursues a strategy of preventing mistakes that create defects.

- **Long-Run Commitment to Continuous Improvement:** TQM requires firms to adopt a focus on making improvements in quality a way of life.

In many cases, American firms using TQM attempt to reduce defects by using **poka-yokes**—the Japanese term for "mistake proofing." Poka-yokes are simple procedures built into the production process that either prevent workers from making mistakes or help workers quickly catch and correct mistakes if they do occur. One simple example of a poka-yoke would be providing assembly workers with "kits" that contain exactly enough parts to complete one unit of work at a time. If the worker

> Quality is the result of a carefully constructed cultural environment. It has to be the fabric of the organization, not part of the fabric.
>
> — Philip Crosby, 20th-century Quality Guru

completes an assembly and sees a part left over, it's clear that a mistake has been made, and he or she can correct it on the spot.[8]

The Move to Six Sigma During the 1990s, another approach to quality improvement, known as **Six Sigma**, became increasingly popular. Six Sigma shares some characteristics with TQM, such as an organization-wide focus on quality, emphasis on finding and eliminating causes of errors or defects (prevention rather than correction), and a long-term focus on continuous quality improvement. Also like TQM, it relies on teams of workers to carry out specific projects to improve quality. At any given time, a firm may have several Six Sigma projects under way, and the goal of each is to achieve the Six Sigma level of quality.

But Six Sigma differs from TQM in other respects. Unlike TQM, it has a single unifying measure: to reduce defects of any operation or process to a level of no more than 3.4 per million opportunities. Attaining this level of quality represents a rigorous and challenging goal. Six Sigma also differs from TQM in its reliance on extensive (and expensive) employee training and reliance on expert guidance. The techniques used in the Six Sigma approach are quite advanced, and their application requires a high level of expertise.

Quality Standards and Initiatives

Another way firms try to improve quality is to launch programs designed to achieve certification or recognition from outside authorities. Two common approaches are participation in the Baldrige National Quality Program and seeking certification under the International Organization for Standardization's ISO 9000 standards.

The Baldrige National Quality Program Congress passed the Malcolm Baldrige National Quality Improvement Act of 1987 in an effort to encourage American firms to become more competitive in the global economy by vigorously pursuing improvements in quality and productivity. Winners of the Baldrige Award must demonstrate excellence in seven areas: leadership; strategic planning; customer and market focus; measurement, analysis, and knowledge management; human resource focus; process management; and business results.

Firms that participate in the **Baldrige National Quality Program** receive benefits even if they don't win the award. Every participating firm receives a detailed report prepared by expert evaluators identifying areas of strength and areas where improvement is needed. Considering the normal fees that high-powered consulting firms charge for similar reports, the information and advice a firm gets for the fee charged to participate in the Baldrige program (which for manufacturing firms, service firms, and small businesses is $7,000) are a tremendous bargain![9]

ISO 9000 Certification Founded in 1947, ISO is a network of national standards institutes from more than 160 nations that have worked together to develop over 18,500 international standards for a wide array of industries. ISO standards ensure that goods produced in one country will meet the requirements of buyers in another country. This benefits buyers by giving them the ability to purchase from foreign sellers with confidence, thus giving them a wider array of choices. It also benefits sellers by allowing them to compete more successfully in global markets.[10]

Most of the standards established by the ISO are industry-specific. But in 1987 the ISO developed and published the **ISO 9000** family of standards. The goal of this effort was to articulate an international consensus on good quality-management practices that could be applied to virtually any company. Similar to the other quality initiatives we've

total quality management (TQM) An approach to quality improvement that calls for everyone within an organization to take responsibility for improving quality and emphasizes the need for a long-term commitment to continuous improvement.

poka-yokes Simple methods incorporated into a production process designed to eliminate or greatly reduce errors.

Six Sigma An approach to quality improvement characterized by very ambitious quality goals, extensive training of employees, and a long-term commitment to working on quality-related issues.

Baldrige National Quality Program A national program to encourage American firms to focus on quality improvement.

ISO 9000 A family of generic standards for quality management systems established by the International Organization for Standardization.

lean production An approach to production that emphasizes the elimination of waste in all aspects of production processes.

just-in-time (JIT) production A production system that emphasizes the production of goods to meet actual current demand, thus minimizing the need to hold inventories of finished goods and work in process at each stage of the supply chain.

discussed, ISO 9000 standards define quality in terms of the ability to satisfy customer preferences and require the firm to implement procedures for continuous quality improvement.

There are several standards in the ISO 9000 family, but the most basic—and the only one for which organizations can be certified—is ISO 9001, which specifies the requirements for a quality-management system. (Other ISO 9000 standards are concerned with the documentation, training, and the economic and financial aspects of quality management.) As of 2009, over one million organizations worldwide had earned ISO 9001 certificates, but the number of U.S. firms with ISO 9001 certification lags that of several other nations. Only about 29,000 U.S. organizations had been certified in 2009, compared to over 257,000 in China and 130,000 in Italy.[11]

LO6 The Move to Be Lean and Green: Cutting Cost and Cutting Waste

Lean production refers to a set of strategies and practices to eliminate waste, which is defined as any function or activity that uses resources but doesn't create value. Eliminating waste can lead to dramatic improvements in efficiency. For example, Sanford, the maker of Paper

Mate® pens and Sharpie® markers and highlighters, used lean thinking to dramatically cut its packaging costs. Before adopting lean thinking, Sanford developed different blister packs for every single product, resulting in literally hundreds of different packages. After applying lean thinking, the company was able to cut the number of package configurations down to 15, reducing setup time for packaging by 50%, cutting tooling costs by up to 80%, and reducing warehousing costs by up to 25%.[12]

Reducing Investment in Inventory: Just-in-Time to the Rescue

One of the hallmarks of lean systems is a tight control on inventories. In part, this reflects recognition of the costs of holding large inventories that we discussed earlier. But the lean approach also offers another reason for minimizing inventories. Large inventories serve as a buffer that enables a firm to continue operations when problems arise due to poor quality, faulty equipment, or unreliable suppliers—making it easier for firms to live with these problems rather than correct them. Advocates of lean production argue that, in the long run, it is more efficient to improve quality, keep equipment in good working order, and develop reliable supply relationships than to continue compensating for these problems by holding large inventories.

Lean manufacturing avoids overproduction and holding large inventories of finished goods by using **just-in-time (JIT) production** methods. JIT produces

© J & L Images/Photodisc/Getty Images

Six Sigma Belts Quality Concerns

Six Sigma quality programs rely on sophisticated techniques that require highly trained and experienced leadership. Much like karate, Six Sigma identifies the proficiency of its practitioners with belt colors:

- ○ *Yellow Belts* have some basic training in Six Sigma concepts, but they are not proficient enough to take responsibility for a project.

- ○ *Green Belts* have a higher level of training than Yellow Belts and work on Six Sigma projects as part of their regular jobs, but they haven't acquired the depth of training needed to become Black Belts.

- ○ *Black Belts* have a high-enough level of training and experience to take charge of a Six Sigma team working on a specific project. They work full-time on Six Sigma projects.

- ○ *Master Black Belts* have achieved the highest level of expertise in the statistical methods, quality improvement strategies, leadership, and other techniques needed to carry out Six Sigma projects. They are the teachers and mentors of Black Belts. Master Black Belts can achieve an almost superstar status within their organizations.[13]

only enough goods to satisfy current demand. This approach is called a *pull system* because actual orders "pull" the goods through the production process. The workers at the end of the production process produce just enough of the final product to satisfy actual orders and use just enough parts and materials from preceding stages of production to satisfy their needs. Workers at each earlier stage are expected to produce just enough output at their workstations to replace the amount used by the processes further along in the process—and in so doing they withdraw just the needed amount of parts and other supplies from even earlier processes.

JIT techniques obviously result in very small inventories of finished goods and work in process. But lean firms also hold only small inventories of materials and parts, counting on suppliers to provide them with these items as they need them to meet current demand. In a lean system, *all* organizations in the supply chain use the JIT approach, so that inventories are minimized at each stage. Clearly, this type of system requires incredible coordination among all parts of the supply chain; in fact, the movement toward JIT is a key reason why supply chain management has become so crucial.

JIT does have some potential drawbacks. The most serious problem is that it can leave producers vulnerable to supply disruptions. If a key supplier is unable to make deliveries due to a natural disaster, labor strike or other problem, the firms further along the supply chain may quickly run out of parts or materials and have to shut down production.

Lean Thinking in the Service Sector

Employing lean principles in the service sector can be quite a challenge because customers often participate in providing the service. This means a service firm usually has less control over how processes are conducted. But many service firms have benefited from creatively applying lean techniques. Southwest Airlines is well known for its efforts to reduce waste. It uses only one type of aircraft (the Boeing 737) to standardize maintenance and minimize training costs. It also has an extremely simple ticketing system (no assigned seating) and, when possible, flies into smaller or older airports where there is less congestion. This means that less time and less fuel are spent circling airports waiting to

"The Greening of Supply Chains"

Several major U.S. companies have gone beyond their own organizations to make their supply chains greener by working closely with suppliers and distributors to reduce waste and improve energy efficiency. Walmart has been the most visible practitioner of this approach. In 2005, the nation's largest retailer announced an ambitious program to improve its environmental impact by focusing on three key goals:

- Be supplied by 100% renewable energy sources
- Create zero waste
- Sell products that sustain our resources and the environment

Walmart initially pursued these goals by focusing on its internal operations. But it soon discovered that to maximize its effectiveness, it had to broaden its focus to look at its supply chain. As the company explained in its 2010 Global Sustainability Report, "In order to know the true impact of our business, we need to look at where products are sourced and manufactured, how they're shipped and packaged, how they are used and ultimately what happens to the product when it's disposed."

One of Walmart's more interesting strategies has been to offer more locally grown agricultural products in its grocery aisles. This reduces the need to ship food long distances, thus lowering the use of fuels and the emission of greenhouse gasses. It also offers customers fresher produce and supports local economies. To achieve this result, Walmart has eliminated middlemen and has begun working directly with small local farmers.

Walmart's local farm initiative is part of a broad plan to cut emissions of greenhouse gasses throughout its supply chain by 20 million metric tons by 2015—the equivalent of removing 3.8 million cars from our nation's highways for an entire year.[14]

land or sitting on runways waiting to take off. Despite a no-frills approach, Southwest almost always ranks near the top of the list in terms of airline customer satisfaction.[15]

Green Practices: Helping the Firm by Helping the Environment

Many of today's leading firms have also tried to become "greener" by finding environmentally friendly ways to carry out the processes needed to produce and distribute their goods and services. Green practices include designing facilities to be more energy efficient, using renewable energy sources such as wind, solar, or geothermal power when possible, making use of recyclable materials, switching to paints, lubricants, cleaning fluids, and solvents that are less harmful to the environment, and even providing labeling to help consumers find out which products are the most environmentally friendly.

The long-term goal of many green practices is to achieve *sustainability*, which means finding ways to meet the organization's current objectives while protecting and preserving the environment for future generations. One impediment to even greater acceptance of sustainability initiatives is that some sustainability efforts—such as switching to renewable sources of energy—add to costs.[16] But many firms have found that other sustainability efforts can actually benefit the bottom line. A recent study by Aberdeen Group, a well-known technology research firm, found that firms employing best-in-class sustainability practices not only saw an 8% drop in sustainability-related costs but also experienced a 16% increase in customer retention.[17]

In the late 1990s, the International Organization for Standardization developed a set of standards called **ISO 14000**. This new set of standards focuses on environmental management. As with ISO 9000, the term ISO 14000 actually refers to a family of standards. The broadest of these is ISO 14001. In order to receive ISO 14001 certification, a firm must:

- demonstrate the ability to identify and control the environmental impact of their activities
- make a commitment to continually improve their environmental performance
- implement a systematic approach to setting environmental targets and to achieving those targets.

It is important to note that ISO 14000 standards do not establish specific goals for environmental performance; doing so would be very difficult, since ISO is intended to be a generic set of standards that apply to all industries, and each specific industry faces different environmental challenges.[18]

One way some firms have tried to make their operations greener is by making use of renewable energy sources.

© Brian A Jackson/Shutterstock.com

THE BIG PICTURE

Operations managers are responsible for "putting it all together" by developing and implementing the processes needed to produce goods and services and distribute them to the target market. Their decisions affect both revenues and costs, going a long way toward determining whether a firm makes a profit or suffers a loss.

The responsibilities of operations managers require them to work closely with other managers throughout their organizations. For example, they must work with marketers and designers to ensure that the desired goods and services move from the drawing board to the final customer on time and within budget. They must work closely with financial managers to ensure that the company invests in the capital goods needed to produce goods and services in the most efficient manner. And they must work effectively with human resource managers to attract and develop workers who possess the knowledge and skills needed to become world-class competitors. Operations managers must even go beyond their own organization and work effectively with the suppliers and distributors who comprise the firm's value chain.

Operations managers must continuously adapt to changes in technology and in competitive conditions. Key challenges in recent years have centered on the need to continuously improve product quality while finding ways to reduce costs and protect the environment. You can expect the goals of becoming ever leaner—and ever greener—to remain a major focus of operations managers in years to come.

Operations management encompasses a number of different specific occupations, including quality management and control, product development, facilities management, and supply chain (or value chain) management. Operations research, which applies mathematical and statistical techniques to solving complex business problems, is a related field that might appeal to you if you have strong quantitative and problem-solving skills.

Operations managers typically need very strong technical skills and must be good problem solvers. Given the increasing use of value chain management software and computerized production methods, they also must be comfortable with information technology. Many companies require bachelor's degrees in operations management or a related field even for entry-level positions.

Job growth in operations management varies according to sector. Positions in the service sector should continue to increase more rapidly than those in the goods-producing sector.

Because operations management encompasses such a wide array of specific occupations, salaries vary widely. For many positions, the entry-level salary is in the $50,000 to $60,000 range. Experienced operations managers often earn base salaries in excess of $100,000 and may also receive substantial performance bonuses.[19]

CAREERS IN OPERATIONS MANAGEMENT

CAREERS

What *else?*
RIP & REVIEW CARDS IN THE BACK
and visit www.cengagebrain.com!

Personal Finance Appendix

©Jose Luis Pelaez Inc/Blend Images/JupiterImages

LEARNING OBJECTIVES
After studying this appendix, you will be able to...

LO 1 Apply the principles of budgeting to your personal finances

LO 2 Identify strategies to help build a sufficient savings

LO 3 Explain the importance of using credit wisely

LO 4 Discuss key wealth-building principles and the financial instruments that may be part of a wealth-building strategy

> IF YOU KNOW HOW TO SPEND *LESS* THAN YOU GET, YOU HAVE THE PHILOSOPHER'S STONE.
>
> — BENJAMIN FRANKLIN

How Do I Get Started?

You can get a good handle on what should be included in your budget by carefully tracking and analyzing all of your financial transactions for several weeks. This takes discipline and careful record keeping, but once you know where your money comes from and where it goes, you'll have what you need to prepare your budget.

> **budget** (personal) A detailed forecast of financial inflows (income) and outflows (expenses) in order to determine your net inflow or outflow for a given period of time.

There are many approaches to setting up your budget. If you don't want to build your budget from scratch, you can check out several free online personal finance sites that can help you get started. Two of the most popular are Mint.com (http://www.mint.com) and Yodlee.com (http://www.yodlee.com). If you want more bells and whistles—and more support—than the free sites provide, you can purchase a commercial program such as Quicken, Moneydance, or AceMoney. Basic versions of these programs typically cost less than $50 and provide a wide range of features, such as online banking services, financial calculators, and stock quotes. Most also give you the ability to export data into tax preparation software, making tax filing much simpler.

If you are comfortable with Excel (or other spreadsheet software), another option is to build your own budget. Excel includes budget templates to help you get started, and even more are available online. These templates are generic, so you may want to tweak them to suit your own circumstances. You won't get all of the features provided by the commercial packages, but that isn't necessarily a bad thing. Some people actually find all of the bells and whistles in the commercial applications overwhelming and prefer the straightforward simplicity of a spreadsheet template. Also, the process of "building" the budget yourself may give you a sense of personal satisfaction and a greater appreciation for the budget relationships than you'd get using online sites or commercial software packages.

Assessing Revenues: Where Does My Money Come From?

A budget starts with a forecast of your income—the money you bring in. This can come from many different sources. For many people, the paycheck from their job is their primary source of income. But the major source of income for entrepreneurs may be the profits they earn from their businesses. Some people also derive a substantial amount of income from financial investments, such as stocks and bonds, while others earn rental income. Retirees often depend on pensions, Social Security, and private investments for much of their income.

Personal financial management issues affect all of us, young and old alike. How successfully we manage our financial resources affects where we live, how well we can provide for our families, and when (or perhaps even if) we'll be able to retire comfortably. The financial decisions you make and habits you develop now will affect your personal and financial future.

New laws and regulations have changed the way many financial markets operate in recent years. The Dodd-Frank Wall Street Reform and Consumer Protection Act of 2010, passed in the wake of the financial crisis of 2008 and 2009, includes several provisions intended to protect the financial rights of consumers. But many of the law's requirements did not go into effect until mid-2011, so it is too soon to evaluate its long-term impact on consumer rights.

One key provision of the Dodd-Frank Act was the establishment of the Consumer Financial Protection Bureau (CFPB). One early goal of the CFPB was to eliminate confusing and deceptive banking practices related to mortgages, credit cards, and other loan agreements.[1]

LO1 Your Budget

One of the first steps in getting control over your financial situation is to develop a **budget**, which is a detailed forecast of your expected cash inflows (income) and cash outflows (expenditures). You can use your budget to develop your financial plan and to monitor your progress toward achieving your financial goals.

Assessing Expenses: Where Does It All Go? Once you have identified the amount of income you expect to receive from various sources, you can turn your focus to the spending side of your budget. In order to set up your budget, you'll need to be very specific about where your money goes. As we've already mentioned, carefully tracking your expenditures over a period of several weeks can help you identify your spending patterns. Many people who do this are surprised by the habits they uncover. You may find that you're spending a lot more than you thought on video games, music downloads, or clothes. Once you discover your spending patterns, you'll be in a better position to determine the categories of spending to include in your budget and to estimate the amount you'll spend in each category.

Understanding Your Spending Habits: Your expenditures can be classified into discretionary and nondiscretionary categories. The payments you have the most control over are called your **discretionary payments**. Perhaps you like dining out, nightclubbing, or shopping. Perhaps you just have expensive taste in coffee. David Bach, author of *The Automatic Millionaire,* challenges us to

He who gathers money little by little makes it grow.

— JEWISH PROVERB

look at our "latté factors," meaning the little vices we each find hard to resist. You'll find that something as seemingly minor as a $4 cup of coffee each workday costs you $1,040 each year ($4 x 5 days per week x 52 weeks). Once you realize the true cost of these "latté factors," you'll have a greater incentive to bring them under control.[2] Your budget can be helpful in imposing the discipline you need to accomplish this goal.

Nondiscretionary payments are those you have little control over, such as your monthly rent or car payment, which are set by contract. Your lifestyle may also lock you into other costs that are at least partly nondiscretionary. Given your need to get to school and work, you may have to spend a significant amount of money on gas and car maintenance every month. But with a little flexibility and creativity, you may find that such costs aren't *completely* nondiscretionary. For instance, you might be able to significantly reduce your expenses for gas and car maintenance by carpooling or using mass transit.

You may also want to consider your attitude toward spending. Are you most likely to spend too much money when you are depressed or stressed out? Look at this aspect carefully, and try to be as honest as possible with yourself. The final thing you should consider is whom you are with

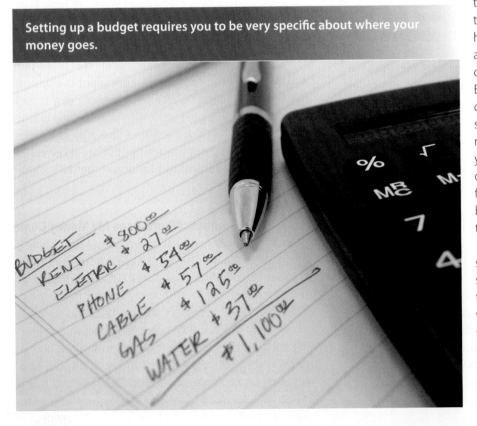

Setting up a budget requires you to be very specific about where your money goes.

when you spend money. You may find that you tend to spend much more money while hanging out with certain friends.

After you have prepared your budget, you'll need to keep track of your actual expenses and compare them to your budget. And you'll need to adjust your budget periodically to reflect significant changes in your lifestyle, employment status, and financial goals.

LO2 Your Savings: Building a Safety Net

A **savings account** is an interest-earning account that is intended to satisfy obligations that your checking account cannot handle. Think of your savings account as a "safety net" for unexpected financial challenges, such as a major plumbing repair, the need to replace your car's transmission, or even the loss of your job. Many financial experts suggest that you have enough money in your savings to cover six months of your expenses. The good news is that if you're lucky enough to avoid major problems, your savings account will earn you a bit of interest income.

One technique for establishing a sizable savings balance is to "pay yourself first." This concept, popularized by David Bach, suggests that you have a predetermined amount from each paycheck automatically deposited into your savings account. Once you've accumulated enough in your savings account to provide an adequate safety net, you can use the "pay yourself first" approach to achieve other financial goals.[3]

Interest rates on savings accounts vary from bank to bank, so you should shop around to find the best rate. In recent years, online savings banks have often provided higher interest rates than traditional banks. Just be sure to look for reputable banks that are insured by the **Federal Deposit Insurance Corporation (FDIC)**. The FDIC is an independent agency created by Congress to maintain stability and public confidence in the nation's financial system, primarily by insuring bank deposits. In recent years the FDIC has insured individual deposits for up to $250,000.[4]

LO3 Your Credit: Handle With Care!

Credit refers to your ability to obtain goods or resources without having to make immediate payment. One of the most important determinants of the amount of credit you can obtain is your **credit score**, which is a numerical indicator of your creditworthiness. Currently, the most commonly used credit scoring system is the Fair, Isaac and Company (FICO) scale. The FICO scale runs from 300 to 850.

Your individual FICO score is based on several factors, including your payment history, the amount you owe, the type of credit used, and the length of time you've held various credit accounts.[5] As Exhibit A.1 shows, about 72% of all Americans have scores between 600 and 800; only 2% have scores below 500 and 13% have scores above 800. A high score makes it easier to get credit on favorable terms. A recent study found that the average interest rate on a mortgage loan offered to someone with a 520 FICO score was more than 4 percentage points higher than the interest rate offered to someone with a score of 720.[6]

savings account An interest-bearing account holding funds not needed to meet regular expenditures.

Federal Deposit Insurance Corporation (FDIC) An independent agency created by Congress to maintain stability and public confidence in the nation's financial system, primarily by insuring bank deposits.

credit Allows a borrower to buy a good or acquire an asset without making immediate payment, and to repay the balance at a later time.

credit score A numerical measure of a consumer's creditworthiness.

EXHIBIT A.1 What FICO Credit Scores Mean

WHAT FICO CREDIT SCORES MEAN		
SCORE	CREDITWORTHINESS	PERCENTAGE OF CONSUMERS
BELOW 500	Very poor	2%
500–599	Poor to below average	13%
600–699	Below average to fair	27%
700–799	Fair to good	45%
800 OR BETTER	Excellent	13%

© Cengage Learning 2013

© Ljupco Smokovski/ Shutterstock.com

Credit Cards: Boon or Bane?

Now let's look at a specific source of credit that is near and dear to many college students' hearts: the **credit card**. A credit card allows its holder to make a purchase now and pay the credit card issuer later.

There are several benefits to having and using credit cards. The most obvious is that credit cards are more convenient and safer than carrying a lot of cash. Credit cards also make it easy to track your expenditures, since you have access to a monthly summary of charges. And many cards offer perks, such as discounts on certain products, extended warranties on purchases, or frequent-flier miles. Another benefit of the *responsible* use of credit cards is that it can improve your credit score by allowing you to establish a history of prompt payments. This can make it easier for you to borrow money when you really need it—such as when you want to buy a car or your first home.

One downside of having a credit card is that the "buy now, pay later" aspect of credit card use makes it hard for some people to maintain financial discipline. Another problem is that interest rates on unpaid card balances tend to be very high. Many card issuers also impose a variety of fees that can make a noticeable dent in your wallet. And making late payments or failing to pay what you owe can damage your credit history, hurting your chances of getting additional credit when you need it.

The Devil in the Details — Understanding Your Credit Card Agreement!

Before you accept a credit card, make sure you read the credit card agreement and understand the main conditions for using that card. Some things to look for include:

- **Grace period:** the period of time that you have to pay your balance before interest or fees are assessed. Some credit card companies expect to receive their payment within 21 days of the credit

In 2008, the average college student owned 4.6 credit cards and owed an average balance of $3,173.

— www.salliemae.com

card statement date. So, it becomes very important to get these bills paid as soon as possible to avoid the interest and other fees.

- **APR (annual percentage rate):** the percentage financing cost charged on unpaid balances. The higher the APR, the greater your interest expense on unpaid balances. Your credit card company may charge different APRs for different types of transactions.

- **Late fees:** may also be assessed if a payment is not received within the grace period. Federal law now caps late fees at $25 for a first offense and $35 for additional late payments.[7]

- **Other fees:** include *annual fees* (a charge just for the privilege of having a card, whether you use it or not), *over-the-credit-limit fees* if your charges exceed your credit limit, and *balance-transfer fees* if you transfer a balance from one card to another. This isn't a complete list, but it does reflect many of the most common types of fees you might incur. Not all cards are subject to all of these charges; the specific types and amounts of fees can vary considerably from one issuer to another—which is why reading the fine print is important!

Protection for Consumers: New Laws and Regulations

Two recent laws have had a significant impact on credit card practices. The Credit Card Accountability, Responsibility and Disclosure Act of 2009 (often called the CARD Act) requires issuers to give a 45-day notice before making significant changes to credit agreements and prohibits them from raising interest rates on existing balances unless the borrower is more than 60 days late in making required payments. It also requires anyone under the age of 21 who applies for a credit card to either verify proof or income or have an older adult cosign the application. And it places caps on certain types of fees that credit card issuers can charge.

As mentioned at the beginning of this appendix, The Dodd-Frank Act created the Consumer Financial Protection Bureau. One focus of the CFPB's early efforts has been to make it easier for consumers to compare the features and costs of various credit cards so that they can select the ones that best meet their needs. The Dodd-Frank Act also requires lenders, insurance companies and others who reject your application to provide you with a free copy of your credit score.[8]

Using Credit Cards Wisely: The Need for Discipline

Although many young adults manage their credit cards without major problems, others are stunned when the credit card bill arrives. Many never read their credit card agreements, so they are taken by surprise by higher-than-expected interest charges and fees. Others simply lack discipline. They succumb to the temptations of a "buy now, pay later" mentality and run up big bills that they can't afford to pay.

The first rule when you have credit card difficulties is to "PUT THE CARD DOWN!" When you find yourself in trouble, stop using the card so you don't compound your difficulties. Make sure you don't use the card again until you've gotten your spending habits under control.

Once you've eliminated the temptation to dig a deeper hole, the next step is to make sure you consistently pay a substantial amount each month toward retiring the debt on that card. Given how high APRs are on the unpaid balances for most credit cards, it is usually a good idea to place a *very* high priority on eliminating these balances as quickly as possible.

If you just can't seem to shake the habit of overspending, consider using cash or a **debit card** instead of a credit card. While a debit card looks like a credit card, there is a big difference. When you use a debit card, money is immediately withdrawn from your bank account, so you "feel the pain" just as if you'd paid in cash. Many people spend less when they use cash or debit cards than when they use credit cards.

© iStockphoto.com/ Burak Can OZTAS

L04 Your Investments: Building for the Future

Investing involves reducing consumption today in order to acquire assets that build future wealth. In a very real way, investing is like the concept of sowing and reaping.

A farmer plants a seed (makes an investment) in anticipation of a harvest (return) that will be much larger than the seed that was planted. When it comes to investing, early is better than late—but late is better than never.

Building Wealth: The Key Is Consistency—and an Early Start!

Don't talk yourself out of investing just because you don't have much to invest. Even if you start with a small amount, your wealth will eventually grow to a significant amount as long as you stick with it. And the earlier you start the better off you'll be. To see this, take a look at Exhibit A.2, which compares how big your retirement nest egg will be at age 65 for different monthly investment amounts beginning at different ages (and assuming you earn an annual return of 8%). A 30-year-old who invests $60 per month will end up with $137,633 at age 65. Compare this to someone who begins investing $60 per month at age 20, and the results are startling. The investor who starts at age 20 only directly invests $7,200 more ($60 per month for 120 more months) than the investor who starts at age 30. But the earlier investor ends up with a nest egg

debit card A card issued by the bank that allows the customer to make purchases as if the transaction involved cash. In a debit card purchase, the customer's bank account is immediately reduced when the purchase is made.

investing Reducing consumption in the current time period in order to build future wealth.

EXHIBIT A.2 Growing Your Investment: Starting Early Makes a Difference

MONTHLY SAVINGS	STARTING AGE			
	20	30	40	50
$30	$158,236	$68,816	$28,531	$10,381
$60	$316,472	$137,633	$57,062	$20,762
$90	$474,709	$206,449	$85,592	$31,143
$120	$632,945	$275,266	$114,123	$41,525
$150	$791,181	$344,082	$142,654	$51,906

© Cengage Learning 2013

Note: Figures in the table show the amount accumulated at age 65. Results are based on an assumed annual rate of return of 8% compounded monthly.

of $316,472—almost $179,000 more than that of the investor who started at age 30.

The reason for this result is that, over time, you earn interest not only on the money you directly invest but also on the *interest* you've earned in *previous* years—a process known as *compounding*. The earlier you begin investing, the more powerful the compounding effect becomes. By the time an investor reaches age 65, any dollars invested at age 20 have been compounded for a *very long* time, resulting in a big increase in the nest egg. The message of Exhibit A.2 is clear: an early start to investing can lead to dramatically more money when it comes time to retire.

Financial Securities: What Are My Investment Options?

Now that we've demonstrated the importance of investing, let's look at some specific types of financial instruments you might want to include in your investment portfolio. Our brief discussion can't hope to cover all of the possibilities, so we'll focus only on some of the most common choices. Keep in mind that, in addition to the financial instruments we describe in this section, many people also hold much of their wealth in other assets. The largest single asset for many households is the equity they have in their home.

Let's begin by looking at *common stock*, which represents ownership in a corporation. Common stock offers the possibility of two types of financial returns. The first, called a *dividend,* is a distribution of profits paid out to the stockholders. Dividends are paid only if the corporation's board of directors declares them—and there is no legal requirement for them to do so. If a corporation is in poor financial shape, its board of directors may decide that it is unable to pay a dividend. But even it a company is highly profitable, its board may decide to reinvest (retain) its profits rather than pay dividends to stockholders.

Investors can earn a second type of return, called a capital gain, if the market price of their stock rises relative to the price they paid for it. But stock prices can go down as well as up—as many investors have painfully discovered in recent years! Thus, it is possible for investors to experience *capital losses* as well as capital gains. Clearly, investing in common stock entails a significant degree of risk. But historically the average rate of return on stocks has been better than the return on many other types of investments.

The best time to plant a tree was 20 years ago. The next best time is now.
— CHINESE PROVERB

In addition to common stock, some corporations also offer another type of stock, called *preferred stock.* The two types of stock have some important differences. From the perspective of many investors, the most important distinction is that owners of preferred stock are more likely to receive a dividend than owners of common stock. Preferred stock is normally issued with a stated dividend, and common stockholders can't be paid *any* dividend until the preferred dividend is paid in full. Still, even preferred stockholders have no guaranteed legal right to receive a dividend.

A *corporate bond* is another type of corporate security, but it is quite different from stock. A bond is a formal IOU issued by a corporation. While stockholders are the owners of a corporation, bondholders are its creditors. Most bonds are long-term debts that mature (come due) 10 to 30 years after they are issued, though bonds with shorter and longer maturities are sometimes issued.

As creditors, bondholders are legally entitled to receive interest payments from the issuing corporation every year until the bond matures, and to receive an amount known as the *principal* (or "face value") when the bond matures. But bondholders don't have to hold their bonds until they mature. Like stocks, bonds can be bought and sold on securities markets, and their price can rise and fall. So, like stockholders, bondholders can experience capital gains or losses.

Because the issuing corporation is legally required to pay interest and principal on a fixed schedule, the returns on bonds are more predictable than returns on stocks. However, even bonds pose some risk. During the recent economic downturn, many firms defaulted on (failed to make) their legally required bond payments.

Government securities are IOUs issued by government entities when they borrow money. As with corporate bonds, government securities normally pay their holders a stated rate of interest until they mature. State and local governments often issue bonds. In fact, many investors like to invest in municipal bonds because interest income earned on these bonds is usually exempt from federal income taxes. But the biggest single issuer of government securities is the federal government. The U.S. Treasury markets a variety of securities, from long-term bonds that mature in 30 years, to short-term treasury bills (popularly called "T-bills") that can mature in as little as four weeks. Historically, securities issued by the federal government have been viewed as very safe investments. But in recent years, the rapid growth in federal debt has led some securities rating services to question this view.[9]

Certificates of deposit are offered by banks and other depository institutions like credit unions. They are similar to savings accounts, but are issued for a fixed term—which could be as short as three months or as long as five years. The rate of interest paid on CDs is often higher than the rate on a regular savings account but usually lower than the interest rate on corporate bonds and most government securities. CDs with longer maturities typically earn a higher interest rate than CDs that have shorter terms. You can cash in a CD before it matures, but you'll incur a substantial penalty if you do.

One advantage of CDs is that they are insured by the FDIC. Because of this insurance and their predictable rate of return, CDs are considered to be among the safest investment options. The trade-off is that they offer lower returns than most other types of investments.

Mutual funds sell shares to investors and pool the resulting funds to invest in financial instruments such as corporate stocks, corporate bonds, government securities, or other assets. Some mutual funds invest mainly in bonds, others invest mainly in stocks, and others in government securities. Some invest in specific sectors of the economy, such as technology, energy, or health care, while others invest in broader portfolios.

Most mutual funds are professionally managed, with the fund's manager selecting the specific securities that the fund will hold. This professional management appeals to many investors who don't have the time or expertise to evaluate investment alternatives. But it is also expensive—mutual funds charge fees to cover the cost of managing the fund and to meet other expenses. Investors must pay these fees even if the funds perform poorly.

Exchange Traded Funds (ETFs) are similar to mutual funds in that they represent ownership in a broad portfolio of securities. However, unlike most mutual funds, they are bought and sold just like shares of corporate stock. ETFs are a relatively new investment vehicle (first marketed in 1993), but they have become quite popular in recent years.

Acquiring Financial Assets: The Role of a Broker

Investors normally acquire many of their financial assets, including shares of common and preferred stocks, corporate bonds and certain other financial assets (such as ETFs), by purchasing them in securities markets. However, individual investors can't directly participate in these markets. Instead, they normally rely on the services of a brokerage firm to buy and sell securities.

When choosing a broker, it's important to consider both the costs and the level of service. In addition to carrying out your trades, a *full-service broker* provides a wide range of services—such as research to identify good investment opportunities, financial planning, and tax advice. Most full-service brokerage firms charge commissions based on the dollar value of the orders their clients place. They also charge fees for the services they provide. In contrast, *discount brokers* buy and sell securities for their clients but offer few additional services. The commissions and fees charged by discount brokers are usually significantly lower than those of full-service brokers. Many discount brokerage firms charge flat fees of a few dollars per trade for simple transactions.

In recent years, competition among brokerage firms has blurred the distinction between full-service and discount brokers. Many full-service firms have lowered their commissions, while many discount brokers have begun offering investment advice and other services. Most major brokerage firms now offer their clients both discount and full-service options.

Before entrusting a brokerage firm with your financial transactions, you should check out its background. The Financial Industry Regulatory Authority's (FINRA's) BrokerCheck website (http://www.finra.org/Investors/ToolsCalculators/BrokerCheck/) is a good place to start. This site offers very detailed background information on over 1.3 million current and former FINRA-registered brokers and over 17,000 FINRA-registered brokerage firms.

Building a Portfolio: A Few Words about Diversification, Risk, and Return

The financial securities we've described are not mutually exclusive. It is possible—and usually desirable—to invest in a diversified financial portfolio consisting of a variety of stocks, bonds, CDs, government securities, and other assets.

The main advantage offered by diversification is that it reduces your risk. If you put a large part of your wealth into one specific investment, you could be wiped out if that investment goes sour. If you invest in several different assets, then losses in some are likely to be offset by gains in others. But diversification also has a downside—it not only reduces risk but also reduces the possibility of earning exceptionally high returns.

One widely accepted financial principal is that a trade-off exists between risk and return; in other words, investments with the potential for generating high returns tend to be riskier than investments that offer lower returns. For example, stock prices sometimes decline sharply, so investing in stocks is considered quite risky. But historically the long-run average return on stocks has been significantly higher than the average return on bonds, which offer safer, more predictable returns.

In general, younger investors are less concerned about risk than older investors. When you are young, you have more time to recover from adverse results, so you may be willing to take more risks and be more aggressive in pursuit of higher returns. If you invest mostly in stocks when you are young, and the stock market crashes, you still have time to recoup your losses and take advantage of future increases in stock prices. But older investors who hold a lot of stock might find that the same crash wiped out much of the wealth just when they were counting on it to supplement their retirement income. Older investors often become more conservative, adjusting their portfolio to include a greater percentage of relatively safe assets such as government securities, bonds of corporations with strong credit ratings, and CDs.

But What Is My Best Investment? (Hint: Look in the Mirror!)

So far, we have focused on investing in financial assets. But in many ways, the most important investment you can make is in yourself, by devoting your time, effort, and money to your education, training, health, and fitness. The Bureau of Labor Statistics reports that the median weekly earnings of high-school graduates in the first quarter of 2011 was $633, while for workers with bachelor's degrees the figure was $1,150—a difference of $517 or 82%.[10] Over a typical worker's forty-year career, this amounts to a difference in earnings of over a million dollars! And higher education not only increases your income, it also gives you more job security. In 2010, the unemployment rate for workers with a high-school education was 10.3% while the unemployment rate for workers with at least a bachelor's degree was 4.7%.[11]

Strategies to become more marketable: One way to increase your marketability and your starting salary is to secure an internship during your college years. Such internships usually offer little or no monetary compensation, but they pay off in other ways. They give students a chance to gain first-hand experience

© iStockphoto.com/ Yunus Arakon

Do You *Really* Need a Broker to Buy Stocks?

Our discussion of how to invest in stocks has emphasized the role of a broker. But it's also possible to buy stocks in many well-known corporations—including Walmart, ExxonMobil, and Coca-Cola—directly from the companies themselves. Companies that offer these direct stock purchase plans (DSPPs) usually provide information about how to make purchases on the investor relations page of their website. Although most direct stock purchase plans charge some fees, they are normally much lower than the commissions and fees charged by brokerage firms.

Many companies also offer dividend reinvestment plans (DRIPs) that allow current stockholders to reinvest their dividends automatically to purchase additional shares of stock. This is a convenient way to purchase shares of stock without paying brokerage fees and commissions, and there usually are no fees charged when purchasing stocks through DRIPs. Some companies allow investors who sign up for dividend reinvestment to buy stock at a discount. (The size of the discount varies, but it is usually between 1 and 10 percent.) One key drawback of DRIPs is that investors must pay taxes on their dividends even though they don't receive any cash.[12]

that supplements what they learn in the classroom and help them determine whether a specific career is right for them. And the internship experience looks great on a résumé. But in 2010, the U.S. Department of Labor issued a ruling that makes it more difficult for profit-seeking firms to offer unpaid or low-wage internships. Many educators, business leaders, and politicians have called on the Department of Labor to modify its stance to make internships easier to establish. But unless and until such modifications are adopted, internships may remain difficult to find.[13]

Other Work Opportunities Don't despair if you are unable to secure an internship. There are other ways to gain experience in your field of interest. Consider taking a (gulp) pay cut from your temporary *job* to get experience in your *career* field. Or perhaps consider doing volunteer work in that field—not only will you be doing a good deed, you'll also be learning the ropes in your chosen field. Taking a temporary pay cut to gain relevant work experience often pays for itself many times over when you leave college and pursue a full-time position.

Investing for the Long Term: Planning for Your Retirement

One of the most important reasons people invest is to build up a nest egg for retirement. While your retirement might seem like it is a long way off, investing for your golden years now can really pay off, since it allows you to take advantage of the compounding effects we talked about earlier.

A key to a comfortable retirement is to start saving early.

© Monkey Business Images/ Shutterstock.com

IRA An individual retirement account that provides tax benefits to individuals who are investing for their retirement.

401(k), 403(b), and 457 plans Employee payroll deduction retirement plans that offer tax benefits.

One of the most popular ways to build wealth for retirement is to set up an individual retirement account, or **IRA**. There are several types of IRAs; the two most popular are the *traditional IRA* and the *Roth IRA*. Both types of IRAs are individual investments—you make the decisions about how much to invest (subject to maximum allowable contributions) and what specific investments to make. You can put your IRA money into stocks, government securities, CDs, mutual funds, or other types of financial securities.

Both traditional and Roth IRAs offer tax advantages intended to provide an incentive for people to invest for their retirement. But the nature and timing of the tax advantages are different. With a traditional IRA, the contributions you make reduce your taxable income in the same tax year, and the earnings on your contributions are tax deferred, allowing them to grow more rapidly.[14] But you must pay taxes on the money received from a traditional IRA when you begin making withdrawals. On the other hand, the contributions you make to a Roth IRA are *not* tax deductible at the time you make them, but earnings on these contributions are tax-free, and you pay no taxes on the distributions you receive from a Roth IRA after you retire.

One drawback to both traditional and Roth IRAs is that the amount that individuals can contribute each year is relatively small. In 2011, the maximum contribution for both types of plans was $5,000. (Individuals over the age of 50 could contribute up to $6,000.)

401(k), 403(b), and 457 plans are employee-contribution retirement plans that are named for the sections of the IRS tax code where they are described. These plans are similar in many respects; the main differences are in who qualifies for each type of plan. 401(k) plans are offered to employees of private-sector businesses, while 403(b) plans are for employees of certain types of nonprofit organizations such as schools, religious organizations, and charities. 457 plans are primarily for state and local government employees and nonprofit organizations. Some employees in the nonprofit sector can qualify for both 403(b) and 457 plans.

Unlike IRAs, all of these plans are implemented through a payroll-deduction process. Also, these plans have much higher contribution limits than traditional and Roth IRAs. In 2011, for example, employees could contribute up to $16,500 in a 401(k) plan, with individuals over 50 allowed to contribute up to an additional $5,500 *if* their

company matching An amount contributed by the employer to an employee's retirement account, matching the employee's retirement contributions either dollar-for-dollar or based on a percentage of each dollar contributed by the employee.

vesting period A specified period of time for which an employee must work for an employer in order to receive the full advantage of certain retirement benefits.

employer's plan contained a "catch-up" provision. Other potential advantages of these plans include:

○ **Tax advantages:** Any income employees invest in traditional 401(k), 403(b), and 457 plans are tax deductible, and the earnings on these investments are tax deferred. This reduces current taxes and allows the funds to grow more rapidly. However, retirees must pay taxes on funds distributed from their fund when they make withdrawals. As with IRAs, there are Roth versions of these plans. Employees who choose the Roth version pay taxes on the income they contribute, but earnings on these contributions and distributions after retirement are tax exempt.

○ **Company matching:** Some employers match employee contribution either dollar for dollar or with a percentage of each dollar you contribute up to a limit. This can be a big advantage of these plans over IRAs. If your company matches your 401(k) or 403(b) or 457 contributions, you should consider contributing as much as you can up to the maximum your company will match—it's like getting free money for your retirement.

There are also some important restrictions on these plans. First, not all employers offer these plans. Second, if your employer does offer a plan that offers matching contributions, you won't be entitled to all of the matching funds unless you've remained employed with the company for a stated period of time called the **vesting period**. The length of time for full vesting varies depending on the employer, but it is usually several years. Finally, keep in mind that these are *retirement* plans. There are restrictions on withdrawing the money in these plans prior to retirement, and you may pay significant penalties if you do.

THE BIG PICTURE

Making sound personal financial decisions requires careful thought and discipline. You should start by establishing a budget; doing so will help you understand your current financial situation, plan for the future, and monitor your progress toward achieving your goals. One of your first goals should be to set aside enough savings to provide adequate protection against unforeseen financial challenges. One good strategy to build your savings is to "pay yourself first." Another key to financial success is to make careful decisions with respect to your use of credit cards and other forms of credit. Next, you should turn your attention to investing to build your wealth over time. You'll discover many different investment opportunities, each with their own pros and cons. No single investment strategy is foolproof, but two principles that have stood the test of time are: (1) start investing early to take full advantage of compounding, and (2) diversify your investments to protect against risk.

What *else?*
RIP & REVIEW CARDS IN THE BACK
and visit www.cengagebrain.com!

BUSN

1

1. 27 Twitter-Ready Consumer Trends you need to know by Matt Carmichael, *AdvertisingAge* magazine, October 20, 2010, accessed January 13, 2010.

2. *Entrepreneurial activity rose to highest rate in 14 years, Kauffman Foundation press release, May 20, 2010, Kauffman Foundation website,* http://www.techjournalsouth.com/2010/05/entrepreneurial-activity-rose-to-highest-rate-in-14-years/, accessed January 13, 2011.

3. *College Freshmen Show Increasing Interest in Entrepreneurship, Kauffman Foundation press release, November 18, 2009, Kauffman Foundation website,* http://www.kauffman.org/newsroom/first-time-college-students-show-increasing-interest-in-entrepreneurship.aspx accessed January 13, 2011; From Books to Business: Student Entrepreneurs by Julia Aubuchon, November 14, 2009, ABC News website, http://abcnews.go.com/Business/SmallBiz/successful-student-entrepreneurs/story?id=9075154, accessed January 13, 2011.

4. State of Entrepreneurship Address, January 19, 2010, Kauffman Foundation website, http://www.kauffman.org/newsroom/entrepreneurs-expect-to-limit-hiring-in-2010-according-to-new-kauffman-foundation-poll.aspx, accessed January 13, 2011.

5. *Business Blunders of the Year 2010* by Adam Horowitz, Martin Douglass, and Mike Grudowski BNET website, http://www.bnet.com/photos/business-blunders-of-the-year/493483?tag=mantle_skin;content, accessed January 13, 2011.

6. Thaler, Richard H. and Sunstein, Cass R, *Nudge: Improving Decisions about Health, Wealth, and Happiness.* (New York: Penguin Group, 2009); "Easy Does It: How to make lazy people do the right thing," by Thaler and Sunstein, *The New Republic,* April 9, 2008, New Republic website; Stephen J. Dubner, "Who will climb the piano stairs? Freakonomics: The Hidden Side of Everything" *New York Times,* October 13, 2009, http://freakonomics.blogs.nytimes.com/2009/10/13/who-will-climb-the-piano-stairs/?pagemode=print, retrieved March 22, 2010. http://articles.latimes.com/2008/apr/02/opinion/oe-thalerandsunstein2 http://www.marcgunther.com/2009/11/16/whats-for-lunch-behaviorial-economics-meets-climate-change/.

7. On the Nonprofit Sector and Community Solutions Act of 2010 by Leonard Jacobs, June 18, 2010, The Clyde Fitch Report, The Clyde Fitch Report Website, http://www.clydefitchreport.com/2010/06/introducing-hr-5533-the-nonprofit-sector-and-community-solutions-act-of-2010/, accessed January 16, 2011; 7.2% of Americans work for nonprofit groups, study finds, by Suzanne Perry, December 19, 2006, The Chronicle of Philanthropy website, http://philanthropy.com/free/update/2006/12/2006121901.htm, accessed January 19, 2009; Wages in the nonprofit sector: management, professional, and administrative support occupations by Amy Butler, October 28, 2008, Bureau of Labor Statistics website, http://www.bls.gov/opub/cwc/cm20081022ar01p1.htm, accessed January 19, 2008; Occupational Employment and Wages, 2007, May 9, 2008, Bureau of Labor Statistics website, http://www.bls.gov/news.release/pdf/ocwage .pdf, accessed January 19, 2009; Nonprofit sector needs to be better understood by Todd Cohen, February 22, 2010, Inside Philanthropy Blog, Philanthropy Journal website, http://philanthropyjournal.blogspot.com/2010/02/nonprofit-sector-needs-to-be-better.html, retrieved March 23, 2010.

8. GNI Per Capita 2007 World Bank Data, revised October 17, 2008, http://siteresources.worldbank.org/DATASTATISTICS/ Resources/GNIPC.pdf, accessed January 19, 2009; CIA World Factbook China, updated December 18, 2008, https://www.cia.gov/library/publications/the-world-factbook/geos/ch.html, accessed January 19, 2009; CIA World Factbook Russia, updated December 18, 2008, https://www.cia.gov/library/publications/the-world-factbook/geos/rs.html, accessed January 19, 2009; CIA World Factbook Hong Kong, updated December 18, 2008, https://www.cia .gov/library/publications/the-world-factbook/geos/hk.html, accessed January 19, 2009.

9. You're checked out but your brain is checked in by Benedict Carey, August 8, 2008, The *New York Times* website, http://www.nytimes.com/2008/08/05/health/research/05mind.html, accessed January 15, 2011; The Hidden Secrets of the Creative Mind, interview with R. Keith Sawyer, January 8, 2006, *Time* magazine website, July 24, 2008, http://www.time.com/time/magazine/article/0,9171,1147152-1,00.html.

10. American Customer Satisfaction Index Scores by Industry, American Customer Satisfaction Index Website, http://www.theacsi.org/index .php?option=com_content&task=view&id=18&Itemid=33, accessed January 15, 2011.

11. Why Webvan drove off a cliff by Joanna Glasner, Wired News, July 10, 2001, http://www.wired.com/news/business/ 0,1367,45098,00.html.

12. Honey, I shrunk the iPod. A lot. by Steven Levy, September 19, 2005, *Newsweek* magazine; Behind Apple's strategy: be second to market by John Boddie, August 29, 2005, Harvard Business School Working Knowledge, http://hbswk.hbs.edu/item.jhtml?id=4970&t=technology. "What's to become of Microsoft's answer to the iPod?" by John Letzing July 29, 2009, Marketwatch website, http://www .marketwatch.com/story/microsofts-zune-continues-to-struggle-2009-07-29, accessed April 1, 2010.

13. See note 12 above.

14. Employee Satisfaction & Stock Performance by Jeffrey Henning on Fri, Aug 06, 2010, Voice of Vovici Blog, http://blog.vovici.com/blog/?Tag=Employee%20Satisfaction%20Surveys, accessed January 17, 2011; Giving employees what they want: the returns are huge, May 4, 2005, Knowledge@Wharton, Human Resources, http://knowledge.wharton.upenn.edu/article/1188 .cfm, accessed January 19, 2009; How Investing in Intangibles—Like Employee Satisfaction—Translates into Financial Returns, January 9, 2008, Knowledge@Wharton website, http://knowledge.wharton.upenn.edu/article.cfm?articleid=1873, accessed January 19, 2009.

15. 10,000—Baby Boomers Retire, Pew Research Center, January 17, 2011, Pew Research website, http://pewresearch.org/databank/dailynumber/?NumberID=1150, accessed January 11, 2011 .

16. Ideas made here by Anne Fisher, Fortune magazine, June 11, 2007, page 35, CNNMoney website, http://money.cnn.com/magazines/fortune/fortune_archive/2007/06/11/100061499/index .htm, accessed January 17, 2011; Editors name the greatest inventions of all time, Encyclopedia Britannica News Release, January 30, 2003, http://corporate .britannica.com/press/releases/invention .html; Encyclopedia Britannica's Great Inventions, accessed October 11, 2005, http://corporate .britannica.com/press/inventions.html.

17. Retail E-Commerce Update by Jeffrey Grau, December 2008, eMarketer website, http://www.emarketer.com/Reports/All/Emarketer_2000545.aspx, accessed January 19, 2009.

18. U.S. Population Projections: 2005–2050, February 11, 2008, by Jeffrey S. Passel and D'Vera Cohn, Pew Research Center website, http://pewhispanic.org/files/reports/85.pdf, accessed January 17, 2011.

19. State and County Quick Facts, Mississippi, U.S. Census, Bureau website, http://quickfacts .census.gov/qfd/states/28000.html Last Revised, February 23, 2010, retrieved March 30, 2010; Hawaii's Asian population at 55% is highest proportion in nation, May 1, 2009, Hawaii 24/7 website, http://www.hawaii247.org/2009/05/01/hawaiis-asian-population-at-55-is-highest-proportion-in-nation/, retrieved March 30, 2010; State and County Quick Facts, New Mexico, U.S. Census Bureau website, http://quickfacts.census .gov/qfd/states/35000.html, Last Revised, February, 23, 2010, retrieved March 30, 2010.

20. Not-so-green jeans by Rebecca Clarren, January 7, 2008, Salon website, http://www.salon.com/life/good_life/2008/01/07/organic_jeans, accessed January 17, 2011; Green Jeans: Levi's Makes Its Denim With Less Water by Bryan Walsh, January 8, 2011, *Time* magazine website, http://www.time .com/time/magazine/article/0,9171,2041116,00 .html, accessed January 17, 2011.

21. Translating Hispanic Marketing into Shareholder Value, Hispanic PR Wire/Business Wire, December 4, 2006, http://www.hispanicprwire.com/print.php?l=in&id=7660.

22. Diversity Awareness, Hershey Foods Corporation website, accessed October 4, 2005, https://www.hersheysjobs.com/Career/ControlPanel.aspx?ModuleCategoryID=1999999.

23. Attitudes of young people toward diversity, CIRCLE fact sheet, February 2005, http://www.civicyouth.org/PopUps/FactSheets/Attitudes%202.25.pdf.

24. U.S. Population Projections: 2005 – 2050, February 11, 2008, by Jeffrey S. Passel and D'Vera Cohn, Pew Research Center website, http://pewhispanic.org/files/reports/85.pdf, accessed January 17, 2011; China's concern over population aging and health by Toshiko Kaneda, Population Reference Bureau website, http://www.prb.org/Articles/2006/ChinasConcernOverPopulationAgingandHealth.aspx, accessed January 17, 2011.

25. Pending job flexibility act received mixed reviews by Sue Shellenbarger, WSJ Career Journal, http://www .careerjournal.com/columnists/workfamily/20010426-workfamily.html, accessed October 4, 2005; Bad attitudes in the workplace by Les Christie, Sept 6, 2005, CNNMoney, http://money.cnn.com/2005/08/24/pf/workplace_morale/?section=money_pf; Inspiring worker loyalty one tough job by John Ellis, July 1, 2005, East Bay Business Times website, http://www.bizjournals.com/eastbay/stories/2005/07/04/focus1.html.

26. Sustainability: Balancing Opportunity and Risk in the Consumer Products Industry, 2007 Report, Deloitte website, http://www.deloitte.com/dtt/cda/doc/content/us_cb _sustainability-study_june2007opt.pdf, accessed January 20, 2009; While Everything Else Stops, Green Still Means Go by Sarah Fister Gale, January 19, 2009, GreenBiz website, http://www.planetthoughts.org/?pg=pt/Whole&qid=2675, accessed June 1, 2011.

27. How Rising Wages Are Changing the Game in China by Dexter Roberts, March 27, 2006, *Business Week* website, http://www.businessweek.com/magazine/content/06_13/b3977049.htm, accessed January 20, 2009; Good Luck Competing Against Chinese Labor Costs, Mfg. Job Growth in China Is Headed Up, Not Down; 109 Million Mfg. Workers in China Dwarfs Number in U.S., by Richard McCormack, May 2, 2006, Manufacturing and Technology News website, http://www.manufacturingnews.com/news/06/0502/art1.html, accessed January 20, 2009; Cost of Chinese labor is on the rise by Scott Tong, July 6, 2007, Marketplace website, http://marketplace.publicradio.org/display/web/2007/07/06/cost_of_chinese_labor_is_on_the_rise/, accessed January 20, 2009; Manufacturing in China Today: Employment and Labor Compensation by Judith Banister, September 2007, The Conference Board website, http://www.conference-board.org/economics/workingpapers.cfm, accessed January 20, 2009.

28. Asian tsunami devastates Sri Lankan fishing industry by Jason Beaubien, January 10, 2005, NPR Morning Edition, http://www.npr.org/templates/story/story.php?storyId=4276161; Phuket tourism industry crippled by mass cancellations by Sally Pook, January 8, 2005, Cyber Diver News Network, http://www.cdnn.info/news/travel/t050111.html; Homeland security scuffle by Veronique de Rugy, October 15, 2004, *National Review* website, http://www.nationalreview.com/comment/rugy200410150840.asp; Bush brushes aside rebuilding cost concerns, September 19, 2005, Reuters News Service, MSNBC website, http://www.msnbc.msn.com/id/9374106/.

29. Pomp and Circumspect by Daniel Pink, June 4, 2005, *The New York Times* website, http://select.nytimes.com/gst/abstract.html?res=F60C1FFD3F5C0C778CDDAF0894DD404482.

Pg. 13 Fact: Your future is on the phone by Steve McKee, *Bloomberg BusinessWeek*, November 12, 2010, *BusinessWeek* website, http://www.businessweek.com/smallbiz/content/nov2010/sb20101112_047190.htm, accessed, January 17, 2011.

Pg. 16 Fact: The rise of a fierce yet agile superpower by Fareed Zakaria, *Newsweek*, January 7, 2008, page 38.

2

1. TABLE B–1.—Gross domestic product, 1959–2008, Economic Report of the President: 2009 Spreadsheet Tables, updated January 14, 2009, Government Printing Office website, http://www.gpoaccess.gov/eop/tables09.html, accessed January 20, 2009.

2. More Foreclosures Expected in 2011 by Amy Hoak, December 12, 2010, *The Wall Street Journal* website, http://online.wsj.com/article/SB10001424052748703518604576014011451160994.html?mod=googlenews_wsj, accessed January 24, 2011; RealtyTrac's James J. Saccacio to Discuss Foreclosure Crisis Fallout at AFSA State Government Affairs Forum by RealtyTrac staff, RealityTrac website, October 1, 2008, http://www.realtytrac.com/ContentManagement/pressrelease.aspx? ChannelID=9&ItemID=5284&acnt=64847, accessed January 22, 2009; "REALTYTRAC® Year-end Report Shows Record 2.8 Million U.S. Properties With Foreclosure Filings in 2009," RealtyTrac Staff, January 14, 2010, RealtyTrac website, http://www.realtytrac.com/contentmanagement/pressrelease.aspx?itemid=8333, accessed April 21, 2010.

3. 7.9 million jobs lost — many forever by Chris Isidore, July 2, 2010, CNNMoney website, http://money.cnn.com/2010/07/02/news/economy/jobs_gone_forever/index.htm, accessed, January 24, 2011.

4. Credit Crisis–The Essentials, Updated January 20, 2009, *The New York Times* website, Automakers say if they go, millions of jobs will vanish by Sharon Silke Carty and Barbara Hagenbaugh, Updated November 21, 2008, *USA Today* website, Auto Industry Bailout Overview, Updated January 20, 2009, *The New York Times* website, http://topics.nytimes.com/topics/reference/timestopics/subjects/c/credit_crisis/index.html, accessed January 21, 2009; http://www.usatoday.com/money/autos/2008-11-17-automakers-bailout-impact_N.htm, accessed January 21, 2009; http://topics.nytimes.com/top/reference/timestopics/subjects/c/credit_crisis/auto_industry/index.html, accessed January 21, 2009.

5. TARP Bailout to Cost Less Than Once Anticipated by Jackie Calmes, *The New York Times* website, October 1, 2010, http://dealbook.nytimes.com/2010/10/01/tarp-bailout-to-cost-less-than-once-anticipated/.

6. One Trillion Dollars by Micheal Grunwald, January 26, 2009, *Time*, pp. 27–31, http://www.time.com/time/politics/article/0,8599,1871769,00.html, accessed February 5, 2011; Economy adds jobs at fastest pace in three years by Jeannine Aversa and Christopher S. Rugaber, April 2, 2010, Associated Press, http://www.google.com/hostednews/ap/article/ALeqM5gNiyJ905Ho0Ur96V2TQhsBX19lGwD9ER6P402, accessed April 20, 2010; Bernanke declares 'recession is very likely over' by Greg Robb, September 15, 2009, MarketWatch website, http://www.marketwatch.com/story/bernanke-declares-the-recession-over-2009-09-15, accessed, April 20, 2010.

7. The Recession Generation by Rana Foorohar, *Newsweek* website, January 9, 2010, http://www.newsweek.com/2010/01/08/the-recession-generation.html, accessed January 27, 2011; "Generation R", aka "The Recession Generation" Dave Manual website, January 27, 2011, http://www.davemanuel.com/2011/01/07/the-recession-generation/, accessed January 27, 2011.

8. Money Stock Measures, Federal Reserve Statistical Release, February 5, 2009, Federal Reserve website, http://www.federalreserve.gov/releases/h6/current/, accessed February 11, 2009.

9. Do We Need $75,000 a Year to Be Happy? by Beliknda Luscombe, *Time* magazine website, September 27, 2010, http://www.time.com/time/business/article/0,8599,2016291,00.html.

10. Money Stock Measures, Federal Reserve Statistical Release, January 22, 2009, http://www.federalreserve.gov/releases/h6/current/, accessed January 23, 2009.

11. Who is the FDIC?, FDIC website, October 27, 2008, http://www.fdic.gov/about/learn/symbol/index.html, accessed January 22, 2009.

12. Historical Changes of the Target Federal Funds and Discount Rates, Federal Reserve Bank of New York website, http://www.newyorkfed.org/markets/statistics/dlyrates/fedrate.html, accessed January 22, 2009.

13. The Secret to Turning Consumers Green by Stephanie Simon, *The Wall Street Journal* website, October 18, 2010, http://online.wsj.com/article/SB10001424052748704575304575296243891721972.html, accessed January 27, 2011.

14. Federal Government, excluding Postal Services, U.S. Department of Labor Bureau of Labor Statistics website, March 12, 2008, http://stats.bls.gov/oco/cg/cgs041.htm, accessed August 16, 2008; Postal Service Workers, U.S. Department of Labor Bureau of Labor Statistics website, December 18, 2007, http://stats.bls.gov/oco/ocos141.htm, accessed August 16, 2008; Job Opportunities in the Armed Forces, U.S. Department of Labor Bureau of Labor Statistics website, December 18, 2007, http://stats.bls.gov/oco/ocos249.htm, accessed August 16, 2008.

15. Russia's flat tax miracle by Daniel J. Mitchell, PhD, The Heritage Foundation, March 24, 2003, http://www.heritage.org/Press/Commentary/ed032403.cfm; Russians do taxes right by Deroy Murdock, *National Review* Online, March 1, 2002, http://www.nationalreview.com/murdock/murdock030102.shtml; Russia: income taxes and tax laws, July 2005, Worldwide-Tax website, http://www.worldwide-tax.com/russia/russia_tax.asp; History of the U.S. taxsystem, U.S. Treasury website, http://www.ustreas.gov/education/factsheets/taxes/ustax.html,accessed March 9, 2006.

16. Central Intelligence Agency. The World Factbook, North America; The United States: Economy: Overview Updated February, 2011, https://www.cia.gov/library/publications/the-world-factbook/geos/us.html, accessed February 5, 2011.

17. Graduates warned of record 70 applicants for every job by Jeevan Vasagar, July 6, 2010, *The*

Guardian website, http://www.guardian.co.uk/education/2010/jul/06/graduates-face-tougher-jobs-fight, accessed January 26, 2011.

18. Labor Force Statistics from the Current Population Survey: Unemployment Rate Table, U.S. Department of Labor Bureau of Labor Statistics website, http://data.bls.gov/PDQ/servlet/SurveyOutputServlet?data_tool=latest_numbers&series_id=LNS14000000, accessed January 22, 2009.

Pg. 32 Fact: Expenditures on Children by Families, 2009, U.S. Department of Agriculture, June 2008, USDA website, http://www.cnpp.usda.gov/Publications/CRC/crc2009.pdf, accessed February 5, 2011.

3

1. CIA – The World Economy Overview, The World Factbook website, updated February, 2011, https://www.cia.gov/library/publications/the-world-factbook/geos/xx.html, accessed February 5, 2011.

2. Zimbabwe: Mobile phone penetration linked to GDP growth, October 28, 2010, AllAfrica Global Media website, http://allafrica.com/stories/201011011088.html, accessed February 7, 2010; Mobile Phone Adoption in Developing Countries, WikiInvest website, http://www.wikinvest.com/concept/Mobile_Phone_Adoption_in_Developing_Countries, accessed February 8, 2011; Cell phones vital in developing world by Malcolm Foster, January 27, 2007, *Washington Post* website, http://www.washingtonpost.com/wp-dyn/content/article/2007/01/27/AR2007012700662.html, accessed January 28, 2009; China's mobile users top 600 million: govt, July 24, 2008, Kioskea website, http://en.kioskea.net/actualites/china-s-mobile-users-top-600-million-govt-10563-actualite.php3, accessed January 28, 2009; Telecom sector regaining momentum by Anand Kumar, August 25, 2008, Dawn website, http://www.dawn.com/2008/08/25/ebr15.htm, accessed January 28, 2009; Adam Hwang, "China market: Mobile phone users increase to nearly 766 million in February, says MIIT," DigiTimes, April 2, 2010, http://www.digitimes.com/news/a20100402vl200.html, accessed May 4, 2010; Telecom Regulatory Authority of India, Press Release No. 20 /2010, New Delhi, April 26, 2010, Telecom Subscription Data as of March 31, 2010, http://www.trai.gov.in/writereaddata/trai/upload/pressreleases/732/pr26apr10no20.pdf, accessed May 4, 2010.

3. Singapore Study finds video game addiction exists globally, The Medical News website, January 20, 2011, http://www.news-medical.net/news/20110120/Singapore-study-finds-video-game-addiction-exists-globally.aspx, accessed February 14, 2011; What they're restricting in South Korea, *Time* magazine briefing, April 26, 2010; U.S. Teens Lag as China Soars on International Test by John Hechinger, December 7, 2010, Bloomberg website, http://www.bloomberg.com/news/2010-12-07/teens-in-u-s-rank-25th-on-math-test-trail-in-science-reading.html, accessed February 14, 2010; South Korea Cracks Down on Gaming Addiction by Geoffrey Cain, *Time* magazine website, April 20, 2010, http://www.time.com/time/world/article/0,8599,1983234,00.html, accessed February 1, 2010.

4. Insperiences, Trendwatching newsletter, http://www.trendwatching.com/trends/insperience.htm, accessed January 12, 2006.

5. Trade to expand by 9.5% in 2010 after a dismal 2009, WTO reports, WTO 2010 Press Release, March 26, 2010, WTO website, http://www.wto.org/english/news_e/pres10_e/pr598_e.htm, accessed February 9, 2010; CIA, The World FactBook, The World Economy: Overview, CIA Website, https://www.cia.gov/library/publications/the-world-factbook/geos/xx.html, updated February 2010, accessed February 9, 2010.

6. What is countertrade? by Neha Gupta, Barter News Weekly website, March 11, 2010, http://www.barternewsweekly.com/2010/03/11/what-is-counter-trade-1851/, accessed February 10, 2010; Countertrade—an innovative approach to marketing by Dan West, Chairman American Countertrade Association, *BarterNews* issue #36, 1996, http://barternews.com/approach_marketing.htm; Global Offset and Countertrade Association website, http://www.globaloffset.org/index.htm, accessed January 27, 2006.

7. Mattel Issues New Massive China Toy Recall, Associated Press, MSNBC website, August 14, 2007, http://www.msnbc.msn.com/id/20254745/ns/business-consumer_news/, accessed February 10, 2010; As More Toys Are Recalled, Trail Ends in China by Eric S. Lipton and David Barboza, June 19, 2007, *The New York Times* website, http://www.nytimes.com/2007/06/19/business/worldbusiness/19toys.html, accessed January 29, 2009.

8. Yellin, E. (2009). *Your call is (not that) important to us.* New York: Simon Schuster, Inc.; Outsourced call centers return, to U.S. homes by Carolyn Beeler, NPR Website, August 25, 2010, http://www.npr.org/templates/story/story.php?storyId=129406588, accessed February 10, 2010.

9. Thinking outside the border by Curtis, Minority Business Entrepreneur, September/October 2005, http://www.export.gov/comm_svc/pdf/MBE_article.pdf.

10. Fiat Nears Stake in Chrysler That Could Lead to takeover by Stacy Meichtry and John Stoll, *The Wall Street Journal* website, January 20, 2009, http://online.wsj.com/article/SB123238519459294991.html, accessed February 10, 2010; eBay to acquire Skype, Press Release, September 12, 2005, Skype website, http://www.skype.com/company/news/2005/skype_ebay.html, accessed February 10, 2010.

11. Intel to Build Advanced Chip-Making Plant in China by David Barboza, March 27, 2007, *The New York Times* website, http://www.nytimes.com/2007/03/27/technology/27chip.html, accessed January 30, 2009.

12. Rethink the value of joint ventures by Cynthia Churchwell, Harvard Business School Working Knowledge, May 10, 2004, http://hbswk.hbs.edu/item.jhtml?id=4113&t=globalization.

13. Hyundai grows up by Michael Schuman, *Time* Global Business, July 2005, http://www.time.com/time/globalbusiness/article/0,9171,1074141,00.html; At 5 feet 10 inches, I was too tall for Tokyo by Cathie Gandel, My Turn, *Newsweek*, December 12, 2005. Hyundai Bets Big On India and China by Moon Ihlwan, January 30, 2008, *Business Week* website, http://www.businessweek.com/globalbiz/content/jan2008/gb20080130_061205.htm, accessed January 30, 2009.

14. The Confucian Consumer by Nouriel Roubini, January 24, 2011, *Newsweek* website, http://www.newsweek.com/2011/01/18/the-confucian-consumer.html, accessed February 16, 2011; Beijing 2010: 90% of Buicks in China bought for cold hard cash by Samuel Abuelsamid, AutoBlog website, April 20, 2010, http://www.autoblog.com/2010/04/26/beijing-2010-90-of-buicks-in-china-bought-for-cold-hard-cash/, accessed February 16, 2010.

15. Rural Market India Brand Equity Foundation, Updated December 10, 2010, IBEF website, http://www.ibef.org/artdispview.aspx?art_id=27581&cat_id=938&in=78, accessed February 10, 2010; Selling to rural India, Springwise Newsletter, June 2003, http://www.springwise.com/newbusinessideas/2003/06/shakti.html; Red herring: selling to the poor, April 11, 2004, The Next Practice website, http://www.thenextpractice.com/news/red_herring_selling_to_the_poor.php; Are you ready for globalization 2.0? by Tim Weber, January 28, 2005, BBC News website, http://news.bbc.co.uk/1/hi/business/4214687.stm.

16. McDonald's country/market sites, http://www.mcdonalds.com/countries.html, accessed February 10, 2011; http://www.dominos.com/Public-EN/Site+Content/Secondary/Inside+Dominos/Pizza+Particulars/International+Speciality+Toppings/; http://slice.seriouseats.com/archives/2008/02/crazy-weird-asian-pizza-crusts-japanese-korean-hong kong.html; http://recipes.howstuffworks.com/fresh-ideas/dinner-food-facts/favorite-pizza-toppings-in-10-countries.htm; http://slice.seriouseats.com/archives/2008/02/crazy weird-asian-pizza-crusts-japanese-korean-hong-kong.htm.

17. Internet Usage Statistics, World Internet Users and Population Stats, June 2010, Internet World Stats Website, http://www.internetworldstats.com/stats.htm, accessed February 16, 2011.

18. Doing Business Economy Rankings 2011 Report, World Bank website, http://www.doingbusiness.org/rankings, accessed February 11, 2011.

19. Who's Winning the Clean Energy Race, G-20 Clean Energy FactBook 2010, The Pew Environmental Group, Pew website, http://www.pewglobalwarming.org/cleanenergyeconomy/pdf/PewG-20Report.pdf, accessed February 15, 2011.

20. 09 Piracy Study in Brief, May 2010, Business Software Alliance website, http://portal.bsa.org/globalpiracy2009/studies/09%20Piracy_In%20Brief_A4_111010.pdf, accessed February 11, 2011.

21. USTR releases 2002 inventory of trade barriers, Press Release, April 2, 2002, http://www.useu.be/Categories/Trade/Apr0202USTRReportForeignTradeBarriers.html; U.S. targets non-tariff barriers to global trade, News Release, April 3, 2002, http://www.usconsulate.org.hk/pas/pr/2002/040301.htm.

22. Debt Relief Under the Heavily Indebted Poor Countries (HIPC) Initiative, Factsheet–December 16, 2010, International Monetary Fund website, http://www.imf.org/external/np/exr/facts/hipc.htm, accessed February 11, 2010.

23. Top 10 Exporting Countries Causing the US Trade Deficit by Daniel Workman, April 27, 2010, Suite101 Website, http://www.suite101.com/content/top-10-exporting-countries-causing-the-us-trade-deficit-a226747, accessed February 11, 2011.

24. CIA The World FactBook European Union: The Economy-Overview: CIA website, https://

www.cia.gov/library/publications/the-world-factbook/geos/ee.html, updated February, 2011, accessed February 11, 2011.

25. American Colleges Set up Shop in India by Elliot Hannon, Time Global Business, November 1, 2010, http://www.time.com/time/photogallery/0,29307,2027210_2203134,00.html, accessed February 15, 2011.

Pg. 39 Fact: This time for Africa? by Stephen Gandel, *Time* magazine website, November 1, 2010, http://www.time.com/time/magazine/article/0,9171,2026897,00.html, accessed February 9, 2010.

4

1. The Ethics of American Youth – 2008 summary, Josephson Institute Center for Youth Ethics website, http://charactercounts.org/programs/reportcard/index.html, accessed February 10, 2009; Josephson Institute, "Character Study Reveals Predictors of Lying and Cheating," October 29, 2009, http://josephsoninstitute.org/surveys/index.html, accessed May 13, 2010; The Ethics of American Youth. What would Honest Abe say? Josephson Institute Press Release, February 10, 2011, Character Counts website, http://charactercounts.org/programs/reportcard/2010/installment02_reportcard_honesty-integrity.html, accessed February 20, 2011.

2. Big Three auto CEOs flew private jets to ask for taxpayer money by Josh Levs, November 19, 2008, CNN website, http://www.cnn.com/2008/US/11/19/autos.ceo.jets/, accessed February 2, 2009.

3. Lawmakers, Questioning Fed Bailout, Seek AIG 'Junket' Refund by Ryan J. Donmoyer – October 9, 2008 Bloomberg website, http://www.bloomberg.com/apps/news?pid=newsarchive&sid=aPlPYw6JXIBU&refer=us, accessed February 21, 2011.

4. Divorce duel reveals Welch's perks, September 6, 2002, CNN Money website, http://money.cnn.com/2002/09/06/news/companies/welch_ge/, accessed February 2, 2009.

5. Why We'll Miss the Disney Trial by Barney Gimbel, *Fortune*, December 27, 2004, retrieved from CNNMoney website, http://money.cnn.com/magazines/fortune/fortune_archive/2004/12/27/8217949/index.htm; Disney's Basket Cases by Peter Bart, *Variety*, March 7, 2004, http://www.variety.com/article/VR1117901299.html?categoryid=1&cs=1.

6. National Business Ethics Survey: How Employees View Ethics in Their Organizations, 1994–2005, Ethics Resource Center, October 12, 2005, http://www.ethics.org/research/2005-press-release.asp; Ethics Resource Center, 2009 National Business Ethics Survey, http://www.ethics.org/nbes/files/nbes-final.pdf, (accessed May 14, 2010).

7. The role of tone from the top by Bob Lane, December 28, 2009, Ethisphere website, http://ethisphere.com/the-role-of-tone-from-the-top/, accessed, February 21, 2011.

8. Complaining Customers Are Good for Business by Bob Leduc, Virtual Marketing Newsletter, May 11, 2004, http://www.marketingsource.com/newsletter/05-11-2004.html.

9. JetBlue paying millions to stranded flyers by John Springer, updated March 4, 2007, MSNBC website, http://www.msnbc.msn.com/id/17237390/, accessed February 3, 2009; jetBlue Airways Ranked 'Highest in Customer Satisfaction

Among Low Cost Carriers...,' June 17, 2008, Press Release on Reuters website, http://www.reuters.com/article/pressRelease/idUS120589+17-Jun-2008+PNW20080617, accessed February 3, 2009.

10. The year in technology industry apologies by Bob Brown, Network World, 12/01/2009, Network World website, http://www.networkworld.com/slideshows/2009/120109-apologies.html#slide2, accessed February 22, 2011; Amazon Erases Orwell Books From Kindle by Brad Stone July 17, 2009, *New York Times* website, http://www.nytimes.com/2009/07/18/technology/companies/18amazon.html, accessed February 22, 2011; The Customer Is Always Right by Daniel Lyons, December 21, 2009, *Newseeek* website, http://www.newsweek.com/2009/12/20/the-customer-is-always-right.html, accessed February 22, 2011.

11. Open letter to iPhone customers, Apple website, http://www.apple.com/hotnews/openiphoneletter/, accessed February 3, 2009; Apple's customer satisfaction up despite struggling industry by Jeff Smykil, August 19, 2008, Ars Technica website, http://arstechnica.com/apple/news/2008/08/apples-customer-satisfaction-up-despite-struggling-industry.ars, accessed February 3, 2009.

12. Giving USA 2010, The Center on Philanthropy at Indiana University, Giving USA Website, http://www.givingusareports.org/products/GivingUSA_2010_ExecSummary_Print.pdf, accessed February 24, 2011.

13. Charitable giving estimated to be $306.39 billion in 2007, June 23, 2008, Planned Giving Center website, http://www.pgdc.com/pgdc/us-charitable-giving-estimated-be-30639-billion-2007, accessed February 4, 2009; Corporate donors adjust to economic slump by Ret Boney, September 15, 2008, Philanthropy Journal website, http://www.philanthropyjournal.org/resources/special-reports/corporate-giving/corporate-donors-adjust-economic-slump, accessed February 4, 2009.

14. The Dirty Little Secrets of Search by David Segal, February 12, 2011, *New York Times* website, http://www.nytimes.com/2011/02/13/business/13search.html, accessed February 28, 2011.

15. Has Green Stopped Giving? by Jack Neff, November 9, 2010, AdvertisingAge website, http://adage.com/article/news/consumer-revolt-sprouting-green-friendly-products/146944/, accessed February 25, 2011; Buzzword: Green fatigue by Kimberly Janeway, Home and Garden Blog, Consumer Reports website, http://blogs.consumerreports.org/home/2010/11/buzzword-green-fatigue-.html, accessed February 25, 2011.

16. Bad and Good Environmental Marks for McDonald's by Donalla Meadows, Sustainability Institute website, http://www.sustainer.org/dhm_archive/search.php?display_article=vn304mcdonaldsed, accessed May 15, 2005.

17. 'Carbon Footprint' Gaining Business Attention, October 18, 2006, Press Release, Conference Board website, http://www.conference-board.org/UTILITIES/pressDetail.cfm?press_ID=2985, accessed February 4, 2009; Green goal of 'carbon neutrality' hits limit by Jeffery Ball, December 30, 2008, *Wall Street Journal* website, http://online.wsj.com/article/SB123059880241541259.html, accessed February 4, 2009; How green is my orange? by Andrew Martin, January 22, 2009, *New York Times* website, http://www.

nytimes.com/2009/01/22/business/22pepsi.html?_r=1&scp=1&sq=How%20green%20is%20my%20orange&st=cse, accessed February 4, 2009.

18. U.S. Corporations Size Up Their Carbon Footprints by Rachel King, June 1, 2009, Bloomberg *BusinessWeek*, *BusinessWeek* website, http://www.businessweek.com/technology/content/jun2009/tc2009061_692661.htm, accessed February 24, 2011.

19. Marketing, Business and Sustainable Development: A Global Guide, Business and Sustainable Development website, http://www.bsdglobal.com/markets/green_marketing.asp, accessed February 4, 2009.

20. Corruption Perceptions Index 2010 Results, Transparency International website, http://www.transparency.org/policy_research/surveys_indices/cpi/2010/results, accessed February 25, 2011.

21. Bribe Payers Index 2008, Transparency International website, http://www.transparency.org/news_room/latest_news/press_releases/2008/bpi_2008_en, accessed February 24, 2011.

22. Sources: BusinessPundit, "25 Big Companies That Are Going Green," July 29, 2008, http://www.businesspundit.com/25-big-companies-that-are-going-green/, (accessed May 17, 2010); CNNMoney, "Ten Green Giants," http://money.cnn.com/galleries/2007/fortune/0703/gallery.green_giants.fortune/8.html (accessed May 17, 2010), Arrowhead website, http://www.arrowheadwater.com/KnowH2O/Be-Green.aspx, accessed February 25, 2011.

23. Selling to the Poor by Kay Johnson, *Time* Bonus Section, May 2005; The Payoff for Investing in Poor Countries by C.K. Prahalad and Allen Hammond, Harvard Business School Working Knowledge website, http://hbswk.hbs.edu/item.jhtml?id=3180&t=nonprofit&noseek=one.

24. Gap, Inc. Social Reporting Award, December 20, 2004, Business Ethics website, http://www.business-ethics.com/annual.htm#Gap%20Inc.

25. Values in Tension: Ethics Away from Home by Thomas Donaldson, Harvard Business Review, September/October 1996.

Pg. 60 Fact: Social Responsibility Weighs Higher in Purchase Decisions for Hispanics and African Americans 9/15/2010, HispanicPRBlog, http://www.hispanicprblog.com/hispanic-market-white-papers-research/social-responsibility-weighs-higher-in-purchase-decisions-for-hispanics-and-african-americans.html, accessed February 28, 2011.

Pg. 65 Fact: Paper Shocking Statistics, TechSoup website, http://www.techsoup.org/greentech/paper/page10834.cfm, accessed February 24, 2011.

5

1. Body Language Tactics That Sway Interviewers by Eugene Raudsepp, *The Wall Street Journal* CareerJournal, December 5, 2002, http://www.careerjournal.com/jobhunting/interviewing/20021205-raudsepp.html.

2. How to dress for an interview by Alison Doyle, About website, http://jobsearch.about.com/od/interviewsnetworking/a/dressforsuccess.htm, accessed March 5, 2011.

3. Social media in China: The same, but different by Thomas Crampton, February 25, 2011, Memeburn Website, http://memeburn.com/2011/02/

social-media-in-china-the-same-but-different/, accessed March 4, 2011.

4. The Listener Wins by Michael Purdy, Monster contributing writer, Monster.com, http://feature-dreports.monster.com/listen/overview/, accessed August 22, 2006; The Human Side of Business by Stephen D. Boyd, *Agency Sales* Magazine, February 2004, page 35, accessed via Infotrac College Edition.

5. We Learn More by Listening Than Talking by Harvey Mackay, *The Daily Herald*, January 16, 2005, page E6[SB14], http://old.heraldextra.com/modules.php?op=modload&name=News&file=article&sid=45313; Listening Factoids, International Listening Association, http://www.listen.org/pages/factoids.html, accessed August 22, 2006.

6. The Human Side of Business by Stephen D. Boyd, Agency Sales Magazine, February 2004, page 35, accessed via Infotrac College Edition; Learn to Listen: Closing the Mouth and Opening the Ears Facilitates Effective Communication by Marjorie Brody, *Incentive*, May 2004, page 57, accessed via Business and Company Resource Center.

7. Andrew Jacobs, "Shanghai Is Trying to Untangle the Mangled English of Chinglish," by Andrew Jacobs *The New York Times*, May 2, 2010, *New York Times* website, http://www.nytimes.com/2010/05/03/world/asia/03chinglish.html?pagewanted=1, accessed May 20, 2010.

8. Location makes a difference in communication even if the same language is spoken, Communication Resource Center 2011, http://www.work911.com/communication/oopslocationalerror.htm, accessed March 5, 2011; How to Speak American by Joan Houston Hall, August 9, 2010, *Newsweek* magazine, http://www.newsweek.com/2010/07/30/how-to-speak-american.html, accessed March 5, 2011; Oh, those idioms will just kill you. Australia idiomatic communication meets U.S. communication, Communication Resource Center 2011, http://www.work911.com/communication/oopsidioms.htm, accessed March 5, 2011.

9. Edward P. Bailey, *Writing and Speaking at Work*, (Prentice Hall, 2005), pages 82–89.

10. Presenting Effective Presentations with Visual Aids, U.S. Department of Labor, Occupational Safety and Health Administration, http://www.osha.gov/doc/outreachtraining/htmlfiles/traintec.html, accessed August 22, 2006.

11. Bringing the cloud with you by Philip Tucker, March 31, 2009, Google Docs Blog, http://googledocs.blogspot.com/2008/03/bringing-cloud-with-you.html, accessed February 13, 2009; Living in the Clouds by Brian Braiker, June 10, 2008, *Newsweek* website, http://www.newsweek.com/id/140864, accessed February 13, 2009; Comparing Google Docs with competing cloud computing applications by Michael Miller, February 9, 2009, InformIT website, http://www.informit.com/articles/article.aspx?p=1323244&seqNum=3, accessed February 13, 2009.

Pg. 77 Fact: *Briefing*, *Time* magazine, February 21, 2011, page 19.

6

1. Why States Should Adopt the Revised Uniform Limited Liability Company Act (2006), National Conference of Commissioners on Uniform State Laws website, http://www.nccusl.org/Update/

uniformact_why/uniformacts-why-ullca.asp, accessed January 28, 2011.

2. U.S. Census Bureau. The 2011 Statistical Abstract of the United States Tables 743 and 744: http://www.census.gov/compendia/statab/2011/tables/11s0744.pdf, accessed January 23, 2011.

3. U.S. Census Bureau. The 2011 Statistical Abstract of the United States Tables 743 and 744: http://www.census.gov/compendia/statab/2011/tables/11s0744.pdf, accessed January 23, 2011.

4. U.S. Census Bureau. The 2011 Statistical Abstract of the United States Table 743: http://www.census.gov/compendia/statab/2011/tables/11s0744.pdf, accessed January 23, 2011.

5. Naming Your Business, Business Owner's Toolkit website, http://www.toolkit.com/small_business_guide/sbg.aspx?nid=P01_4800; Choosing the Right Name for My Corporation or Limited Liability Company, SCORE website, http://www.score.org/leg_choosing_name.html; Business Name Registration (Doing Business As), Business.gov website, http://www.business.gov/register/business-name/dba.html.

6. Delaware Division of Corporations: http://www.corp.delaware.gov/, accessed January 26, 2011.

7. Setting Up a One Person Corporation by Karen Klein, November 7, 2007, *BusinessWeek* website, http://www.businessweek.com/smallbiz/content/nov2007/sb2007117_803605.htm.

8. "The Ben & Jerry's Law: Principles Before Profit," by John Tozzi, *Bloomberg Business Week*, April 26, 2010, pp. 65-66; "Maryland Signs Benefit Corporation Law," by Tasha Petty, Little Green Submarine website, http://www.littlegreensubmarine.com/maryland-signs-benefit-corporation-law/; "Maryland First State in Union to Pass Benefit Corporation Legislation," CSR Newswire website, http://www.csrwire.com/press/press_release/29332-Maryland-First-State-in-Union-to-Pass-Benefit-Corporation-Legislation.

9. "New Law Has Effect on Pay for Executives," by David Nicklaus, St. Louis Post Dispatch, page B1, January 7, 2007; Dodd-Frank's 'say on pay' could impact executive pay by Ronald D. Orol, Marketwatch Website, http://www.marketwatch.com/story/new-say-on-pay-law-could-temper-ceo-pay-2010-08-26; Dodd-Frank: What it Means for Comp and Governance by Daniel J. Ryterband, Bloomberg *Business Week* website, http://www.businessweek.com/managing/content/jul2010/ca20100716_567635.htm.

10. Why States Should Adopt the Revised Uniform Limited Liability Company Act (2006), National Conference of Commissioners on Uniform State Laws website, http://www.nccusl.org/Update/uniformact_why/uniformacts-why-ullca.asp, accessed January 22, 2011.

11. GE: 7000 Tax Returns, $0 US Tax Bill by Annalyn Censky, CNN Money website, http://money.cnn.com/2010/04/16/news/companies/ge_7000_tax_returns/; GE, Exxon Paid No U.S. Taxes in 09 by Christopher Helman, ABC News website, http://abcnews.go.com/Business/Tax/ge-exxon-paid-us-income-taxes-09/story?id=10300167; Why Your Tax Bill Is Higher Than GE's, MSN Money website, http://articles.moneycentral.msn.com/Taxes/Advice/why-your-tax-bill-is-higher-than-ges.aspx.

12. Why States Should Adopt the Revised Uniform Limited Liability Company Act (2006), National Conference of Commissioners on Uniform State Laws website, http://www.nccusl.org/Update/

uniformact_why/uniformacts-why-ullca.asp, accessed January 22, 2011.

13. Franchise Business Outlook: 2011, prepared by PwC for the International Franchise Association Educational Foundation, IFA website, http://emarket.franchise.org/News_Release/Outlook%20report%202011.pdf; Census Bureau's First Release of Comprehensive Franchise Data Shows Franchises Make Up More Than 10% of Employer Businesses, U.S. Census Bureau website, http://www.census.gov/newsroom/releases/archives/economic_census/cb10-141.html, accessed January 30, 2011.

14. Entrepreneur.com website pages for individual franchisors, http://www.entrepreneur.com/franchises/mcdonalds/282570-0.html; http://www.entrepreneur.com/franchises/subway/282839-0.html; http://www.entrepreneur.com/franchises/curves/282265-0.html, accessed January 22, 2011.

15. Fit for Franchising by Taylor Mallory, *Pink Magazine* June/July 2007, pinkmagazine.com website, http://www.pinkmagazine.com/franchise/women/2007/burzynski.html; Franchising Attracts More Women, Minorities by Julie Bennett, Startup Journal, accessed through Entrepreneur.com website, http://www.entrepreneur.com/franchises/franchisezone/startupjournal/article61324.html; Female Franchisors Few and Far Between by Julie M. Young, e-magnify.com website, https://www.e-magnify.com/resources_articlearchiveresults.asp?categoryID=18; Fit to Be a Franchisee: Many Businesswomen Choose Franchises that Connect With Personal Interests by Nancy Lacewell, June 7, 2006 Business First of Louisville website, http://www.bizjournals.com/louisville/stories/2006/05/22/story2.html.

16. Boosting Diversity in Franchising by Joan Szabo, December 5, 2006, *Franchise Update* website, http://www.franchise-update.com/article/188/.

17. Bridging the Gap Between the Minority Community and the Franchising Industry, Minority Franchising website, http://www.minorityfranchising.com/, accessed January 20, 2011; Minority-Fran, International Franchise Association website, http://www.franchise.org/files/MinorityFran%20Broch%20by%20page.pdf, accessed January 20, 2011.

18. Subway, Entrepreneur.com website, http://www.entrepreneur.com/franchises/subway/282839-2.html.

19. Franchise Rule Compliance Guide, Federal Trade Commission website, http://www.ftc.gov/bcp/edu/pubs/business/franchise/bus70.pdf, pages 20, 102-103, and 121.

20. Ben & Jerry's website, http://www.benjerry.com/scoop_shops/partnershops/, accessed August 2, 2009; Nonprofit Owned Franchises: A Strategic Business Approach, prepared by Community Wealth Ventures and IFA Educational Foundation, March 2004, http://www.franchise.org/uploadedFiles/Files/nonprofit_owned.pdf; Franchise Chains, Nonprofits Team Up by Laura Sydell, Morning Edition, February 5, 2004, http://www.npr.org/templates/story/story.php?storyId=1644016; Social Franchise Venture website, http://www.socialfranchise.com/faq.asp?id=128304&page=1, accessed August 2, 2009.

21. U.S. Census Bureau. The 2011 Statistical Abstract of the United States Table 743, http://www.census.gov/compendia/statab/2011/tables/11s0744.pdf, accessed January 23, 2011; Recession, Layoffs Fuel Many to Start Small Businesses, by Laura Petrecca, *USA Today* website,

http://www.usatoday.com/money/smallbusiness/startup/week1-exploring-small-business-options.htm.

22. Franchise Business Outlook: 2011, prepared by PwC for the International Franchise Association Educational Foundation, IFA website, http://emarket.franchise.org/News_Release/Outlook%20report%202011.pdf.

Pg. 90 Fact: MSN Moneycentral website, http://articles.moneycentral.msn.com/Taxes/Advice/why-your-tax-bill-is-higher-than-ges.aspx.

7

1. Despite Recession, Youth Remain Interested in Entrepreneurship, Poll Shows, November 17, 2010, Philanthropy News Digest website, http://foundationcenter.org/pnd/news/story.jhtml;jsessionid=R0ZQZFD52NZNLLAQBQ4CGW15AAAACI2F?id=314900002, accessed March 18, 2011.

2. "Jobless Entrepreneurship" Tarnishes Steady Rate of U.S. Start-Up Activity, Kauffman Study Shows, March 7, 2011, Kauffman website, http://www.kauffman.org/newsroom/jobless-entrepreneurship-tarnishes-steady-rate-of-us-startup-activity.aspx, accessed March 18, 2011.

3. Why Americans start their own business, October 27, 2007, Young Money Talks website, http://www.youngmoneytalks.com/blog/index.php?p=257, accessed February 15, 2008; Study: 72% of workers would rather work for themselves by Rhonda Abrams, October 11, 2008, *USA Today* website, http://www.usatoday.com/money/smallbusiness/columnist/abrams/2007-10-11-workers-survey_N.htm, accessed February 15, 2009.

4. The *Forbes* 400 edited by Matthew Miller and Duncan Greenberg, September 17, 2008, *Forbes* website, http://www.forbes.com/2008/09/16/forbes-400-billionaires-lists-400list08_cx_mn_0917richamericans_land.html, accessed February 15, 2009.

5. Discover Polls Reveal True Character of the American *Entrepreneur*, October 22, 2007, Press Release, Discover Financial Services website, http://investorrelations.discoverfinancial.com/phoenix.zhtml?c=204177&p=irol-newsArticle&ID=1065373&highlight=, accessed February 15, 2009.

6. More than Half of Small Business Owners Work at Least Six-Day Weeks, Still Find Time for Personal Life, Wells Fargo News Release, August 9, 2005, https://www.wellsfargo.com/press/20050809_GallupPersonalLife. Discover Polls Reveal True Character of the American Entrepreneur, October 22, 2007, Press Release, Discover Financial Services website, http://investorrelations.discoverfinancial.com/phoenix.zhtml?c=204177&p=irol-newsArticle&ID=1065373&highlight=, accessed February 15, 2009.

7. Entrepreneurial Risk and Market Entry, by Brian Wu and Anne Marie Knott, SBA Office of Advocacy, January 2005, http://www.sba.gov/advo/research/wkpbw249.pdf.

8. Personality Test for Entrepreneurship Success, by Andy Swan, Small Biz Survival website, http://www.smallbizsurvival.com/2008/08/personality-test-for-entrepreneurship.html, posted August 4, 2008, accessed April 3, 2011.

9. Failure: Use It as a Springboard to Success, U.S. SBA Online Library, no attribution, http://www.sba.gov/library/successXIII/19-Failure-Use-it.doc, accessed December 28, 2005.

10. "Food Truck Nation," by Katy McLaughlin, June 5, 2009, *The Wall Street Journal* website, http://online.wsj.com/article/SB10001424052970204456604574201934018170554.html, accessed June 3, 2010; "How to Open a (Successful) Food Truck," by Christine Lagorio, May 12, 2010, Inc. website, http://preview.inc.com/guides/2010/05/opening-a-successful-food-truck.html, accessed June 3, 2010.

11. Failure: Use It as a Springboard to Success, U.S. SBA Online Library, no attribution, http://www.sba.gov/library/successXIII/19-Failure-Use-it.doc, accessed December 28, 2005.

12. What Makes Them Tick, by Keith McFarland, Inc 500, 2005, Inc website, http://www.inc.com/resources/inc500/2005/articles/20051001/tick.html.

13. How to finance a new business, April 2008, Consumer Reports website, http://www.consumerreports.org/cro/money/credit-loan/how-to-finance-a-new-business/overview/how-to-finance-a-new-business-ov.htm, accessed March 18, 2011.

14. Credit Cards Replace Small Business Loans, by John Tozzi, August 20, 2008, *Business Week* website, http://www.businessweek.com/smallbiz/content/aug2008/sb20080820_288348.htm?chan=smallbiz_smallbiz+index+page_top+small+business+stories, accessed February 15, 2009.

15. Start-up Information, updated April 28, 2008, Delaware Small Business Development Center website, http://www.delawaresbdc.org/DocumentMaster.aspx?doc=1003#6, accessed February 15, 2009.

16. Financial Assistance, Small Business Administration website, http://www.sba.gov/services/financialassistance/index.html, accessed February 15, 2009.

17. Will Angel Investment slowdown hamper recovery? by Anita Campbell, December 26, 2010, Small Business Trends website, http://smallbiztrends.com/2010/12/will-angel-investment-slowdown-hamper-recovery.html, accessed March 18, 2011; "The Angel Investor Market in 2009: Holding Steady but Changes in Seed and Startup Investments," by Jeffrey Sohl, Center for Venture Research, March 31, 2010. http://www.unh.edu/news/docs/2009angelanalysis.pdf, accessed June 4, 2010.

18. The Steady, Strategic Assent of jetBlue Airways, Strategic Management Knowledge at Wharton, December 14, 2005–January 10, 2006, http://knowledge.wharton.upenn.edu/article/1342.cfm; Charging Ahead, by Bobbie Gossage, January 2004, Inc. Magazine, http://www.inc.com/magazine/20040101/gettingstarted.html.

19. Venture capital investment in 2010 grew for first time in three years, by Peter Delevett, February 20, 2011, Mercury News website, http://www.mercurynews.com/rss/ci_17416341?nclick_check=1, accessed March 18, 2011; "'Clean tech' deals among the largest in '09 venture capital spending," by Ben Geman, Jan 22, 2010, *The Hill* website, http://thehill.com/blogs/e2-wire/677-e2-wire/77595-clean-tech-deals-among-the-largest-in-09-venture-capital-spending, accessed June 3, 2010.

20. Amplestuff website, http://www.amplestuff.com/; Kazoo v. Walmart, Reveries Magazine, November 29, 2005, http://www.reveries.com/?p=232.

21. Sustainability Planning for Business Owner, by Kelly Spors, May 9, 2010, Small Business Trends website, http://smallbiztrends.com/2010/05/sustainability-planning-for-business-owners.html, accessed April 3, 2011.

22. E-Commerce Award—June 2002, Anything Left-Handed website, http://www.anythingleft-handed.co.uk/pressreleases.html.

23. Focus on Success, Not Failure by Rhonda Abrams, May 7, 2004, USA Today website money section, http://www.usatoday.com/money/small-business/columnist/abrams/2004-05-06-success_x.htm.

24. Is Entrepreneurship for You? U.S. Small Business Administration, http://www.sba.gov/starting_business/startup/areyouready.html, accessed December 15, 2005.

25. Committee Examines Ways to Ease Growing Regulatory Burden on Small Businesses, July 30, 2008, U.S. House of Representatives Press Release, House of Representatives website, http://www.house.gov/smbiz/PressReleases/2008/pr-7-30-08-regulatory.html, accessed February 15, 2009.

26. Entrepreneurship in the 21st Century, Conference Proceedings, March 26, 2004, SBA Office of Advocacy and the Kauffman Foundation, http://www.sba.gov/advo/stats/proceedings_a.pdf; Health Care Costs Surface in Economic Stimulus Debate by Sharon McLoone, February 10, 2009, *Washington Post* website, http://voices.washingtonpost.com/small-business/2009/02/health_care_costs_surface_in_e.html, accessed February 15, 2009.

27. Business Plan Basics, U.S. SBA, http://www.sba.gov/starting_business/planning/basic.html, accessed February 15, 2009.

28. Top 10 Accidental Inventions, Science Channel website, http://science.discovery.com/brink/top-ten/accidental-inventions/inventions-01.html, accessed March 22, 2011.

29. "Frequently Asked Questions," SBA Office of Advocacy, updated September 2009, SBA website, http://www.sba.gov/advo/stats/sbfaq.pde, accessed June 3, 2010.

30. Frequently Asked Questions, SBA Office of Advocacy, Updated September 2008, SBA website, http://www.sba.gov/advo/stats/sbfaq.pdf, accessed February 17, 2009.

31. Frequently Asked Questions, SBA Office of Advocacy, Updated September 2008, SBA website, http://www.sba.gov/advo/stats/sbfaq.pdf, accessed February 17, 2009.

32. Small Business Drives Inner City Growth and Jobs, NewsRelease, October 11, 2005, U.S. SBA Office of Advocacy, http://www.sba.gov/advo/press/05-32.html.

33. Global Entrepreneurship Monitor, 2008 Executive Report by Niels Bosma, Zoltan J. Acs, Erkko Autio, Alicia Coduras, and Jonathan Levie, Babson College and London School of Economics, http://www.gemconsortium.org/article.aspx?id=76, published January 15, 2009, accessed February 17, 2009.

34. Exclusive Survey Results: Tons of College Students Are Starting Businesses—And A Lot Are Doing It Because They Can't Find Jobs by Alyson Shontell, February 17, 2011, Business Insider website, http://www.businessinsider.com/youth-entrepreneurship-council-2011-2?op=1, accessed March 21, 2011.

Pg. 103 Fact: Study: 72% of workers would rather work for themselves by Rhonda Abrams,

October 11, 2008, *USA Today* website, http://www.usatoday.com/money/smallbusiness/columnist/abrams/2007-10-11-workers-survey_N.htm, accessed February 17, 2009.

Pg. 107 Fact: How Do I... Get Some of That Venture Capital?, by Sharon McLoone, October 6, 2008, *Washington Post* website, http://voices.washingtonpost.com/small-business/2008/10/how_do_iget_some_of_that_ventu.html, accessed February 17, 2009.

Pg. 110 Fact: Global Entrepreneurship Monitor, 2004 Executive Report, http://www.gemconsortium.org/download/1133331987906/GEM_2004_Exec_Report.pdf, published May 27, 2005, accessed August 29, 2008.

Pg. 112 Fact: Slumdog Entrepreneurs, *Time* magazine photo essay, by Daniel Berehulak, *Time* website, http://www.time.com/time/photogallery/0,29307,1877000,00.html, accessed February 17, 2009.

8

1. "Meet Irving Picard, the Lawyer With the Toughest Task in the World," by Vivek Ahuja, December 7, 2010, Financial News website, http://www.efinancialnews.com/story/2010-12-07/madoff-irving-picard; "Half of Madoff Losses Recovered After $7 Billion Settlement," by Josh Nathan-Kazis, The Jewish Daily Forward website, http://www.forward.com/articles/134060/; "Accounting Sleuths on the Trail of Madoff Money," by Rob Scherer, December 22, 2008, Christian Science Monitor website, http://www.csmonitor.com/2008/1222/p01s01-usec.htm; "Post-Madoff, Forensic Accountants Seeing Increase in Business," Shareholders Foundation website, http://shareholdersfoundation.com/news/post-madoff-forensic-accountants-seeing-increase-business, accessed February 17, 2009; "Forensic Accountants Reconstruct Madoff Books," WebCPA website, http://www.webcpa.com/news/Forensic-Accountants-Reconstruct-Madoff-Books-50484-1.html; "Evil Madoff Gets 150 Years in Epic Fraud ,"by Robert Frank and Amir Efrati, Wall Street Journal website, http://online.wsj.com/article/SB124604151653862301.html; "Forensic Teams Dig into Legal Disputes for Clients; Multidisciplinary Investigations Are Now a $6 Billion Business," by Stan Luxenberg, Crain's New York Business, September 25, 2006; "Forensic Accounting: Exponential Growth: The Work Varies Widely, the Credentials to Practice Are Sophisticated, Unique Marketing Is Needed, but the Engagements Are Very Lucrative," by Jeff Stimpson, The Practical Accountant, February 2007.

2. "Scandal Sheet," CBS Marketwatch website, http://www.marketwatch.com/news/features/scandal_sheet.asp; "Corporate Scandal Sheet," Citizen Works website, http://www.citizenworks.org/enron/corp-scandal.php; "The Corporate Scandal Sheet," by Penelope Patsuris, *Forbes*, August 26, 2002, http://www.forbes.com/2002/07/25/accountingtracker.html.

3. "How Parmalat Went Sour," by Gail Edmondson and Laura Cohn, *Bloomberg Business Week* website, http://www.businessweek.com/magazine/content/04_02/b3865053_mz054.htm; "Court: Royal Ahold Scandal Was CFO's Fault," by Stephen Taub and Ronald Fink, CFO website, http://www.cfo.com/article.

cfm/6764238/c_6764367?f=todayinfinance_next; "Royal Ahold's Royal Hold Up," University of Pennsylvania website, http://www.upenn.edu/researchatpenn/article.php?607&bus; "Holier Than Thou: European Sanctimony Over American Accounting Scandals Is Misplaced," *The Economist* website, http://www.economist.com/node/1566871.

4. "Off-Balance Sheet Financing," riskglossary.com website, http://www.riskglossary.com/link/off_balance_sheet_finance.htm; "Enron and the Use and Abuse of Special Purpose Entities in Corporate Structures," by Steven L. Schwarcz, AEI-Brookings Joint Center for Regulatory Studies, reg-markets.org website, http://reg-markets.org/admin/authorpdfs/redirect-safely.php?fname=../pdffiles/phpUH.pdf; "The Fall of Enron," Special Report, the Houston Chronicle website, http://www.chron.com/news/specials/enron/timeline.html; "Accounting Issues at Enron," by Alan Reinstein and Thomas R. Weirich, *The CPA Journal* website, http://www.nysscpa.org/cpajournal/2002/1202/features/f122002.htm; "Causes of the Financial Crisis," by Viral Acharya, the Commission on Growth and Development website, http://www.growthcommissionblog.org/content/causes-of-the-financial-crisis.

5. Mission statement on PCAOB website, http://www.pcaobus.org/index.aspx.

6. "FASB and IASB Rejigger Convergence Plans," by Michael Cohn, Accounting Today website, http://www.accountingtoday.com/news/FASB-IASB-Rejigger-Convergence-Plans-56116-1.html; "IFRS: Current Situation and Next Steps," PricewaterhouseCoopers website, http://www.pwc.com/us/en/issues/ifrs-reporting/transition-to-ifrs-status.jhtml; "Compromise Reached for Financial Instruments; Revenue Recognition and Leases Less Certain," by Matthew G. Lamoreaux, *Journal of Accountancy* website, http://www.journalofaccountancy.com/Web/20113797.htm; "IFRS and US GAAP Similarities and Differences," PricewaterhouseCoopers website, http://www.pwc.com/us/en/issues/ifrs-reporting/assets/ifrs-simdif_book-final-2010.pdf.

7. Albrecht, Stice, Stice, and Swain, *Accounting Concepts and Applications*, 9th ed. (Cengage Learning), p. 758.

8. "It's Time for Triple Bottom Line Reporting," by Daniel Tschopp, *The CPA Journal*, December 2003, http://www.nysscpa.org/cpajournal/2003/1203/nv/nv3a.htm; "Adapting Your Accounting Practices to Triple Bottom Line Reporting," by David Crawford, *CMA Management Magazine*, February 7, 2005, accessed on Greenbiz website, http://www.greenbiz.com/business/research/report/2005/02/08/adapting-your-accounting-practices-triple-bottom-line-reporting; "KPMG: The Triple Bottom Line of People, Planet and Profits," The Big Four Blog website, March 2, 2010, http://bigfouralumni.blogspot.com/2010/03/kpmg-triple-bottom-line-of-people.html; "What is Triple Bottom Line Reporting?," by Shane Thornton, eHow website, http://www.ehow.com/about_5064070_triple-bottom-line-reporting.html, accessed April 28, 2010; "Putting the Triple Bottom Line to Work," by Mark McElroy, November 11, 2009, Greenbiz website, http://www.greenbiz.com/blog/2009/11/11/putting-triple-bottom-line-work.

9. *The Essentials of Finance and Budgeting*, Harvard Business School Press, Boston, MA, 2005, pp. 177–181.

10. "Accountants and Auditors," Occupational Outlook Handbook, 2010-2011 edition, Bureau of Labor Statistics website, http://www.bls.gov/oco/ocos001.htm.

Pg. 116 Fact: Confucius, ChinaCulture.org website, http://www1.chinaculture.org/library/2008-02/08/content_23084.htm, accessed February 18, 2009.

Pg. 125 Fact: A Beginner's Guide to Financial Statements, SEC website, http://www.sec.gov/investor/pubs/begfinstmtguide.htm accessed March 29, 2009. ("Read The Footnotes" finished seventh in the 2004 Kentucky Derby.)

9

1. See, for example, Moyer, McGuigan, and Rao, *Fundamentals of Contemporary Financial Management, 2nd ed.* (South-Western, Cengage Learning), p. 3; Brigham and Houston, *Fundamentals of Financial Management, 11th ed.*, p. 2.

2. Numbers, *Business Week*, February 9, 2009, p. 13.

3. Joseph E. Stiglitz, *Freefall* (W. W. Norton, 2010), pp. 31–32; Financial Crisis Inquiry Commission, *Financial Crisis Inquiry Report*, (Official Government Edition, January, 2011) pp. 109–114.

4. "Green and Social Venture Capital," Green VC website, http://www.greenvc.org/green-and-social-venture-capital.html; "30 Entrepreneurs Who Are Saving the World," by Kelly Fairchild, *Inc. Magazine*, November 1, 2009, http://www.inc.com/magazine/20091101/30-entrepreneurs-who-are-saving-the-world.html; "Do-Gooder Finance," by Natasha Tiku, *Inc. Magazine*, February 1, 2008, http://www.inc.com/magazine/20080201/do-gooder-finance.html; Underdog Ventures website, http://www2.underdogventures.com/, accessed April 19, 2010.

5. The approximate "finance charge" of not taking the discount on credit can be computed using the following formula:

$$\frac{\text{Cost of Not}}{\text{Taking discount}} = \frac{\%\ \text{discount}}{(100 - \%\ \text{discount})} \times \frac{365}{(\text{Credit\_Period} - \text{Discount\_Period})}$$

where % discount is the discount the buyer receives for paying on or before the last day the discount is available, the Credit Discount Period is the number of days before payment of full invoice amount is due.

6. "Financial Services Used by Small Businesses: Evidence from the 2003 Survey of Small Business Finances," by Traci Mack and John D. Wolken, *Federal Reserve Bulletin*, October 2006, p. A181.

7. "Annual Asset-Based Lending and Factoring Surveys, 2009," Commercial Finance Association website, https://www.cfa.com/eweb/docs/2009_survey_nonmember.pdf accessed March 5, 2011.

8. Commercial Paper Funding Facility, New York Federal Reserve Bank website, http://www.federalreserve.gov/monetarypolicy/cpff.htm; New York Fed CPFF FAQs, New York Federal Reserve Bank website, http://www.newyorkfed.org/markets/cpff_faq.html , accessed March 15, 2011.

9. Table B-90: Corporate Profits with Inventory Valuation and Capital Consumption Adjustments, 1962-2010," Economic Report of the President, 2011, GPOaccess website, http://www.gpoaccess.gov/eop/tables11.html.

10. Yahoo! Finance historical stock prices for Apple, Yahoo! Finance website, http://finance

.yahoo.com/q/hp?s=AAPL&a=08&b=7&c=1997&d=02&e=7&f=2011&g=d&z=66&y=0, accessed March 5, 2011. (Note that the stock price for March 1, 2001 has been adjusted for stock splits.).

11. "Why do companies issue debt and bonds? Can't they just borrow from the bank?" Investopedia website, http://www.investopedia.com/ask/answers/05/reasonforcorporatebonds.asp.

12. "Summary: Restoring American Financial Stability," Senate Committee on Banking, Housing and Urban Affairs, http://banking.senate.gov/public/_files/FinancialReformSummaryAsFiled.pdf; "Bernanke: Too Big to Fail a 'Pernicious' Problem," by Christina Cooke, Reuters website March 20, 2010, http://www.reuters.com/article/idUSTRE62J0SM20100320; "Details Still Scarce on WaMu's Failure," by Dan Fitzpatrick and John D. McKinnon, *The Wall Street Journal* website, April 13, 2010, http://online.wsj.com/article/SB10001424052702304506904575180441067747062.html; "Testimony of Chairman Ben S. Bernanke before the Committee on Financial Services of the U.S. House of Representatives," Federal Reserve website, April 20, 2010, http://www.federalreserve.gov/newsevents/testimony/bernanke20100420a.htm.

13. "Financial Sectors' New Buzzword Is Deleverage," by Chris Arnold, NPR website, http://www.npr.org/templates/story/story.php?storyId=94795760, accessed August 9, 2009; Deleveraging, Now Only in Early Stages, Will Transform the Banking Industry by James Saft, *New York Times* website, http://www.nytimes.com/2008/06/26/business/worldbusiness/26iht-col27.1.14006619.html?_r=1, accessed August, 9, 2009; "Deleveraging: A Fate Worse than Debt," *Economist* website, http://www.economist.com/businessfinance/displaystory.cfm?story_id=12306060, accessed August 9, 2009.

14. "Brief Summary of the Dodd-Frank Wall Street Reform and Consumer Protection Act." United States Senate Committee on Banking, Housing and Urban Affairs website, http://banking.senate.gov/public/_files/070110_Dodd_Frank_Wall_Street_Reform_comprehensive_summary_Final.pdf.

15. The World's Biggest Mattress, NPR website, http://www.npr.org/blogs/money/2008/12/worlds_biggest_mattress.html; Treasury Bill Rates Go Negative; Loaning Money at a Guaranteed Loss by Mike Masnick, Techdirt.com website, http://www.techdirt.com/articles/20081210/0329553074.shtml, Zero Return on a T-Bill? Give US a Break by Dan Burrows, SmartMoney.com website, http://www.smartmoney.com/investing/bonds/zero-return-on-a-t-bill-give-us-a-break/; T-Bill rates Can Be Negative, by Karl Smith, http://modeledbehavior.blogspot.com/2008/03/t-bill-rates-can-be-negative.html.

16. Getting Tough with Customers by Matthew Boyle and Olga Kharif, *Business Week* March 9, 2009 p. 30.

17. "Automakers Court Risk with Lean Parts Inventories," by Susan Aluise, Investorplace website, http://www.investorplace.com/33232/automakers-court-risk-with-lean-parts-inventories/.

18. "Hyman Minsky: Why Is the Economist Suddenly Popular?" by Simon Wilson, The Daily Reckoning website, http://www.dailyreckoning.co.uk/economic-forecasts/hyman-minsky-why-is-the-economist-suddenly-popular.html; "The Minsky Moment," by John Cassidy, *New Yorker* website, http://www.newyorker.com/talk/comment/2008/02/04/080204taco_talk_cassidy; "Minsky's Moment," *The Economist* website, April 2, 2009, http://www.economist.com/node/13415233; The Cost of Capitalism, by Robert Barbera, McGraw-Hill, 2009, pp. 26–27.

19. "Financial Managers," Occupational Outlook Handbook, 2010–2011, BLS website, http://www.bls.gov/oco/ocos010.htm#earnings.

20. "Financial Managers," Occupational Outlook Handbook, 2010–2011, BLS website, http://www.bls.gov/oco/ocos010.htm#earnings.

Pg. 134 Fact: "Capitalism for the Long Term," by Dominick Barton, *Harvard Business Review*, March, 2011, p. 89.

Pg. 144 Fact: Financial Crisis Inquiry Commission, *Financial Crisis Inquiry Report*, (Official Government Edition, 2011), p.90.

Pg. 145 Fact: David Skeel, *The New Financial Deal* (John Wiley & Sons, 2010), p. 4.

10

1. "Flow of Funds Accounts of the United States," Table L.109, Federal Reserve Statistical Release, accessed via Federal Reserve website, http://www.federalreserve.gov/releases/z1/Current/z1.pdf.

2. National Credit Union Administration website, http://www.ncua.gov/Resources/ConsumerInformation/aboutJoiningCUs.aspx.

3. "Flow of Funds Accounts of the United States," Table L.115, Federal Reserve Statistical Release, accessed via Federal Reserve website, http://www.federalreserve.gov/releases/z1/Current/z1.pdf.

4. "Flow of Funds Accounts of the United States," Tables L.114, Federal Reserve Statistical Release, accessed via Federal Reserve website, http://www.federalreserve.gov/releases/z1/Current/z1.pdf.

5. See, for example, "Chart 1.1: Numbers and Assets," Office of Thrift Supervision 2009 Fact Book, accessed via Office of Thrift Supervision website, http://www.ots.treas.gov/_files/481165.pdf.

6. "Growth in Hedge Fund Fraud," Securities and Exchange Commission website, http://www.sec.gov/rules/final/ia-2333.htm#IB; "A Brief History of Hedge Fund Adviser Registration and Its Consequences for Private Equity and Venture Capital Advisers," by William J. Sjostrom, Harvard Business Law Review website, http://www.hblr.org/2011/02/a-brief-history-of-hedge-fund-adviser-registration-and-its-consequences-for-private-equity-and-venture-capital-advisers/; The Running of the Hedgehogs by Duff McDonald, *New York Magazine* website, http://nymag.com/news/features/2007/hedgefunds/30341/; "Galleon Wiretaps Rattle Hedge Funds as Insider Trading Targeted," by Katherine Burton and David Glovin, Bloomberg website, http://www.bloomberg.com/apps/news?pid=newsarchive&sid=as8seXJpbDUY; "Some Lessons from the Rescue of Long-Term Capital Management," by Joseph G. Haubrich, Federal Reserve Bank of Cleveland website, http://www.clevelandfed.org/research/POLICYDIS/pdp19.pdf.

7. "The Cost of the Savings and Loan Crisis," by Timothy Curry and Lynn Shibut, FDIC Review December, 2000, accessed on FDIC website, http://www.fdic.gov/bank/analytical/banking/2000dec/brv13n2_2.pdf.

8. Public Company Accounting Oversight Board website, http://pcaobus.org/Pages/default.aspx.

9. "Brief Summary of the Dodd-Frank Wall Street Reform and Consumer Protection Act," United States Senate Committee on Banking, Housing and Urban Affairs website, http://banking.senate.gov/public/_files/070110_Dodd_Frank_Wall_Street_Reform_comprehensive_summary_Final.pdf.

10. "Brief Summary of the Dodd-Frank Wall Street Reform and Consumer Protection Act," United States Senate Committee on Banking, Housing and Urban Affairs website, http://banking.senate.gov/public/_files/070110_Dodd_Frank_Wall_Street_Reform_comprehensive_summary_Final.pdf.

11. Some preferred stock contains a "participating" feature on its dividend. This means that if the dividend paid to common stockholders exceeds some specified amount, the board must also raise the dividend to preferred stockholders. See "Participating Preferred Stock," Investopedia website, http://www.investopedia.com/terms/p/participatingpreferredstock.asp.

12. "Are Bond Buyers This Crazy?" by Dan Caplinger, Motley Fool website, http://www.fool.com/investing/dividends-income/2010/08/26/are-bond-buyers-this-crazy.aspx.

13. The Coming Bond Default Wave, by Richard Lehmann, *Forbes* Magazine website, http://www.forbes.com/forbes/2008/1013/130.html.

14. Defaults Stacking Up in the Junk Bond Market by Tom Petruno, *Los Angeles Times* website, http://latimesblogs.latimes.com/money_co/2009/01/junk-bonds-the.html January 26, 2009; There's Plenty of Juice in Junk Bonds by Mina Kimes, *Fortune* magazine, March 2, 2009, p. 40; Junk Bond Yields Are Crazy High, But Tread Carefully by John Waggoner, *USA Today*, December 5, 2008, Money Section, p. 3b.

15. Finding the Right Green Fund by Eugenia Levenson, *Fortune* magazine website, November 6, 2008, http://money.cnn.com/2008/11/05/magazines/fortune/levenson_greenfunds.fortune/index.htm; Green Investments for Launderers by Will Ashworth, Investopedia website, April 7, 2008, http://community.investopedia.com/news/IA/2008/Green_Investments_For_Launderers.aspx?partner=YahooSA; Winslow Green Growth Fund Performance, Winslow Management Company website, http://www.winslowgreen.com/fund/performance.aspx, accessed April 25, 2011; Portfolio 21 Performance, Portfolio 21 Investments website, http://www.portfolio21.com/in_depth_perf.php, accessed April 25, 2011; New Alternatives Fund Annual Report, December 31, 2010, http://www.newalternativesfund.com/returns/NAF-AR-2009.pdf, accessed April 25, 2011.

16. What Is a Stock Symbol and How Do I Find the Symbol for a Company?, BusinessKnowledgeSource.com website, http://businessknowledgesource.com/investing/what_is_a_stock_symbol_and_how_do_i_find_the_symbol_for_a_company_021903.html, accessed August 29, 2008; Stock Symbol Identifiers, StockMaven.com website, http://www.stockmaven.com/symbols.htm, accessed August 29, 2008; Stock Tickers and Ticker Symbols, Money-zine.com website, http://www.money-zine.com/Investing/Stocks/Stock-Tickers-and-Ticker-Symbols/, accessed August 9, 2009.

17. "Short and Distort Stock Scams," Fraud Guides website, http://www.fraudguides.com/investment-short-and-distort-scams.asp; "What Is Naked Short Selling?" by Annalyn Censky, CNNMoney.com website, http://money.cnn.com/2010/05/19/news/economy/naked_short_selling_wtf/; "The Truth About Naked Shorts" by

Alex Dumortier, Motley Fool website, http://www.fool.com/investing/dividends-income/2008/09/22/the-truth-about-naked-shorts.aspx; "The Short and Distort: Stock Manipulation in a Bear Market," by Rick Wayman, Investopedia website, http://www.investopedia.com/articles/analyst/030102.asp.

18. All information about the nature of work, educational and licensing requirements, earnings and projected growth in employment in this section are based on the Occupational Outlook Handbook, 2010-2011 edition, accessed from the Bureau of Labor Statistics website, http://www.bls.gov/oco/.

Pg. 155 Fact: "Dow Chemical Hikes Quarterly Dividend," Bloomberg Business Week website, http://www.businessweek.com/ap/financialnews/D9MJN2JG0.htm.

Pg. 159 Fact: Investment Company Institute Factbook, the Investment Company Institute website, http://www.icifactbook.org/fb_ch1.html, accessed April 25, 2011.

Pg. 160 Fact: Source: Information provided on p. 1 of Form S1, Securities and Exchange Commission website, http://www.sec.gov/about/forms/forms-1.pdf accessed April 16, 2011.

11

1. Army to Use Webcasts From Iraq for Recruiting, by Stuart Elliott, November 10, 2008, New York Times website, http://www.nytimes.com/2008/11/11/business/media/11adco.html, accessed February 22, 2009; Army Strong! Army Smash! October 11, 2006, Armchair Generalist website, http://armchairgeneralist.typepad.com/my_weblog/2006/10/army_strong_arm.html, accessed April 19, 2011; U.S. Army Searches New Agency, Defines Hispanic Market as Key Target, August 12, 2010, Portada website, http://www.portada-online.com/article.aspx?aid=6604, accessed April 19, 2010.

2. What marketers can learn from Obama's campaign, by Al Ries, November 5, 2008, Advertising Age website, http://adage.com/moy2008/article?article_id=131810, accessed February 22, 2009.

3. Vegas turns to reality show amid recession by Natalie Zmuda, January 2009, Advertising Age website, http://adage.com/abstract.php?article_id=134193, accessed February 22, 2009.

4. American Customer Satisfaction Index Quarterly Scores, Q1—Q4 2008, ASCI website, http://www.theacsi.org/index.php?option=com_content&task=view&id=13&Itemid=31, accessed February 24, 2009.

5. Eight reasons to keep your customers loyal by Rama Ramaswami, January 12, 2005, Mulitchannel Merchant website, http://multichannelmerchant.com/opsandfulfillment/advisor/Brandi-custloyal, accessed February 24, 2009.

6. The psychology of color in marketing by June Campbell, accessed March 19, 2005, UCSI website, http://www.ucsi.cc/webdesign/color-marketing.html; Color psychology in marketing by Al Martinovic, June 21, 2004, ImHosted website, http://developers.evrsoft.com/article/web-design/graphics-multimedia-design/color-psychology-in-marketing.shtml; Colors that sell by Suzanne Roman, November 29, 2004, ImHosted website, http://developers.evrsoft.com/article/web-design/graphics-multimedia-design/colors-that-sell

.shtml; Reinvent Wheel? Blue Room. Defusing a Bomb? Red Room by Pam Belluck, February 6, 2009, New York Times website, http://www.nytimes.com/2009/02/06/science/06color.html, accessed February 26, 2009.

7. Shoe makers gunning for Olympian feat by Andria Cheng, May 9, 2008, Market Watch website, http://www.marketwatch.com/news/story/story.aspx?guid={781CC2E2-2B3F-4FF5-A0C5-0FB962D7E204}, accessed February 24, 2009; Nike Climbs to Record as Orders Surge, Profit Rises by Matt Townsend and Robert Fenne, September 24, 2010, Bloomberg website, http://www.businessweek.com/news/2010-09-24/nike-climbs-to-record-as-orders-surge-profit-rises.html, accessed April 12, 2011.

8. It's true: Food packages shrunk last year by Chris Serres, December 31, 2008, Chicago Sun-Times website, http://www.suntimes.com/news/nation/1356955,w-food-packages-shrinking-general-mills123108.article, accessed February 26, 2008; That Shrinking Feeling by Karen Springen, August 29, 2008, Newsweek website, http://www.newsweek.com/id/156172, accessed February 26, 2009; Shoppers beware: Products shrink but prices stay the same by Bruce Horovitz, June 13, 2008, http://www.usatoday.com/money/industries/food/2008-06-11-shrinking-sizes_N.htm, accessed February 26, 2009; As Food Prices Rise, Packages Get Smaller by Douglas McIntyre, The Street website, http://www.thestreet.com/story/11076912/1/as-food-prices-rise-packages-get-smaller.html, posted April 11, 2011, accessed April 12, 2011.

9. Facebook: Friend, Foe, or Frenemy? May 27, 2010, Newsweek website, http://www.newsweek.com/blogs/techtonic-shifts/2010/05/26/facebook-friend-foe-or-frenemy-.html, accessed April 11, 2010.

10. Hershey stops making mints in coke-like packs, January 24, 2008, MSNBC website, http://www.msnbc.msn.com/id/22827806/, accessed February 26, 2009; Tropicana discovers some buyers are passionate about packaging by Stuart Elliott, February 23, 2009, The New York Times website, accessed February 26, 2009; "Misrepresentation of our nation's ethnic diversity drives us all mad" by Ruth Mortimer, December 10, 2009, MarketingWeek website, http://www.marketingweek.co.uk/misrepresentation-of-our-nations-ethnic-diversity-drives-us-all-mad/3007381.article, accessed June 6, 2010.

11. "Green brands, global insight: Findings from the 2009 ImagePower Green Brands Survey" Landor Staff, September 2009, Landor website, http://www.landor.com/index.cfm?do=thinking.article&storyid=749&bhcp=1, accessed June 7, 2010. Survey Identifies Varied Green Beliefs and Behaviors Among Global Consumers, Landor Press Release, June 8, 2010, Landor Associates website, http://www.landor.com/?do=news.pressrelease&storyid=798, accessed April 14, 2011.

12. Environment a fair-weather priority for consumers, June 3, 2008, Penn, Schoen & Bergland Press Release, Penn, Schoen & Bergland website, http://www.psbresearch.com/press_release_Jun3-2008.htm, accessed February 24, 2009; Green Fashion: Is It More Than Marketing Hype? by Gloria Sin, May 28, 2008, Fast Company website, http://www.fastcompany.com/articles/2008/05/green-fashion-hype.html, accessed February 24, 2009; "Green" Fashion, Formerly Hippie, Now Hip! February 21, 2008, CBS News website,

http://www.cbsnews.com/stories/2008/02/21/earlyshow/living/beauty/main3855868.shtml, accessed February 24, 2009.

13. Smart job picks for 2010 by Michelle Goodman, February 17, 2010, PayScale website, http://blogs.payscale.com/content/2010/02/projected-job-growth-2010.html, accessed April 14, 2011; Best Undergrad College Degrees by Salary, 2010–10 College Salary Report, PayScale Website, http://www.payscale.com/best-colleges/degrees.asp, accessed April 14, 2011.

Pg. 183 Fact: Sustainable Consumption Facts and Trends from a Business Perspective, World Business Council for Sustainable Development Website, December 2008, http://www.wbcsd.org/DocRoot/I9Xwhv7X5V8cDIHbHC3G/WBCSD_Sustainable_Consumption_web.pdf, accessed April 22, 2011.

12

1. Characteristics of a Great Name, The Brand Name Awards by Brighter Naming, http://www.brandnameawards.com/top10factors.html, accessed April 10, 2005.

2. Brand Extensions: Marketing in Inner Space, by Adam Bass, Brand Channel website, http://www.brandchannel.com/papers_review.asp?sp_id=296 accessed March 25, 2007; Brand Extensions We Could Do Without, by Reena Jana, August 7, 2006, Business Week website, http://www.businessweek.com/magazine/content/06_32/b3996420.htm.

3. "Private Label Growing Rapidly" by Alex Palmer, September 22, 2009, BrandWeek website, http://www.brandweek.com/bw/content_display/news-and-features/packaged-goods/e3i7c69fb437bbee15e35345c87bdf679fe, accessed June 14, 2010; Ten Private Label Trends that Shook North America, PlanetRetail website, http://www1.planetretail.net/_data/assets/pdf_file/0016/43063/10-PL-Trends-That-Shook-North-America-Final.pdf, accessed May 2, 2011; IRI: Fewer Shoppers Buying Private Label Versus Last Year, Store Brands Decisions website, http://www.storebrandsdecisions.com/news/2011/04/05/iri-fewer-shoppers-buying-private-label-versus-last-year, posted April 5, 2011, accessed May 2, 2011.

4. "The USA Apparel Market Research Report," June 2010, Fashion, http://www.infomat.com/fido/getpublication.fcn?&type=research&SearchString=apparel&id=737870ST0000927&start=1&tr=17 Infomat, accessed June 14, 2010.

5. The Years 1980, Histomobile website, http://www.histomobile.com/histomob/internet/87/histo02.htm, accessed April 16, 2005; Yugo Redux by Doug Donovan, April 23, 2002, Forbes website, http://www.forbes.com/2002/04/23/0423yugo.html; Worst Cars of the Millennium, CarTalk website, http://www.cartalk.com/content/features/Worst-Cars/results5.html; First Chinese Cars to Hit US Shores by Bill Vlasic, The Detroit News website, January 2, 2005, http://www.detnews.com/2005/autosinsider/0501/02/A01-47455.htm; Yugo Art photos from http://magliery.com/Graphics/YugoArt/diner.jpg.

6. Not on the List? The Truth about Impulse Purchases, January 7, 2009, Knowledge@Wharton website, http://knowledge.wharton.upenn.edu/article.cfm?articleid=2132, accessed February 28, 2009.

7. 3M: Commitment to Sustainability, GreenBiz Leaders website, 1999.

8. "Wacky Warning Labels 2009 Winners Announced," August 16, 2009, Foundation for Fair Civil Justice website, http://www.foundationforfairciviljustice.org/news/in_depth/wacky_warning_labels_2009_winners_announced/, accessed June 14, 2010.

9. U.S. Consumer Online Behavior Survey Results 2007_Part One: Wireline Usage, International Data Corporation website, February 19, 2008, http://www.idc.com/getdoc.jsp?containerId=prUS21096308, accessed March 3, 2009; Why Video On Demand Is Still Cable's Game to Lose by Dan Frommer, September 5, 2008, The Business Insider website, http://www.businessinsider.com/2008/9/why-video-on-demand-is-still-cable-s-game-to-lose, accessed March 3, 2009; Streaming vids boost Netflix profits, by Glenn Abel, January 29, 2009, Download Movies 101 website, http://downloadmovies101.com/wordpress-1/2009/01/29/streaming-vids-boost-netflix-profits/, accessed March 3, 2009; Casting the Big Movie Download Roles, September 7, 2007, eMarketer website, http://www.emarketer.com/Article.aspx?id=1005346, accessed March 3, 2009 Time Watching TV Still Tops Internet posted by Clark Fredricksen, December 15, 2010, eMarketer Blog, http://www.emarketer.com/blog/index.php/time-spent-watching-tv-tops-internet/, accessed May 4, 2011; Average time spent online per U.S. visitor in 2010, posted January 11, 2011, ComScore Data Mine website, http://www.comscoredatamine.com/2011/01/average-time-spent-online-per-u-s-visitor-in-2010/, accessed May 4, 2011. .

10. Permission Marketing by William C. Taylor, December 18, 2007, *Fast Company* website, http://www.fastcompany.com/magazine/14/permission.html, accessed March 3, 2009.

11. 'Two nobodies from nowhere' craft winning Super Bowl ad by Bruce Horovitz, February 4, 2009, *USA Today* website, http://www.usatoday.com/money/advertising/admeter/2009admeter.htm, accessed March 4, 2009.

12. Professor Paul Herbig, Tristate University, International Marketing Lecture Series, Session 6, International Advertising, http://www.tristate.edu/faculty/herbig/pahimadvstg.htm, accessed June 1, 2005; Taking Global Brands to Japan by Karl Moore and Mark Smith, The Conference Board website, http://www.conference-board.org/worldwide/worldwide_article.cfm?id=243&pg=1, accessed June 1, 2005.

13. Search Marketing Trends: Back to Basics, eMarketer website, February 2009, http://www.emarketer.com/Report.aspx?code=emarketer_2000559, accessed June 18, 2010; eMarketer: Display ad growth catching up with search, posted by Leah McBride Mensching on December 16, 2010, sfnblog, http://www.sfnblog.com/advertising/2010/12/emarketer_display_ad_growth_catching_up.php, accessed May 11, 2011.

14. eMarketer: Search Is Vital in a Recession by *Adweek* staff, February 25, 2009, *Brandweek* website, http://www.brandweek.com/bw/content_display/news-and-features/digital/e3i195c363ab252f976a2dabde4d8ef2549, accessed March 3, 2009.

15. U.S. Online Advertising Video Spending 2007–2013, August 2008, eMarketer website, http://www.marketingcharts.com/television/emarketer-revises-online-video-ad-spend-projections-downward-5679/emarketer-online-video-ad-spend-us-2007-2013jpg/, accessed June 18, 2010; Promises, promises: Will online video ads deliver this year? posted by David Hallerman, December 9, 2010, The eMarketer Blog, http://www.emarketer.com/blog/index.php/promises-promises-online-video-ads-deliver-year/, accessed May 11, 2011.

16. Social media claims more of our attention. But email's not dead yet, posted August 2, 2010 by Meghan Keane, eConsultancy website, http://econsultancy.com/us/blog/6366-social-media-might-claim-a-lot-of-our-attention-but-email-s-not-dead-yet, accessed May 11, 2011; "Social Media ROI Examples & Video," by Erik Qualman, posted November 12, 2009, Socialnomics, Social Media Blog, http://socialnomics.net/2009/11/12/social-media-roi-examples-video/, accessed June 28, 2010.

17. Brandchannel's 2004 Product Placement Awards by Abram Sauer, February 21, 2005, http://www.brandchannel.com/start1.asp?fa_id=251; A Product Placement Hall of Fame by Dale Buss, *Business Week* Online, June 22, 1998, http://www.businessweek.com/1998/25/b3583062.htm.

18. Apple tops 2010 film product placement awards, by Eric Slivka, February 22, 2011, MacRumors website, http://www.macrumors.com/2011/02/22/apple-tops-2010-film-product-placement-awards/, accessed May 11, 2011.

19. PQ Media Market Analysis Finds Global Product Placement Spending Grew 37% in 2006; Forecast to Grow 30% in 2007, Driven by Relaxed European Rules, Emerging Asian Markets; Double-Digit Growth in U.S. Decelerates, PQ Media website, March 14, 2007, http://www.pqmedia.com/about-press-20070314-gppf.html, accessed September 4, 2008; DVR Households Swelling Ranks by Jose Fermoso, December 16, 2008, Portfolio website, http://www.portfolio.com/views/blogs/the-tech-observer/2008/12/16/dvr-households-swelling-ranks, accessed March 4, 2009; FCC opens inquiry into stealthy TV product placement, June 26, 2008, *USA Today* website, http://www.usatoday.com/life/television/2008-06-26-fcc-advertising_N.htm, accessed March 4, 2009; "DVRs now in 30.6% of U.S. Households," by Bill Gorman, April 30, 2009, TV by the Numbers website, http://tvbythenumbers.com/2009/04/30/dvrs-now-in-306-of-us-households/17779, accessed June 16, 2010; Product Placement Dipped Last Year for the First Time by Andrew Hampp, June 29, 2010, AdAge website, http://adage.com/article/madisonvine-news/product-placement-dipped-year-time/144720/, accessed May 11, 2011; DVR Penetration grows to 39.7% of households, 42.2% of viewers by Robert Seidman, March 23, 2011, TV by the numbers website, http://tvbythenumbers.zap2it.com/2011/03/23/dvr-penetration-grows-to-39-7-of-households-42-2-of-viewers/86819/, accessed May 11, 2011.

20. The F-Factor Trendwatching May 2011, http://trendwatching.com/briefing/, accessed May 16, 2011.

21. Ford, Coke & AT&T Pay More to Sponsor American Idol by Susan Gunelius, January 18, 2008, Bizzia website, http://www.bizzia.com/brandcurve/ford-coke-att-pay-more-to-sponsor-american-idol/, accessed March 4, 2009; "Global Paid Product Placement to Reach $7.6 billion by 2010: Report," by Amy Johannes, August 17, 2006, PromoMagazine website, http://promomagazine.com/research/paidplacementreport/, accessed June 16, 2010.

22. All Time High: 72% of U.S. Population Plays Video Games, by Matt Peckham, April 3, 2008, *PC World* website, http://blogs.pcworld.com/gameon/archives/006748.html, accessed March 5, 2009; Video Game Advertising report, eMarketer website, http://www.emarketer.com/Report.aspx?code=emarketer_2000485, accessed March 5, 2009.

23. Massive Summary Research—Significant Findings, Massive website, http://www.massiveincorporated.com/casestudiesa.html, accessed March 4, 2009; Google to Buy Adscape by Nick Gonzalez, TechCrunch website, February 16, 2007, http://www.techcrunch.com/2007/02/16/google-to-buy-adscape-for-23-million/, accessed March 5, 2009; IN-game advertising is a massive market, May 15, 2011, The Telegraph website, http://www.telegraph.co.uk/technology/news/5312188/In-game-advertising-is-a-massive-market.html, accessed May 16, 2011.

24. Kid Nabbing, by Melanie Wells, February 2, 2004, *Forbes* website, http://www.forbes.com/free_forbes/2004/0202/084.html; Tremor website, http://tremor.com/index.html, accessed March 5, 2009; General Mills, Kraft Launch Word of Mouth Networks by Elaine Wong, October 5, 2008, *BrandWeek* website, http://www.brandweek.com/bw/content_display/news-and-features/packaged-goods/e3i2db03fb-29d573ec52722456845f5c274, accessed March 5, 2009.

25. Sponsorship Spending To Rise 2.2 Percent in 2009, IEG Press Release, February 11, 2009, Sponsorship.Com website, http://www.sponsorship.com/About-IEG/Press-Room/Sponsorship-Spending-To-Rise-2.2-Percent-in-2009.aspx, accessed March 5, 2009; "Sponsorship Spending To Rise 2.2 Percent in 2009," August 28, 2009, Sommerville Baddley Marketing website, http://www.sbmktg.net/2009/08/sponsorship-spending-to-rise-22-percent-in-2009/ (accessed June 16, 2010); Sponsorship Spending: 2010 Proves Better Than Expected; Bigger Gains Set For 2011, IEG Press Release, January 12, 2011, http://www.prweb.com/releases/2011/01/prweb4958744.htm, accessed May 15, 2011.

26. Publicity from Thin Air (Don't Just Wait for News to Happen), by Bill Stoller, Article Point website, http://www.articlepoint.com/articles/public-relations/publicity-from-thin-air.php, accessed June 15, 2005.

27. The Employment Situation – April 2011, Bureau of Labor Statistics News Release, May 6, 2011, Bureau of Labor Statistics website, http://www.bls.gov/news.release/pdf/empsit.pdf, accessed May 16, 2011.

28. "Grilled Chicken a Kentucky Fried Fiasco" by Emily Bryson York, May 11, 2009, *Advertising Age* website, http://adage.com/article?article_id=136551, accessed June 28, 2010.

Pg. 203 Fact: De-Cluttering your Mailbox by Jeremy Caplan, December 4, 2008, *Time* magazine website, http://www.time.com/time/magazine/article/0,9171,1864428,00.html, accessed May 31, 2011.

13

1. "Supermarket Facts, Industry Overview 2008," Food Marketing Institute website, http://www.fmi.org/facts_figs/?fuseaction=superfact, accessed June 30, 2010.
2. Local Food Statistics, Colorado Local Sustainability website, http://www.localsustainability.net/educate/local-food-statistics/, accessed June 3, 2011; Farmers Markets and Local Food Marketing, USDA website, http://www.ams.usda.gov/AMSv1.0/FARMERSMARKETS, accessed June 3, 2011.
3. Report: Online retail could reach $156B in 2009 by Rachel Metz, January 29, 2009, The Industry Standard website, http://www.thestandard.com/news/2009/01/29/report-online-retail-could-reach-156b-2009, accessed March 13, 2009; eMarketer revises e-commerce forecast by Jeffrey Grau, March 5, 2009, eMarketer website, http://www.emarketer.com/Article.aspx?id=1006948, http://www.emarketer.com/Article.aspx?id=1006948; Inside the Secret World of Trader Joes by Beth Kowitt, August 23, 2010, Fortune website, http://money.cnn.com/2010/08/20/news/companies/inside_trader_joes_full_version.fortune/index.htm, accessed May 30, 2011; Healthy Growth for Ecommerce as Retail Continues Shift to Web, eMarketer Blog, March 17, 2011, http://www.emarketer.com/Article.aspx?R=1008284, accessed May 30, 2011.
4. Fireclick Index, Top Line Growth, Fireclick website, http://index.fireclick.com/fireindex.php?segment=0, accessed March 13, 2009; L.L. Bean Once Again Number One in Customer Service, According to NRF Foundation/American Express Survey, January 13, 2009, National Retail Federation website, http://www.nrf.com/modules.php?name=News&op=viewlive&sp_id=653, accessed May 30, 2011.
5. Sales soften at Costco, March 4, 2009, Retail Analysis IGD website, http://www.igd.com/analysis/channel/news_hub.asp?channelid=1&channelitemid=9&nidp=&nid=5616, accessed March 13, 2009.
6. Loss Leader Strategy, Investopedia website (a Forbes Digital Company), http://www.investopedia.com/terms/l/lossleader.asp, accessed March 14, 2009; Walmart not crying over spilt milk by Al Norman, August 22, 2008, The Huffington Post website, http://www.huffingtonpost.com/al-norman/wal-mart-not-crying-over_b_120684.html, accessed March 14, 2009.
7. "No left turns is actually right on" by Peter DeMarco, April 24, 2008, The Boston Globe website, http://www.boston.com/news/local/articles/2008/04/24/no_left_turns_is_actually_right_on/, accessed June 30, 2010.
8. How Costco Became the Anti Walmart by Steven Greenhouse, July 17, 2005, New York Times website, http://www.nytimes.com/2005/07/17/business/yourmoney/17costco.html?adxnnl=1&pagewanted=1&adxnnlx=1122004143-8Vfn2DFl1MJfernM1navLA; Why Costco is so addictive by Matthew Boyle, October 25, 2006, CNNMoney website, http://money.cnn.com/magazines/fortune/fortune_archive/2006/10/30/8391725/index.htm, accessed March 14, 2009.
9. Spotify cozies up to iPod, takes aim at iTunes by Don Reisinger, May 4, 2011, cNet News

Website, http://news.cnet.com/8301-13506_3-20059630-17.html, accessed June 1, 2011.
10. Why we fall for this by David Kestenbaum, AARP Magazine, May/June 2011 issue, http://www.aarp.org/money/scams-fraud/info-04-2011/marketing-mind-tricks.html, accessed May 29, 2011; "Why the Price Is Rarely Right," by Peter Coy, January 10, 2010, BusinessWeek website, http://www.businessweek.com/magazine/content/10_05/b4165077443953.htm, accessed July 1, 2010.
11. Logistics Management 27th Annual Salary Survey: Ready to Move Up, by Patrick Burnson, Executive Editor of Logistics Management, April 07, 2011, Logistics Management, website, http://www.logisticsmgmt.com/article/27th_annual_salary_survey_ready_to_move_up, accessed June 2, 2011.

14

1. The Importance of Being Richard Branson, Leadership and Change, Knowledge@Wharton, January 12, 2005, http://knowledge.wharton.upenn.edu/article/1109.cfm; Ambition: Why Some People are Most Likely to Succeed, by Jeffrey Kluger, Time magazine, November 14, 2005, p. 48–59, http://www.time.com/time/archive/preview/0,10987,1126746,00.html.
2. The Importance of Being Richard Branson, Leadership and Change, Knowledge@Wharton, January 12, 2005, http://knowledge.wharton.upenn.edu/article/1109.cfm.
3. Hot Topic, Inc. Reports Fourth Quarter EPS Increases 19% to $0.32 Per Diluted Share; Provides Guidance for the 1st Quarter of 2009, March 11, 2009, News Blaze website, http://newsblaze.com/story/2009031112554500001.pz/topstory.html, accessed March 25, 2009.
4. Motivate Your Staff, by Larry Page, How to Succeed in 2005, Business 2.0 magazine, December 1, 2004, http://money.cnn.com/magazines/business2/business2_archive/2004/12/01/8192529/index.htm.
5. A New Game at the Office: Many Young Workers Accept Fewer Guarantees by Steve Lohr, The New York Times, December 5, 2005, http://select.nytimes.com/gst/abstract.html?res=F00F12FE38550C768CDDAB0994DD404482.
6. "100 Best Companies to Work for 2011," Fortune website, http://money.cnn.com/magazines/fortune/bestcompanies/2011/index.html, accessed June 29, 2011.
7. The 100 Best Companies to Work For 2006, Fortune magazine, January 23, 2006, pp. 71–74; Why the Economy Is a Lot Stronger Than You Think by Michael Mandel, BusinessWeek Online, February 13, 2006, http://www.businessweek.com/magazine/content/06_07/b3971001.htm.
8. Don't Get Hammered by Management Fads by Darrell Rigby, The Wall Street Journal, May 21, 2001.
9. A Generation of Slackers? Not So Much by Catherine Rampell, May 28, 2811, New York Times website, http://www.nytimes.com/2011/05/29/weekinreview/29graduates.html, accessed June 29, 2011.
10. Managing Generation Y—Part 1, Book Excerpt by Bruce Tulgan and Carolyn A. Martin, BusinessWeek online, September 28, 2001, http://www.businessweek.com/smallbiz/content/sep2001/sb20010928_113.htm; Managing

Generation Y—Part 2, Book Excerpt by Bruce Tulgan and Carolyn A. Martin, BusinessWeek online, October 4, 2001, http://www.businessweek.com/smallbiz/content/oct2001/sb2001105_229.htm; Generation Y: They've Arrived at Work with a New Attitude by Stephanie Armour, USA Today, November 6, 2005, http://www.usatoday.com/money/workplace/2005-11-06-gen-y_x.htm; The Facebook Generation vs. the Fortune 500 by Gary Hamel, March 24, 2009, The Wall Street Journal Blogs website, http://blogs.wsj.com/management/2009/03/24/the-facebook-generation-vs-the-fortune-500/, accessed March 30, 2009; What Gen Y Really Wants by Penelope Trunk, July 5, 2007, Time magazine website, http://www.time.com/time/magazine/article/0,9171,1640395,00.html, accessed March 30, 2009; Managing Generation Y as they change the workforce by Molly Smith, January 8, 2008, Reuters website, http://www.reuters.com/article/pressRelease/idUS129795+08-Jan-2008+BW20080108, accessed March 30, 2009.
11. The cow in the ditch: how Anne Mulcahy Rescued Xerox, Special Section: Knowledge at Wharton, November 16–29, 2005, http://knowledge.wharton.upenn.edu/index.cfm?fa=viewArticle&id=1318&specialId=41.
12. Green is Virgin Territory by Kerry Capell, August 14, 2006, Business Week website, http://www.businessweek.com/magazine/content/06_33/b3997079.htm, accessed June 29, 2011.
13. Is your boss a psychopath? by Alan Deutschman, July 2005, Fast Company, http://www.fastcompany.com/magazine/96/open_boss.html; Corporate psychopaths at large by Lisa Desai, September 3, 2004, CNN.com International, http://edition.cnn.com/2004/BUSINESS/08/26/corporate.psychopaths/; How Apple does it, by Lev Grossman, October 24, 2005, Time Inside Innovation.
Pg. 227 Fact: Ten Years From Now… The Future of Work—The Poll, August 20, 2007, BusinessWeek website, http://www.businessweek.com/magazine/content/07_34/b4047401.htm, accessed March 30, 2009.

15

1. "Gary Kelly Southwest Airlines CEO on the Business of Building Trust" by Kate McCann, October 11, 2005, McCombs School of Business website, http://www.mccombs.utexas.edu/news/pressreleases/lyceum05_kelly_wrap05.asp, accessed July 2, 2010; "Southwest Airlines Reports Fourth Quarter Profit and 37th Consecutive Year of Profitability," January 21, 2010, PRNewsWire website, http://www.prnewswire.com/news-releases/southwest-airlines-reports-fourth-quarter-profit-and-37th-consecutive-year-of-profitability-82241197.html, accessed July 2, 2010; 1106 HR Magazine: Views from the Top, November 1, 2006, SHRM website, http://www.shrm.org/Publications/hrmagazine/EditorialContent/Pages/1106ceoex.aspx, accessed July 5, 2011.
2. America's jobless recovery. Not again. June 3, 2011, Economist website, http://www.economist.com/blogs/freeexchange/2011/06/americas-jobless-recovery, accessed July 5, 2011; A New Game at the Office: Many Young Workers Accept Fewer Guarantees, by Steve Lohr, New York Times,

December 5, 2005, http://select.nytimes.com/gst/abstract.html?res=F00F12FE38550C768CDDAB0994DD404482.

3. "CEO pay vs. performance – Still a roll of the dice," (WSJ) by Dionysus on April 1, 2010, posted on Economatrix website, http://www.economatix.com/ceo-pay-vs-performance-still-a-roll-of-the-dice-wsj, accessed September 6, 2011; Figure 3AE from Lawrence Mishel, Jared Bernstein, and Heidi Shierholz, *The State of Working America 2009/2009. An Economic Policy Institute Book.* Ithaca, N.Y.: ILR Press, An Imprint of Cornell University Press, 2009, http://www.stateofworkingamerica.org/tabfig/2008/03/SWA08_Chapter3_Wages_r2_Fig-3AE.jpg. accessed July 1, 2010; We Knew They Got Raises. But This?, by Pradnya Joshi, July 2, 2011, *New York Times* website, http://www.nytimes.com/2011/07/03/business/03pay.html, accessed July 5, 2011.

4. In 2011 The Baby Boomers Start To Turn 65: 16 Statistics About The Coming Retirement Crisis That Will Drop Your Jaw, December 30, 2010, The American Dream website, http://endoftheamericandream.com/archives/in-2011-the-baby-boomers-start-to-turn-65-16-statistics-about-the-coming-retirement-crisis-that-will-drop-your-jaw, accessed July 5, 2011.

5. Facing Young Workers' High Job Expectations, from Associated Press, *Los Angeles Times*, June 27, 2005; *Not Everyone* by Bruce Tulgan *Gets a Trophy*, San Francisco: Jossey-Bass (Wiley Imprint), 2009.

6. How Corporate America Is Betraying Women, by Betsy Morris, *Fortune*, January 10, 2005; Jane Drain – women leaving your workforce, Smart Manager website, http://www.smartmanager.com.au/web/au/smartmanager/en/pages/89_jane_drain—women_leaving_workforce.html, accessed July 5, 2011.

7. Featured Employee Rap Sheet, Hot Topic website, http://www.hottopic.com/community/rapsheets/emp_jodi.asp?LS=0&, accessed April 11, 2006; A New Game at the Office: Many Young Workers Accept Fewer Guarantees by Steve Lohr, *New York Times*, December 5, 2005, http://select.nytimes.com/gst/abstract.html?res=F00F12FE38550C768CDDAB0994DD404482; Work-life benefits fall victim to slow economy, by Andrea Shim, April 4, 2009, *Los Angeles Times* website, http://www.latimes.com/business/la-fi-flexible4-2009apr04,0,4344887.story, accessed April 4, 2009; Pending Job Flexibility Act Received Mixed Reviews by Sue Shellenbarger, *WSJ Career Journal*, http://www.careerjournal.com/columnists/workfamily/20010426-workfamily.html, accessed August 9, 2005; Work-life benefits fall victim to slow economy by Andrea Shim, April 4, 2009, *Los Angeles Times* website, http://www.latimes.com/business/la-fi-flexible4-2009apr04,0,4344887.story, accessed April 4, 2009.

8. Why We Hate HR by Keith W. Hammonds, December 19, 2007, *Fast Company* website, http://www.fastcompany.com/magazine/97/open_hr.html?page=0%2C1, accessed April 4, 2009.

9. Table 1. The 30 fastest growing occupations covered in the 2008–2009 *Occupational Outlook Handbook*, Economic News Release, December 18, 2007, Bureau of Labor Statistics website, http://www.bls.gov/news.release/ooh.t01.htm, accessed April 7, 2009; Census Bureau Data Underscore Value of College Degree, U.S. Census Bureau News, October 26, 2006, Census Bureau website, http://www.census.gov/Press-Release/www/

releases/archives/education/007660.html, accessed April 7, 2009; Increasing Share of Adults Have College Degrees, Census Bureau Finds by Derek Quizon, April 26, 2011, *The Chronicle of Higher Education* website, http://chronicle.com/article/Increasing-Share-of-Adults/127264/, accessed July 5, 2011.

10. SHRM Human Capital Benchmarking Study, 2008 Executive Summary, page 14, SHRM website, http://www.shrm.org/Research/Documents/2008%20Executive%20Summary_FINAL.pdf, accessed April 7, 2009; Effective Recruiting Tied to Stronger Financial Performance, Watson Wyatt Worldwide news release, August 16, 2005, Watson Wyatt Worldwide website, http://www.watsonwyatt.com/news/press.asp?ID=14959, accessed April 7, 2009.

11. Top Five Resume Lies by Jeanne Sahadi, December 9, 2004, CNN Money website, http://money.cnn.com/2004/11/22/pf/resume_lies/.

12. "You're Hired. At Least for Now" by Anne Kates Smith, March 2010, Kiplinger website, http://www.kiplinger.com/magazine/archives/employers-choose-temps-contract-workers.html accessed July 13, 2010); Special Report on Contingent Staffing—The Future of Contingent Staffing Could Be Like Something Out of a Movie, by Irwin Speizer, October 19, 2009, Workforce Management website, http://www.workforce.com/section/recruiting-staffing/feature/special-report-contingent-staffingthe-future-contingent/, accessed July 5, 2011.

13. The Questions: How Not to Answer compiled by Barry Shamis of Selecting Winners, Inc., FacilitatorGuy Resume Resource Center, http://resume.bgolden.com/res/interview-bloopers.php, accessed September 1, 2005; Interview Bloopers: What Not to Do! by Maureen Bauer, Channel 3000 website, http://html.channel3000.com/sh/employment/stories/ employment—20001002-144946.html, accessed September 1, 2005; More Interview Bloopers by Maureen Bauer, Channel 3000 website, http://html.channel3000.com/sh/employment/stories/employment—20001002-152818.html.

14. Orientation: Not Just a Once-over-Lightly Anymore, by Matt DeLuca HRO Today, April/May 2005, http://www.hrotoday.com/Magazine.asp?artID=928; New Emphasis on First Impressions by Leslie Gross Klaff, March 2008, Workforce Management website, http://www.workforce.com/archive/feature/25/41/58/index.php?ht=, accessed April 7, 2009; Show and Tell—Disney Institute's Four-Day Seminar on HR Management by Leon Rubis, *HR* magazine, April 1998; New Employee Experience Aims for Excitement Beyond the First Day by Daryl Stephenson, Boeing Frontiers Online, May 2002, http://www.boeing.com/news/frontiers/archive/2002/may/i_mams.html.

15. Labor-Intensive, by Sean McFadden, *Boston Business Journal*, November 19, 2004, http://www.bizjournals.com/boston/stories/2004/11/22/smallb1.html; The Costco Way; Higher Wages Mean Higher Profits. But Try Telling Wall Street by Stanley Holmes and Wendy Zelner, *Business-Week*, April 12, 2004; Study: Moderation in Hiring Practices Boosts Business Performance by Todd Raphael, Workforce Management, August 19, 2005, http://www.workforce.com/section/00/article/24/14/03.html.

16. Appreciating Benefits as Times Gets Tough, by Carroll Lachnit, March 24, 2009, Blog: The Business of Management, Workforce Management

website, http://workforce.com/wpmu/bizmgmt/2009/03/24/benefits_in_tough_times/, accessed April 9, 2009.

17. Perking Up: Some Companies Offer Surprising New Benefits by Sue Shellenbarger, March 18, 2009, *Wall Street Journal* website, http://online.wsj.com/article/SB123733195850463165.html, accessed April 9, 2009.

18. Questions and Answers about Flexible Work Schedules: A Sloan Work and Family Research Network Fact Sheet, updated September 2008, Sloan Work and Family Research Network website, http://wfnetwork.bc.edu/pdfs/flexworksched.pdf, accessed April 9, 2009; Work-life benefits fall victim to slow economy by Andrea Shim, April 4, 2009, *Los Angeles Times* website, http://www.latimes.com/business/la-fi-flexible4-2009apr04,0,4344887.story, accessed April 4, 2009.

19. 100 Best Companies to Work for 2011, Best benefits: Unusual Perks, *Fortune* website, http://money.cnn.com/magazines/fortune/bestcompanies/2011/benefits/unusual.html, accessed July 5, 2011.

20. Home Sweet Office: Telecommute Good for Business, Employees, and Planet by Brendan I. Koerner, September 22, 2008, *Wired* website, http://www.wired.com/culture/culturereviews/magazine/16-10/st_essay, accessed April 11, 2009; Give telecommuting the green light by Ted Samson, June 2, 2007, InfoWorld website, http://www.infoworld.com/d/green-it/give-telecommuting-green-light-628, accessed April 11, 2009; Sun, employees find big savings from Open Work telecommuting program by Ted Samson, June 19, 2008, InfoWorld website, http://www.infoworld.com/d/green-it/sun-employees-find-big-savings-open-work-telecommuting-program-821, accessed April 11, 2009; "National Study Finds Electronics Significantly Reduce Energy," Press Release, September 19, 2007, Telecommute Connecticut! website, http://www.telecommutect.com/employers/pr_9_27_07.php, accessed July 2, 2010.

21. Give telecommuting the green light by Ted Samson, June 7, 2007, InfoWorld website, http://www.infoworld.com/d/green-it/give-telecommuting-green-light-628, accessed April 10, 2009; Home Sweet Office: Telecommute Good for Business, Employees, and Planet by Brendan I. Koerner, September 22, 2008, *Wired* website, http://www.wired.com/culture/culturereviews/magazine/16-10/st_essay, accessed April 10, 2009; Skype: More companies allow telecommuting by Ginger Christ, April 5, 2011, Dayton Business Journal Website, http://www.bizjournals.com/dayton/news/2011/04/05/more-companies-allow-telecommuting.html, accessed July 5, 2011; Costs and Benefits, Advantages of Telecommuting for Companies, Telework Research Network website, http://www.teleworkresearchnetwork.com/costs-benefits, accessed July 5, 2011.

22. The New Job Sharers by Michelle V. Rafter, May 2008, Workforce Management website, http://www.workforce.com/archive/feature/25/53/28/index.php, accessed April 10, 2009; Study Attempts To Dispel Five Myths of Job Sharing by Stephen Miller, May 9, 2007, Society for Human Resource Management website, http://moss07.shrm.org/Publications/HRNews/Pages/XMS_021497.aspx, accessed April 10, 2009.

23. 5.1 million jobs lost in this recession so far by Rex Nutting, April 3, 2009, MarketWatch

website, http://www.marketwatch.com/news/story/51-million-jobs-lost-recession/story.aspx?guid={CF54164C-6F7B-4501-B6FB-D7D1C8D710B9}&dist=msr_8, accessed April 10, 2009; Boost Employee Morale After Layoffs, Workforce Management website, http://www.workforce.com/archive/article/22/14/10.php, accessed April 10, 2009.

24. Sexual Harassment Charges, EEOC & FEPAs Combined: FY 1997–FY 2008, EEOC website, updated March 11, 2009, http://www.eeoc.gov/stats/harass.html, accessed April 10, 2009.

25. Sexual Harassment, updated March 11, 2009, http://www.eeoc.gov/types/sexual_harassment.html, accessed April 10, 2009.

26. 8 Wacky Jobs at Best Companies, 100 Best Companies to Work for 2011, Fortune website, http://money.cnn.com/galleries/2011/pf/jobs/1101/gallery.best_companies_craziest_jobs.fortune/index.html, accessed July 5, 2011; 8 Wacky Jobs, Fortune website, http://money.cnn.com/galleries/2011/fortune/1105/gallery.fortune500_fun_jobs.fortune/index.html, accessed July 5; Strangest jobs in the world; Odd travel industry jobs include bath sommelier, dog surf instructor by Katrina Brown Hunt and Darrin Tobias, June 13, 2011, New York Daily News website, http://www.nydailynews.com/lifestyle/2011/06/13/2011-06-13_strangest_jobs_in_the_world_odd_travel_industry_jobs_include_bath_sommelier_dog_.html, accessed July 12, 2011.

27. Human Resources, Training, and Labor Relations Managers and Specialists, Occupational Outlook Handbook, 2011, Bureau Labor Statistics website, http://www.bls.gov/oco/ocos021.htm, accessed July 5, 2011.

Pg. 253 Fact: Perking Up: Some Companies Offer Surprising New Benefits by Sue Shellenbarger, March 18, 2009, Wall Street Journal website, http://online.wsj.com/article/SB123733195850463165.html, accessed April 10, 2009.

16

1. The iPad in Your Hand: As Fast as a Supercomputer of Yore by John Markoff, New York Times website, http://bits.blogs.nytimes.com/2011/05/09/the-ipad-in-your-hand-as-fast-as-a-supercomputer-of-yore/.

2. The Web Is Dead. Long Live the Internet, by Chris Anderson, Wired website, http://www.wired.com/magazine/2010/08/ff_webrip/all/1.

3. Home Broadband 2010: Trends in Broadband Adoption by Aaron Smith, Pew Internet and American Life Project, http://www.pewinternet.org/Reports/2010/Home-Broadband-2010/Part-1/Little-change-in-home-broadband-in-2010.aspx, accessed May 16, 2011.

4. Internet2 Member and Partner List, Internet2 website, http://www.internet2.edu/resources/listforweb.pdf.

5. Muse website, http://k20.internet2.edu/about/goals.

6. About Us, Internet2 website, http://www.internet2.edu/about/, accessed May 16, 2011.

7. The Web Is Dead. Long Live the Internet by Chris Anderson, Wired website, http://www.wired.com/magazine/2010/08/ff_webrip/all/1; No, Wired, the Web Is Not "Dead" by Rob Pegoraro, Washington Post website, http://voices.washingtonpost.com/fasterforward/2010/08/

no_wired_the_web_is_not_dead.html; The App Is Dead, Long Live the Web App by Paul Anthony, Webdistortion website, http://blog.webdistortion.com/2011/03/18/the-app-is-dead-long-live-the-web-app/; HTML5 and Web Video: Freeing Rich Media from Plugin Prison by Ryan Paul, Arstechnica website, http://arstechnica.com/open-source/news/2009/05/google-dailymotion-endorse-html-5-and-standards-based-video.ars.

8. Inside Amazon's Cloud Disaster by Matt Rosoff, Business Insider website, http://www.businessinsider.com/amazon-outage-enters-its-second-day-lots-of-sites-still-down-2011-4, accessed April 30, 2011; Analysis: Sony Woes May Cause Some to Rethink Cloud Computing by Jim Finkle and Liana B. Baker, Reuters website, http://www.reuters.com/article/2011/05/06/us-sony-cloud-idUSTRE7455C020110506, accessed May 9, 2011; Amazon's Cloud Crash Disaster Permanently Destroyed Many Customers' Data by Henry Blodgett, Business Insider website, http://www.businessinsider.com/amazon-lost-data-2011-4; Google Suffers Major Failure by Sharon Gaudin, InfoWorld website, http://www.infoworld.com/d/cloud-computing/google-suffers-major-failure-454.

9. Self-service, Prorated Super Computing Fun by Derek Gottfrid, The New York Times, November 1, 2007, http://open.blogs.nytimes.com/2007/11/01/self-service-prorated-super-computing-fun/; NY Times AWS Cloud Computing Mistake Costs $240, Green Data Center Blog, November 5, 2008, http://www.greenm3.com/2008/11/nytimes-cloud-c.html; Early Experiments in Cloud Computing by Galen Gruman, InfoWorld website April 7, 2008: http://www.infoworld.com/d/virtualization/early-experiments-in-cloud-computing-020.

10. The Big Switch: Rewiring the World from Edison to Google by Nicholas Carr, W. W. Norton & Company, 2008, Kindle edition, location 1124.

11. Data Mining Ready for a Comeback by Curt Monash, ComputerWorld, September 11, 2006, http://www.computerworld.com/action/article.do?command=viewArticleBasic&articleId=112733&pageNumber=2; A New Market Research Approach in Sport-Data Mining by Chen-Yueh Chen & Yi-Hsiu Lin, The Sport Journal website, http://www.thesportjournal.org/article/new-market-research-approach-sport-data-mining, Volume 12, Number 2, 2009; National Basketball Association, The Data Warehouse Institute website, http://www.tdwi.org/research/display.aspx?ID=5419 accessed May 24, 2009.

12. Management Information Systems, 5th ed. by Effy Oz, Course Technology, Cengage Learning, 2006, pp. 332–338; "Expert Systems," AlanTuring.Net, http://www.cs.usfca.edu/www.AlanTuring.net/turing_archive/pages/Reference%20Articles/what_is_AI/What%20is%20AI07.html.

13. Experiencing MIS by David M. Kroenke Pearson Prentice Hall, 2008, pp. 340–341; What Are Expert Systems? Thinkquest.org website, http://library.thinkquest.org/11534/expert.htm, accessed May 24, 2009.

14. Web 2.0 Definition Updated and Enterprise 2.0 Emerges by Dion Hinchcliffe, ZDnet website, http://blogs.zdnet.com/Hinchcliffe/?p=71; The Ethics of Web 2.0: YouTube vs. Flickr, Revver, Eyespot, Bliptv, and Even Google, Lessig.org website, http://www.lessig.org/blog/2006/10/the_ethics_of_web_20_youtube_v.html, accessed May 24, 2009; Twitter, Blogs and Other Web 2.0 Tools Revolutionize Government Business by Doug

Beizer, Federal Computer Week website, March 6, 2009, http://www.fcw.com/Articles/2009/03/09/Web-2.0-in-action.aspx.

15. 7 Best Green Apps for Mobile Phones by Jaymi Heimbuch, PlanetGreen.com website, http://planetgreen.discovery.com/feature/green-phone/green-apps-mobile-phones.html; The Top Ten Apps to Make You More Green by Matylda Czarnecka, TechCrunch website, http://techcrunch.com/2010/08/10/top-ten-green-apps/; Green Apps that Can Save You Money by Deborah Zabarenko, Reuters website, http://blogs.reuters.com/environment/2011/02/18/green-apps-that-can-save-you-money/.

16. IAB Internet Advertising Revenue Report: 2010 Full Year Results by Pricewaterhouse Coopers, IAB website, http://www.iab.net/media/file/IAB_Full_year_2010_0413_Final.pdf, accessed May 17, 2011; A Milestone for Internet Ad Revenue by Teddy Wayne, New York Times website, April 25, 2010, http://www.nytimes.com/2010/04/26/business/media/26drill.html.

17. Paypal website, https://www.paypal-media.com/aboutus.cfm, accessed May 17, 2011.

18. Walmart to Put Radio Tags on Clothes by Miguel Bustillo, The Wall Street Journal website, http://online.wsj.com/article/SB10001424052748704421304575383213061198090.html?mod=rss_whats_news_us.

19. Crowdfunding and Peer-to-Peer Lending Help Small Business by Laura Petrecca, USA Today website, http://www.usatoday.com/money/smallbusiness/2011-05-06-creative-financing-for-small-businesses_n.htm; Crowdfunding by Kristina Dell, Time magazine website, http://www.time.com/time/magazine/article/0,9171,1838768,00.html; A Guide to Crowdfunding Success, by Brandon Mendelson, Mashable website, http://mashable.com/2009/07/29/crowdfunding-success/; It's Like eBay Meets Match.com by Ray Fisman, Slate website, http://www.slate.com/id/2221372/.

20. Spammers Target Email Newsletters by David Utter, January 19, 2007, WebProWorld Security Forum, http://www.securitypronews.com/insider-reports/insider/spn-49-20070119Spammers TargetEmailNewsletters.html; Spammers Turn to Images to Fool Filters by Anick Jesdanun, USA Today, June 28, 2006, http://www.usatoday.com/tech/news/computersecurity/wormsviruses/2006-06-28-spam-images_x.htm.

21. Pharming: Is Your Trusted Website a Clever Fake? Microsoft website January 3, 2007, http://www.microsoft.com/protect/yourself/phishing/pharming.mspx; Online Fraud: Pharming, Symantic website, http://www.symantec.com/norton/cybercrime/pharming.jsp, accessed May 24, 2009; Advisory: Watch Out for Drive-by-Pharming Attacks, Pharming.org website, http://www.pharming.org/index.jsp, accessed May 24, 2009.

22. "Smishing" Emerges as New Threat to Cell Phone Users by Mark Huffman, Consumer Affairs.com website, http://www.consumeraffairs.com/news04/2006/11/smishing.html accessed May 22, 2009; "SMiShing" Fishes for Personal Data Over Cell Phone by Eleanor Mills, CNet News website, February 24, 2009, http://news.cnet.com/8301-1009_3-10171241-83.html. .

23. Create Strong Passwords, Microsoft Safety & Security Center, Microsoft website, http://www.microsoft.com/security/online-privacy/passwords-create.aspx.

24. The Strong Password Dilemma by Richard E. Smith, PhD., http://www.cryptosmith.com/sanity/pwdilemma.html, accessed May 24, 2009.

25. Passport RFIDs Cloned Wholesale by $250 eBay Shopping Spree by Dan Goodin, *The Register* website February 2, 2009, http://www.theregister.co.uk/2009/02/02/low_cost_rfid_cloner/; Life With Big Brother: Radio Chips Coming Soon to Your Driver's License? by Bob Unruh, World Net Daily website February 28, 2009, http://www.worldnetdaily.com/index.php?fa=PAGE.view&pageId=90008; RFID Driver's Licenses Debated by Mark Baard, *Wired* website October 6, 2004, http://www.wired.com/politics/security/news/2004/10/65243.

26. Email Addles the Mind by Benjamin Pimentel, May 4, 2005, SFGate.com, http://sfgate.com/cgi-bin/article.cgi?file=/c/a/2005/05/04/BU-GOSCJGA41.DTL&type=printable; The Modern Brain, Besieged by Robert MacMillan, April 25, 2005, washingtonpost.com, http://www.washingtonpost.com/wp-dyn/content/article/2005/04/25/AR2005042500342_pf.html.; About the Information Overload Research Group, Information Research Overload Group website, http://iorgforum.org/AboutIORG.htm accessed May 24, 2009.

27. Facebook, Burson discuss role in Google Circle dispute by byron Acohido, Scott Martin and Jon Swartz, *USA Today* website, http://www.usatoday.com/tech/news/2011-05-12-google-whisper-campaign_n.htm; Oops: Facebook Caught Planting Anti-Google Stories to Press by Devindra Hardawar, VentureBeat website, http://venturebeat.com/2011/05/12/facebook-anti-google-smear/; Facebook Busted in Clumsy Smear of Google by Dan Lyons, The Daily Beast website, http://www.thedailybeast.com/blogs-and-stories/2011-05-12/facebook-busted-in-clumsy-smear-attempt-on-google/; Burson-Marsteller Statement, Burson-Marsteller website, http://www.burson-marsteller.com/Newsroom/Pages/Burson-MarstellerStatement.aspx; Burson-Marsteller Caught Deleting Facebook Criticism; Facebook Delivers Statement, by David Murphy, PC Magazine website, http://www.pcmag.com/article2/0,2817,2385394,00.asp.

28. Eighth Annual BSA Global Software 2010 Piracy Study: May 2011, Business Software Alliance website, http://portal.bsa.org/globalpiracy2010/downloads/study_pdf/2010_BSA_Piracy_Study-InBrief.pdf .

29. CESA: Portable Piracy Cost Game Industry $41.5 Billion, Gamasutra website, http://www.gamasutra.com/view/news/28848/CESA_Portable_Piracy_Cost_Game_Industry_415_Billion.php.

30. All information about the nature of work, educational requirements, earnings and projected growth in employment in this section are based on the Occupational Outlook Handbook, 2010–2011 edition, accessed from the Bureau of Labor Statistics website, http://www.bls.gov/oco/ocos287.htm and http://www.bls.gov/oco/ocos306.htm.

Pg. 259 Fact: Internet Speed Record Team Launches Startup by Ben Kuo, Socaltech website, http://www.socaltech.com/internet2_speed_record_team_launches_startup/s-0004916.html.

Pg. 264 Fact: Retailers Turn to Facebook to Sell Their Wares by Bruce Horovitz, *USA Today* website, http://www.usatoday.com/money/industries/retail/2011-05-10-retailers-turn-to-facebook_n.htm.

Pg. 265 Fact: "Vegas Casino Bets on RFID" by Alorie Gilbert, CNet website, http://news.cnet.com/Vegas-casino-bets-on-RFID/2100-7355_3-5568288.html.

17

1. "Establishment Data: Historical Employment," Bureau of Labor Statistics website, ftp://ftp.bls.gov/pub/suppl/empsit.ceseeb1.txt.

2. *OM, 2nd ed.* by David A. Collier and James R. Evans, Mson, OH: South-Western, Cengage Learning, 2010, pages 27–28.

3. Outsourcing: Ripoff Nation, BW Smallbiz Front Line, Winter 2006, *Business Week* website, http://www.businessweek.com/magazine/content/06_52/b4015435.htm?chan=rss_topStories_ssi_5; Outsourcing in China: Five Basic Rules for Reducing Risk by Steve Dickinson, ezinearticles.com website, http://ezinearticles.com/?Outsourcing-in-China:-Five-Basics-for-Reducing-Risk&id=17214.

4. ERP and Cloud Computing: Delivering a Virtual Feast by David Stodder, InformationWeek website, May 20, 2010, http://www.informationweek.com/news/software/bi/224701329, accessed Dec. 6, 2011.

5. Servicescapes: The Impact of Physical Surroundings on Customers and Employees by M. J. Bitner, *Journal of Marketing*, April 1992, pp. 57–71.

6. 3D Printing-An "Industrial Revolution in the Digital Age"? by David Rowan, *Wired Magazine* website, http://www.wired.com/epicenter/2011/05/3d-printing-an-industrial-revolution-in-the-digital-age/; Print Me a Stradivarius, The Economist, February 12th–18th, p. 11; The Next Trillion Dollar Industry: 3D Printing by Pascal-Emmanuel Gobry, *Business Insider* website, http://www.businessinsider.com/3d-printing-2011-2.

7. "Toyota Woes Follow Years of Slipping Quality" by Dan Carney, MSNBC website, http://www.msnbc.msn.com/id/35311172/ns/business-autos/; "Can Toyota Recover Its Reputation for Quality?" by Wendy Kaufman, NPR website, http://www.npr.org/templates/story/story.php?storyId=123519027; "No Big Quality Problems at Toyota?" by Robert E. Cole, *Harvard Business Review* website, http://blogs.hbr.org/cs/2010/03/no_big_quality_problems_at_toy.html; Earthquake Could Further Jolt Toyota and Other Japanese Automakers by David Kiley, AOL Autos website, http://autos.aol.com/article/earthquake-could-stop-car-production/.

8. Poka Yoke Mistake Proofing by Kerri Simon, iSixSigma website, http://www.isixsigma.com/library/content/c020128a.asp; Make No Mistake by Mark Hendricks, *Entrepreneur* Magazine, October 1996, http://www.entrepreneur.com/magazine/entrepreneur/1996/october/13430.html, accessed July 30, 2007.

9. Baldrige FAQs: Applying for the Malcolm Baldrige National Quality Award, National Institute of Standards and Technology website, http://www.nist.gov/baldrige/about/faqs_applying.cfm, accessed June 5, 2011.

10. About ISO, ISO website, http://www.iso.org/iso/about.htm, accessed June 5, 2011; ISO Standards, ISO website, http://www.iso.org/iso/iso_catalogue.htm, accessed June 5, 2011.

11. ISO9001-Quality Management Systems-Requirements, ISO website, http://www.iso.org/iso/survey2009.pdf, accessed June 5, 2011.

12. Sanford "Pens" an Improved Blister-Pack Tale by Lauren R. Hartman, *Packaging Digest*, January 2007, page 43.

13. Six Sigma Training by Charles Waxer, iSix-Sigma website, http://www.isixsigma.com/library/content/c010225a.asp, accessed September 11, 2008; What is Six Sigma?, GE website, http://www.ge.com/sixsigma/SixSigma.pdf, accessed September 11, 2008; Six Sigma Black Belt Certification, ASQ website, http://www.asq.org/certification/index.html, accessed September 11, 2008.

14. Global Sustainability Report: 2010 Progress Update. Walmart website, http://walmartstores.com/sites/sustainabilityreport/2010/environment_overview.aspx; Walmart Unveils Plan to Make Supply Chain Greener by Stephanie Rosenbloom, *New York Times* website, http://www.nytimes.com/2010/02/26/business/energy-environment/26walmart.html; Walmart's CSR Report Shows the Power, and Limits, of Efficiency by Marc Gunther, GreenBiz website, http://www.greenbiz.com/blog/2011/04/25/walmarts-csr-report-shows-power-limits-efficiency.

15. *OM, 2nd ed.* by David A.Collier and James R. Evans, Mason, OH: South-Western, Cengage Learning, 2010, pages 328–330.

16. One reason renewable energy is more expensive than energy from carbon-based sources such as coal or oil is that the market prices of such carbon-based sources do not reflect their environmental costs. .

17. Sustainability Initiatives Cut Costs 6-10%, Environmental Leader website, http://www.environmentalleader.com/2009/06/09/sustainability-initiatives-cut-costs-by-6-10/.

18. ISO 14000 Essentials, ISO website, http://www.iso.org/iso/iso_14000_essentials, accessed June 4, 2011.

19. All information in this section is based on the "Careers in Operations Management" section of the Careers-in-Business website, http://www.careers-in-business.com/om.htm.

Pg. 276 Fact: *Occupational Outlook Handbook*, 2010–2011 Edition, BLS website, http://www.bls.gov/oco/oco2003.htm#industry.

Personal Finance Appendix

1. "Learn About the Bureau," Consumer Finance Protection Bureau website, http://www.consumerfinance.gov/the-bureau/.

2. Bach, David, *The Automatic Millionaire* New York, Broadway Books, 2004.

3. Bach, David, *The Automatic Millionaire* New York, Broadway Books, 2004.

4. "FDIC Insurance Coverage Basics," FDIC website, http://www.fdic.gov/deposit/deposits/insured/basics.html; Note that, in accordance with provisions in the Dodd-Frank Act of 2010, the FDIC provided temporary, unlimited coverage to noninterest-bearing accounts. However, this would not affect coverage on savings accounts, since they do pay interest. Moreover, at the time this text went to print, the unlimited coverage was scheduled to expire on December 31, 2012. (See "Temporary Unlimited Coverage for Noninterest-bearing Transactions Accounts," FDIC website, http://www.fdic.gov/deposit/deposits/insured/temporary.html.).

5. "What's In Your FICO Score?," myFICO website, http://www.myfico.com/CreditEducation/WhatsInYourScore.aspx; 'How Credit Scores Work, How a Score Is Calculated' by Pat Curry, Bankrate.com website, http://www.bankrate.com/brm/news/credit-scoring/20031104a1.asp.

6. "How Credit Scores Work, How a Score Is Calculated" by Pat Curry, Bankrate.com website, http://www.bankrate.com/brm/news/credit-scoring/20031104a1.asp.

7. "Feds Cap Credit Card Late Fees at $25" by Susan Ladika, Creditcards.com website, http://www.creditcards.com/credit-card-news/feds-cap-credit-card-late-payment-fee-25.php.

8. "What the Dodd-Frank Law Means for You" by Leslie McFadden, Bankrate.com website, http://www.bankrate.com/financing/credit-cards/what-the-dodd-frank-act-means-for-you/.

9. "Fresh Downgrade Threat to U.S. Debt" by Carol E. Lee and Janet Hook, *Wall Street Journal* website, http://online.wsj.com/article/SB10001424052702304778304576373992711772366.html.

10. "Table 5: Quartiles and Selected deciles of Usual Weekly Earnings of Full-time Wage and Salary Workers by Selected Characteristics, 1st Quarter 2011 Averages, Not Seasonally Adjusted," BLS News Release (April 19, 2011) BLS website, http://www.bls.gov/news.release/pdf/wkyeng.pdf. .

11. "Table 7: Employment Status of the Civilian Noninstitutional Population 25 Years and Over by Educational Attainment, Sex, Race, and Hispanic or Latino ethnicity," BLS website, http://www.bls.gov/cps/cpsaat7.pdf.

12. "Direct Stock Purchase Plans: A Better Way to Invest" by J. D. Roth, Get Rich Slowly website, http://www.getrichslowly.org/blog/2009/04/07/direct-stock-purchase-plans-a-better-way-to-invest/; "Buying Stock Without a Broker" by Joshua Kennon, About.com website, http://beginnersinvest.about.com/cs/brokers1/a/042501a.htm; "Investment Plans," Computershare Investor Centre website, https://www-us.computershare.com/investor/plans/planslist.asp; "What Are Dividend Reinvestment Plans?" The Motley Fool website, http://www.fool.com/school/drips.htm.

13. "U.S. Department of Labor Advisory" by Janet Oates (Assistant Secretary, Employment and Training Administration) and Nancy Leppink (Deputy Administrator, Wage and Hour Division), U.S. Department of Labor website, http://wdr.doleta.gov/directives/attach/TEGL/TEGL12-09acc.pdf; "The Unpaid Intern, Legal or Not" by Steven Greenhouse, *New York Times* website, http://www.nytimes.com/2010/04/03/business/03intern.html.

14. While earnings on traditional IRA contributions are always tax deferred, there are income-based limits on the deductibility of contributions. Thus, high-income taxpayers are unable to deduct any money they contribute to a traditional IRA. For more specifics, see the IRS guidelines at: http://www.irs.gov/retirement/participant/article/0,,id=202516,00.html.

401(k), 403(b), and 457 plans
Employee payroll deduction retirement plans that offer tax benefits.

absolute advantage
The benefit a country has in a given industry when it can produce more of a product than other nations using the same amount of resources.

accounting
A system for recognizing, organizing, analyzing, and reporting information about the financial transactions that affect an organization.

accounting equation
Assets = Liabilities + Owners' Equity

accredited investor
An organization or individual investor who meets certain criteria established by the SEC and so qualifies to invest in unregistered securities.

accrual-basis accounting
The method of accounting that recognizes revenue when it is earned and matches expenses to the revenues they helped produce.

acquisition
A corporate restructuring in which one firm buys another.

active listening
Attentive listening that occurs when the listener focuses his or her complete attention on the speaker.

active voice
Sentence construction in which the subject performs the action expressed by the verb (e.g., *My sister wrote the paper*). The active voice works better for the vast majority of business communication.

activity-based costing (ABC)
A technique to assign product costs based on links between activities that drive costs and the production of specific products.

administrative law
Laws that arise from regulations established by government agencies.

advergaming
A relatively new promotional channel that involves integrating branded products and advertising into interactive games.

advertising
Paid, nonpersonal communication, designed to influence a target audience with regard to a product, service, organization, or idea.

affirmative action
Policies meant to increase employment and educational opportunities for minority groups—especially groups defined by race, ethnicity, or gender.

agent
A party who agrees to represent another party, called the principal.

agents/brokers
Independent distributors who do not take title of the goods they distribute (even though they may take physical possession on a temporary basis before distribution).

angel investors
Individuals who invest in start-up companies with high growth potential in exchange for a share of ownership.

annual percentage rate (APR)
The interest expense charged on a credit card, expressed as an annual percentage.

applications software
Software that helps a user perform a desired task.

apprenticeships
Structured training programs that mandate that each beginner serve as an assistant to a fully trained worker before gaining full credentials to work in the field.

arbitration
A process in which a neutral third party has the authority to resolve a dispute by rendering a binding decision.

articles of incorporation
The document filed with a state government to establish the existence of a new corporation.

asset management ratios
Financial ratios that measure how effectively a firm is using its assets to generate revenues or cash.

assets
Resources owned by a firm.

autocratic leaders
Leaders who hoard decision-making power for themselves and typically issue orders without consulting their followers.

automation
Replacing human operation and control of machinery and equipment with some form of programmed control.

balance of payments
A measure of the total flow of money into or out of a country.

balance of payments deficit
Shortfall that occurs when more money flows out of a nation than into that nation.

balance of payments surplus
Overage that occurs when more money flows into a nation than out of that nation.

balance of trade
A basic measure of the difference in value between a nation's exports and imports, including both goods and services.

balance sheet
A financial statement that reports the financial position of a firm by identifying and reporting the value of the firm's assets, liabilities, and owners' equity.

Baldrige National Quality Program
A national program to encourage American firms to focus on quality improvement.

Banking Act of 1933
The law that established the Federal Deposit Insurance Corporation (FDIC) to insure bank deposits. It also prohibited commercial banks from selling insurance or acting as investment banks.

behavioral segmentation
Dividing the market based on how people behave toward various products. This category includes both the benefits that consumers seek from products and how consumers use the products.

benefits
Noncash compensation, including programs, such as health insurance, vacation, and childcare.

bias
A preconception about members of a particular group. Common forms of bias include gender bias, age bias, and race, ethnicity, or nationality bias.

board of directors
The individuals who are elected by stockholders of a corporation to represent their interests.

bond
A formal debt instrument issued by a corporation or government entity.

boycott
A tactic in which a union and its supporters and sympathizers refuse to do business with an employer with which they have a labor dispute.

brand
A product's identity—including product name, symbol, design, reputation, and image—that sets it apart from other players in the same category.

brand equity
The overall value of a brand to an organization.

brand extension
A new product, in a new category, introduced under an existing brand name.

breach of contract
The failure of one party to a contract to perform his or her contractual obligations.

breakeven analysis
The process of determining the number of units a firm must sell to cover all costs.

broadband Internet connection
An Internet connection that is capable of transmitting large amounts of information very quickly.

budget (personal)
A detailed forecast of financial inflows (income) and outflows (expenses) in order to determine your net inflow or outflow for a given period of time.

budget deficit
Shortfall that occurs when expenses are higher than revenue over a given period of time.

budget surplus
Overage that occurs when revenue is higher than expenses over a given period of time.

budgeted balance sheet
A projected financial statement that forecasts the types and amounts of assets a firm will need to implement its future plans and how the firm will finance those assets. (Also called a *pro forma* balance sheet.)

budgeted income statement
A projection showing how a firm's budgeted sales and costs will affect expected net income. (Also called a *pro forma* income statement.)

budgeting
A management tool that explicitly shows how firms will acquire and allocate the resources needed to achieve its goals over a specific time period.

business
Any organization that provides goods and services in an effort to earn a profit.

business buyer behavior
Describes how people act when they are buying products to use either directly or indirectly to produce other products.

business cycle
The periodic contraction and expansion that occur over time in virtually every economy.

business environment
The setting in which business operates. The five key components are: economic environment, competitive environment, technological environment, social environment, and global environment.

business ethics
The application of right and wrong, good and bad in a business setting.

business format franchise
A broad franchise agreement in which the franchisee pays for the right to use the name, trademark, and business and production methods of the franchisor.

business intelligence system
A sophisticated form of decision support system that helps decision makers discover information that was previously hidden.

business law
The application of laws and legal principles to business relationships and transactions.

business marketers (also known as business-to-business or B2B)
Marketers who direct their efforts toward people who are buying products to use either directly or indirectly to produce other products.

business plan
A formal document that describes a business concept, outlines core business objectives, and details strategies and timelines for achieving those objectives.

business products
Products purchased to use either directly or indirectly in the production of other products.

business technology
Any tools—especially computers, telecommunications, and other digital products—that businesses can use to become more efficient and effective.

business-to-business (B2B) e-commerce
E-commerce in markets where businesses buy from and sell to other businesses.

business-to-consumer (B2C) e-commerce
E-commerce in which businesses and final consumers interact.

buzz marketing
The active stimulation of word of mouth via unconventional, and often relatively low-cost, tactics. Other terms for buzz marketing are "guerrilla marketing" and "viral marketing."

C corporation
The most common type of corporation, which is a legal business entity that offers limited liability to all of its owners, who are called *stockholders*.

cafeteria-style benefits
An approach to employee benefits that gives all employees a set dollar amount that they must spend on company benefits, allocated however they wish within broad limitations.

cannibalization
When a producer offers a new product that takes sales away from its existing products.

capital budgeting
The process a firm uses to evaluate long-term investment proposals.

capital gain
The return on an asset that results when its market price rises above the price the investor paid for it.

capital structure
The mix of equity and debt financing a firm uses to meet its permanent financing needs.

capitalism
An economic system—also known as the private enterprise or free market system—based on private ownership, economic freedom, and fair competition.

carbon footprint
Refers to the amount of harmful greenhouse gases that a firm emits throughout its operations, both directly and indirectly.

case law (also called common law)
Laws that result from rulings, called precedents, made by judges who initially hear a particular type of case.

cash budget
A detailed forecast of future cash flows that helps financial managers identify when their firm is likely to experience temporary shortages or surpluses of cash.

cash equivalents
Safe and highly liquid assets that many firms list with their cash holdings on their balance sheet.

cause-related marketing
Marketing partnerships between businesses and nonprofit organizations, designed to spike sales for the company and raise money for the nonprofit.

certificate of deposit (CD)
An interest-earning deposit that requires the funds to remain deposited for a fixed term. Withdrawal of the funds before the term expires results in a financial penalty.

channel intermediaries
Distribution organizations—informally called "middlemen"—that facilitate the movement of products from the producer to the consumer.

channel of distribution
The network of organizations and processes that links producers to consumers.

Chapter 7 bankruptcy
A form of bankruptcy that discharges a debtor's debts by liquidating assets and using the proceeds to pay off creditors.

Chapter 11 bankruptcy
A form of bankruptcy used by corporations and individuals that allows the debtor to reorganize operations under a court-approved plan.

Chapter 13 bankruptcy
A form of bankruptcy that allows individual debtors to set up a repayment plan to adjust their debts.

Civil Rights Act of 1964
Federal legislation that prohibits discrimination in hiring, firing, compensation, apprenticeships, training, terms, conditions, or privileges of employment based on race, color, religion, sex, or national origin.

closed shop
An employment arrangement in which the employer agrees to hire only workers who already belong to the union.

cloud computing
The use of Internet-based storage capacity, processing power, and computer applications to supplement or replace internally owned information technology resources.

cobranding
When established brands from different companies join forces to market the same product.

code of ethics
A formal, written document that defines the ethical standards of an organization and gives employees the information they need to make ethical decisions across a range of situations.

cognitive dissonance
Consumer discomfort with a purchase decision, typically for a higher-priced item.

collective bargaining
The process by which representatives of union members and employers attempt to negotiate a mutually acceptable labor agreement.

commercial banks
Privately owned financial institutions that accept demand deposits and make loans and provide other services for the public.

commercial paper
Short-term (and usually unsecured) promissory notes issued by large corporations.

common market
A group of countries that has eliminated tariffs and harmonized trading rules to facilitate the free flow of goods among the member nations.

common stock
The basic form of ownership in a corporation.

communication
The transmission of information between a sender and a recipient.

communication barriers
Obstacles to effective communication, typically defined in terms of physical, language, body language, cultural, perceptual, and organizational barriers.

communication channels
The various ways in which a message can be sent, ranging from one-on-one, in-person meetings to Internet message boards.

communism
An economic and political system that calls for public ownership of virtually all enterprises, under the direction of a strong central government.

company matching
An amount contributed by the employer to an employee's retirement account, matching the employee's retirement contributions either dollar for dollar or based on a percentage of each dollar contributed by the employee.

comparative advantage
The benefit a country has in a given industry if it can make products at a lower opportunity cost than other countries.

compensation
The combination of pay and benefits that employees receive in exchange for their work.

compensatory damages
Monetary payments that a party who breaches a contract is ordered to pay in order to compensate the injured party for the actual harm suffered by the breach of contract.

compressed workweek
A version of flextime scheduling that allows employees to work a full-time number of hours in less than the standard workweek.

computer-aided design (CAD)
Drawing and drafting software that enables users to create and edit blueprints and design drawings quickly and easily.

computer-aided design/computer-aided manufacturing (CAD/CAM)
A combination of software that can be used to design output and send instructions to automated equipment to perform the steps needed to produce this output.

computer-aided engineering (CAE)
Software that enables users to test, analyze, and optimize their designs.

computer-aided manufacturing (CAM)
Software that takes the electronic design for a product and creates the programmed instructions that robots must follow to produce that product as efficiently as possible.

computer-integrated manufacturing (CIM)
A combination of CAD/CAM software with flexible manufacturing systems to automate almost all steps involved in designing, testing, and producing a product.

computer virus
Computer software that can be spread from one computer to another without the knowledge or permission of the computer users.

conceptual skills
The ability to grasp a big-picture view of the overall organization, the relationship between its various parts, and its fit in the broader competitive environment.

conglomerate merger
A combination of two firms that are in unrelated industries.

consideration
Something of value that one party gives another as part of a contractual agreement.

constitution
A code that establishes the fundamental rules and principles that govern a particular organization or entity.

consumer behavior
Description of how people act when they are buying, using, and discarding goods and services for their own personal consumption. Consumer behavior also explores the reasons behind people's actions.

consumer marketers (also known as business-to-consumer or B2C)
Marketers who direct their efforts toward people who are buying products for personal consumption.

consumer price index (CPI)
A measure of inflation that evaluates the change in the weighted-average price of goods and services that the average consumer buys each month.

consumer products
Products purchased for personal use or consumption.

consumer promotion
Marketing activities designed to generate immediate consumer sales, using tools such as premiums, promotional products, samples, coupons, rebates, and displays.

consumerism
A social movement that focuses on four key consumer rights: (1) the right to be safe, (2) the right to be informed, (3) the right to choose, and (4) the right to be heard.

contingency planning
Planning for unexpected events, usually involving a range of scenarios and assumptions that differ from the assumptions behind the core plans.

contingent workers
Employees who do not expect regular, full-time jobs, including temporary full-time workers, independent contractors, and temporary agency or contract agency workers.

contract
An agreement that is legally enforceable.

contraction
A period of economic downturn, marked by rising unemployment and falling business production.

controlling
Checking performance and making adjustments as needed.

convertible security
A bond or share of preferred stock that gives its holder the right to exchange it for a stated number of shares of common stock.

copyright
The exclusive legal right of an author, artist, or other creative individual to use, copy, display, perform, and sell their own creations and to license others to do so.

corporate bylaws
The basic rules governing how a corporation is organized and how it conducts its business.

corporate philanthropy
All business donations to nonprofit groups, including money, products, and employee time.

corporate responsibility
Business contributions to the community through the actions of the business itself rather than donations of money and time.

corporation
A form of business ownership in which the business is considered a legal entity that is separate and distinct from its owners.

cost
The value of what is given up in exchange for something.

countertrade
International trade that involves the barter of products for products rather than for currency.

coupon rate
The interest paid on a bond, expressed as a percentage of the bond's par value.

covenant
A restriction lenders impose on borrowers as a condition of providing long-term debt financing.

craft union
A union comprising workers who share the same skill or work in the same profession.

credit
Allows a borrower to buy a good or acquire an asset without making immediate payment, and to repay the balance at a later time.

credit card
A card issued by a bank or finance company that allows the cardholder to make a purchase now and to pay the credit card issuer later.

credit score
A numerical measure of a consumer's creditworthiness.

credit union
A depository institution that is organized as a cooperative, meaning that it is owned by its depositors.

crime
A wrongful act against society, defined by law and prosecuted by the state.

critical path
The sequence of activities in a project that is expected to take the longest to complete.

critical path method (CPM)
A project-management tool that illustrates the relationships among all the activities involved in completing a project and identifies the sequence of activities likely to take the longest to complete.

current yield
The amount of interest earned on a bond expressed as a percentage of the bond's current market price.

customer benefit
The advantage that a customer gains from specific product features.

customer loyalty
When customers buy a product from the same supplier again and again—sometimes paying even more for it than they would for a competitive product.

customer-relationship management (CRM)
The ongoing process of acquiring, maintaining, and growing profitable customer relationships by delivering unmatched value.

customer satisfaction
When customers perceive that a good or service delivers value above and beyond their expectations.

cybermediary
An Internet-based firm that specializes in the secure electronic transfer of funds.

data
Raw, unprocessed facts and figures.

data mining
The use of sophisticated statistical and mathematical techniques to analyze data and discover hidden patterns and relationships among data, thus creating valuable information.

data warehouse
A large, organization-wide database that stores data in a centralized location.

database
A file consisting of related data organized according to a logical system and stored on a hard drive or some other computer-accessible media.

debit card
A card issued by the bank that allows the customer to make purchases as if the transaction involved cash. In a debit card purchase, the customer's bank account is immediately reduced when the purchase is made.

debt financing
Funds provided by lenders (creditors).

decision support system (DSS)
A system that gives managers access to large amounts of data and the processing power to convert these data into high-quality information, thus improving the decision-making process.

deflation
A period of falling average prices across the economy.

degree of centralization
The extent to which decision-making power is held by a small number of people at the top of the organization.

demand
The quantity of products that consumers are willing to buy at different market prices.

demand curve
The graphed relationship between price and quantity from a customer demand standpoint.

democratic leaders
Leaders who share power with their followers. While they still make final decisions, they typically solicit and incorporate input from their followers.

demographic segmentation
Dividing the market into smaller groups based on measurable characteristics about people such as age, income, ethnicity, and gender.

demographics
The measurable characteristics of a population. Demographic factors include population size and density and specific traits such as age, gender, and race.

departmentalization
The division of workers into logical groups.

depository institution
A financial intermediary that obtains funds by accepting checking or savings deposits (or both) and uses these funds to make loans to borrowers.

depression
An especially deep and long-lasting recession.

direct channel
A distribution process that links the producer and the customer with no intermediaries.

direct costs
Costs that are incurred directly as the result of some specific cost object.

direct investment
(or foreign direct investment) When firms either acquire foreign firms or develop new facilities from the ground up in foreign countries.

discount rate
The rate of interest that the Federal Reserve charges when it loans funds to banks.

discretionary payments
Expenditures for which the spender has significant control in terms of the amount and timing.

disinflation
A period of slowing average price increases across the economy.

distribution strategy
A plan for delivering the right product to the right person at the right place at the right time.

distributive bargaining
The traditional adversarial approach to collective bargaining.

distributorship
A type of franchising arrangement in which the franchisor makes a product and licenses the franchisee to sell it.

divestiture
The transfer of total or partial ownership of some of a firm's operations to investors or to another company.

Dodd-Frank Act
A law enacted in the aftermath of the financial crisis of 2008–2009 that strengthened government oversight of financial markets and placed limitations on risky financial strategies such as heavy reliance on leverage.

Dow Jones Industrial Average
An index that tracks stock prices of thirty large, well-known U.S. corporations.

dynamic delivery
Vibrant, compelling presentation delivery style that grabs and holds the attention of the audience.

e-commerce
Business transactions conducted online, typically via the Internet.

economic system
A structure for allocating limited resources.

economics
The study of the choices that people, companies, and governments make in allocating society's resources.

economy
A financial and social system of how resources flow through society, from production, to distribution, to consumption.

effectiveness
Using resources to create the value by providing customers with goods and services that offer a better relationship between price and perceived benefits.

efficiency
Producing output or achieving a goal at the lowest cost.

electronic bill presentment and payment
A method of bill payment that makes it easy for the customer to make a payment, often by simply clicking on a payment option contained in an email.

electronic communications network (ECN)
An automated, computerized securities trading system that automatically matches buyers and sellers, executing trades quickly and allowing trading when securities exchanges are closed.

e-marketplace
A specialized Internet site where buyers and sellers engaged in business-to-business e-commerce can communicate and conduct business.

embargo
A complete ban on international trade of a certain item, or a total halt in trade with a particular nation.

employment at will
A legal doctrine that views employment as an entirely voluntary relationship that both the employee and employer are free to terminate at any time and for any reason.

enterprise resource planning (ERP)
Software-based approach to integrate an organization's (and in the sophisticated versions, a value chain's) information flows.

entrepreneurs
People who risk their time, money, and other resources to start and manage a business.

environmental scanning
The process of continually collecting information from the external marketing environment.

Equal Employment Opportunity Commission (EEOC)
A federal agency designed to regulate and enforce the provisions of Title VII.

equilibrium price
The price associated with the point at which the quantity demanded of a product equals the quantity supplied.

equity financing
Funds provided by the owners of a company.

equity theory
A motivation theory that proposes that perceptions of fairness directly affect worker motivation.

ethical dilemma
A decision that involves a conflict of values; every potential course of action has some significant negative consequences.

ethics
A set of beliefs about right and wrong, good and bad.

European Union (EU)
The world's largest common market, composed of 27 European nations.

everyday-low-pricing (EDLP)
Long-term discount pricing, designed to achieve profitability through high sales volume.

exchange rates
A measurement of the value of one nation's currency relative to the currency of other nations.

exchange traded fund (ETF)
Shares traded on securities markets that represent the legal right of ownership over part of a basket of individual stock certificates or other securities.

expansion
A period of robust economic growth and high employment.

expectancy theory
A motivation theory that concerns the relationship among individual effort, individual performance, and individual reward.

expenses
Resources that are used up as the result of business operations.

expert system (ES)
A decision-support system that helps managers make better decisions in an area where they lack expertise.

exporting
Selling products in foreign nations that have been produced or grown domestically.

external locus of control
A deep-seated sense that forces other than the individual are responsible for what happens in his or her life.

external recruitment
The process of seeking new employees from outside the firm.

extranet
An intranet that allows limited access to a selected group of stakeholders, such as suppliers or customers.

factor
A company that provides short-term financing to firms by purchasing their accounts receivable at a discount.

factors of production
Four fundamental elements—natural resources, capital, human resources, and entrepreneurship—that businesses need to achieve their objectives.

federal debt
The sum of all the money that the federal government has borrowed over the years and not yet repaid.

Federal Deposit Insurance Corporation (FDIC)
A federal agency that insures deposits in banks and thrift institutions for up to $250,000 per customer, per bank.

Federal Reserve Act of 1913
The law that established the Federal Reserve System as the central bank of the United States.

Financial Services Modernization Act of 1999
An act that overturned the section of the Banking Act of 1933 that prohibited commercial banks from selling insurance or performing the functions of investment banks.

finance
The functional area of business that is concerned with finding the best sources and uses of financial capital.

financial accounting
The branch of accounting that prepares financial statements for use by owners, creditors, suppliers, and other external stakeholders.

Financial Accounting Standards Board (FASB)
The private board that establishes the generally accepted accounting principles used in the practice of financial accounting.

financial budgets
Budgets that focus on the firm's financial goals and identify the resources needed to achieve those goals.

financial capital
The funds a firm uses to acquire its assets and finance its operations.

financial diversification
A strategy of investing in a wide variety of securities in order to reduce risk.

financial leverage
The use of debt in a firm's capital structure.

financial markets
Markets that transfer funds from savers to borrowers.

financial ratio analysis
Computing ratios that compare values of key accounts listed on a firm's financial statements.

Financial Services Modernization Act of 1999
An act that overturned the section of the Banking Act of 1933 that prohibited commercial banks from selling insurance or performing the functions of investment banks.

firewall
Software and/or hardware designed to prevent unwanted access to a computer or computer system.

first-line management
Managers who directly supervise nonmanagement employees.

fiscal policy
Government efforts to influence the economy through taxation and spending.

fixed costs
Costs that remain the same when the level of production changes within some relevant range.

flextime
A scheduling option that allows workers to choose when they start and finish their workdays, as long as they complete the required number of hours.

foreign franchising
A specialized type of foreign licensing in which a firm expands by offering businesses in other countries the right to produce and market its products according to specific operating requirements.

foreign licensing
Authority granted by a domestic firm to a foreign firm for the rights to produce and market its product or to use its trademark/patent rights in a defined geographical area.

foreign outsourcing
(also contract manufacturing) Contracting with foreign suppliers to produce products, usually at a fraction of the cost of domestic production.

franchise
A licensing arrangement under which a franchisor allows franchisees to use its name, trademark, products, business methods, and other property in exchange for monetary payments and other considerations.

franchise agreement
The contractual arrangement between a franchisor and a franchisee that spells out the duties and responsibilities of both parties.

Franchise Disclosure Document (FDD)
A detailed description of all aspects of a franchise that the franchisor must provide to the franchisee at least fourteen calendar days before the franchise agreement is signed.

franchisee
The party in a franchise relationship that pays for the right to use resources supplied by the franchisor.

franchisor
The business entity in a franchise relationship that allows others to operate their business using resources it supplies in exchange for money and other considerations.

free-rein leaders
Leaders who set objectives for their followers but give them freedom to choose how they will accomplish those goals.

free trade
An international economic and political movement designed to help goods and services flow more freely across international boundaries.

General Agreement on Tariffs and Trade (GATT)
An international trade agreement that has taken bold steps to lower tariffs and promote free trade worldwide.

general partnership
A partnership in which all partners can take an active role in managing the business and have unlimited liability for any claims against the firm.

generally accepted accounting principles (GAAP)
A set of accounting standards that is used in the preparation of financial statements.

geographic segmentation
Dividing the market into smaller groups based on where consumers live. This process can incorporate countries, cities, or population density as key factors.

goods
Tangible products.

grace period
The period of time that the credit-card holder has to pay outstanding balances before interest or fees are assessed.

green marketing
Developing and promoting environmentally sound products and practices to gain a competitive edge.

grievance
A complaint by a worker that the employer has violated the terms of the collective bargaining agreement.

gross domestic product (GDP)
The total value of all final goods and services produced within a nation's physical boundaries over a given period of time.

hacker
A skilled computer user who uses his or her expertise to gain unauthorized access to the computer (or computer system) of others, sometimes with malicious intent.

hardware
The physical tools and equipment used to collect, input, store, organize, and process data and to distribute information.

high/low pricing
A pricing strategy designed to drive traffic to retail stores by special sales on a limited number of products, and higher everyday prices on others.

horizontal analysis
Analysis of financial statements that compares account values reported on these statements over two or more years to identify changes and trends.

horizontal merger
A combination of two firms that are in the same industry.

human resource management
The management function focused on maximizing the effectiveness of the workforce by recruiting world-class talent, promoting career development, and determining workforce strategies to boost organizational effectiveness.

human skills
The ability to work effectively with and through other people in a range of different relationships.

hyperinflation
An average monthly inflation rate of more than 50 percent.

implicit cost
The opportunity cost that arises when a firm uses owner-supplied resources.

immediate predecessors
Activities in a project that must be completed before some other specified activity can begin.

importing
Buying products domestically that have been produced or grown in foreign nations.

income statement
The financial statement that reports the revenues, expenses, and net income that resulted from a firm's operations over an accounting period.

independent wholesaling businesses
Independent distributors that buy products from a range of different businesses and sell those products to a range of different customers.

indirect costs
Costs that are the result of a firm's general operations and are not directly tied to any specific cost object.

industrial union
A union comprising workers employed in the same industry.

inflation
A period of rising average prices across the economy.

information
Data that have been processed in a way that makes them meaningful to their user.

infrastructure
A country's physical facilities that support economic activity.

initial public offering (IPO)
The first time a company issues stock that may be bought by the general public.

institutional investor
An organization that pools contributions from investors, clients, or depositors and uses these funds to buy stocks and other securities.

integrated marketing communication
The coordination of marketing messages through every promotional vehicle to communicate a unified impression about a product.

intellectual property
Property that is the result of creative or intellectual effort, such as books, musical works, inventions, and computer software.

intercultural communication
Communication among people with differing cultural backgrounds.

interest-based bargaining
A form of collective bargaining that emphasizes cooperation and problem solving in an attempt to find a "win–win" outcome.

internal locus of control
A deep-seated sense that the individual is personally responsible for what happens in his or her life.

internal recruitment
The process of seeking employees who are currently within the firm to fill open positions.

International Monetary Fund (IMF)
An international organization of 187 member nations that promotes international economic cooperation and stable growth.

Internet
The world's largest computer network; essentially a network of computer networks all operating under a common set of rules that allow them to communicate with each other.

Internet2 (I2)
A new high-tech Internet restricted to dues-paying members of a consortium. I2 utilizes technologies that give it a speed and capacity far exceeding the current Internet.

intranet
A network that has the look and feel of the Internet, and is navigated using a Web browser, but is confined to documents and data located on a single company's servers and is available only to the firm's employees.

inventory
Stocks of goods or other items held by organizations.

investment bank
A financial intermediary that specializes in helping firms raise financial capital by issuing securities in primary markets.

investing
Reducing consumption in the current time period in order to build future wealth.

IRA
An individual retirement account that provides tax benefits to individuals who are investing for their retirement.

ISO 9000
A family of generic standards for quality management systems established by the International Organization for Standardization.

ISO 14000
A family of generic standards for environmental management established by the International Organization for Standardization.

job analysis
The examination of specific tasks that are assigned to each position, independent of who might be holding the job at any specific time.

job description
An explanation of the responsibilities for a specific position.

job enrichment
The creation of jobs with more meaningful content, under the assumption that challenging, creative work will motivate employees.

job specifications
The specific qualifications necessary to hold a particular position.

joint ventures
When two or more companies join forces— sharing resources, risks, and profits, but not actually merging companies— to pursue specific opportunities.

just-in-time (JIT) production
A production system that emphasizes the production of goods to meet actual current demand, thus minimizing the need to hold inventories of finished goods and work in process at each stage of the supply chain.

Labor–Management Relations Act (Taft–Hartley Act)
Law passed in 1947 that placed limits on union activities, outlawed the closed shop, and allowed states to pass right-to-work laws that made union shops illegal.

labor union
A group of workers who have organized to work together to achieve common job-related goals, such as higher wages, better working conditions, and greater job security.

laws
Rules that govern the conduct and actions of people within a society that are enforced by the government.

leading
Directing and motivating people to achieve organizational goals.

lean production
An approach to production that emphasizes the elimination of waste in all aspects of production processes.

leverage ratios
Ratios that measure the extent to which a firm relies on debt financing in its capital structure.

liabilities
Claims that outsiders have against a firm's assets.

licensing
Purchasing the right to use another company's brand name or symbol.

limit order
An order to a broker to buy a specific stock only if its price is below a certain level, or to sell a specific stock only if its price is above a certain level.

limited liability
When owners are not personally liable for claims against their firm. Owners with limited liability may lose their investment in the company, but their personal assets are protected.

limited liability company (LLC)
A form of business ownership that offers both limited liability to its owners and flexible tax treatment.

limited liability partnership (LLP)
A form of partnership in which all partners have the right to participate in management and have limited liability for company debts.

limited partnership
A partnership that includes at least one general partner who actively manages the company and accepts unlimited liability and one limited partner who gives up the right to actively manage the company in exchange for limited liability.

line-and-staff organizations
Organizations with line managers forming the primary chain of authority in the company, and staff departments working alongside line departments.

line extensions
Similar products offered under the same brand name.

line managers
Managers who supervise the functions that contribute directly to profitability: production and marketing.

line of credit
A financial arrangement between a firm and a bank in which the bank pre-approves credit up to a specified limit, provided that the firm maintains an acceptable credit rating.

line organizations
Organizations with a clear, simple chain of command from top to bottom.

liquid asset
An asset that can quickly be converted into cash with little risk of loss.

liquidity ratios
Financial ratios that measure the ability of a firm to obtain the cash it needs to pay its short-term debt obligations as they come due.

lockout
An employer-initiated work stoppage.

logistics
A subset of supply chain management that focuses largely on the tactics involved in moving products along the supply chain.

loss
When a business incurs expenses that are greater than its revenue.

loss leader pricing
Closely related to high/low pricing, loss leader pricing means pricing a handful of items—or loss leaders—temporarily below cost to drive traffic.

M1 money supply
Includes all currency plus checking accounts and traveler's checks.

M2 money supply
Includes all of M1 money supply plus most savings accounts, money market accounts, and certificates of deposit.

macroeconomics
The study of a country's overall economic dynamics, such as the employment rate, the gross domestic product, and taxation policies.

malware
A general term for malicious software, such as spyware, computer viruses, and worms.

management
Achieving the goals of an organization through planning, organizing, leading, and controlling organizational resources including people, money, and time.

management development
Programs to help current and potential executives develop the skills they need to move into leadership positions.

managerial (or management) accounting
The branch of accounting that provides reports and analysis to managers to help them make informed business decisions.

market makers
Securities dealers that make a commitment to continuously offer to buy and sell the stock of a specific corporation listed on the NASDAQ exchange or traded in the OTC market.

market niche
A small segment of a market with fewer competitors than the market as a whole. Market niches tend to be quite attractive to small firms.

market order
An order telling a broker to buy or sell a specific security at the best currently available price.

market segmentation
Dividing potential customers into groups of similar people, or segments.

market share
The percentage of a market controlled by a given marketer.

marketing
An organizational function and a set of processes for creating, communicating, and delivering value to customers and for managing customer relationships in ways that benefit the organization and its stakeholders.

marketing concept
A business philosophy that makes customer satisfaction—now and in the future—the central focus of the entire organization.

marketing mix
The blend of marketing strategies for product, price, distribution, and promotion.

marketing plan
A formal document that defines marketing objectives and the specific strategies for achieving those objectives.

marketing research
The process of gathering, interpreting, and applying information to uncover marketing opportunities and challenges, and to make better marketing decisions.

Maslow's hierarchy of needs theory
A motivation theory that suggests that human needs fall into a hierarchy and that as each need is met, people become motivated to meet the next-highest need in the pyramid.

mass customization
The creation of products tailored for individual consumers on a mass basis.

master budget
A presentation of an organization's operational and financial budgets that represents the firm's overall plan of action for a specified time period.

matrix organizations
Organizations with a flexible structure that brings together specialists from different areas of the company to work on individual projects on a temporary basis.

maturity date
The date when a bond will come due.

mediation
A method of dealing with an impasse between labor and management by bringing in a neutral third party to help the two sides reach agreement by reducing tensions and making suggestions for possible compromises.

merchant wholesalers
Independent distributors who take legal possession, or title, of the goods they distribute.

merger
A corporate restructuring that occurs when two formerly independent business entities combine to form a new organization.

microeconomics
The study of smaller economic units, such as individual consumers, families, and individual businesses.

middle management
Managers who supervise lower-level managers and report to a higher-level manager.

mission
The definition of an organization's purpose, values, and core goals, which provides the framework for all other plans.

mixed economies
Economies that embody elements of both planned and market-based economic systems.

modes of transportation
The various transportation options—such as planes, trains, and railroads—for moving products through the supply chain.

monetary policy
Federal Reserve decisions that shape the economy by influencing interest rates and the supply of money.

money
Anything generally accepted as a medium of exchange, a measure of value or a means of payment.

money market mutual fund
A mutual fund that pools funds from many investors and uses these funds to purchase very safe, highly liquid securities.

money supply
The total amount of money within the overall economy.

monopolistic competition
A market structure with many competitors selling differentiated products. Barriers to entry are low.

monopoly
A market structure with one producer completely dominating the industry, leaving no room for any significant competitors. Barriers to entry tend to be virtually insurmountable.

multichannel retailing
Providing multiple distribution channels for consumers to buy a product.

mutual fund
An institutional investor that raises funds by selling shares to investors and uses the accumulated funds to buy a portfolio of many different securities.

national brands
Brands that the producer owns and markets.

National Labor Relations Act (Wagner Act)
Landmark pro-labor law enacted in 1935. This law made it illegal for firms to discriminate against union members and required employers to recognize certified unions and bargain with these unions in good faith.

natural monopoly
A market structure with one company as the supplier of a product because the nature of that product makes a single supplier more efficient than multiple competing ones. Most natural monopolies are government sanctioned and regulated.

negligence
An unintentional tort that arises due to carelessness or irresponsible behavior.

Net Asset Value Per Share (NAV)
The value of a mutual fund's securities and cash holdings, minus any liabilities, divided by the number of shares of the fund outstanding.

net income
The difference between the revenue a firm earns and the expenses it incurs in a given time period.

net present value (NPV)
The sum of the present values of expected future cash flows from an investment, minus the cost of that investment.

noise
Any interference that causes the message you send to be different from the message your audience understands.

nondiscretionary payments
Expenditures that the spender has little or no control over.

nonprofit corporation
A corporation that does not seek to earn a profit and differs in several fundamental respects from C corporations.

nonprofits
Business-*like* establishments that employ people and produce goods and services with the fundamental goal of contributing to the community rather than generating financial gain.

nonverbal communication
Communication that does not use words. Common forms of nonverbal communication include gestures, posture, facial expressions, tone of voice, and eye contact.

North American Free Trade Agreement (NAFTA)
The treaty among the United States, Mexico, and Canada that eliminated trade barriers and investment restrictions over a fifteen-year period starting in 1994.

observation research
Marketing research that *does not* require the researcher to interact with the research subject.

odd pricing
The practice of ending prices in numbers below even dollars and cents in order to create a perception of greater value.

offshoring
Moving production or support processes to foreign countries.

oligopoly
A market structure with only a handful of competitors selling products that can be similar or different. Barriers to entry are typically high.

on-the-job training
A training approach that requires employees to simply begin their jobs—sometimes guided by more experienced employees—and to learn as they go.

open market operations
The Federal Reserve function of buying and selling government securities, which include treasury bonds, notes, and bills.

open shop
An employment arrangement in which workers are not required to join a union or pay union dues.

operating budgets
Budgets that communicate an organization's sales and production goals and the resources needed to achieve those goals.

operational planning
Very specific, short-term planning that applies tactical plans to daily, weekly, and monthly operations.

operations management
Managing all of the activities involved in creating value by producing goods and services and distributing them to customers.

opportunity cost
The opportunity of giving up the second-best choice when making a decision.

organization chart
A visual representation of the company's formal structure.

organizing
Determining a structure for both individual jobs and the overall organization.

orientation
The first step in the training and development process, designed to introduce employees to the company culture and provide key administrative information.

outsourcing
Arranging for other organizations to perform supply chain functions that were previously performed internally.

out-of-pocket cost
A cost that involves the payment of money or other resources.

over-the-counter (OTC) market
The market where securities that are not listed on exchanges are traded.

owners' equity
The claims a firm's owners have against their company's assets (often called "stockholders' equity" on balance sheets of corporations).

par value (of a bond)
The value of a bond at its maturity; what the issuer promises to pay the bondholder when the bond matures.

partnership
A voluntary agreement under which two or more people act as co-owners of a business for profit.

passive voice
Sentence construction in which the subject does not do the action expressed by the verb; rather the subject is acted upon (e.g., *The paper was written by my sister*). The passive voice tends to be less effective for business communication.

patent
A legal monopoly that gives an inventor the exclusive right over an invention for a limited time period.

penetration pricing
A new product pricing strategy that aims to capture as much of the market as possible through rock-bottom prices.

performance appraisal
A formal feedback process that requires managers to give their subordinates feedback on a one-to-one basis, typically by comparing actual results to expected results.

personal selling
The person-to-person presentation of products to potential buyers.

pharming
A scam that seeks to steal identities by routing Internet traffic to fake websites.

phishing
A scam in which official-looking emails are sent to individuals in an attempt to get them to divulge private information such as passwords, user names, and account numbers.

physical distribution
The actual, physical movement of products along the distribution pathway.

picketing
A union tactic during labor disputes in which union members walk near the entrance of the employer's place of business, carrying signs to publicize their position and concerns.

planned obsolescence
The strategy of deliberately designing products to fail in order to shorten the time between purchases.

planning
Determining organizational goals and action plans for how to achieve those goals.

poka-yokes
Simple methods incorporated into a production process designed to eliminate or greatly reduce errors.

positioning statement
A brief statement that articulates how the marketer would like the target market to envision a product relative to the competition.

preferred stock
A type of stock that gives its holder preference over common stockholders in terms of dividends and claims on assets.

present value
The amount of money that, if invested today at a given rate of interest (called the "discount rate"), would grow to become some future amount in a specified number of time periods.

primary data
New data that marketers compile for a specific research project.

primary securities market
The market where newly issued securities are traded. The primary market is where the firms that issue securities raise additional financial capital.

principal
A party who agrees to have someone else (called an agent) act on his or her behalf.

principal–agent relationship
A relationship in which one party, called the principal, gives another party, called the agent, the authority to act in place of, and bind the principal when dealing with, third parties.

private placement
A primary market issue that is negotiated between the issuing corporation and a small group of accredited investors.

privatization
The process of converting government-owned businesses to private ownership.

probationary period
A specific timeframe (typically three to six months) during which a new hire can prove his or her worth on the job before he or she becomes permanent.

process
A set of related activities that transform inputs into outputs, thus adding value.

producer price index (PPI)
A measure of inflation that evaluates the change over time in the weighted-average wholesale prices.

product
Anything that an organization offers to satisfy consumer needs and wants, including both goods and services.

product consistency
How reliably a product delivers its promised level of quality.

product differentiation
The attributes that make a good or service different from other products that compete to meet the same or similar customer needs.

product features
The specific characteristics of a product.

product life cycle
A pattern of sales and profits that typically changes over time.

product line
A group of products that are closely related to each other, in terms of either how they work or the customers they serve.

product mix
The total number of product lines and individual items sold by a single firm.

product placement
The paid integration of branded products into movies, television, and other media.

productivity
The basic relationship between the production of goods and services (output) and the resources needed to produce them (input), calculated via the following equation: output/input = productivity.

profit
The money that a business earns in sales (or revenue), minus expenses, such as the cost of goods, and the cost of salaries.
Revenue − Expenses = Profit (or Loss)

profit margin
The gap between the cost and the price of an item on a per-product basis.

profitability ratios
Ratios that measure the rate of return a firm is earning on various measures of investment.

promotion
Marketing communication designed to influence consumer purchase decisions through information, persuasion, and reminders.

promotional channels
Specific marketing communication vehicles, including traditional tools, such as advertising, sales promotion, direct marketing, and personal selling, and newer tools, such as product placement, advergaming, and Internet minimovies.

property
The legal right of an owner to exclude non-owners from having control over a particular resource.

protectionism
National policies designed to restrict international trade, usually with the goal of protecting domestic businesses.

psychographic segmentation
Dividing the market into smaller groups based on consumer attitudes, interests, values, and lifestyles.

public offering
A primary market issue in which new securities are offered to any investors who are willing and able to purchase them.

public relations (PR)
The ongoing effort to create positive relationships with all of a firm's different "publics," including customers, employees, suppliers, the community, the general public, and the government.

publicity
Unpaid stories in the media that influence perceptions about a company or its products.

pull strategy
A marketing approach that involves creating demand from the ultimate consumers so that they "pull" your products through the distribution channels by actively seeking them.

pure competition
A market structure with many competitors selling virtually identical products. Barriers to entry are quite low.

pure goods
Products that do not include any services.

pure services
Products that do not include any goods.

push strategy
A marketing approach that involves motivating distributors to heavily promote—or "push"—a product to the final consumers, usually through heavy trade promotion and personal selling.

quality level
How well a product performs its core functions.

quality of life
The overall sense of well-being experienced by either an individual or a group.

quotas
Limitations on the amount of specific products that may be imported from certain countries during a given time period.

radio frequency identification (RFID)
A technology that stores information on small microchips that can transmit the information when they are within range of a special reader.

recession
An economic downturn marked by a decrease in the GDP for two consecutive quarters.

recovery
A period of rising economic growth and employment.

registration statement
A long, complex document that firms must file with the SEC when they sell securities through a public offering.

reserve requirement
A rule set by the Fed, which specifies the minimum amount of reserves (or funds) a bank must hold, expressed as a percentage of the bank's deposits.

retailers
Distributors that sell products directly to the ultimate users, typically in small quantities, that are stored and merchandized on the premises.

retained earnings
The part of a firm's net income it reinvests.

revenue
Increases in a firm's assets that result from the sale of goods, provision of services, or other activities intended to earn income.

revolving credit agreement
A guaranteed line of credit in which a bank makes a binding commitment to provide a business with funds up to a specified credit limit at any time during the term of the agreement.

right-to-work law
A state law that makes union shops illegal within that state's borders.

risk
The degree of uncertainty regarding the outcome of a decision.

risk-return tradeoff
The observation that financial opportunities that offer high rates of return are generally riskier than opportunities that offer lower rates of return.

robot
A reprogrammable machine that is capable of manipulating materials, tools, parts, and specialized devices in order to perform a variety of tasks.

S corporation
A form of corporation that avoids double taxation by having its income taxed as if it were a partnership.

salaries
The pay that employees receive over a fixed period, most often weekly or monthly.

sale
A transaction in which the title (legal ownership) to a good passes from one party to another in exchange for a price.

sales promotion
Marketing activities designed to stimulate immediate sales activity through specific short-term programs aimed at either consumers or distributors.

Sarbanes-Oxley Act
Federal legislation passed in 2002 that sets higher ethical standards for public corporations and accounting firms. Key provisions limit conflict-of-interest issues and require financial officers and CEOs to certify the validity of their financial statements.

savings account
An interest-bearing account holding funds not needed to meet regular expenditures.

savings and loan association
A depository institution that has traditionally obtained most of its funds by accepting savings deposits, which have been used primarily to make mortgage loans.

scope of authority (for an agent)
The extent to which an agent has the authority to act for and represent the principal.

SCORE (Service Corps of Retired Executives)
An organization—affiliated with the Small Business Administration—that provides free, comprehensive business counseling for small business owners from qualified volunteers.

secondary data
Existing data that marketers gather or purchase for a research project.

secondary securities market
The market where previously issued securities are traded.

Securities Act of 1933
first major federal law regulating the securities industry. It requires firms issuing new stock in a public offering to file a registration statement with the SEC.

securities broker
A financial intermediary that acts as an agent for investors who want to buy and sell financial securities. Brokers earn commissions and fees for the services they provide.

securities dealer
A financial intermediary that participates directly in securities markets, buying and selling stocks and other securities for its own account.

Securities and Exchange Commission
The federal agency with primary responsibility for regulating the securities industry.

Securities Exchange Act of 1934
A federal law dealing with securities regulation that established the Securities and Exchange Commission to oversee the securities industry.

services
Intangible products.

servicescape
The environment in which a customer and service provider interact.

sexual harassment
Workplace discrimination against a person based on his or her gender.

Six Sigma
An approach to quality improvement characterized by very ambitious quality goals, extensive training of employees, and a long-term commitment to working on quality-related issues.

skimming pricing
A new product pricing strategy that aims to maximize profitability by offering new products at a premium price.

Small Business Administration (SBA)
An agency of the federal government designed to maintain and strengthen the nation's economy by aiding, counseling, assisting, and protecting the interests of small businesses.

Small Business Development Centers (SBDCs)
Local offices—affiliated with the Small Business Administration—that provide comprehensive management assistance to current and prospective small business owners.

social audit
A systematic evaluation of how well a firm is meeting its ethics and social responsibility goals.

social responsibility
The obligation of a business to contribute to society.

socialism
An economic system based on the principle that the government should own and operate key enterprises that directly affect public welfare.

sociocultural differences
Differences among cultures in language, attitudes, and values.

software
Programs that provide instructions to a computer so that it can perform a desired task.

sole proprietorship
A form of business ownership with a single owner who usually actively manages the company.

spam
Unsolicited email advertisements usually sent to very large numbers of recipients, many of whom may have no interest in the message.

span of control
Span of management; refers to the number of people that a manager supervises.

specific performance
A remedy for breach of contract in which the court orders the party committing the breach to do exactly what the contract specifies.

speed-to-market
The rate at which a new product moves from conception to commercialization.

sponsorship
A deep association between a marketer and a partner (usually a cultural or sporting event), which involves promotion of the sponsor in exchange for either payment or the provision of goods.

spontaneous financing
Financing that arises during the natural course of business without the need for special arrangements.

spyware
Software that is installed on a computer without the user's knowledge or permission for the purpose of tracking the user's behavior.

staff managers
Managers who supervise the functions that provide advice and assistance to the line departments.

stakeholders
Any groups that have a stake—or a personal interest—in the performance and actions of an organization.

Standard & Poor's 500
A stock index based on prices of 500 major U.S. corporations in a variety of industries and market sectors.

standard of living
The quality and quantity of goods and services available to a population.

statement of cash flows
The financial statement that identifies a firm's sources and uses of cash in a given accounting period.

statute of frauds
A requirement that certain types of contracts must be in writing in order to be enforceable.

statute of limitations
The time period within which a legal action must be initiated.

statutory close (or closed) corporation
A corporation with a limited number of owners that operates under simpler, less formal rules than a C corporation.

statutory law
Law that is the result of legislative action.

stock (or securities) exchange
An organized venue for trading stocks and other securities that meet its listing requirements.

stock index
A statistic that tracks how the prices of a specific set of stocks have changed.

stockholder
An owner of a corporation.

store brands
Brands that the retailer both produces and distributes (also called "private-label brands").

strategic alliance
An agreement between two or more firms to jointly pursue a specific opportunity without actually merging their businesses. Strategic alliances typically involve less formal, less encompassing agreements than partnerships.

strategic goals
Concrete benchmarks that managers can use to measure performance in each key area of the organization.

strategic planning
High-level, long-term planning that establishes a vision for the company, defines long-term objectives and priorities, determines broad action steps, and allocates resources.

strategies
Action plans that help the organization achieve its goals by forging the best fit between the firm and the environment.

strike
A work stoppage initiated by a union.

structured interviews
An interviewing approach that involves developing a list of questions beforehand and asking the same questions in the same order to each candidate.

supply
The quantity of products that producers are willing to offer for sale at different market prices.

supply chain
All organizations, processes, and activities involved in the flow of goods from their raw materials to the final consumer.

supply chain management (SCM)
Planning and coordinating the movement of products along the supply chain, from the raw materials to the final consumers.

supply curve
The graphed relationship between price and quantity from a supplier standpoint.

survey research
Marketing research that requires the researcher to interact with the research subject.

sustainable development
Doing business to meet the needs of the current generation, without harming the ability of future generations to meet their needs.

SWOT analysis
A strategic planning tool that helps management evaluate an organization in terms of internal strengths and weakness, and external opportunities and threats.

system software
Software that performs the critical functions necessary to operate the computer at the most basic level.

tactical planning
More specific, shorter-term planning that applies strategic plans to specific functional areas.

target market
The group of people who are most likely to buy a particular product.

tariffs
Taxes levied against imports.

technical skills
Expertise in a specific functional area or department.

telecommuting
Working remotely—most often from home—and connecting to the office via phone lines, fax machines, or broadband networks.

Theory X and Theory Y
A motivation theory that suggests that management attitudes toward workers fall into two opposing categories based on management assumptions about worker capabilities and values.

time value of money
The principle that a dollar received today is worth more than a dollar received in the future.

title
Legal evidence of ownership.

Title VII
A portion of the Civil Rights Act of 1964 that prohibits discrimination in hiring, firing, compensation, apprenticeships, training, terms, conditions, or privileges of employment based on race, color, religion, sex, or national origin for employers with 15 or more workers.

top management
Managers who set the overall direction of the firm, articulating a vision, establishing priorities, and allocating time, money, and other resources.

tort
A private wrong that results in physical or mental harm to an individual, or damage to that person's property.

total quality management (TQM)
An approach to quality improvement that calls for everyone within an organization to take responsibility for improving quality and emphasizes the need for a long-term commitment to continuous improvement.

trade credit
Spontaneous financing granted by sellers when they deliver goods and services to customers without requiring immediate payment.

trade deficit
Shortfall that occurs when the total value of a nation's imports is higher than the total value of its exports.

trade promotion
Marketing activities designed to stimulate wholesalers and retailers to push specific products more aggressively over the short term.

trade surplus
Overage that occurs when the total value of a nation's exports is higher than the total value of its imports.

trademark
A mark, symbol, word, phrase, or motto used to identify a company's goods.

trading bloc
A group of countries that has reduced or even eliminated tariffs, allowing for the free flow of goods among the member nations.

underwriting
An arrangement under which an investment banker agrees to purchase all shares of a public offering at an agreed-upon price.

unemployment rate
The percentage of people in the labor force over age 16 who do not have jobs and are actively seeking employment.

Uniform Commercial Code (UCC)
A uniform act governing the sale of goods, leases, warranties, transfer of funds, and a variety of other business-related activities.

union shop
An employment arrangement in which a firm can hire nonunion workers, but these workers must join the union within a specified time period to keep their jobs.

universal ethical standards
Ethical norms that apply to all people across a broad spectrum of situations.

U.S. Treasury bills (T-bills)
Short-term marketable IOUs issued by the U.S. government.

utility
The ability of goods and services to satisfy consumer "wants."

value
The relationship between the price of a good or a service and the benefits that it offers its customers.

value chain
The network of relationships that channels the flow of inputs, information, and financial resources through all of the processes directly or indirectly involved in producing goods and services and distributing them to customers.

variable costs
Costs that vary directly with the level of production.

venture capital firms
Companies that invest in start-up businesses with high growth potential in exchange for a share of ownership.

vertical integration
Performance of processes internally that were previously performed by other organizations in a supply chain.

vertical merger
A combination of firms at different stages in the production of a good or service.

vesting period
A specified period of time for which an employee must work for an employer in order to receive the full advantage of certain retirement benefits.

viral marketing
An Internet marketing strategy that tries to involve customers and others not employed by the seller in activities that help promote the product.

voluntary export restraints (VERs)
Limitations on the amount of specific products that one nation will export to another nation.

wages
The pay that employees receive in exchange for the number of hours or days that they work.

Web 2.0
Websites that incorporate interactive and collaborative features in order to create a richer, more interesting, and more useful experience for their users.

wheel of retailing
A classic distribution theory that suggests that retail firms and retail categories become more upscale as they go through their life cycles.

whistle-blowers
Employees who report their employer's illegal or unethical behavior to either the authorities or the media.

wholesalers
Distributors that buy products from producers and sell them to other businesses or nonfinal users such as hospitals, nonprofits, and the government.

World Bank
An international cooperative of 187 member countries, working together to reduce poverty in the developing world.

World Trade Organization (WTO)
A permanent global institution to promote international trade and to settle international trade disputes.

World Wide Web
The service that allows computer users to easily access and share information on the Internet in the form of text, graphics, video, apps, and animation.

worm
Malicious computer software that, unlike viruses, can spread on its own without being attached to other files.

LO1 Describe the characteristics of the four basic forms of business ownership

A sole proprietorship is a business that is owned, and usually managed, by a single person. A partnership is a voluntary arrangement under which two or more people act as co-owners of a business for profit. A corporation is a legal entity created by filing a document (known in most states as the "articles of incorporation") with a state agency. A corporation is considered to be separate and distinct from its owners, who have limited liability for the debts of their company. A limited liability company (LLC) is a relatively new form of business ownership that, like a corporation, offers limited liability to all of its owners. However, LLCs offer more flexibility in tax treatment and have simpler operating requirements.

LO2 Discuss the advantages and disadvantages of a sole proprietorship

A sole proprietorship is the simplest and least expensive form of ownership to establish. It offers the single owner the flexibility of running the business without having to seek the approval of other owners. If the business is successful, the sole proprietor retains all of the profits. Finally, the earnings of a sole proprietorship are taxed only as income of the owner, with no separate tax levied on the business itself. One key disadvantage of a sole proprietorship is that the single owner has unlimited liability for the debts of the business. Sole proprietors also often work long hours and assume heavy responsibilities, and they may have difficulty raising funds for expansion. Another drawback of sole proprietorships is their limited life.

LO3 Evaluate the pros and cons of the partnership as a form of business ownership

The most basic type of partnership is a *general partnership, in which* each co-owner may take an active role in management. Compared to the sole proprietorships, a general partnership offers the advantages of pooled financial resources and the benefits of a shared workload that can take advantage of complementary skills. The earnings of general partnerships are taxed only as income to the partners; there is no separate income tax on the business itself. One major disadvantage of a general partnership is that each owner has unlimited liability for the debts of the company. Moreover, disagreements among partners can complicate decision-making. Finally, the death or withdrawal of a partner can create instability and uncertainty in the management and financing of the company.

There are two other common types of partnerships. A *limited partnership,* must have at least one general partner and at least one limited partner. General partners actively manage the company and have unlimited liability for the company's debts. Limited partners have limited liability but may not actively manage the partnership. In a *limited liability partnership,* all partners may manage their company and are protected by some degree of limited liability for the debts of their firm.

LO4 Explain why corporations have become the dominant form of business ownership

The most common form of corporation is the C corporation. All stockholders (the owners of a C corporation) have limited liability for company debts. C corporations can raise financial capital by issuing bonds or shares of stock, giving them an advantage when it comes to financing growth. Other advantages include unlimited life, easy transfer of ownership, and the ability to take advantage of professional management. But forming a corporation can be more complex and expensive than forming a partnership. Another drawback is that any profits distributed to stockholders are taxed twice—once as income to the corporation, then again as income to the stockholders. Corporations are also subject to extensive government regulation.

LO5 Explain why limited liability companies are becoming an increasingly popular form of business ownership

Limited liability companies (LLCs) are attractive because they avoid the problem of double taxation endemic to C corporations, while giving all owners the protection of limited liability. In this sense, LLCs are similar to S corporations, but without the restrictions on ownership. LLCs also face fewer regulations than corporations and give

---

sole proprietorship
A form of business ownership with a single owner who usually actively manages the company.

partnership
A voluntary agreement under which two or more people act as co-owners of a business for profit.

general partnership
A partnership in which all partners can take an active role in managing the business and have unlimited liability for any claims against the firm.

corporation
A form of business ownership in which the business is considered a legal entity that is separate and distinct from its owners.

articles of incorporation
The document filed with a state government to establish the existence of a new corporation.

limited liability
When owners are not personally liable for claims against their firm. Owners with limited liability may lose their investment in the company, but their other personal assets are protected.

limited liability company (LLC)
A form of business ownership that offers both limited liability to its owners and flexible tax treatment

limited partnership
A partnership that includes at least one general partner who actively manages the company and accepts unlimited liability and one limited partner who gives up the right to actively manage the company in exchange for limited liability.

limited liability partnership (LLP)
A form of partnership in which all partners have the right to participate in management and have limited liability for company debts.

C corporation
The most common type of corporation, which is a legal business entity that offers limited liability to all of its owners, who are called stockholders.

corporate bylaws
The basic rules governing how a corporation is organized and how it conducts its business.

stockholder
An owner of a corporation.

institutional investor
An organization that pools contributions from investors, clients, or depositors and uses these funds to buy stocks and other securities.

board of directors
The individuals who are elected by stockholders of a corporation to represent their interests.

S corporation
A form of corporation that avoids double taxation by having its income taxed as if it were a partnership.

statutory close (or closed) corporation
A corporation with a limited number of owners that operates under simpler, less formal rules than a C corporation.

nonprofit corporation
A corporation that does not seek to earn a profit and differs in several fundamental respects from C corporations.

acquisition
A corporate restructuring in which one firm buys another.

merger
A corporate restructuring that occurs when two formerly independent business entities combine to form a new organization.

divestiture
The transfer of total or partial ownership of some of a firm's operations to investors or to another company.

horizontal merger
A combination of two firms that are in the same industry.

vertical merger
A combination of firms at different stages in the production of a good or service.

conglomerate merger
A combination of two firms that are in unrelated industries.

franchise
A licensing arrangement under which a franchisor allows franchisees to use its name, trademark, products, business methods, and other property in exchange for monetary payments and other considerations.

franchisor
The business entity in a franchise relationship that allows others to operate their business using resources it supplies in exchange for money and other considerations.

franchisee
The party in a franchise relationship that pays for the right to use resources supplied by the franchisor.

distributorship
A type of franchising arrangement in which the franchisor makes a product and licenses the franchisee to sell it.

business format franchise
A broad franchise agreement in which the franchisee pays for the right to use the name, trademark, and business and production methods of the franchisor.

franchise agreement
The contractual arrangement between a franchisor and franchisee that spells out the duties and responsibilities of both parties.

the owners the flexibility to either manage the company themselves or hire professional managers.

LO6 Evaluate the advantages and disadvantages of franchising
A franchise is a licensing arrangement under which one party (the *franchisor*) allows another party (the *franchisee*) to use its name, trademark, patents, copyrights, business methods, and other property in exchange for monetary payments and other considerations. The franchisor gains revenue without the need to invest its own money. The franchisee gains the right to use a well-known brand name and proven business methods and often receives training and support from the franchisor. On the downside, franchisors often find that dealing with a large number of franchisees can be complex and challenging. For franchisees, the main drawbacks are the monetary payments (fees and royalties) they must pay to the franchisor and the loss of control over management of their business.

Characteristics of Four Major Forms of Business Ownership

FORM OF BUSINESS	NUMBER OF OWNERS	PARTICIPATION IN MANAGEMENT	OWNERS' LIABILITY	TAX IMPLICATIONS	STATE FILING REQUIREMENTS
SOLE PROPRIETORSHIP	One	Proprietor typically manages the company.	Unlimited	Taxed only as income to the owner.	No special filing required with state.
GENERAL PARTNERSHIP	Two or more (no limit on maximum)	All general partners have the right to participate in management.	Unlimited	Taxed only as income to the owners.	No special filing required with state.
GENERAL (OR C) CORPORATION	No limit on number of stockholders	Most stockholders do not take an active role in management. Stockholders elect a Board of Directors, which sets policy and appoints and oversees corporate officers, who actively manage the corporation.	Limited	Earnings subject to double taxation: all earnings are taxed as income to corporation. Any dividends are also taxed as income to stockholders.	Must file articles of incorporation (or similar document) with state and pay filing fee.
LIMITED LIABILITY COMPANY (LLC)	No limit	May be member- or manager-managed, similar to a corporation.	Limited	Has the option to be taxed as either a partnership or a corporation. If taxed as a partnership, earnings are taxed only as income to owners.	Must file articles of organization (or similar document) with state and pay filing fee.

© Cengage Learning 2013

Franchise Disclosure Document (FDD)
A detailed description of all aspects of a franchise that the franchisor must provide to the franchisee at least fourteen calendar days before the franchise agreement is signed.

LO1 Discuss the objectives, the process, and the scope of marketing

Marketing means delivering value to your customers with the goal of satisfying their needs and achieving long-term profitability for your organization. Goods and services meet customer needs by providing "utility" (or satisfaction) on an ongoing basis. Marketing has moved well beyond the scope of traditional goods and services, to include people, places, events, and ideas. Much nontraditional marketing involves both public and private not-for-profit organizations, which measure their success in nonmonetary terms. Over the last century, marketing has evolved through a number of phases. The marketing era gave birth to the marketing concept, which is still in force today: a philosophy that customer satisfaction—now and in the future—should be the central focus of the entire organization.

The Evolution of Marketing

The focus of marketing has evolved over time.

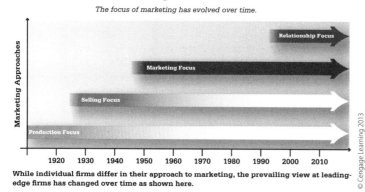

While individual firms differ in their approach to marketing, the prevailing view at leading-edge firms has changed over time as shown here.

© Cengage Learning 2013

LO2 Identify the role of the customer in marketing

Successful marketers always place the customer front and center, with a focus on customer relationship management: acquiring, maintaining, and growing profitable customer relationships by consistently delivering unmatched value. Effective data management and one-on-one personalization are key customer relationship tools. The result of an effective customer-first strategy is loyal customers, who may even be willing to pay more for your product.

LO3 Explain each element of marketing strategy

Marketing strategy essentially involves determining who your *target audience* is and how you will reach it. Choosing the right target begins with *market segmentation*: dividing your market into segments, or groups, of people with similar characteristics. Then you need to determine the best *marketing mix*—the most effective combination of product, pricing, distribution, and promotion strategies to reach your target market. Finally, you must continually monitor each element of the *marketing environment* to ensure that you respond quickly and effectively to change.

Marketing Strategy

© Cengage Learning 2013

---

marketing
An organizational function and a set of processes for creating, communicating, and delivering value to customers and for managing customer relationships in ways that benefit the organization and its stakeholders.

utility
The ability of goods and services to satisfy consumer "wants."

marketing concept
A business philosophy that makes customer satisfaction—now and in the future—the central focus of the entire organization.

customer–relationship management (CRM)
The ongoing process of acquiring, maintaining, and growing profitable customer relationships by delivering unmatched value.

value
A customer perception that a product has a better relationship than its competitors between the cost and the benefits.

customer satisfaction
When customers perceive that a good or service delivers value above and beyond their expectations.

customer loyalty
When customers buy a product from the same supplier again and again—sometimes paying even more for it than they would for a competitive product.

marketing plan
A formal document that defines marketing objectives and the specific strategies for achieving those objectives.

market segmentation
Dividing potential customers into groups of similar people, or segments.

target market
The group of people who are most likely to buy a particular product.

consumer marketers (also known as business-to-consumer or B2C)
Marketers who direct their efforts toward people who are buying products for personal consumption.

business marketers (also known as business-to-business or B2B)
Marketers who direct their efforts toward people who are buying products to use either directly or indirectly to produce other products.

demographic segmentation
Dividing the market into smaller groups based on measurable characteristics about people, such as age, income, ethnicity, and gender.

RIP & REVIEW

CHAPTER 11

geographic segmentation
Dividing the market into smaller groups based on where consumers live. This process can incorporate countries, cities, or population density as key factors.

psychographic segmentation
Dividing the market into smaller groups based on consumer attitudes, interests, values, and lifestyles.

behavioral segmentation
Dividing the market based on how people behave toward various products. This category includes both the benefits that consumers seek from products and how consumers use the products.

marketing mix
The blend of marketing strategies for product, price, distribution, and promotion.

environmental scanning
The process of continually collecting information from the external marketing environment.

market share
The percentage of a market controlled by a given marketer.

consumer behavior
Description of how people act when they are buying, using, and discarding goods and services for their own personal consumption. Consumer behavior also explores the reasons behind people's actions.

cognitive dissonance
Consumer discomfort with a purchase decision, typically for a higher-priced item.

business buyer behavior
Describes how people act when they are buying products to use either directly or indirectly to produce other products.

marketing research
The process of gathering, interpreting, and applying information to uncover marketing opportunities and challenges, and to make better marketing decisions.

secondary data
Existing data that marketers gather or purchase for a research project.

primary data
New data that marketers compile for a specific research project.

observation research
Marketing research that *does not* require the researcher to interact with the research subject.

survey research
Marketing research that requires the researcher to interact with the research subject.

green marketing
The development and promotion of products with ecological benefits.

mass customization
The creation of products tailored for individual consumers on a mass basis.

L04 Describe the consumer and business decision-making process

Understanding how customers make decisions will help you meet their needs. When people buy for their own personal consumption, a number of forces influence them, including cultural, social, personal, and psychological factors. For high-risk decisions, they generally follow a decision process, but for low-risk decisions, they often just follow rules of thumb. When people buy for business, they typically are more methodical, driven by product specifications.

INFLUENCE	DESCRIPTION
CULTURAL	*Culture:* the values, attitudes, and customs shared by members of a society *Subculture:* a smaller division of the broader culture *Social Class:* societal position driven largely by income and occupation
SOCIAL	*Family:* a powerful force in consumption choices *Friends:* another powerful force, especially for high-profile purchases *Reference Groups:* groups that give consumers a point of comparison
PERSONAL	*Demographics:* measurable characteristics such as age, gender, or income
PSYCHOLOGICAL	*Personality:* the mix of traits that determine who you are *Motivation:* pressing needs that tend to generate action *Attitudes:* lasting evaluations of (or feelings about) objects or ideas *Perceptions: how people select, organize, and interpret information* *Learning:* changes in behavior based on experience

© Cengage Learning 2013

L05 Discuss the key elements of marketing research

Marketing research involves gathering, interpreting, and applying information to uncover opportunities and challenges. Primary and secondary data offer complementary strengths and weaknesses. Observation research tools involve gathering data without interacting with the research subjects, while survey tools involve asking research subjects direct questions.

SECONDARY DATA:	PRIMARY DATA:
Existing Data That Marketers Gather or Purchase	New Data That Marketers Compile for the First Time
Tend to be lower cost	Tend to be more expensive
May not meet your specific needs	Customized to meet your needs
Frequently outdated	Fresh, new data
Available to your competitors	Proprietary—no one else has it
Examples: U.S. Census, *The Wall Street Journal*, *Time* magazine, your product sales history	Examples: Your own surveys, focus groups, customer comments, mall interviews

© Cengage Learning 2013

L06 Explain the roles of social responsibility and technology in marketing

The surging social responsibility movement and dramatic advances in technology have had a significant influence on marketing. In addition to seeking long-term profitability, socially responsible marketers actively contribute to meeting the needs of the broader community. Key areas of concern include fair labor practices (especially in foreign markets), environmentalism, and involvement in local communities. The digital boom of the past decade has revolutionized marketing, shifting the balance of power from producers to consumers. The Internet has also created marketing opportunities, helping businesses realize new efficiencies, facilitating more customized service, and generating new promotional opportunities.

LO1 Explain "product" and identify product classifications

A product can be anything that a company offers to satisfy consumer needs and wants; the possibilities include not only physical goods, but also services and ideas. A product also includes all the attributes that consumers associate with it, such as name, image, and guarantees. Goods and services fall along a spectrum from pure goods to pure services. Most products fall somewhere between the two ends, incorporating elements of both goods and services. Products typically encompass three layers: the core benefit, the actual physical good or delivered service, and the augmented product. Customers buy consumer products for personal consumption, and business products to contribute to the production of other products.

LO2 Describe product differentiation and the key elements of product planning

Product differentiation means making your product different from—and better than—the competition. Product planning offers the opportunity to achieve differentiation through elements, such as better quality, better features and benefits, and a stronger brand. These elements are the foundation of an effective product strategy.

Product Quality Indicators

PRODUCT CATEGORY	SOME QUALITY INDICATORS
Internet search engines	Fast, relevant, and far-reaching results
Stylish blue jeans	High-profile designer, high price and celebrity customers
Editing equipment	Reliability, flexibility, and customer service

© Cengage Learning 2013

LO3 Discuss innovation and the product life cycle

Innovation can range from small modifications of existing products to brand-new products that change how people live. Either way, for a business to thrive over the long term, effective new product development is vital. The new product development process is meant to streamline product development. The six steps include idea generation, idea screening, analysis, development, testing, and commercialization. After introduction, successful new products move through a life cycle. During the *introduction* phase, a product first hits the market. Marketing generates awareness and trial. During the *growth* phase, sales rise rapidly and profits usually peak. Competitors enter the category. Marketing focuses on gaining new customers. During the *maturity* phase, sales usually peak, while profits fall. Competition intensifies as growth stops. Marketing aims to capture customers from competitors. During the *decline* phase, sales and profits drop. Marketers consider discontinuing products.

LO4 Analyze and explain promotion and integrated marketing communications

Promotion is marketing communication that influences consumers by informing, persuading, and reminding them about products. The most effective promotion builds strong, ongoing relationships between customers and companies. The current promotional environment is changing rapidly. Thanks to technology, consumers have more control over how, when, and even *if* they receive promotional messages. Media have splintered across entertainment options, and consumer viewing patterns have changed. In response, marketers are seeking increasingly creative means to reach their target consumers. Their goal is to zero in on the right customers, at the right time, with the right message. The goal of integrated marketing communications (IMC) is to ensure that consumers receive a unified, focused message regardless of the message source. To make this happen, marketers must break through the clutter, coordinating their message through various promotional vehicles. Everyone who manages the marketing messages must have information about the customer, the product, the competition, the market, and the strategy of the organization. And clearly, solid teamwork is crucial. The result of effective IMC is a relevant, coherent image in the minds of target customers.

---

product
Anything that an organization offers to satisfy consumer needs and wants, including both goods and services.

pure goods
Products that do not include any services.

pure services
Products that do not include any goods.

consumer products
Products purchased for personal use or consumption.

business products
Products purchased to use either directly or indirectly in the production of other products.

product differentiation
The attributes that make a good or service different from other products that compete to meet the same or similar customer needs.

quality level
How well a product performs its core functions.

product consistency
How reliably a product delivers its promised level of quality.

product features
The specific characteristics of a product.

customer benefit
The advantage that a customer gains from specific product features.

product line
A group of products that are closely related to each other, either in terms of how they work or the customers they serve.

product mix
The total number of product lines and individual items sold by a single firm.

cannibalization
When a producer offers a new product that takes sales away from its existing products.

brand
A product's identity—including product name, symbol, design, reputation, and image—that sets it apart from other players in the same category.

brand equity
The overall value of a brand to an organization.

line extensions
Similar products offered under the same brand name.

brand extension
A new product, in a new category, introduced under an existing brand name.

licensing
Purchasing the right to use another company's brand name or symbol.

CHAPTER 12

cobranding
When established brands from different companies join forces to market the same product.

national brands
Brands that the producer owns and markets.

store brands
Brands that the retailer both produces and distributes (also called private-label brands).

product life cycle
A pattern of sales and profits that typically changes over time.

promotion
Marketing communication designed to influence consumer purchase decisions through information, persuasion, and reminders.

integrated marketing communication
The coordination of marketing messages through every promotional vehicle to communicate a unified impression about a product.

positioning statement
A brief statement that articulates how the marketer would like the target market to envision a product relative to the competition.

promotional channels
Specific marketing communication vehicles, including traditional tools, such as advertising, sales promotion, direct marketing, and personal selling, and newer tools such as product placement, advergaming, and Internet minimovies.

product placement
The paid integration of branded products into movies, television, and other media.

advergaming
A relatively new promotional channel that involves integrating branded products and advertising into interactive games.

buzz marketing
The active stimulation of word-of-mouth via unconventional, and often relatively low-cost, tactics. Other terms for buzz marketing are "guerrilla marketing" and "viral marketing."

sponsorship
A deep association between a marketer and a partner (usually a cultural or sporting event), which involves promotion of the sponsor in exchange for either payment or the provision of goods.

advertising
Paid, nonpersonal communication, designed to influence a target audience with regard to a product, service, organization, or idea.

sales promotion
Marketing activities designed to stimulate immediate sales activity through specific short-term programs aimed at either consumers or distributors.

LO5 Discuss the development of the promotional message

The promotional message should be a big idea—a meaningful, believable, and distinctive concept that cuts through the clutter. Finding the big idea begins with the positioning statement—a brief statement that articulates how you want your target market to envision your product relative to the competition. A creative development team—often spearheaded by advertising agency professionals—uses the positioning statement as a springboard for finding a big idea. The ideas themselves are typically based on either a rational or an emotional premise, with humor as a recurrent favorite.

LO6 Discuss the promotional mix and the various promotional tools

The promotional mix is the combination of promotional tools that a marketer chooses to best communicate the big idea to the target audience. In today's rapidly changing promotional environment, new promotional tools have emerged, and secondary promotional tools have burst into the mainstream. Examples include Internet advertising (especially paid search advertising, search engine optimization), social media, product placement, advergaming, buzz marketing, and sponsorships. Yet traditional promotional tools retain enormous clout in terms of both spending and impact on the market. Mainstream advertising has split among a growing array of media options. Sales promotion, designed to stimulate immediate sales, represents a quickly growing area. Public relations, designed to generate positive, unpaid media stories about a company or its products, also aims to boost brand awareness and credibility. Personal selling, designed to close sales and build relationships, continues to play a dominant role in the promotional mix. Selecting the right mix of promotional tools poses an ongoing challenge for many marketers.

Buzz marketing travels along social networks

BUZZ MARKETING

© Cengage Learning 2013

consumer promotion
Marketing activities designed to generate immediate consumer sales, using tools such as premiums, promotional products, samples, coupons, rebates, and displays.

trade promotion
Marketing activities designed to stimulate wholesalers and retailers to push specific products more aggressively over the short term.

public relations (PR)
The ongoing effort to create positive relationships with all of a firm's different "publics," including customers, employees, suppliers, the community, the general public, and the government.

publicity
Unpaid stories in the media that influence perceptions about a company or its products.

personal selling
The person-to-person presentation of products to potential buyers.

push strategy
A marketing approach that involves motivating distributors to heavily promote—or "push"—a product to the final consumers, usually through heavy trade promotion and personal selling.

pull strategy
A marketing approach that involves creating demand from the ultimate consumers so that they "pull" your products through the distribution channels by actively seeking them.

LO1 Define distribution and differentiate between channels of distribution and physical distribution

Distribution is the element of the marketing mix that involves getting the right product to the right customers in the right place at the right time. A channel of distribution is the path that a product takes from the producer to the consumer, while physical distribution is the actual movement of products along that path. Distributors add value by reducing the number of transactions—and the associated costs—required for goods to flow from producers to consumers. Distributors can also add a range of different utilities:

- *Form Utility:* Provides customer satisfaction by converting inputs into finished products.
- *Time Utility:* Adds value by making products available at a convenient time for consumers.
- *Place Utility:* Satisfies customer needs by providing the right products in the right place.
- *Ownership Utility:* Adds value by making it easier for customers to actually possess the goods and services that they purchase.
- *Information Utility:* Boosts customer satisfaction by providing helpful information.
- *Service Utility:* Adds value by providing fast, friendly, personalized service.

How transactions are reduced through marketing intermediaries

© Cengage Learning 2013

LO2 Describe the various types of wholesale distributors

Wholesalers buy products from the producer and sell them to other businesses and organizations. The two key categories of wholesalers are:

- *Merchant wholesalers,* who take legal title to the goods they distribute. Full-service merchant wholesalers provide a wide array of services, whereas limited-service merchant wholesalers offer more focused services.
- *Agents and brokers,* who connect buyers and sellers in exchange for commissions but without taking legal ownership of the goods they distribute.

LO3 Discuss strategies and trends in store and nonstore retailing

Retailers are the final stop before the consumer on the distribution path. The two main retail categories are *store* and *nonstore*, but the line between the two has blurred as more and more retailers are pursuing a multichannel approach, with online and offline outlets supporting each other. Key nonstore retail approaches include online retailing, direct-response retailing, direct selling, and vending. As competition intensifies, a growing segment of retailers (both store and nonstore) have distinguished themselves by offering their customers an entertainment-like experience.

Retailers Add Value for Consumers

Product Selection
Look and Feel
Customer Service
Location
Promotion
Pricing
TARGET MARKET

© Cengage Learning 2013

RETAILING

Store   Nonstore

distribution strategy
A plan for delivering the right product to the right person at the right place at the right time.

channel of distribution
The network of organizations and processes that links producers to consumers.

physical distribution
The actual, physical movement of products along the distribution pathway.

direct channel
A distribution process that links the producer and the customer with no intermediaries.

channel intermediaries
Distribution organizations—informally called "middlemen"—that facilitate the movement of products from the producer to the consumer.

retailers
Distributors that sell products directly to the ultimate users, typically in small quantities, which are stored and merchandised on the premises.

wholesalers
Distributors that buy products from producers and sell them to other businesses or nonfinal users such as hospitals, nonprofits, and the government.

independent wholesaling businesses
Independent distributors that buy products from a range of different businesses and sell those products to a range of different customers.

merchant wholesalers
Independent distributors who take legal possession, or title, of the goods they distribute.

agents/brokers
Independent distributors who do not take title of the goods they distribute (even though they may take physical possession on a temporary basis before distribution).

multichannel retailing
Providing multiple distribution channels for consumers to buy a product.

wheel of retailing
A classic distribution theory that suggests that retail firms and retail categories become more upscale as they go through their life cycles.

supply chain
All organizations, processes, and activities involved in the flow of goods from their raw materials to the final consumer.

supply chain management (SCM)
Planning and coordinating the movement of products along the supply chain, from the raw materials to the final consumers.

CHAPTER 13

logistics
A subset of supply chain management that focuses largely on the tactics involved in moving products along the supply chain.

modes of transportation
The various transportation options—such as planes, trains, and railroads—for moving products through the supply chain.

penetration pricing
A new product pricing strategy that aims to capture as much of the market as possible through rock-bottom prices.

everyday-low-pricing (EDLP)
Long-term discount pricing, designed to achieve profitability through high sales volume.

high/low pricing
A pricing strategy designed to drive traffic to retail stores by special sales on a limited number of products, and higher everyday prices on others.

loss-leader pricing
Closely related to high/low pricing, loss-leader pricing means pricing a handful of items—or loss leaders—temporarily below cost to drive traffic.

skimming pricing
A new product pricing strategy that aims to maximize profitability by offering new products at a premium price.

breakeven analysis
The process of determining the number of units a firm must sell to cover all costs.

profit margin
The gap between the cost and the price of an item on a per-product basis.

odd pricing
The practice of ending prices in numbers below even dollars and cents in order to create a perception of greater value.

RIP & REVIEW

LO4 Explain the key factors in physical distribution

As marketers manage the movement of products through the supply chain, they must make decisions regarding each of the following factors:

- *Warehousing:* How many warehouses do we need? Where should we locate our warehouses?
- *Materials handling:* How should we move products within our facilities? How can we best balance efficiency with effectiveness?
- *Inventory control:* How much inventory should we keep on hand? How should we store and distribute it? What about taxes and insurance?
- *Order processing:* How should we manage incoming and outgoing orders? What would be most efficient for our customers and suppliers?
- *Customer service:* How can we serve our customers most effectively? How can we reduce waiting times and facilitate interactions?
- *Transportation:* How can we move products most efficiently through the supply chain? What are the key trade-offs?

Elements of the Supply Chain

© Cengage Learning 2013

LO5 Outline core pricing objectives and strategies

Many marketers continually evaluate and refine their pricing strategies to ensure that they meet their goals. Even the goals themselves may shift in response to the changing market. Key objectives and strategies include:

- Building profitability
- Driving volume
- Meeting the competition
- Creating prestige

Pricing Considerations

© Cengage Learning 2013

LO6 Discuss pricing in practice, including the role of consumer perceptions

While most marketers are familiar with economics, they often don't have the information they need to apply the theories to their specific pricing strategies. Because of those limitations, most companies *consider* market-based factors—especially customer expectations and competitive prices—but they *rely* on cost-based pricing: what should we charge to cover our costs and make a profit? Common approaches include breakeven analysis and fixed margin pricing. Many marketers also account for consumer perceptions, especially the link between price and perceived quality, and odd pricing. If no other information is available, consumers will often assume that higher-priced products are higher quality. *Odd pricing* means ending prices in dollars and cents rather than round numbers (e.g., $999.99 versus $1,000) in order to create a perception of greater value.

© Cengage Learning 2013

$$\text{Breakeven Point} = \frac{\text{Total Fixed Costs}}{\text{Price/Unit} - \text{Variable Cost/Unit}}$$

LO1 Discuss the role of management and its importance to organizational success

The formal definition of management is to achieve the goals of an organization through planning, organizing, leading, and controlling organizational resources. Managers provide vision for their company and inspire others to follow their lead. Most medium-size and large companies have three basic management levels: top management, middle management, and first-line (or supervisory) management. Managers must draw on a wide range of skills, but most of their abilities cluster into three key categories: *technical skills, human skills,* and *conceptual skills.* All three skill sets are essential for management success, but in different proportions at each managerial level.

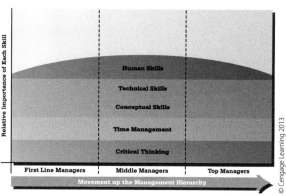

LO2 Explain key theories and current practices of motivation

Research suggests that people's thoughts and feelings play a vital role in motivation. Key theories that incorporate this perspective include Maslow's hierarchy of needs, Theory X and Theory Y, job enrichment, expectancy theory, and equity theory. In today's business environment, leading-edge firms nourish distinctive, positive cultures that tend to create productive employees who are deeply attached to both their work and their companies. Many also focus on training and education, which are especially motivating for the growing cadre of employees who identify themselves based on their field of expertise rather than their organization.

Maslow's Hierarchy of Needs

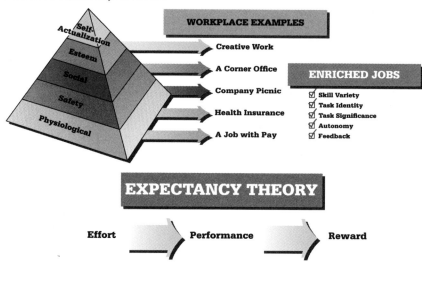

management
Achieving the goals of an organization through planning, organizing, leading, and controlling organizational resources, including people, money, and time.

planning
Determining organizational goals and action plans for ways to achieve those goals.

organizing
Determining a structure for both individual jobs and the overall organization.

leading
Directing and motivating people to achieve organizational goals.

controlling
Checking performance and making adjustments as needed.

top management
Managers who set the overall direction of the firm, articulating a vision, establishing priorities, and allocating time, money, and other resources.

middle management
Managers who supervise lower-level managers and report to a higher-level manager.

first-line management
Managers who directly supervise nonmanagement employees.

technical skills
Expertise in a specific functional area or department.

human skills
The ability to work effectively with and through other people in a range of different relationships.

conceptual skills
The ability to grasp a big-picture view of the overall organization, the relationships among its various parts, and its fit in the broader competitive environment.

Maslow's hierarchy of needs theory
A motivation theory that suggests that human needs fall into a hierarchy and that as each need is met, people become motivated to meet the next highest need in the pyramid.

Theory X and Theory Y
A motivation theory that suggests that management attitudes toward workers fall into two opposing categories based on management assumptions about worker capabilities and values.

job enrichment
The creation of jobs with more meaningful content, under the assumption that challenging, creative work will motivate employees.

expectancy theory
A motivation theory that concerns the relationship among individual effort, individual performance, and individual reward.

equity theory
A motivation theory that proposes that perceptions of fairness directly affect worker motivation.

strategic planning
High-level, long-term planning that establishes a vision for the company, defines long-term objectives and priorities, determines broad action steps, and allocates resources.

tactical planning
More specific, shorter-term planning that applies strategic plans to specific functional areas.

operational planning
Very specific, short-term planning that applies tactical plans to daily, weekly, and monthly operations.

contingency planning
Planning for unexpected events, usually involving a range of scenarios and assumptions that differ from the assumptions behind the core plans.

mission
The definition of an organization's purpose, values, and core goals, which provides the framework for all other plans.

SWOT analysis
A strategic planning tool that helps management evaluate an organization in terms of internal strengths and weakness, and external opportunities and threats.

strategic goals
Concrete benchmarks that managers can use to measure performance in each key area of the organization.

strategies
Action plans that help the organization achieve its goals by forging the best fit between the firm and the environment.

organization chart
A visual representation of the company's formal structure.

degree of centralization
The extent to which decision-making power is held by a small number of people at the top of the organization.

span of control
Span of management; refers to the number of people a manager supervises.

departmentalization
The division of workers into logical groups.

line organizations
Organizations with a clear, simple chain of command from top to bottom.

line-and-staff organizations
Organizations with line managers forming the primary chain of authority in the company, and staff departments working alongside line departments.

LO3 Outline the categories of business planning and explain strategic planning

The four main categories of business planning are *strategic planning, tactical planning, operational planning,* and *contingency planning.* Strategic planning, handled by top managers, sets the broad direction of the organization, typically over a five-year horizon. Strategic planning guides the entire planning process, since all other plans—and most major management decisions—stem from the strategic plan. Given fierce competition and often-unpredictable change, most large firms revise their strategic plans on a yearly basis.

Contingency planning paradigm

Most Probable Issues

Most Harmful Issues

Focus Area for Contingency Plans

EFFECTIVE GOALS
☑ Specific and Measurable
☑ Tied to a Timeframe
☑ Realistic but Challenging

© Cengage Learning 2013

LO4 Discuss the organizing function of management

The organizing function of management means creating a logical structure for people, their jobs, and their patterns of interaction. In choosing the right structure for a specific company, management must consider many different factors, including the goals and strategies of the firm, its products, and its size. Management must also make decisions about the degree of centralization, the span of management control, and the type of departmentalization. Company structures tend to follow one of three different patterns: line organizations, line-and-staff organizations, and matrix organizations.

LO5 Explain the role of managerial leadership and the key leadership styles

Effective business leaders motivate others to achieve the goals of their organization. Most experts agree that true leaders are trustworthy, visionary, and inspiring. Other key leadership traits include empathy, courage, creativity, intelligence, fairness, and energy. While leaders have a range of different styles, three main approaches include autocratic, democratic, and free-rein. The best leaders tend to use all three approaches, shifting style in response to the needs of the followers and the situation.

LO6 Describe the management control process

Controlling means monitoring performance of the firm—or individuals within the firm—and making improvements when necessary. As the environment changes, plans change. And as plans change, the control process must change to ensure that the company achieves its goals. The control process has three main steps:
1. Establish clear performance standards.
2. Measure actual performance against standards.
3. Take corrective action if necessary.

line managers
Managers who supervise the functions that contribute directly to profitability: production and marketing.

staff managers
Managers who supervise the functions that provide advice and assistance to the line departments.

matrix organizations
Organizations with a flexible structure that brings together specialists from different areas of the company to work on individual projects on a temporary basis.

autocratic leaders
Leaders who hoard decision-making power for themselves and typically issue orders without consulting their followers.

democratic leaders
Leaders who share power with their followers. While they still make final decisions, they typically solicit and incorporate input from their followers.

free-rein leaders
Leaders who set objectives for their followers but give them freedom to choose how they accomplish those goals.

Human Resource Management: Building a Top-Quality Workforce

LO1 Explain the importance of human resources to business success

A world-class workforce can lead straight to world-class performance. Human resource managers can directly contribute to that goal by recruiting top talent, promoting career development, and boosting organizational effectiveness. Yet human resource departments typically face numerous challenges in making this happen.

© Cengage Learning 2013

LO2 Discuss key human resource issues in today's economy

As the economy and society continue to change rapidly, a number of issues have emerged that directly affect human resources. As the recession tightened its grip in 2009, massive layoffs thrust human resources into turmoil. The growing wage gap between senior managers and the average employee has created tension for a number of stakeholders. Older workers have begun to retire, while younger workers often bring an unprecedented sense of entitlement. Many women are leaving traditional jobs. Workers are actively seeking more flexibility and a better work–life balance. And the number of costly employee lawsuits has skyrocketed in the last couple of decades.

LO3 Outline challenges and opportunities that the human resources function faces

While HR workers tend to have strong people skills, many lack the business acumen to contribute directly to broad company objectives, and other departments often view HR as either irrelevant or adversarial. HR can respond to these issues by demonstrating that they understand the strategic goals of the company, the core customers, and the competition. The best HR departments use this knowledge to raise the value of the firm's human capital, which in turn increases the value of the firm itself.

LO4 Discuss human resource planning and core human resources responsibilities

Human resource planning objectives must flow from the company's master plan, and the HR strategies must reflect company priorities.

The first step should be to determine where the firm currently stands in terms of human resources and to forecast future needs. Other key areas of focus follow:

- *Recruitment:* The key to recruitment is finding *qualified* candidates who fit well with the organization. The right people can come from either internal or external labor pools.
- *Selection:* Choosing the right person from a pool of candidates typically involves applications, interviews, tests, and references. The terms of the job offer itself play a role as well.
- *Training:* The training process begins with orientation but should continue throughout each employee's tenure. Options include on-the-job training, off-the-job training, and management development.

© Cengage Learning 2013

human resource management
The management function focused on maximizing the effectiveness of the workforce by recruiting world-class talent, promoting career development, and determining workforce strategies to boost organizational effectiveness.

job analysis
The examination of specific tasks that are assigned to each position, independent of who might be holding the job at any specific time.

job description
An explanation of the responsibilities for a specific position.

job specifications
The specific qualifications necessary to hold a particular position.

internal recruitment
The process of seeking employees who are currently within the firm to fill open positions.

external recruitment
The process of seeking new employees from outside the firm.

structured interviews
An interviewing approach that involves developing a list of questions beforehand and asking the same questions in the same order to each candidate.

probationary period
A specific timeframe (typically three to six months) during which a new hire can prove his or her worth on the job before the hire becomes permanent.

contingent workers
Employees who do not expect regular, full-time jobs, including temporary full-time workers, independent contractors, and temporary agency or contract agency workers.

orientation
The first step in the training and development process, designed to introduce employees to the company culture, and provide key administrative information.

on-the-job training
A training approach that requires employees to simply begin their jobs—sometimes guided by more experienced employees—and to learn as they go.

apprenticeships
Structured training programs that mandate that each beginner serve as an assistant to a fully trained worker before gaining full credentials to work in the field.

management development
Programs to help current and potential executives develop the skills they need to move into leadership positions.

performance appraisal
A formal feedback process that requires managers to give their subordinates feedback on a one-to-one basis, typically by comparing actual results to expected results.

compensation
The combination of pay and benefits that employees receive in exchange for their work.

wages
The pay that employees receive in exchange for the number of hours or days that they work.

salaries
The pay that employees receive over a fixed period, most often weekly or monthly.

benefits
Noncash compensation, including programs, such as health insurance, vacation, and childcare.

cafeteria-style benefits
An approach to employee benefits that gives all employees a set dollar amount that they must spend on company benefits, allocated however they wish within broad limitations.

flextime
A scheduling option that allows workers to choose when they start and finish their workdays, as long as they complete the required number of hours.

compressed workweek
A version of flextime scheduling that allows employees to work a full-time number of hours in less than the standard workweek.

telecommuting
Working remotely—most often from home—and connecting to the office via phone lines, fax machines, and broadband networks.

Civil Rights Act of 1964
Federal legislation that prohibits discrimination in hiring, firing, compensation, apprenticeships, training, terms, conditions, or privileges of employment based on race, color, religion, sex, or national origin.

Title VII
A portion of the Civil Rights Act of 1964 that prohibits discrimination in hiring, firing, compensation, apprenticeships, training, terms, conditions, or privileges of employment based on race, color, religion, sex, or national origin for employers with 15 or more workers.

Equal Employment Opportunity Commission (EEOC)
A federal agency designed to regulate and enforce the provisions of Title VII.

affirmative action
Policies meant to increase employment and educational opportunities for minority groups—especially groups defined by race, ethnicity, or gender.

- *Evaluation:* Performance feedback should happen constantly. But most firms also use formal, periodic performance appraisals to make decisions about compensation, promotions, training, transfers, and terminations.
- *Compensation:* Compensation includes both pay and benefits. Interestingly, companies that offer higher compensation generally outperform their competitors in terms of total return to shareholders.
- *Separation:* Employees leave their jobs for both positive and negative reasons. When the separation is not voluntary—e.g., layoffs or termination—fairness and documentation are critical.

Considerations for Compensation

Variable Pay System
- Commission
- Bonuses
- Profit sharing
- Stock options
- Pay for knowledge

EMPLOYEE EVALUATION

Employee   Manager
Feedback should be continual

FLEXIBLE SCHEDULING
- Flextime
- Telecommuting
- Job Sharing

© Cengage Learning 2013

LO5 Explain the key federal legislation that affects human resources

Perhaps the most influential piece of employment legislation is the Civil Rights Act of 1964. Title VII of this act prohibits discrimination in hiring, firing, compensation, apprenticeships, training, terms, conditions, or privileges of employment based on race, color, religion, sex, or national origin. Additional legislation prohibits discrimination based on pregnancy, age, and disability. The Equal Employment Opportunity Commission (EEOC) enforces the provisions of Title VII. Affirmative action programs—while controversial—have received support from the U.S. Supreme Court. And human resource managers must guard against sexual harassment in the organization, since it violates Title VII.

sexual harassment
Workplace discrimination against a person based on his or her gender.

LO1 Explain the basic elements of computer technology—including hardware, software, and networks—and describe the key trends in each area

Hardware is the physical equipment used to collect, store, organize, and process data and to distribute information. Software consists of computer programs that provide instructions to a computer. System software performs the critical functions necessary to operate the computer at the most basic level. Applications software helps users perform a desired task. Most firms (and many households) now use networks to enable users to communicate with each other quickly and efficiently and share both files and hardware resources. The Internet is a vast network of computer networks. The part of the Internet used most by the general public is the World Wide Web, which consists of billions of documents written and linked together using Hypertext Markup Language (HTML). Many organizations have developed intranets that have the same look and feel as the Internet but are limited to servers within an organization. Extranets are intranets that provide limited access to specific stakeholders, such as customers or suppliers.

LO2 Discuss the reasons for the increasing popularity of cloud computing

Cloud computing means going beyond a company's firewall to store data and run applications using Internet-based resources. Cloud computing allows firms to obtain storage space, processing power, and software without investing heavily in internally owned IT resources. Cloud computing also makes it easier for people in different organizations to collaborate, since resources in the cloud are not tied to a specific type of hardware or operating system. But several high-profile security breaches of cloud services in recent years have caused serious concerns. Unless such security lapses are brought under control, they may ultimately limit acceptance of cloud computing.

LO3 Describe how data become information and how decision support systems can provide high-quality information that helps managers make better decisions

Data are raw facts and figures. Data become information when they are processed, organized, and presented in a way that is meaningful to a decision maker. Many companies develop decision support systems (DSS) that give managers access to large amounts of data and the processing power to convert the data into high-quality information. Some firms also develop expert systems to help decision makers when they must deal with problems beyond their expertise. To develop an expert system, programmers ask experts in the relevant area to provide step-by-step instructions describing how they solve a problem. The programmers then write software that mimics the expert's approach and guides the decision maker toward a good solution.

HIGH-QUALITY INFORMATION IS:	
1. Accurate	Free from errors and omissions
2. Relevant	Concerns issues that are important to the decision maker
3. Timely	Available in time to make a difference to the decision maker
4. Understandable	Presented in a way that allows decision makers to grasp its meaning and significance
5. Secure	Stored and presented in a way that prevents hackers and other unauthorized parties from obtaining access to it

© Cengage Learning 2013

LO4 Explain how Internet-based technologies have changed business-to-consumer and business-to-business commerce

Information technology, and especially the Internet, has revolutionized the way firms interact with their customers in both the business-to-consumer (B2C) and business-to-business (B2B) markets. In the B2C market, the Internet has enabled firms to reach broader markets, advertise in new ways, and take customer relationship marketing to a new level. One strategy has been to create more interactive websites that encourage customers to collaborate and provide content—an approach referred to as *Web 2.0*. In the B2B market, e-marketplaces enable firms to negotiate with suppliers or

hardware
The physical tools and equipment used to collect, input, store, organize, and process data and to distribute information.

software
Programs that provide instructions to a computer so that it can perform a desired task.

system software
Software that performs the critical functions necessary to operate the computer at the most basic level.

applications software
Software that helps a user perform a desired task.

Internet
The world's largest computer network; essentially a network of computer networks all operating under a common set of rules that allow them to communicate with each other.

broadband Internet connection
An Internet connection that is capable of transmitting large amounts of information very quickly.

Internet2 (I2)
A new high-tech Internet with access limited to a consortium of member organizations (and other organizations these members sponsor). I2 utilizes technologies that give it a speed and capacity far exceeding the current Internet.

intranet
A private network that has the look and feel of the Internet and is navigated using a Web browser, but which limits access to a single firm's employees (or a single organization's members.

extranet
An intranet that allows limited access to a selected group of stakeholders, such as suppliers or customers.

cloud computing
The use of Internet-based storage capacity, processing power, and computer applications to supplement or replace internally owned information technology resources.

data
Raw, unprocessed facts and figures.

information
Data that have been processed in a way that makes them meaningful to their user.

database
A file consisting of related data organized according to a logical system and stored on a hard drive or other computer-accessible media.

RIP & REVIEW

decision support system (DSS)
A system that gives managers access to large amounts of data and the processing power to convert these data into high-quality information, thus improving the decision-making process.

business intelligence system
A sophisticated form of decision support system that helps decision makers discover information that was previously hidden.

data warehouse
A large, organization-wide database that stores data in a centralized location.

data mining
The use of sophisticated statistical and mathematical techniques to analyze data and discover hidden patterns and relationships among data, thus creating valuable information.

expert system (ES)
A decision-support system that helps managers make better decisions in an area where they lack expertise.

e-commerce
The marketing, buying, selling, and servicing of products over a network (usually the Internet).

business-to-consumer (B2C) e-commerce
E-commerce in which businesses and final consumers interact.

business-to-business (B2B) e-commerce
E-commerce in markets where businesses buy from and sell to other businesses.

Web 2.0
Websites that incorporate interactive and collaborative features in order to create a richer, more interesting, and more useful experience for their users.

viral marketing
An Internet marketing strategy that tries to involve customers and others not employed by the seller in activities that help promote the product.

cybermediary
An Internet-based firm that specializes in the secure electronic transfer of funds.

electronic bill presentment and payment
A method of bill payment that makes it easy for the customer to make a payment, often by simply clicking on a payment option contained in an email.

e-marketplace
A specialized Internet site where buyers and sellers engaged in business-to-business e-commerce can communicate and conduct business.

radio frequency identification (RFID)
A technology that stores information on small microchips that can transmit the information when they are within range of a special reader.

malware
A general term for malicious software, such as spyware, computer viruses, and worms.

customers more effectively and share information that leads to better coordination and collaboration.

LO5 Describe the problems posed by the rapid changes in Internet-based technologies, and explain ways to address these problems

The rapid development of Internet-based technologies has created several challenges and raised some controversial issues. The Internet has made it easier for malware such as computer viruses and spyware to land in your computer, undermining the security of your information and the stability of your system. Performing regular backups and keeping antivirus and antispyware software and operating systems updated can reduce these threats. Spam is unsolicited commercial email, usually sent to vast numbers of people with little regard for whether they have any interest in the message. Spam filters are available, but spammers are good at finding ways to fool the filters. Phishing and pharming are scams that use fake websites to trick people into divulging private information. One of the most controversial impacts of information technology has been the loss of personal privacy. Another issue involves intellectual property. The Internet makes it possible to share videos, music, and computer programs with large numbers of people, leading to a surge in the illegal sharing of copyrighted material.

spyware
Software that is installed on a computer without the user's knowledge or permission for the purpose of tracking the user's behavior.

computer virus
Computer software that can be spread from one computer to another without the knowledge or permission of the computer users by attaching itself to emails or other files.

worm
Malicious computer software that, unlike viruses, can spread on its own without being attached to other files.

spam
Unsolicited email advertisements usually sent to very large numbers of recipients, many of whom may have no interest in the message.

phishing
A scam in which official-looking emails are sent to individuals in an attempt to get them to divulge private information such as passwords, user names, and account numbers.

pharming
A scam that seeks to steal identities by routing Internet traffic to fake websites.

hacker
A skilled computer user who uses his or her expertise to gain unauthorized access to the computer (or computer system) of others, sometimes with malicious intent.

firewall
Software and/or hardware designed to prevent unwanted access to a computer or computer system.

intellectual property
Property that is the result of creative or intellectual effort, such as books, musical works, inventions, and computer software.

Operations Management: Putting It All Together

LO1 Define operations management and describe how its role has changed over the past fifty years

Operations management oversees all the activities involved in producing and distributing goods and services. When operations managers do their job well, their firms produce the *right* goods and services in the *right* quantities and distribute them to the *right* customers at the *right* time—all while keeping quality high and costs low.

Operations management has undergone profound changes over the past half century. One change has been a switch in focus from efficiency to effectiveness. *Efficiency* means achieving a goal at the *lowest cost*. *Effectiveness* means *creating value* by satisfying wants. Other key changes include more emphasis on the provision of services, a switch from mass production to customized production, a focus on global markets (and global competition), reliance on complex value chains, and recognition of the need to protect the environment.

LO2 Discuss the key responsibilities of operations managers

Operations managers often play a role in the design of products by helping designers understand the challenges and constraints involved in producing high-quality products on time and within budget. Once the design is finalized, operations managers must determine the best production processes to convert inputs into outputs, design a facility layout that creates an efficient flow of materials, parts, and work in process through the production process, select the best locations for facilities, make decisions about how much inventory to hold, determine how to allocate resources needed to complete complex projects, and manage value chains to coordinate the functions of all of the organizations and processes directly or indirectly involved in producing goods and services and distributing them to customers.

LO3 Describe how operations managers respond to the special challenges posed by the provision of services

Customers often participate in the provision of services, so service providers have only limited control over ways in which their processes are carried out, how long they take to complete, and whether the result is satisfactory. A *servicescape* is the environment in which the customer and service provider interact. A well-designed servicescape can create a better service experience for both the customer and the provider.

Another challenge facing service providers involves determining the proper capacity of service facilities. If the capacity of a service facility is too small, customers facing long waits during peak periods may take their business elsewhere. But a facility large enough to handle peak capacity is more expensive to build and operate and may have substantial excess capacity during off–peak periods. Many service firms try to spread out demand so that big surges don't occur by offering price discounts to customers during off-peak times.

LO4 Explain how changes in technology have revolutionized operations management

Rapid changes in both machinery and equipment and in software and information technologies have revolutionized operations management. The biggest change in machinery and equipment has been the increasing use of automation, which means replacing human operation and control of machinery and equipment with programmed control. The development of software applications to allow computer-aided design (CAD), computer-aided engineering (CAE), and computer-aided manufacturing (CAM) has given firms the flexibility to design, test, and produce goods more quickly and efficiently than ever before. When these powerful software applications are integrated with robots and other automated equipment, the result is called *computer integrated manufacturing*. This tight integration allows firms to produce customized goods quickly and at low cost, a process called *mass customization*.

LO5 Describe the strategies operations managers have used to improve the quality of goods and services

In recent years, U.S. firms have adopted programs such as total quality management (TQM) and Six Sigma to improve quality. TQM and Six Sigma both view quality

operations management
Managing all of the activities involved in creating value by producing goods and services and distributing them to customers.

efficiency
Producing output or achieving a goal at the lowest cost.

effectiveness
Using resources to create the value by providing customers with goods and services that offer a better relationship between price and perceived benefits.

goods
Tangible products.

services
Intangible products.

process
A set of related activities that transform inputs into outputs, thus adding value.

inventory
Stocks of goods or other items held by organizations.

critical path method (CPM)
A project management tool that illustrates the relationships among all the activities involved in completing a project and identifies the sequence of activities likely to take the longest to complete.

immediate predecessors
Activities in a project that must be completed before some other specified activity can begin.

critical path
The sequence of activities in a project that is expected to take the longest to complete.

value chain
The network of relationships that channels the flow of inputs, information, and financial resources through all of the processes directly or indirectly involved in producing goods and services and distributing them to customers.

vertical integration
Performance of processes internally that were previously performed by other organizations in a supply chain.

outsourcing
Arranging for other organizations to perform supply chain functions that were previously performed internally.

offshoring
Moving production or support processes to foreign countries.

enterprise resource planning (ERP)
Software-based approach to integrate an organization's (and in the sophisticated versions, a value chain's) information flows.

servicescape
The environment in which a customer and service provider interact.

automation
Replacing human operation and control of machinery and equipment with some form of programmed control.

robot
A reprogrammable machine that is capable of manipulating materials, tools, parts, and specialized devices in order to perform a variety of tasks.

computer-aided design (CAD)
Drawing and drafting software that enables users to create and edit blueprints and design drawings quickly and easily.

computer-aided engineering (CAE)
Software that enables users to test, analyze, and optimize their designs.

computer-aided manufacturing (CAM)
Software that takes the electronic design for a product and creates the programmed instructions that robots must follow to produce that product as efficiently as possible.

computer-aided design/computer-aided manufacturing (CAD/CAM)
A combination of software that can be used to design output and send instructions to automated equipment to perform the steps needed to produce this output.

computer-integrated manufacturing (CIM)
A combination of CAD/CAM software with flexible manufacturing systems to automate almost all steps involved in designing, testing, and producing a product.

total quality management (TQM)
An approach to quality improvement that calls for everyone within an organization to take responsibility for improving quality and emphasizes the need for a long-term commitment to continuous improvement.

poka-yokes
Simple methods incorporated into a production process designed to eliminate or greatly reduce errors.

Six Sigma
An approach to quality improvement characterized by very ambitious quality goals, extensive training of employees, and a long-term commitment to working on quality-related issues.

Baldrige National Quality Program
A national program to encourage American firms to focus on quality improvement.

ISO 9000
A family of generic standards for quality management systems established by the International Organization for Standardization.

lean production
An approach to production that emphasizes the elimination of waste in all aspects of production processes.

improvement as a continuous process that is the responsibility of everyone within the organization. Both approaches also empower workers and make use of teams to solve quality-related problems. But Six Sigma incorporates more specific quality goals and relies on more sophisticated techniques that require a higher degree of expertise.

Another way firms have tried to improve efficiency has been to launch programs designed to achieve certification or recognition from outside authorities. Two common approaches are to participate in the Baldrige National Quality Program and to seek certification under the International Organization for Standardization's ISO 9000 standards.

The Deming Chain Reaction

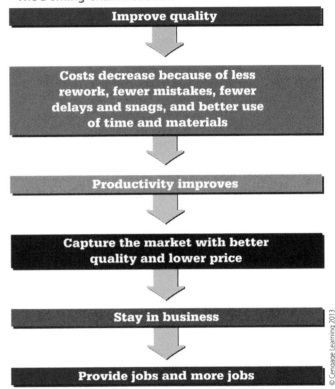

Improve quality

Costs decrease because of less rework, fewer mistakes, fewer delays and snags, and better use of time and materials

Productivity improves

Capture the market with better quality and lower price

Stay in business

Provide jobs and more jobs

© Cengage Learning 2013

L06 Explain how lean and green practices can help both the organization and the environment

Lean production refers to a set of strategies and practices that eliminate waste to make organizations more efficient, responsive, and flexible. Inventory control is one of the key areas where waste often occurs. Many lean firms use just-in-time production methods to minimize the amount of parts, work in process, and finished products they hold in inventory.

Many firms have also become "greener" by finding environmentally friendly ways to produce and distribute their goods and services. Green practices include designing facilities to be more energy efficient; using renewable energy; making use of recyclable materials; switching to paints, lubricants, cleaning fluids, and solvents that are less harmful to the environment; and providing labeling to help consumers find out which products are the most environmentally friendly.

just-in-time (JIT) production
A production system that emphasizes the production of goods to meet actual current demand, thus minimizing the need to hold inventories of finished goods and work in process at each stage of the supply chain.

ISO 14000
A family of generic standards for environmental management established by the International Organization for Standardization.

LO1 Apply the principles of budgeting to your personal finances

A budget is a detailed schedule that documents your expected financial inflows (revenues earned and received) and outflows (expenses incurred and paid) in order to determine your net inflow or outflow for a given period of time. You can use your budget to develop your financial plan and to monitor your progress toward achieving your financial goals. One key part of the budgeting process is accurate estimation of revenues. The other key to setting up a budget is to assess your expenses. Consideration should also be given to understanding factors that affect your spending habits. Certain types of expenditures, called "discretionary costs," can be adjusted fairly easily. Other expenditures, called "non-discretionary costs," are more difficult to cut—at least in the short run.

LO2 Set strategies to help build a sufficient savings and emergency fund

A savings account is an interest-bearing account that is intended to satisfy obligations that cannot be handled by a checking account. Many financial experts suggest that your savings account should be able to cover six months of your expenses. One technique for establishing a sizable savings balance is to "pay yourself first." This technique is accomplished by automatically depositing a predetermined amount into your savings account with each paycheck.

LO3 Understand the importance of building credit history, maintaining good credit, and avoiding unwise credit decisions

Credit refers to your ability to obtain goods or resources without having to make immediate payment. One of the most important determinants of the amount of credit you can obtain is your credit score, which is a numerical indicator of your creditworthiness. Currently, the most commonly used credit scoring system is the Fair, Isaac and Company (FICO) scale. The FICO scale runs from 300 to 850.

A credit card allows its holder to make a purchase now and pay the credit card issuer later. Credit cards are more convenient and safer than carrying a lot of cash. They also make it easy to track your expenditures, since you have access to a monthly summary of charges. And many cards offer perks, such as discounts on certain products, extended warranties on purchases, or frequent-flier miles. Another benefit of the *responsible* use of credit cards is that it can improve your credit score by allowing you to establish a history of prompt payments.

One downside of having a credit card is that the "buy now, pay later" aspect of credit card use makes it hard for some people to maintain financial discipline. Another problem is that interest rates on unpaid card balances tend to be very high. Many card issuers also impose a variety of fees that can make a noticeable dent in your wallet. And making late payments or failing to pay what you owe can damage your credit history, hurting your chances of getting additional credit when you need it.

Before you accept a credit card, you should read and understand all of the main conditions for using that card. Among the major areas to consider are 1) the grace period, the period of time that you have to pay your balance before interest or fees are assessed, 2) the APR (annual interest rate on unpaid balances) as well as any other fees that may be assessed if a payment is not received within a grace period or if credit limits are exceeded when using the credit card, and 3) other fees, such as annual fees, over-the-credit-limit fees, and balance-transfer fees.

The first rule when you have credit card difficulties is to just stop using the card. Then commit to setting up (and sticking to) a budget and putting a consistent amount of money toward retiring the debt on that card. Another useful tip is to use cash or a debit card instead. Many people tend to spend more when they pay with a credit card than if they pay with cash.

budget (personal)
A detailed forecast of financial inflows (income) and outflows (expenses) in order to determine your net inflow or outflow for a given period of time.

discretionary payments
Expenditures for which the spender has significant control in terms of the amount and timing.

nondiscretionary payments
Expenditures that the spender has little or no control over.

savings account
An interest-bearing account holding funds not needed to meet regular expenditures.

Federal Deposit Insurance Corporation (FDIC)
An independent agency created by Congress to maintain stability and public confidence in the nation's financial system, primarily by insuring bank deposits.

credit
Allows a borrower to acquire an asset or to obtain a loan and repay the balance at a later time.

credit score
A numerical measure of a consumer's creditworthiness.

credit card
A card issued by a bank or finance company that allows the cardholder to make a purchase now and pay the credit card issuer later.

grace period
The period of time that the credit-card holder has to pay outstanding balances before interest or fees are assessed.

annual percentage rate (APR)
The interest expense charged on a credit card, expressed as an annual percentage.

debit card
A card issued by the bank that allows the customer to make purchases as if the transaction involved cash. In a debit card purchase, the customer's bank account is immediately reduced at the time the purchase is made.

investing
Reducing consumption in the current time period in order to build future wealth.

IRA
An individual retirement account that provides tax benefits to individuals who are investing for their retirement.

401(k), 403(b), and 457 plans
Employee payroll deduction retirement plans that offer tax benefits.

company matching
An amount contributed by the employer to an employee's retirement account, matching the employee's retirement contributions either dollar for dollar or based on a percentage of each dollar contributed by the employee.

vesting period
A specified period of time in which an employee must be employed in order to receive the full advantage of certain retirement benefits.

RIP & REVIEW

LO4 Discuss key wealth-building principles and outline the various investments that may be part of an effective wealth-building strategy

Investing involves reducing consumption today in order to build future wealth. One key to investing is consistency—make it a habit to invest something every month. Another key is to begin as soon as possible, even if you can only invest a little. The time value of money says that a dollar invested today is worth more than a dollar invested later, because the earlier a dollar is invested, the longer it can earn a return.

There are several different types of financial assets you might want to consider. Each has its own advantages and disadvantages. One trade-off involves risk and return. Investments that offer the potential for high returns tend to be riskier than investments that offer lower returns.

Corporate stock represents shares of ownership in a corporation. Investing in stock offers the possibility of receiving dividends, which are a distribution of a company's profits to its stockholders. It also offers the potential for capital gains, which are increases in the market value of stocks. However, neither dividends nor capital gains are guaranteed. *Corporate bonds* are formal IOUs issued by corporations. Bonds typically pay a stated rate of interest until they mature (come due). Once a bond matures, the issuer is obligated to pay the bondholder an amount known as the "principal" (or face value) of the bond.

Certificates of deposit are offered by banks and other depository institutions. They are similar to savings accounts but are issued for a fixed term—ranging from a few months to as long as five years. One advantage of CDs is that they are insured by the Federal Deposit Insurance Corporation (FDIC). Because of this insurance and their predictable rate of return, CDs are considered to be among the safest investment options. But they generally pay less interest than bonds and most other investments

Government securities are IOUs issued by a government entity. States and municipalities often issue bonds. The federal government issues several types of government securities, ranging from short-term T-bills to long-term bonds. T-bills usually offer relatively low interest rates but have usually been considered very safe investments. The big increase in federal debt in recent years has led some investors to rethink this view.

Mutual funds offer investors shares that represent ownership in a variety of financial securities, such as stocks, corporate bonds, and government securities. These funds are professionally managed. The managers select the specific securities that the fund holds. *Exchange-traded funds* are "market baskets" of securities that are traded much like individual shares of stock.

Investors have several options when it comes to building up wealth for their retirement. One approach is to open an individual retirement account (IRA). There are several types of IRAs, the most popular being the traditional IRA and the Roth IRA. Contributions to a traditional IRA are tax deductible, but withdrawals are taxed. Contributions to a Roth IRA aren't tax deductible, but the distributions paid to retirees are tax exempt. One drawback of IRAs is that the amount investors can contribute each year is relatively small. In 2011, the maximum contribution for both types of plans was $5,000. (Individuals over the age of 50 could contribute up to $6,000.) 401(k), 403(b), and 457 employee contribution retirement plans are named for the sections of the tax code where they are defined. These retirement accounts are funded by payroll deductions. Like IRAs, these plans have both traditional and Roth versions. But compared to IRAs, they have much higher contribution limits. Another possible advantage is that many companies match (contribute) the employee contribution either dollar for dollar or a percentage of each dollar you contribute up to a limit.

Labor Unions and Collective Bargaining

Visit www.cengagebrain.com to find this online appendix.

LO1 Describe how unions in the United States are organized

A labor union is a group of workers who have organized in order to pursue common job-related objectives, such as securing better wages and benefits, safer working conditions, and greater job security. Unions can be organized either as craft unions, which consist of members who share the same skill or profession, or as industrial unions, which consist of workers in the same industry. The most basic unit of a union is the local union. This is the level at which most members have an opportunity to get directly involved in union activities. Most locals belong to a national (or international) union. The national union provides training, legal support, and bargaining advice to locals; organizes new locals; and sometimes takes an active role in the collective bargaining process. Many national unions belong to the AFL-CIO, which serves as the national voice for the labor movement.

LO2 Discuss the key provisions of the laws that govern labor–management relations

Until the 1930s, no federal laws dealt specifically with the rights of workers to organize unions or the way unions could carry out their functions. During the Great Depression of the 1930s, several pro-labor laws were enacted. The most important of these was the National Labor Relations Act, often called the "Wagner Act." This law prevented employers from discriminating against union members and required employers to recognize and bargain with certified unions. It also established the National Labor Relations Board to investigate charges of unfair labor practices. After World War II, Congress enacted the Labor–Management Relations Act, more commonly called the "Taft–Hartley Act." This law sought to limit the power of unions. It identified several unfair labor practices by unions and declared them illegal and allowed workers to vote to decertify a union that represented them. It also made closed shops (in which employers could only hire workers who already belonged to a union) illegal. Finally, it allowed states to pass right-to-work laws that made union shops (in which all workers had to join the union within a specified time in order to keep their jobs) illegal.

LO3 Explain how labor contracts are negotiated and administered

The process by which representatives of labor and management attempt to negotiate a mutually acceptable labor agreement is called "collective bargaining." There are two broad, basic approaches to collective bargaining. In distributive bargaining, the process tends to be adversarial. The sides begin with predetermined positions and an initial set of demands. They then use persuasion, logic, and even threats to gain as much as they can. The other approach is called "interest-based bargaining." In this approach, the two sides do not present initial demands. Instead, they raise issues and concerns and try to work together to develop mutually beneficial solutions.

Negotiations sometimes break down. An impasse occurs when it becomes obvious that a settlement is not possible under current conditions. When an impasse is reached, the union may call a strike, or the employer may call a lockout. However, both sides may agree to either mediation or arbitration to try to settle their differences and reach agreement without resorting to such work stoppages. Mediators can only make suggestions and encourage the two sides to settle. If one or both sides reject the mediator's efforts, then the process is likely to fail. In contrast, an arbitrator has the authority to render a binding decision. Arbitration is common in the public sector but rare in the private sector.

When workers believe they have been unfairly treated under terms of the contract, they may file a grievance. Most labor agreements contain a formal grievance procedure that identifies a specific series of steps involved in settling a complaint. The final step usually involves binding arbitration.

---

labor union
A group of workers who have organized to work together to achieve common job-related goals, such as higher wages, better working conditions, and greater job security.

craft union
A union comprising workers who share the same skill or work in the same profession.

industrial union
A union comprising workers employed in the same industry.

employment at will
A legal doctrine that views employment as an entirely voluntary relationship that both the employee and employer are free to terminate at any time and for any reason.

National Labor Relations Act (Wagner Act)
Landmark pro-labor law enacted in 1935. This law made it illegal for firms to discriminate against union members and required employers to recognize certified unions and bargain with them in good faith.

Labor–Management Relations Act (Taft–Hartley Act)
Law passed in 1947 that placed limits on union activities, outlawed the closed shop, and allowed states to pass right-to-work laws that made union shops illegal.

closed shop
An employment arrangement in which the employer agrees to hire only workers who already belong to the union.

union shop
An employment arrangement in which a firm can hire nonunion workers, but these workers must join the union within a specified time period to keep their jobs.

right-to-work law
A state law that makes union shops illegal within that state's borders.

open shop
An employment arrangement in which workers are not required to join a union or pay union dues.

collective bargaining
The process by which representatives of union members and employers attempt to negotiate a mutually acceptable labor agreement.

distributive bargaining
The traditional adversarial approach to collective bargaining.

interest-based bargaining
A form of collective bargaining that emphasizes cooperation and problem solving in an attempt to find a "win–win" outcome.

strike
A work stoppage initiated by a union.

lockout
An employer-initiated work stoppage.

picketing
A union tactic during labor disputes in which union members walk near the entrance of the employer's place of business, carrying signs to publicize their position and concerns.

boycott
A tactic in which a union and its supporters and sympathizers refuse to do business with an employer with which they have a labor dispute.

mediation
A method of dealing with an impasse between labor and management by bringing in a neutral third party to help the two sides reach agreement by reducing tensions and making suggestions for possible compromises.

arbitration
A process in which a neutral third party has the authority to resolve a dispute by rendering a binding decision.

grievance
A complaint by a worker that the employer has violated the terms of the collective bargaining agreement.

RIP & REVIEW

Major Labor Legislation in the United States

DATE	LAW	MAJOR PROVISIONS
1932	Norris–LaGuardia Act	• Stated that workers had a legal right to organize • Made it more difficult to get injunctions against peaceful union activities
1935	National Labor Relations Act (or Wagner Act)	• Made it illegal for employers to discriminate based on union membership • Established the National Labor Relations Board to investigate unfair labor practices • Established a voting procedure for workers to certify a union as their bargaining agent • Required employers to recognize certified unions and bargain with them in good faith
1938	Fair Labor Standards Act	• Banned many types of child labor • Established the first federal minimum wage (25 cents per hour) • Established a standard 40-hour workweek • Required that hourly workers receive overtime pay when they work in excess of 40 hours per week.
1947	Labor–Management Relations Act	• Identified unfair labor practices by unions and declared them illegal • Allowed employers to speak against unions during organizing campaigns • Allowed union members to decertify their union, removing its right to represent them • Established provisions for dealing with emergency strikes that threatened the nation's health or security
1959	Labor–Management Reporting and Disclosure Act (or Landrum–Griffin Act)	• Guaranteed rank-and-file union members the right to participate in union meetings • Required regularly scheduled secret ballot elections of union officers • Required unions to file annual financial reports • Prohibited convicted felons and Communist Party members from holding union office

© Cengage Learning 2013

LO4 **Evaluate the impact that unions have had on their members' welfare and the economy, and explain the challenges that today's unions face**

Most studies find that union workers earn higher wages and receive more benefits than nonunion workers with similar skills, performing the same type of job. Union contracts and the grievance procedure also provide union members with more protection from arbitrary discipline (including firings) than nonunion workers enjoy. However, unionized industries in the private sector haven't provided much job security. Total employment in many highly unionized industries has fallen dramatically in recent years.

Many critics argue that unions undermine worker productivity by imposing rules and restrictions that reduce the ability of firms to innovate and require employers to use more labor than necessary to produce goods and provide services. But union supporters suggest that unions reduce worker turnover and encourage worker training, thus increasing productivity. Research on this topic has not yielded clear-cut evidence in support of either position.

One of the major problems facing unions is the continuing decline in union membership in the private sector. There are several reasons for this decline. In part, it represents a change in the structure of the U.S. economy. But another reason has been the increasing willingness of employers to use antiunion tactics to discourage union membership. The AFL-CIO and national unions have placed greater emphasis on organizing activities in recent years in an attempt to reverse this trend. Until recently, these efforts met with little success. However, between 2006 and 2007 there was a slight increase in private-sector union membership for the first time in 25 years. This was followed by an even larger increase in membership between 2007 and 2008. These developments raised hopes among union leaders that they had turned the corner. However, union membership fell substantially in both 2009 and 2010. This decline may have been due in part to the severity of the Great Recession. The long-term trend in membership is difficult to determine, but the optimism that existed among union leaders in 2008 is no longer apparent.

Business Law

Visit www.cengagebrain.com to find this online appendix.

LO1 Explain the purposes of laws and identify the major sources of laws in the United States

Laws are those rules—enforced by a government—that set parameters for the conduct and actions of people within a society. These rules promote order and stability, protect individuals from physical or mental harm, protect property from damage or theft, promote behavior that society deems desirable, and deter behavior that society deems undesirable. Laws come from several sources. Constitutional law is based on a constitution, such as the U.S. Constitution or a state constitution. Statutory law is enacted by a legislative body, such as Congress or a state legislature. Administrative laws are established and enforced by government agencies. Case law (also called *common law*) is law based on court decisions known as *precedents*.

There are two branches of law in the United States. *Civil law* deals with disputes between private parties. These disputes are settled in the courts when one of the parties (called the *plaintiff*) initiates a lawsuit against the other (called the *defendant*). *Criminal law* involves cases in which the state investigates and prosecutes alleged wrongdoers accused of a violation of their public duty. The most serious crimes are called *felonies*. Less serious crimes are called *misdemeanors*.

LO2 Describe the characteristics of a contract and explain how the terms of contracts are enforced

A contract is an agreement that is enforceable in a court of law. A valid contract is characterized by (1) mutual assent; (2) consideration; (3) legal capacity; and (4) legal purpose. In addition, according to the *statute of frauds*, certain types of contracts, such as those that will take more than a year to complete, or those involving the sale of goods worth more than $500, must be in writing.

A breach of contract occurs if one of the parties does not live up to the terms of the agreement. When one party breaches a contract, the other party can sue in a civil court. If the court agrees that a party breached the contract, it orders some type of remedy. The most common remedy is compensatory damages, which means the party who breached the contract must pay money to the injured party to compensate for the actual harm suffered. In cases where the contract calls for the sale of a unique good, the courts may apply a remedy known as "specific performance," which requires the party who breached the contract to do exactly what the contract says. Finally, the courts may issue injunctions (court orders) that prevent the party who breached the contract from taking some action.

Differences Between Civil and Criminal Law Cases

	CIVIL LAW	CRIMINAL LAW
Nature of action and parties involved	Lawsuits to settle disputes between private individuals	Federal or state government prosecution of parties charged with wrongdoings against society
Examples of cases	Intentional torts, such as slander, libel, invasion of privacy, wrongful death; unintentional torts arising from negligence; breach of contract	Felonies, such as robbery, theft, murder, arson, identity theft, extortion, embezzlement, as well as less serious crimes called misdemeanors
Possible outcomes	Liable or not liable	Guilty or not guilty
Standard of proof (what is needed for plaintiff to win the case)	Preponderance of evidence (a much less stringent requirement than beyond reasonable doubt)	Proof beyond a reasonable doubt
Goal of remedy	Compensate injured party for harm suffered	Punish wrongdoer and deter similar behavior
Common remedies	Monetary damages (payments of money to compensate the injured party), injunctions against certain types of behavior, or requirements for specific performance	Fines and/or imprisonment; in the most serious felonies, such as premeditated murder, capital punishment (the death penalty) may be imposed

© Cengage Learning 2013

---

laws
Rules that govern the conduct and actions of people within a society that are enforced by the government.

constitution
A code that establishes the fundamental rules and principles that govern a particular organization or entity.

statutory law
Laws that are the result of legislative action.

Uniform Commercial Code (UCC)
A uniform act governing the sale of goods, leases, warranties, transfer of funds, and a variety of other business-related activities.

administrative law
Laws that arise from regulations established by government agencies.

case law (also called common law)
Laws that result from rulings, called precedents, made by judges who initially hear a particular type of case.

tort
A private wrong that results in physical or mental harm to an individual, or damage to that person's property.

negligence
An unintentional tort that arises due to carelessness or irresponsible behavior.

crime
A wrongful act against society, defined by law and prosecuted by the state.

business law
The application of laws and legal principles to business relationships and transactions.

contract
An agreement that is legally enforceable.

consideration
Something of value that one party gives another as part of a contractual agreement.

statute of frauds
A requirement that certain types of contracts must be in writing in order to be enforceable.

breach of contract
The failure of one party to a contract to perform his or her contractual obligations.

statute of limitations
The time period within which a legal action must be initiated.

compensatory damages
Monetary payments that a party who breaches a contract is ordered to pay in order to compensate the injured party for the actual harm suffered by the breach of contract.

specific performance
A remedy for breach of contract in which the court orders the party committing the breach to do exactly what the contract specifies.

sale
A transaction in which the title (legal ownership) to a good passes from one party to another in exchange for a price.

title
Legal of ownership.

principal—agent relationship
A relationship in which one party, called the principal, gives another party, called the agent, the authority to act in place of, and bind the principal when dealing with third parties.

principal
A party who agrees to have someone else (called an *agent*) act on his or her behalf.

agent
A party who agrees to represent another party, called the principal.

scope of authority (for an agent)
The extent to which an agent has the authority to act for and represent the principal.

Chapter 7 bankruptcy
A form of bankruptcy that discharges a debtor's debts by liquidating assets and using the proceeds to pay off creditors.

Chapter 11 bankruptcy
A form of bankruptcy used by corporations and individuals that allows the debtor to reorganize operations under a court-approved plan.

Chapter 13 bankruptcy
A form of bankruptcy that allows individual debtors to set up a repayment plan to adjust their debts.

property
The legal right of an owner to exclude nonowners from having control over a particular resource.

intellectual property
Property that results from intellectual or creative efforts.

patent
A legal monopoly that gives an inventor the exclusive right over an invention for a limited time period.

trademark
A mark, symbol, word, phrase, or motto used to identify a company's goods.

copyright
The exclusive legal right of an author, artist, or other creative individual to use, copy, display, perform, and sell their own creations and to license others to do so.

L03 Describe how both title and risk pass from the seller to the buyer when a sale occurs

A sale occurs when title to a good or a piece of real property passes from one party to another in exchange for a price. Sales of goods are covered by Article 2 of the Uniform Commercial Code, which has been adopted by every state in the United States except Louisiana. Sales of services are based on precedents established by common law. A sales contract must contain the same basic elements as other contracts. However, the UCC has relaxed the requirements for some of these elements. For example, under the UCC, courts may recognize a sales contract even if certain key facts of the agreement (such as the price of the good) aren't explicitly spelled out. In such cases, the UCC provides guidelines for supplying the missing details. One key sales contract issue involves when title actually passes from one party to another. If the contract is silent about this, the UCC generally holds that title passes when the seller has completed all duties related to the delivery of the good. Another key issue involves which party bears the risk if the goods are lost, damaged, or destroyed during the transfer from seller to buyer. If the contract doesn't specify which party assumes the risk, the UCC normally places the risk on the party that is most likely to have insurance against a loss, or on the party that is in the better position to prevent a loss.

L04 Provide an overview of the legal principles governing agency, intellectual property, and bankruptcy

A principal—agent relationship exists when one party (the principal) gives another party (the agent) the authority to act and enter into binding agreements on the principal's behalf. As long as agents act within their scope of authority, principals are legally liable for any contracts their agents enter into while representing them. Not all employees have the authority to act as agents, but many do. A loan officer at a bank and a salesperson at a store are both employees of, and agents for, their companies.

Intellectual property refers to the rights of inventors, innovators, authors, and artists to own their creations and prevent others from copying, distributing, displaying, performing, or selling these creations without their permission. Patents protect the intellectual property rights of inventors. Most patents give the inventor exclusive rights to their invention for 20 years. Copyrights protect the intellectual property rights of authors, artists, and other creative individuals. Copyrights normally extend for 70 years beyond the author's or artist's life. Trademarks, which are marks, symbols, words, phrases, or mottos that identify a company's goods, are another form of intellectual property. Registered trademarks are protected for ten years, and the protection can be extended for an unlimited number of additional ten-year periods.

Bankruptcy provides a way for debtors who are unable to meet their obligations to discharge their debts and get a fresh start. There are several different types of bankruptcy procedures. In a Chapter 7 bankruptcy, the debtor's assets are liquidated, and the proceeds are used to pay the creditors. Once this is done, the debtor's obligations are considered fully discharged, even if (as is almost certainly the case) the proceeds are insufficient to make full payment. Chapter 11 bankruptcy occurs when a debtor reorganizes under a court-approved plan. This approach is usually used by corporations, though it is also possible for individuals to file under Chapter 11. Finally, Chapter 13 bankruptcy allows individuals to adjust their debt payments under a court-approved schedule.

Small Business and Entrepreneurship: Economic Rocket Fuel

LO1 Explain the key reasons to launch a small business

Launching a business is tough, but the advantages of business ownership can far outweigh the risk and hard work. Most people who take the plunge are seeking some combination of greater financial success, independence, flexibility, and challenge. But some are seeking survival and simply have no other options.

For entrepreneurs, the potential rewards outweigh the issues

Risk Hard Work

Financial Success Independence Flexibility Challenge

© Cengage Learning 2013

LO2 Describe the typical entrepreneurial mindset and characteristics

Not all small business owners are entrepreneurs. The difference is attitude: from day one, true entrepreneurs aim to dominate their industry. The entrepreneurial personality typically includes some combination of the following characteristics: vision, self-reliance, energy, confidence, tolerance of uncertainty, and tolerance of failure. While these qualities are very helpful, they aren't essential: it's clearly possible to succeed with a number of different personality types.

Entrepreneurial Characteristics

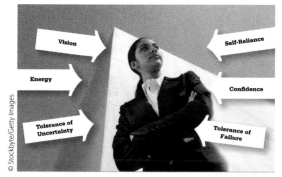

Vision
Self-Reliance
Energy
Confidence
Tolerance of Uncertainty
Tolerance of Failure

© Stockbyte/Getty Images

LO3 Discuss funding options for small business

For many entrepreneurs, finding the money to fund their business is the top challenge of their start-up year. The vast majority of new firms are funded by the personal resources of the founder, including personal accounts (e.g., credit cards), family, and friends. Other key funding sources include bank loans, angel investors, and venture capital firms.

LO4 Analyze the opportunities and threats that small businesses face

Small businesses enjoy some key advantages but also face daunting obstacles as they fight for a foothold in the turbulent marketplace.

Opportunities:

- *Market niches:* Many small firms are uniquely positioned to exploit small, but profitable, market niches.
- *Personal customer service:* With a smaller customer base, small firms can develop much more personal relationships with individual customers.
- *Lower overhead costs:* Many small firms can hold down overhead costs by hiring fewer managers and fewer specialized employees.
- *Technology:* The Web has played a powerful role in opening new opportunities for small business in both local and global markets.

entrepreneurs
People who risk their time, money, and other resources to start and manage a business.

internal locus of control
A deep-seated sense that the individual is personally responsible for what happens in his or her life.

external locus of control
A deep-seated sense that forces other than the individual are responsible for what happens in his or her life.

angel investors
Individuals who invest in start-up companies with high growth potential in exchange for a share of ownership.

venture capital firms
Companies that invest in start-up businesses with high growth potential in exchange for a share of ownership.

market niche
A small segment of a market with fewer competitors than the market as a whole. Market niches tend to be quite attractive to small firms.

Small Business Administration (SBA)
An agency of the federal government designed to maintain and strengthen the nation's economy by aiding, counseling, assisting, and protecting the interests of small businesses.

Small Business Development Centers (SBDCs)
Local offices—affiliated with the Small Business Administration—that provide comprehensive management assistance to current and prospective small business owners.

SCORE (Service Corps of Retired Executives)
An organization—affiliated with the Small Business Administration—that provides free, comprehensive business counseling for small business owners from qualified volunteers.

business plan
A formal document that describes a business concept, outlines core business objectives, and details strategies and timelines for achieving those objectives.

Threats:

- *High risk of failure:* Starting a new business involves a lot of risk, but the odds improve significantly after the five-year mark.
- *Lack of knowledge and experience:* Entrepreneurs often have expertise in a particular area but lack the background to run a successful business.
- *Too little money:* Lack of start-up money is a major issue for most new firms, since ongoing profits don't usually begin for months, or even years.
- *Bigger regulatory burden:* Small firms spend 45% more per employee than big firms, simply complying with federal regulations.
- *Higher health insurance costs:* Small-scale health plans are much more expensive, making it harder to offer employees competitive coverage.

New Business Survival Rates

YEAR IN BUSINESS	SURVIVAL RATE	CHANGE VS. PRIOR YEAR (PERCENTAGE POINTS)
YEAR 1	81%	−19
YEAR 2	66%	−15
YEAR 3	54%	−12
YEAR 4	44%	−10
YEAR 5	38%	−6
YEAR 6	34%	−4
YEAR 7	31%	−3

Source: Business Employment Dynamics data: survival and longevity, II, by Amy E. Knaup and Merissa C. Piazza, September 2007, Monthly Labor Review, Bureau of Labor Statistics website, http://www.bls.gov/opub/mlr/2007/09/art1full.pdf, accessed February 15, 2009.

LO5 Discuss ways to become a new business owner and the tools needed to facilitate success

Many people who are interested in owning their own business prefer to start from scratch and build their company from the ground up. But buying an established business, or even a franchise, can be excellent choices as well. Each choice involves a range of pros and cons, but broadly speaking, it's less risky to buy an established business or franchise, but more satisfying (at least for some people) to start a new venture from scratch. Whichever path you choose—whether you're an ambitious entrepreneur or simply a small business owner—several strategies can help you succeed over the long term: gain experience in your field, learn from others, educate yourself, access SBA resources, and develop a business plan.

BUSINESS LAUNCH OPTIONS

- Starting from scratch
- Buying an established business
- Buying a franchise

STRATEGIES FOR SUCCESS:

- Gain experience
- Learn from others
- Educate yourself
- Access SBA resources
- Develop a plan

© Cengage Learning 2013

LO6 Explain the size, scope, and economic contributions of small business

Small businesses play a vital role in the American economy, generating about half of the U.S. gross domestic product and accounting for 64% of all new jobs over the past 15 years. In addition to fueling employment growth, small businesses contribute innovations to the economy at a much higher rate than their big business counterparts. They also form the backbone of many inner-city economies, finding opportunities—and offering products and services—in places where most large firms opt not to operate. The entrepreneurship rate around the world varies dramatically from country to country, ranging from a high of 31.2% in Vanuatu to a low of 1.3% in Italy. The differences among countries seem to depend largely on the national per capita income, the opportunity costs for entrepreneurs, and the national culture and political environment.

Accounting: Decision Making by the Numbers

LO1 Define accounting and explain how accounting information is used by a variety of stakeholders

Accounting is a system for recognizing, organizing, analyzing, and reporting information about the financial transactions that affect an organization. This information is important to many different stakeholder groups. Owners want to know whether their firm made a profit or suffered a loss. Creditors want to make sure that the firm has the capacity to repay any loans they make. Employees want to know whether their company is performing well enough to provide job security and a good pay raise. The IRS wants to know the amount of taxable income the firm earns during each period.

LO2 Identify the Purposes and Goals of Generally Accepted Accounting Principles

Generally accepted accounting principles (GAAP) are rules that govern the practice of financial accounting. The goal of GAAP is to ensure that the information generated by financial accounting is relevant, reliable, consistent, and comparable.

LO3 Describe the key elements of the major financial statements

The balance sheet shows the firm's financial position at a specific point in time by reporting the value of its assets, liabilities, and owners' equity. The income statement shows the net income (profit or loss) the firm earns over a stated time period by deducting expenses from revenues. The statement of cash flows shows the inflows and outflows of cash that result from a firm's operations, financing activities, and investing activities in a given time period and the net change in the amount of cash the firm has over that time period.

LO4 Describe several methods stakeholders can use to obtain useful insights from a company's financial statements.

In addition to looking at the numbers in financial statements, it's also important to check out the independent auditor's report, read the management discussion, and examine the endnotes that accompany these statements. The auditor's report indicates whether the financial statements were prepared in accordance with GAAP and fairly present the financial condition of the company. The management discussion provides insights by top management to put the numbers in context. Endnotes often disclose key information that isn't directly available in the statements themselves. It's also a good idea to compare the figures reported in current statements to those from earlier statements to see how key account values have changed.

LO5 Explain the role of managerial accounting and describe the various cost concepts identified by managerial accountants.

Managerial accounting provides information to an organization's managers and other internal stakeholders so that they can make better decisions. One key type of information provided by managerial accounting involves the classification and measurement of costs. Explicit (or out-of-pocket) costs involve monetary payments. Implicit costs arise when a company gives up an opportunity to use an asset in an alternative way. Fixed costs don't change when a firm changes its rate of output. Variable costs rise when production increases, and fall when it decreases. Direct costs are tied to the production of a specific good, while indirect costs are incurred as the result of a firm's overall operations and are not tied directly to specific good.

LO6 Explain how the budget process can help managers plan, motivate, and evaluate their organization's performance.

Budgeting facilitates planning by translating goals into measurable quantities and requiring managers to identify the specific resources needed to achieve them. The budgeting process can help with both motivation and evaluation. Employees tend to be more highly motivated when they understand the goals they are expected to accomplish and believe they are ambitious but achievable. Managers can compare actual performance to budgeted figures to determine whether various departments and functional areas are making adequate progress toward achieving their organization's goals.

cash Flows

Standards + reporting

accounting
A system for recognizing, organizing, analyzing, and reporting information about the financial transactions that affect an organization.

financial accounting
The branch of accounting that prepares financial statements for use by owners, creditors, suppliers, and other external stakeholders.

generally accepted accounting principles (GAAP)
A set of accounting standards that is used in the preparation of financial statements.

Financial Accounting Standards Board (FASB)
The private board that establishes the generally accepted accounting principles used in the practice of financial accounting.

balance sheet
A financial statement that reports the financial position of a firm by identifying and reporting the value of the firm's assets, liabilities, and owners' equity.

accounting equation
Assets = Liabilities + Owners' Equity

assets
Resources owned by a firm.

liabilities
Claims that outsiders have against a firm's assets.

owners' equity
The claims a firm's owners have against their company's assets (often called "stockholders' equity" on balance sheets of corporations).

income statement
The financial statement that reports the revenues, expenses, and net income that result from a firm's operations over an accounting period.

revenue
Increases in a firm's assets that result from the sale of goods, provision of services, or other activities intended to earn income.

accrual-basis accounting
The method of accounting that recognizes revenue when it is earned and matches expenses to the revenues they helped produce.

expenses
Resources that are used up as the result of business operations.

net income
The difference between the revenue a firm earns and the expenses it incurs in a given time period.

statement of cash flows
The financial statement that identifies a firm's sources and uses of cash in a given accounting period.

Networking capitals

RIP & REVIEW

Financial Accounting Statements

horizontal analysis
Analysis of financial statements that compares account values reported on these statements over two or more years to identify changes and trends.

managerial (or management) accounting
The branch of accounting that provides reports and analysis to managers to help them make informed business decisions.

cost
The value of what is given up in exchange for something.

out-of-pocket cost
A cost that involves the payment of money or other resources.

implicit cost
The opportunity cost that arises when a firm uses owner-supplied resources.

fixed costs
Costs that remain the same when the level of production changes within some relevant range.

variable costs
Costs that vary directly with the level of production.

direct costs
Costs that are incurred directly as the result of some specific cost object.

indirect costs
Costs that are the result of a firm's general operations and are not directly tied to any specific cost object.

activity-based costing (ABC)
A technique to assign product costs based on links between activities that drive costs and the production of specific products.

budgeting
A management tool that explicitly shows how a firm will acquire and use the resources needed to achieve its goals over a specific time period.

operating budgets
Budgets that communicate an organization's sales and production goals and the resources needed to achieve these goals.

financial budgets
Budgets that focus on the firm's financial goals and identify the resources needed to achieve these goals.

master budget
A presentation of an organization's operational and financial budgets that represents the firm's overall plan of action for a specified time period.

FINANCIAL STATEMENT	PURPOSE	KEY COMPONENTS	BASIC RELATIONSHIP
BALANCE SHEET	Shows the value of a firm's assets at a particular point in time and identifies the claims that owners and outsiders have against those assets.	• Assets: things of value owned by the firm. • Liabilities: claims that outsiders have against the firm's assets. • Owners' Equity: claims that the owners of a firm have against its assets.	Assets = Liabilities + Owners' Equity
INCOME STATEMENT	Reports the profit or loss earned by the firm over a given time period.	• Revenues: increases in cash and other assets that the firm earns from its operations. • Expenses: the cash and other resources used up to generate revenue. • Net Income: the profit or loss earned by a firm in a given time period.	Revenues – Expenses = Net Income
STATEMENT OF CASH FLOWS	Shows how and why the amount of cash held by the firm changed over a given period of time, by identifying the cash flows from the three sources: operations, investments, and financing.	• Operations: the cash flows that arise from producing and selling goods and services. • Investments: the cash flows resulting from buying and selling fixed assets, and from buying and selling financial securities of other companies. • Financing: cash a firm receives from selling its own securities, and cash the firm disburses to pay dividends and interest.	Net change in cash = Total inflow of cash – Total outflow of cash.

© Cengage Learning 2013

Comparison of Financial and Managerial Accounting

FINANCIAL ACCOUNTING	MANAGERIAL ACCOUNTING
Is primarily intended to provide information to external stakeholders, such as stockholders, creditors, and government regulators.	Is primarily intended to provide information to internal stakeholders such as the managers of specific divisions or departments.
Prepares a standard set of financial statements.	Prepares customized reports designed to address specific problems or issues.
Presents financial statements on a predetermined schedule (usually quarterly and annually).	Creates reports upon request by management rather than according to a predetermined schedule.
Is governed by a set of generally accepted accounting principles.	Uses procedures developed internally and is not required to follow GAAP.
Summarizes past performance and its impact on the firm's present condition.	Provides reports dealing with past performance, but also involves making projections about the future when dealing with planning issues.

© Cengage Learning 2013

Finance: Acquiring and Using Funds to Maximize Value

LO1 Identify the goal of financial management and explain the issues financial managers confront as they seek to achieve this goal

Historically, the goal of financial management has been to *maximize the value of the firm to its owners*. But many of today's businesses have adopted a broader perspective, believing that they have responsibilities not just to stockholders but also to customers, employees, and other stakeholders. Treating these other stakeholders well often builds value, which benefits stockholders, but other stakeholder groups also sometimes have goals that conflict with those of stockholders. When this happens, financial managers generally adopt the policies they believe are most consistent with the interests of ownership. Another challenge that financial managers face is the need to find the appropriate balance between risk and return. The *risk-return tradeoff* suggests that sources and uses of funds that offer the potential for high rates of return tend to be riskier than those that offer lower returns.

LO2 Describe the tools financial managers use to evaluate their company's current financial condition and to develop financial plans

One way financial managers evaluate the firm's current financial condition is by computing ratios based on key accounts listed on their firm's financial statements. Financial managers look at four basic types of ratios. *Liquidity ratios* indicate whether the firm will have enough cash to pay its short-term liabilities as they come due. *Asset management ratios* tell financial managers how effectively a firm is using various assets to generate revenues for their firm. *Leverage ratios* measure the extent to which a firm relies on debt in its capital structure. *Profitability ratios* measure the firm's overall success at using resources to create a profit for its owners.

The budgeted income statement, the budgeted balance sheet, and the cash budget are the key tools that financial managers use to develop and present their financial plans. The budgeted income statement develops a forecast of net income for the planning period. The budgeted balance sheet forecasts the types and amounts of assets the firm will need to implement its plans, and the amount of additional financing necessary to obtain those assets. The cash budget identifies the timing of cash inflows and outflows to help the firm identify when it will have shortages and surpluses of cash.

LO3 Evaluate the major sources of funds available to meet a firm's short-term and long-term financial needs

Established firms have several sources of short-term funds, including bank loans, trade credit, factoring, and commercial paper. Trade credit arises when suppliers ship materials, parts, or goods to a firm without requiring immediate payment. Banks extend short-term loans to firms with good credit ratings. Factors provide immediate cash to firms by purchasing their accounts receivable at a discount. Major corporations sometimes raise funds by selling commercial paper, which are short-term IOUs. Firms that want to build up their permanent financial base have two basic options. First, they can rely on equity financing, which consists of funds provided by owners. The second option is long-term debt financing.

Major Financial Planning Tools

TOOL	PURPOSE
BUDGETED INCOME STATEMENT	Forecasts the sales, expenses, and revenue for a firm in some future time period.
BUDGETED BALANCE SHEET	Projects the types and amounts of assets a firm will need in order to carry out its plans, and shows the amount of additional financing the firm will need to acquire these assets.
CASH BUDGET	Projects the timing and amount of cash flows so that management can determine when it will need to arrange for external financing, and when it will have extra cash to pay off loans or invest in other assets.

© Cengage Learning 2013

financial capital
The funds a firm uses to acquire its assets and finance its operations.

finance
The functional area of business that is concerned with finding the best sources and uses of financial capital.

risk
The degree of uncertainty regarding the outcome of a decision.

risk-return tradeoff
The observation that financial opportunities that offer high rates of return are generally riskier than opportunities that offer lower rates of return.

financial ratio analysis
Computing ratios that compare values of key accounts listed on a firm's financial statements.

liquid asset
An asset that can quickly be converted into cash with little risk of loss.

liquidity ratios
Financial ratios that measure the ability of a firm to obtain the cash it needs to pay its short-term debt obligations as they come due.

asset management ratios
Financial ratios that measure how effectively a firm is using its assets to generate revenues or cash.

financial leverage
The use of debt in a firm's capital structure.

leverage ratios
Ratios that measure the extent to which a firm relies on debt financing in its capital structure.

profitability ratios
Ratios that measure the rate of return a firm is earning on various measures of investment.

budgeted income statement
A projection showing how a firm's budgeted sales and costs will affect expected net income. (Also called a *pro forma* income statement.)

budgeted balance sheet
A projected financial statement that forecasts the types and amounts of assets a firm will need to implement its future plans and how the firm will finance those assets. (Also called a *pro forma* balance sheet.)

cash budget
A detailed forecast of future cash flows that helps financial managers identify when their firm is likely to experience temporary shortages or surpluses of cash.

trade credit
Spontaneous financing granted by sellers when they deliver goods and services to customers without requiring immediate payment.

key Financial ratios: big on test

Capital budgeting Pro-forma statements Net present value

spontaneous financing
Financing that arises during the natural course of business without the need for special arrangements.

factor
A company that provides short-term financing to firms by purchasing their accounts receivable at a discount.

line of credit
A financial arrangement between a firm and a bank in which the bank pre-approves credit up to a specified limit, provided that the firm maintains an acceptable credit rating.

revolving credit agreement
A guaranteed line of credit in which a bank makes a binding commitment to provide a business with funds up to a specified credit limit at any time during the term of the agreement.

commercial paper
Short-term (and usually unsecured) promissory notes issued by large corporations.

retained earnings
The part of a firm's net income it reinvests.

covenant
A restriction lenders impose on borrowers as a condition of providing long-term debt financing.

equity financing
Funds provided by the owners of a company.

debt financing
Funds provided by lenders (creditors).

capital structure
The mix of equity and debt financing a firm uses to meet its permanent financing needs.

Dodd–Frank Act
A law enacted in the aftermath of the financial crisis of 2008–2009 that strengthened government oversight of financial markets and placed limitations on risky financial strategies such as heavy reliance on leverage.

cash equivalents
Safe and highly liquid assets that many firms list with their cash holdings on their balance sheet.

U.S. Treasury bills (T-bills)
Short-term marketable IOUs issued by the U.S. federal government.

money market mutual funds
A mutual fund that pools funds from many investors and uses these funds to purchase very safe, highly liquid securities.

capital budgeting
The process a firm uses to evaluate long-term investment proposals.

time value of money
The principle that a dollar received today is worth more than a dollar received in the future.

certificate of deposit (CD)
An interest-earning deposit that requires the funds to remain deposited for a fixed term. Withdrawal of the funds before the term expires results in a financial penalty.

LO4 Identify the key issues involved in determining a firm's capital structure

Capital structure refers to the mix of equity and debt financing a firm uses to meet its financing needs. Debt financing enables the firm to finance activities without requiring the owners to put up more money. When the firm earns more on borrowed funds than it pays in interest, the excess goes to the owners, thus magnifying the return on their investment. And the interest payments on debt are tax deductible. However, the interest payments and the requirement to repay the amount borrowed can put a strain on companies when business conditions are poor. Equity financing is safer and more flexible than debt financing. But dividend payments are not tax deductible. And issuing new stock can dilute the ownership share of existing stockholders.

LO5 Describe how financial managers acquire and manage current assets

Firms must have cash, but cash earns little or no interest. Firms with a surplus of cash often hold cash equivalents such as T-bills, commercial paper, and money market mutual funds to earn interest. Accounts receivable are what customers who buy on credit owe to a firm. Firms must establish credit policies that balance the higher sales generated by accounts receivable against these risks that credit customers might not make their payments. Inventories are the stocks of materials, work in process and finished goods a firm holds. For many firms, the costs of storing, handling, and insuring inventory items are significant. In recent years, many firms have become very aggressive about keeping inventories as low as possible.

Impact of Capital Structure

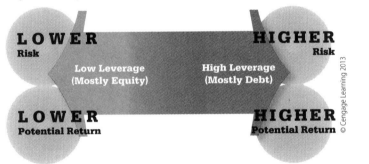

LO6 Explain how financial managers evaluate capital budgeting proposals to identify the best long-term investment options for their company

Capital budgeting is the process financial managers use to evaluate major long-term investment opportunities. Capital budgeting investments are expected to generate cash flows for many years, so financial managers must take the time value of money into account. The time value of money recognizes that the sooner a cash flow is received, the sooner it can be re-invested to earn more money. Financial managers take the time value of money into account by computing the present values of all cash flows the proposal will generate. The present value of a sum of money received in the future is the amount of money today that will become that future amount if it is invested at a specified rate of interest. The net present value (NPV) of the project is the sum of the present values of all the estimated future cash flows, minus the initial cost of the investment. If the NPV of a project is positive, it will increase the value of the firm. If the NPV is negative, it will decrease the value of the firm.

present value
The amount of money that, if invested today at a given rate of interest (called the discount rate), would grow to become some future amount in a specified number of time periods.

net present value (NPV)
The sum of the present values of expected future cash flows from an investment, minus the cost of that investment.

LO1 Define business and discuss the role of business in the economy

A business is any organization that provides goods and services in an effort to earn a profit. *Profit* is the money that a business earns in sales, minus expenses, such as the cost of goods and the cost of salaries. Profit potential provides a powerful incentive for people to start their own businesses, or to become *entrepreneurs*. Successful businesses create wealth, which increases the standard of living for virtually all members of a society.

LO2 Explain the evolution of modern business

Business historians typically divide the history of American business into five distinct eras, which overlap during the periods of transition.

- *Industrial Revolution:* From the mid-1700s to the mid-1800s, technology fueled a period of rapid industrialization. Factories sprang up in cities, leading to mass production and specialization of labor.
- *Entrepreneurship Era:* During the second half of the 1800s, large-scale entrepreneurs emerged, building business empires that created enormous wealth, but often at the expense of workers and consumers.
- *Production Era:* In the early 1900s, major businesses focused on further refining the production process, creating huge efficiencies. The assembly line, introduced in 1913, boosted productivity and lowered costs.
- *Marketing Era:* After WWII, consumers began to gain power. As goods and services flooded the market, the marketing concept emerged: a consumer-first orientation as a guide to business decision-making.
- *Relationship Era:* With the technology boom in the 1990s, businesses have begun to look beyond the immediate transaction, aiming to build a competitive edge through long-term customer relationships.

LO3 Discuss the role of nonprofit organizations in the economy

Nonprofit organizations often work hand in hand with business to improve the quality of life in our society. Nonprofits are business-like establishments that contribute to economic stability and growth. Similar to businesses, nonprofits generate revenue and incur expenses. Their goal is to use any revenue above and beyond expenses to advance the goals of the organization, rather than to make money for its owners. Some nonprofits—such as museums, schools, and theaters—can act as economic magnets for communities, attracting additional investment.

The Relationship Between Nonprofits and Businesses

© Cengage Learning 2013

| Advance Goals of Organization | Generate Revenue Incur Expenses Provide Employment | Create Profit for Owners |

value
The relationship between the price of a good or a service and the benefits that it offers its customers.

business
Any organization that provides goods and services in an effort to earn a profit.

profit
The money that a business earns in sales (or revenue), minus expenses, such as the cost of goods, and the cost of salaries. Revenue – Expenses = Profit (or Loss).

loss
When a business incurs expenses that are greater than its revenue.

entrepreneurs
People who risk their time, money, and other resources to start and manage a business.

standard of living
The quality and quantity of goods and services available to a population.

quality of life
The overall sense of well-being experienced by either an individual or a group.

nonprofits
Business-*like* establishments that employ people and produce goods and services with the fundamental goal of contributing to the community rather than generating financial gain.

factors of production
Four fundamental elements—natural resources, capital, human resources, and entrepreneurship—that businesses need to achieve their objectives.

business environment
The setting in which business operates. The five key components are: economic environment, competitive environment, technological environment, social environment, and global environment.

speed-to-market
The rate at which a new product moves from conception to commercialization.

business technology
Any tools—especially computers, telecommunications, and other digital products—that businesses can use to become more efficient and effective.

World Wide Web
The service that allows computer users to easily access and share information on the Internet in the form of text, graphics, video, apps, and animation.

e-commerce
Business transactions conducted online, typically via the Internet.

RIP & REVIEW

demographics
The measurable characteristics of a population. Demographic factors include population size and density and specific traits such as age, gender, and race.

free trade
An international economic and political movement designed to help goods and services flow more freely across international boundaries.

General Agreement on Tariffs and Trade (GATT)
An international trade agreement that has taken bold steps to lower tariffs and promote free trade worldwide.

LO4 Outline the core factors of production and how they affect the economy

The four factors of production are the fundamental resources that both businesses and nonprofits use to achieve their objectives.

1. *Natural resources:* All inputs that offer value in their natural state, such as land, fresh water, wind, and mineral deposits. The value of natural resources tends to rise with high demand, low supply, or both.
2. *Capital:* The manmade resources that an organization needs to produce goods or services. The elements of capital include machines, tools, buildings, and technology.
3. *Human resources:* The physical, intellectual, and creative contributions of everyone who works within an economy. Education and motivation have become increasingly important as technology replaces manual labor jobs.
4. *Entrepreneurship:* Entrepreneurs take the risk of launching and operating their own businesses. Entrepreneurial enterprises can create a tidal wave of opportunity by harnessing the other factors of production.

LO5 Describe today's business environment and discuss each key dimension

Accelerating change marks every dimension of today's business environment.

- *Economic environment:* In late 2008, the U.S. economy plunged into a deep financial crisis. The value of the stock market plummeted, companies collapsed, and the unemployment rate soared. The president, Congress, and the Federal Reserve took unprecedented steps—including a massive economic stimulus package—to encourage a turnaround.
- *Competitive environment:* As global competition intensifies, leading-edge companies have focused on long-term customer satisfaction as never before.
- *Technological environment:* The recent digital technology boom has transformed business, establishing new industries and burying others.
- *Social environment:* The U.S. population continues to diversify. Consumers are gaining power, and society has higher standards for business behavior. Sustainability has become a core marketplace issue.
- *Global environment:* The U.S. economy works within the context of the global environment. The worldwide recession has dampened short-term opportunities, but China and India continue their rapid economic development.

The Business Environment

© Cengage Learning 2013

LO6 Explain how current business trends might affect your career choices

With automation picking up speed, many traditional career choices have become dead ends. But some things—including empathy, creativity, change management, and great communication—can't be digitized. Having these skills can provide you with personal and financial opportunity.

LO1 Define economics and discuss the evolving global economic crisis

Economics—the study of how people, companies, and governments allocate resources—offers vital insights regarding the forces that affect every business on a daily basis. Understanding economics helps businesspeople make better decisions, which can lead to greater profitability, both short-term and long-term. Macroeconomics is the study of broad economic trends. It focuses on the choices made by smaller economic units, such as individual consumers, families, and businesses.

In September 2008, the United States economy plunged into a deep economic crisis. The banking system hovered on the edge of collapse, property values plummeted, and home foreclosure rates soared. Massive layoffs put more than a million Americans out of work. By the end of the year, the stock market had lost more than a third of its value. To prevent total financial disaster, the federal government and the Federal Reserve intervened in the economy at an unprecedented level by bailing out huge firms that faced total collapse. In early 2009, Congress passed a colossal economic stimulus package, designed to turn around the economy and position the United States for long-term economic growth. In mid-2010, the economy began a painfully slow turnaround, although unemployment remained stubbornly high through mid-2011 with uncertain prospects for a full recovery.

LO2 Analyze the impact of fiscal and monetary policy on the economy

Fiscal policy and monetary policy refer to efforts to shape the health of the economy. Fiscal policy involves government taxation and spending decisions designed to encourage growth and boost employment. Monetary policy refers to decisions by the Federal Reserve that influence the size of the money supply and the level of interest rates. Both fiscal and monetary policies played a pivotal role in mitigating the impact of the recent financial crisis and establishing a framework for recovery. These tools can also help sustain economic expansions.

LO3 Explain and evaluate the free market system and supply and demand

Capitalism, also known as the *free market system*, is based on private ownership, economic freedom, and fair competition. In a capitalist economy, individuals, businesses, or nonprofit organizations privately own the vast majority of enterprises. As businesses compete against each other, quality goes up, prices remain reasonable, and choices abound, raising the overall standard of living.
The interplay between the forces of supply and demand determines the selection of products and prices available in a free market economy. *Supply* refers to the quantity of products that producers are willing to offer for sale at different market prices at a specific time. *Demand* refers to the quantity of products that consumers are willing to buy at different market prices at a specific time. According to economic theory, markets will naturally move toward the point at which supply and demand are equal: the *equilibrium point*.

Equilibrium

© Cengage Learning 2013

LO4 Explain and evaluate planned market systems

In planned economies, the government—rather than individual choice—plays a pivotal role in controlling the economy. The two main types of planned economies are socialism and communism. While planned economies are designed to create more equity among citizens, they tend to be more prone to corruption and less effective at generating wealth than market-based economies.

LO5 Describe the trend toward mixed market systems

Most of today's nations have mixed economies, falling somewhere along a spectrum that ranges from pure planned at one extreme to pure market at the other. Over the past 30 years, most major economies around the world have moved toward the market end of the spectrum, although recently—in the wake of the global financial crisis—the United States has added more planned elements to the economy.

economy
A financial and social system of how resources flow through society, from production, to distribution, to consumption.

economics
The study of the choices that people, companies, and governments make in allocating society's resources.

macroeconomics
The study of a country's overall economic dynamics, such as the employment rate, the gross domestic product, and taxation policies.

microeconomics
The study of smaller economic units such as individual consumers, families, and individual businesses.

fiscal policy
Government efforts to influence the economy through taxation and spending.

budget surplus
Overage that occurs when revenue is higher than expenses over a given period of time.

budget deficit
Shortfall that occurs when expenses are higher than revenue over a given period of time.

federal debt
The sum of all the money that the federal government has borrowed over the years and not yet repaid.

monetary policy
Federal Reserve decisions that shape the economy by influencing interest rates and the supply of money.

commercial banks
Privately owned financial institutions that accept demand deposits and make loans and provide other services for the public.

money supply
The total amount of money within the overall economy.

money
Anything generally accepted as a medium of exchange, a measure of value, or a means of payment.

M1 money supply
Includes all currency plus checking accounts and traveler's checks.

M2 money supply
Includes all of M1 money supply plus most savings accounts, money market accounts, and certificates of deposit.

open market operations
The Federal Reserve function of buying and selling government securities, which include treasury bonds, notes, and bills.

discount rate
The rate of interest that the Federal Reserve charges when it loans funds to banks.

RIP & REVIEW

Federal Deposit Insurance Corporation (FDIC)
A federal agency that insures deposits in banks and thrift institutions for up to $250,000 per customer, per bank.

reserve requirement
A rule set by the Fed, which specifies the minimum amount of reserves (or funds) a bank must hold, expressed as a percentage of the bank's deposits.

economic system
A structure for allocating limited resources.

capitalism
An economic system—also known as the private enterprise or free market system—based on private ownership, economic freedom, and fair competition.

pure competition
A market structure with many competitors selling virtually identical products. Barriers to entry are quite low.

monopolistic competition
A market structure with many competitors selling differentiated products. Barriers to entry are low.

oligopoly
A market structure with only a handful of competitors selling products that can be either similar or different. Barriers to entry are typically high.

monopoly
A market structure with one producer completely dominating the industry, leaving no room for any significant competitors. Barriers to entry tend to be virtually insurmountable.

natural monopoly
A market structure with one company as the supplier of a product because the nature of that product makes a single supplier more efficient than multiple competing ones. Most natural monopolies are government sanctioned and regulated.

supply
The quantity of products that producers are willing to offer for sale at different market prices.

supply curve
The graphed relationship between price and quantity from a supplier standpoint.

demand
The quantity of products that consumers are willing to buy at different market prices.

demand curve
The graphed relationship between price and quantity from a customer demand standpoint.

equilibrium price
The price associated with the point at which the quantity demanded of a product equals the quantity supplied.

socialism
An economic system based on the principle that the government should own and operate key enterprises that directly affect public welfare.

communism
An economic and political system that

L06 Discuss key terms and tools to evaluate economic performance
Since economic systems are so complex, no single measure captures all the dimensions of economic performance. But each measure yields insight on overall economic health.

- *Gross domestic product (GDP):* The total value of all goods and services produced within a nation's physical boundaries over a given period of time.
- *Unemployment rate:* The percentage of the labor force reflecting those who don't have jobs and are actively seeking employment.
- *Business cycle:* The periodic expansion and contraction that occur over time in virtually every economy.
- *Inflation rate:* The rate at which prices are rising across the economy. The government tracks the consumer price index and the producer price index.
- *Productivity:* The relationship between the goods and services that an economy produces and the inputs needed to produce them.

Business Cycle

© Cengage Learning 2013

calls for public ownership of virtually all enterprises, under the direction of a strong central government.

mixed economies
Economies that embody elements of both planned and market-based economic systems.

privatization
The process of converting government-owned businesses to private ownership.

gross domestic product (GDP)
The total value of all final goods and services produced within a nation's physical boundaries over a given period of time.

unemployment rate
The percentage of people in the labor force over age 16 who do not have jobs and are actively seeking employment.

business cycle
The periodic contraction and expansion that occur over time in virtually every economy.

contraction
A period of economic downturn, marked by rising unemployment and falling business production.

recession
An economic downturn marked by a decrease in the GDP for two consecutive quarters.

depression
An especially deep and long-lasting recession.

recovery
A period of rising economic growth and employment.

expansion
A period of robust economic growth and high employment.

inflation
A period of rising average prices across the economy.

hyperinflation
An average monthly inflation rate of more than 50 percent.

disinflation
A period of slowing average price increases across the economy.

deflation
A period of falling average prices across the economy.

consumer price index (CPI)
A measure of inflation that evaluates the change in the weighted-average price of goods and services that the average consumer buys each month.

producer price index (PPI)
A measure of inflation that evaluates the change over time in the weighted-average wholesale prices.

productivity
The basic relationship between the production of goods and services (output) and the resources needed to produce them (input), calculated via the following equation: output/input = productivity.

LO1 **Discuss business opportunities in the world economy**

Advancing technology and falling trade barriers have created unprecedented international business opportunities. Despite the global economic crisis that began in 2008, high-population developing countries—such as China, India, Indonesia, and Brazil—continue to offer the most potential due to both their size and their relatively strong economic growth rates.

LO2 **Explain the key reasons for international trade**

The benefits of international trade for individual firms include access to factors of production, reduced risk, and an inflow of new ideas from foreign markets. Overall, industries tend to succeed on a global basis in countries that enjoy a competitive advantage. A country has an absolute advantage in a given industry when it can produce more of a good than other nations, using the same amount of resources, and a country has a comparative advantage when it can make products at a lower opportunity cost than other nations. Unless they face major trade barriers, the industries in any country tend to produce products for which they have a comparative advantage.

LO3 **Describe the tools for measuring international trade**

Measuring the impact of international trade on individual nations requires a clear understanding of balance of trade, balance of payments, and exchange rates.

- *Balance of trade:* A basic measure of the difference between a nation's exports and imports.
- *Balance of payments:* A measure of the total flow of money into or out of a country, including the balance of trade, plus other financial flows, such as foreign loans, foreign aid, and foreign investments.
- *Exchange rates:* A measure of the value of one nation's currency relative to the currency of other nations. The exchange rate has a powerful influence on the way global trade affects both individual nations and their trading partners.

LO4 **Analyze strategies for reaching global markets**

Firms can enter global markets by developing foreign suppliers, foreign customers, or both. Two strategies for acquiring foreign suppliers are outsourcing and importing. Key strategies for developing foreign markets include exporting, licensing, franchising, and direct investment. Exporting is relatively low cost and low risk, but it offers little control over the way the business unfolds. Direct investment, at the other end of the spectrum, tends to be high cost and high risk, but it offers more control and higher potential profits.

Market Development Options

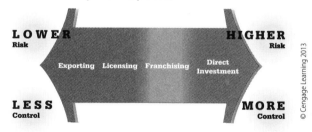

LOWER Risk — **HIGHER** Risk

Exporting · Licensing · Franchising · Direct Investment

LESS Control — **MORE** Control

© Cengage Learning 2013

LO5 **Discuss barriers to international trade and strategies to surmount them**

Most barriers to trade fall into the following categories: sociocultural differences, economic differences, and legal/political differences. Each country has a different mix of barriers. Often countries with the highest barriers have the least competition, which can be a real opportunity for the first international firms to break through. The best way to surmount trade barriers is to cultivate a deep understanding of a country before beginning business. And since conditions change rapidly in many nations, learning and responding are continual processes.

opportunity cost
The opportunity of giving up the second-best choice when making a decision.

absolute advantage
The benefit a country has in a given industry when it can produce more of a product than other nations using the same amount of resources.

comparative advantage
The benefit a country has in a given industry if it can make products at a lower opportunity cost than other countries.

balance of trade
A basic measure of the difference in value between a nation's exports and imports, including both goods and services.

trade surplus
Overage that occurs when the total value of a nation's exports is higher than the total value of its imports.

trade deficit
Shortfall that occurs when the total value of a nation's imports is higher than the total value of its exports.

balance of payments
A measure of the total flow of money into or out of a country.

balance of payments surplus
Overage that occurs when more money flows into a nation than out of that nation.

balance of payments deficit
Shortfall that occurs when more money flows out of a nation than into that nation.

exchange rates
A measurement of the value of one nation's currency relative to the currency of other nations.

countertrade
International trade that involves the barter of products for products rather than for currency.

foreign outsourcing
(also contract manufacturing)
Contracting with foreign suppliers to produce products, usually at a fraction of the cost of domestic production.

importing
Buying products domestically that have been produced or grown in foreign nations.

exporting
Selling products in foreign nations that have been produced or grown domestically.

foreign licensing
Authority granted by a domestic firm to a foreign firm for the rights to produce and market its product or to use its trademark/patent rights in a defined geographical area.

RIP & REVIEW

foreign franchising
A specialized type of foreign licensing in which a firm expands by offering businesses in other countries the right to produce and market its products according to specific operating requirements.

direct investment
(or foreign direct investment) When firms either acquire foreign firms or develop new facilities from the ground up in foreign countries.

joint ventures
When two or more companies join forces—sharing resources, risks, and profits, but not actually merging companies—to pursue specific opportunities.

partnership
A voluntary agreement under which two or more people act as co-owners of a business for profit.

strategic alliance
An agreement between two or more firms to jointly pursue a specific opportunity without actually merging their businesses. Strategic alliances typically involve less formal, less encompassing agreements than partnerships.

sociocultural differences
Differences among cultures in language, attitudes, and values.

infrastructure
A country's physical facilities that support economic activity.

protectionism
National policies designed to restrict international trade, usually with the goal of protecting domestic businesses.

tariffs
Taxes levied against imports.

quotas
Limitations on the amount of specific products that may be imported from certain countries during a given time period.

voluntary export restraints (VERs)
Limitations on the amount of specific products that one nation will export to another nation.

embargo
A complete ban on international trade of a certain item, or a total halt in trade with a particular nation.

free trade
The unrestricted movement of goods and services across international borders.

General Agreement on Tariffs and Trade (GATT)
An international trade treaty designed to encourage worldwide trade among its members.

World Trade Organization (WTO)
A permanent global institution to promote international trade and to settle international trade disputes.

World Bank
An international cooperative of 187 member countries, working together to reduce poverty in the developing world.

L06 Describe the free trade movement and discuss key benefits and criticisms
Over the past two decades, the emergence of regional trading blocs, common markets, and international trade agreements has moved the world economy much closer to complete free trade. Key players include:
- GATT and the WTO
- The World Bank
- The International Monetary Fund (IMF)
- The North American Free Trade Agreement (NAFTA)
- The European Union (EU)

The free trade movement has raised the global standard of living, lowered prices, and expanded choices for millions of people, but critics are troubled by the growing economic gap between the haves and the have-nots, worker abuse, large-scale pollution, and cultural homogenization.

European Union 2011

© Cengage Learning 2013

International Monetary Fund (IMF)
An international organization of 187 member nations that promote international economic cooperation and stable growth.

trading bloc
A group of countries that has reduced or even eliminated tariffs, allowing for the free flow of goods among the member nations.

common market
A group of countries that have eliminated tariffs and harmonized trading rules to facilitate the free flow of goods among the member nations.

North American Free Trade Agreement (NAFTA)
The treaty among the United States, Mexico, and Canada that eliminated trade barriers and investment restrictions over a 15-year period starting in 1994.

European Union (EU)
The world's largest common market, composed of twenty-seven European nations.

1st economy in the world

LO1 Define ethics and explain the concept of universal ethical standards

Ethics is a set of beliefs about right and wrong, good and bad. Who you are as a human being, your family, and your culture all play a role in shaping your ethical standards. The laws of each country usually set minimum ethical standards, but truly ethical standards typically reach beyond minimum legal requirements. Despite some significant cultural and legal differences, people around the globe tend to agree on core values, which can serve as a starting point for universal ethical standards across a wide range of situations: trustworthiness, respect, responsibility, fairness, caring, and citizenship.

Universal Ethical Standards

Trustworthiness, respect, responsibility, fairness, caring, citizenship

© Cengage Learning 2013

LO2 Describe business ethics and ethical dilemmas

Business ethics is the application of right and wrong, good and bad, in a business setting. Ethical dilemmas arise when you face business decisions that throw your values into conflict. These are decisions that force you to choose among less-than-ideal options because whatever choice you make will have some significant negative consequences.

Ethical Dilemma

© Cengage Learning 2013

LO3 Discuss how ethics relates to both the individual and the organization

Ethical choices begin with ethical individuals. To help people make good choices, experts have developed frameworks for reaching ethical decisions. While the specifics vary, the core principles of most decision guides are similar:

- Do you fully understand each dimension of the problem?
- Who would benefit? Who would suffer?
- Are the alternative solutions legal? Are they fair?
- Does your decision make you comfortable at a "gut feel" level?
- Could you defend your decision on the nightly TV news?
- Have you considered and reconsidered your responses to each question?

While each person is responsible for his or her own actions, the organization can also have a dramatic influence on the conduct of individual employees. An ethical culture—which includes ethical leadership from top executives, and accountability at every level of the organization—has an outsized impact on individual conduct. But formal ethics programs also play a crucial role. A written code of ethics—a document that lays out the values and priorities of the organization—is the cornerstone of a formal ethics program. Other key elements include ethics training and a clear enforcement policy for ethical violations.

LO4 Define social responsibility and examine the impact on stakeholder groups

Social responsibility is the obligation of a business to contribute to society. Enlightened companies carefully consider the priorities of all stakeholders—groups who have an interest in their actions and performance—as they make key decisions. Core stakeholder groups for most businesses are listed below, along with key obligations.

- *Employees:* Treat employees with dignity, respect, and fairness. Ensure that hard work and talent pay off. Help workers balance emerging work–life priorities.
- *Customers:* Provide quality products at a fair price. Ensure that customers are safe and informed. Support consumer choice and consumer dialogue.
- *Investors:* Create an ongoing stream of profits. Manage investor dollars according to the highest legal and ethical standards. Support full disclosure.

ethics
A set of beliefs about right and wrong, good and bad.

universal ethical standards
Ethical norms that apply to all people across a broad spectrum of situations.

business ethics
The application of right and wrong, good and bad, in a business setting.

ethical dilemma
A decision that involves a conflict of values; every potential course of action has some significant negative consequences.

code of ethics
A formal, written document that defines the ethical standards of an organization and gives employees the information they need to make ethical decisions across a range of situations.

whistle-blowers
Employees who report their employer's illegal or unethical behavior to either the authorities or the media.

social responsibility
The obligation of a business to contribute to society.

stakeholders
Any groups that have a stake—or a personal interest—in the performance and actions of an organization.

consumerism
A social movement that focuses on four key consumer rights: (1) the right to be safe, (2) the right to be informed, (3) the right to choose, and (4) the right to be heard.

planned obsolescence
The strategy of deliberately designing products to fail in order to shorten the time between purchases.

Sarbanes–Oxley Act of 2002
Federal legislation passed in 2002 that sets higher ethical standards for public corporations and accounting firms. Key provisions limit conflict-of-interest issues and require financial officers and CEOs to certify the validity of their financial statements.

corporate philanthropy
All business donations to nonprofit groups, including money, products, and employee time.

cause-related marketing
Marketing partnerships between businesses and nonprofit organizations, designed to spike sales for the company and raise money for the nonprofit.

corporate responsibility
Business contributions to the community through the actions of the business itself rather than donations of money and time.

sustainable development
Doing business to meet the needs of the current generation, without harming the ability of future generations to meet their needs.

carbon footprint
Refers to the amount of harmful greenhouse gases that a firm emits throughout its operations, both directly and indirectly.

green marketing
Developing and promoting environmentally sound products and practices to gain a competitive edge.

social audit
A systematic evaluation of how well a firm is meeting its ethics and social responsibility goals.

RIP & REVIEW

- *Community:* Support nonprofit groups that improve the community and fit with your company. Minimize the negative environmental impact of your business.

The Spectrum of Social Responsibility

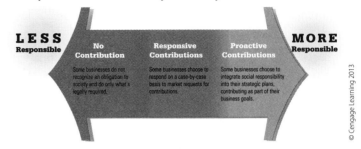

© Cengage Learning 2013

L05 Explain the role of social responsibility in the global arena

Social responsibility becomes more complex in the global arena, largely due to differences in the legal and cultural environments. Bribery and corruption are key issues, along with concern for human rights and environmental standards.

Social Responsibility Issues in the Global Arena

Chapters 1-5

Mid-term

Jan 21?
Mon

L06 Describe how companies evaluate their efforts to be socially responsible

Many companies—even in some entire industries—monitor themselves. The process typically involves measuring objectives for ethics and social responsibility and then measuring actual results against objectives on a systematic, periodic basis. Other groups play watchdog roles as well. Key players include activist customers, investors, unions, environmentalists, and community groups.

- Investors
- Unions
- Environmentalists
- Community Groups

© Cengage Learn

LO1 Explain the importance of excellent business communication

Barriers to communication can be daunting

physical barriers, language barriers, body language barriers, cultural barriers, perceptual barriers, organizational barriers

© Cengage Learning 2013

Effective communication happens when *relevant meaning* is transmitted from the sender to the receiver. Skillful communicators save time and money, and develop deeper, more trusting relationships with their colleagues. Anything that interferes with the correct transmission of your message is a barrier to communication.

Barriers can be physical, verbal, nonverbal, cultural, perceptual, or organizational. To communicate effectively, you should be able to identify and surmount any barriers that stand between you and your audience. The result? Greater chance of long-term success in every aspect of business.

LO2 Describe the key elements of nonverbal communication

The key elements of nonverbal communication include eye contact, tone of voice, facial expressions, gestures, and posture. Studies suggest that, on average, only 7% of meaning during face-to-face communication comes from the verbal content of the message, which magnifies the importance of every element of nonverbal communication. Active listening also plays an influential role. The starting point is empathy: a genuine attempt to understand and appreciate the speaker. You should signal your focus to the speaker through verbal cues, such as "I understand your point," and nonverbal cues, such as nods, eye contact, and leaning forward. The result will be better relationships and better information for you.

eye contact
tone of voice
facial expressions
gestures
posture

93% of meaning comes from nonverbal communication

© Cengage Learning 2013

LO3 Compare, contrast, and choose effective communication channels

Communication channels differ significantly in terms of richness: the amount of information that they offer the audience. The spectrum ranges from written communication at the low end to face-to-face meetings at the high end. The best choice depends on your objective, your message, and your audience. To ensure that your communication achieves your goals, always consider the needs and expectations of your audience. If you tailor each message with the audience in mind, you'll give yourself a competitive edge in terms of the time, attention, and response of your audience.

Communication Channels Have Different Levels of Richness

Teambldg

Very High · High · Moderate · Low · Very Low

Face-to-Face Meeting · In-Person Presentation · Telephone · Voice Mail · Instant Message · Email · Memos/Reports

© Cengage Learning 2013

---

communication
The transmission of information between a sender and a recipient.

noise
Any interference that causes the message you send to be different from the message your audience understands.

communication barriers
Obstacles to effective communication, typically defined in terms of physical, language, body language, cultural, perceptual, and organizational barriers.

＊intercultural communication
Communication among people with differing cultural backgrounds.

nonverbal communication
Communication that does not use words. Common forms of nonverbal communication include gestures, posture, facial expressions, tone of voice, and eye contact.

active listening
Attentive listening that occurs when the listener focuses his or her complete attention on the speaker.

communication channels
The various ways in which a message can be sent, ranging from one-on-one, in-person meetings to Internet message boards.

bias
A preconception about members of a particular group. Common forms of bias include gender bias; age bias; and race, ethnicity, or nationality bias.

active voice
Sentence construction in which the subject performs the action expressed by the verb (e.g., *My sister wrote the paper*). The active voice works better for the vast majority of business communication.

passive voice
Sentence construction in which the subject does not do the action expressed by the verb; rather the subject is acted upon (e.g., *The paper was written by my sister*). The passive voice tends to be less effective for business communication.

dynamic delivery
Vibrant, compelling presentation delivery style that grabs and holds the attention of the audience.

Always be honest

LO4 Choose the right words for effective communication

The right words can make the difference between a message your audience absorbs and a message your audience ignores. Keep these considerations in mind: analyze your audience, be concise, avoid slang, avoid bias, and use active voice.

LO5 Write more effective business memos, letters, and emails

Here, too, you should begin with the needs of your audience; their anticipated response should drive the structure of your writing. Determine the "bottom line" of your communication, and be sure to deliver it up front. Your message itself should have a natural tone and must be completely free of grammatical errors.

Sample Emails: Same Message, Different Approach

If the recipient will feel positive or neutral about your message...

Subject line specifies the key issue

Main point in the first sentence

Inbox — TO: Online Poker Team / FROM: Yumi Tanaka, VP Product Development / RE: Game Development Team Restructuring

To help meet our goal of developing three more innovative games this year, I plan to reassign each member of the online poker team to a new team that needs to brainstorm more effectively. Please let me know sometime in the next two days if you have a preference regarding your new assignment.

Thank you for arranging to present the new version of your online poker game to the sales force last week. I am confident that this game your team developed will be a huge hit with our key customers.

Positive close reinforces goodwill

If the recipient will feel negative about your message...

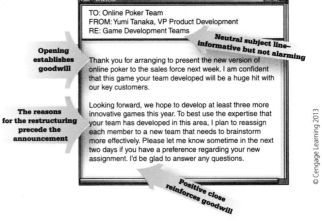

Neutral subject line—informative but not alarming

Opening establishes goodwill

The reasons for the restructuring precede the announcement

Inbox — TO: Online Poker Team / FROM: Yumi Tanaka, VP Product Development / RE: Game Development Teams

Thank you for arranging to present the new version of online poker to the sales force next week. I am confident that this game your team developed will be a huge hit with our key customers.

Looking forward, we hope to develop at least three more innovative games this year. To best use the expertise that your team has developed in this area, I plan to reassign each member to a new team that needs to brainstorm more effectively. Please let me know sometime in the next two days if you have a preference regarding your new assignment. I'd be glad to answer any questions.

Positive close reinforces goodwill

© Cengage Learning 2013

LO6 Create and deliver successful verbal presentations

A great presentation begins with a hook that draws your audience in and engages their attention. The body of the presentation typically focuses on three key points, supported by credible information and persuasive arguments. The close summarizes the key points and often refers back to the opening hook. Dynamic delivery is simply a matter of practice, with a focus on knowing your material.